Map of **S0-DRD-525**

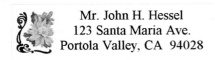

Mr. John H. Hessel
123 Santa Maria Ave.
Portola Valley, CA 94028

FIELD GUIDE TO THE
BIRDS OF
East Africa

Kenya Tanzania Uganda Rwanda Burundi

Terry Stevenson and John Fanshawe

FIELD GUIDE TO THE
BIRDS OF
East Africa
Kenya Tanzania Uganda Rwanda Burundi

Terry Stevenson and John Fanshawe

Illustrated by
Brian Small, John Gale and Norman Arlott

T & A D POYSER
London

First published in 2002 by T & A D Poyser Ltd
Harcourt Place, 32 Jamestown Road, London NW1 7BY, UK
http://www.academicpress.com

Reprinted 2002.

ISBN 0-85661-079-8

A catalogue record for this book is available from the British Library

Library of Congress Card Number: 00-110863

Typeset by J&L Composition Ltd, Filey, North Yorkshire
Colour Separation by Tenon & Polert Colour Scanning Ltd
Printed and bound in Spain by Grafos SA Arte Sobre Papel, Barcelona

02 03 04 05 06 GF 9 8 7 6 5 4 3 2

Dedicated to

Jane, Jay & Amory
Clare, Jack & Holly

CONTENTS

List of Plates

Preface

The East African countries of Kenya, Tanzania, Uganda, Rwanda and Burundi shelter some of Africa's most spectacular landscapes and wildlife, and this guide is an attempt to share our fascination and enthusiasm for birding in the region. Flick through the 286 plates and it is quickly obvious why – the area has a stunning avifauna. During our work leading bird tours and in conservation, we have been lucky enough to see most of the region's 1388 species. Here, we have tried to use this experience to package the information you need for bird identification in a simple layout that brings the text, maps and plates together in a comprehensive but reasonably small and lightweight book. Given that many modern guides are now devoted to single groups, like raptors and gulls, this has been quite a challenge, and we hope we have managed a reasonable compromise. We would nevertheless welcome suggestions and observations that would improve this work.[1]

INTRODUCTION

Landscapes

East Africa's extraordinary biodiversity is inextricably linked to a remarkably diverse and complex landscape. The region's habitats range from coastal beaches, reefs and creeks, through deserts, arid and semi-arid country, a great range of grass, bush and woodland, lowland to montane forests (some ancient, some very young in evolutionary terms), and extensive freshwater and alkaline lake systems (see habitats map: figure 1). The eastern and western arms of the Rift Valley cut through the region from north to south. Climate radically influences habitats, from the deserts of the drier north-east to moist lowland forests in the west, and rainfall patterns, including localised storms, can radically influence local movements of resident and migratory birds. Altitude also plays a major role in bird distributions, ranging from sea-level to the peak of Kilimanjaro at 5825m (see topographic map: figure 2).

Many species are characteristic of particular habitats or biomes (for example, Scarlet-tufted Sunbird is restricted to alpine moorlands from 3000–4500m). East Africa also contains important centres of endemism, like the Albertine Rift (running along the extreme west of the region), the Kenyan mountains, the Serengeti Plains, all the coastal forests, and Pemba Island. Such areas shelter species with extremely restricted world ranges (less than 50,000 km^2 and marked with a black dot in the text ●): they are often the quarry of keen birders.

Sites

Although birds dominate the landscape virtually everywhere in East Africa, a rapidly changing environment means that some areas are particularly

---

[1] Please send any recommendations to the authors via T. & A.D. Poyser.

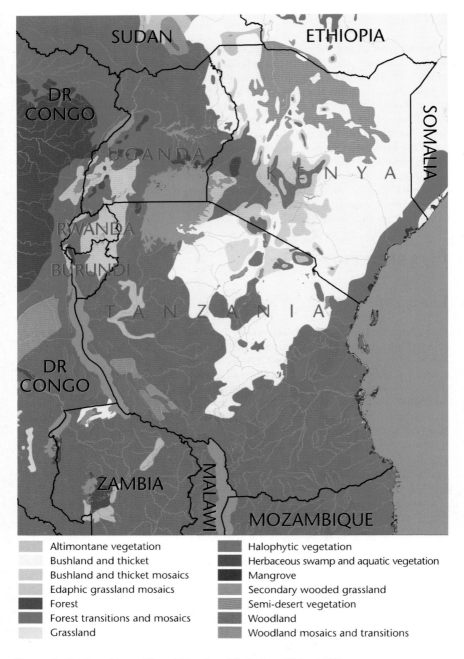

Figure 1: Habitats Map of East Africa (modified after White 1983)

Legend:

- Altimontane vegetation
- Bushland and thicket
- Bushland and thicket mosaics
- Edaphic grassland mosaics
- Forest
- Forest transitions and mosaics
- Grassland
- Halophytic vegetation
- Herbaceous swamp and aquatic vegetation
- Mangrove
- Secondary wooded grassland
- Semi-desert vegetation
- Woodland
- Woodland mosaics and transitions

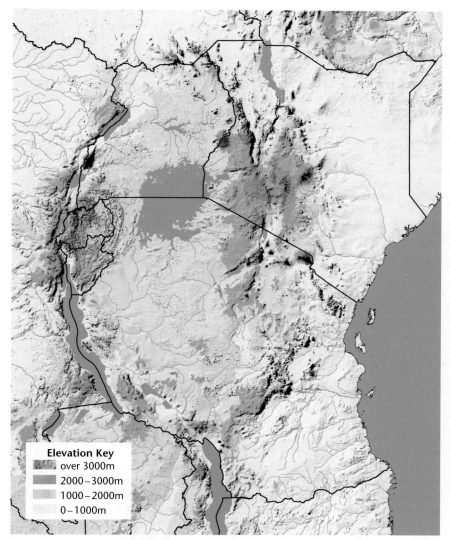

Figure 2: Topographic Map of East Africa (modified from US Geological Survey data)

important. Such sites range from the world's greatest protected areas (like Tanzania's Serengeti National Park), to smaller and highly fragmented sites, like Kakamega Forest in western Kenya, and unprotected, vulnerable and often small areas like the Mukurweini Valleys of Nyeri District in central Kenya (a stronghold for the endemic Hinde's Babbler). Often these sites are oases of natural habitats in a landscape that is being rapidly altered.

Since 1993, conservationists have been identifying these Important Bird Areas (IBAs) in the region, using criteria developed by the BirdLife International Partnership. So far 182 have been identified (they are mapped on the inside back cover). IBAs are recognised for sheltering populations of birds that are endemic, threatened, or restricted to particular biomes (like the 'Afrotropical highlands'), or because they are places where exceptionally large numbers of birds congregate. All are assessed against agreed global thresholds with an overarching philosophy that seeks to recognise and protect a network of sites worldwide and aims to ensure the conservation of all bird species. Moreover, IBAs harbour a phenomenal wealth of other fauna and flora, and so contribute to global biodiversity conservation.

Any birding safari into East Africa inevitably visits many of these areas – be it Lake Nakuru National Park in Kenya to see the massed flocks of Lesser Flamingos, or Bwindi Forest NP in Uganda to try and track down that gem, the African Green Broadbill. One of the joys of birding this region is that the sheer diversity of species and habitats forces us to visit a real range of areas. Please find time to interact with the people who live in and around these places, be they guides or waiters, farmers or schoolchildren, and share some of your sense of discovery. Details of the more formal networks of people who have identified and monitor these sites are given in the conservation section.

Species

Our book covers 1388 species, more than 80% of the birds that have been recorded in sub-Saharan Africa. This includes families, like turacos and mousebirds, and species, like Secretary Bird and Hamerkop, which are found only in the Afrotropics. Although our knowledge is steadily increasing, there is still a huge amount to find out about East Africa's birds. New species and races are still being discovered: Udzungwa Forest-partridge, not only a new species but also a new genus to science, was found in the highland forests of south-central Tanzania in 1991.

Alongside new discoveries, existing taxa are regularly re-assessed and changes in status debated. For example, the Grey-headed Sparrow species complex has often been treated as a single species but is currently split into five: Grey-headed, Parrot-billed, Swainson's, Swahili, and Southern Grey-headed sparrows. There are numerous other examples where evolving knowledge leads to taxonomic changes. We have tried to take account of this, often including proposed common names for races in an overall account where that race might be considered a good species. An example is the north-eastern race of Lilac-breasted Roller *Coracias caudata lorti*, which is treated as a good species by some authorities. We have bracketed and emboldened its proposed common name (**Lilac-throated Roller**) in the text.

In East Africa, sub-species and races are numerous. In the species accounts, we have mentioned those races which we consider important or distinctive. It is likely that a number of well-marked and restricted races are actually good species. This is not just an academic issue, as a species' conservation ranking may be strongly influenced by these decisions. The restricted and threatened Taita Thrush, for example, is merely treated as a race of Olive Thrush by some authors, and, as such, may not receive the protection its critically threatened status warrants. In 2000, the BirdLife network reviewed threatened birds worldwide and red-listed 49 in East Africa (out of a global total of 1186): they have a red spot opposite their names in the text (●). Following IUCN criteria, four categories of threat are recognised: critical, endangered, vulnerable, and near-threatened. Those too poorly known to be assessed may be listed as 'data deficient'. Some species, like Lesser Kestrel, are primarily threatened in their Palearctic breeding areas. In the region covered here, three birds, Taita Thrush, Taita Apalis and Long-billed Tailorbird, are treated as critical; meaning they face an extremely high risk of extinction in the wild in the immediate future.

Seasonality

Unlike the temperate Palearctic where seasons, like spring and summer, are reasonably distinct, East Africa's tropical weather systems often seem far more difficult to predict. Nevertheless, resident and migrant bird distributions are strongly influenced by equatorial seasons. Dry and wet season patterns vary a great deal across the region and between years. Most of the north has rains that typically fall from March to November. Over much of Kenya and southern Uganda, heavier 'long rains' fall from March to May, with a second, smaller peak in October and November. In southern and western Tanzania, Rwanda and Burundi, the main rainy season is from October to April or May. But complex local patterns occur, and are often influenced by topography, proximity to the coast or Lake Victoria, etc. The basic rule is that bird activity, especially in more arid areas, is strongly influenced by the presence or absence of rain. Many species nest during and shortly after the rains, when food is often most abundant, though some (such as sandgrouse) prefer the dry season.

Passage and visiting migrant species from both the Palearctic (like Yellow Wagtail) and southern Africa (like Southern Pochard) are a regular feature of East African birding. Timings of their arrivals and departures are, where known, outlined in the species accounts, but these birds and many residents also move in response to local weather, often reacting with astonishing speed to rain and its consequences (like the emergence of winged termites). In extended dry seasons natural or lit fires also attract birds (like bee-eaters) to feast on insects driven ahead of the flames. Within the dry and wet season framework outlined, the best advice about the links between East Africa's weather patterns and bird activity is – always expect the unexpected!

Taxonomy and names

Our nomenclature is based on the official East African list, originally published in 1980 (Britton, P.L. (Ed) 1980 *Birds of East Africa*, East Africa Natural History Society) and revised regularly and most recently in 1996. We have made a number of changes based on more recent information. Each species has a common name, for example 'White-headed Barbet', and a scientific one that has two parts: the genus, e.g. *Lybius*, followed by the species, e.g. *leucocephalus*. For many species, we have also described a number of races (also sometimes known as sub-species). White-headed Barbet has four: *Lybius leucocephalus leucocephalus* (called the nominate race because the same name is used for both the species and race), and *senex*, *albicauda* and *lynesi*, three additional races. Where possible, we have also provided alternative East and South African common names.

Species accounts

The bulk of the book is made up of 286 plates opposite the species accounts and maps. In developing the book, we worked closely with the artists to design the plate layouts. Using field notes, museum specimens and a wide range of still and video reference material, they have taken immense care to ensure that the images painted are as accurate as possible. We have tried to show every species recorded in the region in all its major plumages, taking account of sex, age, and geographic variation.

Plates are arranged around similar-looking species, with commoner birds usually at the top, and most have a short introduction outlining the main features of the birds. Species might be linked to a key habitat, like dry country plovers, or to a part of the region, like western greenbuls, and in some cases the introduction refers to more than one plate (e.g. large forest hornbills). Notoriously complex groups like the greenbuls, have introductions outlining particular identification issues in more detail. Design constraints have meant that a few species appear out of place and they are typically separated from the other species on the page with a simple line.

Each species account begins with a section describing how to identify the bird in the field. It usually starts with an adult male, leading on to adult female, and working through to immature and juvenile plumages. For most Palearctic species, the account starts with the non-breeding plumage that is most frequently encountered in our area. Birds in flight are also described. Key identification features are italicised. Line drawings on the following pages show the terms used to describe the parts of perched and flying birds.

In the **HH** section, we describe how the birds are likely to be encountered, as pairs, flocks, etc., outline the habitat and, where appropriate, the altitudinal range in metres. For non-resident birds, a period in months is given, e.g. Nov–Mar (meaning November to March). As well as mapping distributions (see below) we often refer to particular place names. The majority of these can be found on the maps inside each cover. Particular habits or behaviours are noted when they aid identification.

Describing bird calls and songs in a confined space is fraught with problems, and in most cases learning vocalisations is only really achieved through listening to birds in the field or to recordings. For many skulking and similar species, however, voice is a vital clue to identity, and for all the species a description of the main calls and songs is given in the **Vo** section. Wherever possible, these accounts include transliterations: Eastern Nicator, for example, is described as extremely vocal, invariably from dense cover, with a loud song that starts hesitantly with a *yu-ik-wit-wer-trrr* and bubbles into a jumbled *cho-chou-choou-chueeee*. Such descriptions are subjective, but we hope give a sense of the sound of the songs and calls. A set of companion CDs with recordings of East African bird songs and calls is to be published alongside this book by our friend and colleague, Brian Finch.

We have tried to make sure that similar species (**SS**) are on the same plate. In a few cases, the name of a confusing similar species on another plate is listed at the end the account, for example Black-backed Puffback and Tropical Boubou.

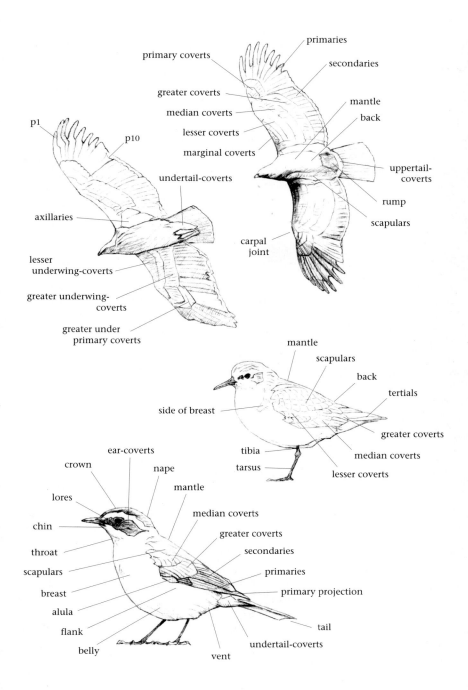

primaries

primary coverts

secondaries

greater coverts

mantle

median coverts

back

lesser coverts

marginal coverts

p1

p10

undertail-coverts

uppertail-coverts

axillaries

rump

scapulars

lesser underwing-coverts

carpal joint

greater underwing-coverts

greater under primary coverts

mantle

scapulars

back

tertials

side of breast

greater coverts

median coverts

tibia

lesser coverts

tarsus

ear-coverts

crown

nape

mantle

lores

median coverts

chin

greater coverts

throat

secondaries

scapulars

primaries

breast

primary projection

alula

flank

tail

belly

undertail-coverts

vent

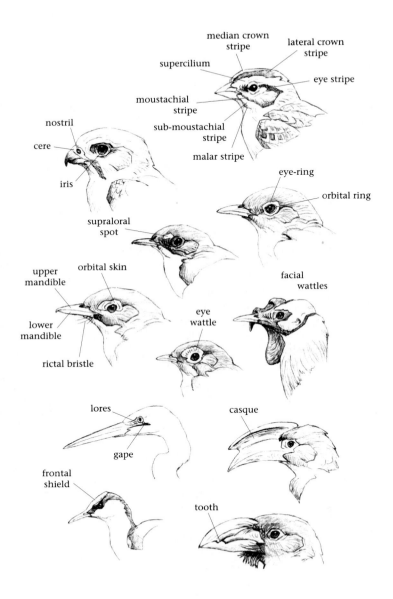

median crown stripe

lateral crown stripe

supercilium

eye stripe

moustachial stripe

sub-moustachial stripe

malar stripe

nostril

cere

iris

eye-ring

orbital ring

supraloral spot

upper mandible

orbital skin

facial wattles

lower mandible

eye wattle

rictal bristle

lores

casque

gape

frontal shield

tooth

Abbreviations

Ad = adult
Sub-ad = sub-adult
Imm = immature
Juv = juvenile
1st year = first year
2nd year = second year
♂ = male
♀ = female
Br = breeding
Non-br = non-breeding
Mel = melanistic
N = North

S = South
E = East
W = West
C = Central
Ke = Kenya
Tz = Tanzania
Ug = Uganda
Rw = Rwanda
Bu = Burundi
HH = Habits and habitats
Vo = Voice
SS = Similar species

Maps

Knowledge of bird distributions in East Africa varies from country to country. Kenya is the most widely travelled and studied area and an excellent atlas was published in 1988. Uganda is also reasonably well known and we have been fortunate to have access to newly drafted maps that will form the basis of the Uganda Bird Atlas to be published in 2001. With the thumbnail scale of our maps, the presence or absence of a species in Burundi and Rwanda provides a useful clue since natural forests and wetlands in both countries are usually well-defined and surrounded by intensively managed farmland. In Tanzania, the north and much of the east are reasonably well known, but the south, west and centre are not. The forthcoming Tanzania bird atlas will greatly improve the situation, but our maps are based on the literature, information from colleagues, and our field visits. In a few cases, we have used question marks in areas where the distribution is unresolved.

Species ranges vary from tiny well-defined areas, like that of Taita Thrush, a threatened endemic confined to forest patches in the Taita Hills of south-east Kenya, to the entire region, like that of the widespread and common Cattle Egret. For many migrant species, like Isabelline Wheatear and African Pitta, we have shown the limits of their range, not every recorded site. A tired and hungry migrating Greenshank, for example, may alight on virtually any ephemeral pool in the region.

For vagrants, we have used one or more crosses to mark the actual locations of records (up to a maximum of 10 records).

Recent Records

New birds are constantly being found in the region. During the latter days of preparing this book, seven were discovered, either in the field, or as old records previously overlooked. They are described and illustrated here. In the very last days of writing, two others, Eurasian Griffon Vulture *Gyps fulvus*, and South African Cliff Swallow *Hirundo spilodera*, have also been seen in Kenya. It was too late to illustrate them. Inevitably more new birds will be found in the future. If you are lucky enough to encounter one, please send your record to the relevant national organisation (see conservation section for details).

Mallard *Anas platyrhynchos* 60cm, 23.5"
Br ♂ is distinctive with a *yellow bill, glossy green head, narrow white neck band and a purplish-brown breast*. ♀ is largely brown with darker brown mottling and streaks, usually darker on the crown and through the eye: *bill is dull orange with a blackish smudge on the upper mandible*. Eclipse ♂ similar to ♀ but with an all yellow bill and a rufous-brown breast. In flight, both sexes reveal a *blue speculum conspicuously bordered with white*. **HH** Palearctic vagrant; birds shot near Marsabit, Ke, in 1928–29 are the only definite records, but there was an unsubstantiated record from Lake Turkana, Ke, in the mid-1980's. **Vo** not recorded in the region but elsewhere the ♂ calls a soft low raspy *raehb* and the ♀ a series of harsh loud quacks.

Congo Serpent-Eagle *Dryotriorchis spectabilis* 60 cm, 2.5"
A small eagle which at first glance may suggest a large *Accipiter*. Ad is largely brown above but greyer on the head; at close range shows darker barring in the primaries and across the tail. Underparts white, with a dark throat streak and variable dark bars on the flanks. Eyes yellow in ♂ and brown in ♀: legs yellow. Imm browner above than ad with mottled white feathering on the nape and mantle, heavy blackish bars across the wings and variable dark spotting on the underparts. **HH** in our area only known from Semliki Forest, WUg, where there have been several sight records, but it is undoubtedly a rare bird. **Vo** reported as a cat-like miaowing and a repeated low nasal *cow-cow-cow*.

Grey-throated Rail *Canirallus oculeus* 30 cm, 12"
Ad is a dark olivaceous-brown and chestnut forest rail with a grey face and throat, and buff and brown barred flanks: bill dark with greenish lower mandible, legs brown. If flushes shows extensive white spotting in flight feathers. Sexes alike, imm similar but face and throat brown. **HH** in our area only known from the Semliki Forest, WUg, where it is presumed to be resident in small numbers. **Vo** reported as a loud snore, soft coos and short *chunk* notes.

Common Crane *Grus grus* 112cm, 44"
A grey crane with *scruffy bustle-tailed appearance* caused by the elongated and dishevelled tertials. *Face and foreneck black with a narrow red band across the crown*, a broad white stripe extends from behind each eye and down the hind-neck, and they usually show some brownish smudges to the back and wing-coverts. In flight, blackish flight feathers contrast with the paler grey body and wing-coverts. Sexes similar, imm has a variable pale buff head and upper neck. **HH** Palearctic vagrant, in our area only known from a single ad near Eldoret, WKe, in Oct 1999. **Vo** migrating birds call *krro* or *karr*.

Spotted Sandpiper *Actitis macularia* 20cm, 8"
Very similar to Common Sandpiper, but ad easily distinguished in br plumage by *prominent black spots on the underparts*. Non-br ad far more difficult but slightly greyer above with plain edges to the tertials (barred on Common), and the *tail projects only slightly beyond the wing tips* (Common appears longer-tailed). In flight, *white wing bar fades on inner-wing* (across most flight feathers on Common). Spotted often has a paler base to the bill and brighter yellow legs than Common Sandpiper, but these characteristics are variable. **HH** vagrant from the Americas, with one record from Mt Kenya, Ke, in Sep 1999. **Vo** often flushes silently, but may call a slightly rising *peet* either singly, or repeated twice.

Black-throated Coucal *Centropus leucogaster* 54cm, 21"
A distinctive large coucal with the *head, neck and breast black*, mid-breast to vent buff-white (or rich cinnamon on some individuals); wings chestnut, rump and uppertail variably barred rufous and black. **HH** in our area only known from Semliki Forest, WUg, where it is a shy resident of dense undergrowth. **Vo** calls include a series of very deep typical coucal notes which descend and slow towards the end, while another series descends and then rises. Both songs may be heard together in duet.

Bush Petronia *Petronia dentata* 13cm, 5"
Ad ♂ is similar and browner that Yellow-spotted Petronia with a paler throat and a *rufous line extending from the eye to behind the ear-coverts*; the yellow throat spot is often concealed. Ad ♀ is a rather nondescript sparrow except for a long pale buffy supercilium. Imm like ♀ but browner. **HH** in our area only known from a single specimen collected in the Labwor Hills, EUg, in Dec 1993. It may have previously been overlooked. **Vo** not recorded in the region, but elsewhere sings fast repeated phrases, including *triup-triup-triup*, and also calls a soft sparrow-like *chewee*.

♀

♂

Mallard

Imm

♂

Congo
Serpent-
Eagle

non-br

Common Crane

Ad

Imm

br

Spotted
Sandpiper

Grey-throated Rail

Black-throated
Coucal

♀

♂

Bush Petronia

Conservation

As in most parts of the world, birding and bird conservation activity is growing apace in East Africa, with an increasingly determined and articulate lobby keen to ensure that the species this book covers have a secure future. Good information on the status of birds can help these conservation efforts – so records from resident and visiting birders are important. To send in your records (especially of unusual or threatened species), or to find out more about how you can get involved in working with networks of bird conservationists in the region, please contact the following organisations:

Nature Kenya
P.O. Box 44486
Nairobi
Kenya

Website: www.naturekenya.org

Nature Uganda
P.O. Box 27034
Kampala
Uganda

Wildlife Conservation Society of Tanzania
P.O. Box 70919
Dar es Salaam
Tanzania

Association pour la Conservation de la Nature au Rwanda (ACNR)
P.O. Box 4290
Kigali
Rwanda

Association Burundaise pour la Protection des Oiseaux (ABO)
P.O. Box 7069
Bujumbura
Burundi

The regional ornithological journal, *Scopus*, is published twice a year. Material thought suitable for publication can be submitted to the Editor, Scopus, P.O. Box 44486 Nairobi, Kenya.

Birders interested in conservation activity in East Africa and elsewhere, can also contact BirdLife International, Wellbrook Court, Girton Road, Cambridge CB3 0NA, United Kingdom. National BirdLife Partners provide a focus for bird conservation activity in more than a hundred countries worldwide, and can also be reached via a website (www.birdlife.net). BirdLife is the global authority on threatened species.

The African Bird Club provides another excellent focus for birders interested in the region, and can be contacted care of the BirdLife International address above or via its website (www.africanbirdclub.org).

Additional reading

East Africa is increasingly well-supplied with relevant books on birds and bird conservation. The region's species are comprehensively tackled in *Birds of Africa*, a seven volume series edited by Hilary Fry, Stuart Keith, and Emil Urban, and illustrated by Martin Woodcock, which has been successively published by Academic Press since 1988 (volume six appeared in 2000).

Several guides have been published including Dale Zimmerman, Don Turner and David Pearson's excellent *Birds of Kenya and Northern Tanzania* (published in 1996 in a handbook and in 1999 in a compact version by Princeton and Helm). Ber van Perlo's illustrated checklist to the region was published by Collins in 1995, and Collin's also published John Williams' original and several times revised and reprinted *Field Guide to the Birds of East Africa* illustrated by Norman Arlott.

Comprehensive atlases include those to Kenya (by Adrian Lewis and Derek Pomeroy and published in 1989 by Balkema) and Uganda (by Margaret Carswell, Derek Pomeroy, Jake Reynolds, and Herbert Tushabe that was published jointly in 2001 by the British Ornithologists' Union and Club). An atlas to the birds of Tanzania is being prepared.

BirdLife's Important Bird Areas programme has seen national guides published in Kenya in 1999 (edited by Leon Bennun and Peter Njoroge), and Uganda in 2001 (edited by Achilles Byahuranga, Panta Kasoma, and Derek Pomeroy). IBAs of Tanzania is also being prepared, and all of Africa's IBA's will be published in a continental directory by the Council of BirdLife International's Africa Partnership in 2001. This huge task covers all of Africa, and has been edited by Lincoln Fishpool. The IBA directories act, in many ways, as planning tools for concerted conservation action, but also as informal guides on where to watch birds. A more specific example is Jonathan Roussow and Marco Sacchi's very useful and well illustrated *Where to Watch Birds in Uganda* published by the Uganda Tourist Board in 1998.

Acknowledgements

Numerous people have contributed to this book. We would like to start with two: the late Phoebe Snetsinger who, at the time of her death, had seen more species of birds in the world than any other person. Her spirit and commitment to global birding was an inspiration to all who knew her. And to David Ngala, whose passion for the forest besides which he was born, Arabuko-Sokoke, means future generations of birders are more likely to be able to enjoy unique birds like the Sokoke Pipit and Sokoke Scops-Owl.

The three artists who have provided the plates that dominate this book have worked extraordinarily hard to make sure that they are accurate: Brian Small, John Gale, and Norman Arlott. We owe them an immense debt.

We would like to give a special mention to our friend and colleague Brian Finch, who in the latter stages of the project came on board and worked tirelessly on our voice section. He also gave up a good holiday to read through all the species accounts adding his comments and ideas. Many thanks, Brian.

Special thanks are also due to our patient colleagues: Rose Ann Rowlett,

Richard Webster, John Coons and all the team at Field Guides; Gary Allport, Dave Capper, Nigel Collar, Lincoln Fishpool, Richard Grimmett, Frank Hawkins, Mike Rands, Sue Shutes, Martin Sneary, Alison Stattersfield, David Thomas, and all the team at BirdLife International; Leon Bennun, Paul Matiku, Solomon Mwangi, Oliver Nasirwa, Peter Njoroge, Shriti Rajani, Edward Waiyaki, and all the staff and volunteers at Nature Kenya and in the National Museums of Kenya; Alex Mwalimu, Wellington Kombe, Francis Charo, and all the members of the Arabuko-Sokoke Forest Guides Association, Robert Prys-Jones, Mark Adams and Peter Colston at the British Museum. Margaret Carswell, Derek Pomeroy, Jake Reynolds, and Herbert Tushabe, for their support and permission to use unpublished maps from the *Bird Atlas of Uganda*.

Many, many others have also provided advice, support and encouragement at various stages, and we apologise for anyone inadvertently missed from this list: Barbie Allen, Ken Arber, Marie Arlott, Graeme Backhurst, Neil and Liz Baker, Mark Beaman, Simon Blyth, Markus Borner, Nik Borrow, Paul Buckley, Lucy Camm, Clide Carter, Gail and Doug Cheeseman, Gary Claydon, Norbert Cordeiro, Miles Coverdale, John Croxall, Harvey Croze, Bob Dowsett, Francoise Dowsett-Lemaire, Jon Fjeldsa, David Fisher, Pat and Mona Frere, the late Robin Fuggles-Couchman, Alec Forbes-Watson, Fay Gale, Paul Gale, Yves Gaugris, Nathan and Cecilia Gichuki, Roy Gregory, Jenny Horne, Hussein adan Isack, Colin Jackson, Sam Kanyamibwa, Martin Kelsey, Margaret Kullander, Leo and Lala Kunkel, Mike Langman, Chris Lear, Adrian Lewis, David Macdonald, Duncan Macdonald, Clair Mathews, Duncan McCrae, the late Roland McVicker, David Moyer, Fleur Ng'weno, the late Jimmy Onslow, Craig Packer, Robert Payne, David Pearson, Derek Pomeroy, Tony Potterton, Richard Porter, Anne Pusey, Richard Ranft, Nigel Redman, Dave Richards, Andy Roberts, Jamie Roberts, Ann and Ian Robertson, Iain Robertson, Alan Root, Jonathan Roussow, Jonathan Scott, Lester Short, Barbara Simpson, Ian Sinclair, Janet Small, the late Chum van Someren, Bob Sternsjedt, Neil Stronach, Chris Thouless, Don Turner, Tom Whiley, Jean Pierre Vande weghe and Dale Zimmerman.

At T. & A.D. Poyser, tremendous back-up has been provided by a team that includes Sam Fallon, Sutapas Bhattacharya and our editor Andrew Richford. Andy kindly took this project on in the first place and has provided unwavering support throughout.

Finally, this book is dedicated to our long-suffering families, particularly to Jane Roberts and Clare FitzGibbon, and to our parents, Bill and Marjorie Stevenson, and Peter and Clemency Fanshawe.

Species Accounts and Plates

OSTRICHES

Endemic to Africa, ostriches are huge flightless birds with small wings, massive legs and two large forward pointing toes. The small wings are mainly used for fanning, dusting and in spectacular dancing displays. Ostriches walk at an average of 4kph, but can sprint at speeds of up to 60kph, and act as early warning of predators to a range of plains game. They often dust bathe.

Common Ostrich   *Struthio camelus*   height 2.5m, 96"
[Ostrich]

Two basically similar races occur: in both ad ♂ has blackish body feathering, white wings and tail (often stained with local soil colour), and a *pink neck and legs* (which are brighter in br birds): *eyes brown*. Northern nominate also has a small white collar at base of neck which is lacking in much more widespread race *massaicus*. Nominate ad ♀ is largely brown, while *massaicus* is grey-brown. Both races have dull pinkish-brown or brown legs. Imm ♂ like ad ♀, but gains black colour in second year. Imm ♀ is similar to ad ♀. Chicks have striped buff and black heads and necks and mottled backs. **HH** race *massaicus* is sometimes common as singles, small groups and occasionally much larger flocks in drier grassland, bushed and wooded grassland, mainly below 2000m. Nominate is an uncommon bird of the far north. Ostriches have a complex breeding system with one major and 5-6 minor hens laying an average total of 25 eggs in the same nest (which the major hen incubates during the day, and the cock at night). Chicks hatch after around 6 weeks and leave nest after 4 days. They join other young birds to form crèches that can number more than a hundred. Ostriches mature at 3–4 years, but male unlikely to achieve mating status until 6–7. Eggs are eaten by the tool-using Egyptian Vulture (which uses stones to break them open), as well as other predators like hyaenas. **Vo** generally silent but displays a repertoire of roars, booms and hisses during breeding. ♂ well known for booming call, which is a little like a distant lion's roar, a deep vibrant three or four note *hooo booo hooooomph hooo* (which can be heard over 1km). ♀ utters a subdued contact *twoo*.

Somali Ostrich   *Struthio molybdophanes*   height 2.5m, 96"

Ad ♂ is similar to Common Ostrich, but has blacker plumage and a *blue-grey neck and legs*. In br plumage the blue parts are brighter blue, but note bill and front of legs become bright pink: *eyes pale grey-brown*. Ad ♀ is darker brown than widespread ad ♀ *massaicus*, and similar to nominate Common, but *always has blue-grey eyes*. Imm browner than ad ♀, otherwise as Common Ostrich. Chicks similar. **HH** singles and pairs, and less often groups, are widespread but rarely common in semi-arid and arid grassland, bush and woodland in N and NEKe. Less social than Common, more often encountered alone or in pairs, and regularly in much denser bush habitat. Introduced Somali Ostrich hybridised with resident Common Ostrich in Nairobi NP in 1970s, but natural range overlap is limited. **Vo** similar to Common.

Plate 1

♀

Imm ♂

chicks

Common Ostrich
massaicus

♂

♂

Somali Ostrich

GIANT-PETRELS
Large heavy-bodied petrels, which are virtually the size of a small albatross. Flight is stiff-winged, only gliding over short distances. The two species are hard to identify from each other at sea, with all dark immatures gradually becoming white on the face: identification dependent on colour of bill tip. Although giant petrels have been seen in our area, the species has not been determined. Either could occur as vagrants from the southern oceans.

Southern Giant-Petrel *Macronectes giganteus* 98cm, 38": wingspan c 200cm, 78"
Has two distinct colour morphs. Ads of the more common dark morph are grey-brown with a whitish face; imms are all dark. At all ages they can by identified by a *heavy, pale horn bill with a greenish tip*. The rare white morph (not known in Northern Giant-Petrel) is all white with random small black spots: it has not been reported from our area. **HH** possibly occurs as a vagrant along the EA coast. **Vo** silent, unless squabbling over food.

Northern Giant-Petrel *Macronectes halli* 94cm, 37": wingspan c 200cm, 78"
Extremely similar to dark morph Southern Giant-Petrel at all ages. At close range birds show a *heavy, pale horn bill with a dark reddish-brown tip*. No white morph occurs. **HH** possibly occurs as a vagrant along the EA coast. **Vo** silent, unless squabbling over food.

ALBATROSSES
Spectacular seabirds from the southern oceans, with long narrow wings, short tails, and legendary gliding flight. Width of black underwing margins key to identification, but also note head and bill colour. Sexes alike, but immatures have greyer heads and bills.

Shy Albatross *Diomedea cauta* 98cm, 38": wingspan c 244cm, 96"

Ad shows a *narrow black margin to white underwing and a black thumb-print where the leading edge of the wing joins the body*. At close range shows a dark eyebrow, pale grey cheeks, and a *yellowish-grey bill with a yellow tip*. Imm has a grey head and grey bill with a black tip: underwing pattern same as ad. **HH** vagrant off the EA coast, but may be annual. **Vo** silent when not breeding, at times gives a low nasal *squark*.

Black-browed Albatross *Diomedea melanophris* 95cm, 37": wingspan c 224cm, 88"

Slightly smaller than Shy Albatross, ad has *wide black margins on the underwing*. *Dark eyebrow and yellow bill with reddish tip* are only visible at close range. Imm has variable grey head and sides to neck and an all dark underwing which whitens centrally with age. **HH** vagrant to coastal waters. **Vo** calls when squabbling over food, a goose-like honking laugh.

PRIONS
Delicate blue-grey seabirds from the southern oceans, with a black line forming an 'M' pattern across wings and back. Buoyant flight, with fast wing beats and short glides. Hard to separate but face, upperpart and tail pattern help. Sexes alike, immatures similar to adults.

Antarctic Prion *Pachyptila desolata* 30cm, 12": wingspan 61cm, 24"

Blue-grey above with a *well marked quite broad 'M' pattern and a fairly broad black tip to the tail*. At close range shows white supercilium and a dark line through the eye. White below *with dusky grey patches on sides of breast*. **HH** vagrant to EA, occasional sightings at sea appear to be this species, also known from beach-cast birds: two specimens at Watamu, Ke, Aug 1988. **Vo** silent at sea.

Slender-billed Prion *Pachyptila belcheri* 26cm, 10": wingspan 56cm, 22"

Very similar to Antarctic Prion, but *paler with a less distinct 'M' across the back and wings and slightly less black on the tail tip*. At close range shows a larger white supercilium and lores giving a white-faced look, smudges at sides of breast are smaller, and bill thinner. **HH** vagrant: one found dead at Watamu, Ke, Aug 1984. **Vo** silent at sea.

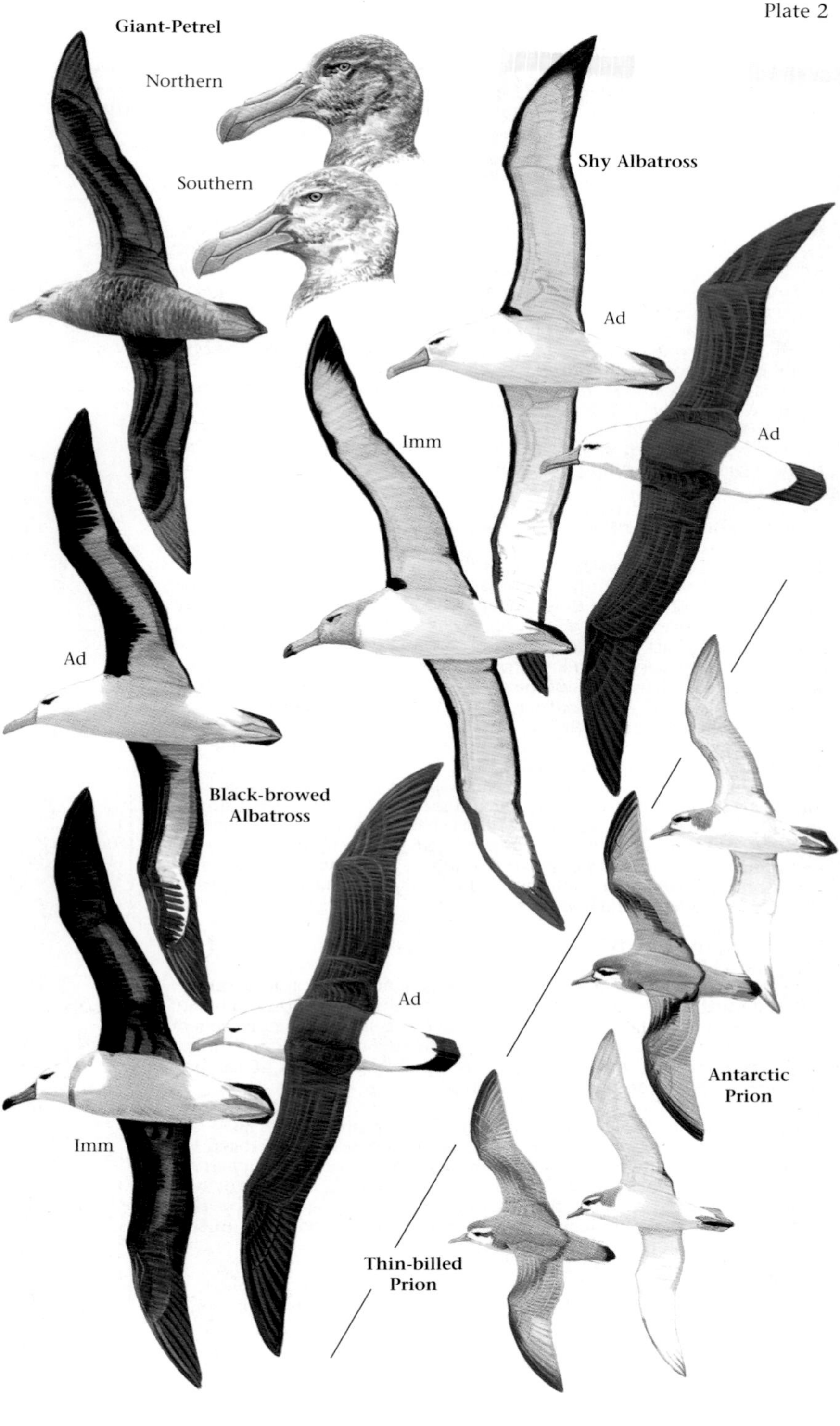

Giant-Petrel

Northern

Southern

Shy Albatross

Ad

Imm

Ad

Ad

Black-browed
Albatross

Ad

Antarctic
Prion

Imm

Thin-billed
Prion

Plate 2

SHEARWATERS & PETRELS

A varied group of blackish or black and white seabirds. At close range most are easily identified, but can be difficult at distance, and can also be confused with noddies (plate 80). With experience, some can be identified by flight characteristics. Sexes and immature plumage alike in all species.

Audubon's Shearwater *Puffinus lherminieri* 30cm, 12": wingspan 69cm, 27"

Small rather thickset shearwater which is *blackish-brown above and white below*. The races (perhaps species?) involved are unclear, but race *bailloni* certainly occurs. It has a dark cap stopping just below eye level, *extensive white in the underwing and a white vent*. Race *persicus* (**Persian Shearwater**) is *dark brown above, narrowly dark brown along the sides of breast and flanks*, while the white on the underwing is limited to a *narrower central band, and the vent is dark*. Both races have rapid fluttering flight, interspersed by short glides. Feeding birds may rest on the sea surface with slightly raised wings, and then dive and swim underwater. Another taxon described in 1995 as *atrodorsalis* (**Mascarene Shearwater**) is now believed to be the imm plumage of *bailloni*. It is blackish above and white below including the vent. **HH** solitary birds or small flocks are uncommon but regular. They occur offshore in most months in Ke, but are vagrants to Tz. One exceptional record was at Limuru, Ke, 550km inland, in Oct 1963. **Vo** silent at sea.

Wedge-tailed Shearwater *Puffinus pacificus* 46cm, 18": wingspan 102cm, 40"

Fairly large *all dark brown* shearwater with rather broad secondaries, and a wedge-shaped tail (which looks long and pointed at sea). Bill is all dark grey; legs are pale but hard to see. Wings are well-bowed and held forward and slightly above the body. Flaps up slowly (but not usually very high) and then glides back towards water, speeding up as wind strengthens, and often progressing forward in low arcs, before rising on the wind and gliding down again. **HH** singles and small groups are very uncommon visitors to Ke coastal waters, perhaps from the Seychelles, and most records are from Aug–Feb. **Vo** silent at sea.

Jouanin's Petrel *Bulweria fallax* 31cm, 12": wingspan 82cm, 32"

Slender all dark petrel with narrow wings and a long wedge-shaped tail. Significantly smaller than Wedge-tailed Shearwater with a *shorter heavy-looking bill*, and (in worn individuals) a pale bar on the upperwing coverts. Also has a very different flight, sweeping over the sea in a series of wide arcs, climbing perhaps 15m above the waves, wings held forward and slightly bowed. **HH** vagrant to coastal Ke from the NW Indian Ocean, with three Dec records. **Vo** silent at sea.

White-chinned Petrel *Procellaria aequinoctialis* 58cm, 23": wingspan 147cm, 58"

Very large *broad-winged, wedge-tailed, blackish-brown petrel, with a creamy bill*, and usually a white chin (hard to see at distance). Large size and broad wings impart powerful feel, with slow steady wheeling flight interspersed with long glides; if windy may glide high. **HH** vagrant to coastal Ke from the southern oceans, with one record in Sep 1990. **Vo** silent at sea, but squabbles noisily over food.

Pintado Petrel *Daption capense* 40cm, 16": wingspan 92cm, 36"

Uniquely marked *black and white petrel*. Black upperparts are broken by white patches in the wings, and by the chequered back and uppertail. Below, white with black wing margins and tail band. Flight is distinctive, interspersing rapid shallow flaps with longer stiff-winged glides. **HH** vagrant to coastal Ke from the southern oceans, with one record in Sep 1974. **Vo** silent unless feeding.

Plate 3

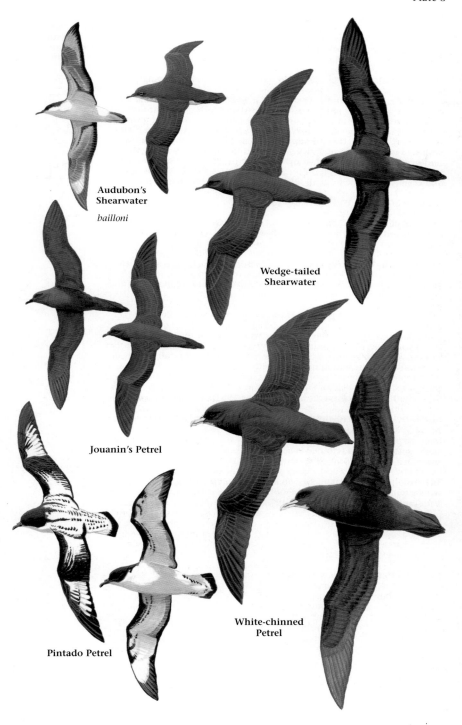

Audubon's
Shearwater

bailloni

Wedge-tailed
Shearwater

Jouanin's Petrel

White-chinned
Petrel

Pintado Petrel

STORM-PETRELS

Diminutive seabirds with characteristic flight patterns. Small size and usually a white rump means little confusion with other groups, but separating storm-petrels as species can be difficult. Note should be taken of flight and feeding patterns, as well as distribution of white in the plumage, shape and length of wing, tail and legs. Sexes alike: immatures similar to adults.

Wilson's Storm-petrel *Oceanites oceanicus* 18cm, 7":
wingspan 41cm, 16"

Smallest storm-petrel in the region, with a *square cut or slightly rounded tail beyond which the feet just protrude*. Upperwing shows paler band across coverts and an *extensive white rump crescent wraps round on to the lower flanks. Legs are long and foot-webbing is yellow* (but rarely visible). Rather weak flight is distinct, being dipping and swallow-like, with rapid wing beats and occasional short glides; sometimes halts to feed, pattering the sea surface with long legs. **HH** annual visitors in small numbers from the southern oceans, occurring off the Ke coast from Apr–Dec, lack of records from Tz probably due to small number of observers. **Vo** silent at sea.

Leach's Storm-petrel *Oceanodroma leucorhoa* 23cm, 9": wingspan 47cm, 19"

Larger than Wilson's Storm-petrel with longer more pointed wings and a *forked tail* (only seen when spread), *white rump* with a greyish centre (rarely visible). *Upperwing shows more distinct pale band on the secondary coverts. Dark legs and feet do not protrude beyond tail tip in flight*. Stronger and more buoyant flight than Wilson's, with deeper wing beats, moves erratically with regular changes of direction and unexpected dancing jerky movements. **HH** vagrant to Ke waters from the Atlantic (three sight records and one beached corpse) from Oct–Apr. **Vo** silent at sea.

Matsudaira's Storm-petrel *Oceanodroma matsudairae* 26cm, 10": wingspan 56cm, 22"

Only all dark storm-petrel in the region, wings show a distinct pale band across the upperwing-coverts and at very close range *white shafts to the bases of the outer primaries*. Also has a deeply forked tail (but often difficult to see). Flight generally rather slow, with flaps and short glides giving a tired impression, but occasionally makes surprise dashes, twists and turns. Dips to sea surface to feed, raising wings in a 'V'. **HH** vagrant to Ke from the western Pacific (two records, Jul and Aug 1981). **Vo** silent at sea.

Black-bellied Storm-petrel *Fregetta tropica* 20cm, 8": wingspan 46cm, 18"

Distinctive if seen well, with an *all black head* and upperparts, except for a white rump; *breast to belly and underwings striking white, the belly bisected by a narrow black line* (sometimes surprisingly hard to see). In flight, looks heavy-bodied, swerves and zigzags low over the ocean, may splash breast first into the water, breaking free on long legs and pattering on the surface. **HH** vagrant to Ke waters from the southern oceans (two beach-cast records, both June, 1994 and 1998). **Vo** silent at sea.

Plate 4

Wilson's
Storm-petrel

Leach's
Storm-petrel

Matsudaira's
Storm-petrel

Black-bellied Storm-petrel

BOOBIES & GANNETS

Striking seabirds with long wings, wedge-shaped tails and long sharp bills. Extent of black, brown, and white in the wings and tail aids identification. Transition from immature to adult plumage acquired over 3–4 years. Sexes alike, but females are slightly larger than males. Graceful slow flapping and gliding flight, often high over the sea. Make spectacular vertical or angled plunge dives to capture prey.

Masked Booby   *Sula dactylatra*   c 92cm, 36": wingspan 152cm, 60"

Ad has a white head and body contrasting with *all black flight feathers and a black tail, a yellowish bill, small bare black face patch*, and pale grey legs. No yellow wash on the head. Imm is similar to Brown Booby with a brown head, throat and upperparts, but with a *whitish collar at base of hindneck, and brown at base of neck does not join with brown at leading edge of wings.* With age begins to show *white mottling on back and wing-coverts.* In flight, imm shows *more white in underwing than other boobies.* **HH** most regular in the vicinity of Latham Island, SE of Zanzibar, Tz, where they are known to breed. Elsewhere off the coast of Ke and Tz, they are usually encountered as single birds. **Vo** on breeding grounds birds give a nasal barking.

Brown Booby   *Sula leucogaster*   c 74cm, 29": wingspan 142cm, 56"

Ad has the *upperparts, neck and throat dark chocolate-brown, clearly cut off across upper breast, and remainder of underparts* pale yellowish. Separated from similar imm Masked Booby by *lack of a white collar on hindneck*, and less clearly defined white on underwing. Imm similar to ad, but with dull brown feathering below and a grey bill. Never shows white spotting above like sub-ad Masked. *At all ages brown of lower neck joins with brown at leading edge of wing.* Appears lighter on the wing and smaller and more slender than Masked, with a comparatively longer tail. **HH** singles are rare visitors off the Ke coast from Aug–Feb. Not recorded in Tz waters. **Vo** resting birds maintain an abrupt rather rapid nasal barking.

Red-footed Booby   *Sula sula*   c 74cm, 29": wingspan 142cm, 56"

Graceful booby: ads are highly variable with white, brown and intermediate morphs – in our area, most are white, brown is very rare. Typical white morph ad resembles ad Masked Booby but is smaller, with a narrower black trailing edge to the secondaries, *a white tail and red feet and legs* (hard to see at distance). Crown may have slight yellowish wash: *bill blue-grey.* In flight, from below, wing shows black trailing edge and diagnostic *black carpal patch* contrasting with the white underwing-coverts. Brown morph is entirely dull brown with red feet. Intermediates vary from white head, body and tail with a brown back and wings, to mostly brown with a white belly, rump and tail. All ads have pale blue-grey bills and *red feet.* Imms are largely dull brown with paler brown underparts and all brown underwings, or with poorly defined rather dirty brown underwing-coverts: bill brownish. **HH** vagrant off coastal Ke from Aug–Mar, and one record in Tz. **Vo** silent at sea.

Cape Gannet   *Morus capensis*   c 94cm, 38": wingspan 180cm, 71"

Ad is similar to Masked Booby but with a *narrower black trailing edge to the secondaries*, and at close quarters *a blue-grey bill and yellow wash to the crown and nape.* Imm varies from wholly dark brown with fine white speckles (1st year), gradually gaining white on body and wing-coverts, and attaining ad plumage over 4 years. **HH** singles are rare visitors from South Africa, with several old records off the Tz coast from Jul–Sep, and no Ke records. **Vo** silent at sea.

Plate 5

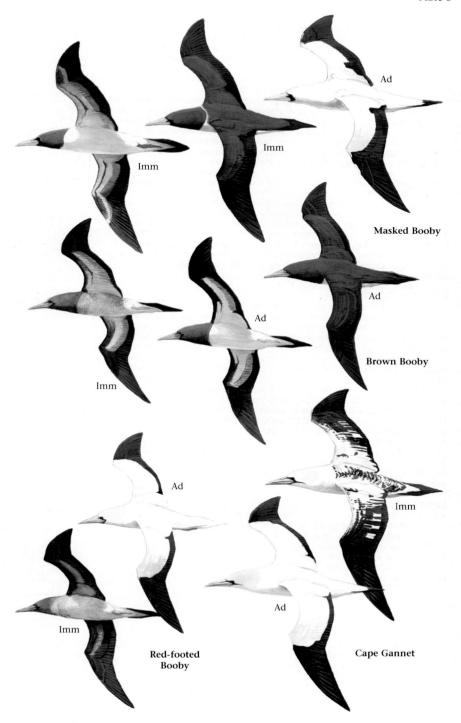

Imm

Imm

Ad

Masked Booby

Imm

Ad

Ad

Brown Booby

Ad

Imm

Imm

Ad

Red-footed Booby

Cape Gannet

TROPICBIRDS

Spectacular graceful largely white seabirds, resembling large terns with very long tail streamers. Often seen 15–30m above the sea, mixing fluttery flight with circling and soaring glides, before hovering and plunge diving to capture food on the sea surface. Sexes are similar, but immatures lack tail streamers. Best identified by amount of black in the wings, bill and tail colour.

White-tailed Tropicbird   *Phaethon lepturus*   81cm, 32": wingspan 94cm, 37"

Ad has a *black diagonal bar across wing-coverts, black bases to the outer primaries, long white tail streamers and a yellow bill*; at close range shows a small black eye mask. Imm has a black patch in the outer primaries, and variable black barring from crown to rump and on the upperwing-coverts. It lacks the long tail streamers and has a black-tipped yellowish bill. **HH** singles are reasonably regular from Sep–Mar, usually far offshore, especially off the SKe coast. Vagrant to Tz (two records). **Vo** silent at sea.

Red-tailed Tropicbird   *Phaethon rubricauda*   81cm, 32": wingspan 100cm, 40"

Large and rather broad-winged *mainly white* tropicbird. At close range shows a *red bill, black smudge through the eye, elongated bright-red central tail streamers*, and blackish shafts to the outer primaries. Red tail can be surprisingly hard to see against bright blue sky. Imm is similar to imm Yellow-billed Tropicbird, but *lacks heavy black patches in primaries*, and has no tail streamers: bill is black, before turning through yellow to red of ad. **HH** this distinctive species is occasionally recorded off the Ke coast by deep sea fishing enthusiasts. **Vo** silent at sea.

FRIGATEBIRDS

Large aerial seabirds with long narrow wings, deeply forked tails, and hooked bills. Soar and glide easily, often chasing other birds to steal food. Males are easily identified, but all other plumages are difficult. Pay attention to pattern of white on underparts and underwing. Immatures distinguishable, but vary considerably through 4–6 years of sub-adult plumages. Females slightly larger than males.

Greater Frigatebird   *Fregata minor*   c 100cm, 39": wingspan c 208cm, 82"

Ad ♂ *looks all black* (but has a scarlet throat sac which can be inflated in courtship display). Ad ♀ has a *grey throat; white on breast does not extend on to the axillaries*. Imm has a tawny or white head, separated from white belly by a blackish breast band. As imm ages, all white is lost in ♂, and breast band becomes mottled black and white, with less white on belly in ♀. In flight, *white of underparts never extends onto axillaries* as in Lesser Frigatebird (but can be hard to judge at distance). **HH** regular sightings of single frigatebirds, mainly from Aug–Dec, are usually this species, but are often far offshore (and some are imms hard to identify with certainty). **Vo** silent at sea.

Lesser Frigatebird   *Fregata ariel*   c 80cm, 32": wingspan c 192cm, 76"

Ad ♂ is entirely black *with two small white patches extending from flanks to the axillaries* — white armpits! Ad ♀ has a *black throat, extensive white on the breast extends as a collar on to the neck and axillaries*. Imm has a russet or whitish head, white breast with or without a dark breast band, and *white axillaries*. The axillaries are an important distinguishing feature in all ages, but can be hard to observe accurately at sea or distance. **HH** extreme vagrant; one Watamu, Ke, in Jan 1980, and two Dar es Salaam, Tz, Oct 1974 and May 1982. **Vo** silent at sea.

Plate 6

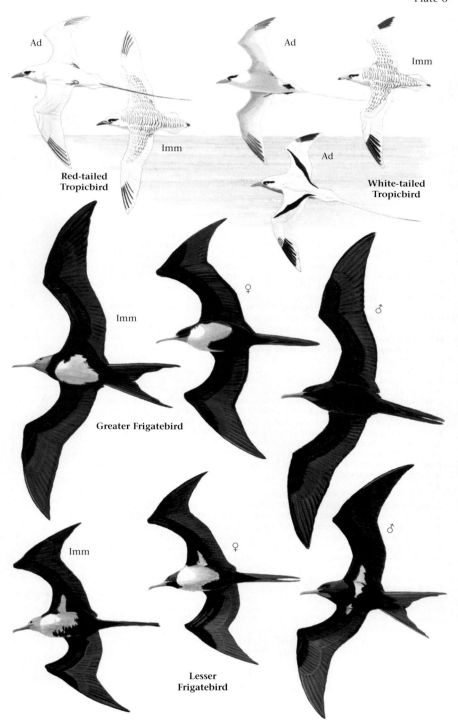

Red-tailed
Tropicbird

White-tailed
Tropicbird

Greater Frigatebird

Lesser
Frigatebird

PELICANS
Well-known, distinctive bulky birds easily identified both at rest and in flight. Separated from each other by size, colour and behaviour. Soar and glide easily, often in large skeins, and regularly circle at height. Fishing technique is unique, gracefully plunging their bills into the water to catch prey.

Great White Pelican   *Pelecanus onocrotalus*   c 178m, 70"
[Eastern White Pelican]
Ad is a *massive black and white pelican with a yellow bill pouch.* Br ad has pinkish hue and a short ragged crest: ♂ has purplish facial skin, ♀ orange-yellow. Bill yellow with a pink tip and both sexes gain an orange knob where bill joins forehead. Duller non-br ad has a greyish bill. Imm grey-brown with dull bare parts. Juv much darker and browner. In flight, shows extensive *black flight feathers contrasting with white coverts above and below.* HH singles to large flocks are widespread on a wide range of fresh, alkaline and coastal salt waters, with concentrations on the Great Rift Valley lakes. Common and gregarious, often fishing together in large flocks. Vo silent, but on breeding grounds gives a continuous cacophony of low growling.

Pink-backed Pelican   *Pelecanus rufescens*   c 146cm, 56"
Smaller and duller than Great White Pelican with an *overall grey appearance and usually a pink bill pouch.* Small pointed crest gives head a peaked look. Br ad develops yellow pouch and brighter pink and yellow facial skin. Imm like dull ad with a grey-brown head and back and paler below. *In flight, wings are mostly grey with darker flight feathers, but never strongly contrasting black and white as in Great White.* Pink back can be visible in flight, but variable and may be absent. HH singles, pairs and small flocks are widespread and common on a range of fresh, alkaline and coastal waters. Much more solitary than Great White and exploits smaller lakes and ponds. Vo silent, but in tree-tops colonies maintain a constant guttural croaking.

GREBES
Low slung aquatic diving birds with sharp bills and distinct silhouettes. Virtually never seen away from water. Sexes alike.

Little Grebe   *Tachybaptus ruficollis*   28cm, 11"
[Dabchick]
Small buoyant short-necked grebe with a short bill, rounded head, and rather square tail. Br ad has *chestnut sides to the face and neck, and a swollen creamy gape spot.* Non-br ad has face and neck duller buffy-brown and a smaller gape. Juv has grey white face and throat and may show some striping on the neck. HH pairs, family groups and large concentrations are widespread and common on wide range of fresh and alkaline water from sea-level to 3000m. Vo call is a loud and carrying giggling bray. Juvs maintain a persistent piping.

Great Crested Grebe   *Podiceps cristatus*   56cm, 22"
Large, long-necked slender grebe. Br ad has a *black crest and reddish and black ruff around face.* Non-br birds are similar, but the crest and ruff are smaller and paler. Juv has black and white striping on the head and neck. HH singles and pairs, less often groups, are scarce and possibly declining on higher alkaline and freshwater lakes from 1500-3000m. Vo breeding birds give a goose-like descending growl and a nasal bugling.

Black-necked Grebe   *Podiceps nigricollis*   33cm, 13"
Larger than Little Grebe, with a rather bigger head and slightly upturned bill. Br ad is dark, with *golden tufts behind red eyes* and mottled rufous flanks. Non-br birds lose tufts and are much duller. Imm like non-br ad, but head tinged brown and buff. HH rather local above 1500m on the higher Great Rift Valley lakes in Ke and NTz, but may gather in large non-br flocks on larger lower soda lakes. Vo usually silent, but breeding birds give loud repeated whistles.

Plate 7

Ad

Imm

Ad

Great White Pelican

Imm

Ad

br

Pink-backed Pelican

non-br

Juv

br

Little Grebe

Imm

br

Juv

Great Crested Grebe

br

Black-necked Grebe

CORMORANTS
Black or black and white waterbirds with slightly hooked bills. Easily identified by size and plumage. Sexes similar, but male slightly larger than female. Often stand to dry their wings after swimming and diving.

Great Cormorant   *Phalacrocorax carbo*   c 100cm, 40"
[White-breasted Cormorant]

Br ad is glossed dark green-black with a white throat and neck and white thigh patches (majority), white chin (some western birds), or all black (rarely). Non-br duller black with no flank patches. Imm is dark brown above with off-white underparts. Appears long-necked, short-tailed and heavy in flight. **HH** singles to large flocks are common on larger freshwater and alkaline lakes in the Great Rift Valley, preferring more open shores, but disperse in small numbers elsewhere including the coast. **Vo** silent away from nesting colonies where birds maintain a low reverberant growling.

Long-tailed Cormorant   *Phalacrocorax africanus*   c 53cm, 21"
[Reed Cormorant]

Much smaller than Great Cormorant *with a shorter neck (and bill) and proportionately longer tail*. Br ads are black (glossed green) with a short crest, and silvery black-edged wing-coverts and scapulars giving wing a scaly appearance. Non-br ad lacks the crest and is dull brown-black with a white chin, dirty white throat and dull off-white underparts. Imm similar to non-br ad, but duller brown above, and whiter below. **HH** singles, small groups and flocks are common on a wider range of waters than Great Cormorant, often dispersing to temporary floods, and preferring waterside vegetation and trees for perches. **Vo** breeding birds give a strange, variable high musical barking.

DARTER
Darters are similar to cormorants, but are more slender and smaller-headed, and spear fish with their dagger-like bills. They are often called snakebirds on account of swimming with just their slender necks visible above the water.

African Darter   *Anhinga rufa*   79cm, 31"

A large cormorant-like bird with a *long thin neck, pointed bill* and large tail. Ad ♂ has a dark rufous foreneck and a thin white line from below the eye down sides of neck. Otherwise blackish above with fine white streaks on the wing-coverts and elongated scapulars. Ad ♀ is browner above with a less distinct neck stripe. Imm is much paler brown, lacks neck line, and is whitish-buff below. *Fly and often soar showing distinctive cross-like silhouette.* **HH** single birds, pairs and less often groups are rather shy on a wide range of still or slow moving fresh, alkaline and coastal waters, usually well-fringed with vegetation. **Vo** calls a series of staccato gradually descending nasal barks.

FINFOOT
Superficially like cormorants and darter, but is reclusive and has a bright red bill. Swims low, moving head back and forth, and may partially submerge and slip quietly into dense cover if detected.

African Finfoot   *Podica senegalensis*   66cm, 26"

Large blackish and brown waterbird, with *bright red bill and legs*. ♂ has a blacker head and brighter bill than ♀, with an obvious thin white line from eye down side of neck, and a more conspicuous white spangled back. ♀ duller with browner head, whitish eye-ring and throat. Imm like ♀, but duller and less spotted. **HH** singles and pairs are uncommon, secretive and may be overlooked on permanent rivers, streams and pools with overhanging vegetation. **Vo** rarely heard call is a series of sharp cracks, similar to African Darter but sharper.

Plate 8

Imm

non-br

Imm

Great Cormorant

br

br

Long-tailed Cormorant

Imm

African Darter

br

Imm

African Finfoot

♂

♂

Imm

♀

BITTERNS

Short-legged herons with comparatively thick necks which are often held upright in a freeze position. If seen well identification should not be difficult.

Little Bittern *Ixobrychus minutus* 38cm, 15″

A small distinctive bittern with a conspicuous *cream upperwing patch*. Two fairly similar races occur: ad ♂ *payesii* has a rich chestnut face and neck, while the slightly larger nominate has the face and neck buffy. In both races, ad ♀ is browner above with some streaking below. Imms like ♀♀, but more heavily streaked below. *All reveal pale upperwing-coverts in flight.* **HH** singles and small groups can be locally common at permanent or seasonal water where good vegetation cover occurs, including on the coast. Local *payesii* breeds occasionally inland, while nominate birds are visitors from the Palearctic from Oct–May. **Vo** calls a short *rrah* when flushed and br ♂ gives low long barks at about two second intervals.

Dwarf Bittern *Ixobrychus sturmii* 30cm, 12″

A small dark slate-grey bittern, *strikingly striped black on buff-white below, with bright orange-yellow legs*. Sexes alike. Imm is darker with a tawny-fringed back and wings, and warm buff below with pale legs. **HH** singles and small groups are widespread but uncommon in well-vegetated permanent and seasonal waters, including tiny pools to which they may disperse after rains. Those occurring in Apr–Nov may be intra-African migrants from the south, but their movements are poorly known. **Vo** br ♂ gives a rhythmical repeated *kwark-a-kwark kwark kwark kwark*, the last three notes being louder.

Great Bittern *Botaurus stellaris* 75cm, 30″
[Bittern]

Well-camouflaged large thick-necked bittern streaked throughout with brown and buff; cap and well-marked moustachial stripes blackish-brown. Sexes alike, imm less boldly marked than ad with a browner crown. **HH** extremely scarce: southern race *capensis* has been recorded in permanent swamps and marshes of the Lake Rukwa area in SWTz. Sight records of nominate Palearctic birds require confirmation. **Vo** breeding birds call a far-carrying deep foghorn-like boom *mm-oom*.

NIGHT-HERONS

Big-headed, hunched, stocky crepuscular or nocturnal herons (hence name). Flight silhouette is stump-necked and wide-winged. Both roost during the day, often in trees close to water.

Black-crowned Night-Heron *Nycticorax nycticorax* 61cm, 24″

Ad has a black crown and back contrasting with dove-grey wings, a whitish face and underparts. Imm is brown and buff with extensive white spots on the back and wing-coverts, and well-streaked underparts. **HH** small and sometimes large groups are widespread and may be locally common on permanent water and rivers, generally with fringing vegetation for roosting. Some birds probably being of Palearctic origin. **Vo** distinct and far-carrying *kwuk* or *kwark* barked when disturbed and in flight.

White-backed Night-Heron *Gorsachius leuconotos* 56cm, 22″

Slightly smaller than Black-crowned Night-Heron. Ad has a black head with *huge reddish eyes, prominent white eye-rings, pale-yellow lores*, and a rich rufous neck to upper breast. Wings and back are blackish-brown, with a patch of white plumes on the back only easily seen in flight. Imm is very similar to imm Black-crowned, but differs in being smaller with a blackish crown, pale lores, and large red-brown eyes. **HH** singles and pairs are uncommon and secretive residents of secluded rivers and mangrove creeks, where they are probably overlooked. Crepuscular and nocturnal, liking to roost in dense waterside vegetation during the day. **Vo** calls egret-like quick low barks *kruk kruk kruk*, which are quite unlike Black-crowned.

Plate 9

Imm

Ad

**Dwarf
Bittern**

Ad

Imm

**Little
Bittern**
payesii

Ad

Ad

Imm

**Great
Bittern**

**Black-crowned
Night-Heron**

Imm

Ad

**White-backed
Night-Heron**

SMALLER HERONS

Varied group of smaller short-legged herons which, with the exception of the squacco herons, are all easily identified. Sexes alike, immatures generally similar to non-breeding adults.

Cattle Egret *Bubulcus ibis* 56cm, 22"

Br ad is white with a buff-orange wash on the head, back and breast, a short bright yellow bill and lores, and short yellow legs (which flush orange in courtship). Non-br ad is all white, with a paler yellow bill and yellowish-green legs. Imm is similar to non-br ad, but may have darker legs. **HH** classic game-hugging heron: small to large flocks are very common and widespread, often with plains game or domestic stock, preferring damper grasslands and cultivation. Flocks often fly in disorderly lines with rapid direct wing beats. **Vo** breeding and roosting birds maintain a constant, variable and musical barking. Gives a short bark when disturbed.

Common Squacco Heron *Ardeola ralloides* 46cm, 18"

Hunched heron which is *brownish-buff and cryptic at rest, but reveals bright white wings and tail in flight*. Br ad is rather plain buff above and below, with some dark streaking on the head, and a dark-tipped blue bill. Non-br ad is darker brown above (but not so dark as Madagascar Squacco Heron), with brown streaking on the buff underparts, and a pale greenish-yellow base to the bill. Imm is like non-br ad but more heavily streaked below. **HH** singles and small groups are widespread and common on a range of well-vegetated water from coastal mangroves to small highland freshwater pools. **Vo** disturbed birds call a harsh *skwok*, while breeding birds maintain a constant musical barking and growling.

Madagascar Squacco Heron *Ardeola idae* 48cm, 19" ●

[Malagasy Pond-Heron]
Non-br ad is very similar to non-br ad Squacco Heron, but much darker above (lacking the warm buff tones), with broader blacker streaking below (contrasting with a white lower belly), and a slightly heavier bill. Br plumage (rarely seen in EA) is pure white with a black-tipped blue bill and orange-red legs. **HH** singles are fairly regular non-br visitors to coastal and inland waters from May–Oct (less often Apr–Nov). Invariably fly into trees when flushed. **Vo** the call *krrrrk* is more rattling and reverberant than Squacco Heron.

Striated Heron *Butorides striatus* 40cm, 16"

[Green-backed Heron]
Small, short and typically crouching heron: ad is dark grey above with a blue-green sheen, a black crown (erected when alarmed), and greyish below with some rufous streaks, and yellow legs (orange when br). Imm is much browner grey above, with a paler crown, light tips to wing-coverts, broad brown and buff-brown streaks below, and duller legs. Typically make short flights close to water with distinct jerky wing beats. **HH** singles are rather secretive but widespread and common residents of inland and coastal waters. **Vo** flying birds give a loud, high-pitched pinched musical bark, that can be single or given in series where it drops in tone.

Rufous-bellied Heron *Ardeola rufiventris* 46cm, 18"

Ad ♂ is a small rather *thickset charcoal-grey heron* with rufous-chestnut wing patches, belly and tail: bill is yellow with a dark tip, legs yellow. At rest, *rufous-chestnut plumage can be very hard to see, but it is obvious in flight*. Ad ♀ duller grey, with a whitish streak on the chin. Imm is much browner, being dark buff-brown grey above, with some white streaking below. **HH** singles and small flocks are secretive residents of abundant cover in temporary and permanent freshwater swamps at scattered localities. **Vo** usually silent even when flushed, but breeding birds give a rasping *kraak* or *caw*.

Plate 10

Cattle Egret

br

non-br

br

br

non-br

Common Squacco Heron

Imm

Madagascar Squacco Heron

Ad

Imm

br

non-br

Striated Heron

Ad

Ad

Imm

Rufous-bellied Heron

WHITE AND BLACK EGRETS

A confusing group: Little, Dimorphic and Western Reef egrets have light and dark morphs and are hard to identify (and sometimes considered conspecific). Intermediate, Great and Black egrets are more easily identified. Breeding adults have head, back and breast plumes which are lacking in non-breeding birds. Note size and shape of bill, colour of lores, legs and feet (bare parts often flush when breeding but are variable). Also consider habits and range. Sexes alike, immatures resemble non-breeding adults.

Little Egret *Egretta garzetta* 64cm, 25"

Medium-sized, elegant white egret with a *slender black bill, black legs, and bright yellow feet.* Lores are usually blue-grey, but may turn yellowish or orange in br birds. Rare dark morph is all slate-grey with a white chin and throat and best told from dark Dimorphic Egret by black legs and *clear cut yellow feet.* **HH** singles to small groups are common and widespread in fresh and alkaline wetlands throughout the region, including the coast. **Vo** call is rather crow-like, a deep throaty growl *rrraaahhhh.*

Dimorphic Egret *Egretta dimorpha* 64cm, 25"

Very similar to Little Egret, but dark morph is more numerous than white. Dark birds are mostly dark grey with a white chin and throat, and a variable white patch near bend of wing (obvious in flight). *Yellow foot colour often extends a little up front of black legs* (feet more sharply defined in Little). Lores are usually grey, but may be yellow, and turn pinkish in br birds (as do feet). White morph is like Little, but may show some dark streaking. Imm is paler grey, splotchy grey and white, or white. **HH** singles and small groups are mainly confined to the coast where it is locally common. Feeds by actively running on shore and stabbing at prey. **Vo** call is a short low bark *rah,* rather than the long growl of Little Egret (but breeding birds sound similar).

Western Reef-Egret *Egretta gularis* 66cm, 26"

[Western Reef Heron]
Both white and dark morphs differ from Little and Dimorphic egrets in having a *slightly decurved yellowish-brown bill. Yellow foot colour extends half-way up the dark-green legs.* Lores are yellow. Dark morph is very dark grey with a white throat and a variable amount of white in the wing-coverts. Imm is variable grey, grey and white, or all white. **HH** uncommon but regular at Lake Turkana, Ke, rare elsewhere including the Ke coast. **Vo** not reliably reported due to past confusion with Dimorphic.

Black Egret *Egretta ardesiaca* 51cm, 20"

[Black Heron]
Smaller than dark morphs of the other egrets and *entirely plain slaty-black* with a ragged short crest, black bill and black legs with orange-yellow feet. Imm is slightly paler blackish-brown and lacks the head plumes. **HH** singles and small flocks are generally uncommon but widespread preferring marshy lake fringes, but also on open tidal flats. *In unique umbrella feeding action birds throw their wings forward, creating a canopy over the water.* **Vo** breeding birds give a long gargling growl, otherwise usually silent.

Intermediate Egret *Mesophoyx intermedia* 69cm, 27"

[Yellow-billed Egret]
Similar to Great Egret, but smaller, with a *shorter yellow bill and gape line which stops below the eye.* Neck shorter than Great and not so kinked, legs and feet often yellowish, but black in br birds. Lores usually yellow, but green when breeding. **HH** singles and small groups are widespread but never common favouring marshy grassland and lake fringes. **Vo** a quiet egret but disturbed birds sometimes give a series of low crow-like short growls.

Great Egret *Casmerodius albus* 92cm, 36"

[Great White Egret]
Largest white heron, with a long neck (often held kinked), and a *dark gape which extends well behind the eye.* Long dagger-like bill is yellow in non-br and black in br birds, while lores turn from yellow to green. Imm is very similar to ad, but has duller black-tipped yellow bill. **HH** singles and groups are widespread and common in a wide range of wetlands throughout the region. **Vo** in flight, commonly gives a repeated drawn-out wooden descending growl.

Plate 11

Dimorphic Egret

non-br

dark morph br

Little Egret

br

dark morph non-br

Black Egret

Ad

dark morph br

Western Reef-Egret

non-br

Great Egret

br

non-br

br

Intermediate Egret

LARGE HERONS
Classic long-necked, long-legged large herons: widespread in wetlands (but Black-headed Heron is also frequently seen in open grasslands). All are easily identified. Sexes alike. They have loud throaty calls when disturbed, but are otherwise largely silent. Flight is powerful and leisurely, with necks retracted onto shoulders.

Goliath Heron   *Ardea goliath*   152cm, 60"
Massive heron which is grey above with a heavy spear-like bill, a warm chestnut head and hindneck, white foreneck streaked with black, and a dark chestnut-maroon belly. Imm similar to ad, but rather paler grey above with chestnut fringes and paler below with dark streaking: belly washed tawny. In laboured flight, ad shows a uniform grey upperwing, and rich chestnut underwing-coverts that contrast with grey flight feathers. Imm has less well-defined and mottled underwing. **HH** world's largest heron: singles and rarely small groups are widespread, but never common at major lakes, swamps, and larger coastal estuaries. **Vo** disturbed birds give a loud and descending, musical barked series *krrw krowkrowkrowkrowkrow kroww.*

Purple Heron   *Ardea purpurea*   84cm, 33"
Slender, elegant and slim-necked heron, dark blue-grey above, with a yellowish bill, black crown and striking rich chestnut-rufous face and neck with a black stripe on either side, chestnut flanks, and a black belly. Can be confused with Goliath Heron, but is darker, far smaller and paler billed with a two-toned upperwing. Imm is similar, but rather duller and paler grey-brown above with paler brown feather edgings, and lacks the chestnut flanks and black belly. **HH** singles are solitary residents of well-vegetated swamps and lake edges where they tend to feed in cover. Uncommon in the open, although often seen flying to communal roosts in evenings. **Vo** generally silent, flight call is similar to Grey Heron, but sounds more cross and pinched.

Grey Heron   *Ardea cinerea*   100cm, 38"
A predominantly grey, black and white heron: ad is pale grey above with a thick black eye-stripe extending as a wispy plume, a white face and foreneck with black streaks, and is grey-white below. In flight, *underwings appear uniform dark grey.* Imm is darker and plainer than ad, with overall dingy grey plumage: lacks well-defined black eye-stripe of ad, but crown often dark grey. **HH** singles are rather solitary but widespread and reasonably common residents in a wide range of habitats from the coast (including open shores), to soda and freshwater lakes (including temporary water). **Vo** disturbed and flying birds give a loud, sudden nasal *kraahnk*, either singly or in a series.

Black-headed Heron *Ardea melanocephala* 92cm, 36"
Ad similar to Grey Heron, but *black head and hindneck contrast markedly with white throat and foreneck.* Imm is dingy grey above including crown and hindneck, not contrasting strongly with white foreneck as in ad. *In flight, all birds show strong contrast of white underwing-coverts and black flight feathers.* **HH** singles to flocks are widespread and common residents in a wide range of wetlands from coastal lagoons, to lakes and rivers inland. Notable, however, for its preference for drier habitats including cultivation and grassland sites, often far from water. **Vo** breeding birds maintain a constant noise of various barks and snaps. In flight, call is similar to Grey, but lower pitched, shorter and not so nasal.

Plate 12

Goliath Heron

Imm

Ad

Imm

Purple Heron

Ad

Ad

Imm

Imm

Ad

Black-headed Heron

Grey Heron

HAMERKOP

Extraordinary species in monotypic family restricted to Africa. Easily identified from any other bird by unique shape. In rather buoyant flight, may suggest a small eagle. Pairs build several vast tree nests which they often share or lose to species like Grey Kestrel, Verreaux's Eagle-Owl and Egyptian Goose. Often confiding and unafraid of man. Considered magical or birds of ill omen, but only occasionally persecuted. Hamerkop is derived from the Afrikaans name for hammer-head.

Hamerkop *Scopus umbretta* 56cm, 22"

Medium-sized all dull-brown waterbird with a long crest and flattened bill giving a *hammer-headed appearance.* Sexes and imm all similar, but ♂ may be slightly larger. In distinctive buoyant flight appears largely brown with tawny bases to the flight feathers. Can look rather raptor-like when soaring, but long-billed silhouette rules out confusion. **HH** single birds, pairs, and sometimes flocks are common and widespread beside a wide range of waters from tiny temporary roadside pools to the largest Rift Valley lakes. Often nomadic in drier country responding to local rains. **Vo** loud distinctive trilling incorporating dominant *yip pruurr* notes, often with several birds calling together. Also a sharp far-carrying *kyip* in flight.

LARGE MAINLY WHITE STORKS

Mainly white storks with black flight feathers, easily identified by bill colour, habitat and behaviour. White Stork is the classic stork nesting on buildings in Europe, and wintering in grasslands throughout sub-Saharan Africa. Yellow-billed Stork is a wetland bird, resident in Africa, but wanders far from breeding grounds.

White Stork *Ciconia ciconia* 122cm, 48"

Large white stork with black flight feathers, a *white tail, red bill and red legs* (which are often splattered with droppings and may appear partially white). A small black line through the dark eye is visible at close range. Sexes are alike. Imm has darker-tipped red bill, duller legs and brownish flight feathers. Some birds are tinged greyish. Flying birds appear white with long black and white wings and a *white tail.* Flocks regularly soar on thermals. **HH** singles to gatherings of many thousands are widespread and common winter visitors and passage migrants, preferring moist grasslands usually above 1600m. Large passages occur east and west of Lake Victoria (especially northward movements from Feb–May). They are less common in EKe and ETz, but are also widely nomadic in response to the rains, burning and at outbreaks of army worms and locusts. Often associate with other species, like Abdim's Storks. **Vo** usually silent on wintering grounds, except for occasional bill clattering.

Yellow-billed Stork *Mycteria ibis* 108cm, 42"

Large white stork with black flight feathers and a *black tail, red face, slightly decurved yellow bill,* and pinkish legs. Ad has pink blush to back and wing-coverts which is brighter in br birds. Neck often stained brown from muddy water. Imm is dull brown, with darker flight feathers, a dirty brownish-yellow bill, and matt-brown legs. In flight, appears white with black flight feathers, and a *black tail.* They also regularly thermal. **HH** single birds or groups are widespread and common on larger and permanent fresh and alkaline water throughout the region. Also visit temporary waters, but rarely stay long. Feed on fish by standing or walking slowly in water, bills open and partially submerged. **Vo** breeding birds give squarks and squeals, and also clatter bills.

Plate 13

Hamerkop

Ad

Imm

White Stork

Yellow-billed
Stork

br

non-br

Imm

LARGE MAINLY BLACK STORKS
Similar black storks are easily identified at close range, but for distant birds note colour of neck, back and belly. Sexes alike or virtually so.

Abdim's Stork   *Ciconia abdimii*   81cm, 32"

Medium-sized black stork glossed purple-green, with lower-back to rump and lower breast to vent white. Rather *small greenish-grey bill, with powder-blue facial skin, red lores and eye-ring,* and greenish-grey legs (with a reddish knee joint). All bare parts brighten when breeding. Sexes alike, though ♀ slightly smaller. Imm is similar but blackish-brown, lacking gloss, with a reddish bill and rather darker legs. In flight, appears quite small and short-winged, and is mainly black but white belly extends as wedge onto the underwing, and *shows a white rump from above.* **HH** nomadic and gregarious with tens of thousands following recent rains, burns and insect emergences. Prefers open grasslands, but visits a wide range of habitats including agricultural lands in search of food gluts. Leaves breeding grounds in the northern tropics to be present in EA from Oct to May (moving south Oct–Nov and north from Mar–May). **Vo** usually silent in region.

Black Stork   *Ciconia nigra*   102cm, 40"

Large black stork glossed with purple-green with just lower breast to vent white: *long bill, facial skin, eye-ring, and legs all bright red.* Sexes alike, but ♀ slightly smaller. Imm duller brown-black with yellow-green bill tipped orange and greenish legs. In flight, has white belly extending into underwing (like Abdim's Stork), but is *entirely black above including the rump.* **HH** singles, pairs and rarely small groups are rather infrequent uncommon Palearctic migrants from Oct–Apr, to habitats fringing lakes and pools, and are rarely seen far from freshwater. Much more solitary than other migrant storks. Birds in SWTz may be from southern Africa. **Vo** mainly silent in region, but occasionally gives hisses and bill clattering.

Woolly-necked Stork   *Ciconia episcopus*   86cm, 34"

A distinctive black stork with a glossy purple-blue and green sheen, *striking white woolly neck and head,* a blue-black crown, red-eyes, a black bill with a reddish tip, and grey-black legs. Sexes alike. Imm is duller above, with a slightly blacker crown, dark eyes and dull pinkish legs. In flight, *white head and neck* are obvious, but also shows long white undertail-coverts which hide black tail from below. **HH** singly or in pairs on coastal waters, including lagoons, the open shore and salt-works, but wanders widely and may occur throughout the region in marshes, swampy hollows and grasslands. **Vo** breeding birds maintain a rhythmical growling and bill clattering, otherwise silent.

African Open-billed Stork   *Anastomus lamelligerus*   81cm, 32"
[Open-billed Stork]

Medium-sized shaggy all-black stork with a purple-green gloss and diagnostic *greyish open-bill* (gap near tip visible at close quarters). Sexes are alike. Imm is duller, with some white speckling on the hindneck, and a straighter shorter bill. In flight, all black from above and below with a strange pterodactyl-like silhouette. **HH** singles to large groups are widespread and locally common in wetlands below 1500m including freshwater swamps and lakes, inundated grasslands and coastal saltwater creeks and lagoons. Specialised diet of snails and bivalves. **Vo** breeding birds call a loud braying, otherwise usually silent.

Plate 14

Ad

Imm

Black Stork

Imm

**Abdim's
Stork**

Ad

Imm

Imm

Ad

African Open-billed Stork

Ad

Woolly-necked Stork

GIANT STORKS
Highly distinctive and characterful storks that should not be confused with any other species. Saddle-billed Stork is a solitary bird of large swamps and river valleys, while Marabou is a fearless, widespread, successful, flocking scavenger.

Saddle-billed Stork *Ephippiorhynchus senegalensis* 142cm, 57"

Very large black and white stork with a very long tri-coloured bill (red and black with a yellow saddle and two small pendulous yellow or red wattles) and very long grey legs with pink knees and feet. ♂ has dark eyes, while slightly smaller ♀ has yellow eyes. Imm is largely dingy grey-brown with some white patches on the back, a blackish bill which lacks the saddle, and duller legs. **HH** singles and pairs are uncommon to locally common in suitable permanent freshwater swamps and wetlands, sometimes in the midst of dry country, and usually below 1500m but may occur as high as 3000m. Hunts with a slow walk through flooded vegetation where it captures fish and frogs, which are often tossed in the air before swallowing. **Vo** usually silent, but breeding birds give descending squealing wheezes.

Marabou Stork *Leptoptilos crumeniferus* 152cm, 60"

Huge stork with grey back and wings and white underparts. Naked head and neck pink or reddish showing scabby black spots at close range, and a downy white neck ruff. Birds have two inflatable air sacs: a bright red one at base of hindneck, and a pinkish pendulous balloon which is variable in size and hangs below the neck. Bill massive and horn-coloured. Legs dark grey but often appear white as splattered with excrement. Sexes alike, but ♀ is slightly smaller. Br ad has light greyish wings, white-edged wing-coverts, and a fluffier undertail. Non-br ad is darker grey. Imm is duller than ad with brown not grey wings. Massive in flight, soaring on broad wings with neck retracted, but will makes short flights with neck extended. **HH** singles to gatherings of hundreds are common and widespread in a range of habitats from city rubbish dumps to lakeshores and also at predator kills. **Vo** silent away from the nest, but breeding birds give a wide range of bleating, grunting and squealing noises, as well as bill clattering.

SHOEBILL
Extraordinary-looking scarce and atypical stork-like bird (which may be related to the pelicans). Generally considered monotypic in a family confined to Africa. Nowhere common, preferring remote, secluded and extensive permanent swamps. Walks across floating vegetation or stands silently watching for prey. Usually flies slowly and low with neck retracted, but will soar to very great heights, and occasionally wanders.

Shoebill *Balaeniceps rex* 124cm, 48"

Giant stork-like *grey bird with a massive fat hooked bill*. Ad has a slightly erect crest, pale grey eyes, a mottled horn-coloured bill, and grey legs. Sexes alike, but ♀ is slightly smaller. Imm fringed with brown. **HH** singles and pairs are confined to the interior of permanent and undisturbed swamps. While small numbers are widespread in Ug and Rw, the only real EA stronghold is in the remote Moyowosi–Kigozi wetland complex of WTz. It has not been seen in Bu, but there is one record from Ke, a wandering bird recorded from three sites between Sep 1994 and mid-1995. **Vo** breeding birds make a hollow reverberant hammering sound, donkey-like brays and pig-like squeals. Otherwise silent away from the nest.

Plate 15

Saddle-billed Stork

♀

♂

Imm

pouch inflated

Marabou Stork

Imm

Ad

Shoebill

IBISES

Medium-sized to large terrestrial and wetland birds with long decurved bills. Most are dull or dark brown with a green (or purple and green) sheen on the wing, they are best identified by head shape, calls and range. Sacred Ibis is unique among ibises in being black and white. Some have loud diagnostic calls, often given in morning or evening flights to and from their roosts. Sexes similar, immatures mainly dull versions of adults.

Sacred Ibis   *Threskiornis aethiopicus*   82cm, 32"
Largely *white ibis with a bare black head and neck, long black bill* and black legs. Br ad grows black plumes from scapulars and inner secondaries, and bare skin on underwing turns bright red. Imm is similar to ad, but rather dull with some white feathering on the neck. **HH** singles, small groups and larger flocks are widespread and common in many habitats, including cultivated lands, often near fresh or salt-water from sea-level to 3000m. **Vo** breeding birds give high squealing yelps and short barks, otherwise silent away from the nest.

Hadada Ibis   *Bostrychia hagedash*   82cm, 32"
[Hadeda Ibis]
Stocky dark ibis with a *green-purple glossed wing, and short legs*. Bill heavy and down-curved with a red culmen (which may brighten in br ad). Diagnostic buff-white malar stripe is visible at close range. Imm is duller than ad without red in the bill or wing gloss. In flight, appears dark, broad-winged and short-tailed: legs do not project beyond tail. **HH** pairs and small flocks are common and widespread in grasslands, marshy areas, and damp forest edges, as well as gardens and cultivation, mainly in the highlands, but ranging from sea-level to 3000m. **Vo** very, very noisy, most often heard at dawn and dusk, calling a varying bugled and onomatopoeic *haa haa ha-aaa* with the last notes downslurred.

Glossy Ibis   *Plegadis falcinellus*   65cm, 26"
Similar to Hadada Ibis, but far more *slim and elegant with a slender bill and neck and long legs:* always appears dark at distance. Br ad is largely rich dark chestnut with well glossed greenish-purple back, wings and tail (close views reveal two cobalt-blue lines on face). Non-br ad has the head and neck speckled with white-grey. Imm duller brown. In rather rapid flight, *wings look narrow and feet extend well beyond tail.* **HH** singles, pairs and small groups are common and widespread, but often rather skittish, in wetlands of all types including lakes, rivers and coastal lagoons. Many birds probably originate from outside the region, possibly including the Palearctic. **Vo** usually silent, but flying parties commonly utter a nasal quack-like growling *ehhk ehhk ehhk...*

African Green Ibis   *Bostrychia olivacea*   74cm, 29"
[Olive Ibis]
Dark olive-green ibis with a long bushy crest, short only slightly decurved red bill, and dull reddish legs: wings glossed bronze, green and rose. Imm duller than ad with a shorter crest. Usually seen flying at dawn or dusk when appears all dark. **HH** singles, pairs and occasionally small flocks are uncommon, retiring and rarely seen (despite loud calls) in remote forest from 2000–3700m on Mt Kenya and the Aberdares, Ke, and Mt Kilimanjaro, NTz, 160–1100m in East Usambara Mts, NETz and at 700m in Semliki Forest, WUg. **Vo** in flight, calls a loud goose-like nasal downslurred bugling *ahhnk ahnk...*

Spot-breasted Ibis   *Bostrychia rara*   60cm, 24"
Smaller than Olive Ibis, with a similar crested head and only slightly decurved red bill. Spotted neck and underparts are hard to see in the field. Imm duller than ad. **HH** pairs are dense forest dwellers and in our area only known from 700m in Semliki Forest, WUg. **Vo** flight call is mainly a rhythmical high-toned double bugling intermingled with single notes *a-a-hahn a-hahn a-hahn a-hahn...* second note of each pair is a couple of tones higher.

Plate 16

Imm

Ad

Sacred Ibis

Ad

Imm

Hadada Ibis

br

Imm

Glossy Ibis

Ad

African Green Ibis

Ad

Spot-breasted Ibis

SPOONBILLS

Largely white birds with unique spatulate spoon-like bills. Reasonably easily told apart by bill, leg and bare part colour. Confusion with other species unlikely. Elegant feeders which walk in the shallows and scythe the water with their bills.

African Spoonbill *Platalea alba* 91cm, 36"

Ad is all white with an *extensive bare red face, a blue-grey pink-edged bill, pale blue eyes, and bright pink-red legs*. Sexes similar. Imm lacks red face, has a dusky yellow bill, dark eyes, dark-tipped primaries, and blackish legs and feet. In flight, ad shows all-white plumage, a spoon-shaped bill and long red legs: imm has dark tips to the primaries. **HH** singles, pairs and small groups are common in a wide range of freshwater and alkaline wetlands, including coastal lagoons from sea-level to 3000m. **Vo** noisy at nest, giving a crane-like bugling, which is similar but softer when feeding or resting.

Eurasian Spoonbill *Platalea leucorodia* 89cm, 35"

Very similar to African Spoonbill, but ad has a *black bill with a yellow spot near the tip, black legs* (not red), a very small area of yellow facial skin (not red), and feathering between red eyes (not bare skin). Br ad (rare in EA) has a yellowish crest and wash to centre of breast. Sexes alike. Imm similar to ad, but has black-tipped wings, a dull pinkish-grey bill, and dark legs. **HH** very rare visitor to wetland areas in Ke and Ug. **Vo** silent in region.

FLAMINGOS

Tall pink wading birds which mass in thousands (even millions) on the Great Rift Valley lakes: easily identified by size, plumage and bill colour. Specialist bills allow food to be filtered from lake water and bottom ooze. Greater Flamingo eats a wide variety of minute aquatic animals, while Lesser Flamingo almost always feed on blue-green algae. Regularly swim and upend, and fly with their necks extended.

Greater Flamingo *Phoenicopterus ruber* 140cm, 55"

Much larger than Lesser Flamingo: *big bent bill is pink with a black tip*. Ad appears largely pale pink or white at distance with a line of bright coral pink in the folded wing. Legs are also bright coral pink. Sexes are similar, but the ♀ is slightly smaller. Imm grey-brown and only attains ad plumage in second year: bill two-toned (pale grey with a black tip). In flight, ad reveals brilliant coral wing-coverts and black flight feathers, contrasting with a paler body. Lesser has a dark almost concolorous bill at all ages. **HH** singles to flocks of thousands are found mainly on muddy fringed alkaline lakes and coastal lagoons, less often on fresh water. Exploits a greater range of habitats than Lesser Flamingo, and benefits more from man-made lakes, dams, and sewage settlement ponds. **Vo** flocks maintain a constant low angry goose-like growling.

Lesser Flamingo *Phoeniconaias minor* 90cm, 36"

Smaller than Greater Flamingo: *with a blackish-red bill appearing all dark at distance*. Wing-coverts blotched bright pink-red and flight feathers black (hidden at rest). Legs red. Sexes alike, but slightly smaller ♀ is often paler (although br plumage brighter in both sexes). Imm is grey-brown turning through white and attaining pink ad plumage after two years: bill uniform blackish-grey. **HH** gregarious often with huge flocks congregating on alkaline lakes in the Great Rift Valley. Regularly makes nomadic local movements, including to and from main breeding grounds at Lake Natron, NTz. Rare elsewhere, including at the coast. Associates freely with Greater Flamingo, but specialist algal diet confines birds to alkaline lakes (where they often feed at night). **Vo** very noisy, constantly making a muffled goose-like babble with occasional high-pitched whistles. At night flying birds keep contact with a soft goose-like honking.

Plate 17

Imm

Eurasian Spoonbill

Imm

Ad

br

African Spoonbill

Greater Flamingo

Imm

Imm

Ad

Ad

Lesser Flamingo

LARGE RESIDENT WATERFOWL

Easily distinguished by size and plumage. Most often seen around or on freshwater, but not restricted to it, and also frequent in marshy grasslands.

Egyptian Goose   *Alopochen aegyptiacus*   ♂ 74cm, 29"

A bulky brown goose with a richer and darker rufous-brown back: *rich brown eye-patches and breast spot* distinctive. Sexes similar, although ♀ is usually slightly smaller. In flight, *shows large white oval wing patches.* Imm is dusky brown, lacking the eye patches and breast spot. **HH** pairs, family groups and flocks are common and widespread beside a wide range of wetlands including fresh, alkaline and coastal waters below 3000m. Swims with a high posture and upends, and also frequently grazes on shore. **Vo** on ground, ♂ gives an agitated nasal rather high-pitched honking, whilst ♀ accompanies him with low muffled growls. In flight, this can be accelerated as the birds become excited.

Spur-winged Goose   *Plectropterus gambensis*   ♂ 100cm, 39"

Ad ♂ is a *massive long-necked goose with a bare warty red face, and iridescent patchy black and white plumage*, which shows green reflections in good light. ♀ is quite similar but smaller and lacks red knob on forecrown. In slow and laboured flight, shows a *long white bar along leading edge of wing.* Imm similar to ♀, but is duller and browner. **HH** pairs, family groups and flocks are widespread beside inland wetlands to 3000m, preferring freshwater, including flooded grasslands. They are local at the coast close to larger rivers. **Vo** ♂ flight call is a repeated variably rapid double wheezy note, almost a hiccup.

Knob-billed Duck   *Sarkidiornis melanotos*   ♂ 76cm, 30"

[Comb Duck]

Ad ♂ is a bulky boldly marked black and white duck with a large knob (or comb) on top of the bill (which is smaller in non-br birds). In good light back shows green and purple iridescence. ♀ is much smaller, lacks knob on bill, and has the head more speckled with black and white than ♂. In flight, all dark wings contrast with whiter underparts. Imm is like ♀ but duller and washed with dingy brown. **HH** pairs and small flocks are common and widespread on freshwater wetlands from sea-level to 3000m, but wanders extensively. **Vo** ♂ quite vocal, either on the ground or more usually in flight, when he gives a soft burry bark.

PYGMY-GOOSE

A misleadingly named very small colourful duck which is reasonably widespread, but rather elusive. Birds often hide in dense floating vegetation.

African Pygmy-goose   *Nettapus auritus*   31cm, 12"

[Pygmy Goose]

Br ♂ easily distinguished from all other ducks by *small size, green and white head, yellow bill, dark green back and mostly chestnut underparts.* Non-br or eclipse ♂, ♀ and imm are more subdued, with grey-brown face smudges, crown and hindneck. In fast and direct flight is the only duck showing combination of white face, secondary patches and belly. **HH** pairs and small groups are widespread but rather local and shy, preferring quiet and well vegetated waters, invariably with an abundance of water-lilies, from sea-level to 2000m (wanders to a wide range of sites). **Vo** a variety of rather irritated whistles and clucks and an occasional explosive *tak.*

Plate 18

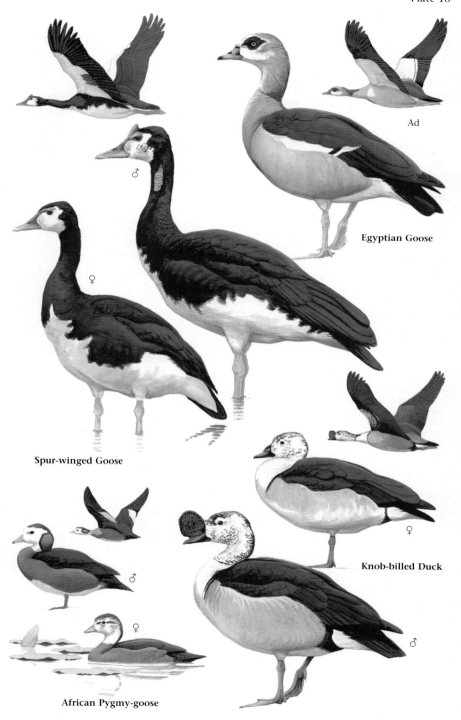

Egyptian Goose

Ad

Spur-winged Goose

♂

♀

Knob-billed Duck

♀

♂

African Pygmy-goose

♂

♀

WHISTLING-DUCKS

Whistling or tree ducks are long-necked, long-legged ducks, giving an about-to-spring-into-the air impression which is distinctive even at distance. Well-named since they frequently attract attention with their loud far-carrying whistling, with lots of birds often calling together. Sexes similar; immatures duller versions of adults.

White-faced Whistling-Duck *Dendrocygna viduata* 48cm, 19"
[White-faced Duck]

A *dark white-faced duck* with a chestnut neck and breast (face is often soiled dirty brown by muddy waters). In flight, appears largely dark (except for white face), with limited body to wing contrast. **HH** gregarious with small to large flocks gathering together beside a wide range of waters throughout the region. Local movements occur, but many birds are resident. **Vo** calls frequently, often the whole flock together, with a whistled *wi wi-wi-yu*, the last three notes descending and slurring into each other.

Fulvous Whistling-Duck *Dendrocygna bicolor* 51cm, 20"
[Fulvous Duck]

A *cinnamon-brown duck with a dark brown back and wings*. Dark line down hindneck and white flank stripes are obvious at close range. In flight, shows conspicuous *buff-white rump crescent* and strong contrast between body and wing. Imm duller and lacks the white flank streaks. **HH** small to large flocks are found in a wide range of wetlands including shallow inundated grasslands, rice fields, and coastal areas, mainly below 1500m. Local movements occur and many birds are non-br visitors from southern Africa. **Vo** call is a repeated well-spaced explosive double whistle *wi-whiu* with the second part higher though descending and ending abruptly.

RESIDENT DUCKS

A mixed group of waterfowl which move about locally, but are mainly considered resident within the region. Three are in distinctive genera: Maccoa Duck is the only stiff-tail, Hartlaub's Duck a large forest species, and White-backed Duck a large-headed species which swims very low in the water. The others are typical ducks, all easily identified if seen well.

Maccoa Duck *Oxyura maccoa* 51cm, 20"

Br ♂ is an attractive *chestnut stifftail with a black head and bright blue bill*. Eclipse ♂, ♀ and imm are duller brown with a *white line below the eye, a broad dark cheek stripe, and a whitish throat*. Silhouette distinctive if tail is cocked. Only rarely flies to escape disturbance, preferring to dive or submerge. **HH** pairs or family groups are rather local mainly on highland and Great Rift Valley lakes. Larger numbers may club together on soda lakes, notably in Arusha NP in NTz. **Vo** generally quiet, but br ♂ gives a low slurred snore that lasts about three seconds, gradually falling then rising again. This is repeated at 5–7 second intervals.

Hartlaub's Duck *Pteronetta hartlaubii* 58cm, 23"

Br ♂ is a striking, rather large dark chestnut duck with a blackish head, pale blue shoulders, and an obvious white patch on the forehead (which varies and may extend to entire crown, even sides of face). Ad ♀ is duller and lacks white on head. Imm duller still and may appear mottled at close range. All birds have a dark grey bill with a pale band near tip. **HH** pairs, less often small flocks, are uncommon on well-vegetated and secluded forest pools and rivers in Semliki Forest, WUg and Nyungwe Forest, SWRw. **Vo** on the ground, agitated birds give a low growled quacking, but in flight, utter a soft whistling intermingled with the quacking.

Plate 19

White-faced Whistling-Duck

Ad

Fulvous Whistling-Duck

Ad

♀

♂

Maccoa Duck

♀

♂

Hartlaub's Duck

Red-billed Teal *Anas erythrorhyncha*   48cm, 19"
Only *red-billed duck with a dark crown and nape* contrasting clearly with pale cheeks and foreneck. Remainder of plumage largely brown above with pale feather edges producing a scaly effect. Sexes alike. Imm similar to ad, but bill rather pinker. In flight, shows striking creamy-white secondaries contrasting with otherwise dark upperwing. **HH** pairs, family parties and large flocks are common and widespread on shallow freshwater lakes, marshes and pools. Less common on alkaline waters, and rare on the coast away from major estuaries. **Vo** ♂ gives a rising, nasal drawn-out *yuuuw*, while ♀ responds with a harsh quacking.

Hottentot Teal *Anas hottentota*   36cm, 14"
Small neat duck with a dark cap and pale cheeks similar to Red-billed Teal, but easily separated by size, *pale blue sides to bill and neck smudge.* ♀ duller with less clear-cut head and neck pattern. Imm even duller than ♀. In flight, dark upperwing shows green speculum and white trailing edge to secondaries (much less white than in Red-billed). **HH** pairs, family parties, and small flocks, are widespread and common on fresh and alkaline waters of all sizes from sea-level to 3000m, but rare at the coast. Prefers areas with fringing vegetation and often dabble close to the water's edge. **Vo** call is similar to Common Moorhen, a nasal series *kekekeke...* given rapidly.

Cape Teal *Anas capensis*   48cm, 19"
[Cape Wigeon]
Elegant *mottled pale grey duck with a pink bill.* Closer views reveal a finely speckled head and more boldly mottled underparts. Sexes similar. Imm duller and less clearly spotted. In flight, shows two white bars on secondaries separated by a broad dark green bar. **HH** pairs, family groups and occasionally flocks are typical of shallower Great Rift Valley soda lakes, and more rarely to nearby freshwater. **Vo** ♂ calls a short whistle followed by a longer upslurred whistle, and also a low growling quack. In flight, utters a strong but burry quack.

White-backed Duck *Thalassornis leuconotus*   41cm, 16"
A large-headed brown duck which swims very low in the water. Close views reveal *vertical white spot between base of bill and eye* contrasting strongly with a dark face and tawny-brown neck: back and flanks tiger-striped rufous-brown and blackish. Sexes alike. Imm duller with less pronounced face spot. In flight, appears dark and short-tailed with a white back (a feature which, despite name, is not visible at rest). Birds prefer to submerge if disturbed and swim away partially hidden. **HH** pairs, family parties (and rarely flocks) are local and unobtrusive on well-vegetated freshwater of all sizes from the coast to 3000m. **Vo** generally silent, but ♂ calls a loud, piercing and explosive double whistle *swit-sweet.*

Plate 20

Red-billed Teal

Ad

♀

♂

Hottentot Teal

Cape Teal

Ad

Ad

White-backed Duck

Yellow-billed Duck   *Anas undulata*   59cm, 23"

A large dark duck with a *bright yellow bill* (visible even over long distances). Closer views reveal a blackish stripe on top of the bill, and mostly pale fringed and scalloped upperparts (except for dark brownish-grey head). Sexes alike. Imm similar, but with broader buff feather edges. In flight, dark upperwing shows green speculum (narrowly edged with black and white). **HH** pairs, family parties or flocks are common on a wide range of wetlands mainly above 1600m, but often wanders (and occasionally occurs at the coast). **Vo** variety of mallard-like quacks, some with a trumpeting quality.

African Black Duck   *Anas sparsa*   56cm, 22"

Large blackish duck with variable bold white spots on the back and rump, and a pale pink and blackish bill. Sexes similar. Imm much duller with limited or no spotting above. In flight, upperwing shows blue-green speculum narrowly bordered with black and white. **HH** singles, pairs and family parties are shy on well-wooded streams and fast flowing rivers (less often ponds), in the highlands up to 4250m, but may wander to lower levels, especially in NETz. **Vo** a harsh, low-pitched, clipped quacking.

PALEARCTIC MIGRANT DUCKS

Large numbers of Palearctic waterfowl winter in the region (mainly end–Oct to early–Apr), notably on the Great Rift Valley and highland lakes. All can be identified reasonably easily on water or in flight, by a combination of plumage and silhouette. Note many migrant male ducks wear a dull eclipse plumage, moulting into this before arriving in East Africa, and remaining in eclipse until at least Dec when they begin to acquire the familiar northern breeding plumage.

Northern Shoveler   *Anas clypeata*   51cm, 20"
[European Shoveler]

Br ♂ is a distinct green-headed, chestnut and white duck with a *long spade-like bill*. ♀ entirely mottled light and dark brown with an orange-sided shoveler-bill. Eclipse ♂ similar to ♀, but darker with a more mottled breast and rufous-toned flanks. Imm similar to ♀ but duller. In flight, ♂ has obvious big-billed rather front-heavy silhouette, and reveals large pale blue shoulder patches, and a wide green speculum with a white front edge. ♀ has paler shoulders. **HH** small to large flocks are very common Palearctic passage migrants and visitors to a wide range of fresh and alkaline lakes mainly from Oct–Apr, with concentrations in Great Rift Valley and highland lakes above 1500m. They are less common elsewhere. **Vo** silent in region.

Northern Pintail   *Anas acuta*   ♂ 66cm, 26"
[Pintail]

Elegant small-billed, slender-necked duck with a pointed tail. Br ♂ has a dark chocolate head, offset by a fine white neck stripe, throat and breast, and very long central tail feathers. ♀ is all mottled browns with a paler plainer head (and a shorter pointed tail). Eclipse ♂ similar to ♀, but has greyer upperwing. Imm like ♀. In flight, shows slender neck and pointed tail: ♂ has a dark green speculum narrowly bordered with rufous and white; ♀ has a brown speculum with a white trailing edge. **HH** flocks are common visitors from Nov–Apr occurring mainly on highland freshwaters in W and CKe above 1400m, but also wandering to a wide range of other wetlands. **Vo** silent in region.

Plate 21

Yellow-billed
Duck

♀

♂

African Black Duck

♂

Northern Shoveler

♀

♀

♂

Northern Pintail

Garganey *Anas querquedula* 41cm, 16"
Small, neat duck: br ♂ has a *broad bright white stripe which curves from above eye to lower nape*, otherwise mainly mottled browns with silver-grey flanks. ♀ is extremely similar to ♀ Common Teal, but has a *slightly longer all grey bill with a more contrasting face pattern* (including a paler loral spot), *and no pale bar below sides of tail*. Eclipse ♂ is like ♀, but retains ad ♂ wing. Imm is similar to ♀. In flight, ♂ reveals *pale grey shoulders* and a green speculum bordered white; while ♀ has a more uniform grey-brown wing and brownish speculum (also edged white). **HH** small groups to large flocks are widespread and common Palearctic visitors from Oct–Apr on pools, lakes and other wetlands, up to 3000m (particularly at higher altitudes, but also near the coast). **Vo** usually silent in EA, but prior to departure ♂ may give a rattling display call, a harsh *hrrrroorrrr*, which sounds like a stick being run rapidly along a fence.

Common Teal *Anas crecca* 38cm, 15"
Br ♂ has a *bottle green (cream-rimmed) eye mask set against a rich chestnut head*, a white line along grey flanks, and a cream-buff undertail. ♀ is similar to ♀ Garganey, but has a *slightly shorter dark bill with an orangey base, a less distinct face pattern, and a short pale bar below sides of tail*. Eclipse ♂ and imm are very like ♀, but slightly darker. Rises easily straight from water into flight, revealing a green speculum with white borders similar to Garganey, but *more uniform brown-grey upperwings* (including the shoulder). **HH** singles and small groups are uncommon winter visitors to shallow and secluded freshwater in the highlands of Ke, with smaller numbers in Ug, and stragglers elsewhere. **Vo** silent in region.

Eurasian Wigeon *Anas penelope* 51cm, 20"
Br ♂ has a rounded *rich chestnut head with a broad buffy-cream forehead*, a neat black-tipped blue-grey bill, and is otherwise grey with a pinkish breast and black vent. ♀ is mottled brown tinged with silver or rufous, with a plainer browner head. Eclipse ♂ is similar to ♀, but has a more rufous tone. Imm is like ♀. In flight, ♂ has a white forewing patch and green speculum edged with black, while ♀ has a duller wing, the speculum edged white: both sexes have white bellies. **HH** singles and small groups are irregular visitors to highland freshwater lakes above 1600m from Nov–Feb, mainly to Ke, and infrequently elsewhere. **Vo** silent in region.

Gadwall *Anas strepera* 56cm, 22"
Br ♂ is a subtle *dusky grey duck*, with a mottled breast, finely vermiculated flanks, and a *black vent and lower rump*. ♀ is much browner, with a dark eyeline, and yellow-orange sides to the bill. Eclipse ♂ is like ♀, but retains ♂ wing pattern. Imm is similar to ♀. In flight, both sexes show a white speculum, with additional black and rufous patches in the ♂. **HH** rare vagrant to freshwater lakes in Ke and NTz. **Vo** silent in region.

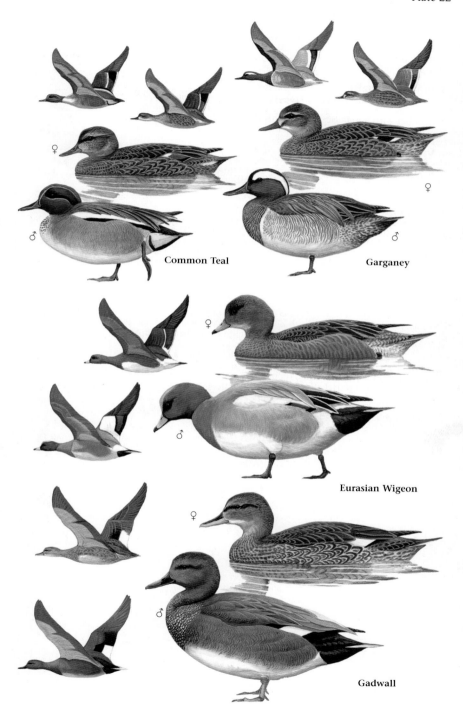

Plate 22

♀

♂ Common Teal

♀

♂ Garganey

♀

♂ Eurasian Wigeon

♀

♂ Gadwall

MIGRANT DIVING DUCKS

A group of diving ducks with longish bills, steep foreheads, and white wing bars. Distinctive breeding males are easily identified, but other plumages require careful observation of face pattern and vent colour. All dive for food, exploiting deeper water than other ducks. Southern Pochard is mainly an intra-African migrant, while the others are uncommon or rare Palearctic visitors.

Southern Pochard *Netta erythrophthalma* 51cm, 20"

Large dark diving duck: ♂ is *blackish-brown, with paler chestnut-brown flanks, red eyes, and a blue-grey bill* (no eclipse plumage). ♀ is more uniform drab brown, but with a *well-defined face pattern* (white patch at base of bill and crescent behind eye) and a white vent (blackish in ♂). Imm is similar to ♀, but with less white on the face. In flight, both sexes show a clear white bar across all flight feathers. **HH** small to large flocks are common on alkaline and freshwater Rift Valley lakes and elsewhere to 3000m. Although small numbers breed, most are visitors from southern Africa, appearing mainly from Oct–Mar. **Vo** usually silent, but br ♂ calls a loud low churring *prrrrr*, and an explosive wheeze.

Ferruginous Duck *Aythya nyroca* 41cm, 16"

Br ♂ often appears *very dark with a white vent*, but at close range shows ferruginous (rust-coloured) head, breast and flanks, and *white eyes*. ♀ is duller and browner than ♂ with dark eyes. Eclipse ♂ is like ♀ but pale-eyed. Imm is like ♀, but even duller brown. In flight, both sexes reveal a wide white wing bar, well-defined white belly, and clear white vent. **HH** singles are very scarce Palearctic visitors to highland lakes in CKe from Nov–Mar (vagrant to WUg). **Vo** silent in region.

Common Pochard *Aythya ferina* 48cm, 19"

Distinctive br ♂ is *silver-grey, with a chestnut-red head and neck, and black breast and rear-end*: black bill has a wide pale grey-blue band. Eclipse ♂ is duller than br ♂ with a browner head, breast and rear. ♀ has a brown head with a diffuse pale loral patch, contrasting slightly with a greyer tinged back and flanks: dark bill with narrower pale band near tip. Imm is similar to ♀, but has a plainer face and dark bill. In flight, both sexes show largely pale grey upperwings. **HH** stragglers are Palearctic vagrants with scattered records from Dec–Mar. **Vo** silent in region.

Tufted Duck *Aythya fuligula* 46cm, 18"

Br ♂ is a striking handsome duck being *black with bright white flanks, a drooping black crest, and yellow eyes*. Eclipse ♂ is duller, with dingy grey-brown flanks and a reduced crest. ♀ is dull dark-brown, with a short tuft on rear of crown (not a crest), a pale belly, and yellow eyes. Imm is similar to ♀, but has brown eyes. In flight, both sexes show extensive white wing bar, a white or pale belly, and a dark vent. **HH** singles and small flocks are uncommon annual visitors from Nov–Mar on lakes in Ke, SWUg, and NTz. **Vo** silent in region.

Plate 23

Southern
Pochard

Ferruginous
Duck

Common
Pochard

Tufted Duck

KITES
Black Kite is a fairly large, long-winged, fork-tailed brown bird of prey which is often very common, especially in towns and cities. The two white kites are smaller and more elegant, and they are easily separable on wing pattern and tail shape.

Black Kite *Milvus migrans* 61cm, 24"

Fairly large brown raptor with angled wings and a *long slightly forked tail*. Three races occur and are sometimes considered as two distinct species: if so, the dark-billed nominate race remains **Black Kite**, while the yellow-billed African races *parasiticus* and *aegyptius* become **Yellow-billed Kite**. Resident *parasiticus* is mostly brown (including the head) and has a neat *yellow bill*. Sexes are alike, but the imm is rather warmer brown, with some dark streaking below, and a *dark bill*. Race *aegyptius* (mainly present from Jul–Mar) is similar to ad *parasiticus*, but with more distinct barring on the tail. Palearctic migrant race *migrans* (Sep–Apr) is *much paler-headed with black streaking on the throat and neck, and a black bill with a yellow cere*. Sexes alike, imm may be paler still (almost white-headed) and pale streaked below. In graceful and wheeling flight, shallow forked tail which it frequently twists and turns. Some birds (particularly nominate) show a pale bar across the upperwing-coverts and a variable pale patch in the primaries from below. **HH** singles to large groups are seasonally very common from sea-level to over 3000m. They inhabit villages, towns and open country with trees, often near water. **Vo** vocal and fairly musical two-part call starts with a rising whistle and breaks into a downslurred trilling *wi-yrrrrrrrrrw*. Also a whistled rising *tiew...te te te ti* with an explosive opening note.

Black-shouldered Kite *Elanus caeruleus* 35cm, 14"

A whitish hawk with grey back and wings, *contrasting black shoulders*, and a short white tail. In flight from below, primaries mostly blackish. Sexes alike. Imm is browner with a heavily scaled back and wings, and a buff wash across the breast. Flight soft and elegant, often beating into the wind with head down, soars on raised wings and regularly hovers. **HH** singles, pairs and occasional small groups are common in a wide range of moister open bushed and wooded grassland from sea-level to 3000m. Responds rapidly to local insect and rodent plagues. **Vo** usually an explosive, harsh *w-eeyah*, which is repeated after brief pauses.

African Swallow-tailed Kite *Chelictinia riocourii* 30cm, 12"

Rather tern-like elegant raptor. Ad is *grey above, and pure white below, with a long deeply forked tail, and a small black bar on the underside of the carpal joint* (not visible at rest). Sexes alike. Imm is washed brown above with buff edges to the coverts and back, and a *shorter tail*. Superbly graceful in flight, riding winds with a spread tail, wheeling and hovering. **HH** highly social intra-African migrant from the north breeding in our area, most records are Mar–Oct, but recorded in all months. Prefers semi-arid and arid bushed and wooded country in NKe and NUg, but birds also disperse south, to the Great Rift Valley and rarely to northern coastal lowlands in Ke. **Vo** breeding pairs give an almost tern-like *keek keek...* which breaks into a rapid rising and rattling series.

SECRETARY BIRD
Endemic to Africa, the Secretary Bird is an extraordinary long-legged raptor, adapted to a specialist terrestrial predatory lifestyle. Walks through grassland hunting prey like snakes which are stamped to death with hardened pads on the small scaled feet. Name may be derived from long pen-like quills on the nape, or from the Arabic *saqr-et-tair* or hunter-bird.

Secretary Bird *Sagittarius serpentarius* 150cm, 60"

Large striding grey and black bird with a bare orange-red face, thick eagle-like bill, long plumes on nape, long legs with black leggings, and a long narrow centre-tail. Unlike any other bird. Sexes alike. Imm is similar but browner with duller facial skin. If disturbed will often run rather than fly away: flight rather laboured, although soars easily and presents a very distinctive silhouette. **HH** singles, pairs, and pairs with young, are locally common in open bushed and wooded grasslands from near sea-level to 3000m. **Vo** at nest pairs make long low burping growls.

Plate 24

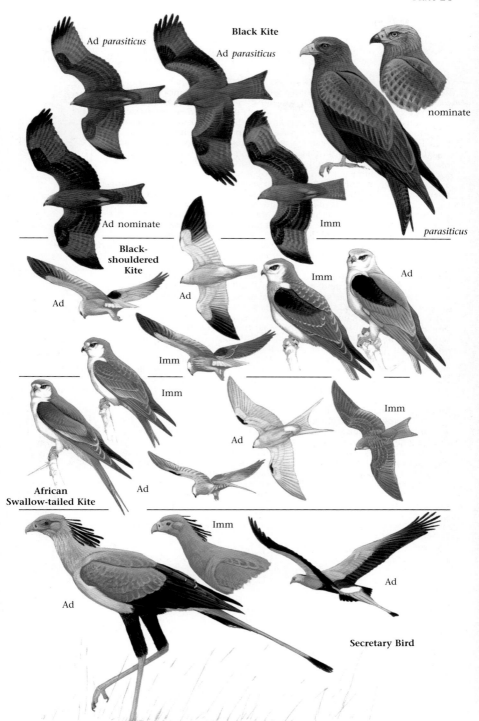

Ad *parasiticus*

Black Kite

Ad *parasiticus*

nominate

Ad nominate

Imm

parasiticus

Black-shouldered Kite

Ad

Ad

Imm

Ad

Imm

Imm

Imm

African Swallow-tailed Kite

Ad

Ad

Imm

Ad

Ad

Imm

Ad

Secretary Bird

FISH-EATING RAPTORS

Three large pied raptors usually associated with water. African Fish Eagle and Osprey are spectacular, aggressive, fishing birds. Palm-nut Vulture (also known as Vulturine Fish Eagle) is often seen scavenging on the sea-shore, but is also strongly associated with oil palms particularly in the west. With good views, all reasonably easy to distinguish, but take care with immature birds.

African Fish Eagle   *Haliaeetus vocifer*   ♀ 73cm, 29"

Ad is a striking fishing eagle with a gleaming *white head, breast and tail, chestnut shoulders and underparts,* and mostly *black back and wings.* Sexes alike, but ♀ is larger than ♂. Juv scruffy, largely dark brown with a dark cap and whitish face, variable dark streaking on the nape, throat and breast, and white patches at primary bases on underwings: whitish tail is broadly tipped with black. Sub-ad gains a whiter head and white under- wing-coverts attaining full ad plumage in fifth year. In flight, appears broad-winged and short-tailed, flapping with shallow beats and soaring on flat wings. **HH** pairs and pairs with young are common throughout the region on a wide range of fresh, alkaline and salt waters, from sea-level to 3000m. They can be particularly numerous on the lakes of both rift valleys and at Lake Victoria. **Vo** a very familiar waterside sound. Most calls are attractive yodels *weee........wu wu wu* with the last three notes accelerating and falling. Pairs also duet, one calls *wi* and the other immediately replies *oo.* Also calls a low nasal *ahnk-ank-ank-ank.*

Palm-nut Vulture   *Gypohierax angolensis*   ♀ 60cm, 24"
[Vulturine Fish Eagle]

Ad is a boldly marked black and white raptor, with large black patches in the wings (secondaries and primary tips) and a *white-tipped black tail.* Perched bird has a rather hunched appearance, with a long bill and large area of bare pinkish skin around the eyes. Sexes alike, but ♀ is slightly larger than ♂. Juv scruffy and all brown, except for dull yellow-green orbital skin, and whitish greater coverts on the underwing. Sub-ad attains more white, including primary patches on both upper- and underwings. In flight, has a *round-winged and short-tailed silhouette,* with a unique bold black and white wing pattern visible at great distance. **HH** singles and pairs are resident and locally common from WUg to SWTz in the west, and in the east throughout the coastal belt and inland along major rivers up to 1400m. **Vo** a downslurred wheezy screaming whistle. **SS** Egyptian Vulture.

Osprey   *Pandion haliaetus*   59cm, 23"

A slender brown and white raptor with uniquely shaped narrow angled wings. Dark brown above and pearly white below, with a rather small flat head, a white crown and broad black band through the yellow eyes. Sexes are alike, but ♀ often has a fuller chest band. Juv has a less well-defined head pattern, with some narrow dark streaking on the crown and pale fringes to the back and wings. In flight, appears mainly white below with striking long angled wings, and distinctive *black carpal patches, primary tips, and dark edges to the underwing-coverts.* Often hovers with dangling legs and plunges into water after fish. **HH** singles are regular visitors and passage migrants to a wide range of freshwater lakes and rivers, as well as salt-water creeks, shores and estuaries, from Aug–Apr (but mainly Oct–Mar). Some are present all year round. **Vo** silent in region.

Plate 25

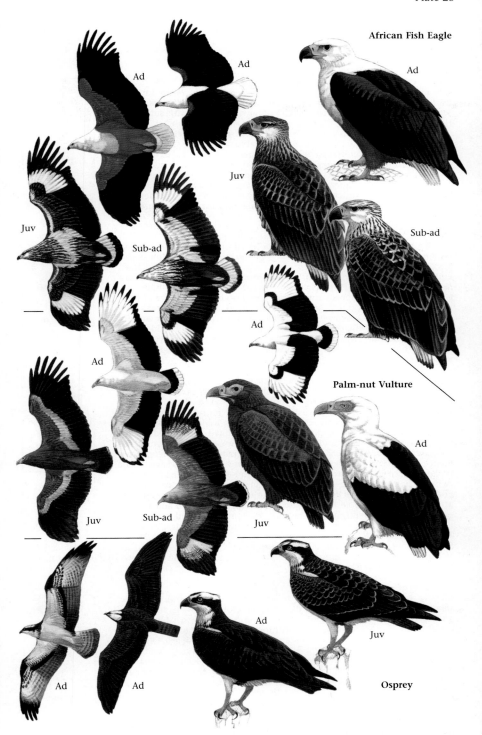

African Fish Eagle

Ad

Ad

Ad

Juv

Ad

Sub-ad

Juv

Juv

Sub-ad

Ad

Palm-nut Vulture

Ad

Juv

Sub-ad

Juv

Ad

Ad

Ad

Juv

Osprey

SOLITARY VULTURES

Three vultures which are usually solitary or found in pairs. In recent times, however, Hooded Vulture has adapted to feeding in villages and towns where it may be quite numerous. All are attracted to kills. Adults are distinctive, but care should be taken in identifying immature birds.

Egyptian Vulture *Neophron percnopterus* ♀ 71cm, 28"

Ad is a conspicuous medium-sized *white or buffy-yellow and white vulture, with black flight feathers, a bare orange-yellow face* (surrounded by long lax feathers which form a shaggy halo), and a slender bill with a black tip. Sexes are similar, but ♀ is slightly larger. Imm is brown and similar to imm Hooded Vulture, but may show some yellow on the face, and has *longer feathers on the back of its head*. In flight, ad has obvious black and white plumage, while imm is all brown. All birds have rather long straight wings and a *wedge-shaped tail*. **HH** solitary birds, pairs, or family groups are widespread but nowhere common, inhabiting arid, semi-arid, and bush country from near sea-level to 3000m: rarely found far from their nesting cliffs. Attend kills, but feeds after more numerous larger vultures. Specialist tool-user, breaking open ostrich eggs by repeatedly throwing stones at them. **Vo** breeding birds give high-pitched rattled trills and scratchy wheezes. **SS** Palm-nut Vulture.

Hooded Vulture *Necrosyrtes monachus* ♀ 75cm, 30"

Size is similar to Egyptian Vulture, but ad is all brown with a *naked pink head and some sparse white-grey down on the hindneck*. Slender bill is also pinkish-brown and may brighten if excited. Sexes alike. Imm is darker, with dark grey facial skin and dark brown down on the head. *In flight, easily identified from imm Egyptian by more square-ended tail*. **HH** singles and small groups are widespread and may be common in a wide range of habitats including arid country, grassland, cultivation, and coastal areas from sea-level to 3000m. Much more gregarious than Egyptian Vulture and (in the west) occurs in villages and towns, where attracted to rubbish dumps. Tree nester, so not constrained by rocky cliffs. **Vo** calls a variety of high-pitched complaining *peei-u peei-u peei-u peei-u...* and various scratchy squeals.

White-headed Vulture *Trigonoceps occipitalis* ♀ 84cm, 33"

Attractive large blackish vulture with a colourful angular head, white crop, and white belly. At close quarters ad shows rather peaked triangular shaped head, with thick white down on the crown, bare pink facial skin, and a red bill with a pale blue cere. Imm is duller, with a brownish top to the head and all dark underparts. In broad-winged flight, ads show conspicuous white bellies and legs, extending as a narrow white line along rear of underwing-coverts; ♀ also has large white patches in the secondaries. Flying imm is all dark with a narrow white line along rear edge of the underwing-coverts. **HH** singles and pairs are the most solitary and least common of the large vultures, but widespread at low densities from semi-arid open country to wooded grasslands between sea-level and 3000m. Regularly attends kills, but unable to compete with larger species. **Vo** squeals and chitters when squabbling at a carcass, but is not as vocal as smaller vultures.

LAMMERGEIER

Striking giant vulture of remote areas and rocky cliffs. Name derived from German for Lamb Vulture. Unlikely to be confused with any other species, in distant views may recall immature Egyptian Vulture, but much bigger.

Lammergeier *Gypaetus barbatus* 110cm, 43"

Massive *very long-winged black and orange vulture with a distinct diamond shaped tail*. Face appears white at distance, but close-up reveals black lores and beard which hangs below base of bill, underparts invariably stained russet (with iron oxide during dust bathing). Sexes are alike. Imm entirely dark brown, but becoming paler on face and underparts with age. Flight silhouette distinct from all except Egyptian Vulture. **HH** singles and pairs occur at low densities in high mountain areas and at volcanic craters, but wanderers (notably imms) may turn up unexpectedly elsewhere. Requires precipitous cliffs for breeding, but range considerable distances to scavenge from kills and take all sorts of carrion. Bones are broken by dropping from heights onto rocky outcrops. **Vo** quite silent, but at nest gives a long downslurred wheezy and rather burry whistle.

Plate 26

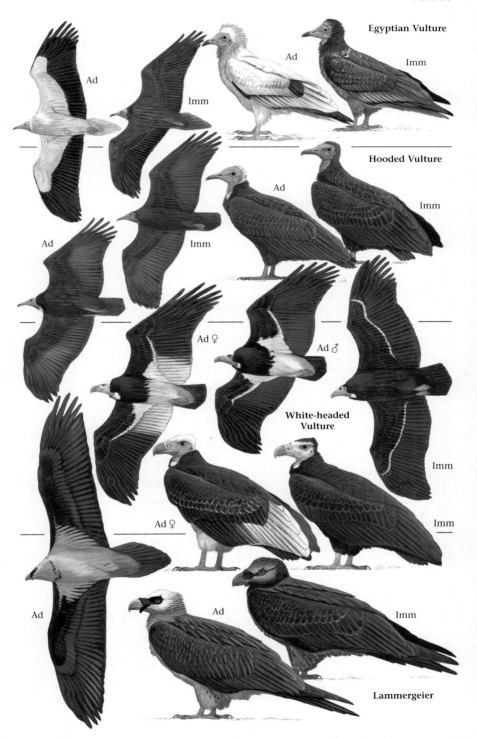

Egyptian Vulture

Ad

Imm

Ad

Imm

Hooded Vulture

Ad

Imm

Ad

Imm

Ad ♀

Ad ♂

White-headed Vulture

Imm

Ad ♀

Imm

Ad

Ad

Imm

Lammergeier

LARGE PLAINS VULTURES

Classic East African vultures commonly seen associating together at carcasses (and often with the species on plate 26). All three are easily distinguished on the ground, but immature (and sometimes adult) African White-backed and Rüppell's Griffon may be difficult on the wing. All are resident, but make long distance movements in search of food.

African White-backed Vulture *Gyps africanus* 98cm, 39″

Ad is only likely to be confused with Rüppell's Griffon Vulture, but on the ground is easily separated by *entirely blackish bill, darker brown eyes, and essentially rather plain body and wings* (which lighten considerably with age): white back is usually concealed. Sexes alike. Imm is dark at first, with narrow pale streaking on the back and wings (never scalloped), extensive down on neck, and a dull brownish ruff. Birds gradually lighten attaining ad plumage (with white back) in six years. In flight, ad shows *tapering white lower back and rump from above, and wholly white underwing-coverts from below*. Underwing of imm shows a long thin white crescent just inside the leading edge and is thus identical to imm Rüppell's Griffon. **HH** small to large groups are widespread and may be numerous in open grassland and woodland from sea-level to 3000m, usually associating with plains game, and generally outnumbering Rüppell's Griffon. **Vo** often silent, but make an expressive range of hisses, cackles and wheezy rattles at kills.

Rüppell's Griffon Vulture *Gyps rueppellii* 104cm, 41″

In close views ad is easily identified from African White-backed Vulture by *yellowish-cream tip to the bill, yellowish eyes, and by whitish edges to back feathers and wing-coverts giving a thickly scaled appearance*. Longer and thicker necked, slightly more heavily billed, as well as a little larger than African White-backed, giving a rather heavier feel when seen together. Sexes alike. Imm is very similar to imm African White-backed with a blackish bill, dark eyes, rather plain back and wings, and variable pale streaking below. At kills can be separated by slightly larger and heavier appearance: ad plumage gained over about 6 years, with scaling, pale bill tip and yellowish eyes all acquired gradually. In flight, from below, ad shows thin white crescent near leading edge of wing, and may have parallel concentric bars on the wing-covert edges (but are often hard to see). Mottled belly and pale bill tip may be visible at distance. Imm is dark below, with a single white crescent on the underwing and cannot be safely separated from imm African White-backed. **HH** groups are widespread, gregarious, and in a few areas – like the Serengeti – numerous at kills. Often associate with cliff and rocky outcrop colonies, although birds forage far from nest sites. **Vo** largely silent, but more vocal than White-backed at kills, uttering an extraordinarily varied range of loud screamed hisses, groans, grunts and low guttural rattles.

Lappet-faced Vulture *Torgos tracheliotus* 115cm, 45″ ●

Thickset squarish head, enormous bill, and broad often spread wings, give this species a massive and brooding presence at kills. Ad is largely blackish-brown with extensive whitish streaking on the breast, and large white leggings. Head and neck bare and pink (may flush brightly) with fleshy lappets on sides of face. Sexes similar. Imm darker, almost black, with duller facial skin and black leggings which become progressively whiter over approximately 6 years. In flight, looks huge and broad-winged, ad shows a conspicuous narrow white crescent on underwing and white leggings. Imm is entirely dark below. **HH** singles and pairs are reasonably widespread and common residents of open grassland and woodland with plains game from sea-level to 3000m. Densities are generally lower than other large vultures, and it is rare to see more than four or five together at kills, although small groups do occasionally gather. **Vo** quiet, but unusual calls include a low growling *churr* and a series of various metallic spitted notes.

Plate 27

Imm

Ad

Imm

Ad

**African
White-backed
Vulture**

Ad

Ad

**Rüppell's Griffon
Vulture**

Ad

Imm

Imm

Ad

Ad

**Lappet-faced
Vulture**

Ad

Imm

Ad

SNAKE-EAGLES

Medium-sized eagles with large rounded heads, striking yellow eyes, bare legs, and (when perched) a rather upright stance. Sexes are similar, but immatures often differ, and gain adult plumage over about three years. Underwing, tail patterns and range aid identification. All feed on snakes and other reptiles.

Black-chested Snake-Eagle *Circaetus pectoralis* 68cm, 27"

Ad is blackish-brown above, on the head, throat and upper breast, and otherwise plain white below. Imm is totally different, being dark brownish above with some pale fringes, and paler rufous below, often with a whitish face and narrow streaking on throat. In flight, ad is all dark above and on the upper breast, contrasting with a white belly and underwings, which show narrow black bars across the flight feathers: the undertail has three black bands. Imm is brown above and mainly rufous below with rufous underwing-coverts, and indistinctly barred flight feathers. **HH** singles are largely resident, widespread and sometimes common in bushed and wooded grassland from sea-level to 3400m. They sometimes hover. **Vo** usually quiet, but calls a piercing whistled downslurred *peeeu...*, a monotone *peee...*, and a loud *pee pee pee pee...* **SS** Martial Eagle.

Short-toed Snake-Eagle *Circaetus gallicus* 68cm, 27"

Two very similar races (perhaps species?) occur: nominate *gallicus* (**Short-toed Snake-Eagle**) is medium-brown above, but very variable below – typically the upper breast is brown and the remainder of the underparts are white with some crescent-shaped barring. Paler birds are almost entirely white below, some with a few brown breast streaks. Imm is similar. Ad of race *beaudouini* (**Beaudouin's Snake-Eagle**) is darker than all the other forms, with continuous crescentic barring from breast to vent. Imm has the underparts and underwing-coverts rufous-brown. In both races the tail has three or four narrow dark bars. **HH** race *gallicus* is a very rare visitor from the Palearctic (Oct–Mar), while *beaudouini* occurs infrequently in NUg and perhaps in NWKe. **Vo** silent in region.

Brown Snake-Eagle *Circaetus cinereus* 71cm, 28"

Large-headed all dark brown eagle, with conspicuous yellow eyes and pale legs. Imm similar, but may be paler. In flight, appears all dark above, except for narrow bars on tail. From below, *silver-white greater coverts and flight feathers contrast strongly with the brown body and other underwing-coverts.* Tail shows three light bars both above and below, and a narrow pale tip. **HH** singles and pairs are widespread at low densities in bush and woodland from sea-level to 2000m. **Vo** calls a drawn-out wheeze and high-pitched metallic *kwink*.

Western Banded Snake-Eagle *Circaetus cinerascens* 60cm, 24"

Ad is grey-brown above with extensive brown from throat to belly and *barring restricted to lower belly and lower flanks:* single broad white band across tail. Imm is much paler and browner above with a whitish lightly streaked head, and largely dirty white below with variable brown bars and smudges. In flight from above a broad white tail bar is conspicuous. From below, ad shows *dark chin to belly, mainly white underwing-coverts, and a single broad whitish band in the tail.* **HH** singles and pairs are rather uncommon residents of riverine forest, woodland and forest edge, from Ug to NTz, and extending eastwards to CKe, between 400–2000m. **Vo** commonly calls in display over territory, a far-carrying nasal *ayaaah ka-haaa* with the first note rising and last note falling.

Southern Banded Snake-Eagle *Circaetus fasciolatus* 60cm, 24"

Ad is similar to Western Banded Snake-Eagle, *but barring on the underparts extends from breast to vent; tail rather longer with four dark and three light bands.* Imm is similar to imm Western Banded, but often more marked below and has different tail barring. In flight, ad shows more extensive barring on underparts and underwing-coverts than other snake-eagles. **HH** singles and pairs are shy but widespread at low densities in coastal forest, lowland forest close to the coast (to 1500m in NETz) and along major river systems inland. **Vo** birds are vocal and display high over the canopy with a far-carrying nasal *woop ta'ta'ta'taaa*, with first note rising and leisurely, last notes rapid, and final note falling. Also a loud clanging *kyan kyan kyan kyan...* sometimes given at end of display.

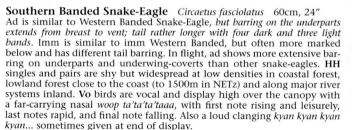

Plate 28

Black-chested Snake-Eagle

Ad

Imm

Ad

Ad

Short-toed Snake-Eagle

gallicus

Ad

beaudouini

Ad

Imm

Ad

Ad

gallicus

Ad

Imm

Ad

Brown Snake-Eagle

Ad

Imm

Ad

Imm

Ad

Ad

Ad

Ad

Western Banded Snake-Eagle

Ad

Southern Banded Snake-Eagle

HARRIERS

Elegant raptors of open country which are similar in shape and character. Females and immatures are hard to identify, and we concentrate on separating birds in flight. Adult female and immature Montagu's and Pallid harriers are particularly difficult to tell apart. In all cases, note should be taken of head, rump, and wing patterns. With experience, subtle differences in flight action aid identification, even at long distances.

African Marsh Harrier *Circus ranivorus* 50cm, 20"

Ad is mostly dark brown above and paler brown below with dark streaking (some are washed rufous on rump, flanks and legs). Extent of pale areas on face and throat varies individually. Imm is similar, but darker, with a cream-buff nape and throat (not crown), and a pale breast band (again extent varies). In flight, birds are overall slender and dark (without a white rump). Ad is brown above with a whitish leading edge to the wing, *boldly barred underwings, and a narrowly barred tail*. Imm in flight is darker still, but with a buff-white leading edge to the wing, a pale patch on nape and throat, and often a whitish breast bar. **HH** singles and pairs are rather local and often uncommon over marshes and swamps, including seasonal wetlands, from the coast to 3000m. **Vo** vocal on breeding grounds where it gives a rough upslurred *weeey*, at intervals of about 4–6 seconds.

Eurasian Marsh Harrier *Circus aeruginosus* 56cm, 22"

Heaviest looking harrier: ad ♂ is dark brown, grey and black, with a pale cream crown, nape and throat, variable dark streaking across the chest, and a rufous-brown lower breast to vent. Ad ♀ is largely dark brown, with leading edge of wings and head creamy (face is variably brown and some show a cream patch across the breast). Imm is similar, but the crown and throat are buffier, and cream in wing is reduced or absent. In flight, appears sedate and is bigger and broader winged than other harriers. Ad ♂ is brown, grey and black above, with a grey tail, the underwings are silvery-grey with black tips, and the lower body rufous-brown. Ad ♀ is rich brown with a cream cap, forewing and shoulders, and a *plain tail*. Rare dark morph ad ♂ is blackish with a grey tail and white bases to flight feathers on the underwing. Ad ♀ lacks cream on forewing, but has white bases to primaries on underwing. **HH** singles and small groups are reasonably common and widespread Palearctic visitors to lakes and marshes, flooded grassland and cultivation from Sep–Apr. **Vo** silent in region.

Montagu's Harrier *Circus pygargus* 46cm, 18"

Ad ♂ has smoke-grey upperparts, head and upper breast, with a whiter belly, *chestnut flank streaking, and a short black bar in the closed wing*. Ad ♀ is dark brown above, streaked brown on buff-white below. *Close views of face reveal thin stripe through eye, and dark ear-coverts, not prominently edged by a whitish collar*. Imm has similar face pattern, but is plain bright rufous below. In flight, slightly heavier and more sedate than Pallid Harrier, with a rather bulging-crop-look. Ad ♂ also appears *darker grey, with a thin black bar on the secondaries, larger black wing tips, and chestnut streaked flanks and underwing-coverts*. In the underwing, ad ♀ shows *two broad pale bars across the secondaries, dark tipped primaries and rufous barring on the coverts*. Ad ♀ and imm both have white rumps. **HH** singles to small groups are fairly common Palearctic passage migrants and visitors to grasslands, especially in the highlands, from Oct–Apr. **Vo** silent in region.

Pallid Harrier *Circus macrourus* 46cm, 18"

Very similar to Montagu's Harrier, but of slighter build with a longer tail which projects beyond the wing tips at rest. Ad ♂ is an ethereal pale grey above and very white below, with *no black bar across the closed wing*. Ad ♀ differs from ad ♀ Montagu's by having a *thicker black line through the eye and a whitish collar around the ear-coverts*. Imm is also similar to imm Montagu's except for more distinctive face pattern. Has a buoyant, lithe flight. Ad ♂ is plain ghostly grey with *less black in wing tips*, and no secondary bar or chestnut streaking. Ad ♀ has *darker secondaries, and paler primaries, especially towards tips*. Ad ♀ and imm both have white rumps. **HH** singles and small groups are common Palearctic passage migrants and visitors to grasslands from Oct–Apr. **Vo** silent in region.

Plate 29

African
Marsh
Harrier

Eurasian
Marsh Harrier

Montagu's
Harrier

Pallid Harrier

Ad

Imm

Ad

Ad

Imm

Imm

Imm

Imm

♂

♂

♀

♂

♀

♀

♂

♂

♀

♂

♀

CHANTING-GOSHAWKS, GABAR GOSHAWK AND LIZARD BUZZARD

Four quite similar grey raptors (most adults) which have a rather upright and bold stance. Adult chanting-goshawks are easily told apart by bare part and rump colour, but immatures can be much more difficult – consider range. Gabar Goshawk and Lizard Buzzard are smaller and should not be confused if seen well.

Eastern Chanting-Goshawk *Melierax poliopterus* ♀ 61cm, 24"

Medium-sized grey raptor which is barred grey and white from breast to vent. Generally paler than Dark Chanting-Goshawk (but not always so), and best identified by a *yellow cere, long orange-red legs, and a white rump*. ♀ is similar, but larger than ♂. Imm is brown above with pale (not dark) eyes, a whitish supercilium, and a *mainly white rump* (beware, some show narrow barring at sides). Breast brown with variable darker streaking; barred brown and white from breast to vent. Cere grey, legs dull yellowish. In character-ful stiff-winged, direct flight, ad appears grey above, with black outer pri-maries and an *obvious narrow white rump*. **HH** singles and pairs perch prominently and are widespread and common in arid and semi-arid bush, dry grasslands and woodland, from sea-level to 2000m. **Vo** calls a loud and piercing *pee..peepeepeepeepeepeeepeepeep* which slowly rises in tone, a rather mewing *peeyuh*, and a rhythmical *weeu wi-wu-wu-wu-wu* with the first note rising and last notes falling and accelerating like a bouncing ball.

Dark Chanting-Goshawk *Melierax metabates* ♀ 56cm, 22"

Similar to Eastern Chanting-Goshawk, but usually slightly darker grey, with a *grey and white barred rump, and orange-red cere and legs*. ♀ is similar, but larger than ♂. Imm is very similar to imm Eastern Chanting, but some birds are less heavily streaked on the breast: best separated by *extensive bar-ring on the white rump*. **HH** singles and pairs are common residents of sim-ilar but moister habitats than Eastern Chanting, occurring up to 3000m. Also typically flies low with stiff beats interspersed with glides, swooping up onto exposed perches. **Vo** quite vocal, with a gull-like downslurred *peeeyuh* and a repeated *whee-pee-pee-pee...*

Gabar Goshawk *Micronisus gabar* ♀ 36cm, 14"

Superficially resembles a small chanting-goshawk. Typical ad is grey above with a bold white rump: head to upper breast also grey, mid-breast to belly barred grey and white, cere and legs orange-red, and eyes dark. Reasonably common melanistic ad is mostly black (when perched), with no white rump, and a grey and black barred tail. ♀ is similar, but larger than ♂. Imm largely dull brown above with a white rump, pale throat and breast streaked warm-brown, and mid-breast to belly banded warm-brown. Cere, eyes and legs are pale yellowish. Dashing and rather accipiter-like flight on short rounded wings: typical ad shows striking narrow *white rump* and heavily barred underwings and tail. Melanistic birds are black above and below with silvery white bars in underwing and tail. **HH** singles are wide-spread and common residents of bush and woodland from sea-level to 2000m, often in drier country. **Vo** common call is rising *wi-we-we* (rather like Diederik Cuckoo), while a longer series consists of this call with the last note repeated *wi-we-we wiwiwiwiwiwiwi...*

Lizard Buzzard *Kaupifalco monogrammicus* 35–37cm, 14–15"

Small upright and rather stocky raptor which is grey above and across the breast with a *vertical black stripe down centre of white throat*, and mid-breast to belly well-barred dark grey and white. Cere and legs are red, eyes dark. Sexes alike. Imm is slightly browner version of ad with a duller cere and less distinct throat stripe. Compact and neat on the wing, flying low with shal-low beats before swooping up onto perches. From above shows mainly grey upperparts contrasting strongly with a white rump and blackish tail which has a single thin white bar and tip. From below, appears barred, but under-wing-coverts are quite plain, with barring mainly confined to the body and flight feathers. **HH** pairs are common and widespread residents of bush, woodland, cultivation and gardens from sea-level to 3000m, but with a patchy distribution away from the coast. Often on posts or wires where it can be both unobtrusive and confiding. **Vo** very vocal, shouting a distinc-tive *wioo...wu wu wu wu wu wu wu wu wu...* with the first note rising and then falling and the remainder slightly lower and on the same pitch.

Plate 30

Ad

Ad

Ad

Ad

Imm

Imm

Eastern Chanting-Goshawk

Imm

Ad

Ad

Ad

Imm

Imm

Dark Chanting-Goshawk

Imm

Imm

Imm

mel

Ad

Ad

Ad

Gabar Goshawk

melanistic

Ad

Ad

Ad

Ad

Ad

Lizard Buzzard

OPEN COUNTRY SPARROWHAWKS
Four similar sparrowhawks of open country. All are built for dashing manoeuvrable flight. Shikra is a common and widespread resident, Ovambo is rare, and the others are vagrants. Best identified by head, cheek and throat pattern, as well as underwing and eye colour: none have obvious white rumps. Adults similar, but females are often larger than males.

Shikra   *Accipiter badius*   ♀ 30cm, 12"
[Little Banded Goshawk]

Small classic sparrowhawk: *grey above* (sometimes with a few white spots on back), with grey cheeks, and a largely plain grey centre tail (may be dark-tipped on ♀). *Lightly barred pinkish or light rufous-brown below,* except for whitish throat and vent. ♂ has bright red eyes, ♀ bright orange: cere and legs yellow. Imm dark brown above, whitish below with a rufous-brown central throat streak, heavily streaked breast, and barred lower breast and flanks. Eyes and bare parts pale yellow. In flight, ad may appear very pale at a distance with black wing tips. Appears similar to Levant Sparrowhawk, but the wings are slightly more rounded and it is more extensively barred below. Tail mostly plain above, but barred from below. **HH** singles and pairs are common residents in a wide range of woodland and edge habitats from sea-level to 3000m, including towns, gardens and cultivation. **Vo** various (sometimes woodpecker-like) calls are shrill and querulous; either single upslurs *k-wi* or a chittered series *kwikwikwikwikwi...*

Ovambo Sparrowhawk   *Accipiter ovampensis*   ♀ 40cm, 16"

Slightly *small-headed* sparrowhawk with two distinct colour morphs. Normal grey birds are all grey above *often with a few white marks on the rump* and a barred tail with *white streaks on central feather shafts.* Below *finely barred grey or grey-brown from throat to belly.* Eyes dark wine red, cere and legs vary from yellowish to red. Rare melanistic morph is dull black above except for *white streaks on tail shafts.* In flight, black underwing-coverts contrast with pale bars on flight feathers and tail. At close range both morphs show *exceptionally long middle toes.* Imm rather variable, but all show the *white streaks on tail shafts.* Typical birds are dark brown above with a white supercilium and *chestnut-brown below* with a streaked breast and barred belly and flanks: others are whiter on the crown and underparts. Eyes brown, cere and legs yellow. **HH** singles are very scarce residents of riverine and open woodland, with scattered records suggesting that birds may wander. **Vo** calls 7–12 rapidly delivered notes, a wader-like *kweh-kwehkwehkweh...* with a nasal upslur.

Eurasian Sparrowhawk   *Accipiter nisus*   ♀ 38cm, 15"

Ad ♂ is slate-grey above (sometimes with slight white supercilium), with *buff-orange sides to the face,* and barred rusty-orange underparts. Ad ♀ is often much larger, grey-brown above with a more prominent supercilium contrasting with a dark cap, and barred dark brown below. Eyes, cere and legs yellow. Imm is like ad ♀, but browner-grey above, and dark barring below is much more mottled and broken. In compact dashing flight, ad ♂ is dark grey above with a barred rusty-orange body and leading edge to the underwing: longish tail shows four or five bars both above and below. Ad ♀ has looser flight, is grey-brown above and well barred below. **HH** very rare Palearctic visitor to Ke from Nov–Feb, with scattered records typically from wooded country; vagrant to NETz. **Vo** silent in region.

Levant Sparrowhawk   *Accipiter brevipes*   ♀ 38cm, 15"

Ad ♂ is similar to Shikra, with grey cheeks and plain upperside to centre tail. Best separated by Levant's slightly darker upperparts, dark red eyes (not bright red), and richer chestnut-orange underparts (which may be plain or barred or both). In flight, *more pointed wings show black ends from above and distinct black tips from below.* Slightly larger ad ♀ is browner above, and shows more barring on underwing-coverts in flight. Imm is browner above than ♀, with a *dark stripe on the throat and heavily spotted underparts.* **HH** singles are vagrants from the Palearctic to woodland and bush, with the few records occurring Nov–Apr. **Vo** silent in region.

Plate 31

Shikra

melanistic

Ovambo Sparrowhawk

Ad ♂

Eurasian Sparrowhawk

Ad ♀

Ad ♂

Imm ♀

Ad ♀

Levant Sparrowhawk

WOODLAND AND FOREST SPARROWHAWKS

Six sparrowhawks of woodland and forest (African Little Sparrowhawk and Black Goshawk are on Plate 33). Their secretive nature, similarity in plumages, and (in some) different races and morphs make identification difficult. Size (beware females are often larger), markings on the underparts and tails, and range, aid identification.

African Goshawk *Accipiter tachiro* 38–46cm, 15–18"

The most common large *Accipiter* in the region, with highly variable plumage. Typical ad ♂ is very dark grey above with a whitish throat and finely barred rufous and white underparts; tail indistinctly barred black and dark grey above (occasionally with small white spots), undertail greyish and lightly barred. Larger ad ♀ is dark brown above and more heavily barred black-brown on white below. Melanistic birds are all blackish with dark grey bands in the tail and contrasting flight feathers in the underwing. Race *pembaensis* (Pemba Is. Tz) is small, pale grey above and rufous or pinkish-brown below. All ads have eyes and feet yellowish (imms are dark eyed). Imm (typical) is dark brown above with rufous fringes, a whitish supercilium (and often a pale nape); below, heavy spots on breast and barred flanks, some have a dark throat streak. In flight, ad ♂ (typical) is dark above with a rufous body and wing-coverts. Ad ♀ is more heavily barred on the body and underwings. Imm also heavily marked, but with spots not bars. Race *canescens* (WUg) sometimes known as **Red-chested Goshawk** is grey above with three white bars on uppertail, and *all plain rufous below* with a greyish throat, and chestnut underwing-coverts. Imm is brown above and mostly white below with a few dark spots. **HH** singles are common in a wide range of forest, woodland and gardens, from sea-level to 3000m. **Vo** calls a sharp snappy *chutt* like a smacking of lips, often in high aerial circling display.

Chestnut-flanked Goshawk *Accipiter castanilius* 30–35cm, 12–14"

Ad is dark-grey or blackish above with three bold white bars on a black tail. Below, white throat (sometimes barred grey) blends to centre of *chestnut and white barred breast; sides of breast, flanks and thighs plain chestnut*, vent white. Eyes, cere and legs yellow. Imms are brown-black above with a whitish supercilium, sometimes with white on the nape. Below, whitish with dark tear-drop spots on the breast, becoming bars on the flanks and thighs. Eyes brown, cere and legs yellow. Flying ad very similar to *canescens* race of African Goshawk being dark above with three white bars in the tail, but differs in having chestnut and white bars down centre of the breast, and white underwing-coverts. **HH** in our area known only from the Semliki Forest in WUg (1 record). **Vo** unknown.

Rufous-breasted Sparrowhawk *Accipiter rufiventris* 33–40cm, 13–16"

[Red-breasted Sparrowhawk]

Ad is dark slate-grey above with a dark grey and black barred tail. Below, throat buffy, *plain rich rufous from cheeks to belly*; vent white. Eyes, cere and legs yellow. Imm dark brown above with a pale supercilium and some rufous feather edges. Below, breast and flanks streaked and barred rufous becoming plain rufous on the legs. In flight, ad shows striking contrast between *darkslate upperparts and plain rufous body and underwing-coverts*. Imm has streaked and barred rufous underparts. **HH** singles are widespread residents of highland forest, forest edge and mature gardens, from 1200–3000m. Often hunts in open country. **Vo** calls a loud downslurrred *kiu-kiu-kiu-kiu...*

Red-thighed Sparrowhawk *Accipiter erythropus* 25–30cm, 10–12"

A small forest sparrowhawk. Ad is black above with white spots on scapulars, a narrow white rump and white spots in the outer tail. Below, chestnut sides of breast and thighs, contrast with a white throat; centre-breast plain grey, chestnut, or chestnut banded. Eyes orange-red, cere and legs orange-yellow. Imm is dark brown above with rufous fringes and a white supercilium; below, white with dark spotting on the breast and light chestnut barred flanks. Eye pale orange, cere and legs yellow. In flight, ad is *blackish above with a narrow white rump and white spots in outer tail*. Chestnut barring on underparts extends to underwing-coverts. Imm shows indication of white rump, spots on the breast and *chestnut bars on the flanks*. **HH** singles are secretive dense forest dwellers, in our area only known from Semliki Forest, WUg, from 700–900m. **Vo** calls a shrill reedy *kew-kew-kew...* similar to Little Sparrowhawk.

Plate 32

African Goshawk

Imm

Ad ♀

♂

♂

mel

♀

melanistic

Ad ♂

canescens

Ad ♂

**Chestnut-flanked
Goshawk**

Ad

Imm

Ad

Imm ♀

**Rufous-breasted
Goshawk**

Imm ♀

Ad ♂

Ad

Imm

Ad ♂

Ad

Imm

Imm ♀

Ad

Imm

♀

Ad ♂

Red-thighed Sparrowhawk

Little Sparrowhawk *Accipiter minullus* ♀ 28cm, 11"

Very small woodland sparrowhawk: ad is slate grey above with a white rump and white spots in a black tail. Grey head and cheeks contrast with white throat, remainder of underparts white with fine brown barring, and a variable rufous wash to sides of breast and flanks. Eyes orange-yellow: cere and legs yellow. Imm is brown above, with some white on rump and white tail spots. Below, extensive dark brown spots on breast variably becoming bars on flanks. Strikingly small, compact and agile on the wing. From above, *ad shows white rump and two white spots in centre of very black tail*. From below, barring of body and wings contrast with pale rufous underwing-coverts. Imm differs from imm Red-thighed Sparrowhawk with white spots in centre of uppertail and more extensive spotting on underparts. **HH** singles and pairs are usually local and uncommon, and also rather secretive residents of forest, dense woodland and woodland edge, as well as gardens and plantations, from sea-level to 3000m. **Vo** calls 8–10 rather full sounding and hurried *tiu-tiu-tiu-tiu...* low-pitched for size of bird.

Great Sparrowhawk *Accipiter melanoleucus* ♀ 58cm, 23"
[Black Sparrowhawk]

Very large black and white sparrowhawk: ad is *charcoal black above and white below, with conspicuous heavy black barring from sides of breast to flanks*. Rare melanistic form is all black with a white throat and shows contrasting barred flight feathers in the underwing. Eyes red to brown: cere and legs yellow. Imm is browner above, and *heavily streaked black-brown below on either white or rich rufous-brown*. Flying birds show huge but typical accipiter shape. Ad is black above, with faint greyer bars in tail: *largely white below, with black flank patches*, and barring in flight feathers and tail. Imm is dark brown above, with *dark streaking on white or rufous underparts* and either whitish or rufous underwing-coverts (imm African Goshawk is spotted and smaller). **HH** singles are widespread and sometimes common in a wide range of forest, woodland and woodland edge, including stands of exotics and well-wooded towns, from sea-level to 3000m. **Vo** calls a single loud rising and then falling buzzard-like slur *seeeuur* and a repeated sharp *keek-keek-keek-...*

African Cuckoo-Hawk *Aviceda cuculoides* 40cm, 16"
[African Baza]

Odd short-crested raptor: slender, with long wings reaching almost to tail tip at rest. Ad ♂ is dark grey-brown above, with a grey head, throat and upper breast, small rufous patch on nape, and *bold broad rufous barring from white mid-breast to belly*. Eyes red-brown or yellow: cere and legs yellow. Sexes similar, but ♀ is warm brown above with lighter barring below. Imm is dark brown above with buff fringes and a distinct white supercilium, white below with variable dark spotting. Eyes grey-brown: cere and legs pale yellow. In flight, looks long-winged and rather cuckoo-like. Ad is dark above with pale bands in the tail and *barred rufous below from breast onto the underwing-coverts*. Imm has varied spots on body, and black and white underwing coverts. **HH** singles and pairs are uncommon, in forest edge, woodland and wooded bushland from sea-level to 3000m. Status uncertain, but occurs as a regular non-br visitor to the Ke coast from May–Nov. **Vo** calls a slowly repeated downslurred squealed *peeuu*. Also duets: one bird whistles a series of rising downslurs *pek-t-wioo k-t-wioo k-t-wioo...* and the other answers with a rapid rising *pipipipipipi*.

Bat Hawk *Macheiramphus alcinus* 45cm, 18"

Atypical crepuscular *large falcon-like raptor* with a slightly crested head. Ad is mostly sooty black with a white throat bisected by a thin black line (but variably shows white on nape, breast and vent). At close range shows white lines above and below bright yellow eyes: cere and legs grey. Imm is similar, but has much more white on the throat and lower belly. Flight is languid and easy-going, but swift and dashing when hunting. Ad appears black at a distance, but imm often shows white below. **HH** singles are rather uncommon residents of forest edge, woodland, cliffs, urban areas and off-shore islands, from sea-level to 2000m. Birds emerge alongside bat prey at dusk, but occasionally kill small birds and may be active during the day. **Vo** breeding birds call a slow piercing *wii wii wii wii...*

Plate 33

Little Sparrowhawk

Great Sparrowhawk

African Cuckoo-Hawk

Bat Hawk

African Harrier-Hawk *Polyboroides typus* ♀ 66cm, 26"
[Gymnogene]

Large, floppy grey raptor with a *rather small slim head and bare yellow facial skin* (turns red if excited). Ad is grey above, with long lax nape feathers and a single broad white band across a black tail. Head and upper breast also grey, but remainder of underparts are densely barred black on white: long yellow legs. ♀ is slightly larger. Imm is highly variable from dark to light brown above, with pale feather edges, and from dark to light brown below, either mottled or plain. Facial skin grey-green. In flight, wings and tail appear broad and long. Ad is *grey with a black band along outer and trailing edge of wing, and a white-banded black tail.* Imm has barred flight and tail feathers and brown underwing-coverts which contrast with pale primary bases. *Best feature overall is slow, measured flight.* **HH** singles and pairs are widespread but local residents of forest edge, riverine woodland, well-wooded grassland and cultivation, from sea-level to 3000m. Regularly steal young from cavity nests like those of swifts and weavers, using their long flexible legs to probe for and grab nestlings. **Vo** calls a high-pitched upslurred whistle with the accent on the second half *piiiii'iii*. Also a monotonous *piiii* on one note.

European Honey-Buzzard *Pernis apivorus* 60cm, 24"

Highly variable plumage can cause considerable confusion. Ads are typically grey-brown above with *obvious yellow eyes:* all morphs have a *distinctive tail with a broad band near tip and two narrow bands near base.* Underparts are often heavily barred, but may also be lightly barred, all white, rufous, or blackish. Imms even more confusing, as in addition to varied morphs they have four or five tail bars and dark eyes. In flight, has slow deep wing beats, but soars with wings flat, and glides with wings slightly lowered. Ad in flight is like a *small-headed, long-tailed buzzard,* with dark carpal patches, a blackish trailing edge to the wing, and a distinctive barred tail. Imm has more barring on underwing and a shorter more barred tail, but protruding head and flight action useful with experience. **HH** uncommon but regular Palearctic migrant, with records across the region, mainly Oct–Apr (but also Jun–Aug). **Vo** silent in region.

Grasshopper Buzzard *Butastur rufipennis* 44cm, 17"

Perched ad looks largely grey-brown above and light rufous with narrow black streaking below. At close range shows white throat bisected by black stripe and yellow eyes, cere and legs. Sexes alike. Imm is browner above, with a pale chestnut-brown head and underparts, and a brownish or white throat bordered by dark stripes. In low buoyant gliding flight *reveals unmistakable rufous patches in upperwing.* From below, pale chestnut body contrasts with dark-tipped whitish wings. **HH** singles are non-br visitors from the northern tropics to open dry bush country, and bushed and wooded grassland from Oct–Apr. Groups may gather near fires, perching in the open, and dropping to forage for insects on the ground. **Vo** silent in region.

Long-tailed Hawk *Urotriorchis macrourus* ♀ 60cm, 24"

Extraordinary large long-tailed hawk: ad ♂ is dark grey above with a white rump and a *very long boldly marked tail. Mainly rich chestnut below,* with a pale grey throat. Eyes, cere and legs yellow. ♀ is slightly larger. Imm dark brown above, with blackish and rufous bands in the wings and tail. Below, white with variable dark spots on breast and flanks. *In flight, long-tailed silhouette is unique.* Ad appears blackish above with a white rump and bars in tail. Below chestnut body and underwing-coverts contrast with barred flight feathers. Imm has whitish underwing-coverts. **HH** in our area only known 700–900m in Semliki Forest, WUg, where they are scarce and shy occupants of the high canopy. **Vo** cries a long high scream *weeeee-ah* from a high perch.

Plate 34

African Harrier-Hawk

Ad

Ad

Ad

Ad

Imm

Imm

European
Honey-Buzzard

Ad

Imm

Imm

Imm

Ad

Ad

Ad

Ad

Ad

Ad

Ad

Grasshopper
Buzzard

Imm

Ad

Ad

Imm

Ad

Ad

Ad

Imm

Long-tailed Hawk

Ad

BUZZARDS

Five true buzzards in the genus *Buteo*. Variation in plumage (of most) can lead to confusion, but underpart markings, wing pattern, and tail colour aid identification. Additionally some are migrants, so time of year should also be considered: Common and Long-legged are from the Palearctic, Red-necked from the northern tropics, Augur and Mountain are resident. Sexes similar, but females are slightly larger.

Augur Buzzard *Buteo augur* ♀ 60cm, 24″

Stocky, red-tailed buzzard, with two distinct colour morphs. Light ad is black above with a chequered panel across the flight feathers, and white below with a brick-red tail. Perched dark morph ad is similar, but entirely blackish below. Pale imm is brown above, with heavy streaking on the throat, and narrowly dark barred brown or dull rufous tails, while dark imm is darker overall including underparts. Dark birds are particularly associated with highland areas. In flight, silhouette is highly characterful with broad wings and a short tail. **HH** singles and pairs are common residents of open country, rocky outcrops, and treed cultivation, from 400–4600m, generally above 1500m. May be confiding and often seen on roadside poles and trees. **Vo** calls a repeated barking *k'wenk k'wenk k'wenk k'wenk...*, usually in flight.

Mountain Buzzard *Buteo oreophilus* ♀ 50cm, 20″

Small well-marked buzzard: ad is brown above, with narrow bars on tail and broader dark band near tip. Below, heavily blotched dark brown on white, legs and vent barred. Sexes alike, but some individual variation. Imm is softer brown above, buff-tinged below with lighter blotching. In flight, heavily spotted body and underwing-coverts contrast with the flight feathers, thus very similar to some morphs of Common Buzzard, but never shows warm rufous tones to the tail often found in that species. **HH** singles and pairs are moderately common in and over montane forest areas from 2000–3800m. **Vo** noisy pairs indulge in display flights giving a short descending *peeu* repeated by both birds.

Common Buzzard *Buteo buteo* ♀ 50cm, 20″
[Steppe Buzzard]

Race *vulpinus* is a highly variable small buzzard with grey-brown, rufous, and dark morphs. Typical birds are brown or warm brown, with some barring below, and usually a pale band across the lower breast. In flight, typical ads have brown or rufous underwing-coverts, a *dark smudged or thin comma-like carpal patch,* and pale flight feathers with black tips and trailing edges: tail is grey-brown or rufous (often finely barred and may show dark sub-terminal band). Imms have less distinct trailing edge to wings. Scarce dark morphs are blackish-brown on the body and underwing-coverts. **HH** singles to large flocks are common passage migrants and winter visitors from Sep–Apr, but mainly on passage in Sep–Nov and Feb–Mar. Occurs across a wide range of open, bushed and wooded habitats. **Vo** silent in region.

Long-legged Buzzard *Buteo rufinus* ♀ 65cm, 26″

Large, long-winged buzzard with variable pale, rufous and dark morphs. Typical birds have a *pale cream head and breast blending to a dark rufous belly, and a plain orange-white tail.* In flight from above, ad shows contrasting *white primary bases, rufous or pale wing-coverts, and a plain pale-orange tail.* From below, rufous body and underwing-coverts (darker on belly), *large black carpal-patches,* and a black trailing edge to the wings. Soars with wings well-raised and often hovers when hunting. Rufous and rare dark morphs, and all imms very similar to corresponding morphs of Common Buzzard, and best separated by larger size, longer wings, and usually larger black carpal patches. **HH** uncommon migrant from the Palearctic, with scattered records mainly in NUg and Ke from Nov–Apr. **Vo** silent in region.

Red-necked Buzzard *Buteo auguralis* ♀ 50cm, 20″

Ad has *red-brown sides of head and nape and a rufous tail with a black sub-terminal band.* Variable below, but usually shows a white throat, dark breast band, and black spots on remainder of white underparts. Imm is boldly fringed rufous above, with a greyer tail, paler underparts, and a less distinct or no breast band. **HH** irregular visitor to NWUg from Dec–Mar. **Vo** silent in region.

Plate 35

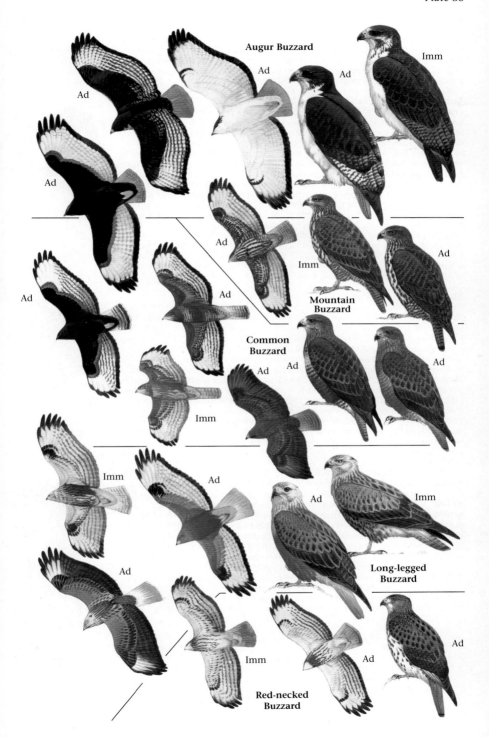

Augur Buzzard

Mountain Buzzard

Common Buzzard

Long-legged Buzzard

Red-necked Buzzard

LARGE BROWN EAGLES

Six similar large brown eagles (three on plate 37) with long broad wings, broad rounded tails (mostly), and feathered legs. Most adults are rather plain, immatures can have distinctive wing patterns: overall shape and silhouette also help with identification. Females slightly larger than males. Tawny Eagle is the most common and widespread, familiarity with it, from imm to ad, and its range of browns – from buff to dark, form a good basis for comparison with less well-known birds. Four are migrants from the Palearctic.

Tawny Eagle   *Aquila rapax*   ♀ 74cm, 29"

Overall colour varies from dark to very pale brown or creamy-buff, some are vaguely streaky and present a rather scruffy appearance, and a few show random rufous splotches: flight feathers and (plain-looking) tail always darker. At close range, gape is short, only extending back to below middle of eye. Eyes yellowish-brown on ad, dark on imm. Perched imm shows two very narrow bars (pale fringes) across closed wing. In soaring flight, wings held flat, and tail is broad and rounded. Ad shows browner or paler wing-coverts, contrasting with flight feathers on both wing surfaces (never as plain and dark as ad Steppe Eagle). Imm above, shows narrow bands across coverts and along trailing edge of wing, a small whitish flash in inner primaries, and a pale buffy rump crescent. From below, shows narrow white trailing edge, pale line between coverts and flight feathers is obscure. **HH** singles, pairs, and small groups at kills, are the most frequently encountered large brown eagle. Occurs throughout the region, including all game parks, and often feeds on road kills. **Vo** vocal, especially near nest and when scavenging at kills. Calls consist of deep barks and growls, and a series of quite varied *rrooh, kwo, kwow* and *uh-uh*.

Steppe Eagle   *Aquila nipalensis*   ♀ 80cm, 31"

Ad is slightly larger and darker than Tawny Eagle, *often with a buff nape patch and, at close range, gape extends back to rear edge of dark eye*: tail can show even spaced barring. Imm paler with *two conspicuous bars across the closed wing*. In flight, silhouette similar to Tawny, with flat wings and a broad rounded tail. Ad often looks all dark but closer birds may show small flashes at primary bases in upperwing, a small pale back spot, and a dark trailing edge to underwing. Paler imm has a white band along the upper-wing-coverts, *broad white trailing edges*, a small whitish flash in inner primaries, and a white rump crescent. *From below, shows a very conspicuous broad white band along centre of wing and a broad white trailing edge.* **HH** common passage migrant and visitor from the Palearctic from Oct–Apr. Can occur in flocks on migration, but more frequently found as singles, or in small groups in a variety of open country, including game parks, farmland, and grassland. **Vo** occasionally gives a deep growl or bark, which is lower pitched than Tawny.

Wahlberg's Eagle   *Aquila wahlbergi*   ♀ 60cm, 24"

Smaller than other brown eagles with a *small pointed crest on back of head*. In flight, dark morph (common) differs from similar plain brown eagles in having a *longish narrow, square-ended tail;* wings long straight and flat. Intermediate and pale (rare) morphs occur: they have buffy or white under-parts and underwing-coverts, white birds also have black flight feathers. Imms similar to ads. Could be confused with either pale or dark morphs of Booted Eagle, but upperparts always lack the pale rump and band across wing-coverts of that species. **HH** common throughout the region in a wide variety of open country, but most numerous from Aug–Apr when migratory birds are also present. Many are known to come from the northern tropics, but birds from southern Africa are also probably involved. **Vo** breeding birds call a long series of sharp chittering *chitchitchit* sometimes rising in pitch, and a loud whistled downslurred *seeeeeee...* **SS** Booted Eagle.

Plate 36

Imm

Ad

Imm

Imm

Ad

Imm

Tawny Eagle

Ad

Ad

Ad

Imm

Ad

Ad

Steppe Eagle

Imm

Ad

Imm

Wahlberg's Eagle

Ad

Ad

Ad

Lesser Spotted Eagle *Aquila pomarina* ♀ 66cm, 26"

Ad is a medium-sized brown eagle with darker wings and tail, close perched birds show *narrow feathering on lower legs (and a round nostril which is distinctive of the spotted eagles)*. Imm is darker than ad, with white spots across the wings (those on coverts often worn away) and usually a small golden or white nape patch. In gliding and soaring flight, the wings arch slightly downwards. Compared with Greater Spotted Eagle, ad has the *head, body and wing-coverts paler than the flight feathers* on both wing surfaces. There is a small white flash in the primaries on the upperwing, often two pale commas at the carpal joint in the underwing, and a variable white crescent on the rump. Imm above, shows a white rump crescent and usually a *white spot on the back;* white wing flash is often strong on inner primaries. Below, the wing-coverts may be paler than flight feathers or almost as dark, whitish tips to wing-coverts and trailing edge quickly wear off. **HH** regular visitor and passage migrant from the Palearctic from Oct–Apr. Migrating flocks recorded from WUg and CKe, but generally only occur as singles, or in small groups, often near lakes in high country. **Vo** silent in region.

Greater Spotted Eagle *Aquila clanga* ♀ 76cm, 30"   ●

Ad is *dark and plain looking,* close perched birds also reveal *narrow feathering on lower legs*, and round nostrils. Imm also dark, with prominent white spots on wings, often including (but not always) large white spots on coverts. Like Lesser Spotted Eagle glides with wings arched slightly downwards, but looks *broader-winged and shorter-tailed.* Ad looks all dark above, with *coverts not contrasting strongly with flight feathers,* and with just a hint of pale in primaries: rump crescent indistinct, but some may show white. Below, *wing-coverts similar to or darker than flight feathers,* usually with a single whitish comma at carpal joint. Imm is dark above with a white rump crescent and may show distinctive heavy spotting on wing-coverts. Below the *underwing-coverts are darker than flight feathers.* A rare pale morph known as 'fulvescens' could occur, it is most like a pale Tawny Eagle, but differs in having narrow feathering on lower legs, a round nostril, broader wings and a shorter tail. **HH** vagrant from the Palearctic with scattered records in Ke between Oct–Feb and two records in Tz (one of a bird tracked over the country by satellite). Status in Ug uncertain. **Vo** silent in region.

Imperial Eagle *Aquila heliaca* ♀ 84cm, 33"   ●

Largest *Aquila* eagle. Ad is very dark with an *extensive golden nape and white shoulders.* Imm like large pale morph Tawny Eagle, but with numerous *dark streaks on body and large pale spots on wing-coverts.* In flight, ad looks massive, with *white shoulders* and a *greyish tail broadly tipped black;* underwing-coverts darker than flight feathers. Imm has pale streaked body and wing-coverts strongly contrasting with blackish flight feathers, a *conspicuous pale wedge in inner primaries,* and a creamy-buff rump. Soars on flat wings with its tail held slightly closed, appearing longish and square-ended. **HH** uncommon Palearctic visitor from Nov–Mar, with virtually all records from Ke (perhaps reflecting the greater number of observers there). **Vo** silent in region.

Plate 37

Lesser Spotted Eagle

Greater Spotted Eagle

Imperial Eagle

HAWK-EAGLES

Varied group of medium-sized eagles. Several are similar, with black and white adults and brown and tawny immatures. They are best identified by colour and markings on the underparts and underwings, although habitat and range should also be taken into account. All have feathered legs, and females are slightly larger than males.

African Hawk-Eagle   *Hieraaetus spilogaster*   ♀ 66cm, 26"

Black and white open-country eagle with streaked underparts. Close views of ad reveal black and grey banding in the secondaries and tail, and, if perched upright, *long white feathered legs*. Imm is dark brown above including sides of face and rufous below with narrow streaking across the breast. In flight, tail looks rather long and wings are pinched-in at base. From above ad shows *large white patches in primaries*, and black and grey barring in the secondaries and tail. Below, body and wing-coverts are streaked black, *flight feathers are mostly white with narrow black tips and trailing edge*, and the tail is broadly tipped black. Imm similar to imm Ayres's Hawk-Eagle, but richer rufous below, and may show indication of white patches at primary bases. **HH** pairs are common and widespread in open woodland, bush, and semi-arid country, from near sea-level to about 1500m (rarely wandering to 3000m). **Vo** loud, punctuated repeated upslurs or downslurs *kwee kwee kwee...* often ending on a lower note.

Booted Eagle   *Hieraaetus pennatus*   ♀ 51cm, 20"

Variable eagle, with two distinct morphs, plus intermediates and a rufous variant of dark birds. When perched often just looks rather odd! Typical pale morph has a brownish head, streaked upperparts, often a pale band across wing-coverts, and white underparts with narrow dark streaking. Dark morph has a darker head and all brown underparts. *More easily identified in flight, when both morphs show a broad buffy band across the wing-coverts, buffy scapulars, and a pale crescent on the rump*. From below pale morph has a largely white body and wing-coverts (some lightly streaked), contrasting with black flight feathers and a greyish tail. Dark morph is quite uniform brown below, except for a paler tail, and slightly paler inner primaries (rufous birds have the body and leading edge of underwing-coverts rufous-brown). Both morphs usually show a white spot at base of leading edge of each wing: so-called landing lights. Imm pale morph has pale rufous wash to underparts. **HH** reasonably common Palearctic migrant occurring in a variety of open country from Oct–Apr. **Vo** silent in region. **SS** Wahlberg's Eagle.

Ayres's Hawk-Eagle   *Hieraaetus ayresii*   ♀ 56cm, 22"

Black and white forest eagle with spotted underparts. Close views of ad reveal short crest on rear of crown (some have a narrow white supercilium), black and grey barred tail, and *heavily spotted legs*. Imm is brown above with extensive pale fringes, tawny-buff on forecrown, sides of face and underparts. In flight, ad differs from ad African Hawk-Eagle in having *all dark upperwings*, and from below, in *spotted (not streaked) underparts, and well-barred flight feathers*. Some birds show a white spot at base of leading edge of wing. Imm has pale tawny-buff underparts and underwing-coverts, and extensively barred flight feathers. **HH** singles and pairs are rather local and uncommon in forest and riverine woodland from sea-level to 3000m. **Vo** breeding birds call loud and squealed notes that rise and then fall *weeyah weeyah weeyah...*

Cassin's Hawk-Eagle   *Spizaetus africanus*   ♀ 56cm, 22"

Black and white forest eagle with mostly white underparts, a black and grey barred tail, and some black spotting on the legs. Imm has a rather rufous head and pale-fringed dark brown back and wing-coverts. Below variably washed pale rufous with blackish spotting. In flight, from above, ad looks largely black, but from below *heavily marked black flanks and underwing-coverts contrast strongly with the mostly white underparts*. Imm has the body and underwing-coverts paler tawny than similar species, with variable dark spotting. **HH** in our area restricted to the forests of W and SUg, Rw and Bu, where it is locally common from 1500–2500m. One collected at Mt Elgon, Ke, in 1926 was exceptionally far east of its usual range. **Vo** a repeated two-part high-pitched *kiuu-wi*.

Plate 38

African Hawk-Eagle

Imm

Ad

Imm

Ad

Ad

Ad

Booted Eagle

Ad

Ad

Ad

Imm

Ad

Ad

Ayres's
Hawk-Eagle

Ad

Ad

Ad

Imm

Imm

Ad

Cassin's Hawk-Eagle

Bateleur
Terathopius ecaudatus ♀ 70cm, 28"

Stocky cowl-headed and short-tailed eagle: ad is largely black with extensive bright red facial skin and cere, grey wing-coverts, and a very short chestnut tail (hidden by wings at rest): legs bright red-orange. Most have chestnut backs, but a minority are creamy-white or light brown, a form which is more common in arid areas. Perched ad ♂ shows all-black flight feathers; ad ♀ differs in having a pale grey panel across the closed wing, and is slightly larger. Imm is dark brown with variable paler brown areas on the head and underparts, dull blue-grey or greenish facial skin and cere, and pale legs. Change from imm to full ad plumage takes 6–7 years. Flight is direct and sailing with a few flaps (after take-off) and the tilting action of a tightrope walker. From below, both sexes have black and white underwings, but ad ♂ shows a broad black trailing edge (all flight feathers except outer primaries), and ad ♀ shows a narrow black trailing edge. Orange-red legs project beyond chestnut tail. Imm has similar silhouette, but is brown and may have a slightly longer tail. Imm ♂ shows wider dark trailing edge to wing than imm ♀, presaging ad pattern. **HH** singles and pairs, more rarely small groups, are widespread and often common in a wide variety of open grassland, bushland and woodland, including arid and semi-arid country, from sea-level to 3000m. Individuals range over wide areas, seeking out carcasses, as well as hunting, and often patrol over roads for kills. May make local seasonal movements. **Vo** quite vocal, a loud explosive *yaaaow* often followed by sound of beating wings. Also a high-pitched squealed and slightly downslurred *wee weeye weeye weeye...*

Long-crested Eagle
Lophaetus occipitalis ♀ 58cm, 23"

Striking *small blackish eagle with a long lax crest and bright yellow eyes*. At rest ad appears largely black with pale feathered legs (whiter in ♂, browner, or brown and white in ♀): long crest often waves in the wind. ♀ slightly larger than ♂. Imm is browner, with a shorter crest and dull brown eyes. In rather stiff-winged flight, shows *large white patches in primaries* (from both above and below). Underwing also boldly barred black and grey across the secondaries: tail shows three pale bands. Small size, straight wings, dark rump and barred tail distinguish Long-crested from superficially similar, but massive, Verreaux's Eagle. Imm very similar in flight, but dark brown and white not black and white. **HH** singles are widespread and common residents of moister wooded country from sea-level to 3000m, including forest edge, and settled areas with fields and isolated trees. Commonly perches on roadside poles and trees, swooping to pounce on rodents. **Vo** calls a single downslurred *wiiyuu* in flight. This note is repeated frequently at the nest. **SS** Verreaux's Eagle.

Plate 39

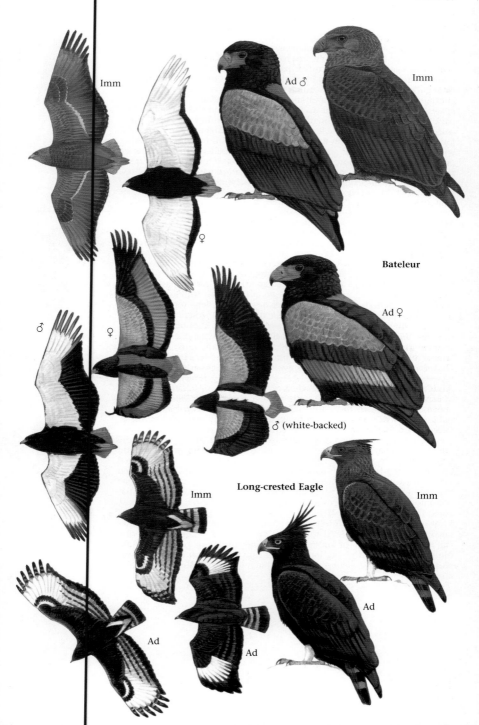

Imm

Ad ♂

Imm

♀

Bateleur

Ad ♀

♂

♀

♂ (white-backed)

Imm

Long-crested Eagle

Imm

Ad

Ad

Ad

Verreaux's Eagle *Aquila verreauxii* ♀ 96cm, 38"

[Black Eagle]

Massive black eagle with a white back and rump extending as a white V around the upper back: bright yellow eye-ring, cere and feet. Sexes similar, but ad ♀ larger. Imm has buff-cream crown and nape, and variable blackish-brown back and wings with much pale fringing, especially to the wing-coverts. Face, neck and breast blackish, becoming browner on belly with large dark streaks and spots. Acquires ad plumage over 4 years. In leisurely gliding and soaring flight (rarely flapping) shows distinctive *broad wings pinched markedly towards the body*. From above, black ad shows bright white back and rump, and prominent white patches at primaries bases. From below, birds are entirely black, except for white primary patches (and yellow feet). Imm is dark with white primary patches and distinct narrowing wings. **HH** pairs are local and rather uncommon residents in a wide range of rocky and mountainous country from 900-3500m, often in drier areas, near inaccessible cliff nesting sites, and in association with their main prey, rock hyrax. **Vo** displaying birds give a far-carrying, loud upslurred and high-pitched scream *iiy'iii*, interspersed with low barking notes *auw auw auw*... **SS** Long-crested Eagle.

Martial Eagle *Polemaetus bellicosus* ♀ 84cm, 33"

Very large and powerful eagle: ad has dark grey-brown upperparts, throat and upper breast, all clearly separated from *pure white underparts, variably peppered with black spots*. Eyes yellow: cere and feet grey. Imm is pale-fringed grey-brown above, with a white face and white underparts including the leg feathering. Attains ad plumage over 5–6 years. In flight, ad shows dark underwings and a black head and throat clearly separated from the white body (spots can be hard to see at distance). Similar, but much smaller Black-chested Snake-Eagle has a white underwing with black bands. Imm has a white body and underwing-coverts which contrast with the black flight feathers. **HH** singles and pairs are widespread and occasionally common in a wide range of bush, wooded grassland, and semi-arid country from sea level to 3500m. May also occasionally range over woodland and forested areas. **Vo** breeding birds give a rising series of loud *kiu kiu kiu kiu* notes, and rasping barks *enk enk enk*... **SS** Black-chested Snake Eagle.

African Crowned Eagle *Stephanoaetus coronatus* ♀ 92cm, 36"

Massive heavily marked eagle with a rough crest. Ad is blackish-brown above, with a brown head and throat, and is *heavily barred and blotched rufous, black and white below:* feathered legs are boldly marked with black. Cere, eyes and feet yellow. Imm is white-headed except for dark-tipped crest, with a heavily scaled grey-brown back and wings, and is largely white below (with a variable pale buff-orange wash across the upper breast), and bold blackish spots on the legs. In flight, appears massive, broad winged and quite long-tailed. Ad is dark above, with grey bands in the wings and tail, and heavily barred below, with *chestnut underwing-coverts*, a broad black trailing edge to the wing, and a strongly barred undertail. Imm has pale chestnut underwing-coverts, more prominently barred flight feathers, and a largely white body. **HH** singles and pairs are rather uncommon and local residents of dense forest and woodland, including riverine and isolated patches, from sea-level to 3500m. **Vo** unique, loud and far-carrying call is a familiar sound of forests. Pairs or single birds engage in aerial tumbling displays whilst giving loud ringing calls that rise and fall in waves *phewee-phewee-phewee-phewee-phewee*... (much-loved by mimicking robin-chats!).

Plate 40

Verreaux's Eagle

Imm

Ad

Imm

Ad

Ad

Ad

Imm

Martial Eagle

Imm

Ad

Ad

Imm

Imm

African Crowned Eagle

Ad

Ad

Ad

BROWN KESTRELS
Slim attractive falcons of open country which, though lacking the spectacular flight of some fal-cons, are still adept at riding the wind, and frequently hover. These four species are predomi-nantly brown, though some have grey heads. Back, tail and underwing markings aid identifica-tion. Females are slightly larger than males.

Common Kestrel   *Falco tinnunculus*   ♀ 33cm, 13"
[Rock Kestrel]

Four distinct races occur. In resident *rufescens*, ad ♂ has a grey head, *rufous upperparts that are well-spotted with black*, a lightly barred blue-grey tail with a broad black sub-terminal band, and strongly washed rufous underparts streaked with black. Ad ♀ is largely brown, with a pale face, more obvious moustache stripes, rufous-brown upperparts heavily spotted and barred black, and rufous underparts streaked blackish. Imm is like ad ♀. Nominate Palearctic race is similar, but much paler. Coastal race *archeri* is smaller and more barred above. In STz race *rupicolus*, ad ♂ is plainer below with a whiter underwing, while ad ♀ is similar, including a grey head and a grey and black barred tail. Imm has browner head and tail. In all races, eyes are dark, cere and legs yellow, and *claws black*. In flight, ad ♂ resembles Lesser Kestrel but lacks blue-grey in upperwing, and the underwing is usually more heav-ily marked (except in *rupicolus*). **HH** singles and pairs of race *rufescens* are rather uncommon residents, often in rocky areas, from sea-level to 4300m; *archeri* is known from coastal NEKe; and *rupicolus* around Songea, STz. Nominate race is a common and widespread winter visitor, often in flocks in a variety of open country from Oct–early May. **Vo** race *rufescens* gives a penetrating *ki-ki-ki-ki...* often followed by a burry squeal. Nominate birds are silent in the region.

Lesser Kestrel   *Falco naumanni*   ♀ 33cm, 13"   ●

Very similar to Common Kestrel, but ad ♂ has a *paler blue-grey head, plain chestnut back, blue-grey greater coverts, and warm chestnut-buff underparts with discrete dark spotting*. Perched ad ♀ and imm only reliably told from nomi-nate ad ♀ Common by *white (not black) claws*. In flight, both sexes show a rather wedge-shaped tail, with central tail feathers slightly protruding, and from below, paler silver-grey underwings with limited speckling. From above ad ♂ has a *blue-grey bar on the greater coverts*. **HH** small groups to large flocks are widespread and common Palearctic migrants and winter visitors to open bushed and wooded grassland, as well as fields and pastures, from Oct–early May, though commoner on northern passage. Often associates with herds of plains game. **Vo** usually silent in the region, but may give a sharp chatter at roosts.

Greater Kestrel   *Falco rupicoloides*   ♀ 36cm, 14"
[White-eyed Kestrel]

Rather thick-set warm-brown kestrel, with dark streaks on head and breast, a *heavily barred back, wings and flanks, and grey tail broadly barred black*. Ad has *creamy-white eyes* and a yellow cere and legs. Imm is similar but more rufous, with a brown and black barred tail, streaked underparts, and brown eyes. In slightly heavy flight, shows obvious *grey and black barred rump and tail from above*, and largely white underwings that contrast with the warm-brown underparts and barred undertail. **HH** singles and pairs are rather uncommon in semi-arid country with scattered trees, and in dry bushed grasslands below 1800m. **Vo** calls loud squeals and barking notes, unlike Common Kestrel.

Fox Kestrel   *Falco alopex*   ♀ 38cm, 15"

Large bright chestnut kestrel with a long rather tapering tail. Ad is *all chestnut-red, finely streaked with black both above and below*. Eyes brownish-yellow: eye-ring, cere, and legs yellow. Imm is similar, but has a more heavily barred tail and blue-grey eye-ring. In flight, appears long-winged with a long slightly graduated tail. From above, looks strikingly rich chestnut with black flight feathers, but from below chestnut body contrasts with paler chestnut underwing-coverts, and silvery-white flight feathers. **HH** pairs are uncommon and local residents of arid and semi-arid cliff and rocky country in NEUg and NWKe, occasionally wandering southwards. **Vo** breeding birds give a high-pitched rasping screech *kreee-kreee-kree*, similar to Common Kestrel.

Plate 41

Common Kestrel

♂

nominate

♀

Ad ♂

rufescens

♀

♂

Ad ♀

♂

♀

Lesser Kestrel

Ad ♂

Ad ♀

Imm

♂

Greater Kestrel

Ad

Ad

Ad

Fox Kestrel

Ad

Ad

Ad

GREY KESTRELS

Two similar kestrels separated on plumage and range (but also consider Sooty Falcon, plate 43). Both species are rather thickset kestrels, with comparatively short, blunt wings. Sexes alike.

Grey Kestrel *Falco ardosiaceus* ♀ 33cm, 13"

Stocky, rather large-headed *all grey kestrel, with yellow skin around the eyes,* yellow cere and legs: eyes dark brown. Appears all slate-grey at distance, but close views reveal fine black streaking, particularly on the head and breast. *Wing tips do not reach tail tip at rest.* ♀ is slightly larger than ♂. Imm is similar to ad but tinged brownish. Eye-ring and cere bluish-green on juv, but quickly turn yellow. Often flies rather slowly on stiff wings, but can be dashing, and sometimes hovers. May appear all grey in flight, but in good light primaries look blacker, and may show slightly barred flight feathers and tail from below. Similar Sooty Falcon (a scarce passage migrant) has uniform slimmer and longer wings which extend beyond the tail tip at rest. **HH** pairs are rather uncommon residents of bushed and wooded grassland, mainly in the north and west below 1800m, but has wandered to coastal NETz. Breeds in Hamerkop nests. **Vo** calls a harsh burry downslurred scream, and a muffled *keek-keek-keeek*. **SS** Sooty Falcon.

Dickinson's Kestrel *Falco dickinsoni* ♀ 31cm, 12"

Rather thickset, large-headed appearance is similar to Grey Kestrel, but ad is easily separated by *pale grey head and rump, and strongly barred pale grey and black tail.* Yellow eye-ring, cere and legs are conspicuous at close range: eyes dark brown. Imm similar, but brown-grey, with less contrasting head and rump, noticeably barred flanks, and blue-green cere. Flies on stiff wings with shallow beats, and occasionally hovers. From above, *pale grey rump and banded tail* are obvious, and from below has more distinctly barred flight feathers and tail than Grey Kestrel. **HH** singles and pairs are locally common residents of lowland open wooded country mainly in the south and east, often associating with palms, and liking to hunt from tall bare trees. Wanderers recorded as vagrants to S and CKe between Jun–Aug. **Vo** screams and burry squeals more like Common than Grey Kestrel.

Pygmy Falcon *Polihierax semitorquatus* 20cm, 8"

Tiny, attractive little raptor with a *white face and underparts.* Ad ♂ is pale-grey above with blacker wings and a short rather conspicuous black and white barred tail. Eye-ring, cere and legs are reddish-pink: eyes brown. Ad ♀ is similar, but with a chestnut-brown back. Imm is duller than ad, with a buff wash across the breast and variable dark grey-brown streaking: sexes also distinguished by back colour. Birds have direct, undulating and rapid flight, revealing a *bright white rump, white spotted black wings, and a black and white barred tail.* **HH** pairs and family groups are common residents of semi-arid bush and dry acacia grasslands, from near sea-level to 1800m. Often seen conspicuously perching on the tops of small bushes. Breeds in White-headed Buffalo-Weaver nests. **Vo** breeding birds call a discordant rather loud screaming squeal, recalling a woodpecker.

Plate 42

Grey Kestrel

Ad

Ad

Ad

Imm

Dickinson's Kestrel

Ad

Ad

Ad

Imm

Pygmy Falcon

Ad

Imm

♀

Imm ♂

Imm ♀

Ad ♀

Ad ♂

MEDIUM-SIZED DARK FALCONS

Dark dashing falcons with rather long sickle-shaped wings, although Red-footed and Amur also have leisurely kestrel-like hunting behaviour (including hovering). Taita Falcon should also be considered (plate 45). Head and underwing markings aid identification. Migrant species often associate with storm fronts and may gather to feed at termite emergences. Most have females slightly larger than males.

African Hobby   *Falco cuvieri*   ♀ 31cm, 12"

Small neat falcon: ad is dark grey-black above and *rufous-chestnut below* with fine blackish breast streaks at close range. Beware some ads have a small patch of chestnut on nape and are similar to Taita Falcon. Imm is similar, but duller and browner above, with a paler throat, and *more heavily streaked underparts*. In flight, appears dashing, slender, and rather short-tailed. Ad has rufous underparts extending onto underwing-coverts, flight feathers and tail paler buffy-rufous with much barring. Imm is similar, but more heavily streaked below. **HH** singles and pairs are uncommon residents and local wanderers from forest edge and woodland, typically in highlands in the west, but lower in ETz, recorded from sea-level to 3000m. **Vo** breeding birds give screaming and shrill *ki ki ki ki...* and a burry *kree kree kree...* **SS** Taita Falcon.

Eurasian Hobby   *Falco subbuteo*   ♀ 36cm, 14"
[European Hobby]

Ad is dark grey above and whitish below heavily streaked with black: *legs and vent chestnut*. Neat face pattern with white cheeks curving round the ear-coverts like an inverted comma. Imm is similar, but browner above with buff fringes, and mostly buff below with heavy dark streaking. Agile in flight, with long slender wings like a giant swift; at a distance it can appear all dark with a white throat. Closer birds show heavily streaked underparts, a densely barred underwing, and a *chestnut vent*. Imm is paler and lacks distinct vent colour of ad. **HH** singles or small groups are common passage migrants and winter visitors from the Palearctic, from late Sep–May. **Vo** silent in region.

Eleonora's Falcon   *Falco eleonorae*   ♀ 41cm, 16"

Medium-large, long-winged, long-tailed falcon with two distinct colour morphs. Pale morph is all dark above with a hobby-like face pattern (but more rounded cheek patch), and breast to vent strongly washed rufous with black streaking. Dark morph appears all brownish-black. Imm is dark above with pale fringing, heavily blotched and streaked on buff below. Flight varies from relaxed with elastic wing beats to agile and dashing when hunting. Long wings and tail always apparent. On both morphs *blackish underwing-coverts* are distinctive. Imm differs from imm Eurasian Hobby in longer wings and tail, and pale bases to flight feathers. **HH** singles and small groups are uncommon but regular passage migrants in the east, with some wintering in STz. Can occur over any habitat on passage, southwards in Oct–Nov, and northwards in Mar to early May. **Vo** silent in region.

Sooty Falcon   *Falco concolor*   ♀ 36cm, 14"

Slim all grey falcon with *long wings reaching to or beyond tail tip* (much shorter in similar Grey Kestrel). Ad has a yellow eye-ring, cere and feet. Imm is dark grey above (pale-fringed), with a hobby-like face pattern, and is creamy-buff below with variable blackish streaking: eye-ring and cere pale bluish. Ad in flight looks very long-winged (sometimes with slightly protruding central tail feathers), and often appears all dark grey, but outer wing and tail end darker in good light. Imm differs from similar imms in having a dark band near tip of undertail. **HH** singles and small groups are uncommon but regular passage migrants from North Africa and the Middle East, from Oct–Dec (passing through to wintering grounds in Madagascar and southern Africa), and less often Feb–May (returning northwards). **Vo** silent in region. **SS** Grey Kestrel.

Plate 43

African Hobby

Ad

Imm

Ad

Imm

Ad

Ad

Ad

Imm

Ad

Imm

Eurasian Hobby

Ad

Imm

Ad

Imm

Ad

Ad

Eleonora's Falcon

Imm

Ad

Ad

Ad

Ad

Imm

Imm

Ad

Sooty Falcon

Amur Falcon   *Falco amurensis*   30cm, 12"
[Eastern Red-footed Falcon]
Perched ad ♂ appears dark slate-grey above and slightly paler below, with a chestnut vent and leg feathering: eye-ring, cere and legs orange-red. Ad ♀ is grey above with black barring, a white forehead, cheeks and throat, remainder of underparts whitish-buff with black streaks and barring, and a plain buff vent. Bare parts as in ♂. Imm is similar to ad ♀, but paler above with brown fringes, and streaked dark below on white (without barring). In flight, ad ♂ shows *striking white underwing-coverts contrasting with dark flight feathers*, and a chestnut vent. Ad ♀ *also has largely white underwing-coverts*, but flight feathers and tail barred with black from below. Imm has darker crown and whiter underparts than imm Red-footed Falcon. 2nd year ♂ has mixed imm-ad plumage like Red-footed Falcon, but with white in underwing-coverts. **HH** singles, small groups, and less often large flocks, are passage migrants from the Eastern Palearctic, moving south through SEKe, E and STz in Nov–Dec; and returning north on a wider front (but rare in the west) Mar to early May. Some overwinter in STz, often associating with other migrant falcons, like Lesser Kestrels. **Vo** mainly silent in region but roosting birds maintain burry squeals.

Red-footed Falcon   *Falco vespertinus*   30cm, 12"
[Western Red-footed Falcon]
Perched ad ♂ is very similar to ad ♂ Amur Falcon, but is a more uniform slate-grey above and below. Ad ♀ has a *blackish eye mask, white cheeks and throat, and orange-buff crown, nape and underparts*: back, wings and tail grey barred blackish. In imm dark eye mask stands out against whiter face, and underparts are buffy with blackish streaking. In flight from above, ad ♂ is dark grey with silvery-grey flight feathers, and from below shows *black underwing-coverts*, and a chestnut vent. Ad ♀ is orange-buff below and on underwing-coverts, contrasting with the heavily barred flight feathers. Imm usually more buff below than imm Amur Falcon. 2nd year ♂ shows a mixture of imm and ad plumage. **HH** rare migrant from the Palearctic, passing mainly to the west of our area, from Oct–May. **Vo** silent in region.

Red-necked Falcon   *Falco chicquera*   36cm, 14"
Ad is distinctive if seen well. The only falcon with a *rich rufous crown and nape and black and white barred underparts*. Close views reveal dark brown moustache stripes, black barring on the upperparts, and a rufous band across the upper breast. Imm is dull on the crown and browner above, with buffy or pale rufous underparts, narrowly streaked on the breast, with heavier blackish barring on flanks and belly. Flight is fast and dashing. From above, ad shows a rufous crown, dark ends to the wings, and a black sub-terminal tail bar, and from below the pale throat and chest contrasts with a well-barred body and wings. Imm has a pale rufous body and underwing-coverts which are largely barred, not streaked as on other medium-sized falcons. **HH** singles and pairs are widespread but rather local from sea-level to 1250m, showing a marked preference for palm country, especially *Borassus*. **Vo** breeding birds call a burry downslur and a more barking *kikikiki...*

Saker Falcon   *Falco cherrug*   ♀ 56cm, 22"
Very large brown and white falcon with a *whitish crown* (very narrowly streaked black). Underparts variably streaked, but usually broadly, brown on white: *leg feathering heavily blotched with brown*. Can be almost identical to some (pale-crowned) imm Lanner Falcons, but closer views show Saker lacks dark band across forecrown, and has a less defined face pattern: Lanner also usually has paler leg feathering. Saker has spots in outer-tail, and incomplete bars on upperside of centre-tail, suggesting centre-tail is plain (all barred on ad Lanner). In flight, long wings are broad-based, and *show whitish bases to flight feathers from below*. **HH** vagrant from the Palearctic with about a dozen records, mainly from the Great Rift Valley, Oct–Apr. **Vo** silent in region.

Plate 44

Amur Falcon

Imm

♂

♂

♂

♀

Imm

Ad ♀

Ad ♂

Imm

Imm

Sub-ad ♂

♂

♀

Ad ♀

Ad ♂

Red-footed Falcon

Imm

Ad

Ad

Ad

Ad

Ad

Imm

Red-necked Falcon

Imm

Ad

Ad

Ad

Ad

Imm

Ad

Saker Falcon

LARGE FALCONS
The three raptors on this plate, together with Saker Falcon (plate 44) are a confusing group of large powerful falcons which often soar, but chase prey with diving stoops, or fast low flight. Best identified by head, body and underwing markings. Taita Falcon should also be compared to species on plate 43. Females are larger than males.

Lanner Falcon   *Falco biarmicus*   ♀ 46cm, 18"

Ad has a *rufous crown and nape, comparatively narrow moustache streaks*, grey upperparts (variably mottled), and a barred tail. Mostly plain buff or pinkish-buff below, lightly spotted on the flanks (widespread nominate race) or with some streaks and bars (northern *abyssinicus*). Imm is much browner above with a pale brown crown, and buffy below with heavy dark streaking. Beware, some imms have rather white crowns and look like the rare Saker Falcon, but Saker usually has *darker leg feathering*. Also, all barred tail distinctive from most Sakers, but some Lanners have a plain centre tail. In flight, wings are narrower than Saker but have similar rather blunt tips. From below, ad has quite plain underwings and on nominate race pale almost plain underparts. Imm is very heavily streaked below and on the underwing-coverts. **HH** by far the most common large falcon in the region, inhabiting semi-arid bush, open rocky hill country, the vicinity of cliffs, and woodlands, from near sea-level to 3200m. **Vo** breeding birds call a deep harsh *kak-kak-kak...* and loud quivering squeals and barks.

Peregrine Falcon   *Falco peregrinus*   ♀ 48cm, 19"

Ad has a *black crown, nape, and broad moustache stripes*. Resident race *minor* is dark grey above with extensive *black and white barring below,* while slightly larger Palearctic migrant race *calidus* (from Oct–Apr) is paler above, and less barred below. Imm *minor* is dark grey-brown above and buffy below, with streaking on the breast, becoming more blotched and barred on flanks and vent. Imm *calidus* is paler brown above (including the crown) and buff below with narrow dark streaking. In flight, appears compact and broad-chested, wings look broad at base and pointed at tips: tail rather short. Ad shows very black and white head, and barred underparts. Imm has under wing-coverts and flight feathers evenly dark barred, not contrasting. **HH** resident *minor* is uncommon throughout the region, usually in the vicinity of cliffs or tall buildings, while *calidus* occurs in the east, including coastal sites, from Oct–Apr. **Vo** race *minor* gives a loud slow and deliberate series of barked gull-like downslurs *kew-kew-kew....* Migrant *calidus* is silent in the region.

Barbary Falcon   *Falco pelegrinoides*   ♀ 46cm, 18"

Suggests a Peregrine × Lanner hybrid, but compact shape is much more like Peregrine in flight. Close views reveal a *rufous hind-crown and nape* (with two dark smudges) and slightly narrower moustache stripes than Peregrine. Paler above than Peregrine and *buffier below, with a few small spots on the breast and fine bars on the flanks and leg feathers*. Imm has a paler nape patch, browner upperparts, and a darker crown than Lanner. Underparts are less boldly streaked than either Lanner or Peregrine. In flight, ad often shows a dark 'comma' on greater underwing-coverts. Imm is separated from imm Lanner by evenly barred underwing. **HH** rarely recorded and presumed migrant from north Africa to NKe, from Nov–Feb. However, reports of ads and imms together, and sightings in June, could indicate a small undetected breeding population. **Vo** calls similar to Peregrine but higher pitched.

Taita Falcon   *Falco fasciinucha*   ♀ 30cm, 12"

Ad is dark slate above with *rufous nape patches divided by a blackish line.* Below, the *white throat contrasts with remainder of rich rufous underparts*. Imm is browner above with pale fringes and streaked below. Often flies with stiff wings, but also makes spectacular diving stoops: looks short-tailed and pale-rumped. From below, ad shows mainly *rich rufous underparts and underwing-coverts*. Imm has an evenly barred underwing. **HH** a very uncommon resident, usually found on high cliffs at scattered localities, but occasionally wanders to nearby open woodland. **Vo** breeding birds call a low-pitched slightly slurred *krieer-krieer-krieer.* **SS** African Hobby.

Plate 45

Lanner Falcon

nominate

Imm

Ad

Imm

Ad

Ad

Ad

Imm

Peregrine Falcon *minor*

Ad

Ad

Imm

Ad

Ad

Barbary Falcon

Imm

Ad

Ad

Imm

Ad

Ad

Ad

Taita Falcon

GUINEAFOWLS

Endemic to Africa, guineafowls are distinctive spotted gamebirds of forest and bush. All are highly gregarious, foraging, chasing and dust-bathing together. They respond to danger with loud far-carrying rattling and trilling calls. Sexes are alike.

Helmeted Guineafowl *Numida meleagris* 61cm, 24"

Ads are easily identified by an upright *bony casque on top of the head*. Races vary mainly in the shape and colour of the casque and gape wattles. Across Ug and NKe nominate birds have a variable-sized casque and rounded blue gape wattles. In NEKe *somaliensis* has pointed blue wattles with red tips, and a prominent tuft of bristles extending from the bill base. From CKe to CTz *reichenowi* has a long casque and pointed red wattles. In WTz, and in coastal Ke and ETz *mitrata* has blue wattles with red tips like *somaliensis* but lacks long facial bristles, and in SWTz *marungensis* is like *mitrata* but has a shorter paler casque. Imms are duller than ads with smaller casques and wattles. Juvs are spotted and barred with rufous, buff and black. **HH** family groups to large flocks are widespread and sometimes very common in a wide range of grassland, bush country, woodland and cultivation from sea-level to 2200m. **Vo** calls a trumpeted loud rattling *kruh-kruh-kruh-krahhhhh krr krr krr...*, and a piped squeaky *pi-pi'oo* first two notes identical, the last falling.

Vulturine Guineafowl *Acryllium vulturinum* 71cm, 28"

A tall and elegant guineafowl with a *long pointed tail*, a bare blue-grey head and neck with a bristly russet hind-cap, and a *bright cobalt-blue breast covered by long lanceolate black and white feathers*. Imm is largely dull grey-brown with rufous and buff mottling. **HH** small groups to large flocks are locally common in arid and semi-arid bush country and grassland, from sea-level to 1900m. **Vo** rattled call is faster and higher-pitched than Helmeted Guineafowl, a piped *wi-yi-wi-yi-wi-yi-wii*, the *yi* notes being slightly higher creating a see-saw effect.

Crested Guineafowl *Guttera pucherani* 54cm, 21"

A *shaggy-crested forest guineafowl* which is spotted with pale-blue. In EKe and ETz the nominate race (**Kenya Crested Guineafowl**) has bright red skin around the eyes and on the throat, and entirely spotted neck feathering. Further west race *verreauxi* has red skin only on the throat and plain black neck feathering. In SETz race *barbata* has similar plain black neck feathers, but lacks any red skin on the head or neck. Imms are much duller with extensive rusty, buff and black bars, spots and mottling. **HH** family groups and flocks of the nominate race are widespread and locally common in forest and dense thickets from near sea-level to 1800m; *verreauxi* is less common in montane forest from 1700–3000m; and *barbata* inhabits coastal forest in SETz. **Vo** nominate calls a very harsh rhythmical clucking with descending churrs; while *verreauxi* gives a crack followed by a distinct rapid piping *krk pu-pu-pu-pu-pu*, as well as drawn-out nasal unmusical growls.

Stone Partridge *Ptilopachus petrosus* 28cm, 11"

A *dark bantam-like gamebird which frequently cocks its tail*. At close quarters shows a slightly scaly head, faint barring on the flanks, and red facial skin. Sexes similar, but ♀ may be paler on the breast. Imm similar to ad but rather more barred. **HH** pairs and small groups are rarely common on rocky hillsides from 600–2300m. If disturbed usually runs over rocks to cover. **Vo** a well orchestrated duet, rising and falling like a whistled wave *oo-wirr'oo-wirr'oo-wirr...*, while other birds utter soft trilled churrs. **SS** Crested Francolin (when tail is cocked).

Udzungwa Forest-partridge *Xenoperdix udzungwensis* 28cm, 11" ● ●

A dark forest-dwelling partridge-like bird with a red bill, rufous sides to the head and throat, olive-brown upperparts (variably barred rufous and black), and blackish spotted underparts: legs yellow. Sexes similar. **HH** Tz endemic discovered in 1991 and only known from Ndundulu and Nyumbanitu in the west Udzungwa mountains, where it is locally common in montane forest from 1350–1900m. **Vo** subdued high-pitched peeping notes and a whistled song have been reported.

Plate 46

Helmeted Guineafowl

nominate

somaliensis

reichenowi

Imm

Vulturine Guineafowl

Crested Guineafowl

nominate

barbata

Stone Partridge

Udzungwa Forest-partridge

verreauxi

FOREST FRANCOLINS

These rather dark francolins are typical of western and highland forests, although often shy and difficult to observe. They draw attention to themselves with their loud calls (notably in the morning and evening) when they may also appear at forest edge or on trails.

Scaly Francolin *Francolinus squamatus* 31cm, 12"

Medium-sized olive-brown francolin with variable pale buff-brown feather edges giving a scaly effect. Bill red, and legs red or orange-red. ♂ may have one or two spurs. In addition to individual variation eastern birds are darker overall than those west of the Great Rift Valley (and may appear almost plain brown if only seen briefly). Imm has a duller bill than ad, is warmer rufous-brown flecked with black above and lightly barred black and white below. **HH** pairs and small groups are widespread and locally common, in forest, bamboo and secondary areas from 800–3000m. **Vo** crescendo call begins with soft, rising and grating churrs that get louder *k-rrrk k-rrrrk...* and end in a set of hysterical screamed and rasping *kereeeek kereeeek kereeeek.*

Forest Francolin *Francolinus lathami* 20cm, 8"

[Latham's Forest Francolin]
Striking small dark forest francolin. Ad ♂ is distinct with *pale grey sides to the face*, rich chestnut-brown upperparts, and *black underparts heavily marked with white heart-shape spots*. Ad ♀ is largely brown, with warm-rufous cheeks, and brown underparts with small buff and white spots. Both sexes have blackish bills and yellow legs. Imm is similar to ♀ but with blackish streaking above, a pale throat, and brown underparts speckled with white and black. **HH** singles, pairs and small groups are very shy and uncommon in primary forests of W and SUg and NWTz (at Minziro Forest), from 700–1400m. **Vo** repeated hollow and burry calls *krr-krou krr-krou...* the second note falling and fading.

Nahan's Francolin *Francolinus nahani* 20cm, 8" ●

Most similar to Forest Francolin but darker blackish-brown above with *red skin around the eyes*, and *black and white streaked underparts*: bill and legs red. Sexes alike. Imm is darker than ad with greyish legs. **HH** an unusual francolin occurring in small groups and walking around with cocked tails recalling Stone Partridge. In our area appears to be restricted from 1000–1400m in the Budongo, Bugoma and Mabira forests of W and SUg, but it may be overlooked. **Vo** unfrancolin-like call is a rising-falling wave similar to Stone Partridge. Parties erupt into a series of rapid growls that break into long complex whistles, which grow louder and then stop abruptly.

Jackson's Francolin *Francolinus jacksoni* ♂ 46cm, 18" ●

Very large rufous-brown francolin with a whitish throat and bright chestnut underparts each feather fringed in white: bill and legs red. Sexes similar, but ♀ is smaller than ♂. Imm is duller than ad, with some dark barring on the upperparts and from the lower breast to vent. **HH** almost endemic to Ke where pairs are locally common in moorland, bamboo and forest edge from 2300–3500m. It is most numerous on Mt Kenya and the Aberdares, less common in the Cherangani Mts and Mau plateau, and rare on Mt Elgon (including one Ug record). **Vo** calls a loud, rasping and slowly delivered *kirr-kee-kik.*

Handsome Francolin *Francolinus nobilis* ♂ 46cm, 18" ●

Most similar to Jackson's Francolin but has red-skin around the eyes, more grey feathering on the neck, and a totally different range. Scaly Francolin is smaller, duller brown and lacks red around the eyes. Sexes similar, but ♀ is smaller and slightly duller. Imm is like ad, but duller, with dark grey and tawny barred upperparts. **HH** pairs and small groups inhabit dense forest and bamboo thicket from 2150–2500m, in WUg, Rw and Bu. They are most often seen on forest tracks at dawn and dusk. **Vo** loud and musical call for a francolin, a rising repeated *kor-kik'ik*, and then a scratchy descending *kikek kikeyk kikoik kikoyk.*

Plate 47

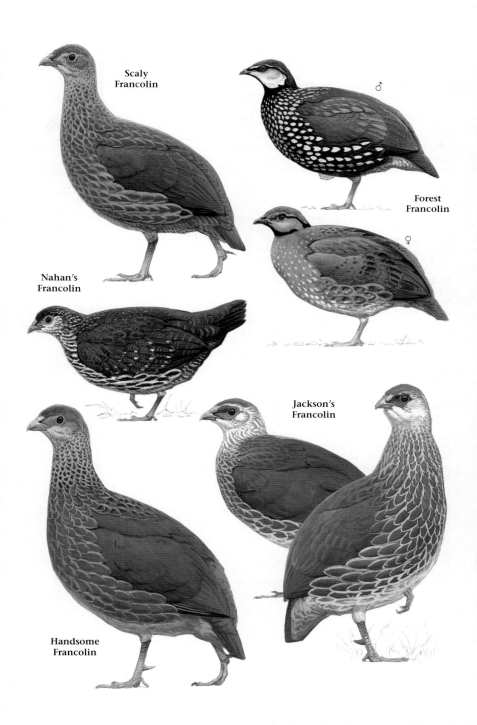

Scaly
Francolin

Forest
Francolin

♂

♀

Nahan's
Francolin

Jackson's
Francolin

Handsome
Francolin

RED-WINGED FRANCOLINS

Often known as the red-winged group (although the closely related Ring-necked Francolin lacks this feature). All have rather strong head patterns and white throats and can be difficult to identify in the field. Careful attention to head, neck and breast markings, together with distribution and habitat aid identification. Sexes alike in all except Ring-necked. Immatures are duller versions of adults. All occur as pairs or in small coveys.

Shelley's Francolin *Francolinus shelleyi* 33cm, 13"
Best identified from similar francolins by a *narrow black-edged (or speckled) white line extending from the eyes down sides of neck.* Underparts pale buffy-white with blotchy chestnut streaks, *belly barred black and white.* Darker birds (sometimes considered a distinct race *macarthuri*) occur in the Chyulu Hills, Ke. **HH** locally common in grassland and wooded grassland from 700–3000m, mainly from CKe to NTz, but with scattered records from further south, and in SWUg, Rw and Bu. Usually shy so perhaps overlooked. **Vo** calls a repeated short and unhurried *tirich-chi-che'e* which rises and falls.

Moorland Francolin *Francolinus psilolaemus* 38cm, 15"
Larger than Shelley's Francolin with a basically similar face pattern, but *line behind the eye and throat are buffy-orange or pale buff* (not white). *Underparts are warmer rufous-buff with small black spots across the upper breast, less extensive chestnut streaking, and no strong black and white barring on the belly.* **HH** local and uncommon in moorland on Mt. Kenya, the Aberdares and Mau Narok in Ke, but rather more common on Mt. Elgon in both Ke and Ug, from 2300–4000m. **Vo** call is virtually identical to Shelley's Francolin.

Red-winged Francolin *Francolinus levaillantii* 38cm, 15"
[Red-wing Francolin]
More rufous on sides of face and neck than similar francolins, with a *rufous-orange supercilium extending broadly down side of neck, a rufous band also across the throat and a black and white barred collar extending around the upper breast and hindneck*: breast largely rufous with buff streaking. **HH** inhabits open woodland, grassland, scrub and cultivation from 600–3000m. In WUg, Rw and Bu it is locally common, but uncommon further east due to habitat loss, while its status in STz is unclear. **Vo** calls like Shelley's Francolin, a sharp *kik-kik-kik-kik-kik...*, and then a short rapidly delivered and repeated *kik-ker-ri-ku...*

Orange River Francolin *Francolinus levaillantoides* 33cm, 13"
Similar to Shelley's Francolin, but lacks a white line behind the eye, and the underparts are a stronger buff without obvious black and white barring on the belly. Birds in our region are the race *archeri* and it is possible they are specifically distinct from nominate birds in southern Africa. **HH** in our area poorly known and presumed to be scarce in grassland and wooded grassland at Kidepo and Mt Moroto in NUg and in the Huri Hills and Mt. Kulal in NKe. **Vo** call is similar to Shelley's Francolin, but a more urgent and higher-pitched *ki-keet ki-kit*.

Ring-necked Francolin *Francolinus streptophorus* 33cm, 13"
Quite a dark francolin with rufous-chestnut sides to the face and neck, a *long white supercilium*, white throat, and a *wide black and white collar across the upper breast and hindneck*. Sexes quite similar but ♀ has a darker crown and more barring both above and below. **HH** very shy and local in NUg, Rw, Bu and NWTz, where they inhabit open woodland and grass-covered rocky hillsides from 600–1800m. It is now extremely scarce in WKe. **Vo** call is reported to be a rather pigeon-like double *cooo-cooo* with a higher second note, and also a trill and a loud flight call.

Plate 48

Shelley's
Francolin

Moorland
Francolin

Orange River
Francolin

Red-winged
Francolin

♂

♀

Ring-necked
Francolin

OTHER FRANCOLINS
A mixed group of francolins that are mainly associated with bushed grasslands.

Coqui Francolin *Francolinus coqui* 28cm, 11"

Small well-marked francolin. In nominate race the ad ♂ has a *chestnut-rufous head and neck*, and entirely black and white barred underparts. ♂♂ of rather similar races *maharao* and *hubbardi* have barring on the underparts confined to the breast and flanks, the belly is plain buff. Nominate ad ♀ has a buff-chestnut head, throat and breast, a black line above and behind the eye, and another around the throat: the flanks and belly are barred. ♀ *hubbardi* has a darker crown, greyish breast and a plain belly, ♀ *maharao* is similar but with finer barring. Imms are similar to ♀♀ but paler. **HH** pairs and family parties are widespread and often common in wooded and bushed grassland from sea-level to 2200m. Nominate birds are particularly associated with open *Brachystegia* woodland from SWUg to STz, and locally in coastal Ke. Race *maharao* is found from NKe to NETz, and *hubbardi* in CKe to NTz. **Vo** two very different calls are heard mainly at dawn and dusk, an onomatopoeic and repeated see-sawing *co-kee co-kee co-kee...* which is delivered leisurely and increases in volume, and a growled burry *ke-ke-ke-kekeke kuh* which falls away gradually.

Chestnut-naped Francolin *Francolinus castaneicollis* 43cm, 17"

A large red-billed francolin with a *black forehead and short black supercilium*. In our area, race *atrifrons* is largely dull brown above with pale feather shafts and fringes, and little or no chestnut on the nape or back: underparts are largely buffy with some darker speckling across the upper breast. Sexes are similar but legs spurred in ♂. **HH** a single bird on a rocky hillside near Moyale, NKe, is the only record. **Vo** reported to be a harsh *kek-kek-kek-kerak*, often in a duet.

Hildebrandt's Francolin *Francolinus hildebrandti* ♂ 41cm, 16"

Some local variation but typical ad ♂ is dark brown above and heavily spotted with black and white below: bill dark with a orange-yellow base and legs orange-red. Smaller ad ♀ is like ♂ above but the underparts are mainly rufous-buff, often with some darker speckling to sides of upper breast. Imm is similar to ad ♀ but more heavily marked above and below with bars and streaks. **HH** pairs or small groups are locally common from 1000–2500m, in varied habitats which include thick bush country, grassed areas on rocky hillsides, acacia woodland and the edges of montane heath. **Vo** calls a wooden crescendo of rapid notes *tunk-unkunkunk* with first one loudest. May continue for long periods breaking into an insane bout of screaming, often given in duet.

Heuglin's Francolin *Francolinus icterorhynchus* 36cm, 14"

A very streaky, mottled and scalloped brown francolin with a yellowish base to the lower mandible, a dark brown crown, long pale supercilium, and a bare patch of yellowish-brown skin behind the eyes. Sexes alike but ♀ may be smaller. Imm is like ♀, but more heavily barred above. **HH** pairs are locally common in grassland, bushed grassland and cultivation, from 500–1400m in Ug. **Vo** calls harsh grating rasps, growls and churrs which are similar to several species of spurfowl.

Clapperton's Francolin *Francolinus clappertoni* 43cm, 17"

Most similar to Hildebrandt's Francolin but easily identified by the red-based blackish bill, *bare red skin around the eyes* and a white throat. Sexes alike but ad ♀ is smaller. Imm is like ♀ but duller. **HH** pairs and family parties are common and widespread in bushed grassland in Kidepo NP and south towards Mt Elgon in NEUg. **Vo** calls a loud grating *kerak...* repeated 4–6 times.

Plate 49

Coqui Francolin

♀

♂

nominate

hubbardi

♂

Chestnut-naped
Francolin

♂

♀

Hildebrandt's
Francolin

Clapperton's
Francolin

Heuglin's
Francolin

Crested Francolin *Francolinus sephaena* 30cm, 12"

Small brown francolin with a long white supercilium and some white streaking on the upperparts: *often cocks tail and raises crown feathers when agitated or alarmed* (does not look crested if relaxed). Widespread race *grantii* has small bold dark brown spots across the breast, while in NKe *spilogaster* and in EKe and ETz *rovuma* are more streaky brown below. ♀♀ and imms are slightly more barred above. *In flight, mostly black tail is conspicuous.* **HH** pairs and family groups are widespread and often common in a wide range of bush country, wooded grasslands and thickets from sea-level to 2100m. **Vo** calls are monotonous repeated and very rapid short rising squeals followed by descending scratchy notes *kik-kera'ra kik-kera'ra kik-kera'ra...* **SS** Stone Partridge

SPURFOWLS

Bare-throated spurfowls or francolins are characteristic of rather open bushed and wooded grassland. All three can be easily identified by the colour of their naked throats. Females are generally smaller than males and lack leg spurs.

Yellow-necked Spurfowl *Francolinus leucoscepus* ♂ 40cm, 16"

[Yellow-necked Francolin]
Large francolin with a blackish bill, distinctive *bare yellow throat* and red-orange skin around the eyes. Brown upperparts have some narrow buff streaking, underparts more heavily streaked brown and white. Imm is similar, but generally greyer with narrow black barring above and with a paler yellow throat. In flight, reveals a large pale patch in the primaries. **HH** pairs and family parties are common residents in drier bushland, bushed and wooded grassland and cultivation, from sea-level to 2400m. In game parks often becomes rather tame and easy to observe, dusting and searching for food in the open and along tracks. **Vo** calls a loud grating series of up to seven descending scratchy upslurs that fade away *k-wirrrk...k-wirrrrrrk... k'wirrrrrrkk'wirrrrrrkk'wirrrrrrk.*

Grey-breasted Spurfowl *Francolinus rufopictus* ♂ 40cm, 16"   ●

[Grey-breasted Francolin]
Similar in size to Yellow-necked Spurfowl, but has a *red base to the bill*, orangey or reddish skin around the eyes, *white malar stripes*, and *pinkish-red or orange throat skin*: legs dark brown. *Underparts are largely greyish with narrow black barring, becoming boldly streaked chestnut, black and white on the flanks.* Imm is similar, but with duller bare parts and more barring both above and below. In flight, shows pale primaries patches. **HH** endemic to NTz, especially in the Mwanza to Serengeti area where pairs and family groups are locally common in acacia country, bushed grasslands and in riverine woodland. Occasionally hybridises with Yellow-necked Spurfowl. **Vo** calls are similar to Yellow-necked but slightly more hurried.

Red-necked Spurfowl *Francolinus afer* ♂ 38cm, 15"

[Red-necked Francolin]
A dark francolin with the *bill, skin around the eyes, throat and legs all red*. Four races occur in two distinct groups: from WUg and Rw east to WKe and south to SWTz race *cranchii* is brown above, and rather plain grey-brown below with some chestnut streaks on the flanks and belly. In NWTz and Bu *harterti* is similar but the rufous streaking is darker. In the other group, eastern birds are much more boldly streaked black and white on the underparts. Coastal Ke *leucoparaeus* has some white to the sides of face, while in C and ETz *melanogaster* has a blacker face. Intergrades occur in several areas. Imms are duller with dark, not red, bills. In flight, appears all dark above, lacking the pale primary patches of other spurfowls. **HH** pairs and family groups are widespread but local and often shy, in bushed and wooded grassland, thickets and in cultivation, from sea-level to 1500m. **Vo** often calls a harsh rhythmical *ker-ker-kek...* or *ker-kek-kek...* and a rapid *kekekekek*, becoming more urgent and accelerating into a descending series of whistled upslurs that fade away.

Plate 50

Crested Francolin
grantii

♀

♂

**Yellow-necked
Spurfowl**

cranchii

**Grey-breasted
Spurfowl**

leucoparaeus

Red-necked Spurfowl

QUAILS

Small rotund grassland birds which are rarely seen unless flushed, when they tend to fly low and straight, before dropping to cover and hiding. Most often encountered in pairs, although Harlequin Quail may occur in large numbers on migration.

Harlequin Quail *Coturnix delegorguei* 15cm, 6"

Ad ♂ is a dark brown quail with a *bold black and white face pattern and a long white supercilium*. Underparts are rich-rufous and black, with black streaking extending on to the flanks. Ad ♀ and imm are very similar to Common Quail but generally darker and less streaked on the flanks. **HH** common and widespread in grassland and cultivation from sea-level to 3000m, often appearing in large numbers during the rains. **Vo** calls a sharp but rather quiet, rhythmical and insect-like *swit-wit-wit wit-wit-wit wit-wit...*

Common Quail *Coturnix coturnix* 19cm, 7.5"

Very difficult to identify from ♀ Harlequin Quail, and particularly so as they are usually only seen in flight. In resident race *erlangeri* ad ♂ is distinctive with a dark chestnut face, but ♀ differs in being paler overall with heavier streaking on the flanks. Both sexes of nominate Palearctic race are also similar and paler than Harlequin, especially on the cheeks. Ad ♂ may show a black throat patch. **HH** sometimes common in moist grassland and cultivation from 1200–3000m, but down to 600m in Ug. Small numbers of nominate birds reach the north of the area between Nov–Apr. **Vo** ♂ calls a three-part soft but far-carrying *twi twi'wit twi twi'wit twi twi'wit...* and the ♀ answers with a soft nasal *nrah*.

Blue Quail *Coturnix adansonii* 14cm, 5.5"

Ad ♂ is a *small dark quail without a white supercilium*. Black and white throat contrasts with *dark slate-blue body plumage and rufous wing patches*. Ad ♀ is generally dark brown with much mottling, a paler throat and *strongly barred underparts*. Appears very small and dark on the wing. **HH** widespread, scarce and erratic migrant, occasionally recorded during the rains in wet grasslands from sea-level to 1800m. **Vo** calls a trisyllabic whistled piping *kew kew yew*, descending in half-tones, the first note slightly louder, and sometimes a soft *ki-rik-ik* when flushed.

BUTTON-QUAILS

Tiny secretive quail-like birds which are usually only seen when flushed (and hard to flush a second time). Small size and whirring flight identify them as button-quails, rump colour separates species. ♂ is responsible for incubation and rearing the young.

Common Button-quail *Turnix sylvatica* 14cm, 5.5"
[Kurrichane Buttonquail, Little Button-quail]

If seen well ad shows pale eyes, very scaly upperparts, a rufous-orange wash across the breast, and black spots on the sides of the breast and flanks. Ad ♀ is brighter than ♂. Imm is like ♂ but more spotted across the breast. In flight, *pale upperwing-coverts contrast with darker flight feathers: rump and tail barred brown*. **HH** locally common resident and wanderer to dry and moist grassland, and rough cultivation, from sea-level to 2000m. Single birds and pairs are most often seen, but they can be more numerous during influxes. **Vo** ♀ calls a soft resonant fog-horn-like bugle that increases in volume *whoooooooooo*.

Black-rumped Button-quail *Turnix hottentotta* 14cm, 5.5"

Very similar to Common Button-quail, but often more rufous on sides of head (especially in ♀), spots may extend right across the breast. Imm is duller than ♂ with dark barring on the breast and flanks. Best identified in flight when *black rump and tail are obvious*. Our birds are the race *nana*. **HH** locally common in wet grassland from 1200–1800m in WUg, but always shy and hard to see. Now very rare in WKe. **Vo** ♀ gives a soft but carrying *ooooo...* (once per second) that increases slightly in volume and then fades, very similar to Namaqua Dove.

Quail-plover *Ortyxelos meiffrenii* 13cm, 5"
[Lark Button-quail]

A very small strange bird which may suggest a tiny courser or even a lark. Standing birds are well camouflaged but in flight shows a *unique bold black and white wing pattern*. ♀ is brighter than ♂, and imm is paler. **HH** very local and uncommon in semi-arid grasslands, and perhaps partially migratory. Disturbed birds run, freeze, or may rock forwards in a slow walk. **Vo** reported to call a soft low whistle, but silent when flushed.

Plate 51

Harlequin
Quail

♀

♂

Blue
Quail

♂

Common
Quail

nominate

erlangeri

Common
Button-quail

♀

Quail-plover

♀

♀

♀

Black-rumped
Button-quail

FLUFFTAILS

Tiny secretive rails which are extremely difficult to see. Usually, in fact often only, located by call. All males have chestnut on the head, but colour of tail, and presence of spots or streaking on the body and wings aid identification. Females are even harder to observe and identify and are described below.

White-spotted Flufftail *Sarothrura pulchra* 17cm, 6.5"

Ad ♂ has head, upper back, breast and tail bright chestnut-red, the remainder of the plumage is black *peppered with white spots*. Ad ♀ has the head and breast similar to ♂, but the body and wings are barred blackish-brown and rufous-buff, and the tail has some blackish barring. Imms like ads but duller and browner. **HH** pairs are locally common residents of swampy areas within forest, along streams in thickets, and in dense overgrown cultivation, from 700–2000m. **Vo** throughout the year, calls a ventriloquial *pooh-pooh-pooh-pooh…* varying in speed and volume. Excited birds call a rapid piercing *keekeekeek*.

Buff-spotted Flufftail *Sarothrura elegans* 17cm, 6.5"

Ad ♂ has a bright chestnut-red head and breast, a blackish-brown back and wings *heavily spotted with buff* (sometimes appearing very dense and mottled), and a rufous and black banded tail. Ad ♀ is brown above spangled with pale buff and black, and largely dingy olive-brown below with a whitish throat and extensive darker brown and buff barring. Imm is like ad ♀ but plainer and duller. **HH** uncommon resident of forest, bamboo and dense thicket (not necessarily near water), mainly in the highlands below 2600m. Also occurs as an erratic wanderer, turning up in unexpected places, like city gardens. **Vo** commonly heard after rain and sometimes throughout the night: its distinctive fog-horn note grows in volume and is a far-carrying *mmm ooooooooooo*. Each call lasts about 3 seconds and is given about every 10.

Red-chested Flufftail *Sarothrura rufa* 17cm, 6.5"

Ad ♂ has a deep chestnut-red head, upper back and breast; remainder of plumage is black with narrow white streaks, and small white spots on the tail. Ad ♀ is dark brown above, spotted or lightly barred with buff, and brown below scaled and barred buff with a whitish throat and belly. Imm is similar to ad ♀ but plainer and darker. **HH** common but secretive resident of bogs, swamps and marshes from sea-level to 2700m. **Vo** calls all year with a long series of accelerating *e-wump…* notes, and also a nasal upslurred *wiiwiiwiiwii…*

Streaky-breasted Flufftail *Sarothrura boehmi* 17cm, 6.5"

Ad ♂ is similar to Red-chested Flufftail above, but below has less extensive chestnut on the breast and *largely white black-streaked breast to vent*. Ad ♀ is very dark above, with fine buff streaks and fringes and pale below with a white throat and boldly scaled flanks. Imm is blackish with a whitish throat and belly. **HH** poorly known, presumed intra-African migrant to seasonally flooded grasslands, which is mainly recorded in our area from Apr–Jul. **Vo** calls a muffled series of identical *whooo* notes, given about every 2 seconds. Also gives more rapid and nasal *woo*, *e-woo* or *goo* calls, sometimes with a rising and then falling effect.

Striped Flufftail *Sarothrura affinis* 17cm, 6.5"

Ad ♂ is most like Streaky-breasted Flufftail but has a *chestnut tail (not black)*. Ad ♀ is dark-brown above mottled and fringed with buff and buffy-white below spotted and barred with brown: tail is barred dull rufous and black. Birds in our area are the race *antonii*. **HH** rarely recorded presumed resident of montane grasslands and moorland, mainly above 3000m in Ke, but down to 1500m in STz. **Vo** repeatedly calls a muffled drawn-out *wooooo* which increases in volume, and also an excitable machine-gun-like rattle.

Chestnut-headed Flufftail *Sarothrura lugens* 15cm, 6"

Ad ♂ has *chestnut restricted to the top and sides of head*, a white throat, and black and white streaked breast to vent: tail black with small white spots. Ad ♀ is largely dingy blackish-brown finely speckled with white above, with browner sides to the head, and a paler throat and belly. Imm blackish with a white throat. **HH** rare and little known, it was collected in Ugalla, WTz in 1883, and reported from Rw in the mid-1980s. It is thought to favour rank vegetation and grassy marshes. **Vo** calls a long series of increasingly loud but muffled *poohpoohpoohpooh* notes, that rise very slightly in tone. Also a longer drawn out single *pooooh*.

Plate 52

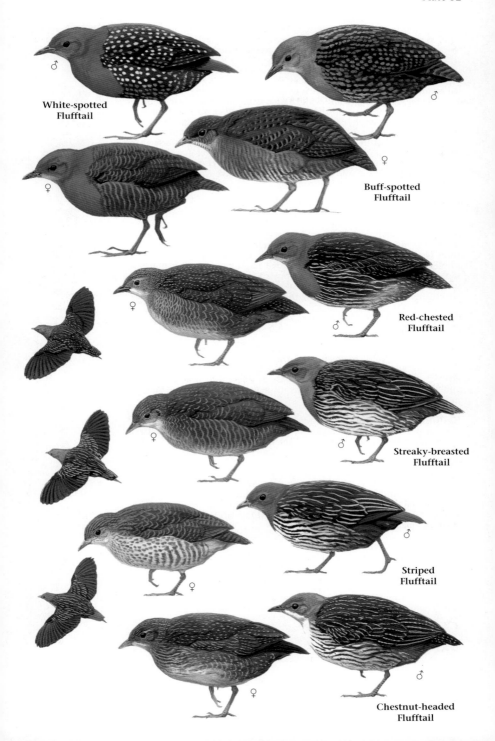

White-spotted
Flufftail

♂

♂

♀

Buff-spotted
Flufftail

♀

♀

Red-chested
Flufftail

♂

♀

♂

Streaky-breasted
Flufftail

♀

♂

Striped
Flufftail

♀

♂

Chestnut-headed
Flufftail

CRAKES AND RAILS

A varied and mostly secretive group of terrestrial birds inhabiting moist grasslands, rank vegetation, as well as temporary and permanent swamps. Invariably brief views hinder identification. With similar species look for bill and leg colour, extent of spots and streaks above, and barring (if any) on the flanks.

African Crake   *Crex egregia*   23cm, 9"

Ad is similar to several other crakes with mottled brown upperparts, a grey face and breast, and black and white barred flanks and belly. Best identified by yellow-green or grey bill with a pinkish-red base, *narrow white supercilium and no white streaking or spots on the upperparts*. Sexes are similar. Imm is duller, with a fainter supercilium and brown bill, a brownish face and throat, and less distinct barring on the flanks. **HH** shy and local intra-African migrant to marsh and swamp edges, rank and wet grass, from sea-level to 2000m, breeding in STz from Oct–May, rarely elsewhere. **Vo** calls a dry *krik-krik-krik-krik...*, and also a quiet francolin-like *chi-co* with the second note lower and rather questioning.

Corncrake   *Crex crex*   27cm, 10.5"   ●

Larger than African Crake, but overall tone is much more buffy-brown, with a pale pinkish-brown bill, broad grey supercilium, greyish throat to breast, and remainder of the underparts pale and barred russet on the flanks. *Striking warm-rufous wings* obvious in flight. Sexes similar, but ♀ may show less grey on foreneck. Imm is duller and less heavily patterned. **HH** singles or small groups are seldom recorded and uncommon Palearctic passage migrants to both dry and wet grasslands in Oct–Dec and Mar–May, from sea-level rarely to 3000m. **Vo** silent in Africa, but ♂ utters repeated advertising *crek-crek* when breeding (hence scientific name).

Spotted Crake   *Porzana porzana*   24cm, 9.5"

Small dark-brown crake *with extensive white spots and flecks above and below*, barred flanks, and *plain buff undertail coverts: in flight shows diagnostic white leading edge to wing*. Ad ♂ has grey face and throat well spotted with white and a short thick yellow-green bill with a red base. Similar ♀ has less grey on the face and throat. Imm is browner including sides of face and breast. **HH** very scarce Palearctic visitor and passage migrant to swamps, marshes and wet grasslands with scattered records mainly from Oct–May. **Vo** silent in region.

Baillon's Crake   *Porzana pusilla*   18cm, 7"

Very small brown and grey crake: ad ♂ is best identified from Little Crake by *plain greenish bill, slightly heavier white streaks, rings and squiggles, on back and wing-coverts, and more strongly barred flanks*. Also has shorter primaries. Ad ♀ is similar, also grey below, but paler on the throat and breast. Imm is buff-brown below, with a pale throat, and buff-brown barred flanks. **HH** resident race *obscura* is uncommon in marshes and dense lakeside vegetation; they are known to wander locally and are probably joined by migrant Palearctic race *intermedia* from Nov–Apr. **Vo** calls a frequent very sharp *tik*, various rasping noises, a loud wooden rattling, and other calls with a laughing quality.

Little Crake   *Porzana parva*   19cm, 7.5"

Very similar to Baillon's Crake, but ad has a *red base to pale green bill*. Ad ♂ is duller above with fewer solid white streaks, *almost plain brown wing-coverts, longer primaries, and less distinct barring confined to the lower flanks and vent*. Ad ♀ is buff-brown below with a whiter throat and breast. Imm is like ♀, but whiter below, more spotted above, and with more extensive barred flanks. **HH** vagrant from the Palearctic with few records in WUg and possibly CKe. **Vo** silent in region.

Plate 53

Imm

Ad

African
Crake

Corncrake

Ad

Imm

Ad

Baillon's
Crake

♀

♂

Spotted
Crake

♂

♀

Little
Crake

Black Crake *Amaurornis flavirostris* 20cm, 8"

Small distinctive *black crake with a yellow-green bill, and red eyes and legs.* Sexes alike. Imm is browner above and greyer below with a whitish throat, and duller bill and legs. **HH** pairs and small groups are widespread and often common on virtually any lake or small pool with fringing and floating vegetation from sea-level to 3000m. Often walks in the open at any time of day. **Vo** call is a frequently heard and noisy duet: one bird makes a complex and musical bubbling while the other responds with low growls.

Purple Swamphen *Porphyrio porphyrio* 46cm, 18"

[Purple Gallinule]
Enormous purply-blue and green crake with white undertail-coverts, a *heavy red bill and frontal shield,* thick red legs and long toes. Sexes alike. Imm is duller grey-blue, especially pale on the belly, with a browner, not green, back and innerwings: bill, frontal shield and legs are duller. **HH** pairs and small groups are widespread, but rarely common in larger marshes and swamps from sea-level to 3000m. Generally shy and retiring, but feeds in the open where not disturbed. **Vo** loud and varied repertoire, consisting of strong trumpeting and bugling calls.

Allen's Gallinule *Porphyrio alleni* 30cm, 12"

[Lesser Gallinule]
Similar to Purple Swamphen, but *much smaller with a red bill and greenish-blue frontal shield.* Sexes similar. Imm is largely brown with buff fringes to the back and wings, a whiter throat and belly, and rich buff undertail-coverts. In good light shows *blue-green centres to some wing-coverts and flight feathers.* Bill is dark with a red base, legs dull olive or red-brown. **HH** widespread but generally scarce, although in years of good rains large influxes may occur. Inhabits well-vegetated swamps, marshes and lakes from sea-level to 1900m. **Vo** vocal, calling a loud clucking *kuk kuk kuk...* and nasal moans.

Striped Crake *Aenigmatolimnas marginalis* 22cm, 8.5"

Small brown crake with narrow white streaks on the back and wings, a *greenish bill and legs, and cinnamon undertail-coverts that contrast with the white belly.* Sexes differ, ad ♂ is rufous-brown on sides of head and across the breast; ad ♀ has head, breast and flanks grey. Imm has a *plain dark brown back and wings,* rufous-brown sides to the head and breast, and a white throat, belly and undertail-coverts. **HH** small numbers are scarce intra-African migrants to marshes and seasonal pools from May-Nov, occasionally breeding during the rains. **Vo** call is a rarely heard rapid dry rattle (lasting about 10 seconds), and also utters various low growling notes.

African Water Rail *Rallus caerulescens* 30cm, 12"

[African Rail]
Dark brown and grey rail with a *long red bill,* red legs and black and white barred flanks. The only rail in the region with a long bill. Sexes alike. Imm is similar but browner on the head and breast, with diffuse bars on the flanks and a duller bill and legs. **HH** widespread, but generally uncommon resident and wanderer to a wide range of swamps and marshes from sea-level to 3000m. **Vo** calls a forced series of squealed notes that break into a long trilled and descending *pipipipipipipipi....pi pi pi,* the last notes being slower and downslurred.

Nkulengu Rail *Himantornis haematopus* 43cm, 17"

Large dark brown forest rail, with a heavy greyish bill and red legs. Ad plumage is variable but typically has some grey-brown on the crown and nape, scaly fringes to the upperparts, and a whitish throat. Sexes alike. Imm is generally plainer and warmer brown, with variable whitish patches on the throat and belly. **HH** in our area known only from Semliki Forest, WUg, where it is resident in small numbers. **Vo** calls pre-dawn and after dusk a repeated rhythmical growling *ooo a-aa-a* that sounds like a dancing conga-line going through the forest.

Plate 54

Black Crake

Imm

Ad

Imm

Purple
Swamphen

Imm

Ad

Allen's
Gallinule

Imm

♂

♀

Striped Crake

Imm

Imm

Ad

Nkulengu
Rail

Ad

African Water
Rail

COOTS AND MOORHENS
Bulky-bodied, small-headed, black rails which are widespread and familiar. Colour of bill and head shield easily identifies adults, but care should be taken with immature plumages. Sexes are alike.

Red-knobbed Coot *Fulica cristata* 46cm, 18"

Very dark grey-black rail with a *striking white bill and frontal shield*. Br ad has two swollen red knobs above the frontal shield, but these are hard to see at distance, and quickly become reduced and darker after breeding. Imm lacks the frontal shield and is more brown-grey above, with paler grey underparts and a variable amount of white on the face and throat. **HH** small flocks are common on lakes and pools across the region (though rare near the coast). Non-br flocks of hundreds may gather on freshwater lakes in the Great Rift Valley and in the nearby highlands. **Vo** varied single calls include a nasal *krrk*, a reverberating *iuenk*, and a deeper *ernh*, and also utters an occasional metallic chinking.

Common Moorhen *Gallinula chloropus* 36cm, 14"

A blackish rail with a *yellow-tipped red bill and rounded red frontal shield*, white stripes along the flanks and white undertail-coverts: *legs yellow-green with red above the 'knee'*. Imm has a dark olive bill, no frontal shield, and is generally all dull brown above, and paler below with a whitish throat and buffy flank stripes: legs dull greenish. **HH** singles, pairs and family groups are most common above 1200m, but smaller numbers occur in scattered pockets throughout much of the region, including the coast. Prefers well-vegetated freshwaters, and frequently swims in the open. **Vo** highly vocal and quarrelsome. Calls are nasal, loud and explosive, either single notes or rattled series.

Lesser Moorhen *Gallinula angulata* 27cm, 10.5"

Smaller than Common Moorhen with a *mostly yellow bill* (red only along the top) and a *small pointed red frontal shield: legs greenish-yellow*. Imm is dull brown above with paler underparts and a yellowish bill. **HH** uncommon local resident and intra-African migrant, with numbers increasing from Apr–Aug. Much shier than Common Moorhen keeping to cover in well-vegetated wetlands and seasonal pools. **Vo** calls are similar to Common Moorhen, but more bubbly and querulous.

JACANAS
Jacanas or lily-trotters are striking, long-legged, long-toed waterbirds which walk and feed on floating vegetation, especially water-lilies. Adults are easily identified, but beware confusion between Lesser Jacana and half-grown immature African Jacana.

African Jacana *Actophilornis africanus* ♀ 31cm, 12"

Ad is a striking chestnut and white waterbird, with a *powder-blue bill and frontal shield,* a black hindneck, and *dark chestnut from the lower breast to vent*. Sexes similar but ♀ is slightly larger than ♂. In rather weak flight, wings are all *chestnut and black*. Imm is paler and duller brown above, with a white supercilium and a small greyish frontal shield (hard to see): underparts are mostly white washed yellowish at sides of breast. **HH** widespread and common residents of freshwater ponds and lakes with good surface cover, from sea-level to 3000m. **Vo** noisy, calling a series of rapid repeated rattling notes, shrill squeals, and aggressive trills.

Lesser Jacana *Microparra capensis* 17cm, 6.5"

Very small jacana which looks brown above and white below at distance. Close birds show a rufous crown and nape (some are black on the fore-crown), a white supercilium, narrow rufous eye-stripe, and golden-yellow and rufous patches at sides of breast. Sexes are alike. In flight, reveals conspicuous *white trailing edge to most of wing and a rufous rump and tail*. Imm is paler and duller than ad with a black rump. **HH** widespread but generally scarce and local, with scattered records from vegetated lakes and pools across the region. **Vo** calls a simple series of rattled chitters that rise and fall in tone.

Plate 55

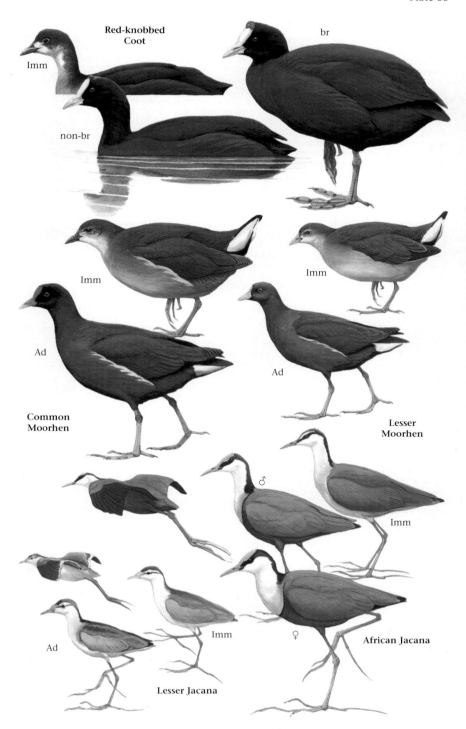

Red-knobbed Coot

Imm

br

non-br

Common Moorhen

Imm

Ad

Imm

Ad

Lesser Moorhen

♂

Imm

Ad

Imm

♀

African Jacana

Lesser Jacana

CRANES

Attractive tall birds of wetlands and moist agricultural land, all easily identified if seen well. Crowned cranes are separated by overall colour and face pattern, Wattled and Demoiselle cranes by head and neck pattern, and by size. Sexes very similar, but females are slightly smaller. Immature birds tend to be duller than adults. Resident cranes all perform elaborate courtship dances.

Grey Crowned Crane *Balearica regulorum* 112cm, 44"
[Southern Crowned Crane]

Ad is *largely grey* with dark-chestnut, black and white wings, a bristly golden crown, and a *bare white cheek edged above with a small red wattle*. In flight, looks hunched and laboured with lowered neck and bowed wings revealing extensive white on the upperwing contrasting with black and chestnut flight feathers. Imm smaller than ad with a shorter crest, rufous head and neck, and rufous fringed body plumage. **HH** pairs, family groups and larger flocks are widespread and common in a wide range of wetter habitats, including swamps, inundated grasslands, and moister agricultural lands from sea-level to 3000m, but will range well away from wetter areas to feed. **Vo** calls a loud atmospheric bugling *ooh-eyannh* or *oh-wang*.

Black Crowned Crane *Balearica pavonina* 112cm, 44"

Ad is very similar to Grey Crowned Crane, but *blacker with a mostly pink-red cheek patch edged above in white*. Imm has reduced crest and extensive brown edges to back feathers, darker than similar imm Grey Crowned. Flight also similar to Grey Crowned but blacker body plumage obvious even at distance. **HH** in our area singles, pairs and occasionally small flocks are very uncommon and only occur in the extreme north of Ug and Ke. **Vo** calls are similar to Grey Crowned, but perhaps deeper-toned.

Wattled Crane *Bugeranus carunculatus* 120cm, 47"

Very large stately grey crane with a dark cap, *bare red face and well-feathered white wattles*; largely white face and *gleaming white neck* visible even at great distance. Remainder of plumage black or grey, with elongated secondaries drooping below tail. Imm is duller and rather browner, with a pale not a dark grey crown, duller face and smaller wattles. In flight, white neck contrasts strongly with dark wings and body. **HH** pairs, family groups and occasionally larger flocks are resident on permanent swamps, rivers and wet grasslands in the Moyowosi-Kigozi swamp complex, WTz, and the Usangu Flats, SWTz. **Vo** a high-pitched burry bugling.

Demoiselle Crane *Anthropoides virgo* 96cm, 38"

A black-necked grey or dark grey crane with long black breast feathers, white plumes extending from eye to hindneck and elongated inner secondaries drooping over tail. Imm much duller than ad, with less defined plumes behind the eyes, and only an indication of the black foreneck. In flight, appears mainly blackish and grey, lacking the striking contrast of other cranes. **HH** extreme vagrant from the Palearctic with just one record of nine birds, first on the Ke coast and later at Mt Kenya from Jan–Mar 1986. **Vo** not recorded in the region, but migrating birds call *grro*.

Plate 56

Black Crowned
Crane

Grey Crowned
Crane

Ad

Imm

Ad

Imm

Demoiselle
Crane

Wattled
Crane

Ad

Imm

Ad

Imm

LARGE BUSTARDS
Stately bustards which prefer to walk purposely, only taking to wing when disturbed. Males have spectacular balloon displays, visible over long distances, and are larger than females. All are easily identified if seen well.

Heuglin's Bustard   *Neotis heuglinii*   ♂ 89cm, 35"

Large black-faced bustard: ad ♂ has a *black crown, mask and chin,* a blue-grey neck, and a chestnut band on the lower breast separated from the white belly by a narrow black line. Ad ♀ is smaller, more subdued, and face is striped, not black. Imm is like ♀. In flight, reveals a white primary wedge in the dark upperwing. **HH** singles and pairs are uncommon in arid and semi-arid country, including desert edge, in N and NEKe, although birds will wander well to the south, including to Tsavo East NP. **Vo** not known.

Denham's Bustard   *Neotis denhami*   ♂ 118cm, 46"

[Stanley's Bustard]
Ad ♂ is large with an *extensive triangular chestnut-rufous patch on hindneck,* a black and white striped crown and face, pale grey neck, extensive black and white coverts, and a white belly. Ad ♀ is smaller with a brown centre to crown, and slightly paler rufous hindneck. Imm is similar to ♀. **HH** occurs at low densities in open and lightly bushed or wooded grassland from 600–3000m in much of the west, and is seasonal in some areas (like the Serengeti). Displaying ♂ inflates white throat and chest hugely and expands chestnut nape, either striding with tail raised or standing tall with tail lowered. **Vo** usually silent, but br ♂ gives low resonant booms. Also a barked *kaa-kaa* given as alarm.

Kori Bustard   *Ardeotis kori*   ♂ 128cm, 50"

Largest bustard: crested head and extensive *black and white patterning at bend of closed wing* is distinctive. Sexes similar, but ad ♀ is smaller and more lightly built. Imm is like a less clearly marked ♀. Prefers to walk, but will occasionally fly and ad ♂ is Africa's heaviest flying bird. **HH** singles and small groups are widespread and sometimes common in open grassland from 700–2000m in NEUg to NTz, with strongholds in the grasslands of SWKe (like the Maasai Mara) and NTz (like the Serengeti: where it may be common). Displaying ♂ inflates throat ruff and chest, lowers wings, and lifts tail to reveal mass of soft white undertail-coverts. **Vo** ♂ gives a low resonant *voomp* at intervals of up to 10 seconds and both sexes may utter harsh *craark* when disturbed.

Arabian Bustard   *Ardeotis arabs*   ♂ 92cm, 36"

Significantly smaller, more elegant version of Kori Bustard, but has *white chequered covert pattern at close of wing* (not black and white). Sexes similar, but ad ♀ smaller and rather greyer. Imm is similar to ♀, but much duller, lacking the contrast in the wing. **HH** singles and pairs are extremely rare visitors to NKe (where may be overlooked), in arid and desert border country. **Vo** rasping or honking croaked *pah pah* when displaying.

Plate 57

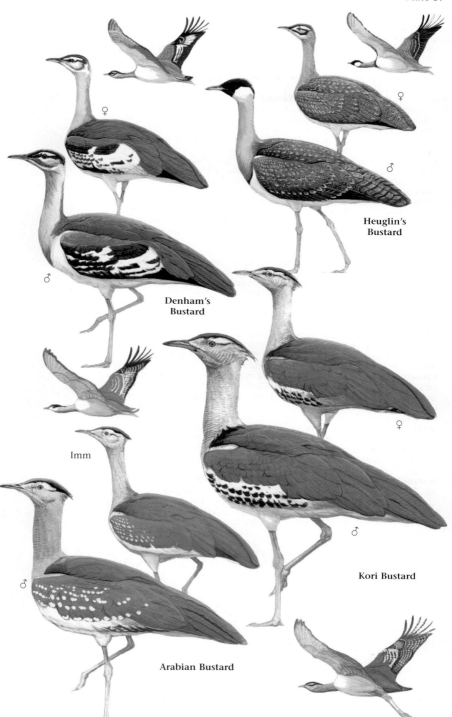

♀

♂

Heuglin's
Bustard

Denham's
Bustard

Imm

♀

♂

Kori Bustard

♂

Arabian Bustard

SMALLER BUSTARDS

Smaller bustards: males can be easily identified by plumage and call, while females and similar immatures present more of a challenge. Most call and perform aerial displays which are strikingly different from the ground-based displays of larger bustards (plate 57). These bustards are known as korhaans in southern Africa.

White-bellied Bustard *Eupodotis senegalensis* 61cm, 24″

[White-bellied Korhaan]

Ad ♂ has a rather plain brown back and wings, blue-grey neck, and a *black and white face pattern with a pinkish-red base to bill*, and a white belly. Ad ♀ is similar, but browner and more washed out, with blue-grey confined to hindneck. Imm is browner, lacking the blue-grey tones. **HH** pairs and family groups are common in a wide range of open grassland below 2000m, usually with bush or tree cover. Ad ♂ has a subdued display where he walks near ♀, raising his crest, craning his neck, and puffing up his throat. **Vo** calls a loud and far-carrying rather goose-like cackling duet: ♂ gives *ah-nghaa-nghaa*, whilst ♀ replies *eh-e-e-er*.

Buff-crested Bustard *Eupodotis gindiana* 54cm, 21″

A small short-legged bustard: ad ♂ has a warm buff-brown back marked with darker brown spots and bars, a *pale rufous crown and cheeks, black throat line and belly*. Crest only visible in display. Ad ♀ is similar, but crown is mottled and buff neck well-barred, and black confined to belly. Imm like ♀. From above, flying birds show well-patterned flight feathers and a small white wedge on the coverts. **HH** singles and pairs are common in arid and semi-arid bushland to 1800m from NEUg, through EKe to NETz. Ad ♂ has a rocket display, flying up and tumbling on closed wings, to stall and land at the last minute. **Vo** loud, shrill and piercing calls may lead to an aerial display in which ♂ calls an accelerating series *kri-kri-kri*. slowing down towards the end.

Black-bellied Bustard *Eupodotis melanogaster* 64cm, 25″

[Black-bellied Korhaan]

Ad ♂ is a medium-sized black-bellied bustard which is very similar to Hartlaub's Bustard. Identified by *less black on face, greyer-brown cheek, a brown-backed neck*, and a brown and buff rump and tail barred dark brown. Ad ♀ is separated from extremely similar Hartlaub's by a *finely vermiculated brown neck*. Imm similar to ad ♀. In flight, ad ♂ is black below with a large white patch in primaries and *black trailing edge to secondaries*. **HH** singles and pairs are widespread and common in wetter open, bushed and wooded grassland to 2500m. In display flight, climbs with exaggerated wing beats and glides to ground. **Vo** displaying ♂ starts with an intake of breath, makes a loud nasal upslur (followed by a pause of up to 10 seconds) before a short low growl and an explosive pop.

Hartlaub's Bustard *Eupodotis hartlaubii* 71cm, 28″

Ad ♂ is more thickset and crisply marked than Black-bellied Bustard. Identified by *white thumb print over ear-coverts which contrast with a blacker face*, a *silver-grey-backed neck*, and a black rump and barred dark brown tail. Ad ♀ is separated from extremely similar Black-bellied by rather darker tones, *cream line down foreneck, and speckled (not vermiculated) brown hindneck*. Imm similar, but duller. In flight, ad ♂ shows a blackish rump and tail and *only the inner secondaries have a black trailing edge*. **HH** pairs and family parties are not uncommon in bushed grassland, in drier areas to 1600m, in NEUg, and then separately from NKe to CTz. ♂ has a striking parachute display similar to Black-bellied. **Vo** displaying ♂ utters a quiet click, then a slightly louder *pop* (not unlike a cork being pulled) followed by a quiet deep drawn out moaning *booooom*.

Plate 58

Buff-crested
Bustard

♀

♂

White-bellied
Bustard

♀

♂

Black-bellied
Bustard

♀

♂

Hartlaub's
Bustard

♀

♂

LARGE BLACK AND WHITE SHOREBIRDS

Four boldly marked large black and white shorebirds which can be identified by plumage, shape of bill, and leg colour. All have distinct flight calls.

Black-winged Stilt *Himantopus himantopus* 38cm, 15"

Tall elegant black and white wader with a *thin bill and very long pinkish-red legs*. In ad, the crown and hindneck varies from pure white, to white with variable amounts of dark grey. ♀ differs from ♂ in having a browner back. Imm is duller with pale fringes to the brownish back and a narrow white trailing edge to the wing. In flight, *stiff black wings contrast with white body, and long trailing pink legs*. **HH** common at a wide range of waters, including alkaline and freshwater lakes, flooded fields and coastal lagoons. Numbers increase from Aug–Apr, but their origin is unknown. **Vo** sharp distinct pinking call, based around *kek-kek-kek…* or *kik-kik-kik-…*

Pied Avocet *Recurvirostra avosetta* 43cm, 17"

Distinct black and white shorebird with a *slender upcurved black bill, black cap and hindneck, and long blue-grey legs*. Sexes similar, but ♂ has a longer bill than ♀. Imm has browner markings with some grey-brown mottling to the back and wings. In stiff-winged flight, shows distinct black and white pattern, and long trailing legs. **HH** local but widespread on a range of alkaline and freshwaters, especially on alkaline lakes in the Great Rift Valley of Ke and NTz. Uncommon in Ug, Rw and Bu. Has distinct feeding action, walking in shallow water and sweeping the bill from side to side. **Vo** quite vocal, a metallic sharp *ink-ink-ink…*

Crab-plover *Dromas ardeola* 41cm, 16"

Rather big-headed black and white shorebird with a *heavy black bill and blue-grey legs*. Sexes alike. Imm has some dark streaking to the crown and mantle, and wings washed grey. In slow and heavy flight, large bill is distinctive. **HH** singles and flocks are present all year round on coastal flats, but mainly from Aug–Apr at regular sites, notably Lamu and at Mida Creek, Ke, and at Dar es Salaam, Tz. Feeds plover-like, with a stalk, short run, stop and stab. **Vo** noisy, calling a musical and mournful *kerrui* or *kirruerk*, either single notes or in a long series.

Eurasian Oystercatcher *Haematopus ostralegus* 43cm, 17"

Thickset black and white shorebird with a *bright orange-red bill and pinkish-orange legs*. Sexes similar. Non-br ad has white bar across throat. Imm dirtier than non-br ad with brown-tinged upperparts: bill and legs less bright. In flight, bold white wing bar and bright orange-red bill highly distinctive. **HH** singles and small groups are uncommon annual visitors to coasts of Ke and Tz; rare inland, including occasionally to Ug. **Vo** gives an occasional high-pitched piping.

PAINTED-SNIPE

A somewhat crepuscular dumpy snipe-like bird, which often hides in dense vegetation during the day. Polyandrous, with duller ♂ responsible for nest building, incubation and raising young.

Greater Painted-snipe *Rostratula benghalensis* 24cm, 9.5"

Unmistakable if seen well, with a *long slightly drooping bill, rotund tail-less appearance, and a pronounced stripe around and behind the eye*. Noticeable light saddle-like ring separates fore and hind body. ♂ much duller than ♀, but with more conspicuous buff-gold spots on wing-coverts; lacks her rich chestnut head, neck and upper breast. Imm similar to ♂, but paler and less spotted. Flies weakly on rounded wings, often with dangling legs. **HH** singles and pairs are erratic wanderers to well-vegetated fresh and alkaline water margins, including near the coast. **Vo** ♀ has a long call during the rains, commencing with a series of dove-like slurred *oo-o* rising then falling in tone, followed by a series of hiccup-like notes.

Plate 59

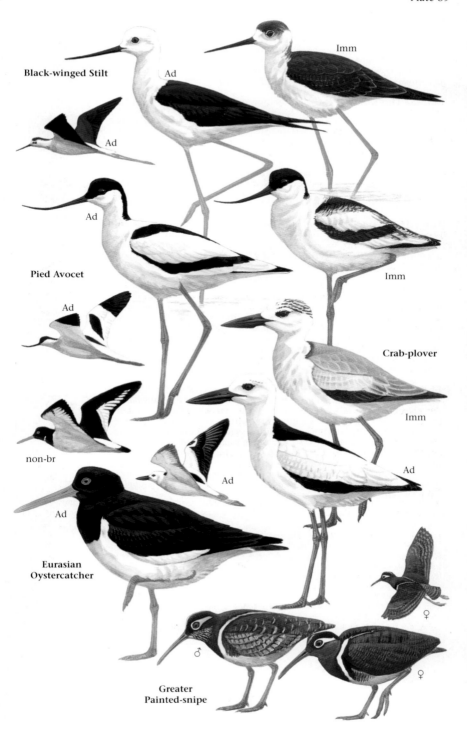

Black-winged Stilt

Imm

Ad

Ad

Pied Avocet

Ad

Imm

Ad

Crab-plover

Imm

non-br

Ad

Ad

Eurasian
Oystercatcher

♀

♂

♀

Greater
Painted-snipe

THICK-KNEES

Thick-knees, dikkops, or stone curlews, are easily identified as a group by their well-camouflaged brown plumage, large yellow eyes, and long thickly jointed yellowish legs (hence name). Mainly nocturnal, they seek shade and stand hunched and inactive during most of the day, freezing or squatting if disturbed. Identification of streaked species can be difficult: note markings across wing-coverts, extent of yellow on bill, as well as habitat and range. Sexes and immatures are all very similar. Loud far-carrying calls are often heard at night.

Spotted Thick-knee *Burhinus capensis* 43cm, 17"
[Spotted Dikkop]

Only spotted species, with *bold black spots over most of the upperparts and wings, and no bar across the wing-coverts.* Ground colour varies from buff-brown in widespread nominate race, to brighter warm tawny in race *maculosa* (NUg to NKe). In flight, shows limited white in upperwings. **HH** pairs or family groups are widespread at low densities, but may also be locally numerous. Inhabits dry open, bushed and wooded grassland from near sea-level to 2000m, and is regularly seen on dirt roads at night. **Vo** call is a long series of identical notes (not rising and falling) that break into a punctuated series *pipipipipi.....pi pi pi pi pi pi pi...*

Water Thick-knee *Burhinus vermiculatus* 41cm, 16"
[Water Dikkop]

Typical thick-knee with streaked brown-grey plumage; closed wing usually shows a *wide grey panel bordered above with a narrow white bar,* and above that a thicker blackish bar: *there is no second black bar immediately below the white.* At close range shows fine vermiculations to the upperparts (not present on other thick-knees). Bill has small dull yellowish-green patches at the base and a black culmen. Eyes and legs often more greenish-yellow than similar species. Beware – some birds have the narrow white bar indistinct or even lacking, and can only be told from Senegal Thick-knee by their greener bill and legs. **HH** pairs and small groups are widespread and locally common near water of all types, including lake shores, river sandbanks, coastal creeks and lagoons, and offshore islands. **Vo** call is a long rising then falling series of shrill notes, unlike Senegal they are unhurried and slur together *wi-wi-wi-wi-wi-wi-wi-wi-wi... wii wii wii.*

Senegal Thick-knee *Burhinus senegalensis* 38cm, 15"

Very similar to Water Thick-knee, but wide *grey wing panel is bordered above with a black bar only; no narrow white band.* Bill similar to Water Thick-knee with black culmen ridge, but slightly longer and heavier, with more extensive and often brighter yellow patches near base, eyes and legs also usually brighter yellow. **HH** singles, pairs and small groups associate with water mainly to the north and west of Water Thick-knee. In recent years appears to be extending its range south to areas like Lake Baringo, Ke, where it is now regular. **Vo** calls similar to Water Thick-knee, but all notes shriller, distinctly separate and hurried (not slurred together) *pi-pi-pi-pi-pi-pi-pi-pi-pi* with no slower terminal notes.

Eurasian Thick-knee *Burhinus oedicnemus* 43cm, 17"

Most similar to Water Thick-knee, but *narrow white wing bar is bordered both above and below with black bars.* Bill comparatively small with *extensive yellow base,* including the basal half of the culmen ridge. **HH** possibly an annual visitor from the Palearctic to NUg and NKe between Oct–Mar. Occurs in open country, including grasslands and recently burnt areas. Vagrant to NTz. **Vo** silent in region.

Plate 60

Spotted Thick-knee

Water Thick-knee

Senegal
Thick-knee

Eurasian Thick-knee

COURSERS
Delicate, subdued birds of open country. All are crepuscular to some extent, but vary from near diurnal Temminck's, to near-nocturnal Violet-tipped. All have upright stance, especially when alarmed, and prefer to run to cover, rather than fly. Often exploit burnt areas. Reasonably easily told apart by head, breast and underwing markings. Sexes similar: immatures have pale fringes to the wing-coverts and back.

Temminck's Courser *Cursorius temminckii* 21cm, 8"
Slightly smaller than similar species with a *rufous cap. Lower breast dull rufous*, with a *blackish smudge in centre of belly* (can be hard to see). Pale lores, dark eye lines, and whitish superciliary stripes, give neat 'capped' head pattern. Easily flushed into rather jerky flight, when shows dark underwing with no white trailing edge. **HH** pairs and small groups are widespread and common in a wide range of drier open bushed and occasionally wooded grassland, mainly from sea-level to 2000m, but wanders to 3000m. **Vo** strange repeated rather mournful and nasal *peeu* notes some with a reverberating quality.

Somali Courser *Cursorius somalensis* 22cm, 8.5"
Larger, longer-legged and paler than Temminck's Courser, with a white lower belly. Whitish superciliary stripes and black eye lines join to form clear 'V' on the back of the head: cap is sandy on the forecrown and blue-grey on the hindcrown. In flight, *underwing shows black outer half, and paler sandy innerwing with a white trailing edge*. **HH** pairs and small groups may be locally common in arid and semi-arid desert, grassland and scrub, mainly below 1500m. **Vo** scratchy descending slurred *pyau* and a muffled *pip*, often with several birds calling together.

Cream-coloured Courser *Cursorius cursor* 24cm, 9.5"
Very similar to Somali Courser, but slightly larger and more sandy-buff with a slightly shorter bill and legs. In flight, shows an *entirely black underwing*, with strong contrast to the sandy body. **HH** vagrant from the Palearctic, with only one definite record of several birds on the east shore of Lake Turkana, NKe, from Jan-Feb 1987. **Vo** may call *quett* or *kritt* when disturbed.

Two-banded Courser *Rhinoptilus africanus* 24cm, 9.5"
[Double-banded Courser]
Distinctive, with heavily scaled upperparts and *two clear narrow black breast bands*. In flight, shows a rufous band across the secondaries and inner primaries. **HH** pairs and small groups are local, but may be common in semi-arid open and bushed habitat, often in bare and stony areas, below 1800m. **Vo** rapid shrill trill that rises and falls (rather like a Water Thick-knee) and continues with sharp often paired *keek-eek* notes.

Heuglin's Courser *Rhinoptilus cinctus* 27cm, 10.5"
[Three-banded Courser]
Cryptic beautiful courser, with *unique pattern of black, white and chestnut bands running above and below a broad mottled brown breast band*. In flight, underwing largely white with black tips to outer primaries. **HH** singles and pairs may be common in semi-arid bush and wooded country, including miombo, from near sea-level to 2200m. **Vo** a spectacular call that starts with a sharp *keek-keek* and then breaks into an accelerating rising and then falling wave of sharp *kik* notes.

Violet-tipped Courser *Rhinoptilus chalcopterus* 28cm, 11"
[Bronze-winged Courser]
Largest courser which may suggest Crowned Lapwing but *bold face pattern around large dark eyes*, *two breast bands* (upper one wide, lower one narrow) and dull purple-red legs are distinctive. Violet tips to primaries are rarely visible in the field. In flight, reveals broad white band across underwing, with creamy coverts, black primaries and trailing edge. **HH** pairs are widespread but local, uncommon, and nocturnal, in bushed and wooded country below 2200m, especially in miombo. Wanders widely, but exact status as an intra-African migrant poorly known. **Vo** mournful rather thick-knee-like call which starts with a downslur, then three notes that slur into each other *w'yo yor wee waah*, the middle note higher.

Plate 61

Temminck's
Courser

Somali
Courser

Two-banded
Courser

Cream-coloured
Courser

Heuglin's
Courser

Violet-tipped
Courser

PRATINCOLES

Pratincoles are graceful and rather tern-like on the wing, but squat and short-legged on the ground. Best identified by throat and underwing markings, but also consider range. Sexes alike.

Collared Pratincole *Glareola pratincola* 26cm,10"
[Red-winged Pratincole]
Br ad has a pale buff throat surrounded by a narrow black line (streaks in non-br birds); at rest, wing tips and tail are approximately the same length. In flight, shows a white rump, deeply forked tail, and a dark underwing with *chestnut-red coverts*. Secondaries are very narrowly edged in white, but beware this may be worn off. Imm is heavily mottled above, with a less defined throat and shorter tail. **HH** widespread and locally common on flat sparsely vegetated land around lakes, rivers and at the coast. **Vo** utters a wide range of sharp creaky high-pitched and rather tern-like *krik* and *keek* calls.

Madagascar Pratincole *Glareola ocularis* 25cm, 10"
A stocky and dark pratincole with a white streak below and behind the eye, chestnut patch on belly and a short tail. In flight, shows *short, shallow forked tail, chestnut-orange underwing-coverts*, and a clear white belly. **HH** non-breeding migrant from Madagascar which flocks in large numbers from Apr–Oct on the coasts of NTz and Ke, notably near Malindi. It is very rare inland. **Vo** calls a short sharp *twik twik twik*, and a whinnying rising and falling series of *kik* notes.

Black-winged Pratincole *Glareola nordmanni* 25cm, 10"
Very similar to Collared Pratincole, but has *black underwing-coverts*, no white trailing edge to wing, a shallower, shorter forked tail and, at rest, wings extend well beyond tail tips. Overall darker than Collared with a more extensive black loral patch, and less red at base of bill (not reaching nostrils). Imm also dark with ill-defined throat patch and *black underwing-coverts*. **HH** visitor from the Palearctic with records from Oct–Apr, but only frequent in the west (WUg, Rw, Bu), where large numbers may pass through particularly in Mar–Apr. **Vo** calls are very similar to Collared Pratincole, but with a more bubbling quality.

Rock Pratincole *Glareola nuchalis* 19cm, 7.5"
Small and dark with a *neat white stripe extending from behind eyes and across hindneck*; legs bright red. In flight, dark underwing shows white central line. Imm is buff-fringed above and lacks collar on hindneck. **HH** pairs or small parties are locally common on rocks in fast-flowing rivers, and on rocky islets in Lake Victoria. Although mainly a bird of the west it occurs in the Selous GR, SETz, and on the Tana River, Ke. **Vo** a rapid sharp series of tern-like *kik-kik-kik…* notes, and a softer *kip-kip*.

Grey Pratincole *Glareola cinerea* 19cm, 7.5"
A small beautiful *grey and white pratincole with a buff-chestnut wash to the hindneck and breast*. In flight, shows striking black, white and grey wing pattern. **HH** vagrant to our area from west-central Africa, with just one record of a single bird at Rusizi NP, Bu, in Oct 1991. **Vo** calls an accelerating series *zi-zi-zi…*

Egyptian-plover *Pluvianus aegyptius* 21cm, 8"
A chunky striking shorebird: largely black and white and blue-grey above, with bold head markings, a black and white breast band, and orange-buff washed underparts. Sexes similar; imm duller with brown mottling on wing-coverts. In flight, reveals *striking white and grey wings, with a diagonal black band and tips*. **HH** in our area, pairs and small groups are restricted to sandbanks along the Aswa River in NUg, and as a vagrant (once) to NKe. Sedentary, but responds to water level changes with local movements. **Vo** noisy, calling a loud *cherk cherk…* or *chee-chee-chee…* in flight.

Plate 62

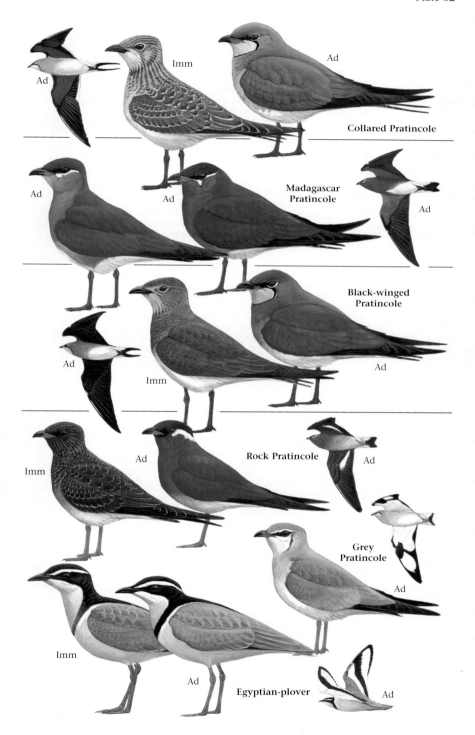

Collared Pratincole

Madagascar Pratincole

Black-winged Pratincole

Rock Pratincole

Grey Pratincole

Egyptian-plover

WETLAND LAPWINGS

Wetter country lapwings are all easily identified if seen well. Noisy and conspicuous (calling by both day and night), they are often seen in aggressive territorial encounters. Sexes alike. Immatures have similar basic pattern to adults, but are often browner, with less clear-cut markings and pale fringed upperparts. Only described below if markedly different. All are known as plovers in Southern Africa.

Blacksmith Lapwing *Vanellus armatus* 31cm, 12"

Striking black, white and grey lapwing, with a *white skull cap set off against a black face and breast*. Imm browner and dark-capped with pale fringed upperparts. In flight, upperwing black and grey without a white wing bar. **HH** pairs, families and small parties are widespread, common and largely resident around most highland fresh and alkaline waters in Ke and Tz. Wanders to some extent to lower altitudes, and once as a vagrant in Bu. **Vo** noisy, calls sound like metal hitting an anvil *tink-tink-tink*, accelerating and given at speeds denoting levels of excitement.

Spur-winged Lapwing *Vanellus spinosus* 28cm, 11"

Black, white and brown lapwing, with a *white cheek and sides of neck set off against a black crown, throat and breast*. Name derived from curved carpal spur which is very hard to see. In flight, shows white bar across upperwing-coverts. **HH** common and widespread on shorter turf beside both fresh and alkaline waters, particularly in WUg and NKe, but becoming progressively less numerous in Rw, Bu and on the southern Ke coast, generally uncommon in Tz. **Vo** calls are piercing *keek* notes that become scratchy as the bird gets more excited.

Long-toed Lapwing *Vanellus crassirostris* 31cm, 12"

Large upright lapwing with a *white face and foreneck* standing out clearly against black nape and breast band; bill pinkish with a black-tip, legs red. Imm similar to ad but duller with brown fringed upperparts. In flight, large white shoulders contrast strongly with black flight feathers. **HH** locally common below 2200m on permanent waters with extensive floating vegetation, notably in the west, but non-br birds wander widely in response to flooding, including to the coast. **Vo** noisy, call is metallic and spitted, starting slowly then speeding up, almost sounding like a rattle *kik kik kik kik-kik-kik kikikikikik...*

African Wattled Lapwing *Vanellus senegallus* 34cm, 13.5"

Large brown lapwing with a black-tipped yellow bill and bright yellow legs: pin-stripe streaks on throat and neck, small white forehead patch, and prominent yellow wattles at sides of bill. Two races occur: black-bellied *lateralis* (widespread) and brown-bellied nominate (in NUg). Imm has smaller wattles and a brown forecrown. **HH** pairs and small groups are widespread but not numerous in damp grasslands and marsh edges from 250–2200m. More easterly and lower altitude birds are wanderers. **Vo** calls are a pinched and non-metallic *kip-kip-kip...*, repeated for long periods.

White-crowned Lapwing *Vanellus albiceps* 32cm, 12.5"

Spectacular long-spurred, *grey-headed lapwing with a white crown stripe*, and long dangling yellow wattles at sides of bill. Imm has brown crown stripe. In flight, from above, shows largely white wings with a black diagonal bar and tips. **HH** pairs and small parties are locally common along permanent rivers with sandbars in C and STz; reported as vagrants in NTz and Rw. **Vo** very noisy, with sharp *ki* notes commencing singly and accelerating into long metallic trills *ki-ki-ki...kreechy-kreechy-kreechy...*

Plate 63

Ad

Ad

Imm

Blacksmith Lapwing

Ad

Spur-winged Lapwing

Imm

Ad

Long-toed Lapwing

nominate

lateralis

Ad

African Wattled Lapwing

Ad

White-crowned Lapwing

DRY COUNTRY LAPWINGS

Lapwings more associated with dry country and grasslands than those on plate 63. They are best identified by head, breast and wing markings. Sexes alike: immatures are generally duller with some paler fringes on upperparts. All resident species are known as plovers in Southern Africa.

Crowned Lapwing *Vanellus coronatus* 31cm, 12"
Smart head pattern with a *black cap and white crown ring* standing out at long distance; ring accentuates flat head and steep forehead. Alert and upright, with yellow eyes and bright red legs. Imm similar, but head pattern less well-defined, upperparts fringed with buff, eyes, bill and legs dull. **HH** pairs, small parties and flocks are common residents (and local wanderers) in a wide range of drier grasslands, including bushed and wooded areas, from sea-level to 3000m. **Vo** noisy and aggressive, calls consist of scratchy upslurs *kir, kiree, kree* either singly or in series.

Black-headed Lapwing *Vanellus tectus* 26cm, 10"
Nominate race is an attractive *spike-crested* lapwing, with a white chin, forecrown and nape patches (forecrown patch larger in EKe race *latifrons*). In front view shows *narrow black 'tie' from throat to breast*. Bill is red with a black tip; small loral wattles and legs are also red. **HH** pairs and small parties are resident and often approachable and tame in semi-arid and arid open and bushed plains from near sea-level to 1800m. Largely crepuscular or nocturnal, often standing in shade during the day. **Vo** quite vocal, more so in flight: call is a burry, muffled and tinny series that develops into a loud rattle *kreek-kreek...krkrkrkrkrkr...*

Northern Lapwing *Vanellus vanellus* 30cm, 12"
Classic lapwing with *long curving crest, dark green upperparts*, a broad black breast band, and a white belly. Br ad has a black face, non-br shows paler face and narrow buff fringes to upperparts. Imm duller, with more heavily scalloped upperparts and a shorter crest. In flight, reveals *wide dark wings*, appearing all dark above and black and white below. **HH** vagrant from the Palearctic with only one record, at the Sabaki River estuary, Ke, from Jan 1995 to early 1996. **Vo** flight and alarm call is a strange high-pitched downslurred *wee'y* given singly.

Black-winged Lapwing *Vanellus melanopterus* 27cm, 10.5"
Very similar to Senegal Lapwing, but thicker-set and shorter-legged; hard to tell at distance. At close range typically shows slightly wider white forehead and broader black breast band, but this is not consistent. *Reddish eye-ring* is a good field mark at very close quarters. In flight, *upperwing shows diagonal white bar fully across coverts, and a black trailing edge to the secondaries*. **HH** flocks may be common above 1300m, especially in higher altitude grasslands and cultivation from CKe to NTz. Non-br birds occasionally wander to lower altitudes. **Vo** calls a harsh, strident and staccato upslurred *ki-ki-ki-ki-krrrrrri*.

Senegal Lapwing *Vanellus lugubris* 26cm, 10"
[Lesser Black-winged Plover]
Slightly smaller, more slender, and longer-legged than Black-winged Lapwing, often with a more clear-cut but smaller white patch on forecrown, black breast band is usually narrower, yellowish eye-ring indistinct. In flight, shows *white trailing edge to the secondaries*. **HH** pairs, small groups and flocks may be common below 1500m (rare to 3000m) preferring moist grasslands, including at the coast. Wanders widely in response to rains, often exploiting burnt areas. **Vo** calls a fluty and attractive *tyu-u* or *tyu* repeated singly, never in series.

Brown-chested Lapwing *Vanellus superciliosus* 23cm, 9"
Attractive and distinctive ad has a *rufous-brown forehead, black crown and yellow loral wattles; sides of face to breast grey, bordered below with a broad chestnut band*. Imm is much duller, with a brownish capped appearance, a variable wash of brown across the lower breast, and no loral wattles. **HH** singles and small flocks are intra-African migrants from West Africa, occurring in the western part of our region from Jul–Dec, often on burnt areas or lakeshores (vagrant to CKe and SETz). **Vo** calls a pinched scratchy series *kreek-kreek-kreek-kreek*, rather similar to Black-winged Lapwing.

Plate 64

Black-headed
Lapwing

Crowned
Lapwing

Ad

nominate

Imm

Ad

Imm

Black-winged
Lapwing

Northern
Lapwing

Ad

Senegal Lapwing

Imm

Ad

Imm

Ad

Brown-chested Lapwing

SMALLER RESIDENT PLOVERS

These plovers are mainly resident in our area, although Forbes's occurs as an intra-African migrant from the west. The three smaller species run whirringly fast, almost floating over the ground. All can be confiding and may allow close approach, they are best identified by head and breast markings.

Kittlitz's Plover *Charadrius pecuarius* 15cm, 6"

Br ad is a slightly long-legged *buff-breasted* plover with *black stripes extending across the forecrown, through the eyes and meeting on the hindneck*. Non-br ad is muted, and may lose black head stripes and breast colour. Imm as non-br ad, but more buffy on face and hindneck collar, upperparts are buff -fringed, and some show dark breast patches. In flight, shows limited white wing bar and *toes project beyond tail*. **HH** locally common and widespread resident on short grass and muddy fringes to a wide range of inland waters below 2300m. Also on temporary pools and coastal salt pans. **Vo** calls are rather variable, most commonly heard is a loud, harsh downslurred trill *trit-tri-rit-rit*.

White-fronted Plover *Charadrius marginatus* 17cm, 6.5"

Similar to Kittlitz's Plover but generally paler, with *bright white forecrown giving a peak-headed look*. Br ad has a blackish frontal bar and eye-stripes, and a short white supercilium. Breast and hindneck often with tawny-buff wash (but sometimes restricted to patches at sides of breast). Non-br (especially ♀) may lack black head markings. Imm lacks any black on the head, has buff-fringed upperparts, and is whiter below. Tail projects beyond wing tips at rest, and *toes do not extend beyond longish tail in flight*. **HH** pairs and loose groups are common at the coast, extending inland along major rivers, and they are also widespread at lower densities on some inland lakes, particularly those with sandy shorelines. Makes localised non-breeding movements. **Vo** calls a low confiding *chut*, as well as a loud dry, churred trill in flight. **SS** Kentish Plover.

Chestnut-banded Plover *Charadrius pallidus* 14cm, 5.5"

Small grey-brown and white plover with a *narrow chestnut breast band*. Ad ♂ has a black bar above the white forehead and short black eye-stripes. Ad ♀ is similar but lacks black markings. Imm has a broken (or complete) narrow grey breast band and lacks all black and chestnut. **HH** pairs and small groups are rather local residents along the fringes of alkaline lakes in the Great Rift Valley south from S Turkana in NKe, to Dodoma in CTz, including lakes Magadi and Natron, with wanderers elsewhere, e.g. Amboseli NP. **Vo** calls a sharp *pii* in flight, with breeding birds giving a complex series of strange trilled nasal notes.

Three-banded Plover *Charadrius tricollaris* 18cm, 7"

Curiously named plover, with *only two black breast bands (separated by a third white band), and a broad white forehead*; sides of face grey with obvious red eye-ring surrounding pale eyes: legs orange-red. Sexes alike. Imm is more weakly marked with pale fringed upperparts and duller legs. In flight, longish dark wings reveal *thin white wing bar* and trailing edge to secondaries. **HH** pairs are common and widespread beside wide range of fresh and alkaline water from sea-level to 3000m, often on soft muddy margins with some cover. Flies with irregular stiff wing beats. **Vo** in flight utters a rising *phiuu-eet,* and displaying birds give a long rising and falling series of rapidly spitted notes that slow down and become gravelly in quality.

Forbes's Plover *Charadrius forbesi* 19cm, 7.5"

Very similar to Three-banded Plover, but slightly larger, with a *dark brown forehead*, and browner sides to the face. Sexes alike. Imm is similar to ad but has buff-fringed upperparts. In flight, dark wings look uniform except for narrow white tips to the secondaries. **HH** scarce non-br visitor to WUg, Rw, Bu, and WTz from Apr–Oct, often in drier areas than Three-banded Plover including burnt grasslands. **Vo** calls are smoother and less metallic than Three-banded Plover.

Plate 65

Kittlitz's Plover

Imm

br

Imm

White-fronted Plover

br

Ad ♀

Imm

Chestnut-banded
Plover

Ad ♂

Ad

Imm

Three-banded Plover

Ad

Forbes's Plover

MIGRANT PLOVERS

Plovers which visit East Africa from their Palearctic breeding grounds, mainly from Oct–Apr, but a few are present all year round. All easily identified in breeding plumage, but need care otherwise: note head, breast, and wing markings.

Common Ringed Plover   *Charadrius hiaticula*   20cm, 8"
[Ringed Plover]
Non-br ad is brown above, with a single blackish breast band and a dull white forehead: bill dark, legs dull orange. Br ad is crisper, with a jet black breast band, bright white forehead, a brighter *orange bill base (with a black tip) and orange legs*. Imm like dull non-br ad, with reduced or broken breast band. In flight, shows a *prominent white wing bar*. **HH** common visitors and passage migrants mainly to coast and major lakes from Sep–May, a few remain all year round. **Vo** calls a sad rising then falling *pweoo*, usually in flight.

Little Ringed Plover   *Charadrius dubius*   17cm, 6.5"
Very similar to Common Ringed Plover, but smaller and slimmer with a dark bill, *narrow yellow eye-ring and pale pinkish or yellowish legs*. Br ad has dark forecrown stripe separated from brown crown by a narrow white band. Imm like dull non-br ad, with broken breast band and less distinct eye-ring. In flight, *wing is entirely dark* (without a white bar). **HH** not uncommon, but fairly solitary visitor to the fringes of mainly inland waters in Ke, much less often to the coast, and scarce in NTz, Ug, Rw and Bu. Likes grasslands near to lakeshores; rare outside Oct–Apr. **Vo** calls a short downslurred *peeu* in flight, not rising and falling as in Common Ringed.

Kentish Plover   *Charadrius alexandrinus*   16cm, 6"
Small plover with *dark patches at sides of breast and blackish legs*. Non-br ad could be confused with White-fronted Sandplover, but has whiter hindneck and underparts, and wings extend slightly beyond tip of tail. Br ♂ has black frontal bar, eye-stripe, and chest patches, and may show rufous wash on nape (variable). Br ♀ as non-br ad, while imm is slightly buffier. In flight, shows narrow white wing bar and white outer-tail. **HH** annual to Lake Turkana, Ke, Oct–Apr, but very scarce elsewhere. **Vo** usually quiet in region, but flying birds may give a scratchy upslur *bipip*. **SS** White-fronted Plover.

Lesser Sandplover   *Charadrius mongolus*   21cm, 8"
[Mongolian Sandplover]
Non-br ad is very similar to Greater Sandplover, but *smaller, more slender, with a rounder head, shorter bill and shorter blacker legs*. Br ad has a mostly black forecrown and eye-patch, and a broad chestnut breast band. Imm like non-br ad, but slightly washed buff on the head. In flight, *toes hardly show beyond tail tip*. **HH** flocks are very common visitors and passage migrants to the coast Sep–Apr, with some throughout the year, Much less common, but still regular, inland. **Vo** flight call is a hard, short dry trill on one note *treet*.

Greater Sandplover   *Charadrius leschenaultii*   25cm, 10"
Non-br ad is distinguished from very similar Lesser Sandplover by *larger size, more angular head, a longer heavier bill, and longer grey-green legs*. Br ad has a *white forecrown*, and a usually narrower more clear-cut chestnut breast band. In flight, *toes project well beyond tail*. **HH** very common along the coast from Sep–Apr with some remaining all year, generally uncommon inland, apart from Lake Turkana, NKe. **Vo** flight call extremely similar to Lesser Sandplover, but may be slightly softer and more rolling.

Caspian Plover   *Charadrius asiaticus*   21cm, 8"
A fine-billed, rather elegant plover. Non-br ad has a *broad white supercilium and a broad grey-brown breast band*. Br ♂ has a white-faced look, with a smart chestnut breast band narrowly banded below with black. Br ♀ similar to non-br ad; imm has buff fringed upperparts, and a more mottled breast band. **HH** flocks are common from Aug–May on short grasslands in WUg to CKe and NTz (particularly in the Serengeti-Mara ecosystem), and less often at the coast. **Vo** calls a repeated dry *chip* or *tchup* in flight.

Plate 66

Common Ringed Plover

non-br

br

Little Ringed Plover

non-br

br

Kentish Plover

br ♂

non-br

Lesser Sandplover

non-br

non-br

br

Lesser

Greater Sandplover

non-br

br

Greater

Caspian Plover

non-br

br ♂

Caspian

non-br

Grey Plover *Pluvialis squatarola* 31cm, 12"
[Black-bellied Plover]
A large, stocky, heavy-billed plover. Non-br ad is silvery grey-brown above, and grey-mottled below, with a broad but weak supercilium, and often with a dusky face or eye-patch. Br ad is black from face to belly, and brightly spangled silver, grey and black above. Sexes alike. Imm similar to non-br ad, but with slightly stronger buffy-yellow wash. In flight, *black axillaries, white rump and obvious wing bar* are diagnostic. **HH** very common passage and winter visitor to the coast, mainly Sep–May, but some oversummer. Much less common inland, and rare in Ug, Rw and Bu. **Vo** very vocal, atmospheric and mournful slurred whistle that rises and falls *pee-yu-eeee.*

Pacific Golden Plover *Pluvialis fulva* 26cm, 10"
Slimmer and smaller than Grey Plover: non-br ad always shows some golden-yellow above, a *stronger buff-yellow supercilium*, and mottled dusky grey-yellow underparts. Br ad is *spangled black and gold above*, with a black face to belly. Sexes alike. Imm similar to non-br ad, but with stronger buffy-yellow wash. In flight, *pale grey underwing and axillaries* are diagnostic, along with a *golden mottled (not white) rump, and an indistinct wing bar:* feet extend beyond tail tip. **HH** uncommon (but regular) visitor to the coast, especially the Tana River delta and nearby grassy areas in Ke. Less common to CKe and vagrant to Bu. **Vo** in flight, gives a loud, shrill and spaced *tu-whi'yu.*

Ruff *Philomachus pugnax* ♂ 30cm, 12", ♀ 23cm, 9"
Highly variable, *small-headed, short-billed, scaly-backed* shorebird: ads with bright orange legs. Usual non-br ♂ and ♀ brown or grey-brown, scaly above, with lightly mottled head to breast. ♀ (reeve) is smaller. Some ♂♂   are extensively white on the head, back and underparts. Br ♂♂ gain exotic ruffs after leaving Africa. Imm is boldly scaled above with bright buffy fringes. In rather powerful long-winged flight, shows narrow white wing bar, and *white oval patches at sides of tail.* **HH** very common winter visitor and passage migrant to both fresh and alkaline waters (especially with muddy fringes) from Aug–May. A few stay all year round. **Vo** unlike most shorebirds, ruffs are silent in EA.

Buff-breasted Sandpiper *Tryngites subruficollis* 20cm, 8"
Like a small imm Ruff with a short bill, small head and boldly scalloped upperparts; differs in having a more *uniform buff face and underparts, a conspicuous dark-eyed look, and yellow legs*. In flight, shows *no white in upperwing or tail,* underwing mostly white with a dark comma on primary coverts. **HH** rare Nearctic vagrant recorded at Lake Turkana, Ke, in Dec 1973, and Rusizi NP, Bu, in Mar 1992. **Vo** quiet for a wader, but flushed birds may give a low *chwup* or *prreet.*

Red-necked Phalarope *Phalaropus lobatus* 18cm, 7"
[Northern Phalarope]
Small slender-necked swimming shorebird with a *needle-thin black bill.* Non-br ad is grey above and white below with a black smudge behind the eye. Br ♀ has a dark grey face, upperparts and breast, with a white chin and *rufous sides to neck*; br ♂ similar but duller. **HH** reasonably common along the Ke coast from Oct–Apr, especially in floating seaweed. Irregular inland. Often feeds by swimming in circles and pecking at the water surface. **Vo** flying birds utter a low, churred trill of four identical notes *trrt-trrt-trrt-trrt.*

Grey Phalarope *Phalaropus fulicarius* 20cm, 8"
[Red Phalarope]
Non-br ad is very similar to Red-necked Phalarope but larger, with a *heavier broader bill*, and a paler and plainer mantle. Br ♀ has black-tipped yellow bill, black cap, white cheeks and brick-red underparts. Br ♂ similar, but duller. **HH** vagrant inland to Rift Valley lakes in Ke and Bu. **Vo** rarely calls a simple *chit* in flight.

Plate 67

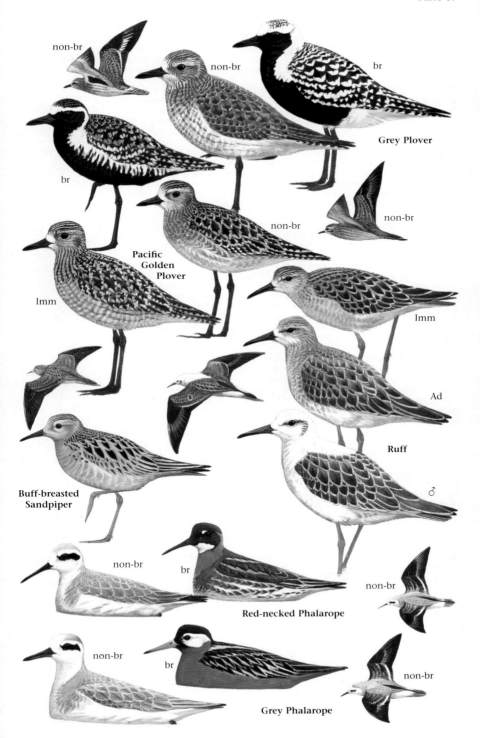

non-br

non-br

br

Grey Plover

br

non-br

non-br

Pacific Golden Plover

Imm

Imm

Ad

Ruff

Buff-breasted Sandpiper

♂

non-br

br

non-br

Red-necked Phalarope

non-br

br

non-br

Grey Phalarope

SANDPIPERS

A highly varied group of Palearctic shorebirds which mainly occur in East Africa during the period Sep–May, although smaller numbers remain throughout the year (includes four species on plate 67 and all the plates 68–73). Species vary in size from small stints (plate 70) to curlews (plate 72). Sandpipers exploit a wide range of wetland and coastal habitats, often in large numbers. Many moult into their striking breeding plumages towards the end of their stay.

Common Sandpiper *Actitis hypoleucos* 20cm, 8"
Short-legged *rather plain brown and white* sandpiper with an obvious horizontal stance: *white underparts peak to form a white wedge at shoulder*, and tail is noticeably longer than wing tips. Non-br ad has a whitish throat and centre of breast. Legs variable greenish-yellowish-olive. Br ad has some black streaking above and a fuller breast band. Imm has buff barred wing-coverts. Flight diagnostic, with shallow beats and glides on bowed wings, showing a clear white bar. **HH** very common winter visitor and passage migrant to lakes, rivers, and the coast from Jul–May, with a few throughout the year. Ever-bobbing tail is good feature even at long distance. **Vo** noisy, calling a piercing series of rapidly delivered virtually identical notes which run together *pipipipipipipipipipipi…*, as well as a plaintive long *siiu-uu*.

Wood Sandpiper *Tringa glareola* 20cm, 8"
Similar to Green Sandpiper, but more graceful and *browner above with a longer white supercilium, a well spotted back, and slightly longer yellowish legs*. Br ad is more mottled above, with a *streaked neck and sides to the breast which mix gradually with the white underparts*. Imm is warmer brown above with buff speckles. Flying birds reveal a small squarish white rump and *pale underwings*: feet extend well beyond tail tip. **HH** very common passage migrant and winter visitor to a wide range of inland waters from Jul–May (only inshore at the coast). Some birds are present all year round. **Vo** noisy, a loud and piercing *chi-chi-chi-chi-chi…* on one tone. Flushed birds call for long periods often in towering flight.

Green Sandpiper *Tringa ochropus* 23cm, 9"
Dumpier and *much darker than Wood Sandpiper with finer spotting on the upperparts* (non-br ad appears almost plain above), supercilium confined to front of eye, *eye-ring more obvious. Dark mottling on breast always ends in a more clear-cut line*. Legs grey-green. Br ad is similar but head and breast with stronger streaking. In flight, *blackish wings and underwing contrast strongly with a brilliant white rump and underparts*. **HH** single birds are common on passage and as winter visitors between late Jul and Apr. Most common at inland freshwaters, from extensive marshy lakeshores, to temporary pools, and even on road puddles, inshore at the coast. Shyer than Wood Sandpiper, bursting into erratic zig-zagging flight when flushed. **Vo** noisy, calling a distinctive rather brazen *tiu-yiu-yiu-yiu…*

Terek Sandpiper *Xenus cinereus* 25cm, 10"
Non-br_ad is striking and unusual with a *long orange-based upswept bill, and short orange legs*. Br ad similar but has blackish scapular lines, and brighter legs. In flight, wing shows a strong white trailing edge across the secondaries. **HH** common passage migrant and winter visitor to the coast, rarely inland, from Aug–Apr, with a few all year round. Feeding birds rush around rapidly, often switching direction. **Vo** flight call is a rapid rather dry and monotone *tu-yer'yer*.

Plate 68

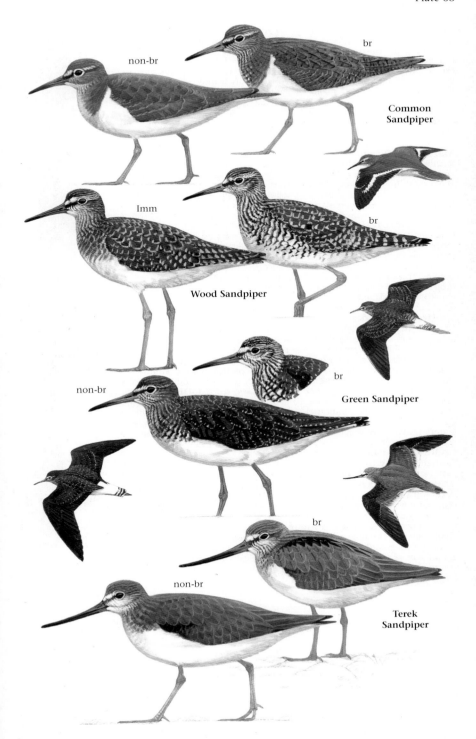

non-br

br

Common Sandpiper

Imm

br

Wood Sandpiper

non-br

br

Green Sandpiper

br

non-br

Terek Sandpiper

Common Greenshank *Tringa nebularia*   32cm, 13"
Large grey-brown and white sandpiper with a *long bill which tapers from a heavy base and is slightly upturned*, and long greenish or grey-green legs. Non-br ad has crown and sides of neck lightly streaked with grey, and rest of underparts white. Br ad is more heavily streaked on the head, neck and breast, with white-fringed blackish and grey scapulars giving a rather spangled appearance. Imm browner above with buff feather edges. In flight, dark wings contrast with a *long white wedge up the back*, and toes just project from tail tip. **HH** common on a wide range of both inland and coastal waters, mainly Sep–Apr, but some are present in all months. Alarmist, towering up and calling when flushed. **Vo** calls a memorable loud, ringing and clear downslurred *tiu* variously repeated 2–6 times, often *tiu-tiu-tiu.*

Marsh Sandpiper *Tringa stagnatilis*   25cm, 10"
Smaller, slimmer, and altogether more delicate than Common Greenshank, with a *fine straight bill and proportionally longer legs.* Non-br ad is grey-brown above, with light streaking from crown to sides to breast; face, supercilium and underparts white, legs greenish-yellow. Br ad shows black streaking on head and neck, and some black spotting on back and flanks: legs brighter yellow. Imm is browner above, with pale feather edges. In flight, shows contrast between dark wings and paler body, with a *long white wedge on back, and toes extending well beyond tail tip.* **HH** common inland on a wide range of waters, from large Great Rift Valley lakes to small pools, mainly from Aug–Apr but some are present throughout the year. At the coast more confined to river estuaries and brackish pools. Often feeds very actively, pecking at water surface and rushing about. **Vo** noisy, calling a squealed, unmusical and sharp *kiu kiu kiu...,* which lacks the ringing effect of Common Greenshank.

Spotted Redshank *Tringa erythropus*   32cm, 13"
Tall attractive wader with *long red legs and a long straight bill with a striking red base.* Non-br ad is mostly grey above and whitish below, with a prominent supercilium *notably white in front of the eye.* Br ad is largely black, with fine white spotting above, variably showing white bars below as plumage changes. Imm similar to non-br ad, but finely spotted and rather browner above, lightly barred brown-grey below. In powerful rising flight, shows dark upperwing, *white wedge on back, and trailing red feet.* **HH** singles and small groups are regular visitors to a wide range of inland waters from Sep–May, but very uncommon at the coast. Birds are alert and shy, with a distinctly tall character, often feeding in small groups, swimming and upending. **Vo** noisy, a diagnostic questioning and rising double *tch'wit.*

Common Redshank *Tringa totanus*   28cm, 11"
Smaller and slightly dumpier than Spotted Redshank with browner upperparts, and a *shorter bill* (with more extensive red at base), and striking *orange-red legs.* Non-br ad has short white supercilium and a grey-brown head and breast. Br ad is extensively mottled, streaked and barred with brown. Imm similar but more streaky below with paler yellow-orange legs. In rather jerky flight, shows *broad white trailing edge to most of wing,* and a white wedge up the back: red feet partially exposed. **HH** uncommon but regular in very small numbers to the coast, especially Mida Creek, Ke, between Oct–Mar. Rare inland, but with records in most months. **Vo** calls a loud ringing *teu-uu-uu* all on the same note.

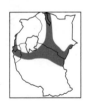

Plate 69

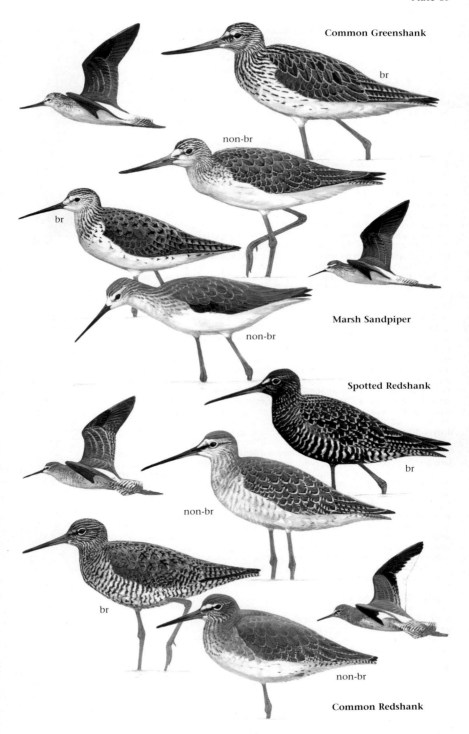

Common Greenshank

br

non-br

br

Marsh Sandpiper

non-br

Spotted Redshank

br

non-br

br

non-br

Common Redshank

STINTS AND SMALLER SANDPIPERS

Stints and smaller migrant sandpipers (including species on plate 71). Best identified by careful attention to markings on head, upperparts, rump and tail, and by leg colour (beware of mud).

Little Stint *Calidris minuta* 15cm, 6"

Non-br ad is grey-brown above with dark feather shafts, pale below with mottled greyish breast patches (which may form a band), bill and legs black. Br ad has much rufous on the head and upperparts (may extend on to sides of breast, but throat always white), *a creamy-buff 'V' at sides of mantle*, and chestnut and buff feather edges with blackish centres giving a strong scaly effect. Imm also mottled above with black and rufous, 'V' on back, forecrown and supercilium whiter. In flight, reveals narrow white wing bar, white sides to rump, and *grey outer-tail*. **HH** very common Palearctic migrant and winter visitor, occurring in flocks on a wide variety of fresh and alkaline waters inland, as well as on the coast, from Aug–May. **Vo** calls a dry *chit*, either singly or running into a trill.

Temminck's Stint *Calidris temminckii* 15cm, 6"

Similar to Little Stint, but *plainer grey-brown above, with a fairly clear-cut grey-brown breast and shorter yellow-green legs* (resembles mini Common Sandpiper). Br ad has some rufous-fringed black-centred feathers on back and scapulars. Imm has scaly buff-fringed wing-coverts. At take off and landing may show white outer-tail, but this is hard to see in typical towering flight. **HH** Palearctic winter visitor from Aug–May; occurs singly or in small loose associations, especially at freshwater lakes and pools with muddy fringes and some cover. Rare in NTz. **Vo** calls a series of 4 or 5 dry rather high notes given so rapidly as to form an insect-like trill *tititit*.

Broad-billed Sandpiper *Limicola falcinellus* 17cm, 6.5"

Non-br ad suggests a large stint with a *longish broad-based bill, which droops at tip*. Grey upperparts show darker shaft streaks, and there is some faint streaking on breast. *Diagnostic double or forked supercilium varies and may not be so obvious in non-br birds*. Br ad is dark above with golden-buff and white fringes, merging as a 'V' on the mantle, *white below with strong black arrow marks on breast and flanks*. Imm similar but brighter. In flight, shows dark leading edge to wing and narrow white wing bar. **HH** generally uncommon Palearctic migrant to coastal mudflats from Aug–May, with small flocks annual at the Sabaki River mouth, Ke. Rare inland. **Vo** not very vocal, calls in flight with a dry *chut chut...*, that can run into a brittle *churr*.

Long-toed Stint *Calidris subminuta* 15cm, 6"

Scaly upperparts may suggest Little Stint, but *often more upright, with a longer neck, dark forecrown, longer yellow-brown legs, and a very long middle toe* (hard to see). In flight, looks very similar to Little, but *toes project slightly beyond tail tip* (flight action often more erratic and may tower). **HH** eastern Palearctic vagrant mainly to marshy fringes of Great Rift Valley lakes in Ke, Nov–May. **Vo** flight call is a deep trill, much deeper than Temminck's Stint.

Red-necked Stint *Calidris ruficollis* 15cm, 6"

Non-br ad is virtually identical to Little Stint, but may have a slightly fatter-based bill, shorter legs, and longer wings and tail. Br ad, however, is very distinctive with a *bright rufous head, throat and breast, bordered below with short black streaks*. **HH** eastern Palearctic vagrant to coastal and inland Ke, three records, May–Aug. **Vo** calls a slow fairly deep *chit chit*, similar to but stronger and slower than Little Stint.

White-rumped Sandpiper *Calidris fuscicollis* 17cm, 6.5"

Non-br ad is rather mottled dull grey above with a slightly drooping bill (with a paler base to lower mandible), a whitish supercilium, greyish streaked breast (usually) and *long wings extending beyond tail tip*. Br ad gains some rufous above. All ages identified by *white uppertail-coverts* (Curlew Sandpiper is larger and longer-billed). **HH** Nearctic vagrant with one record in Rusizi NP, Bu. **Vo** calls a high-pitched thin *jeeet* in flight.

Plate 70

non-br

br

Little Stint

Ad moulting

Temminck's Stint

br

Broad-billed Sandpiper

non-br

Long-toed Stint

non-br

br

Red-necked Stint

Ad

White-rumped Sandpiper

non-br

br

Sanderling *Calidris alba*   21cm, 8"
Small sandpiper which may be confused with either Little Stint or Broad-billed Sandpiper. Non-br ad is usually *pale grey above and very white below*, often with a black smudge at bend of folded wing: bill and legs black. Br ad (rare in EA) is spangled black, silver and chestnut above with a rufous head and breast. Imm mottled above silvery and black with a buff wash at sides of breast. In flight, shows *much black in wing with a strong white wing bar*, and a black centre to tail. **HH** very common passage and winter visitor to the coast, with a few inland, mainly Aug–May. Small numbers over-summer. Hyperactive, constantly running and foraging along the water's edge. **Vo** flying and feeding birds call a rhythmical sharp *twik twik twik...*

Curlew Sandpiper *Calidris ferruginea*   22cm, 8.5"
Slender medium-sized sandpiper with a *long evenly decurved bill*. Non-br ad has distinct white supercilium, and is grey-brown above variably extending on to the upper breast. Br ad gains chestnut head and underparts in Mar–May, with many showing mottled intermediate plumage. Imm more like non-br ad, but browner above with pale feather fringes, and a buffy wash on sides of breast. In flight, clearly shows a *white rump* and wing bar. **HH** flocks are widespread winter visitors and passage migrants from Aug–May, very common at the coast and inland, with some over-summering. **Vo** very noisy in flight, where birds call with a frequent cheerful trilled *chrrut...*

Dunlin *Calidris alpina*   c 21cm, 8"
Non-br ad is similar to Curlew Sandpiper, but *slightly smaller and dumpier, with shorter legs, a darker breast, and decurved bill which curves only towards tip*. Br ad is largely black and rufous above, with a streaked breast, and a *black belly patch*. Imm is more streaky and gingery-brown above than non-br ad, with streaks on breast extending on to flanks as small black spots. In flight, shows *black centre to rump and tail*, and a white wing bar. **HH** vagrant, with only five records, Oct–Apr. **Vo** flight call is a dry trilled *kreeet* or *kreeee* that falls in tone at the end.

Pectoral Sandpiper *Calidris melanotos*   23cm, 9"
Medium-sized sandpiper which at all ages shows a *short slightly decurved bill and streaky brown upperparts extending across the breast in a well-defined dark band*: legs and feet dull yellowish. If alarmed looks long-necked with upright stance suggesting Ruff. In flight, also ruff-like, with black centre-tail and white ovals on sides of rump. **HH** rare vagrant with only three records, Sep–May. **Vo** calls a harsh, low scraping and dry trill *krrt* in flight.

Red Knot *Calidris canutus*   25cm, 10"
[Knot]
Thickset sandpiper with a rather short bill and neck, and short dull-greenish legs. Non-br ad is largely grey and faintly scaled above, pale below and lightly mottled, and streaked grey on the breast and flanks. Br ad is mottled black, chestnut and grey above and chestnut below. In flight, shows narrow white wing bar and *pale grey rump*. **HH** vagrant to EA, with five records from coastal Ke and Tz. **Vo** calls a regularly spaced, paired upslurred nasal *kiu-kiu*.

Ruddy Turnstone *Arenaria interpres*   23cm, 9"
[Turnstone]
Stout short-billed shorebird with *short orange legs*. Non-br ad is dark brown and black above, with a dark breast band contrasting with a white throat and belly. Br ad is a striking mix of black, white and chestnut. Imm is like non-br ad, but with pale feather edges above, and duller legs. In flight, reveals *obvious bold pattern of white bars on wings, back and tail*. **HH** very common passage migrant and winter visitor to the coast from Aug–Apr, with a small number over-summering, regular but much less numerous inland. Rare in Rw and Bu. **Vo** flight call is a hurried *tuk'a'tuk*, and also gives a low throaty and musical churred trill.

Plate 71

Sanderling

non-br

br

Curlew Sandpiper

non-br

br

Dunlin

br

non-br

Pectoral Sandpiper

Red Knot

non-br

br

Ruddy Turnstone

non-br

br

GODWITS AND CURLEWS

Large Palearctic migrant shorebirds. Best identified by size and shape of bill, head, wing and tail markings, and by distinctive calls.

Black-tailed Godwit   *Limosa limosa*   40cm, 16"

Tall elegant wader, with a striking *long straight bill* (with a wide pink base) and very long legs. Non-br ad has a *uniform fairly dark grey-brown back, head, neck and breast*, mottled gradually into a white belly. Br ♂ has rust-red from sides of face to breast, black and white barred lower breast, and a white belly. Br ♀ variable, usually with less rufous. In flight, shows a *broad white wing stripe, a white rump and a wide black tail bar* (hence name): long legs and toes trail markedly. **HH** small and large flocks are sometimes common on larger lakes and wetlands, especially in the Great Rift Valley from Aug–Apr, with some over-summering. Seemingly more common than formerly, but still very uncommon in Rw, Bu and at the coast. **Vo** flying birds call *wika-wika-wik*.

Bar-tailed Godwit   *Limosa lapponica*   38cm, 15"

Similar to Black-tailed Godwit, but with notably *shorter upper leg,* and a shorter *slightly upcurved bill* (which also has a striking pink base in non-br birds). Non-br ad also has paler grey-brown *mottled and streaked upperparts, throat, and sides of breast*, and more extensive white underparts. Br ♂ has a mostly dark bill and a deep *chestnut-red head, neck and underparts*. Br ♀ and imm are rather like non-br ad, but with a buff wash to the neck and breast. In flight, reveals *plain upperwing*, a white rump extending as a wedge onto back, and a *barred tail* from which the feet barely extend. **HH** small numbers occur regularly on passage and as wintering birds, mainly on the coast from Aug–Apr, very uncommon inland. **Vo** flying birds call a nasal *kweek-eek*.

Whimbrel   *Numenius phaeopus*   40cm, 16"

Smaller than Eurasian Curlew with a long bill (but still comparatively short) that decurves suddenly towards the tip, and a *bold striped head pattern*. Sexes and imm are all similar. In rather fast-winged flight, shows white wedge extending from base of tail to centre of back. **HH** very common visitor to the coast, including estuaries, mudflats, and tidally exposed coral reefs, mainly Aug–Apr, but with many over-summering. Scarce inland, mainly to the large Great Rift Valley lakes. **Vo** very noisy, both on the ground and in flight. Distinctive tittering 7–12 note whistle is a characteristic sound of the coast *bi'bi'bi'bi'bi'bi...* Also calls an attractive curlew-like bubbling of rising and falling slurs.

Eurasian Curlew   *Numenius arquata*   ♀ 59cm, 23"

Much larger and generally a warmer brown than Whimbrel, with a *much longer more evenly decurved bill, and no head stripes*. Considerable size range of both body and bill length, from larger ♀ to smaller ♂. In flight, shows similar white wedge on back as Whimbrel, but wing beat slower, stronger and more even. **HH** generally rather uncommon visitor and passage migrant mainly to the coast from Aug–Apr, with occasional birds oversummering. Most frequent on larger estuaries and creeks, uncommon on larger lakes inland, and rare in the west. **Vo** in flight calls a distinctive and very loud *cour-lii,* and a bubbling call is also occasionally heard.

Plate 72

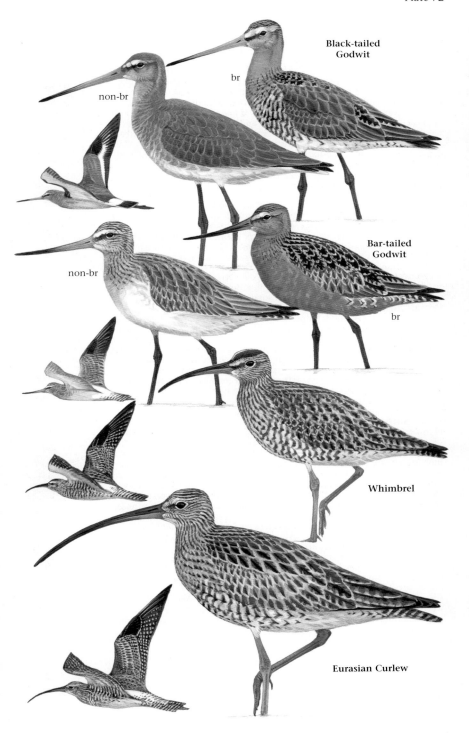

Black-tailed
Godwit

br

non-br

Bar-tailed
Godwit

non-br

br

Whimbrel

Eurasian Curlew

SNIPES

Well-camouflaged, long-billed cryptic birds of marshes and swamps. Because of their often skulking behaviour all five can be hard to see well. Note of back, underwing and tail patterns, as well as behaviour, habitat and calls aid identification. Sexes and immature plumages are all similar.

Common Snipe *Gallinago gallinago* 27cm, 10.5"
The classic snipe, with a long bill and a striking buff-yellow and black-brown striped head and back, brown and buff striped breast, darkly barred flanks, and a white belly. In towering and twisting flight, reveals *white trailing edge to secondaries and broad rufous tips to tail feathers with limited white at sides*. **HH** common winter visitor and passage migrant from the Palearctic, occurring in large marshes and swamps, smaller ponds and seasonally flooded grasslands south into CTz, mainly below 2000m from late-Sep–early May. **Vo** calls a harsh *schhp* with an upslur at the end, less dry than other snipes.

African Snipe *Gallinago nigripennis* 30cm, 12"
[Ethiopian Snipe]
Similar to Common Snipe, but *longer-billed, and much darker above, with more contrast between the dark breast and white belly, and more heavily barred flanks*. Flushed birds tower less than Common, often flying closer to the ground, revealing *darker more rounded wings* (with a white trailing edge to the secondaries), *a whiter belly, and much more white in the outer-tail feathers*. **HH** reasonably common and widespread but local resident in highland and montane wetlands from 1700–4000m, although non-br birds may wander to lower altitudes. **Vo** call is similar to Common Snipe, but harsher and drier, and longer than Pintail Snipe.

Pintail Snipe *Gallinago stenura* 25cm, 10"
Very similar to Common Snipe, but has a slightly shorter bill, a more bulging supercilium in front of the eye, a finer loral line, and shorter tail that barely projects beyond the folded wings. If preening unique *pin-like outer-tail feathers* may be noticeable. In flight, shows, *rather pale wing-coverts contrasting with flight feathers, no obvious white trailing edge to secondaries, and a well-barred dark underwing*. Birds take off more leisurely than Common, towering and zig-zagging less. **HH** vagrant from Asia with three records from Ke wetlands, Oct–Jan. **Vo** calls a short harsh *schht* similar but drier than Common Snipe.

Great Snipe *Gallinago media* 28cm, 11"
Plumper, darker and shorter-billed than Common Snipe, with *rows of white spots on wing-coverts, and more strongly barred flanks and belly*. Imm has less obvious wing-covert spots. Appears *heavy and rather pot-bellied* in flight, flushing tightly and usually flying low and direct over a short distance before dropping back into cover. Upperwing shows white bars across the coverts and a very limited white trailing edge to the secondaries. *Underwing and belly are dark and closely barred; outer-tail is white*. **HH** widespread but generally uncommon Palearctic migrant to flooded grassland, swamps and marshes, mainly late Sep–Dec and Apr–May. **Vo** when flushed calls a low *etch*, followed by a deep and distinct *crork crork...*

Jack Snipe *Lymnocryptes minimus* 19cm, 7.5"
Small dark snipe with a short bill, *a broad buff supercilium which splits above the eye, no central crown stripe*, and golden lines on the back. Hard to flush, rising quietly from near feet, and only flying a short distance before rushing to settle quickly; appears short-billed in flight, with narrow wings, and a wedge-shaped dark tail. Tends to bob up and down when feeding. **HH** scarce and occasional (perhaps overlooked) Palearctic visitor to marshes and wetlands from Oct–Mar, vagrant to NTz. **Vo** silent away from breeding grounds.

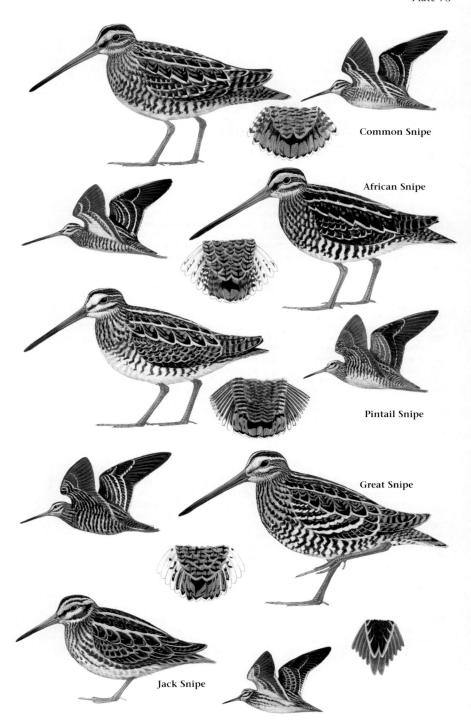

Plate 73

Common Snipe

African Snipe

Pintail Snipe

Great Snipe

Jack Snipe

SKUAS

Two genera of fierce gull-like seabirds which regularly steal food (often from gulls and terns) by forcing them to regurgitate. All are difficult to identify, with both pale and dark morphs and intermediates. Careful note should be made of overall shape and proportions, shape and length of tail streamers (if present), and the extent of white in the primaries. All are very uncommon in East Africa, with *Stercorarius* visiting from their Arctic breeding grounds, and Sub-Antarctic Skua from the southern oceans.

Arctic Skua *Stercorarius parasiticus* c 41cm, 16" + br tail 5–8.5cm, 2–3.5"
[Parasitic Jaeger]

Neat, rather elegant and of slighter build than Pomarine Skua, but heavier-bodied than Long-tailed. In both morphs br ad has *elongated and pointed central tail feathers, and prominent white wing flashes*. Additionally pale morph has a dark cap and pale underparts, and may, or may not, have a breast band. Dark morph is all dark grey-brown (with white wing flashes). Intermediates also occur. Non-br ad may lack tail streamers and show barring on the back and uppertail-coverts. Imm (which also has pale and dark morphs) has variable barring both above and below, and on the underwing-coverts. With experience can be told by proportions, and if seen well shows *short pointed projections to centre-tail*. Juv usually warmer brown than other juvs, with pale rufous feather edges. Flight is very *falcon-like*, chasing other seabirds on rapid wings. **HH** very rare visitor with few records, mainly at Lake Turkana and the Ke coast, Sep–Apr. One reported Rusizi NP, Bu. **Vo** silent in region.

Long-tailed Skua *Stercorarius longicaudus* c 38cm, 15" + br tail 12–24cm, 5–9.5"
[Long-tailed Jaeger]

More delicate than other skuas, with comparatively *slender wings*, and on br ad *very long tail streamers*. Pale morph has a neat black cap, contrasting with largely white underparts, but birds changing to non-br plumage gain dark throats and barred undertail coverts. *Lacks extensive white wing flashes*, and from above shows a *grey-brown back and wing-coverts contrasting with darker primaries and trailing wing edge*. Non-br ad gains barring on rump and underparts (sometimes extensively), and has a shorter tail. Rare dark morph has not been recorded in our area. Imm varied, as with other species, but often grey-toned, with *strongly barred undertail-coverts, and rather blunt projections to centre tail*. Flight more *tern-like* than the other skuas. **HH** a br ad at Lake Turkana, Ke, in Aug 1961 is the only EA record. **Vo** silent in region.

Pomarine Skua *Stercorarius pomarinus* c 46cm, 18 " + br tail 5.5–11cm, 2–4.5"
[Pomarine Jaeger]

Bulky and deep-chested with a heavier bill than other similar skuas. Br ad has *long spatulate central tail feathers* (may be worn or lost) and *prominent white wing flashes*. Commoner pale morph usually (but not always) has a dark breast band and barring on the flanks and undertail. Dark morph is all blackish-brown, except for white wing flashes. Imm barred and varied as others, but looks more bulky: tail looks square-ended or with slight blunt projections. Non-br ad is like imm, but with plain dark underwing-coverts. Flight *steadier, heavier, and slower* than Arctic Skua. **HH** uncommon visitor, mainly to Lake Turkana and the coast, from Oct–Mar. **Vo** silent in region.

Sub-Antarctic Skua *Catharacta antarctica* 63cm, 25"

A *large, bulky, powerful brown skua* with a thick bill, broad wings, and a comparatively *short broad tail*. Shows extensive white wing flashes in flight. Birds in our area are presumed to be the race *lonnbergi* which is numerous in South African waters. **HH** easily confused with other *Catharacta* skuas: at least five sightings have been reported off the Ke coast, and a single was seen very well near Kilifi, Ke, in Dec 1990. **Vo** silent in region.

Plate 74

pale morph br

Arctic Skua

Imm

dark morph br

Long-tailed Skua

Imm

non-br

pale morph br

Imm

dark morph br

Pomarine Skua

pale morph br

Sub-Antarctic Skua

SMALLER GULLS

One resident and two Palearctic migrant gulls which are easily identified in breeding plumage, but are otherwise more difficult. Note head and eye colour, and, in flight, wing markings. Sexes alike. Plumage changes from immature to adult in just over one year.

Grey-headed Gull   *Larus cirrocephalus*   c 41cm, 16"

Br ad is a neat *grey-headed gull, with pale yellow eyes surrounded by a pink-red ring*, a thickish dark-red bill, and red legs. At close range light-grey hood shows a darker grey edge, and the underparts may have a pale pink wash. Non-br ad has a much paler poorly defined hood, or a whitish head with a smudge behind the eye. 1st year is similar to 1st year Black-headed Gull, with smudges on the crown and behind the dark eyes, and a narrow black tail band. It differs in being slightly larger, having more black in the primaries, and a darker underwing. The bill is pinkish with a dark tip; legs dirty orange-brown. In flight, upperwing of ad shows black outer primaries (with two white spots), and a *dark-grey underwing*. **HH** flocks are common and widespread on both fresh and alkaline waters inland. Wanders widely, though very rare at the coast. **Vo** utters a loud rasping downslurred *graarr*, typical of smaller gulls.

Common Black-headed Gull   *Larus ridibundus*   c 38cm, 15"
[Black-headed Gull]

Slightly more slender and smaller than Grey-headed Gull, with *dark brown eyes at all ages*. Br ad has a neat *dark-brown hood and a partial white eye-ring*, a dark red bill, and red legs. Non-br ad has a white head with a *conspicuous dark spot behind the eye*; and a paler-red bill with a dark tip. 1st year very similar to 1st year Slender-billed Gull, but that species has a longer bill and a slender-necked appearance. Differs from 1st year Grey-headed in having more white in primaries and a paler underwing. In flight, from above, ad shows a conspicuous white leading edge to the outer wing, while from below, darker inner primaries contrast with the mostly light-grey underwing. **HH** sometimes common Palearctic winter visitor to a wide range of waters, particularly inland from Oct–Apr, with a few over-summering. **Vo** occasionally cries a shrill, but low-pitched raspy downslurred *kreeeeaa*.

Slender-billed Gull   *Larus genei*   c 40cm, 16"

Most similar to Black-headed Gull, but has a *long-necked look, with a gently sloping forehead and a long bill*. Br ad has a pure white head, and may have pink-washed underparts: bill varies from dark blood red, to paler orange-red, legs bright red. Eyes appear small, and are usually pale yellowish-white (but dark on very young birds): there is a small reddish eye-ring. Non-br ad may have a light grey smudge behind the eye. 1st year has paler yellowish-brown bill and legs. In flight, best told from similar plumages of Black-headed by overall shape, especially the long-billed, long-necked look. **HH** scarce Palearctic migrant to major lakes along the Great Rift Valley, particularly lakes Turkana and Nakuru from Oct–Mar. Rare at the coast: vagrant to Ug. **Vo** calls a deep throaty *rraaaa*.

Plate 75

1st year

Grey-headed Gull

br

1st year

br

non-br

1st year

non-br

br

Common Black-headed Gull

br

1st year

br

br

non-br

br

Slender-billed Gull

LARGE DARK-BACKED GULLS

Three rather large dark-backed gulls. Taxonomy of Palearctic Lesser Black-backed and Heuglin's is highly complex, contentious, and liable to change. Kelp Gull is a vagrant from southern Africa. All change through a range of plumages from immature to adult in just over three years; being very brown and dark-tailed in 1st year, greyer or blacker above in 2nd year, tail mostly white and wing tips gaining adult pattern in 3rd year, followed by adult plumage (non-breeding and breeding) after that. All have black bills in 1st year, becoming yellow with a red spot as adults, leg colour varies and is described below. Familiarity with the common Lesser Black-backed Gull forms a good basis for comparison, note overall size and shape, wing markings, and back and leg colour.

Lesser Black-backed Gull   *Larus fuscus*   c 56cm, 22"

Slightly smaller and slimmer than the other black-backed gulls, and standing birds often have a drawn-out attenuated look. In our area, br ad of the nominate race is *black-backed* with a white head, a fairly slender yellow bill with a red spot, and yellowish legs. Non-br ad is very similar (including the white head). Imm passes through age groups as described in introduction, but note legs are pinkish until second year. Best identified from similar-aged large gulls by smaller and more slender appearance. In flight, appears *slimmer-winged* than others, with ad showing small white tips to primaries, and a single white spot on the outer most feather. **HH** common Palearctic visitor from Oct–Apr, with a few present throughout the year. Most numerous at the larger lakes and on the coast. **Vo** usually silent in EA.

Heuglin's Gull   *Larus heuglini*   c 63cm, 25"

Large, bulky, dark-backed gulls, which were formerly considered to be Herring Gull *Larus argentatus*. Imm and ad plumages are very similar to Lesser Black-backed Gull, but Heuglin's always looks *bigger* especially when seen together, and is also slightly larger-billed. The situation is further confused as both pale and dark backed birds occur. Br ad has a white head, a yellow bill with a red spot (which may also have a narrow blackish band), pale yellow eyes, and usually yellow legs. Non-br birds have some grey streaking on the head and either yellow or pinkish legs. **HH** Palearctic winter visitor especially around the Sabaki River mouth and the NKe coast, from Oct–Mar. Appears to have become more common in recent years, with birds reported from lakes Turkana and Victoria, and some birds over-summering. **Vo** usually silent in EA.

Kelp Gull   *Larus dominicanus*   c 60cm, 24"

Large *black-backed* gull, with a *thick and heavy yellow bill with red spot*, white head (in both br and non-br ad plumages) and *olive-yellow, or olive legs*. Imm is also large and robust, but the thick bill is black, and the legs are grey: plumage changes to ad as for previous species. **HH** a single ad at Malindi, Ke, in Jan 1984 is the only EA record. **Vo** unknown in EA.

Plate 76

1st year

Ad

2nd year

Lesser Black-backed Gull

Ad

1st year

1st year

Ad

dark backed

1st year

Heuglin's Gull

Ad

pale backed

Ad

2nd year

Ad

Ad

1st year

Kelp Gull

LARGER DARK-HEADED GULLS

Three large dark-headed gulls. Massive Great Black-headed is distinctive in all plumages, changing from immature to adult in just over three years. Sooty and White-eyed are both similar, and identification (particularly for immatures) requires careful attention to size, shape and colour of bills. They attain adult plumage in just over two years. Sooty is common on the coast: the others are vagrants.

Sooty Gull *Larus hemprichii* 47cm, 18.5"

Br ad is *dark brownish-grey above and across the breast, with a darker sooty-brown head, and a striking white collar around the hindneck*, breast to vent white. At close range shows a *white mark above the eye* (a second faint mark below the eye may also be present); *bill is greenish-yellow with a narrow black band and red tip*, legs yellowish. Non-br ad has generally less well defined markings, and a duller bill and legs. 1st year is paler, plainer, and browner above with pale fringes to the wing-coverts, and no white hind-collar; *bill pale grey with a black tip*, legs dull grey-green. In rather slow and laboured flight, ad appears dark above with a white trailing edge to the wing; dark head and breast contrast strongly with the white underparts and tail. Imm shows similar (but duller pattern), with a wide black band across the tail. **HH** flocks are common on the coast, with small numbers breeding on offshore islands in NEKe, but most numerous as non-br visitors from Oct–May, and many are present all year round. **Vo** single birds are rather quiet, but flocks are very noisy, with all members calling a nasal downslurred *weeooo...weeooo...*, and creating a loud chorus.

White-eyed Gull *Larus leucophthalmus* 43cm, 17"

Br ad is similar to Sooty Gull, but slightly smaller and more slender with *paler grey upperparts and breast, a black head, and a long, slender slightly drooping red bill with a black tip. White crescents both above and below the eye* more obvious; legs yellow. Non-br ad is similar, but duller with some pale flecking on the head. 1st year is similar to 1st year Sooty, but darker and browner (lacking extensive pale fringes to the wing-coverts): *slender bill is all dark*. In light and buoyant flight basic pattern is similar to Sooty at all corresponding ages, but wings appear narrower and more pointed. **HH** vagrant from the Middle East although exact status is unclear. It was reported from the NKe coast in the 1950s and 60s, and there are three records from Lake Turkana, Ke (Dec and Apr). **Vo** similar to Sooty Gull but less harsh.

Great Black-headed Gull *Larus ichthyaetus* c 66cm, 26"
[Pallas's Gull]

Br ad is a *spectacular massive gull with a black hood, and a large yellow bill with black and red bands near the tip:* conspicuous white crescents above and below eye are visible at close range. In non-br ad the hood is reduced to dark smudges around the eye. 1st year differs from other 1st year large gulls (like Heuglin's) in having a *dark smudge behind the eye, a dark-tipped pale bill, white underparts and a clear-cut black tail band*. In flight, ad appears very large and very pale, with *black on the wings restricted to primary tips*. 1st year differs from other large gulls in having a *grey panel across the wing-coverts* and a solid black tail band. **HH** scarce, but almost annual Palearctic visitor to the Ke coast and Lake Turkana, mainly from Dec–Apr. Vagrant to Ug and Bu. **Vo** silent in region.

Plate 77

br

1st year

Sooty Gull

1st year

1st year

br

White-eyed Gull

non-br

1st year

br

Great Black-headed Gull

LARGER TERNS

These large or fairly large terns are mainly non-br visitors to the coast (except Gull-billed). All are grey above and white below, with black caps in breeding plumage. They can all be identified by size and bill colour. Sexes alike.

Lesser Crested Tern   *Sterna bengalensis*   39cm, 15.5"

Smaller and slimmer than Greater Crested Tern with a *straight rich orange-yellow bill*. Br ad has a *black cap stretching from bill to nape* and forming a short crest. Non-br ad has a white forecrown, with black confined to above and behind eye, and to the nape. 1st year has a duller bill and dark outer flight feathers. Flight, lighter, more dipping and buoyant than Greater Crested, with slightly darker outer primaries (noticeably darker in 1st year) and uniform pale-grey back, rump and centre-tail. **HH** very common non-br tern at the coast from Nov–Apr, with some present throughout the year. Occurs as singles, or in small to large flocks, both offshore and in creeks and estuaries, and occasionally further inland along larger rivers. Vagrant to Great Rift Valley lakes, including in Rw and Bu. **Vo** quite noisy, with feeding parties maintaining a high descending *krreek*.

Greater Crested Tern   *Sterna bergii*   49cm, 19"

[Swift Tern]

Larger than Lesser Crested Tern, with a *heavier pale yellow bill*, decurved at tip. Br ad has crested black cap *separated from bill by a narrow white forehead*. Non-br ad has black confined to behind the eye and around nape. Two races occur: *velox* is distinctly darker grey above with a paler grey rump and tail; while *thalassina* is similar to Lesser Crested but obviously larger, with a longer paler bill. 1st year has speckled blackish-brown crown, a grey-brown back and wings with much pale fringing, and a dark carpal bar. Flight is more forceful and shallower than Lesser Crested. **HH** non-br birds of race *velox* occur along the Ke coast throughout the year, but are most numerous from Nov–Jun particularly north of Mombasa. Race *thalassina* breeds in large numbers on Latham and other islands off the Tz coast, but non-br birds are widespread. **Vo** calls low slightly descending scrapy rasps *krrekk* or *krreerrk*.

Caspian Tern   *Sterna caspia*   54cm, 21"

Largest tern with a *massive red bill* (tipped black). Br ad has a short crested black cap, pale grey back and wings, and a rather short forked tail. Non-br ad has a white streaked forecrown. 1st year is similar to non br ad but has a duller orange bill. Flight is strong and steady, showing distinct *blackish ends to underwings* in all plumages. **HH** singles and small groups of non-br birds are regular along the Ke coast (Jul–Apr), especially at the Sabaki River mouth, but becoming progressively rarer south into Tz. It is seasonally common at Lake Turkana, but rare elsewhere inland, and vagrant to lakes in Ug, Rw and Bu. **Vo** calls a variable high-pitched *sqeeweewoo* and a harsh *krre-ahk*.

Sandwich Tern   *Sterna sandvicensis*   41cm, 16"

Similar proportions to Lesser Crested Tern with pale grey upperparts and a *long slender yellow-tipped black bill* (tip hard to see at distance); rump white, tail has a shallow fork. Br ad has a black cap with a short crest and well-marked bill; black confined to nape and behind eye in non-br. 1st year has virtually all dark bill, some brownish fringes on the wing-coverts, and a darker tail. Flight is powerful and deep, showing a variable darker grey wedge in primaries. **HH** singles and small groups are uncommon but annual Palearctic visitors to the NKe coast and Dar es Salaam, Tz, mainly from Aug–Apr, vagrant inland. **Vo** utters a high-pitched scratchy, slightly wavering *kirrireek*.

Gull-billed Tern   *Sterna nilotica*   38cm, 15"

Solid medium-sized tern, with a *short heavy gull-like black bill*, pale grey back, wings and rump, short shallow forked tail, and longish dark legs. Br ad has neat glossy black cap and no crest; non-br ad has a *black smudge just behind the eye*. 1st year like non-br ad with some brown scaling on wing-coverts. In buoyant and lithe flight, wings often reveal a narrow dark trailing edge to primaries. **HH** singles, and flocks are common Palearctic winter visitors mainly from Jul–Apr, but some oversummer. Occurs around major inland lakes and at the coast, and also often over grasslands (like the Serengeti). Does not plunge dive, but swoops and picks food from surface. **Vo** call is a loud raspy *crr-aarp* with an accent on the second syllable.

Plate 78

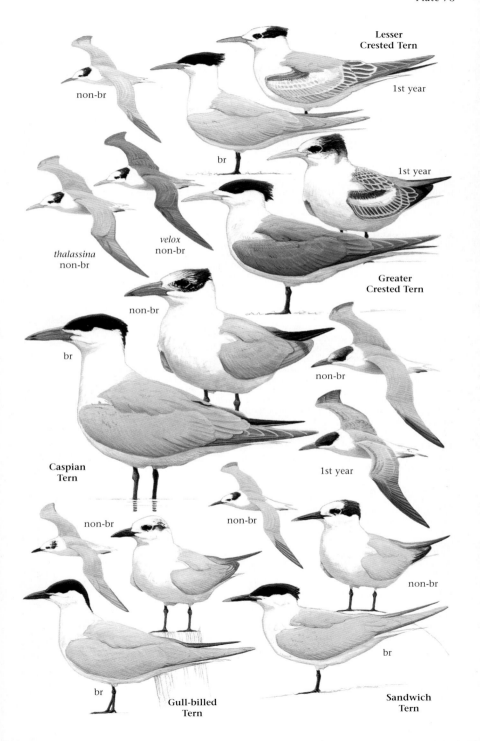

non-br

Lesser Crested Tern

1st year

br

1st year

thalassina non-br

velox non-br

Greater Crested Tern

non-br

br

non-br

Caspian Tern

1st year

non-br

non-br

non-br

br

Gull-billed Tern

br

Sandwich Tern

SWALLOW TERNS

Three medium-sized marine terns which are difficult to identify except in full breeding plumage. Particular attention should be paid to the shape and colour of the bill, distribution of black and grey in the wings, and to rump colour. Sexes alike.

Common Tern *Sterna hirundo* c 35cm, 14"

Classic swallow tern. Br ad has a black cap and pale grey upperparts contrasting with a whiter rump and tail, the latter having elongated, but not very long outermost feathers: underparts are *washed pale grey. Bill usually black in EA,* but may be red with a black tip. Non-br ad has a white forecrown, less contrast between the back and rump, and a blackish bar across the lesser wing-coverts. 1st year is similar but may show a few brown fringes above, darker primaries, and a dark bar across the secondaries. In flight, br ad shows a mostly *white underwing with a dark grey trailing edge to the primaries,* and a medium length forked swallow-tail. Non-br has a paler rump than very similar White-cheeked Tern. HH flocks are very common along the coast from Aug–Apr, with some recorded all year round. Large numbers may occur, both in offshore mixed-species feeding flocks, and at estuarine roosts. Rare inland: vagrant to Ug and Bu. Strong and confident flight action, hovers and dives directly to catch fish. Vo calls a descending *skreeoo* with accent on the first syllable.

White-cheeked Tern *Sterna repressa* c 35cm, 14"

Br ad is *dark-grey above and below* with a black cap, and an obvious *white cheek: back, wings and forked tail are uniform dark grey.* Non-br ad is very similar to non-br Common Tern with a white forehead and underparts and a dark carpal bar, but the *rump and tail are always greyer than on Common,* and there is more grey in the underwing. 1st year is like non-br ad but with paler silvery-grey primaries. HH breeds on islands off the NKe coast, but is typically marine and uncommon inshore, except at the Sabaki River mouth: scarce in NTz. Vo calls a harsh *kee-errr,* similar to Common Tern. SS Whiskered Tern.

Roseate Tern *Sterna dougallii* c 38cm, 15"

Br ad is similar to Common Tern but appears *much whiter with very long tail streamers and a long slender bill* which varies from bright red, to black, or a mixture of both: *underparts may be washed pink.* Non-br ad and 1st year have a less distinct carpal bar and a longer bill than similar Common. In flight, shows narrow dark primary wedge from above, but *underwing is always very white.* HH locally common resident breeding on islands in NKe, less common and somewhat more erratic further south. Vo calls a distinctive, scratchy almost wader-like *kirurit.*

LITTLE TERNS

Two tiny terns, flying with rapid wing beats and much hovering before diving to catch fish. May be conspecific and exact status is unclear as they look almost identical except in breeding plumage.

Saunders's Tern *Sterna saundersi* 23cm, 9"

Br ad has a *white forehead patch that does not extend behind the eye,* and three or four black outer primaries appearing as a slightly larger dark wedge than on Little Tern. Black-tipped yellow bill is similar to Little, but legs are brownish or olive. In the field, non-br ad and imm cannot be separated from Little Tern. HH very common along the Ke coast from Oct–Apr but with some throughout the year: less numerous further south. One has also been collected at Lake Turkana, Ke. Vo calls a frequent *plik plik...,* not obviously different from Little Tern.

Little Tern *Sterna albifrons* 23cm, 9"

Very similar to Saunders's Tern but br ad has a *white forehead patch that extends just behind the eye,* with only two or three black outer primaries, and brighter orange-yellow legs. Other plumages cannot be distinguished in the field. HH status uncertain, but singles to small flocks have been reported on the Great Rift Valley lakes, and occasionally at the coast. Vo not recorded in region.

Black-naped Tern *Sterna sumatrana* 30cm, 12"

Distinctive handsome very white tern with a slender black bill and a well-defined black band running through the eyes and across the nape. Crown and underparts pure white, back and wings pale grey except for black outer web of the outermost primary. HH vagrant with only one record in our area, nine together at Latham Island, Tz , in Nov 1987. Vo a short raspy and low *kirit.*

Plate 79

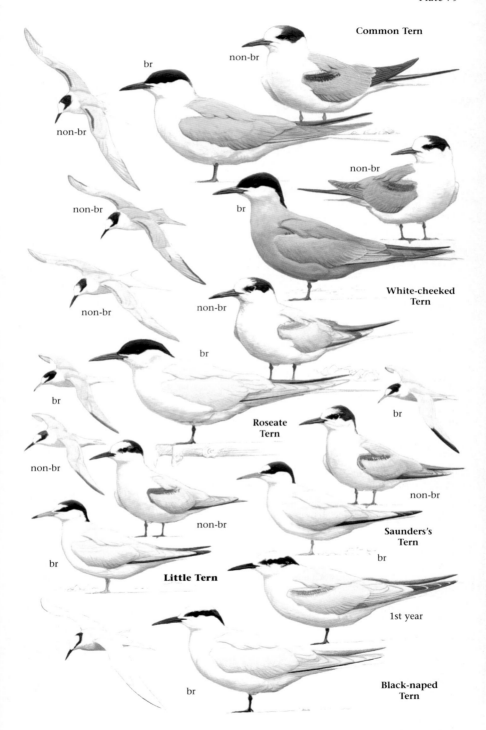

Common Tern

non-br

br

non-br

non-br

non-br

non-br

White-cheeked
Tern

br

non-br

br

Roseate
Tern

br

br

non-br

non-br

Saunders's
Tern

br

Little Tern

br

1st year

br

Black-naped
Tern

DARK-BACKED SEA TERNS
Two dark-backed fork-tailed sea terns which can be difficult to identify at distance. Note extent of white on forecrown, nape and back contrast, and overall colour of upperparts. Sexes alike, but immature plumage is quite different.

Bridled Tern *Sterna anaethetus* 35cm, 14"

Smaller than Sooty Tern, with dark grey-brown upperparts, a narrow white forehead, and, at close range, a *thin white supercilium which invariably extends behind the eye. Dark crown contrasts with paler back*, and often a paler grey hindneck. In buoyant flight, underwing may show less contrast than Sooty, with grey-white coverts grading into the dark wing tip. 1st year has a greyish forecrown, pale fringes to the back and wing-coverts, and mostly white underparts with a grey wash to the flanks. **HH** singles and flocks occur offshore all along the coast, with breeding on NKe coastal islands Jul–Aug. **Vo** noisy on breeding grounds where birds give an almost gull-like barking.

Sooty Tern *Sterna fuscata* 43cm, 17"

Larger than Bridled Tern with *uniform sooty-black upperparts*, no paler hind-neck, or contrast between the crown and back. Brilliant white forehead does not extend behind the eye. In flight, underwing white and black, the coverts contrasting clearly with the wing tip. 1st year is largely dark brown flecked with white above, and with an off-white belly. **HH** singles to very large flocks (many hundreds) are usually encountered well offshore, often feeding over active fish shoals. Breeds on islands off the NKe coast Jul-Aug, and off Tz mainly in Nov. **Vo** breeding birds cry a strange three-part waver-ing *waa-a-aa*, the entire colony making a considerable din!

NODDIES
All-brown sea terns, with pale caps, well-angled wings and broad slightly forked tails (when spread). If seen together should not present identification problems, but solitary birds more dif-ficult, note extent of pale cap, bill size and any contrasting pale areas in the upperwing. Sexes and immature plumages are similar.

Brown Noddy *Anous stolidus* 41cm, 16"
[Common Noddy]

Larger, browner and altogether a heavier bird than Lesser Noddy, with a pale cap clearly demarked from the blackish lores, and a thicker bill. In flight, upperwing looks two-toned, a paler brown band contrasting with the darker brown coverts and flight feathers. **HH** quite common off the coast throughout the year, with hundreds breeding near Lamu, NKe, and on Latham Island, Tz, in Jun–Oct. Usually feeds well offshore. **Vo** breeding birds call a rather unmusical rasp.

Lesser Noddy *Anous tenuirostris* 33cm, 13"

Darker, smaller and more elegant than Brown Noddy, with a thinner bill and a silver-grey cap which grades into the pale lores. In flight, appears very dark brown-black without contrast in the upperwing. Looks narrow-winged, with more rapid wing beats and a lighter feel than Brown. **HH** for-merly considered rare but may have been confused with Brown Noddy, and now seen regularly offshore. **Vo** silent in region.

SKIMMER
Black and white tern-like bird, with graceful, elastic, measured flight. Feeds in calm water, skim-ming the surface with its flexible thin lower mandible partially submerged, and snapping up small prey with remarkable accuracy.

African Skimmer *Rynchops flavirostris* 41cm, 16"

Attractive long-winged, short-tailed tern-like bird most noted for its later-ally compressed red bill (with a pale tip), lower mandible longer than upper. Br ad is all black-brown above and white below. Non-br ad is duller with a greyish-brown collar across the hindneck. Imm paler brown above, with a shorter blackish bill and dull yellow legs. **HH** singles to small flocks occur sporadically throughout, but are only regular on the Great Rift Valley lakes, especially at Lake Turkana where many hundreds may gather and occasionally breed. Smaller numbers are resident on larger rivers in STz. **Vo** often silent, but groups give a high-pitched quavering contact *kreek kreek kreek*.

Plate 80

1st year

Ad

Bridled Tern

Ad

1st year

Ad

Sooty Tern

Ad

1st year

Ad

Lesser Noddy

Ad

Brown Noddy

br

non-br

br

African Skimmer

MARSH TERNS

Three closely related small slight terns which are mainly found over inland lakes and marshes. All are easily identified in breeding plumage, but much more difficult in variable non-breeding and immature plumages. Key features to note are extent of black on crown, rump and tail colour, presence of a shoulder 'peg', and, at close range, bill size. Sexes alike. White-winged Tern (curiously named given it has extensive black on the underwing) vastly outnumbers the others throughout the region.

White-winged Tern   *Chlidonias leucopterus*   23cm, 9"
[White-winged Black Tern]

Br ad is a stunning boldly patterned tern with a *black head, body and under-wing-coverts* contrasting strongly with the *mainly white wings, rump, tail and vent*. Non-br ad varies, but is largely grey and white with some blackish markings on the hindcrown and behind the eyes. *Rump and tail whitish contrasting with a pale grey back and wings;* primaries may show a darker grey wedge, and some show distinctive *black feathering in the underwing-coverts*. Does not show small black peg at sides of breast. Shorter-billed than either Whiskered or Black terns. 1st year similar to non-br ad, but may have a slightly more extensive dark cap, and a darker grey-brown back. In flight, looks light and bouncy. **HH** very common passage migrant and winter visitor to inland lakes and dams from Aug–May, although a good number over-summer. Highly gregarious and may occur in flocks of thousands, especially on the larger Great Rift Valley lakes. It is much rarer at the coast apart from on freshwaters just inland. **Vo** feeding parties utter short *plik plik...* calls.

Whiskered Tern   *Chlidonias hybridus*   26cm, 10"

Slightly larger and stronger-billed than White-winged and Black terns. Br ad has a striking combination of black cap, white sides to the face and dark grey underparts. Non-br ad has a black patch behind the eye and fine black streaking on the rear of the crown (suggesting a *Sterna* tern): *rump, tail and back uniform pale grey*. Also beware confusing *Sterna*-like birds which lose the grey underparts before moulting the black cap. 1st year is similar to 1st year White-winged, but the back is more boldly spangled with brown and buff and the rump is grey, not white. Flight action stronger and more steady than White-winged Tern. **HH** common, but not numerous, on a wide range of fresh and alkaline inland waters, although breeding confined to only a few areas, like Lake Naivasha, Ke. **Vo** vocal, giving unpleasant low rasps and churrs, unlike most terns. **SS** White-cheeked Tern.

Black Tern   *Chlidonias niger*   23cm, 9"

Br ad has a largely black head and underparts, with grey wings and whitish underwing-coverts (black in White-winged Tern), back, rump and tail uniform grey. Non-br ad is similar to non-br White-winged, but with more extensive and solid black on the crown, and a diagnostic *dark peg at sides of breast;* rump, tail and back uniform grey. Rather longer-billed and shorter-legged than White-winged. 1st year best identified from other similar 1st years by dark breast patches. Flight action light and buoyant. **HH** vagrant to the region, but may be overlooked amongst the large marsh tern flocks on the Great Rift valley lakes. **Vo** silent in region.

Plate 81

non-br

br

non-br

non-br

White-winged Tern

br

br

non-br

non-br

non-br

br

Whiskered Tern

non-br

br

non-br

non-br

SANDGROUSE
Well-camouflaged rather dove-like ground birds of dry country. Most active in the early morning and evening when large flocks congregate at waterholes. Head and underpart markings aid identification. Immatures generally resemble females but with narrower barring.

Black-faced Sandgrouse *Pterocles decoratus* 23cm, 9"

Ad ♂ has a neat face pattern with a vertical *black stripe from the forecrown to the throat, and narrow black and white stripes curving above and behind the eye.* Underparts have a *narrow black breast band above a broader white band.* Ad ♀ is almost entirely barred, mottled and streaked except for a plain yellowish-buff lower face and breast band. In flight, shows grey-buff underwings contrasting with the dark belly. Three races occur, varying mainly in general tone: *ellenbecki* in the north and *loveridgei* in SWKe to CTz are paler than nominate birds in SKe to NTz. **HH** pairs and small flocks are common in areas of dry open and bushed grassland from near sea-level to 1600m. Gathers at water holes in the early mornings and late afternoons. **Vo** flight-call is an explosive *wop'dela wiiiii,* the last note being a fading whistle.

Chestnut-bellied Sandgrouse *Pterocles exustus* ♂ 28cm, 11"

Ad ♂ has a *yellow-buff head, neck and breast, dark chestnut belly* (which may look black at distance) and a *long pointed tail.* Ad ♀ is largely mottled and streaked except for yellowish-buff sides to the head and throat, and a broad buffy breast band. In flight, shows dark underwings and belly and a pointed tail. **HH** pairs and flocks are often common in dry open country and dry bushed grassland below 1700m. Frequently flocks together with Black-faced Sandgrouse. **Vo** flight-call vaguely resembles gobbling turkeys, a mixed set of musical pops and gurgles *etchup-ga-googooliga...*

Lichtenstein's Sandgrouse *Pterocles lichtensteinii* 28cm, 11"

Rather stout sandgrouse with extensive barring both above and below. Ad ♂ has black and white bands on the forecrown and a small white spot behind the eye. A *broad buff-brown breast band is traversed by two narrow black bands* (one centrally and one below). Ad ♀ is entirely barred with narrow blackish lines. In flight, looks bulky, the pale innerwing contrasting with darker flight feathers. **HH** pairs and small flocks are rather uncommon in the arid north, preferring stony and sparsely bushed country below 1800m. Drinks before dawn or just after dusk. **Vo** flight-call is a high-pitched whistled and bubbling *wicky-wi-wheo-wickiwicki-weeo...* and also a low churr.

Four-banded Sandgrouse *Pterocles quadricinctus* 28cm, 11"

Ad ♂ is similar to Lichtenstein's Sandgrouse with black and white bands on the forecrown, and best identified by *bands of chestnut, white and black across the breast and a plain buff-brown neck and upper breast.* Ad ♀ is extensively barred, except for the face, throat and upper breast which are plain rich buffy-brown. In flight, shows a pale underwing. **HH** pairs and flocks are rather uncommon residents and wanderers across the north-west, inhabiting open and bushed grasslands below 2000m. Drinks before dawn and after dusk. **Vo** flight-call is a repeated piercing rhythmic whistle *wi-ti-wi'wrreee* with the last note tremulous.

Yellow-throated Sandgrouse *Pterocles gutturalis* 31cm, 12"

Large bulky sandgrouse. Ad ♂ has a *pale yellow face and throat encircled by a black band.* Remainder of upperparts rather plain grey-brown, with some dark spotting on the scapulars and broad rufous fringes to the wing-coverts: belly dark chestnut. Ad ♀ is heavily mottled with black, brown and buff, with a paler yellowish face and throat and a dark chestnut belly. In flight, looks large and bulky with dark underwings and belly. **HH** pairs, small groups and occasionally larger flocks are locally common residents and wanderers on open short grasslands and highland plains from 800-2000m. Drinks in the mid-morning. **Vo** flight-call is a strange musical cawing *ah-oo-op-oo-ah-er-aap...*

Plate 82

Black-faced
Sandgrouse

Chestnut-bellied
Sandgrouse

Lichtenstein's
Sandgrouse

Four-banded
Sandgrouse

Yellow-throated
Sandgrouse

GREEN-PIGEONS

Green-plumaged tree-dwelling pigeons which, with their cryptic plumage, can be very hard to see. Often first located by their yapping rather un-pigeon-like calls. Pointed-winged appearance and fast, direct flight can suggest parrots. Sexes alike.

African Green-Pigeon *Treron calva* 27cm, 10.5"

A rather stout pigeon with seven races occurring in our area. Basic ad has a *yellow-green head, neck and breast*, a purple shoulder patch on green wings, and a yellow belly with dark centres to the undertail-coverts. Grey or green tail: western birds are generally greyer, while eastern and southern birds are greener. Imm duller than ad and lacks purple shoulder patch. **HH** common in a wide range of woodland, forest edge, open country and cultivation at fruiting trees, from sea-level to 2200m. **Vo** very complex and un-pigeon-like call that usually begins with a series of rising crackling notes, and continues with varied whinnying notes and lower musical growls. Often several birds calling together.

Bruce's Green-Pigeon *Treron waalia* 28cm, 11"

Differs from African Green-Pigeon in having a *greyish head, neck and upper breast sharply separated from striking yellow lower breast and belly*; large purple shoulder patches, and a chestnut central undertail. *In flight, clearly shows the yellow breast and belly.* Duller imm lacks the purple patch in wing. **HH** small flocks are local in wooded river valleys and semi-arid grassland where it typically occurs in fruiting fig trees. **Vo** similar to African Green-pigeon, but notes crisper and more crackling, with an insane churring and laughing quality.

Pemba Green-Pigeon *Treron pembaensis* 25cm, 10"   ●

Dull green pigeon with an *entirely grey head, neck and underparts*, a large purple shoulder patch, and boldly scalloped yellow, chestnut and grey vent and undertail coverts. Imm plumage duller and lacks shoulder patch. **HH** endemic to Pemba Is off NTz coast where flocks are not uncommon and frequently occur in fruiting trees. **Vo** similar to African Green-Pigeon, but tends to sound slightly softer and less grating.

BRONZE-NAPED PIGEONS

Very dark arboreal pigeons of forested areas. Difficult to locate when high in canopy, but draw attention to themselves with their frequent calls.

Eastern Bronze-naped Pigeon *Columba delegorguei* 27cm, 10.5"
[Delegorgue's Pigeon]

Ad ♂ appears all dark slate-grey with a *striking white half-collar* on lower nape. If seen well shows iridescent green, purplish-pink and bronze sheen to hindneck. Ad ♀ is duller, lacks the collar, and is washed rufous-bronze on crown and nape. Imm is similar to ♀, but darker brown above and dark rufous below. **HH** pairs and flocks are locally common in highland forest mainly above 1500m, with birds occasionally wandering to coastal forests. **Vo** quite a complex call *oo-oo-oo oo-oo-oo-oo-oo-oo-ah'ah'ah* after three see-sawing introductory notes, a descending series of *oo*'s is followed by a more rapid series of deeper notes with a peculiar effect like a voice breaking. **SS** Lemon Dove.

Western Bronze-naped Pigeon *Columba iriditorques* 27cm, 10.5"

Similar to Eastern Bronze-naped Pigeon, but ad ♂ has a greyer head, a red base to the upper mandible, a *broad ginger-bronze (not white) half-collar and bright chestnut (not grey) undertail-coverts*. Ad ♀ is similar to ♀ Eastern Bronze-naped, but mainly rufous below, with a chestnut belly and undertail. Imm is similar to ♀, but duller. In flight, appears very dark with broad buff corners to tail. **HH** in our area, restricted to forest from 700–1500m in far WUg. **Vo** call is like the final part of Eastern Bronze-naped Pigeon, but slower with the last deeper notes fading. **SS** Lemon Dove.

Plate 83

Ad

African Green-Pigeon

Bruce's Green-Pigeon

Ad

Ad

Pemba Green-Pigeon

Eastern Bronze-naped Pigeon

♂

♀

Western Bronze-naped Pigeon

♀

♂

LARGE PIGEONS

Large *Columba* pigeons have a small-headed large-bodied appearance. Flight is swift and direct and birds often take to the air with loud wing claps. Sexes similar (except White-naped); immatures are like dull versions of adults.

Speckled Pigeon   *Columba guinea*   34cm, 13.5″
[Rock Pigeon]

Robust grey and maroon-brown pigeon with *conspicuous white spots on wing-coverts, a patch of bare red skin round eyes*, and a pink and white striated neck. In flight, reveals a distinct pale grey rump and broad black end to tail. Imm is duller grey-brown with a greyish eye patch. **HH** widespread and common from 500–3000m, occurring in open country with cliffs and in many towns. **Vo** two main calls, a throaty *woopor...woooo* first note rising then falling and last note falling and fading. Also a monotonous *woo-woo-woo-woo...* given for long periods.

Afep Pigeon   *Columba unicincta*   33cm, 13″

Large rather pale grey pigeon with contrasting darker wings, a pinkish breast, and a white belly and undertail-coverts. In flight, appears pale and reveals striking wide grey-white band above a broad black tail tip. Imm is darker above and brownish below. **HH** pairs and small flocks are not uncommon in forests and dense remnant forest patches from 1100–1600m. Most likely to be detected by call or in flight over the canopy. **Vo** calls a monotonous and deep throaty *oorrrooo-oorrrooo...* the middle part is tremulous.

Olive Pigeon   *Columba arquatrix*   38cm, 15″
[Rameron Pigeon]

Very large dark grey pigeon with a *bright yellow bill, yellow eye-ring and feet*. Conspicuously spotted with white on the wing-coverts and across the breast. Pale grey nape (sometimes very pale) may suggest White-naped Pigeon, but that species has plain dark wings. ♀ is slightly duller and imm is rather browner. In flight, simply appears very dark with a yellow bill and feet. **HH** flocks are common in highland forest and woodland, as well as in adjacent country with isolated fruiting trees, mainly above 1500m (but down to 700m in WUg). **Vo** a deep vibrating *churr* is followed by a sequence of rising *oo* notes.

White-naped Pigeon   *Columba albinucha*   34cm, 13.5″

Slightly smaller than similar Olive Pigeon, but ♂ has a well-defined *bright white hindcrown, a yellow-tipped dark bill, red-brown legs, and all dark wings*. ♀ similar, but hindcrown soft grey. In flight, appears largely dark and has paler grey outer corners to the tail. Imm is duller brown above than ad with a greyer nape. **HH** in our area, only known from forests in WUg from 700–1800m, but may overlap and flock to feed and drink with Olive Pigeon. **Vo** call is a deep quavering and deliberate *tuu-uu* followed by 3–4 *tuu-tu-tu* notes which decrease in volume.

Feral Pigeon   *Columba livia*   33cm, 13″

Highly variable introduced urban pigeon which varies from grey with pale wings, glossed purple neck and two grey-white wing bars, through to brown and white birds, and to all sooty black individuals. **HH** flocks are widespread and abundant in cities, towns and larger villages throughout the region where they nest on buildings. **Vo** bubbling rising and falling *churrs,* interspersed with wing-clapping.

Plate 84

Speckled Pigeon

Ad

Afep Pigeon

Ad

Olive Pigeon

♀

♂

White-naped Pigeon

♂

Feral Pigeon

WOOD-DOVES
Small, delicate grey-brown doves, with banded rumps, rufous wing patches, and iridescent spots in their wings. Characterised by attractive long cooing songs which die away. Sexes alike (except in Tambourine). Immatures have much duller wing spots and lightly barred upperparts.

Emerald-spotted Wood-Dove   *Turtur chalcospilos*   20cm, 8"
[Green-spotted Dove]

Typical wood-dove which is grey-brown above and paler below with a pinkish breast, and *iridescent green spots in the wings*. Bill varies from blackish to dark red. Flaps noisily into flight, showing a warm rufous panel in the wing, two bold black bars over the lower back, and a broad band near tail tip. **HH** single birds and pairs are widespread and common in dry bush, scrub, woodland and cultivated lands from sea-level to around 2100m. **Vo** slow long call of all muffled *poo* notes lasting up to 10 seconds: first two or three are hesitant upslurs, then three see-sawing notes, and a long slow series of 15 descending *poo*'s which accelerate as they fade.

Blue-spotted Wood-Dove   *Turtur afer*   20cm, 8"
[Blue-spotted Dove]

Very similar to Emerald-spotted Wood-dove, but rather darker brown above and warmer buff below, with *dark blue wing spots* (which may appear blackish), and a *purply-red bill with a yellow tip*. In flight, overall tone is browner than Emerald-spotted. **HH** common generally in moister habitat than Emerald-spotted Wood-dove including forest edges, woodland, gardens and secondary areas, from sea-level to around 2000m. **Vo** similar to Emerald-spotted, but final notes are all on one tone not descending.

Black-billed Wood-Dove   *Turtur abyssinicus*   20cm, 8"

Slightly paler and cleaner-looking than the other wood-doves, with a *black bill and dark blue wing spots*. Similar in flight to others, but appears greyer and colder toned. **HH** in our area pairs are locally common in the northwest, occurring in a wide range of habitats, from woodland to dry scrub, including cultivation. **Vo** similar to Emerald-spotted Wood-dove, but slightly higher toned and often repeats three faster rhythmic notes amongst the descending *poo*'s.

Tambourine Dove   *Turtur tympanistria*   22cm, 8.5"

Ad ♂ is rich dark rufous-brown above with a *brilliant white face and underparts*, and blue-black wing spots (very hard to see). Ad ♀ is duller with whitish sides to face, mostly grey underparts, and white in centre of belly. In flight, ♂ appears dark brown above with rufous wings, and white below. **HH** singles and pairs are widespread and common in a wide range of forest, dense woodland and thickets, as well as gardens in wetter areas from sea-level to 2500m. **Vo** similar to Emerald-spotted Wood-Dove, but typically lacks slurred notes of introduction and all the final *poo* notes are on same tone not descending.

Namaqua Dove   *Oena capensis*   25cm, 10"

Delicate small dove with a *long graduated tail*. Ad ♂ is *black on the face and upper breast* with a yellow-tipped purplish bill, two black bands cross the lower back, and dark purple-black spots on the wings. Ad ♀ has a pale buff-grey or whitish face and a dark grey bill. Imm is similar to ♀, but the back and wing-coverts are spotted and edged in pale rufous, grey, black and white. Flight is swift and direct, revealing rufous wings and a slender tail. **HH** widespread and common in drier bush and cultivated areas from sea-level to 2000m, rarely to 3000m, but wanders widely. **Vo** calls a plaintive descending *oooo* given about every 2 seconds.

Plate 85

Emerald-spotted Wood-Dove

Emerald

Black

Blue

Black-billed Wood-Dove

Blue-spotted Wood-Dove

♀

♂

Tambourine Dove

♂

Imm

♀

♂

♂

Namaqua Dove

RING-NECKED DOVES
Grey-brown and pinkish-grey medium-sized doves with black half-collars on their hind-necks. Best identified by eye colour and voice. They all have distinctive songs and calls on alighting. All spend considerable time feeding on the ground. Sexes are alike. Immatures similar (unless described) with buffy fringes above.

Ring-necked Dove *Streptopelia capicola* 25cm, 10"
[Cape Turtle Dove]

Most common and widespread ring-necked dove. Basic appearance is *grey with small but prominent black eyes* (obvious even at distance). Two races occur: widespread *tropica* is brownish-grey, and north-eastern *somalica* is a cooler grey. **HH** pairs and flocks are widespread and may be very common at forest edge, in open woodland, dry bush, and cultivation, mainly from sea-level to 2200m, less often to 3000m. **Vo** a three-note call *oo-oo-rrooo* repeated fairly rapidly (saying 'ring-necked-dove' over and over), as well as other coo's and growling calls, and a nasal crooning *err-waaaa* on alighting.

Red-eyed Dove *Streptopelia semitorquata* 32cm, 12.5"

Larger and darker than Ring-necked Dove with *dark red eyes surrounded by a small diamond-shaped area of dull maroon skin*. Steep pale grey forehead contrasts with otherwise mainly plain brown upperparts and dark pinkish underparts. In flight, rather dark and uniform above with a wide grey band across end of tail. Imm has brown eyes, rufous fringed upperparts, and a rather obscure hind-collar. **HH** solitary birds and pairs, less often flocks, are widespread and common in moist forest, woodland and gardens from sea-level to 3000m. **Vo** call varies slightly, but is typically a very rhythmical *oo-oo-oo-oo-oo-oo* which sounds like 'I-am-a-red-eyed-dove!' (with the third and fifth notes lower). Also has various other growling calls, and a single or double moan *uu-raaow* on alighting.

African Mourning Dove *Streptopelia decipiens* 29cm, 11.5"

A grey-brown ringed-necked dove with a *whitish or pale yellow eye and narrow pink eye-ring*. Three races occur and vary in overall tone: western *logonensis* is browner above and wine-pink below, central *perspicillata* is grey-brown above and pale pink below, and rather bleached eastern *elegans* is grey above and whitish below. Browner imms have dull brown eyes. **HH** pairs and flocks are widespread and sometimes abundant in arid and semi-arid bush and wooded country, typically including acacias, from sea-level to 1500m. **Vo** most distinctive call is a cheerful descending rolling *churr rrrrrrrooooooo,* and an *oo-rrrrrrrr* on landing (with last note very tremulous and throaty).

Vinaceous Dove *Streptopelia vinacea* 25cm, 10"

Extremely similar to Ring-necked Dove race *tropica* (with which it overlaps in NWUg). Usually has a *pale pink not grey forehead*, and is variably washed pink below, but can only be safely separated on call. **HH** pairs and flocks are locally common in dry wooded and bushed grassland, and old cultivation below 2000m in NWUg, occasionally wandering further afield. **Vo** calls a rapid monotonous four-note *oo-oo-o'oo* with the third note higher and all the notes clear, lacking the tremulous quality of Ring-necked. Also a three-note *oo'o-oo* with a lower third note.

African White-winged Dove *Streptopelia reichenowi* 25cm, 10" ●

Grey-toned ring-necked dove with a brownish back: *pale yellow eye surrounded by a white eye-ring is obvious at close range*. In flight, shows distinctive white bar across upperwing-coverts. ♀ like ♂, but slightly browner below. **HH** in our area restricted to extreme NEKe, where it is common in riverine woodland, palm stands and adjacent scrub along the Daua River at around 250m. **Vo** calls a monotonous rising and rolling *churr rrrooke'r-rrooke'rrrooke'...* sometimes followed by a long series of descending short *oo* notes that may rise to form the rolling call again.

Plate 86

Ring-necked Dove

tropica

Red-eyed Dove

Ad

African Mourning Dove

logonensis

Vinaceous Dove

African White-winged Dove

LAUGHING AND TURTLE DOVES

Three doves with rufous scalloping in the upperparts or wings. Laughing Dove has a mottled breast; the turtle doves have characteristic dark neck smudges, none have black hind-collars. Sexes similar, immatures duller than adults.

Laughing Dove   *Streptopelia senegalensis*   23cm, 9"

A fairly small slender pinkish dove which is pale rufous above with *pink and black mottling across the upper breast and steel blue wing-coverts* (no black collar or neck smudges). ♀ is slightly paler below. Appears slender in flight, revealing blue band across wings and white corners to tail. Imm significantly duller and plain below (lacks the black breast mottling). **HH** pairs and flocks are very common throughout the region in a wide range of habitats, usually below 2000m, occasionally to 3000m, including gardens, villages and towns. **Vo** calls a strange and laughing 5–6 note refrain *oo-oo-oo-oo-oo* with fourth note highest and fifth lowest.

Dusky Turtle Dove   *Streptopelia lugens*   30cm, 12"

Very dark grey dove with slightly paler grey face and *distinct black patches on sides of neck*. Broad rich rufous edges to some wing-coverts and tertials. In flight, appears very dark with dull grey corners to tail. Imm is paler with more extensive rufous feather edges. **HH** singles, pairs and flocks are widespread and sometimes common in the highlands from 1800–3200m, including forest edge, wooded areas, farmland and gardens. Birds wander widely, sometimes to lower altitudes. **Vo** calls a very deep gargling and scraping *oo-oo orrrrr-orrrrrr* with all notes descending.

European Turtle Dove   *Streptopelia turtur*   28cm, 11"

Much paler and slightly smaller than Dusky Turtle Dove with distinctive *black and white patches on either side of neck*, broad and extensive rufous edges to wing-coverts, and a blue-grey edge to closed wing. In flight, suggests Laughing Dove but cleaner, brighter and longer-winged. **HH** vagrant from Palearctic with scattered records mainly in dry bush country in the north. **Vo** silent in region.

Lemon Dove   *Aplopelia larvata*   24cm, 9.5"

[Cinnamon Dove]

Plump brown dove with a *greyish-white face and cinnamon-brown underparts*. If seen well, shows green and purple sheen to nape and back. Sexes alike. Imm similar, but duller below with some rufous edgings to breast feathers. **HH** singles and pairs are shy and uncommon (except locally), often walking on the ground in the shade of forest undergrowth and exploding into noisy flight when disturbed. Occurs mainly in areas of dense highland forest from around 1800–3000m. **Vo** calls with very low notes, either a pulsating *poopoopoopoopoo...* or a slow rising moan *ooooo*. **SS** Eastern and Western Bronze-naped pigeons.

Plate 87

Laughing Dove

Ad

Ad

Dusky Turtle Dove

Ad

European Turtle Dove

Lemon Dove

Ad

WOODLAND PARROTS
Medium-sized mainly brown and green parrots, best identified by presence or absence of yellow on head, colour of underwing-coverts and belly. Also note ranges which barely overlap. Sexes alike (except African Orange-bellied Parrot). Immatures like dull adults. All attract attention with loud calls, but are often hard to find in canopy.

Brown Parrot *Poicephalus meyeri* 23cm, 9"
[Meyer's Parrot]

Ad is mainly grey-brown on head and upperparts with a green (or bluish-green) rump, and lower breast to vent: *band on forecrown, shoulders and underwing-coverts are bright yellow*. Close views reveal wholly dark bill and brown-red eyes. In flight, clearly shows yellow underwing-coverts. Imm is duller than ad and lacks yellow crown and thighs. **HH** pairs and small parties are widespread and sometimes common in woodland, bushland, scrub and cultivation below 2200m. **Vo** similar to Brown-headed Parrot, but screeches are not so metallic and interspersed with slurred chattering.

Brown-headed Parrot *Poicephalus cryptoxanthus* 24cm, 9.5"

Ad is mainly green (brighter on rump and lower breast to vent) with a greyish-brown head: *yellow confined to the underwing-coverts* (absent from crown, shoulders and thighs). At close range shows blackish upper and cream lower mandibles and pale yellow eyes. In flight, note bright yellow underwing-coverts and green rump. Imm is duller. **HH** pairs and small groups are rather local, but may be common residents in a wide range of well-wooded and baobab country throughout coastal Ke and ETz. **Vo** very loud, high-pitched and strangely metallic calls.

African Orange-bellied Parrot *Poicephalus rufiventris* 25cm, 10"

Ad ♂ is rather striking with a *broad bright orange band across the breast*, a grey-brown head, and a blue-green rump and vent. In flight, ad ♂ shows orange underwing-coverts. Ad ♀ is very similar to imm Brown Parrot, but lacks yellow on shoulder and has brown not yellow underwing-coverts. At close quarters, the bill is black and eyes are deep orange-red. Imm is slightly paler than ad ♀. **HH** pairs and small groups are locally common in wide range of semi-arid and arid bushed and wooded grassland below 1200m, often in association with baobab trees. **Vo** intermingles quiet chattering with rather muffled screeches.

Plate 88

Brown Parrot

Imm

Ad

Brown-headed Parrot

Ad

African Orange-bellied Parrot

♀

♂

LARGER FOREST AND WOODLAND PARROTS

Large parrots mainly found in forest, but Brown-necked Parrot also occurs in miombo woodland. All have far-carrying calls which are made frequently during long flights over the forest canopy. Usually seen in small groups, but may gather at fruiting trees, and often follow regular paths to roosting and feeding areas.

Grey Parrot *Psittacus erithacus* 30cm, 12"

A large broad-winged grey parrot with a *short square-ended scarlet-red tail* (which can be surprisingly difficult to see except in good light). At close range shows creamy-yellow eyes, whitish sides to face, and scaly dove-grey fringes to head and neck. Sexes alike. Flying birds show darker, near-black primaries, but red tail always diagnostic. Imm similar to ad, but has dark trailing edge to scarlet tail, and grey eyes. **HH** pairs or small parties are locally common in suitable forest from 700–2300m in Ug, but now very scarce elsewhere in its EA range. **Vo** in flight and perched, gives a great variety of loud slurs and raucous notes, some as explosive.

Red-fronted Parrot *Poicephalus gulielmi* 28cm, 11"

Large green parrot with a red or red-orange forecrown, shoulders and thighs. At close range, shows pale upper and dark lower mandibles, and reddish-orange eyes. Sexes similar. In flight, appears largely green with dark flight feathers and a bright red forecrown. Imm duller with buff-brown forecrown. **HH** pairs and sometimes large flocks are common in highland forest, particularly *Podocarpus*, from 1800–3250m in W and CKe and NTz. **Vo** calls a shrill but not usually piercing warbling and chattering.

Brown-necked Parrot *Poicephalus suahelicus* 33cm, 13"

Robust green parrot with a silvery-grey head and massive pale bill. Ad ♂ has striking red carpal joints and thighs; ♀ similar but with red on the forecrown. Imm lacks red at bend of wing and on thighs. In flight, despite the grey head, overall green plumage, red carpal joints and forecrown (on ♀ and imm) could lead to confusion with Red-fronted Parrot (but ranges do not overlap). Birds in our area are sometimes treated as conspecific with South African Cape Parrot *Poicephalus robustus*. **HH** pairs to small flocks are uncommon in two different habitats, occupying highland forest in the extreme north-west of its range and a variety of woodland including miombo further south. **Vo** north-western birds call a variety of screeched and rather unpleasant notes, and elsewhere a loud double ringing *creeee-creeee* with shrill squeaks.

Rose-ringed Parakeet *Psittacula krameri* 36cm, 14"

All emerald-green parrot with a diagnostic *long graduated tail*. Ad ♂ has a black throat and rose-pink collar narrowly bordered above with blue. Ad ♀ is largely bright green. In flight, shows long pointed tail, and blackish flight feathers contrasting with bright yellow-green underwing-coverts. Imm is similar to ad ♀. **HH** in our area the nominate race is restricted to woodland and wooded grassland in Kidepo NP, NEUg, where it is uncommon. Escaped cage-birds, probably of Asian origin, are sometimes seen around cities like Nairobi and Mombasa, Ke (and formerly on Zanzibar, Tz). **Vo** calls a variety of metallic churrs and chatters

Plate 89

Red-fronted Parrot

Grey Parrot

Ad

Imm

Ad

Rose-ringed Parakeet

Imm

♂

♀

Brown-necked Parrot

♂

♀

LOVEBIRDS

Small bright green parrots (name a consequence of regular mutual preening) with distinctive head or rump markings. Much smaller than other parrots and often seen feeding on the ground, or in cultivation, sometimes in large flocks. All are rather sedentary within their natural ranges, but Fischer's and Yellow-collared (both virtually endemic to Tz) occur as introduced birds elsewhere where they commonly hybridise.

Fischer's Lovebird   *Agapornis fischeri*   15cm, 6"

Bright green with a rather dull orange-red face, red bill, white eye-ring, and a yellow collar which extends round hindneck and across breast: *uppertail-coverts azure-blue*. Sexes alike: imm duller. In flight, looks bright green with an orange face and a blue rump. Interbreeding occurs between Fischer's and Yellow-collared lovebirds with hybrids showing characteristics of both. **HH** EA endemic: pairs and flocks can be common in wooded grassland from 1100–2000m in NTz, including the Serengeti, occasionally west to Rw and Bu. Hybrids are now widespread elsewhere and expanding their range, especially around towns. **Vo** calls a chattering of squeaks, lacking any shrill notes (unlike the hybrids).

Yellow-collared Lovebird   *Agapornis personatus* ·   15cm, 6"

Similar to Fischer's Lovebird with a red bill, white eye-ring, and blue upper-tail-coverts, but head mostly *dark brown contrasting with broad rich yellow collar*. Sexes similar: imm is duller. In flight, appears darker headed and paler green than Fischer's. **HH** pairs and flocks are sometimes common in woodland and wooded grassland in NCTz from 1100–1800m to the east of Fischer's (overlaps in some areas). Hybrids with Fischer's are now common (see above). **Vo** calls are similar to Fischer's Lovebird, but more shrill and squeaky.

Lilian's Lovebird   *Agapornis lilianae*   15cm, 6"

Ad is green with an orange-red face blending into the yellow head, a red bill, broad white eye-ring, and *green (not blue) uppertail-coverts*. In flight, appears uniform green with an orange-red face. Sexes similar: imm duller with dusky marks on head, and a darker bill. **HH** in our area pairs and flocks just reach extreme STz in mopane and acacia woodland. **Vo** very similar to Fischer's Lovebird, calling with high-pitched squeaks and chitters.

Black-collared Lovebird   *Agapornis swindernianus*   15cm, 6"

Striking bright green lovebird with a diagnostic *black hind-collar around base of nape*, and a dark blue rump. At close range shows yellow eyes and a thin red eye-ring. In flight, appears all green and shows dark green underwings and dark blue rump. Sexes similar: imm duller and lacks collar. **HH** pairs and flocks occur locally in dense lowland forest and secondary growth in extreme SWUg from 700–1200m. **Vo** call is described as a shrill rattling.

Red-headed Lovebird   *Agapornis pullarius*   13cm, 5"

Vivid green lovebird with a pale blue rump: ad ♂ has a *cherry-red face and black underwing-coverts;* ad ♀ has an orange face and green underwing. In flight, clearly reveals bright red or orange face and dark underwings. Imm similar to ad ♀, but face all greenish. **HH** pairs and small flocks are sometimes common in a wide range of secondary forest, wooded grassland, more open moist bush and cultivation from 900–2000m in the west. **Vo** calls are different from all other lovebirds, a rapid fire high-pitched metallic chinking *tink tinktink tink tink...*

Plate 90

Imm

Ad

Fischer's Lovebird

hybrid

Imm

Lilian's Lovebird

Ad

Imm

Ad

Yellow-collared Lovebird

Imm

Ad

Ad

Red-headed Lovebird

Black-collared Lovebird

Imm

LARGE BLUE TURACOS

Turacos are an endemic African family. These two large, but very different-looking species, have mainly blue plumage. Both easily distinguished even if seen only briefly. Like other turacos they are most frequently seen in the canopy, running and jumping along large branches before gliding weakly to the next tree. Sexes alike.

Great Blue Turaco *Corythaeola cristata* 75cm, 30"

An enormous and spectacular blue turaco: ad has a red-tipped yellow bill and obvious ragged black crest. Colourful, but rather muted blue from head to upper breast, upperparts and wings, lower breast greenish-yellow, belly to vent chestnut: long tail has yellow side panels and a broad black band near tip. Imm is duller with a smaller crest. Great Blue does not have the red wings of other turacos. **HH** pairs and small parties are locally common in good forest, relict forest patches, secondary growth, and well-treed farmland nearby, from 700–2500m. **Vo** far-carrying hollow wooden rattle of rapid *gonk-gonk-gonk-gonk-* notes, which may continue for a long period, building to an excited crescendo with several individuals joining in. Also a rolling *prrru* call.

Ross's Turaco *Musophaga rossae* 54cm, 21"
[Ross's Lourie]

Deep-blue glossed turaco, with a bulbous bright yellow bill, yellow eye patches, and a brilliant crimson crest and outer wings. Imm is duller with a blackish bill and small dull frontal shield. In slow buoyant flight, reveals extensive crimson in the wings. **HH** singles, pairs and small groups are widespread and locally common in riverine forest, forest edge, woodland, and mature gardens from 700–2300m. **Vo** often duets with a series of musical growls slowly rising in tone to climax in a rolling bubbling for up to 15 seconds which then descends before ending abruptly.

Purple-crested Turaco *Tauraco porphyreolophus* 43cm, 17"
[Purple-crested Lourie]

Dark turaco with a rounded glossy dark purple crown, bright green forecrown and sides of face, and a red eye-ring. Overall dark appearance due to much blue in back, wings and tail. **HH** widespread and locally common, although often at low densities, in a variety of riverine forest, woodland, thickets and moist bush, from near sea-level to 1300m. Now absent from much of its former eastern range in Ke. **Vo** calls a rising series of staccato and then grating *kok-kok-kok-* notes, before a pause and then a faster descending set of *kok* notes which may end with a musical *purr*.

Rwenzori Turaco *Tauraco johnstoni* 45cm, 18" ●

Superb, painted turaco with a glossy green-blue crest, orange-yellow lores and eye-ring, blue-black chin and throat, and maroon nape. Otherwise is green-blue above and lighter green below, with a rosey-orange blush on centre of breast. **HH** endemic to the Albertine Rift, with pairs and small groups locally common in montane forest in SWUg, Rw and Bu from 2200–3400m. **Vo** calls an odd descending series of high-pitched chipping notes (more like a squirrel than a turaco), as well as low growling *kok* notes.

White-crested Turaco *Tauraco leucolophus* 40cm, 16"

Distinctive green turaco with a gleaming white crest and neck, black forecrown, yellow bill and red eye-ring. Body largely bottle-green with a purple-blue wash over back, wings and tail. **HH** singles and pairs are locally common in woodland (especially well-wooded valleys), thickets and bushed country from 1000–2200m. **Vo** call starts with a single long laughing upslur and, after a distinct short pause, continues with a rapid sequence of gruff *khow* notes that slur into each other.

Plate 91

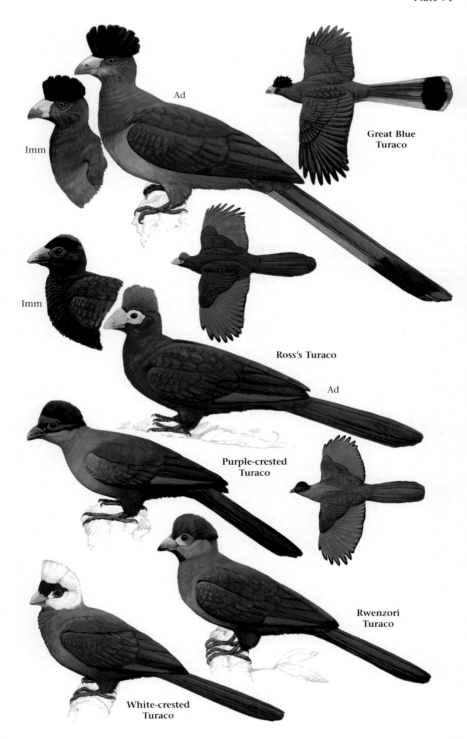

Imm

Ad

Great Blue Turaco

Imm

Ross's Turaco

Ad

Purple-crested Turaco

Rwenzori Turaco

White-crested Turaco

GREEN TURACOS

Eight mainly bottle-green and dark blue turacos which reveal scarlet wing patches in flight (three are on plate 91). Identification is mainly based on the colour and pattern of head markings. Sexes are alike. Immatures like subdued adults, often with less red in wings. Within wooded and forested habitat birds run and bound through the canopy, often with their tails raised, before swooping to trees nearby. Their raucous calls are characteristic sounds of many forests.

Hartlaub's Turaco   *Tauraco hartlaubi*   43cm, 17"

Dark-crowned turaco with a *short rounded blue-back crest, obvious oval white loral spot*, red eye-ring and white line below the eye: bill very dark red. Wings and tail rather dark violet-blue. **HH** EA endemic: widespread and sometimes common, singles and pairs occur in a range of highland forest areas from massive blocks like Mts Kenya and Kilimanjaro, to more isolated patches like the Taita Hills, Ke as well as well-wooded country and gardens, from 1600-3000m. **Vo** calls with loud, but gruff and muffled *khaws*, the first few notes quiet, rapid and ascending, then a set of 3–4 slower identical notes.

Black-billed Turaco   *Tauraco schuetti*   40cm, 16"

Neat mainly green turaco with a peaked crest edged in white, *bill appears all black in the field*. Short white line above and a longer one below and behind the red-ringed eyes. Wings and tail dark green, tail often darker blue-green. **HH** singles and pairs are shy and hard to see, occupying dense forest canopies from 700–2800m. Although now rare in the east of its range, it can be common in the far west, including Rw and Bu. **Vo** calls a harsh roaring series of *rrrerr* notes, the first few slow and rising, then a long faster set of up to 15, slightly descending.

Livingstone's Turaco   *Tauraco livingstonii*   40cm, 16"

[Livingstone's Lourie]

Largely green turaco, with a *peaked white-tipped crest and bright red bill*. Short white line above, and a longer one below the red-ringed eyes. Wings green and tail dark green-blue. **HH** pairs and singles are reasonably common in mature woodland and riverine forest in much of S and ETz, with a isolated population around Biharamulo, NWTz. **Vo** series of gruff notes, first few slow and rising, then a faster slightly descending series of about eight notes.

Schalow's Turaco   *Tauraco schalowi*   40cm, 16"

Similar to and often considered conspecific with Livingstone's Turaco: best identified by *very long, white-tipped, floppy forward-pointing crest*. Also has a bright red bill, and short white line above, and a longer one below the red-ringed eyes. Wings green washed blue and tail dark glossed purple-black. **HH** singles and pairs are common in forest and riverine woodland in SWKe and NTz; with a separate population from western to SWTz. **Vo** call is a slightly descending series of growls preceded by an introductory growl and a short pause *rrow... rrow- rrow-rrow-rrow-rrow*.

Fischer's Turaco   *Tauraco fischeri*   40cm, 16"   ●

Attractive green turaco with a *peaked crest edged dull red and thinly fringed white* (red of crest extends on to nape). Has a bright red bill and white lines above and below the red-ringed eyes. Wings green-blue and tail dark blue-green. **HH** singles and pairs are locally common in dense coastal forest, woodland and remnant forest patches mainly in the lowlands but up to 1500m in the Usambara Mts., NETz. **Vo** call is similar to Schalow's Turaco, but burrier, rising notes commence slowly and progress as a rapid series of up to 12 identical notes.

Plate 92

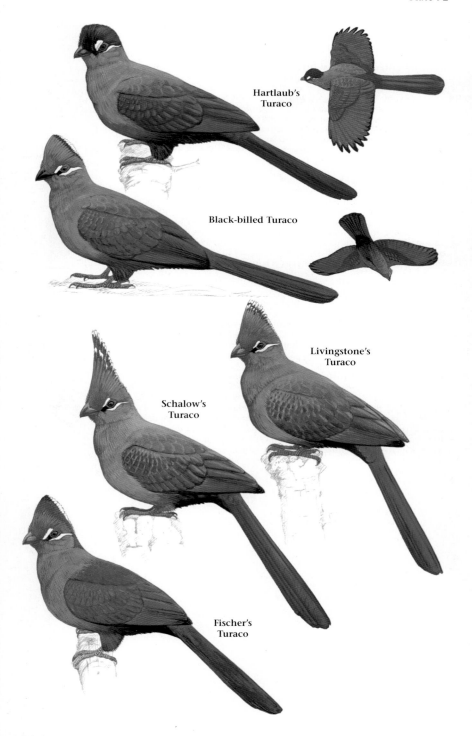

Hartlaub's Turaco

Black-billed Turaco

Livingstone's Turaco

Schalow's Turaco

Fischer's Turaco

GO-AWAY-BIRDS AND PLANTAIN-EATER

Large grey and white birds which are the dull open country relatives of turacos. Like turacos, sexes are similar and immatures are like subdued adults. All often sit exposed in the canopy of trees, and some utter loud onomatopoeic calls (hence go-away-bird).

White-bellied Go-away-bird *Corythaixoides leucogaster* 50cm, 20"

Large slender grey and white go-away-bird with a tall grey crest. Grey upperparts, throat and breast are sharply separated from a white lower breast to vent: long tail is grey, black and white. Sexes largely alike, but bill black in ad ♂ and green in ad ♀. Imm is duller than ad with plainer wings. In ragged undulating flight reveals white bars in wings and broad white band in tail. **HH** pairs and family groups are common, widespread and often confiding in arid and semi-arid wooded and bush country to 2200m. **Vo** calls a repeated *waah*, a more rapid hollow *wop-wop-wop...* and occasionally a drawn-out *ga-warr.*

Bare-faced Go-away-bird *Corythaixoides personata* 48cm, 19"

A black-faced go-away-bird: widespread race *leopoldi* is largely grey-brown with a contrasting white neck and breast. Close views reveal a green breast smudge which is larger on northern nominate race. Sexes are alike, but imm has duller face, brownish crest, and lacks green on breast. **HH** pairs and small groups are locally common in open woodland, bush and cultivation, preferring wetter country west of White-bellied Go-away-bird, mainly below 1400m, but occasionally to 2200m. **Vo** usual call is a rather surprised *corrr!*, and less often heard is a loud, insane cackling duet.

Grey Go-away-bird *Corythaixoides concolor* 50cm, 20"
[Grey Lourie]

Entirely dark ash-grey go-away-bird with a tall crest and long plain grey tail. Imm is paler grey-brown with a shorter crest. Appears all grey in flight. **HH** pairs and groups are locally common in bushed grassland and woodland, including miombo in S and SETz. **Vo** call is a wonderful drawn-out *gu'way* (go-away), and also a loud, harsh, pinched and interrogatory descending *wherrrrrrrr?*

Eastern Grey Plantain-eater *Crinifer zonurus* 50cm, 20"

A thick-set grey-brown turaco with an ashy head and shaggy white-tipped crest. Conspicuous bill is light-green in ad ♂ and yellowish in ad ♀. In rather ragged flight, reveals white bar in primaries and bold grey, black and white tail pattern. Imm is like ad. **HH** pairs and groups are sometimes common in a wide range of wooded and bushed grassland, including cultivation and gardens from 700–1800m. **Vo** calls with loud, querulous and nasal notes which build up into a maniacal laughter.

Plate 93

Bare-faced
Go-away-bird

White-bellied
Go-away-bird

♂

♀

leopoldi

Grey Go-away-bird

Ad

♀

Eastern Grey
Plantain-eater

CRESTED CUCKOOS

Large long-tailed, long-winged crested cuckoos with loud, stirring calls. All are at least partially migratory, mainly within the Afrotropics, but their movements are poorly known. Sexes are alike. *Oxylophus* have light and black morphs. All are brood parasites: Great Spotted on starlings and crows; Levaillant's on babblers (notably Arrow-marked); and Black-and-white on bulbuls and babblers.

Great Spotted Cuckoo   *Clamator glandarius*   38cm, 15"

Largest crested cuckoo: ad has a *shaggy pale grey crest*, is dark grey-brown above with *bold white spotting across the wings*, and whitish below with a buff throat. Tail is long, dark, graduated and tipped white. Strikingly different imm has black crown and cheeks, and reveals a clear chestnut primary patch in flight. **HH** widespread and sometimes common passage migrant in woodland, bushed and wooded grassland, and cultivation from sea-level to 3000m throughout region, mainly from Oct–Mar, with a notable passage in NTz, Jan–Mar. Some birds are present all year round and there are scattered local breeding records. **Vo** migrants are silent, but breeding birds give a loud woodpecker-like rattling *chhhtrtrtrtrrr-titititititit*.

Levaillant's Cuckoo   *Oxylophus levaillantii*   40cm, 16"

[Striped Cuckoo]
Large, crested black and white cuckoo with two distinct morphs: widespread light morph is black (glossed green) above and white below with heavy black streaking on throat and breast. Coastal dark morph is entirely black except for a white patch at base of primaries and tips to tail. In flight, the white wing patches and tail spots are conspicuous on both forms. Imm is duller brownish above, with the throat and underparts washed buff. **HH** sometimes common intra-African migrant to moist woodland, bush and forest edge from sea-level to 2100m, shunning drier areas. Birds appear to associate with the rains, not simply calendar months. A pattern seems to exist: from SETz through to Ug birds occur from Oct–Jun, and in WKe from May–Sep, with the black morph being mainly present in NETz and coastal Ke, Mar–Nov. Breeds sporadically throughout the region. **Vo** calls are loud single-spaced squealed and rattled notes *ttttttttttt kweer kweer kweer ttttttttt tttttt...*

Black-and-white Cuckoo   *Oxylophus jacobinus*   33cm, 13"

[Jacobin Cuckoo]
Similar to but smaller and shorter-tailed than Levaillant's Cuckoo: two races occur, widespread *pica* is *black above and entirely white below (or hair streaked), with a white wing patch and white-tipped tail*. Light morph of southern *serratus* is similar, but washed pale grey and finely streaked below. Dark morph *serratus* is jet black (including tail) except for a white wing patch. Imm is brownish-black above and washed buff below. **HH** sometimes common in bush, wooded grassland, scrub and cultivation from sea-level to 3000m, often in the rains. Breeds sporadically across the region. Migrations not well known, but race *pica* can be common moving south Nov–Jan and less common moving north from Mar–Apr. Southern *serratus* is uncommon from Apr–Sep. **Vo** migrants are silent, but breeding birds give squealed double and single notes *kwir'kik kwir'kik...kwir...kwir...*

Thick-billed Cuckoo   *Pachycoccyx audeberti*   36cm, 14"

Large accipiter-like cuckoo: ad is uniform slate-grey above and pure white below with a dark banded tail. At close range a yellow eye-ring and base to bill are visible. Sexes are alike. Imm has brown back scalloped white and patchy scaled with white crown and cheeks. **HH** uncommon resident and wanderer in canopy of forest and woodland, notably miombo, from sea-level to 1200m. Performs fluttering display over canopy while calling loudly (and parasitises Retz's and possibly Chestnut-fronted helmet-shrikes). **Vo** call is a rising series of paired high-pitched *wirr-wi... wirr-wi... wirr-wi*, which may break into an excited shrill babbling.

Plate 94

Great Spotted Cuckoo

Imm

Ad

Imm

Ad

Black-and-white Cuckoo

pica

Ad

Imm

Ad

Ad

Imm

Levaillant's Cuckoo

Ad

Imm

Ad

Thick-billed Cuckoo

GREY CUCKOOS
Very similar-looking grey and barred cuckoos: all are hard to distinguish. Careful note should be taken of size, tail pattern, extent of yellow on the bill, barring and rufous colours, and calls. In dashing flight often resemble small raptors and may flush other birds. Three are long distance migrants; while one, African, is a partial intra-African migrant that parasitises African Drongo.

African Cuckoo *Cuculus gularis* 33cm, 13″
A large grey cuckoo: ad ♂ is grey above, on throat and breast, and thinly barred black and white below. From Common Cuckoo by *more yellow-orange on bill (usually almost all rear half)* and by complete white bars on two outer-tail feathers (usually very hard to see). Ad ♀ is brown-grey above, with a paler barred breast (often with a buff wash), but can be very similar to ad ♀ Common. Imm is barred throughout including rump. **HH** widespread and rather uncommon intra-African migrant to drier woodland, wooded and bushed grassland from sea-level to 3000m. Movements unclear, but records occur in all months in some areas, often during the rains, and birds may be overlooked when silent. **Vo** calls a quiet repeated *pooh-pooh* which is very similar to Hoopoe, but slightly slower.

Common Cuckoo *Cuculus canorus* 33cm, 13″
[European Cuckoo]
Extremely similar to African Cuckoo: ad ♂ is best distinguished by having *yellow-orange confined to base of bill* and outer-tail feathers spotted not barred (also very hard to see). Ad ♀ has two distinct colour morphs: either grey-brown (normal) or brick-rufous (hepatic); both are barred below with a strong rufous wash to sides of breast. Imm strongly barred like African, but crown and rump plain (not barred). **HH** widespread and common Palearctic migrant to forest edge, woodland, wooded and bushed grassland on southward passage from Oct–Dec, and more common moving north from Mar–Apr (when it may be very common along the coast). **Vo** silent in region.

Asian Lesser Cuckoo *Cuculus poliocephalus* 28cm, 11″
[Lesser Cuckoo]
Smaller and more distinctly marked than larger grey cuckoos, and extremely similar to Madagascar Lesser Cuckoo: ad ♂ is grey above, on throat and breast, and *well-barred black on white below*. Ad ♀ has two distinct colour morphs: one form is grey-brown with a buff tinge to breast and flanks, and the other is bright brick-red or hepatic. Imm is grey-brown barred white and buff above and is well-barred dark below. **HH** migrates from South Asia, occurring from Nov–Apr in forest edge, woodland and bush on the coast in Ke and Tz (and further inland): it is sometimes common when moving north in Mar–Apr. **Vo** usually silent in region, but flushed birds may utter a loud staccato rattle.

Madagascar Lesser Cuckoo *Cuculus rochii* 28cm, 11″
[Madagascar Cuckoo]
Note range and season, since very hard to distinguish from Asian Lesser Cuckoo: ad ♂ is darker grey above, with a contrasting paler grey head, slightly longer wings and tail, and has thinner dark bars below. Ad ♀ also has buff tinge to chest and flanks (but no hepatic phase occurs). Imm slightly darker above, and well-barred above and below. **HH** uncommon migrant from Madagascar to dense habitats including forest edge and thicket from Apr–Sep in the west of our region, and rarely as a wanderer elsewhere. **Vo** silent in region.

Plate 95

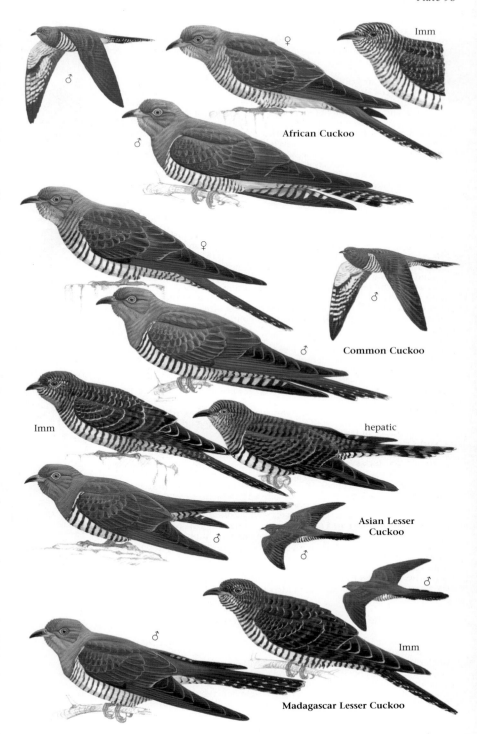

♂

♀

Imm

African Cuckoo

♂

♀

♂

Common Cuckoo

Imm

hepatic

Asian Lesser Cuckoo

♂

♂

♂

Imm

Madagascar Lesser Cuckoo

DARK CUCKOOS

Two confusing cuckoos with dark grey or black upperparts and (in some plumages) rufous across the upper breast. Hard to see, but best identified by location of rufous in underparts (if any) and calls. Black Cuckoo mainly parasitises bush-shrikes, and Red-chested mainly scrub-robins and robin-chats (which regularly mimic their calls).

Red-chested Cuckoo *Cuculus solitarius* 30cm, 12″

Ad ♂ is dark grey above (sometimes lighter on head), with black and white banding from upper breast to belly, and a *broad rufous band across breast, and grey throat*. Ad ♀ similar but has a whitish-buff throat. Imm is charcoal black above (with scaly pale fringes in fresh birds) and with a black throat and black and white barring below. **HH** common and widespread resident in forest edge, woodlands and gardens from sea-level to 3000m, wandering widely in rains, but also occurs as an intra-African migrant from the south to SETz from Oct–Apr. **Vo** call is a familiar seasonal sound, usually a three half-tone descending whistle *fwi-fwi-few* (often rendered it-will-rain!), but it also has a rising bubbling call.

Black Cuckoo *Cuculus clamosus* 30cm, 12″

Two races occur: more easterly and widespread nominate is often entirely black (blue-black in good light), but may show some pale barring below. Western *gabonensis* is black above and rather dingy black and buff below, with a strong wash of rufous across the breast and onto the throat. Similar Red-chested Cuckoo has a plain grey or whitish-buff throat. Sexes alike and imms are duller. **HH** nominate is a common and widespread intra-African migrant to forest edge, woodland, wooded grassland and thickets, from sea-level to 2000m; while *gabonensis* is a less common resident of forest in the west. **Vo** usual call is a three-note rising whistle, first two identical, third note an upslur commencing a half-tone higher *for for-fier*, sometimes leading into a cheerful rising bubbling call.

LONG-TAILED CUCKOOS

Three very similar looking elusive forest cuckoos with long graduated tails. All are extremely difficult to see and are best identified by call. Believed to parasitise akalats, illadopses and ant-thrushes. Sexes alike.

Barred Long-tailed Cuckoo *Cercococcyx montanus* 33cm, 13″
[Barred Cuckoo]

Dark olive-brown and well-barred with rufous-buff above, whitish below and sharply barred black, with narrower denser barring on throat. Extent of buff on throat and vent varies. Imm similar, but more barred above, with a darker throat, and less defined below. **HH** in the west it is resident and locally common in montane forest to 2800m. In the east and south it inhabits lower forest and woodlands and is present seasonally at the coast from Jun–Sep. Calls from canopy throughout the day, but forages at all levels. **Vo** calls a long sequence of slowly accelerating slurred and wheezy *weeeyu weeeyu weeeyu…*, then a more clipped *wee-we'yu, wee-we'yu…*, often ending with a fast *wit-wit-wu wit-wit-wu* (recalling Red-chested Cuckoo).

Olive Long-tailed Cuckoo *Cercococcyx olivinus* 33cm, 13″

Plain olive-brown above (often with a slight bronze gloss), well-barred black-brown on white below, with a buff wash on vent. Imm well-barred with rufous above and similar to ad below. **HH** common resident in forest from 900–1800m in WUg, usually high in the canopy and calls at dawn and dusk. **Vo** a far-carrying series of whistled *feee-uu, feee-uu, feee-uu…* (slowly rising in quarter-tones); and less often a lazy descending *fi-fio-fiau, fi-fio-fiau…*

Dusky Long-tailed Cuckoo *Cercococcyx mechowi* 33cm, 13″

Very similar to Olive Long-tailed Cuckoo, but sootier dark-grey above, with slightly broader darker barring below, and a warm orange-buff wash to lower flanks and vent. Imm is dark above, lightly barred with rufous, and similar if duller to ad below. **HH** common resident in lowland forest from 900–1600m in W and SWUg, and NWTz, where it calls all day and chiefly inhabits the mid-canopy and undergrowth. **Vo** calls a repeated three-note whistle, similar to Red-chested but higher-pitched and all notes identical *fwi-fwi-fwi*. Also makes a slow descending whistle that rises and falls *fwo-fwo-fwo* or *fwi-fwo-fwo-fwo…* given in a long series of about 25 notes.

Plate 96

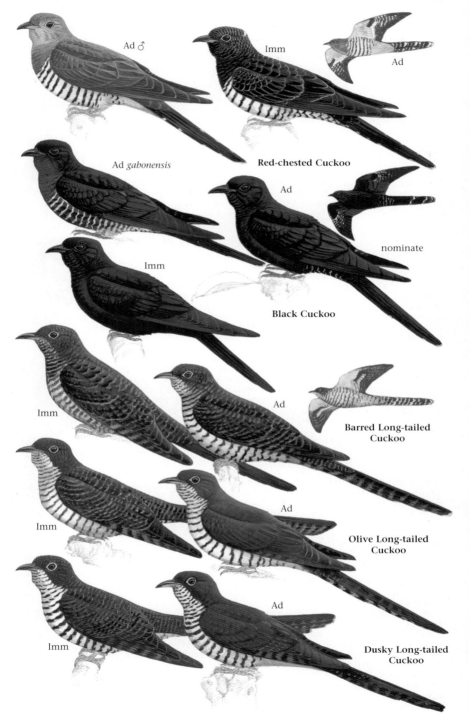

Ad ♂

Imm

Ad

Red-chested Cuckoo

Ad *gabonensis*

Ad

nominate

Imm

Black Cuckoo

Imm

Ad

Barred Long-tailed Cuckoo

Imm

Ad

Olive Long-tailed Cuckoo

Imm

Ad

Dusky Long-tailed Cuckoo

SHINING CUCKOOS

Small, slender cuckoos with distinctive partially iridescent male plumages, but rather confusing barred females and immatures. Extent of green and brown in plumage and colour of outer-tail aid identification. Females are secretive, but males are extrovert and vocal. Diederik Cuckoo largely parasitises weavers; Klaas's Cuckoo warblers and sunbirds; African Emerald Cuckoo robins and smaller thrushes; Yellow-throated Cuckoo's hosts are not known.

Diederik Cuckoo   *Chrysococcyx caprius*   19cm, 7.5"
Ad ♂ is metallic bronze-green above, with a *bold green and white face pattern, obvious red eye, and white spots in the wing-coverts*. White below with barred flanks and *outer-tail spotted black and white*. In flight, shows spotted outer-tail and entirely barred underwing. Ad ♀ more brown and green above, with a russet throat and upper breast, and thickly barred flanks: eyes dull brown. Imm has two colour morphs: most common is similar to ad ♀, but with rufous barring on the upperparts and a heavily streaked throat. Less common form is largely rufous above and below. Both have bright red bills. **HH** common resident and partial migrant in a wide range of bushed and wooded grassland, and cultivation from sea-level to 2200m, often appearing during rains. **Vo** memorable onomatopoeic *dee-dee-dee-dee-derik...* which can be clear, but is often wildly accelerated and slurred.

Klaas's Cuckoo   *Chrysococcyx klaas*   18cm, 7"
Ad ♂ is *iridescent bright green above, with plain wings, a small white bar behind a dark eye*, and snow white below with dark green patches on sides of breast. Ad ♀ is bronze-green above with fine russet barring below: eyes pale brown. In flight, ad ♂ shows white underwing-coverts and largely white outer-tail, ♀ and imm also show the white outer-tail. Imm is similar to ad ♀, but more heavily barred above and below, with a subdued bar behind the eye, and a dark bill. **HH** common and widespread resident in more moist and often denser habitats than Diederik Cuckoo, including woodland, forest edges, bush and gardens, from sea-level to 3000m. **Vo** calls a repeated high-pitched slurred whistle *fwiii-fi, fwiii-fi...*

African Emerald Cuckoo   *Chrysococcyx cupreus*   23cm, 9"
Ad ♂ is a stunning, gaudy *emerald-green and yellow cuckoo* unlike any other bird. In flight, shows black and white underwing-coverts, and dark not barred flight feathers. Ad ♀ is extensively barred rufous and green above and green and white barred below. Imm is very similar to ad ♀, but both lack white face of Diederik and Klaas's cuckoos. **HH** solitary, but widespread and common resident of moist forest, dense woodland and thickets from sea-level to 2000m. Males call regularly from high canopy and are surprisingly hard to see despite their bright colours. **Vo** very distinctive set of four whistles *whi'twau wor-wee* (often translated as 'hel-lo geor-gie'), with first two notes descending, a short pause, and then two accentuated rising slurs.

Yellow-throated Cuckoo   *Chrysococcyx flavigularis*   18cm, 7"
Ad ♂ is a rather dark bronzy cuckoo with a *bright yellow stripe down throat to upper breast*, and noticeable pale yellow eyes. In flight, shows obvious white outer-tail feathers. Ad ♀ is similar, but lacks the yellow throat, and is entirely finely barred below. Imm is duller and thinly barred tawny above. **HH** solitary and uncommon resident in thick primary forest or dense secondary stands from 700–1200m in Semliki and Maramagambo forests in SWUg. **Vo** a series of high-pitched first slightly rising then descending wispy whistles *fi-fi-fifififififi*.

Yellowbill   *Ceuthmochares aereus*   33cm, 13"
[Green Coucal]
Odd large long-tailed cuckoo, with a bright yellow bill, and pale blue skin around the red eyes. Two races occur: nominate is dark grey above and paler below, while *australis* is generally greener-toned with a pale throat. Both appear dark at distance. Sexes alike: imm is duller with a brownish throat, pale horn bill, and brown eyes. **HH** inhabits dense thickets, forest patches and edges from sea-level to 2000m. Nominate is local in the west, while *australis* is mainly a migrant from the south to the coast and less often inland. **Vo** call typically starts with paired clicking notes which accelerate into a rapid series of descending *tic*'s, terminating in a long rattle. Also has a loud and rising whistle with an accent on the last part *weee-eeeeeee*.

Plate 97

Imm

♀

♂

Diederik Cuckoo

♂

♂

♀

Imm

Klaas's Cuckoo

♀

♂

African Emerald Cuckoo

♂

♂

♀

Yellow-throated Cuckoo

nominate

Yellowbill

COUCALS
Cumbersome non-parasitic cuckoo-relatives easily identified as a group, but difficult to separate as species. All are bulky with short rufous or chestnut wings, long tails, red eyes (except Black Coucal), weak flight, and loud bubbling calls (hence alternative name of water-bottle birds). Note range, size, head and tail colour. Sexes alike, but immatures vary.

White-browed Coucal *Centropus superciliosus* 41cm, 16"
Dark crown and face separated by long white eyebrow, with pale streaking extending onto brown-rufous back. Pale below, streaked and barred darker. Imm similar, but supercilium, streaking above and underparts suffused buff. **HH** pairs are widespread and common in a wide range of rank vegetation, thickets, bushed and wooded grassland, often near water, from sealevel to 2300m. **Vo** much more hurried series of descending hollow notes than other coucals (except Burchell's). Also has a variety of harsh *kak* notes.

Burchell's Coucal *Centropus burchelli* 41cm, 16"
In our area, the race *fasciipygialis* has a blue-black crown and nape, rufous back and wings, and is white below, with a barred lower back and base of tail. Imm is identical to imm White-browed Coucal. **HH** common in rank waterside vegetation in S and SETz, including Mafia Island. **Vo** call is not believed to be separable from White-browed Coucal.

Blue-headed Coucal *Centropus monachus* 46cm, 18"
Large, robust coucal with a glossy blue-black crown extending over nape (may look black in the field), off-white to buff below, with a long black tail slightly glossed green. Imm like ad, but has a dull faintly streaked crown, barred primaries, buffy underparts, and a black-brown tail. **HH** residents are locally common close to water in marshes, papyrus swamps and other dense wet areas from 700-2000m, rarely to 2700m. Also occurs in highland bush in CKe. **Vo** call is a typical coucal descending series, lower and slower than White-browed.

Senegal Coucal *Centropus senegalensis* 41cm, 16"
Very similar to Burchell's Coucal but rump and tail are plain black (not barred). Imm is similar to White-browed Coucal, but has a browner crown, only a faint buff supercilium, and buffy not grey-white underparts. Blue-headed and Coppery-tailed coucals are much larger. **HH** common and widespread resident of drier habitats, like forest clearings, thickets and bushed grassland (being the least water-dependent coucal). **Vo** call varies locally, but is typically descending after an initial two-note introduction, rather minor-key, ending on a higher series of identical notes.

Coppery-tailed Coucal *Centropus cupreicaudus* 48cm, 19"
Largest coucal: black crown and nape have slight purple sheen, and long loose blackish-brown tail is glossed copper (hard to see in field). Imm similar, but crown duller, and back olive not reddish-brown, with some barring in primaries. **HH** pairs are localised residents in dense reeds and papyrus swamps, as well as rank grass, and other thickets near water in SWTz. **Vo** a deep, reverberant and pulsating typical large coucal call, with notes given more rapidly than similar Blue-headed Coucal.

Black Coucal *Centropus grillii* 38cm, 15"
Smallest coucal: br ad is highly distinctive being *all black with bright chestnut wings*. Non-br ad is heavily streaked with buff and brown on the head and upper back, with barred rufous and black wings and tail, and mottled brown and buff below. Imm like non-br ad, but has more extensive barring over crown and forehead (resembles White-browed Coucal but smaller and always lacks the white brow). **HH** generally uncommon and localised in swamps, river valleys, and flooded grasslands from sea-level to 2700m. Mainly in the west and coastal lowlands, although wanders widely during the rains. **Vo** calls a regular, rather hollow-sounding *kuk-uk kuk-uk kuk-uk...* both notes are identical and rhythmic, and a subdued typical descending coucal series.

Plate 98

White-browed Coucal
Imm

Burchell's Coucal
Ad

Ad

Blue-headed Coucal
Imm

Ad

Imm

Imm

Senegal Coucal

Imm

Ad

non-br

br

Coppery-tailed Coucal
Ad

Black Coucal

MEDIUM-SIZED OWLS AND BARN OWLS

A mixed group of medium-sized owls, including the barn owls with their characteristic heart-shaped faces. All can be identified by a combination of plumage, habitat and calls. Sexes are alike, but females may be larger than males. Immatures tend to be similar to, but a little darker than adults.

African Wood Owl *Strix woodfordii* 36cm, 14"

Attractive round-headed owl which lacks ear-tufts, with a pale lightly barred facial disc, dark brown eyes and heavily barred rufous-brown and white underparts. **HH** pairs are common in a wide range of forest and forest edge, woodland, and mature gardens, from sea-level to 2700m. **Vo** ♂ gives a rhythmic *oo-hoo-oohu-hu-hu-hu,* ♀ often replies with identical series on lower tone. ♂ also gives a long rising and then falling slurred *oo-oooooo.*

Barn Owl *Tyto alba* 36cm, 14"

A ghostly owl patterned golden-buff and pale grey above (finely speckled black and white), with small dark eyes set in a pale heart-shaped facial disc, and white to creamy-buff underparts. In buoyant flight appears largely pale golden-buff and white. **HH** pairs are uncommon but widespread residents from sea-level to 3000m, often near settlements, and in buildings, old wells, and Hamerkop nests, but tends to be absent from forest and arid country. **Vo** calls frequently, although bird usually unseen, a high-pitched screamed *churr* given singly or in series *chrirrrr.*

African Grass Owl *Tyto capensis* 38cm, 15"

Similar to Barn Owl, but with much *darker brown back and wings*, which contrast with paler buff underparts. Flying birds are dark brown above with a small buff patch at base of primaries (much smaller than in Marsh Owl). **HH** pairs are scattered, uncommon and very local residents of highland grassland and moorland mainly from 1500–3200m. Rarely seen in daylight unless flushed. **Vo** usual call is a harsh, but short raspy scream *kreee,* also gives various dry rasps and chitterings near the nest.

Marsh Owl *Asio capensis* 38cm, 15"

Warm uniform brown above and buff-brown below, with penetrating *dark eyes set in a paler facial disc*. In flight, resembles African Grass Owl, but shows *obvious larger rich buff patch at base of primaries*. **HH** singles and sometimes small groups are not uncommon in grassland, as well as moorland and marshes below 3000m. Birds are often active just before dusk and flush easily in daylight. **Vo** usual call is a rising rasp *krrrik* or a series of rasps.

Short-eared Owl *Asio flammeus* 38cm, 15"

An extensively streaked and mottled owl with *yellow eyes*. In flight, can look very similar to Marsh Owl, but appears more patterned above, and has yellow (not obvious dark eyes). **HH** Palearctic vagrant with a few scattered records in Ke (including Lake Naivasha) and NTz (in the Serengeti). **Vo** silent in region.

African Long-eared Owl *Asio abyssinicus* 43cm, 17"

A heavily mottled and streaked dark brown owl, with *fierce orange-yellow eyes, and conspicuous long ear tufts*. **HH** in our area the race *graueri* is an extremely scarce resident of giant heathland and montane forest in the Rwenzori Mts, SWUg and at 3350m on Mt Kenya, Ke. **Vo** call unknown.

Plate 99

African
Wood Owl

Barn Owl

African Grass Owl

Marsh Owl

Short-eared
Owl

African Long-eared
Owl

SCOPS-OWLS

Small owls with ear tufts (though often lowered and hard to see). Cryptic, often roost close to tree trunks, and when disturbed respond by raising their ears tufts and adopting a thin, elongated posture. Sexes and immatures are similar.

African Scops-Owl *Otus senegalensis* 17cm, 6.5"

A well-camouflaged scops-owl entirely streaked and mottled grey-brown, but some individuals are lightly washed warmer brown or pale rufous. Bright yellow eyes are set in a narrowly black-edged grey facial disk. Sometimes considered conspecific with Eurasian Scops-Owl. **HH** pairs are common and widespread in dry bush and woodland, including large trees along river courses, from sea-level to 2000m. **Vo** calls for long periods, a musical *krrrou* given at varying regular intervals of 4–8 seconds. Eastern birds tend to be more reverberant than western populations.

Eurasian Scops-Owl *Otus scops* 18cm, 7"

Very slightly larger than African Scops-Owl, but otherwise almost identical and probably not separable in the field. **HH** singles are scarce Palearctic migrants, but are almost certainly overlooked, in wooded habitats and forest edge from Nov–Apr. Dispersed records are of captured birds and specimens in Ke and Ug, and from one specimen in the Pare Mts, NTz. **Vo** silent in region.

White-faced Scops-Owl *Otus leucotis* 26cm, 10"

[White-faced Owl]

Larger, paler and greyer than other scops-owls with variable yellow to red eyes and a *white face mask with black borders*. Some authors split northern nominate birds (approximately north of the equator) from the more southerly race *granti*, stating that basic plumage colour (paler in northern birds), and voice differ, but both criteria vary widely across Africa. **HH** pairs are local and rarely common residents from sea-level to 1700m, preferring dry woodland, bushed and wooded grassland, often in acacias. **Vo** northern populations call a hollow dove-like *kuk-koo'ooh* with the last note descending, birds in EUg make a simple descending *pooor* and southern birds call a reverberating *wu-wu-wu-wu-wu-wu-wu woo!* the last note explosive.

Sokoke Scops-Owl *Otus ireneae* 15cm, 6" ●●

Very small with light grey, grey-brown and bright rufous morphs. All are lightly speckled with black and white above, and vermiculated and speckled black and white below. **HH** EA endemic: pairs are confined to the red soil *Cynometra* area of coastal Arabuko-Sokoke Forest, Ke, and, at low densities in the foothill forests of the East Usambara Mts, NETz, at 200–400m. **Vo** a noisy scops-owl giving a hollow rather high-pitched and ventriloquial *hooh* at about 2 second intervals for long periods without pause.

Pemba Scops-Owl *Otus pembaensis* 21cm, 8" ●

A medium-sized scops-owl which varies from pale rufous-brown (with some light streaking on head and faint barring below) to bright rich russet (with virtually no markings). **HH** Tz endemic: pairs are confined to thick forest, woodland and plantation on Pemba off the NTz coast. **Vo** monosyllabic call *hu* is uttered singly at irregular intervals. Pairs call to each other: ♀ with a lower pitch.

Plate 100

Eurasian
Scops-Owl

African
Scops-Owl

White-faced
Scops-Owl

grey-brown
morph

rufous
morph

Sokoke
Scops-Owl

Pemba
Scops-Owl

EAGLE-OWLS

A striking group of large heavily built owls. Verreaux's Eagle-Owl is distinct, but the other four are all similar; general colour, range and calls aid identification. Sexes are similar, but females may be larger than males. Immatures resemble adults unless described.

Verreaux's Eagle-Owl *Bubo lacteus* ♀ 66cm, 26"
[Giant Eagle Owl]

Massive finely barred pale grey-brown eagle-owl with a *paler face broadly edged black and dark brown eyes with pink eyelids* (only clearly visible when eyes closed). Smallish ear tufts are often laid flat and inconspicuous. Imm has duller face with narrower black borders and shorter ear-tufts. **HH** pairs and family groups are common in wooded grassland and woodland, including riverine acacia groves, from sea-level to 3000m, but mainly below 2000m. Occurs widely, but is only locally common in N and NEKe, W and SETz. **Vo** very deep grunted *huh-huh, huhhu, huh*, which is far-carrying, but often absent-mindedly halting. Imm calls a loud piercing scream that rises then falls and fades.

Spotted Eagle-Owl *Bubo africanus* ♀ 48cm, 19"

Variable dull brown eagle-owl which is heavily spotted brown, buff and cream above, and lightly barred below with slightly darker rather mis-shapen blotches on the upper breast. Ear tufts are often prominent. Three races occur, but are sometimes split as two species: north of the equator *cinarescens* (**Greyish Eagle-Owl**) is generally brown with *dark brown eyes,* while to the south the widespread nominate (**Spotted Eagle-Owl**) is grey-brown with *yellow eyes* and black rimmed facial discs, similar yellow-eyed *tanae* (interior EKe), is paler and greyer with indistinct facial discs. **HH** pairs are widespread and sometimes common from sea-level to 2100m in a wide variety of bushed and wooded country often with cliffs and rocky hills. **Vo** northern birds give a single low hoot, while southern birds call with an emphasised *ooh*, followed by a pause and then a lower and quieter *oh*, like an echo.

Cape Eagle-Owl *Bubo capensis* ♀ 61cm, 24"

In our area, the race *mackinderi* (**Mackinder's Eagle-Owl**) is a large dark eagle-owl, splotched buff and dark brown above, and *very heavily marked dark brown and orange-buff below*, with intense orange eyes set in a grey-brown facial mask with narrow black edges. Ear tufts are pronounced. **HH** pairs are uncommon residents above 2400m (sometimes as low as 1800m), in rocky moorland and montane country mainly in W and CKe (but with a number of known and probable records from Tz, including on Mts Kilimanjaro and Luhoto). **Vo** calls a repeated deep hooting *oooo...oo ooyuoo ooo.*

Fraser's Eagle-Owl *Bubo poensis* ♀ 48cm, 19"

Large *bright rufous* eagle-owl extensively barred dark brown and black above and below, with large ear tufts over black-edged reddish-brown facial disk: eyes dark brown. **HH** pairs are poorly known residents of Bwindi Forest, SWUg (from 1500 and 2150m) and Nyungwe Forest, Rw. **Vo** strange high-pitched rather bugled *yor-wah* or *iyor-wah* first note downslurred, second upslurred and shorter. Also has a low muffled bubbling rumble *grrrrooooo.*

Usambara Eagle-Owl *Bubo vosseleri* ♀ 48cm, 19" ● ●

Large eagle-owl with russet-brown back barred with dark brown, warm pale-buff to white underparts barred reddish-brown with *larger dark brown bars and splotches on upper sides of breast.* **HH** pairs are rare residents of low-land and montane forest, as well as some plantation edges from 200–1500m, in Usambara Mts of NE and Uluguru Mts of ETz. **Vo** calls a rather dove-like high-pitched *ho-ro-roo* all slurred together, with the middle part rising and then falling. Also has a rising low rumbled purr.

Plate 101

Verreaux's
Eagle-Owl

Spotted
Eagle-Owl

cinarescens

nominate

Fraser's
Eagle-Owl

Cape
Eagle-Owl

Usambara
Eagle-Owl

OWLETS

Small round-headed owls which are streaked, spotted or barred below with longish tails: none have ear tufts. Several, particularly Pearl-spotted Owlet, are partially diurnal, and often mobbed by small birds. Sexes alike and immatures resemble adults, but are less well marked.

Pearl-spotted Owlet *Glaucidium perlatum* 19cm, 7.5"
[Pearl-spotted Owl]

Brown above with small white spots on crown and back, larger white spots on scapulars (forming a white line), and two dark eye-spots (false eyes) on the nape. Intimidating yellow eyes. Underparts are variably streaked and spotted rufous-brown with broad streaking extending to the lower flanks. **HH** singles and pairs are widespread and very common in bushed and wooded grasslands, preferring drier areas with acacias, mainly below 2200m (sometimes to 3200m). **Vo** call starts with a long series of short piped *fwoo-fwoo-fwoo…* notes that gradually rise in pitch and volume and, after a pause, a shorter sequence of whistled downslurs *fweeu-fweeu-fweeu…* often given in a see-sawing duet.

African Barred Owlet *Glaucidium capense* 22cm, 8.5"
[Barred Owl]

Three races occur: all have *narrowly barred crowns and napes and well barred and spotted underparts*, but differ in back pattern. Race *ngamiense* (C and STz) has a barred back, *scheffleri* (EKe and ETz) has the back lightly barred or plain, while *castaneum* (**Chestnut Owlet**) (WUg) is plain rufous-backed. **HH** singles and pairs of *ngamiense* are widespread and common in interior woodlands, while *scheffleri* is local and uncommon in coastal forest and woodlands. In our area, *castaneum* has only been collected once in the Semliki Forest, WUg. **Vo** long series commences with regular identical piped downslurs then, after a pause, a set of peculiar vibrato downslurs that seesaw towards the end.

Albertine Owlet *Glaucidium albertinum* 21cm, 8" ● ●

Very similar to African Barred Owlet, but with *fine cream spotting on the crown and nape* and a largely plain rufous-brown back. **HH** a rare and little known forest owlet endemic to the Albertine Rift, in our area known only from Nyungwe Forest, Rw, at c 2000m. **Vo** call unknown.

Red-chested Owlet *Glaucidium tephronotum* 21cm, 8"

Rather plain owlet with a greyish head, dark reddish-brown back and wings, a *rufous washed chest and flanks with variable dark spots,* and a boldly white-spotted tail. **HH** pairs are uncommon residents of forests in WUg from 700m, but more confined to highland forest in W and CKe from 1500–2350m. **Vo** gives a piped series of 3–6 identical notes *phoo-phoo-phoo…*, and also a regular high-pitched and descending slurred *feeeeeeo.*

Pel's Fishing-Owl *Scotopelia peli* 61cm, 24"

Huge owl which is unlikely to be confused with any other bird. Bright orange-rufous heavily barred dusky above, and a little paler below with variable dark spots and bars (usually more concentrated on flanks). Sexes similar; ♀ little less rufous than ♂, but there is considerable individual variation. Imm much paler orange-rufous, and head may be almost white. **HH** singles and pairs are very uncommon beside well-wooded slow-flowing larger rivers, as well as lakes and mangroves from sea-level to 1700m. Occurrence is scattered, but ranges from Murchison Falls NP, WUg to Ruvubu NP in Bu, from the Maasai Mara, SWKe to the Tana River in EKe, and on major rivers in STz, like those in the Selous GR. **Vo** common call is a deep booming *oom…oom…oom…* at 4–5 second intervals, and also cries an eerie downslurred scream.

Plate 102

Pearl-spotted Owlet

African Barred Owlet

scheffleri

castaneum

Albertine Owlet

Pel's Fishing-Owl

Red-chested Owlet

NIGHTJARS

Nightjars are a notoriously difficult group to identify: not only do the species look alike, several have different colour morphs, and they are most frequently encountered at night. Many are best told by call, although the amount of white in the wings and tail, range and habitat, all help identification. Many also have white throat marks, but these are variable. Most females have a similar wing and tail pattern to males, but these areas are coloured buff. Immatures resemble adults. During the day, nightjars are inactive and perfectly camouflaged, hiding in the shade along branches, or on the ground in leaf litter.

NIGHTJARS WITH WHITE SIDES TO THE TAIL

Square-tailed Nightjar   *Caprimulgus fossii*   23cm, 9"
[Gabon Nightjar, Mozambique Nightjar]
A typical *Caprimulgus* nightjar, mainly differing from Slender-tailed and Long-tailed nightjars in having a *square-ended tail*. ♂♂ of all three have white spots on the primaries (4 or 5 feathers in Square-tailed), a *white bar across the lesser wing-coverts, narrow white outer-tails, and white tips to the secondaries forming a white bar along the trailing edge of the wing*. ♀ has the wing spots and outer-tail buff. **HH** common and widespread in bushed grassland, clearings within woodland, and open cultivated areas, from sea-level to 1800m. Some intra-African movements appear to occur, but are poorly understood. **Vo** calls a long low continuous churring, typically about 20 notes per second, but which often changes in speed and pitch. Also gives a *whoop* in flight.

Slender-tailed Nightjar   *Caprimulgus clarus*   25cm, 10"
Similar to Square-tailed Nightjar, with white spots on the primaries (6 or 7 feathers), a *white bar across the lesser wing-coverts, a narrow white outer-tail, and white tips to the secondaries forming a white bar along the trailing edge of the wing*. Both sexes have *slightly elongated central tail feathers* (typically ♂ 2cm, 3/4" and ♀ 1cm, 3/8"), but in ♀ this can be hard to see. ♀ has the wing spots and outer-tail buff. **HH** common and widespread in dry bush country, coastal scrub, and untended cultivation, often near water, from sea-level to 2000m. **Vo** calls a slower, steadier churr than Square-tailed Nightjar, typically about 8 notes per second *kwoikwoikwoikwoi...* (like the pulsating of a generator), and also a rapid *kwip-kwip* or *kwip-kwip-kwip* called in flight.

Long-tailed Nightjar   *Caprimulgus climacurus*   40 cm, 16"
Similar to both Square-tailed and Slender-tailed nightjars with white spots on the primaries (5 feathers), a *white bar across lesser wing-coverts, narrow white outer-tail, and white tips to the secondaries forming a white bar along the trailing edge of the wing*. Both sexes have very long centre-tail feathers (up to 28cm, 11" in ♂), but moulting birds have shorter tails and are very similar to Slender-tailed. ♀ has the wing spots and outer-tail buff. Southern birds often washed with rufous. **HH** seasonally common within range, preferring bushed grasslands and semi-arid country, and breeding in NUg from Mar–Jul. **Vo** calls with a very fast and constant, almost reeling, churr of 40 plus notes per second (much faster than other churring species), and also a nasal *chyaw* flight call.

Swamp Nightjar   *Caprimulgus natalensis*   23cm, 9"
[African White-tailed Nightjar, Natal Nightjar]
Could be confused with Square-tailed Nightjar, but ♂ has *broad white outer-tail*, and lacks white bars on lesser wing-coverts and trailing edge of wing. Looks short-tailed in flight when ♂ also shows white spots on the primaries (4 or 5 feathers). ♀ has wing spots and outer-tail buff. With good views both sexes reveal *dark cheeks* and a buff collar. Montane Nightjar is similar but darker, with a more obvious tawny collar and a more easterly distribution. **HH** locally common with a preference for wet grasslands and marshy areas from 600–2200m. **Vo** calls a repeated simple and monotonous *chok-chok-chok...*, and a melodious laughing *whip hulululu* in flight.

Plate 103

Square-tailed
Nightjar

Slender-tailed
Nightjar

Long-tailed
Nightjar

Swamp Nightjar

WHITE-TAILED MONTANE NIGHTJARS

Three closely related nightjars variously lumped and split as one to three species. Each occupies a different highland area. Males of all have extensive white outer-tails, tawny-buff or rufous hindnecks, and quavering whistled songs. Best identified from each other by range, and the amount of white in their outer-tails.

Montane Nightjar *Caprimulgus poliocephalus*   23cm, 9"
[Abyssinian Nightjar]

A rather dark nightjar: ♂ has white spots on the primaries (4 feathers) and a *mostly white outer-tail*. ♀ has buffy wing spots and less white in the outer-tail. ♂ has a similar tail to Swamp Nightjar, but that more westerly species is paler overall and occupies different habitat. **HH** common and widespread in highland areas, usually in the vicinity of forest, but also in nearby farmland and well-wooded urban areas, mainly between 1500–3000m. **Vo** a nasal *ank-ank-ank* often precedes a haunting high-pitched and whistled *piiiyu-pirrrrr* (first note a falling and then rising upslur, the last note slightly falling and tremulous). Higher-pitched than Fiery-necked Nightjar.

Rwenzori Nightjar *Caprimulgus ruwenzorii*   23cm, 9"

Darker than Montane Nightjar: ♂ usually has smaller white spots on the primaries, and white on outer-tail only extends roughly half way up from the tips (not all white). ♀ has buffy wing spots and less white in the outer-tail. In areas of overlap with Swamp Nightjar, Rwenzori occurs mainly in more forested higher altitudes, and has less white in the outer-tail. **HH** common in highland areas of the west, usually near forest, but also ranges in to nearby open areas, from 1800–2800m. **Vo** similar to Montane Nightjar whistle, but higher-pitched and less musical *p'iiiii-pwiiiirr* (first note barely rising, the last note only slightly falling and less tremulous).

Usambara Nightjar *Caprimulgus guttifer*   23cm, 9"

Very similar to Rwenzori Nightjar: ♂ differs mainly in having slightly less white in the outer-tail. ♀ has buffy wing spots and even less white in the outer-tail than ♂. **HH** occurs in two widely separated areas, in the Usambara Mts, NETz, and the highlands north of Lake Malawi, STz. It is locally common around highland forest from 1000–2500m. **Vo** very like Rwenzori Nightjar, a high-pitched whistled *pwii-pwirrrr* (first note only slightly upslurred, last note almost monotone and slightly tremulous).

NIGHTJARS WITH WHITE TAIL CORNERS

A large group of nightjars with white on the outer-tail restricted to the distal half or less (includes species on plates 105 and 106). Call, range, and exact amount of white in tail aid identification.

Fiery-necked Nightjar *Caprimulgus pectoralis*   24cm, 9.5"

In flight, ♂ shows white spots on primaries (4 feathers) and large white tail corners (approximately one third). Rich rufous ear-coverts and hind-collar may be visible in daylight. ♀ has smaller wing spots and tail corners sometimes washed buffish. In STz, a rufous morph occurs: it has the head and variably the back, tail and breast cinnamon-rufous. **HH** common and widespread in forest and woodland (especially miombo), throughout the south and in coastal Ke from sea-level to 1300m. **Vo** calls with a slow *woi- woi-woi-...* preceding a dramatic whistled *t'woy-wirrrrr* (the first note a falling then slightly rising upslur, the last note very tremulous).

Black-shouldered Nightjar *Caprimulgus nigriscapularis*   24cm, 9.5"

Very similar to Fiery-necked Nightjar (and sometimes considered conspecific). Differs in having slightly smaller white spots on the wings, *blackish-brown lesser wing-coverts* (only visible in daylight), and in voice and range. ♀ wing and tail spots smaller and may be tinged buff. **HH** locally common in the west, inhabiting forest edge, woodland along streams, and neglected cultivation from 700–1450m. **Vo** very similar to Fiery-necked Nightjar, but the song is preceded by a monotonous rapid *kwoip-kwoip-kwoip-...* which then breaks into a whistled *choy-chrrrrr* (first note a rising slur, second all on the same tone).

Plate 104

Montane
Nightjar

♂

♀

♂

♀

Rwenzori
Nightjar

♂

♀

♂

♀

Usambara Nightjar

♂

♀

Fiery-necked
Nightjar

Black-shouldered
Nightjar

♀

♂

Dusky Nightjar *Caprimulgus fraenatus* 23cm, 9"
Similar to Fiery-necked Nightjar with a rufous hindneck, white spots on the primaries (3-4 feathers) and fairly large white tail corners. Differs in being generally darker, including the ear-coverts, with larger creamy-buff spots on the wing-coverts, and a very different voice. ♀ has spots on wings and tail smaller and washed brownish. **HH** locally common resident and migrant most often found in grasslands and on rocky slopes, but always with some cover. Mainly at medium altitudes, but range extends from near sea-level to 3200m. **Vo** calls a long series of a deep hollow-sounding churrs, lacking any rising or falling inflections, and often commences with a pair of hurried hiccup-like notes *kwi-kuk kwi-kuk*.

Nubian Nightjar *Caprimulgus nubicus* 23cm, 9"
Slightly variable colour morphs complicate identification of this species even more than usual! Typical ♂♂ are very similar to Dusky Nightjar, but with smaller white tail corners. In daylight appears paler, more grey-brown, but in flight shows more rufous in the wings. ♀ has wing spots washed buffy, tail spots slightly smaller. **HH** occurs in dry bush and semi-desert in the north and east from 600–1250m. Exact status is uncertain: it has occurred throughout the year, but most records are for Nov–Mar. **Vo** call has never been satisfactorily recorded in the region, although elsewhere gives a barking and paired *wow-wow* very similar to Freckled Nightjar (but less musical and more rushed).

Plain Nightjar *Caprimulgus inornatus* 23cm, 9"
A rather plain looking nightjar with grey-brown, brown, and rufous morphs. ♂♂ of all have white spots on primaries (4 feathers), large white corners to tail, and no white on the throat (may show small black spots on crown and scapulars like Star-spotted Nightjar). ♀♀ have buffy-brown wing spots, and no white in the tail. **HH** a seasonally common non-br migrant, occurring in our area mainly from Oct–Apr. Others (possible breeding birds) occur in the far north from May–Aug. Recorded from a wide variety of bush country and grassland from sea-level to 1800m. **Vo** largely silent in the region, but gives a *chuck* call when flushed: breeding birds call with a long mechanical churr that is similar but higher pitched than Dusky Nightjar.

Star-spotted Nightjar *Caprimulgus stellatus* 23cm, 9"
Very similar to Plain Nightjar, with similar plain overall appearance. Colour morphs include brown, grey-brown, rufous, and buff forms. Best identified from Plain Nightjar by *smaller white corners to tail* on both sexes and by voice. Roosting day time birds show white patches on either side of throat, and very small black spots on the crown and scapulars. **HH** locally common up north, particularly in areas of lava and nearby sandy scrub, mainly from 350–1000m, and rarely wandering to higher areas. **Vo** calls a steady yelping *pweu, pweu, pweu...*

Donaldson-Smith's Nightjar *Caprimulgus donaldsoni* 19cm, 7.5"
A *small* boldly patterned species with grey-brown and rufous morphs. In flight, has white spots on primaries (4 feathers), and small white corners to tail on both sexes (slightly tinged buffy on ♀). Birds seen in daylight often show a large white throat patch and boldly edged creamy-buff scapulars. **HH** locally common in dry bush country from sea-level to 1250m. **Vo** calls a monotonous whistled rather tremulous *t-weer-tweeu* (first note a rising upslur, last notes descending).

Plate 105

Dusky
Nightjar

Nubian
Nightjar

Star-spotted
Nightjar

Plain Nightjar

Donaldson-Smith's
Nightjar

Eurasian Nightjar *Caprimulgus europaeus*   27cm, 10.5"
[European Nightjar]

A large migratory nightjar: in flight ♂ shows white spots on primaries (3 or 4 feathers) and white tail corners. Four races occur, varying in overall tone from grey-brown to cinnamon-buff, but this is difficult to judge in the dark. In daylight, shows narrow black streaks on the crown, blackish mottled shoulders, and a pale bar on the lesser wing-coverts; it lacks the rufous hindneck of many nightjars. ♀♀ lack white in wings and tail. **HH** common Palearctic winter visitor and passage migrant which occurs in a wide range of more open habitats from Oct–Apr, from sea-level to 2000m, and which tends to roost on branches during the day. **Vo** usually silent in EA, but occasionally calls *quoik* when flushed.

Freckled Nightjar *Caprimulgus tristigma*   25cm, 10"

A large and dark grey-brown nightjar, mottled all over with fine greyish or buffy speckles, sometimes shows whitish throat markings. No rufous hindneck. In flight, ♂ shows white spots primaries (4 feathers) and small white corners to tail. ♀ has white spots on wings, but the tail is barred dark brown on brown. **HH** locally common on rocky hills and escarpments from 600–2000m. **Vo** paired, musical and whiplashed *kow-wow...kow-wow...* often interspersed with irregular nasal upslurs *wup-wup-wup...*

Bates's Nightjar *Caprimulgus batesi*   29cm, 11.5"

A large, dark forest species. In flight, ♂ shows white on primaries (2 or 3 feathers) and small white corners to tail. If seen well has a greyish crown and blackish forewing. ♀ lacks white on wings and tail. **HH** very rare in our area and only known from forest in the Semliki Valley, WUg, at 700m. **Vo** calls while perched upright on branches, a repeated *kwup kwup*, recalling Freckled Nightjar. This may speed up into a rather muffled barking *kwup kwupkwupkwupkwupkwupkwupkwup.*

SPECTACULAR NIGHTJARS

Males of these *Macrodipteryx* nightjars develop dramatic wing projections in breeding plumage.

Standard-winged Nightjar *Macrodipteryx longipennis*   20cm, 8"

Br ♂ unique and spectacular with large flags at ends of long wires (the elongated shafts of second primary feathers). In flight, looks like a nightjar being chased by two smaller birds. Non-br ♂ and ♀ are more like typical-female nightjars, but without white wing spots or tail corners. If seen in good light the combination of a rufous hindneck, and strongly barred blackish and rufous flight feathers and tail distinguish it from all except larger ♀ Pennant-winged Nightjar. **HH** locally common within breeding range in NWUg mainly Sep–Apr, but scarce elsewhere. Inhabits bushed grasslands and marshy lakeshores from 600–1400m. **Vo** a very high-pitched and rapid insect-like *titititititit...*

Pennant-winged Nightjar *Macrodipteryx vexillarius*   28cm, 11"

Br ♂ is unmistakable with a broad white flash right across the wing and long white wing streamers (elongated second primaries). Non-br ♂ loses long pennants, but still distinctive with broad white flash and black ends to wings. ♀ has a rufous hindneck, and strongly barred blackish and rufous flight feathers and tail (without any white): similar to non-br ♂ and ♀ Standard-winged Nightjar, but larger. **HH** breeds in southern Tz (Aug–Mar) and then migrates north where it may be locally common (particularly in the west). Prefers bushland and bushed grassland between 1000–2800m, but may wander to near sea-level. **Vo** breeding birds utter a rapid insect-like *chitchitchitchit...* which is similar to but slower than Standard-winged Nightjar.

Plate 106

Eurasian
Nightjar

Freckled Nightjar

Bates's Nightjar

Standard-winged
Nightjar

Pennant-winged
Nightjar

WHITE-RUMPED SWIFTS

Three similar black swifts with white rumps which mainly differ in tail shape. Sexes and immatures are similar.

Little Swift *Apus affinis* 14cm, 5.5"
Small swift with a rectangular white rump patch (extending onto lower flanks), a *square-ended tail,* and an obvious white throat patch. Seems stocky in flight, with fairly broad wings, interspersing rather fluttery wing beats with short glides. **HH** small to large flocks are common and widespread from the coast to 3000m. Often seen in small screaming parties. Nests under bridges, in villages and towns, as well as in natural sites, like cliffs and gorges. Widespread away from dry NEKe, but local and uncommon in W, C and STz. **Vo** a very noisy swift which frequently calls with musical twittering downslurs.

White-rumped Swift *Apus caffer* 15cm, 6"
Slender and slightly longer than Little Swift, with a *forked tail and narrow crescent-shaped white rump* (which hardly wraps onto lower flanks). Throat is clearly white. In fluid flight looks slim-winged with a pointed tail which only appears forked when spread (often while banking). **HH** more solitary than Little Swift, but pairs and small flocks are common from sea-level to 3000m in villages and towns, as well as near rocky cliffs and gorges. Nests in crevices and often in old mud swallow nests. Widespread at low densities away from arid NEKe, and largely absent from W and CTz. **Vo** breeding birds give rapid short burry and buzzy rattled churrs lower-pitched than most other swifts.

Horus Swift *Apus horus* 15cm, 6"
Stocky dark swift with a *shallow forked tail,* but broad white band on rump (wrapping around flanks like Little Swift), and large white throat (which may extend onto upper breast). Flying birds are shorter tailed than White-rumped Swift, and spread tail may appear only slightly notched. **HH** pairs and small flocks are mainly intra-African migrants occurring in our area from Mar–Sep, and breeding in unused holes in bee-eater colonies in the highlands from 1600–2000m, occasionally to 3000m. Wanderers may occur almost anywhere, but confusion with similar species means exact extent of range and seasonality are unclear. **Vo** low pitched, burry and downslurred screams have a unique nasal and pinched quality.

VERY LARGE SWIFTS

Large swifts with broad wings and thickset bodies, and deep and powerful flight (noisy at close quarters). Single Mottled Swifts can be hard to judge for size and both species wander far from nest sites. Sexes and immatures are very similar.

Mottled Swift *Apus aequatorialis* 21cm, 8"
Very large grey-brown swift with mottled underparts (only visible at close range and in good light) and a small dingy white throat. When nearby, striking and impressive on long wings with rather pointed forked tail. **HH** single birds to large flocks, often with other swifts, and screaming parties at craggy cliff nest sites (like Hell's Gate Gorge NP, Ke). Only common in highlands to 3000m, but birds wander widely often feeding over wetlands. **Vo** around breeding colonies gives dry twittered trills, almost screamed in excited aerial chases.

Alpine Swift *Apus melba* 22cm, 8.5"
Distinctly patterned huge swift: uniform brown above and *largely white below with a well-defined brown breast band.* Powerful in flight, with deep wing beats. **HH** singles or small groups are fairly uncommon away from their highland nesting sites, but are widespread and often associate with other swifts. Palearctic birds occur in NUg (Sep–Apr) and may wander elsewhere (but patterns are poorly understood). **Vo** at breeding colonies, gives a twittered trill and a soft trilled scream.

Plate 107

Little Swift

White-rumped
Swift

Horus Swift

Mottled
Swift

Alpine
Swift

PLAIN SWIFTS
Similarly sized largely plain black or dark brown swifts presenting serious identification problems. Subtle plumage differences are often muddled by light conditions and some, particularly lone birds, cannot be identified with confidence. Mixed-species flocks allowing comparisons help. Try to watch swifts against dark backgrounds and avoid strong back-lighting. Particular attention should be paid to presence or lack of contrasts in upperwing and underwing, extent of white on throat and forehead, and to location, season and calls. All the species have similar short well-forked tails. Sexes and immatures are similar.

African Black Swift *Apus barbatus* 18cm, 7"
[Black Swift]

Dark *blackish swift with a slightly paler blackish-brown patch on inner upperwing* (secondaries and greater coverts) which contrasts with a darker body and rest of wing. Birds always have a dark forehead, with a variable white or whitish-grey throat. **HH** small parties and flocks are sometimes common, often with other swifts, in the highlands from WUg to Bu, from NEUg through Ke into NETz, and in SWTz, from 1000–2400m (but may wander to other areas). **Vo** near breeding sites calls an excited rasped trill which lacks any musical quality.

Nyanza Swift *Apus niansae* 17cm, 6.5"

Widespread nominate race is a dark brown swift which is similar to African Black Swift, but in good light is *always obviously brown* (not black). It also shows a *contrasting lighter innerwing patch* from above (slightly more extensive than in African Black), but this is also visible from below and often appears translucent. Forehead is dark brown, with a variable but usually poorly defined whitish throat. Paler race *somalicus* has been collected once in NKe. **HH** singles, small and sometimes large flocks are locally common often in drier country, breeding in rocky cliffs below 2800m from NEUg through W and CKe to NTz (abundant at roosts in Hell's Gate Gorge NP, Ke). Occasionally wanders. **Vo** in flight gives short dry and rasping trilled downslurs and high-pitched twittering notes.

Eurasian Swift *Apus apus* 18cm, 7"
[European Swift]

Nominate race is an *entirely sooty black-brown swift, lacking the contrast in wings* of African Black and Nyanza swifts. Forehead is dark (paler in imm) and has a small but prominent white throat patch. Eastern race *pekinensis* is paler and browner, with a slightly larger brighter throat patch. **HH** small to sometimes huge flocks associate with weather fronts throughout: main passage is Sep–Dec (south) and Mar–Apr (north), but also occurs Aug–Apr in areas with lots of insect prey, often over wet grassland. Race *pekinensis* has been recorded in Ug and Ke, but its status is unclear. **Vo** usually silent in EA, but may call with harsh high-pitched screams.

Forbes-Watson's Swift *Apus berliozi* 18cm, 7"

Very similar to Eurasian Swift (especially paler race *pekinensis*): being uniform sooty brown with a prominent white throat. Dark-headed birds may be indistinguishable from *pekinensis* (except on call), but some have an obvious white forehead (when only confusion is with blacker imm nominate Eurasian). Extremely close views may reveal faint scaly underparts. **HH** small to large flocks visit coastal Ke and NTz from breeding sites in NE Africa in Oct–Feb (often over forests like Arabuko-Sokoke and the Shimba Hills, Ke). **Vo** in flight birds give musical trilled downslurs.

Pallid Swift *Apus pallidus* 18cm, 7"

Vagrant all-brown swift with a prominent white throat, pale forehead and dark eye patch. From above, hindneck and rump are paler than mantle giving a saddle effect. From below, pale inner underwing contrasts with a darker wing tip (and good views may reveal light scaling on body). **HH** only recorded specimen is from Mt Moroto, NEUg, but recent sight records in Ke suggest it may have been overlooked. **Vo** a down-slurred scream.

Plate 108

African Black
Swift

Nyanza
Swift

nominate

Eurasian
Swift

somalicus

pekinensis

nominate

Forbes-Watson's
Swift

Pallid
Swift

SLIM SWIFTS

Two slender swifts (in different genera) which are relatively easy to identify from all other swifts and from each other. Note slender pointed tail and rather uniform plumage. Sexes alike. Immatures are similar to adults with a slightly shorter tail.

Scarce Swift *Schoutedenapus myoptilus* 17cm, 6.5"
A slender dark brown (or grey-brown) swift with a slightly paler throat (beware birds often look very dark against bright sky). *Rather long tail is often held closed and appears narrow and pointed, only showing deep fork when spread.* **HH** flocks are widespread over highland forest and grasslands, usually above 2000m, but wander as low as 1000m. Patchy distribution is centred on highlands from WUg to Bu, and from NEUg through CKe to the mountains of NE and ETz. **Vo** does not scream like other dark swifts, but flocks chitter like spinetails during aerial chases and near breeding colonies.

African Palm Swift *Cypsiurus parvus* 18cm, 7"
Very slim uniform mouse-brown swift, with long scimitar wings, and a long very deeply forked tail. Highly characterful flickering flight, with the tail invariably held closed and needle-like. **HH** more solitary than other swifts, but pairs and small flocks are common and widespread residents from sea-level to 1400m (less often to 2000m), invariably associating with the palm trees. **Vo** breeding birds call a thin high-pitched twittering and rattled trills.

SPINETAILS

Atypical swifts with broad wings and short tails, usually in pairs or small groups. Fairly easy to identify: special note should be taken of extent of white in plumage, range and habitat. Sexes and immatures are similar.

Böhm's Spinetail *Neafrapus boehmi* 10cm, 4"
[Bat-like Spinetail]
Extremely short-tailed spinetail, with broad black wings narrowing close to the body: extensive white belly and narrow white rump contrast with a blackish-brown throat and upper flanks. Flight is uncertain, fluttery and bat-like with much slow-wheeling and chasing, often low over the canopy. **HH** pairs and small groups are local and uncommon in forest and woodland, including miombo, through the coastal lowlands of Ke (inland on major rivers), but much more wide-ranging in Tz. **Vo** distinctive musical twittering.

Mottled Spinetail *Telacanthura ussheri* 14cm, 5.5"
Closely resembles Little Swift (plate 107), but white rump extends as a *narrow whitish band across the lower belly* (can be hard to see). Indistinct mottling across the throat and breast also obscure in the field. Flight swift-like, without the fluttering of other spinetails. **HH** pairs and small groups are rather uncommon and local residents of W and SUg forests, but are more widespread in woodland, open forest and edges, from CKe south into Tz (often associating with baobabs). **Vo** flying birds give a variety of rhythmic chitters and squeaks.

Sabine's Spinetail *Rhaphidura sabini* 11cm, 4.5"
A small spinetail with an *extensive white lower back and rump (elongated uppertail-coverts cover the dark tail)*, and clean white below with a black throat. Has typical wheeling spinetail-like flight over canopy. **HH** locally common over mature forest from 700–2000m in W and SUg (and formerly in WKe). **Vo** calls a variety of metallic chinks and chittering in flight.

Cassin's Spinetail *Neafrapus cassini* 15cm, 6"
Large tail-less spinetail: black-brown above and on throat, with extensive white underparts and a clear narrow white rump band. Close views reveal fine brown streaks below. Flight is powerful, wheeling and circling over canopy. **HH** in our area, only known from Budongo and Mabira forests, Ug. **Vo** flying birds call with rasping tuneless chitters and crackles.

Plate 109

Scarce Swift

African Palm Swift

Böhm's Spinetail

Mottled Spinetail

Cassin's Spinetail

Sabine's Spinetail

MOUSEBIRDS

Endemic to Africa: social, crested, and long-tailed mousebirds scramble through bushes and trees using both their feet and bills (hence family name). All call regularly to maintain contact. *Colius* have rather weak and floppy flight, while *Urocolius* fly strongly, fast and direct. Sexes alike: immatures are duller than adults.

Speckled Mousebird *Colius striatus* 33cm, 13"

Ad is a scruffy buff and brown bird with a brown crest, whitish cheeks, a blackish patch around the eye, and fine dark barring on the throat and breast. Bill black above and pink below. Similar imm has shorter crest and paler duller bill. **HH** small flocks are widespread and common in a variety of moister bush from thicket to forest edge, including gardens, from sea-level to 2600m. **Vo** scratchy and unpleasant raspy churrs given perched and in flight.

White-headed Mousebird *Colius leucocephalus* 31cm, 12"

Ad has a *white crest* and face, an obvious small blackish eye-mask, and a finely barred throat, nape and hindneck. Bill is pale with a dark tip. Imm has a duller crest and less pronounced barring. **HH** flocks are uncommon in arid and semi-arid bush from sea-level to 1400m. **Vo** calls rapid, spitted metallic notes *tititititititit...*

Blue-naped Mousebird *Urocolius macrourus* 35cm, 14"

Slender, thin-tailed and crested ad is grey with a red mask, black-tipped red bill, and a *blue nape patch*. Imm duller, with less distinct blue nape, greenish facial skin and pale bill. **HH** flocks are widespread and common in arid and semi-arid bushland, woodland and sparsely bushed grassland from sea-level to 1900m. **Vo** calls a single loud and rather mournful *piiiyew* and softer short nasal slurred notes, rather wader-like in quality.

Red-faced Mousebird *Urocolius indicus* 35cm, 14"

Ad is very similar to Blue-naped Mousebird with the same bare red facial patch and black-tipped red bill, but differs in having a buff forecrown, and no blue on the nape. Duller imm has a shorter crest, greenish facial skin and a pale bill. **HH** small flocks are common, but often shy in bush and coastal scrub in SW and SETz. **Vo** mournful slurred notes given by all members of group, also a short rapid series of shorter notes, rather wader-like.

TROGONS

Spectacular long-tailed birds which, despite bright green and red plumage, are hard to see. Both species make short silent undulating flights, but are unobtrusive and sit still for long periods, often high in the canopy. Undertail pattern and calls are diagnostic.

Narina Trogon *Apaloderma narina* 30cm, 12"

Ad ♂ is vivid green above with a green throat and upper breast, startling red belly, and a blue-green tail with *white outer-tail feathers (tail looks all white from underneath)*. Ad ♀ duller and has varied buff-brown, not green forecrown, throat and breast. Imm like ad ♀, but has white tips to wing-coverts. **HH** singles and pairs are widespread and reasonably common residents of forest and richer woodland from sea-level to 3000m. **Vo** calls a pulsating, repeated and crooned *krooo-krrrou* with strong accent on the second note. Each long series commences with short purred notes and increases in volume.

Bar-tailed Trogon *Apaloderma vittatum* 28cm, 11"

Ad ♂ is similar to Narina Trogon, but somewhat darker with a blue band across the breast. From behind shows *narrow black and white tail edges, but from underneath tail is entirely barred*. Ad ♀ has dull brown head and breast. Imm similar to ad ♀, but has pale-tipped wing-coverts. **HH** singles and pairs are uncommon in highland forest from 900–2600m (usually occurs at higher altitudes than Narina Trogon where their ranges overlap). **Vo** calls a series of up to a dozen identical upslurred or downslurred reedy notes *fweu-fweu-fweu...*, with pauses between each set, and also a single far-carrying *yaow* from high in the canopy.

Plate 110

White-headed Mousebird
Ad

Speckled Mousebird
Ad

Ad

Blue-naped Mousebird

Ad

Red-faced Mousebird

♀

♀

♂

♂

Narina Trogon

Bar-tailed Trogon

KINGFISHERS

Stocky, dagger-billed, colourful birds. Despite the family name, only a few species catch fish, and many are not dependent on water, inhabiting bush country, woodland and forest. Displays and calls make some conspicuous, but forest birds are shy and cryptic despite their bright colours.

Pied Kingfisher *Ceryle rudis* 25cm, 10"

Characterful large *crested black and white kingfisher*: ad ♂ has two complete breast bands; ad ♀ has a single broken band. Imm is similar to ad ♀, but has brown fringing to the face and throat, and a duller band. Uniquely fish from hovering flight, enabling birds to exploit open water. **HH** highly social: singles and groups are widespread and common residents beside all types of water, from sea-level to 2300m, including coastal shallows. **Vo** calls an explosive and rather tern-like *chit-chit*, which often breaks into a metallic, musical and rhythmic chittering with many birds joining in excitedly.

Striped Kingfisher *Halcyon chelicuti* 17cm, 6.5"

Small dumpy rather drab kingfisher with a dark eye-stripe, pale throat and collar, and a variably streaked crown, lower breast and flanks. Bill is black with a red lower mandible. Sexes similar, although ♂ has a black band on the underwing (seen when flashes open wings in display), and a greyer crown than ♀. In rapid direct flight shows a turquoise-blue back, rump and tail. Imm has dull reddish bill, is less streaked and can be darkly scaled below. **HH** singles and pairs are common and widespread from sea-level to 2300m in a wide range of bushed and wooded grassland, often far from water. **Vo** regularly repeated call is an emphatic introductory note then, after a very short pause, a descending series of trills *fi-frrrrrrr... fi-frrrrrrr... fi-frrrrrr...*

Grey-headed Kingfisher *Halcyon leucocephala* 21cm, 8"
[Grey-hooded Kingfisher]

Ad of nominate race has a pale grey head, black upper back and chestnut belly, a red bill, and bright blue lower back, wings and tail. Sexes are similar. Imm is duller with dusky barring on the head and breast, a very pale chestnut belly, and dark-tipped red bill. Race *pallidiventris* has a greyer head and paler chestnut belly. **HH** singles and pairs are common and widespread in a wide range of woodland, bush and cultivation from sea-level to 2200m, often near water. Race *pallidiventris* is a resident of C and STz, and a visitor elsewhere from Apr–Sep. **Vo** song is a rising, falling, then rising wave of notes that become very strident *ti-ti-ti-tit-tit-tit-tiu-tiu-tiu-ti-tit-tit-tit...* Call is a series of identical sharp notes *tchk, tchk, tchk...*

Brown-hooded Kingfisher *Halcyon albiventris* 21cm, 8"

Similar to Grey-headed Kingfisher: race *prentissgrayi* has a faintly streaked brownish crown, pale collar, and a pale buff belly with a buff-chestnut wash confined to flanks: bill bright red. Sexes differ: ♂ has black back; ♀ dark brown. Coastal race *orientalis* has a plainer crown (no obvious collar) and plain buff flanks. Darker-billed imm has a browner crown and light barring on the breast. In flight, shows *warm rufous-chestnut underwing*. **HH** pairs are fairly common in bushed and wooded habitats mainly in the east from sea- level to 1800m, often near water, with some local movements. **Vo** call is a monotonous repeated and whistled sequence of four descending notes with an emphasis on the first note, and the next three gradually fading *wi-ti-ti-tu*.

Giant Kingfisher *Megaceryle maxima* 43cm, 17"

A spectacular massive kingfisher: blackish above with fine white speckles and bars. Ad ♂ has a broad chestnut breast band; ad ♀ has chestnut restricted to the belly. Imms resemble ads, but chestnut bands are speckled and broken. **HH** single birds or pairs are shy and local, but widespread on highland lakes, rivers and streams, mainly from 1500–2700m, but wanders widely including to deeper coastal creeks. **Vo** loud, far-carrying raucous laugh followed by single notes *kiau-kiau-kee-ee-ee-ee-ee-ee- kiau-kiau-kiau-kiau...* often called in flight.

Plate 111

Pied Kingfisher

Imm

♀

♂

♂

Striped
Kingfisher

Grey-headed
Kingfisher

Imm

Ad

nominate

Imm

Brown-hooded
Kingfisher

Giant Kingfisher

♂

♀

Ad

orientalis

WOODLAND KINGFISHERS

A varied group of woodland and forest kingfishers (which include Striped, Grey-headed and Brown-hooded on plate 111). Often found well away from water, they feed on insects, lizards and occasionally small birds. All have loud trilling calls and striking displays. Sexes are similar, immatures tend to be duller than adults and often scaled on the breast. Half-collared is related to species on plate 113.

Woodland Kingfisher *Halcyon senegalensis* 22cm, 8.5"
A rather thick-set kingfisher: ad of nominate race is dove-grey, black and bright blue with a *striking red and black bill, and no blue on breast.* Migrant southern race *cyanoleuca* has a grey head washed blue, and black extends slightly behind the eye. Imm is similar to ad, but has buff wash on head, lightly scaled breast and flanks, and a dark bill. **HH** singles and pairs are widespread and common in a range of wooded and bushed grassland, cultivation and gardens mainly from sea-level to 1500m (but up to 3000m), with southern race *cyanoleuca* breeding in STz and migrating further north (Apr–Sep). **Vo** song is a descending rattled series that starts with an explosive note, followed by a short pause, *chit chtchtchtchttitititchrrrrrrr.* Birds also call with a repeated musical rattled upslur.

Mangrove Kingfisher *Halcyon senegaloides* 23cm, 9"
Very similar to Woodland Kingfisher, but has a slightly darker grey head and *bright all red bill.* Imm duller than ad with buff-brown wash on head, breast and flanks, and a dark bill. Flying birds reveal a black carpal crescent in the underwing. **HH** common resident of coastal areas in a wide range of bush to forest, mangroves and gardens, with some local movements occurring. **Vo** song is similar in structure to Woodland Kingfisher, but after introductory *chink* followed by a short pause, the series is much slower and more emphatic *chink trrt trrt trrt trrt trrt trrt trrt trt trtt trtrtrtrtrtrtrtrt.*

Blue-breasted Kingfisher *Halcyon malimbica* 25cm, 10"
Larger than similar Woodland Kingfisher, with blacker wings and a *blue breast band* (which contrasts with white throat and belly), blue hind-crown and neck: *bill red and black.* Imm has buff underparts and a dark red-brown bill. **HH** pairs and singles are reasonably common in forest and dense riverine woodland from 700–1800m in the west of region. **Vo** song is a loud whistled series of rising and then falling notes, which usually finishes on the same tone as the opening note *fih fi fi fi fififififififi fi fi fi.*

Chocolate-backed Kingfisher *Halcyon badia* 21cm, 8"
A spectacular forest kingfisher which is *dark chocolate above and white below,* with a bright blue wing panel, rump and tail, and a bright red bill. Sexes are alike, while the imm is duller, with a black red-tipped bill, and brownish-grey scaling on the upper breast and flanks. **HH** pairs are local and uncommon residents of the mid and high canopy in dense forests from 700–1400m in WUg. **Vo** song is a distinctive loud series given from high in forest canopy *wi-wi-wi-wi-wi-wi-wi-wi-wiu-wiu-wiu-wiu-wiu-wiu-wu-wu-wu* first rising then falling in downslurs towards the end, and finally fading away with single notes. Very musical and mournful with long breaks between each series.

Half-collared Kingfisher *Alcedo semitorquata* 18cm, 7"
A black-billed short-tailed kingfisher: blue-green above and pale rufous-orange below with a white throat and spot on side of neck, *dark blue patches at sides of breast* are diagnostic. Sexes are alike, and imm is similar but paler below with dark scaling across the breast, and dark legs. Similar Shining Blue Kingfisher is larger and darker; imm Malachite Kingfisher is also dark-billed, but smaller, and lacks the blue breast patches. **HH** singles and pairs are shy and uncommon on well-wooded streams, rivers and lakes mainly in STz, but also in other widely scattered localities. **Vo** in flight or while perched, calls a simple single or repeated metallic *chink.*

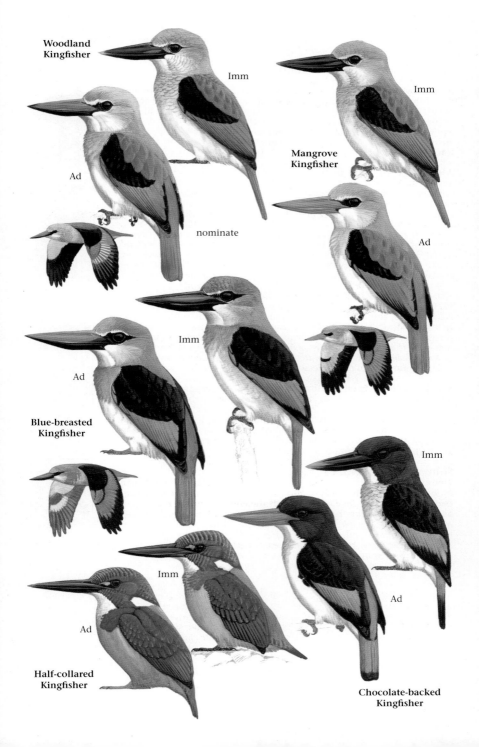

Plate 112

Woodland
Kingfisher

Imm

Imm

Ad

Mangrove
Kingfisher

nominate

Ad

Imm

Ad

Imm

Blue-breasted
Kingfisher

Imm

Imm

Ad

Ad

Half-collared
Kingfisher

Chocolate-backed
Kingfisher

BLUE AND RUFOUS KINGFISHERS

Small kingfishers, all essentially dark blue and rufous with white throats and neck spots. Head pattern, bill and underpart colour, habitat and range aid identification. Sexes are alike: immatures are duller with black bills, some scaling on the breast, and dark legs.

Malachite Kingfisher *Alcedo cristata* 12cm, 5"

Ad is blue above and rufous below with a *slightly shaggy blue-green and black barred crown which extends down to the eye,* and a bright red bill. Imm is similar, with a shorter black bill, brownish-rufous underparts, and a whitish belly. **HH** pairs and singles are common and widespread throughout most of the region from sea-level to 3000m, occurring beside all types of water where fringed with vegetation. Some local movements appear to occur, but are not well known. **Vo** calls a short sharp rather unmusical *chht,* that may run on into a dry chitter.

African Pygmy Kingfisher *Ispidina picta* 11cm, 4.5"

Slightly smaller but similar to Malachite Kingfisher: ad of nominate race has a *small dark blue crown which does not extend down to the eye* and orange cheeks with a purple-pink wash to ear-coverts. Imm like ad but duller, with a darker face, breast scaling, and a shorter blackish bill. The similar southern race *natalensis* has a paler belly with a small barred blue patch above the white neck spot. **HH** nominate is widespread, often far from water, in forest and denser thickets in bushed and wooded grassland, and woodland, usually below 1500m (less often to 2000m); migrant *natalensis* breeds in C & STz from Sep–Apr, before travelling north to forests and dense coastal thickets in Ke. **Vo** calls a high-pitched *tsi-tsi...* and a squeaky chittering.

African Dwarf Kingfisher *Ispidina lecontei* 10cm, 4"

Very similar to African Pygmy Kingfisher, but ad has *all rufous crown and black forehead,* and a paler belly. Imm duller with a blackish crown, a shorter black and reddish bill, and dark scaling on the cheeks and breast. **HH** singles and pairs inhabit lowland forest from 700–1400m in W and SUg, preferring to keep low in gloom of undergrowth: Africa's smallest kingfisher. **Vo** calls a high-pitched whistled *sisiseu sisiseu sisisi...* quite unlike other small kingfishers.

White-bellied Kingfisher *Alcedo leucogaster* 12cm, 5"

Ad is ultramarine-blue above, with chestnut-orange flanks, a *white blaze from throat through breast to undertail,* and a red bill. Imm has blue spotting on upperparts and a black bill. **HH** pairs and singles are rather shy and uncommon residents of dense forest and forest pools in W and SUg from 700–1200m and in NWTz in Minziro Forest, usually close to the ground. **Vo** sharp flight call is similar to Malachite Kingfisher.

Shining-blue Kingfisher *Alcedo quadribrachys* 17cm, 6.5"

A beautiful kingfisher of forest rivers with a dark blue cap and wings contrasting with an electric blue back, a long black dagger bill, rich chestnut underparts, and dark blue breast smudges. Duller imm has a shorter black bill and dark scaling on the breast. **HH** singles and pairs are shy inhabitants of rivers and streams within forest from 700–1200m, rarely to 1800m, mainly in the west, and very rare in extreme WKe. **Vo** usually calls a single and not particularly sharp *tint,* which may be repeated.

Plate 113

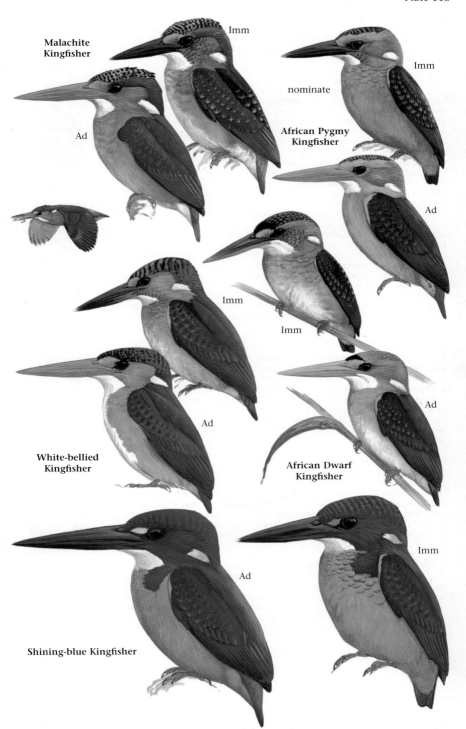

Malachite Kingfisher

Imm

Ad

nominate

African Pygmy Kingfisher

Imm

Ad

Imm

Imm

Ad

White-bellied Kingfisher

Ad

African Dwarf Kingfisher

Ad

Shining-blue Kingfisher

Imm

GREEN AND CINNAMON BEE-EATERS

A group of largely green and cinnamon bee-eaters usually encountered in pairs or small groups in open country (except for forest Cinnamon-chested). Colour of underparts, face pattern and tail shape aid identification, along with limited range overlap. Sexes are similar and immatures resemble adults but are duller. Sit fairly upright with slowly wagging tails and leave perches to sally out after insects, snapping them up with an audible click. Often associate with bush fires and termite emergences.

Little Bee-eater *Merops pusillus* 15cm, 6"

Small neat bee-eater: ad is green above with a yellow throat, a well-defined black gorget, and dull cinnamon-rufous underparts. Two races are common: *meridionalis* (widespread) has a short, narrow blue stripe just over the eye-mask and a blue top edge to the gorget; *cyanostictus* (in Ke) has longer blue superciliary stripes joining over the bill, and a thin purplish-blue top edge to the gorget. Imms are duller and paler than ads, washed variably pale green below. Larger Cinnamon-chested Bee-eater is a much richer and darker bird of forests. **HH** pairs or family groups are common in bushed and wooded grassland, and more open woodland from sea-level to 2200m. **Vo** calls a sharp high-pitched *tsip tsip...*, and when excited these break into a long metallic sequence interspersed with some quite musical nasal skirls.

Cinnamon-chested Bee-eater *Merops oreobates* 22cm, 8.5"

Similar to Little Bee-eater but much larger: *dark green above and deeper rufous-cinnamon below* (with variable white edge to rear of yellow cheek). Little or no blue above mask. Imm is paler, lacks black gorget, and is variably washed green below. In flight, tail appears longer, broader and largely green from above with a broad black tip. **HH** pairs and small groups are common in highland forest, forest edge and gardens from 1800–2300m, generally perching high in the canopy. **Vo** calls from excited birds are a very varied mixture of metallic chinks, slurs and trills, often rather cheerful in quality.

Blue-breasted Bee-eater *Merops variegatus* 18cm, 7"

Very like Little Bee-eater, but slightly larger and stockier: ad has a noticeable *white wedge on the cheek*, separating the yellow throat from the black eye mask. Blue in the eyebrow varies from limited to obvious. Blue-breasted is a confusing name, since the gorget varies from very dark blue to blackish, and often appears black in the field. Imm lacks the gorget, is duller green below, and has a less defined white cheek. **HH** pairs and small groups occupy reedbeds and damp areas fringing lakes and swamps from about 600–1800m. **Vo** calls with short dry and deep throaty trills suggestive of a small plover.

Böhm's Bee-eater *Merops boehmi* 23cm, 9"

A slender, distinctive bee-eater: ad has a *chestnut-rufous crown and lighter orange-rufous throat* with long black-tipped tail streamers. Imm is similar to ad, but has a yellowish throat fading to green and very short or no elongated central tail feathers. **HH** pairs or small groups are uncommon and local residents of dense bush, woodland, and forest edge preferring the vicinity of rivers and streams from 200–1400m in Tz. **Vo** call is a long attractive ramble of sharp high-pitched metallic notes that rise and fall.

Little Green Bee-eater *Merops orientalis* 24cm, 9.5"

Ad is a *very bright green streamer-tailed* bee-eater, with a narrow eye-mask and very narrow black gorget. Imm is similar, but paler, lacking the gorget and tail streamers. **HH** singles and small groups are rare visitors to sparsely wooded dry country in NUg from Aug–Sep (also recorded in May). **Vo** calls an uninteresting ramble of scratchy metallic notes with little variation.

Plate 114

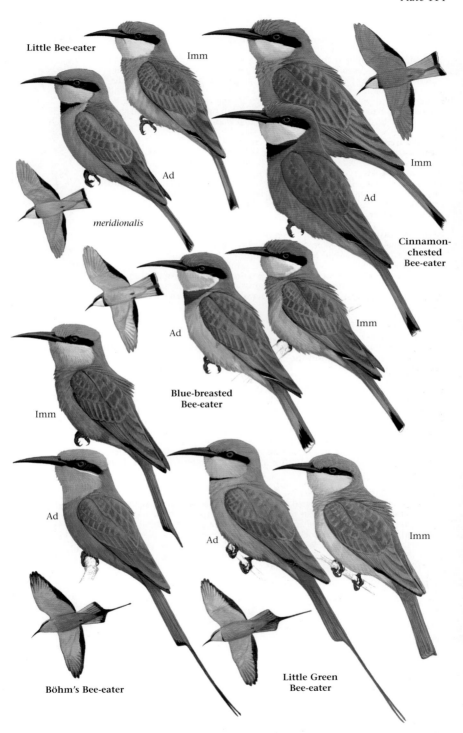

Little Bee-eater

Imm

meridionalis

Ad

Cinnamon-
chested
Bee-eater

Imm

Ad

Ad

Imm

Blue-breasted
Bee-eater

Imm

Ad

Imm

Böhm's Bee-eater

Little Green
Bee-eater

White-throated Bee-eater *Merops albicollis* 28cm, 11"
Ad is a pale blue-green bee-eater with a *striking black and white head pattern*, tawny nape, and long central tail feathers. Sexes are similar, but ♂ has slightly longer tail streamers. Imm is similar to ad, but has yellow wash over throat, is duller with many buff-edged feathers, and lacks the tail streamers. **HH** a common intra-African migrant from the southern Sahara (rarely breeding in NUg and Ke). Highly gregarious and vocal flocks disperse to woodland, bush and grassland, as well as more open forest and gardens mainly Aug–Apr from sea-level to 2000m (less often 3000m). **Vo** calls a rather harsh and throaty *chep*, which often breaks into musical slurs with several birds taking apart in an excitable wader-like chorus.

Somali Bee-eater *Merops revoilii* 17cm, 6.5"
Washed-out, slightly unkempt bee-eater: ad is pale blue-green above, with a *white throat, and pale apricot underparts*. Imm is duller version of ad. In flight, reveals silvery-blue rump and undertail. **HH** singles and pairs are shy, solitary and sedentary residents below 1000m in arid and semi-arid bushland in EKe (away from the coast), and vagrant to Tz. **Vo** rarely heard call consists of a long ramble of musical and excitable though rather mournful chits and whistled slurs.

Swallow-tailed Bee-eater *Merops hirundineus* 22cm, 8.5"
Elegant blue-green bee-eater: ad has a yellow throat, narrow blue gorget and a *long deeply forked blue tail*. Sexes are similar, but ♀ is paler with a thinner gorget, and shallower fork. Imm is also similar, but has a whitish throat and no gorget with a less forked tail. **HH** pairs and small groups are never common in drier bushed and wooded grassland below 1500m. **Vo** sweet musical slurs and trills with a rather wader-like quality are called for long periods.

FOREST BEE-EATERS
Shy, confiding and dark forest-dependent bee-eaters: launch for levels, but are usually high in the canopy. Typical stance is up wagging tails.

Blue-headed Bee-eater *Merops muelleri* 19cm, 7.5"
Ad is largely dark blue with a black-rimmed scarlet throat forehead, and *rufous-brown back and wings*. Sexes alike, imm is m duller blue-green below without the scarlet throat. **HH** in o gles and pairs are uncommon and local residents of forest and ings restricted to Kakamega and South Nandi forests in W consist of a repeated simple *swir-swi swi* starting with a raspy sl spersed with metallic tinks, resulting in a medley punctuate pauses.

Black Bee-eater *Merops gularis* 20cm, 8"
Ad is a stunning scarlet-throated black and turquoise bee-eater with *brilliant turquoise-blue streaks across the lower breast*: wings and back are black. Sexes are similar. Imm duller and lacks scarlet throat. **HH** solitary birds, pairs and sometimes small flocks are residents of primary and riverine forest, including clearings, in WUg. **Vo** calls are extremely hard, very high-pitched, and often paired, with a short first note *siit sit s'sit...p'sit p'sit seet...*, the whole sequence sounding quite random.

Plate 115

White-throated Bee-eater

Ad

Imm

Imm

Somali Bee-eater

Ad

Imm

Ad

Imm

Swallow-tailed Bee-eater

Imm

Imm

Ad

Blue-headed Bee-eater

Ad

Black Bee-eater

LARGE MIGRANT BEE-EATERS

Elegant long-winged migrants with confident loose-wheeling flight. Blue-cheeked and Madagasar bee-eaters differ mainly in head-colour, while European is unmistakable if seen well. Sexes are similar: duller immatures have brown, not red, eyes.

European Bee-eater *Merops apiaster* 28cm, 11"

A striking *chestnut and golden bee-eater with a yellow throat and pale blue underparts*. In fresh plumage, ad ♂ has broad golden sides to chestnut back: non-br ♂ and ♀ are much duller and greener above. At rest or in flight, ads show projecting central tail feathers which are slightly shorter in ♀, and absent in young birds. Imm is greenish above, with a brown washed crown, dull green sides to back, a pale yellow throat and blue underparts. **HH** small to large flocks on passage are harbingers of Palearctic migration even in Jul, but main southward movement is Sep–Nov, with a more sporadic northward passage Mar–May. Prefers open country from sea-level to 3000m. **Vo** far-carrying, loud and attractive calls are very fluid and deep throaty trills and churrs *prrutt, prrutt prrutt* often with many birds calling together.

Blue-cheeked Bee-eater *Merops persicus* 30cm, 12"

Slender vivid emerald-green bee-eater: ad has a *green crown, blue borders to the eye-mask*, and a yellow chin blending with the orange-brown throat. ♀ has shorter tail streamers. Imm is duller with less blue around the eye and no tail streamers. Particularly obvious cinnamon underwings in banking flight. **HH** small parties are regular throughout the region from Oct–Apr, preferring bushed and wooded grassland below 1500m, often close to water. **Vo** calls an attractive fluid trill *preepp, preepp, preepp*, which is repeated for long periods with slight changes in tone.

Madagascar Bee-eater *Merops superciliosus* 30cm, 12"

[Olive Bee-eater]
Overall slightly duller than similar Blue-cheeked Bee-eater, with a *smoky olive-brown cap, white borders to the eye-mask*, and a dull brick-red throat. ♀ has shorter tail streamers. Imm is much duller than ad and lacks the bold head pattern. It is very similar to imm Blue-cheeked, but is less green with a more uniform throat. In flight, shows plain cinnamon underwings like Blue-cheeked. **HH** small flocks are non-br visitors from the south, mainly from Apr–Sep below 1500m (but up to 2300m) in bushed and wooded country, often near water. A few breed in the coastal lowlands, and some may be present all year round. **Vo** very similar to Blue-cheeked Bee-eater, but slightly higher-pitched and less fluid.

RED-THROATED BEE-EATERS

Closely related, attractive, resident highly social and colonial bee-eaters identified by head pattern and range. Sexes alike.

White-fronted Bee-eater *Merops bullockoides* 23m, 9"

Colourful rather upright bee-eater: ad has a *white forecrown and stripe separating red throat from the eye-mask*, is green above, warm buff-cinnamon below, with a deep cobalt-blue vent. Imm is similar but subdued with an orange-yellow, not red, throat. **HH** pairs and flocks are widespread and sometimes common (notably in the Rift Valley and STz), associating with open water and rivers, bushed and wooded country to 2000m. **Vo** utters a distinct rather nasal and muffled *gaaar,* and a variety of other pinched slurred notes which may rise and fall.

Red-throated Bee-eater *Merops bulocki* 23cm, 9"

Similar to White-fronted Bee-eater, but ad has an *entirely red throat and blue-green forecrown*. Imm is duller with a red-orange throat and a green stripe below the eye-mask. **HH** pairs and flocks are local, but also common and gregarious residents of bushed and wooded grassland, near lakes and rivers, below 1000m in NWUg. **Vo** calls with a variety of short musical yaps, churls and trills, which are usually higher pitched than those of White-fronted.

Plate 116

European
Bee-eater

Imm

Blue-cheeked
Bee-eater

Imm

Ad

Ad

Madagascar
Bee-eater

Ad

Imm

Imm

Imm

Ad

Ad

White-fronted Bee-eater

Ad

Red-throated Bee-eater

CARMINE BEE-EATERS

Large long-tailed carmine-red and turquoise-blue bee-eaters easily separated by throat colour (they are considered conspecific by some authors). Intra-African migrants which move south (Northern) and north (Southern) towards the Equator after breeding. Both species have similar powerful, wheeling flight. Sexes are similar.

Northern Carmine Bee-eater   *Merops nubicus*   38cm, 15"

Ad is bright carmine above, with a turquoise-blue rump, lower belly and vent, a *well-defined green-blue crown and throat*, and long central tail feathers. Imm is much duller with a strong olive-brown wash, mottled head and throat, and short tail streamers. **HH** single birds and flocks are regular visitors to bushed and wooded grassland, as well as cultivation in N and EKe, NUg, and ETz from Sep–Apr, usually below 1200m. Sometimes very common in coastal districts and a few birds linger throughout the year. Occasionally breeds in extreme NKe. **Vo** calls unattractive loud skirls, chitters and complaining notes, lacking the sweetness or variation of smaller bee-eaters.

Southern Carmine Bee-eater   *Merops nubicoides*   38cm, 15"
[Carmine Bee-eater]

Very similar to Northern Carmine Bee-eater, but *throat is brilliant carmine: green-blue is restricted to crown.* Imm is much duller and browner, lacks any blue on the throat, and has short tail streamers. **HH** small to large flocks are regular visitors to bushland, bushed and wooded grassland in WTz as far north as Lake Victoria and Akagera NP in Rw from Mar–Aug (and as a vagrant in SKe). Often associate with bush fires and plains game. **Vo** calls are similar to Northern Carmine, but more musical and varied.

BROAD-BILLED ROLLERS

Compact bright chestnut rollers (which appear dark at distance) with broad bright yellow bills. Acrobatic, agile and slender in flight, often appearing rather falcon-like. Always choose to perch conspicuously at the top of tallest trees. Sexes alike.

Broad-billed Roller   *Eurystomus glaucurus*   28cm, 11"

Ad is a *bright chestnut roller* (variably washed lilac below) with a *broad yellow bill.* Imm is much duller brown above with a dusky yellow bill and pale blue underparts. In flight, birds show a strong contrast between chestnut back and deep azure-blue outerwing and tail. **HH** singles, pairs or small groups are sometimes common residents and intra-African migrants in bushed and wooded grassland, woodland and forest edge from sea-level to 2200m. **Vo** calls deep and raspy single *ahk* or *wak*, and a *uh-uh-uh-uhuhuhuhuh* in rapid sequence.

Blue-throated Roller   *Eurystomus gularis*   25cm, 10"

Very similar to Broad-billed Roller, but slightly smaller with a *blue throat patch* (which can be hard to see) and rufous, not blue, vent. Imm is duller and browner with a dusky bill and pale blue underparts. In flight, may appear darker and less contrasting than Broad-billed. **HH** singles and pairs are resident, local and often rather uncommon in forest and associated dense woodland below 1800m. **Vo** calls a nasal trumpeted squeak repeated slowly or excitedly, and tern-like laughing which may be given in chorus.

Plate 117

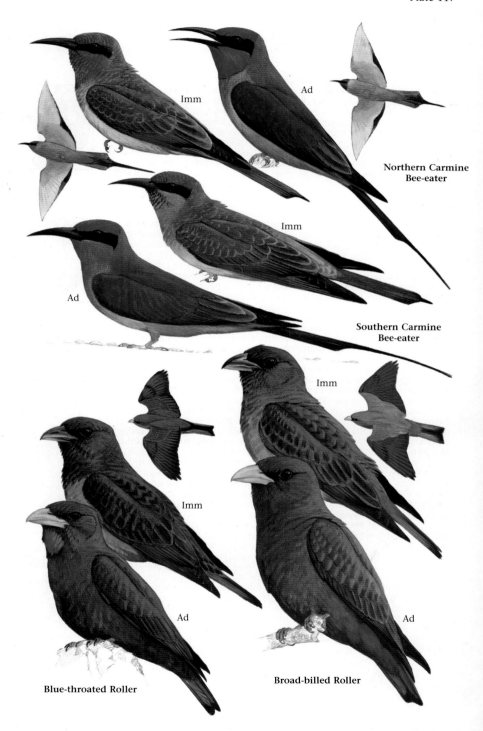

Imm

Ad

Northern Carmine Bee-eater

Imm

Ad

Southern Carmine Bee-eater

Imm

Imm

Ad

Blue-throated Roller

Ad

Broad-billed Roller

BLUE AND CHESTNUT ROLLERS

Striking blue and chestnut rollers: best identified by presence or absence of lilac on throat and by tail shape and length. Bold and confiding, they drop onto prey on the ground from prominent perches like roadside poles. All have raucous calls and perform rolling display flights. Sexes alike.

Lilac-breasted Roller *Coracias caudata* 38cm, 15"

A striking blue roller: the nominate race has a lilac throat and breast, light olive-chestnut back, dark blue wing-coverts, and deep blue underparts. Outer-tail streamers are slender and straight. Race *lorti* (**Lilac-throated Roller**) differs in having a small lilac throat patch. Imm is much duller and greener above, with a brownish wash to throat and breast, and no tail streamers. **HH** pairs are widespread and common residents in open bush country, wooded grassland, woodland and cultivation from sea-level to 2000m (less often 3000m). Race *lorti* is largely confined to NEKe, but wanders occasionally to NTz. **Vo** displaying birds give loud dry rasps breaking into a long series that develops into a harsh rattle. Calls of race *lorti* are similar but possibly more nasal.

Racket-tailed Roller *Coracias spatulata* 38cm, 15"

In our area, race *weigalli* is very similar to Lilac-breasted Roller, but has a richer chestnut back, largely chestnut wing-coverts, and *elongated outer-tail feathers terminating in small rackets* (often hard to see at distance). Imm is duller with a muddy crown and nape: largely brown, not blue, wing-coverts and greenish not purple throat separate it from imm Lilac-breasted. **HH** pairs and occasionally small groups are fairly uncommon in miombo woodland in C and STz. Shy and less inclined to perch in open. **Vo** more musical than other East African rollers, breeding birds give a complex series of accelerated downslurs with a rather raptor-like quality.

Abyssinian Roller *Coracias abyssinica* 41cm, 16"

Slender vivid blue roller with a rufous-brown back and very long outer-tail streamers. Appears bluer than other species, like a slim long-tailed European Roller. Imm is duller than ad, with an olive-brown tinge to the back, and a squared tail without any streamers. **HH** singles and less often small groups are common local residents and less common wanderers in semi-arid bush and woodland across NUg and NKe below 1000m. **Vo** calls are very harsh and unpleasant variable loud rasps.

European Roller *Coracias garrulus* 31cm, 12"

Robust, thickset roller with a blue head, chestnut-brown back, blue underparts and a rather short square cut tail (without streamers). On arrival in Oct, non-br ads and 1st year birds are very pale with washed out green-blue heads and underparts, and muddy brown backs. Prior to departure in Apr, ads are a striking blue, with bright chestnut backs, purplish-blue wing-coverts and rumps. **HH** singles (often moving together in loose associations) are common Palearctic visitors and passage migrants from Oct–Apr, typically in bushed and wooded grassland below 1500m. **Vo** usually silent in region, but may occasional utter a deep croak.

Rufous-crowned Roller *Coracias naevia* 33cm, 13"

[Purple Roller]

Big-headed thickset roller which lacks the blue underparts of other species. Ad has a rufous crown with a broad white supercilium and is rufous-purple below broadly streaked with white. In flight, dark purple-blue flight feathers contrast sharply with the rufous wing-coverts and a greenish back. Imm similar, but duller and greener both above and below. **HH** singles and pairs are local but never numerous, often associating with rocky areas and large trees in drier wooded and bushed grassland to 2000m (sometimes up to 3000m). Erratic and occasional influxes of non-residents occur. **Vo** calls a loud, harsh and throaty *ouw*, and in display flight a strident *ak-ak-ak-aka-aka-aka-aka…kiau-kiau-kiau...*

Plate 118

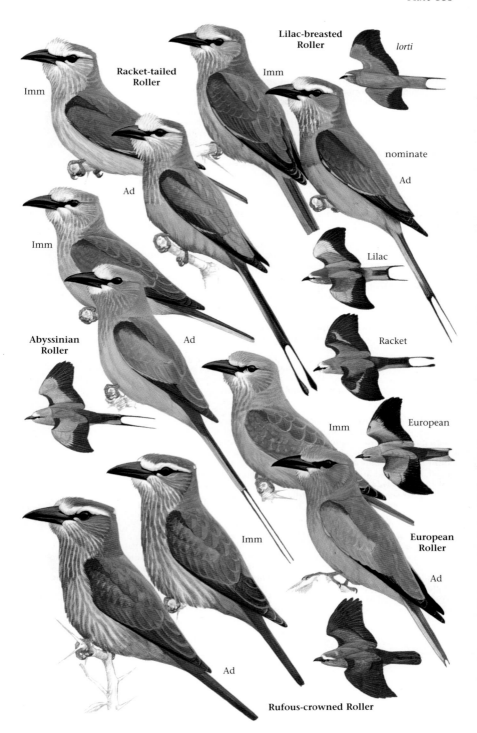

Imm

Racket-tailed
Roller

Imm

Lilac-breasted
Roller

lorti

Ad

nominate

Ad

Lilac

Imm

Abyssinian
Roller

Ad

Racket

European

Imm

Imm

European
Roller

Ad

Ad

Rufous-crowned Roller

WOOD-HOOPOES

Wood-hoopoes are endemic to Africa, and are closely related to the scimitarbills (see plate 120). They are a similar group of clumsy, glossy, long-tailed social birds best identified by careful attention to the exact colour of head, back and bill, as well as range and habitat. Sexes similar, but males are slightly larger than females with longer more decurved bills.

Green Wood-hoopoe *Phoeniculus purpureus* 37cm, 14.5"
[Red-billed Wood-hoopoe]

Ad is a large red-billed iridescent bird with a white spot and bar in the wing, and a long graduated white-tipped tail. Two races occur: widespread *marwitzi* is relatively easy to identify with a *green head and back* (although the wings may shine violet and blue), while northern *niloticus* is generally more violet-blue and very similar to Violet Wood-hoopoe, but will always shows *some green on the head* (if watched for several minutes). Imms are dull blackish, with brownish throat patches, straighter and shorter black bills, and dark legs. **HH** extended family groups are common and widespread in a wide range of wooded and forested habitats from sea-level to 2800m, with race *niloticus* occurring in NWKe as far south as Lake Bogoria. **Vo** nasal, bubbling and maniacal cackling in which group members engage in noisy displays (calls probably indistinguishable from Violet and Black-billed wood-hoopoes).

Violet Wood-hoopoe *Phoeniculus damarensis* 37cm, 14.5"

In our area, ad of race *granti* is very similar to Green Wood-hoopoe race *niloticus*, but head, nape and back only shine violet-blue, with *green restricted to the throat*. Imm is duller with a brown-buff streaked throat and shorter black bill. **HH** family groups are local and uncommon in semi-arid and arid bush and woodland, often associating with rivers and doum palms. **Vo** probably not distinguishable from Green Wood-hoopoe.

Black-billed Wood-hoopoe *Phoeniculus somaliensis* 37cm, 14.5"

Very similar to Green Wood-hoopoe (formerly considered a race), but has a more violet and blue gloss, and a black bill (sometimes with limited red to base). Imm is duller with some buff on the throat, a shorter black bill, and black legs. **HH** family groups are fairly common but confined to NEKe, where they occupy semi-arid bushed and wooded areas, often in larger acacias and riverine woodland. **Vo** probably not distinguishable from Green Wood-hoopoe.

Forest Wood-hoopoe *Phoeniculus castaneiceps* 25cm, 10"

Smaller wood-hoopoe which lacks white in either wings or tail and has a dark grey bill, with a *creamy-yellow cutting edge*. In ♂ head colour is highly variable being brown, white or glossy dark green. ♀ is always brown-headed. Imm is duller than ad, lacking the gloss, and always with a dark brown head. **HH** singles and family groups are rather uncommon residents of forest from 1200–2300m in WUg east to Mt Elgon (but apparently lost from extreme WKe), Rw (Nyungwe), and in NWTz (Miniziro). **Vo** group members maintain contact with a very high-pitched *sii-sii-sii* call, also in flight.

White-headed Wood-hoopoe *Phoeniculus bollei* 35cm, 14"

Ad has a *white head (extent of white varies between individuals), red bill* and plain blue and green glossed wings and tail. Imm has a black bill and gains white head quickly. Red bill and legs separate them from the white-headed form of Forest Wood-hoopoe. **HH** family groups are common and widespread in forest from 900–3000m in the west (but mainly restricted to highland forest above 2000m in Ke and extreme NTz). **Vo** similar to Green Wood-hoopoe, but notes are fuller, less nasal and more of a rattle.

Plate 119

marwitzi

Ad

Imm

**Green
Wood-hoopoe**

Green

**Violet
Wood-hoopoe**

Imm

Ad

Violet

Imm

Imm

Ad

**Forest
Wood-hoopoe**

**White-headed
Wood-hoopoe**

Ad

**Black-billed
Wood-hoopoe**

HOOPOES

Bizarre crested rufous-cinnamon and black and white birds. Often seen in buoyant butterfly-like flight, or walking on the ground where they dig for food with slightly decurved bills. Name derived from calls. The two taxa are often considered conspecific.

African Hoopoe *Upupa africana* 28cm, 11"

Ad is most easily identified from Eurasian Hoopoe in flight when it reveals *all black primaries*, but also differs in being darker and more richly rufous-cinnamon, and having plain black tips to the crest (not the black and white, or black and buff of Eurasian). Sexes very similar. Imm is also similar to ad, but is darker and rather browner. **HH** singles and pairs are common residents, as well as local wanderers, in a wide range of bushed and wooded grassland, and open woodland from sea-level to 2200m, including gardens and cultivation. Often on ground, crest usually closed, but fanned up when alarmed or excited. **Vo** a double *pooh-pooh* given at about 3 second intervals (which is very similar to African Cuckoo).

Eurasian Hoopoe *Upupa epops* 28cm, 11"

Three races occur: all are quite similar to African Hoopoe, but differ in having a *bold white band across the primaries* and a narrow band of white (nominate) or pale buff *(waibeli* and *senegalensis)* below the black tips of the crest. These races differ from each other in the overall tones of the back, head and underparts: *waibeli* is the darkest, *senegalensis* intermediate, and nominate the palest. Imms are duller versions of ads. **HH** race *waibeli* is resident in extreme NWKe, but migrates south as far as Entebbe, Ug, and Nairobi, Ke; *senegalensis* occurs in extreme NKe; while nominate birds are uncommon visitors from the Palearctic south into drier northern areas of Ug and Ke, and rarely into NETz from Oct–Mar. **Vo** calls may be indistinguishable from African Hoopoe.

SCIMITARBILLS

Like small slim wood-hoopoes (plate 119), but recent evidence suggests they are not related. Scimitarbills are less social, usually occurring as pairs. They can be identified by bill colour, presence or absence of white in wing, and range. Females are slightly duller than males, and often washed brown on the throat and breast.

Abyssinian Scimitarbill *Rhinopomastus minor* 24cm, 9.5"

Small and neat, ad has a sharply decurved bright *orange-red bill and all black glossed blue-purple plumage* (lacking any white in the wings or tail). Imm similar, but all brownish below with a dull brownish-red bill. **HH** pairs are locally common but widespread in drier bushed and wooded grassland to 1400 (less often 2000m), including acacia scrub, preferring more arid and open areas than Common Scimitarbill. **Vo** usual call is a hollow rattle of identical notes, terminating on a single or double lower note *k-k—k-k-k-k-k-k-k-kiow,* and also a *kreekreekreekree...* given as a piercing burry scream.

Common Scimitarbill *Rhinopomastus cyanomelas* 30cm, 12"

[Greater Scimitarbill]

Larger than Abyssinian Scimitarbill, but with a slight violet gloss: ad has a decurved black bill, a white wing bar across the primaries, and white tips to the tail (may also show a little white in the coverts). Imm similar, but has a shorter straighter bill, and less violet gloss. **HH** pairs are fairly common and widespread in bush and bushland, and riverine forest, from sea-level to 2400m. **Vo** normal call is a loud repeated downslurred sequence *quee-quee-quee-kirr-kirr-quee...,* also a hollow wooden rattle and a high pitched *sisisisisi* while foraging.

Black Scimitarbill *Rhinopomastus aterrimus* 27cm, 10.5"

Similar to Common Scimitarbill, but in our area race *emini* is black lightly glossed blue, with a shorter less decurved black bill (sometimes with creamy sides), a white band across the primaries, *variable small white bar in the primary coverts*, and a less graduated tail with white tips. Imm similar to ad, but duller and less iridescent. **HH** pairs are uncommon below 2000m in woodland and bushland N and NWUg only. **Vo** call is a carrying fluty but mournful *kwee-kwee-kwee...* given as a descending sequence with a muffled short last note.

Plate 120

senegalensis

nominate

African Hoopoe

Eurasian Hoopoe

Ad

Imm

Abyssinian Scimitarbill

Abyssinian

Black

Black Scimitarbill

Common Scimitarbill

Imm

Ad

Ad

Imm

Common

HORNBILLS

Noisy and characterful birds of many habitats from semi-arid bush to lowland forest. Most are black and white varying in size from diminutive dwarf to giant casqued hornbills. Unique breeding behaviour involves the female being encased within a cavity and fed by her mate while she incubates the eggs and rears the young.

DRY BUSH HORNBILLS

Smaller hornbills which are widespread and characteristic birds of the African bush. Genus name *Tockus* is derived from the atmospheric *tok tok* calls made by some. Colour of bill and wing markings aid identification.

Eastern Yellow-billed Hornbill   *Tockus flavirostris*   51cm, 20"

Typical bush hornbill easily identified by a combination of *banana-yellow bill* and white-spotted wing-coverts. Ad ♂ has a slightly larger bill with a thicker casque than ad ♀, and rich rose-pink rather than black bare throat patches. Imm has smaller dusky yellow bill and is less clearly marked. **HH** pairs and family groups are widespread at low densities in semi-arid bush country and drier wooded grassland mainly below 1400m. Form associations with groups of Dwarf Mongoose, acting as look-outs for birds of prey, and benefiting from the insects flushed. **Vo** regularly calls a gently rising and falling series of very low pitched and throaty rasping notes *kruk-kruk-krukrukrukruk-krakrakrark-kerkrukrukruk...*

Red-billed Hornbill   *Tockus erythrorhynchus*   45cm, 18"

Much smaller than similar Eastern Yellow-billed Hornbill with a *slender more decurved red bill* and a whiter face and neck. Ad ♂ has slightly heavier bill than ad ♀, often with a blacker base to the lower mandible. Imm is duller, with buff spots on the wing-coverts and a smaller dull red bill. **HH** pairs, family parties and sometimes larger flocks are common and widespread residents in dry bush and woodland up to 1400m, less often 2000m. **Vo** calls a rather urgent rising and falling series of nasal *kankankankankankank-kik-hahaha-kik-hahaha...* which is higher pitched than other similar hornbills.

Von der Decken's Hornbill   *Tockus deckeni*   48cm, 19"

Striking pied hornbill that is similar to Jackson's Hornbill, but has *unspotted black wing-coverts*. Ad ♂ *has a large red-orange bill with a well-defined creamy-yellow tip*, ad ♀ has an all-black bill. Imm resembles ♀, but has a duller bill and indistinct white spotting on the wing-coverts. **HH** pairs and family parties are widespread and common in dry bushed and wooded grassland from sea-level to 1700m. **Vo** calls a long series of low-pitched *kuk-kuk-kukukukukukukuk-kuk...* all on the same tone.

Jackson's Hornbill   *Tockus jacksoni*   48cm, 19"

Similar to Von der Decken's Hornbill, but has *boldly spotted wing-coverts*. Ad ♂ also has a red bill, but with a smaller less defined creamy tip, ad ♀ has an all-black bill. Imms are duller than ads. **HH** pairs and family groups are common in semi-arid and arid country in NWKe and NEUg from 350–2000m (where they replace Von der Decken's Hornbill). **Vo** calls a long sequence of low rasping *krukrukrukrukruk...* all on much the same tone.

Hemprich's Hornbill   *Tockus hemprichii*   59cm, 23"

Larger rather scruffy bush hornbill which is blackish above with pale fringes to the wings and a dusky red bill (brighter lower mandible in ad ♂, largely black in ad ♀). Imm is similar to ♀. In undulating and buoyant flight, appears dark above and white-bellied with *white stripes inset from the black outer-tail*. **HH** pairs and family groups are local to dry bush and woodland with rocky outcrops and cliffs from 950–1300m in NEUg and NKe. Birds wander, but depend on rock crevices in cliffs and gorges for nesting. **Vo** calls a dramatic long series of loud whistled *kek-kek-kek...* notes that start slowly and then accelerate into a frantic piping *pip-pip-pip-pipip...ipip-ipipipi...* before fading away.

Plate 121

Eastern Yellow-billed Hornbill

♀

♂

Red-billed Hornbill

♀

♂

Von der Decken's Hornbill

♀

♂

♀

Jackson's Hornbill

♀

♂

♀

♂

Hemprich's Hornbill

WOODLAND HORNBILLS
Largely woodland species with loud piping calls, and dramatic courtship displays in which they rock on perches, point their bills skywards, and flick open their wings. Primarily arboreal, but agile, and will drop to the ground to feed.

African Grey Hornbill *Tockus nasutus* 51cm, 20"

Dull grey-brown hornbill with pale edges to the wing feathers and a *long pale supercilium which extends down side of neck to nape*. In nominate race, ad ♂ has a dark bill with a slender flat casque and a striking creamy-white wedge at base; ad ♂ of smaller race *epirhinus* has a casque ending in a slim raised tube. In both races, ad ♀ has no casque, a purplish-red bill tip and a larger yellow-white wedge. Imm similar to ads, but duller with buff feather edges and a smaller blackish bill. In undulating flight, reveals white corners to its long grey-brown tail. **HH** pairs and groups are widespread and common residents in woodland, bushed and wooded grassland, from sea-level to 1700m. Nominate in most of Ug and Ke, while *epirhinus* is widespread from SUg, through Tz into SEKe. **Vo** calls a sharp *pi pi pi...* that accelerates and develops into a descending rather sad piping *pipipipipipi pieu pieu*. In flight, also often calls a single far-carrying *pieu*.

Pale-billed Hornbill *Tockus pallidirostris* 51cm, 20"

Very similar to African Grey Hornbill, but has a *pale creamy-yellow bill* with an orangey tip. Ad ♂ has a slightly longer casque than ad ♀. Imm resembles ad, but is duller with a smaller duskier bill. Similar buoyant flight to African Grey. **HH** pairs and family groups are local (almost endemic) to miombo woodland below 1200m in C and STz, and rarely further N. **Vo** call is very similar to African Grey Hornbill, but piping whistles are slightly deeper and fuller.

Crowned Hornbill *Tockus alboterminatus* 55cm, 21.5"

Slender dark hornbill with a *bright red bill and long black tail with white corners*. Two races occur: eastern and paler-backed *suahelicus* and more western black-backed *geloensis*. Despite name, no obvious crown, but white streaks behind the eyes create a dark capped effect. Ad ♂ is slightly larger than ad ♀ with a heavier casque. Imm is similar to ♀, but duller, with a dull yellowish bill. In rather floppy undulating flight, birds show the obvious white tips to outer-tail. **HH** pairs and family groups are quite widespread and common in woodland and forest edges from the coast to 3000m. **Vo** calls a very sharp high-pitched *kip-kip-kip* and a long piercing refrain that rises and falls *kwi-kwi-kwikwikwi* which is more musical than African Pied Hornbill.

African Pied Hornbill *Tockus fasciatus* 55cm, 21.5"

Similar to Crowned Hornbill, but markedly pied with a *pale yellow bill* tipped reddish-black. Ad ♂ has a slightly larger casque than ad ♀. Imm is similar to ♀ with a plain yellow bill. Flight is swooping and buoyant revealing *white stripes inset from black outer-tail*. **HH** pairs and small groups are common residents in W and SUg, from 700–1200m. Occupy primary and secondary forest where they are often encountered slowly working through the forest canopy, but also exploit more open areas to visit isolated fruiting trees. **Vo** calls a high-pitched squealed series of *kwi-kwi-kwi-kwikwikwikwik-wi-kwi-kwi...* that accelerates in the middle.

Plate 122

Imm

nominate

♀

epirhinus ♂

♂

African Grey Hornbill

♀

Imm

♂

Pale-billed Hornbill

Imm

♀

♂

suahelicus

Crowned Hornbill

♀

♂

African Pied Hornbill

WESTERN FOREST HORNBILLS

A mixed group of forest-dependent hornbills. All are easily identified: dwarf hornbills are very small, White-crested is extremely long-tailed, and Piping is the smallest of the *Bycanistes* hornbills (see plate 124). Along with African Pied Hornbill (on plate 122) all these species are restricted to the west in our area.

Piping Hornbill   *Bycanistes fistulator*   61cm, 24"

Ad ♂ is glossed black above with a black throat and breast, and a gleaming white belly. Bill is creamy-white with a dusky patch in the centre. Ad ♀ is slightly smaller with a paler bill and a greenish not black eye-ring. Imm is duller with a darker bill and no casque. In flight, reveals *white secondaries and small white primary tips, and a black tail with mainly white sides.* **HH** pairs and small groups are sometimes common in primary forest, often associating with fruiting trees, in Semliki and Budongo forests in extreme WUg. **Vo** calls with trumpeted nasal notes which are given slowly and then accelerate into a laugh *ah-ah-ah-ah-hahahahahaha-ah-ah...*

Red-billed Dwarf Hornbill   *Tockus camurus*   36cm, 14"

A very small rufous-brown and white hornbill with a red bill. Close views reveal broad white scaling on the wing-coverts, a white breast to vent, and a dark brown tail with white tips to the corners. Ad ♀ is a little smaller than ad ♂, with a black-tipped bill. Both have pale yellow eyes. Imm is similar to ad, but has grey eyes, and duller orangey bill. **HH** small groups are sometimes common in primary forest at 700m in Semliki Forest, WUg, and less commonly in secondary forest. Fairly inconspicuous, but birds are often seen in mixed-species flocks or associating with ant-swarms. **Vo** utters a rising and falling fluty and mournful series of downslurs *we-we-we-we-we-weeo-weeo-weeow-weeow.*

Black Dwarf Hornbill   *Tockus hartlaubi*   36cm, 14"

A very small black and grey-white hornbill with a dark bill and an obvious broad white supercilium. Tail is black with all but the central tail feathers tipped white. Ad ♂ has a black bill with a dark red tip; ad ♀ has an all-black bill. Imm resembles ad ♀. **HH** singles, pairs or small family groups are uncommon residents at 700m in Semliki Forest, WUg. Birds prefer the canopy, often sitting still for long periods as they scan for prey. **Vo** calls consist of clucks followed by a short pause and then two rising piping squeals *kukukukuk kwi-kor kwi-kor.*

White-crested Hornbill   *Tropicranus albocristatus*   71cm, 28"

Highly distinctive and un-hornbill-like with a *rounded white crest and very long graduated, white-tipped tail* (like a giant wood-hoopoe). Ad ♂ has a small casqued black bill with a variable pale wedge at base; ad ♀ is similar but slightly smaller. Imm is similar to ads, but has a dingy green bill. **HH** pairs and family groups are scarce in primary forest at 700m in Semliki Forest, WUg. Despite long tail, birds are graceful on the wing weaving through forest middle-storey with ease. **Vo** call starts with a nasal trumpet that rises in tone ending in a explosive high-pitched bark *errrrrrrrr-yow,* which may then be repeated at a higher pitch finishing with various warped squeals.

Plate 123

Piping Hornbill

Red-billed Dwarf
Hornbill

Black Dwarf
Hornbill

White-crested
Hornbill

LARGE FOREST HORNBILLS

Large, exuberant forest hornbills (includes Piping Hornbill on plate 123 and Black-casqued Hornbill on plate 125). All are black and white with large casques, but can be identified by the extent of white in plumage, and by range. They often roost and sunbathe together, sometimes in mixed-species flocks. Despite their size, they are agile in flight, twisting and turning through the canopy. Calls are raucous and far-carrying, but they also utter soft clucks, bleats and grunts when feeding.

Trumpeter Hornbill *Bycanistes bucinator* 66cm, 26"

Mainly black above, with a black throat and upper breast very clearly separated from a white lower breast and belly. Ad ♂ has a heavier bill with a longer casque than ad ♀. Both sexes have bright pink eye-rings. Imm is similar to ♀ with an insignificant casque. Flying birds show *narrow white trailing edge to most of wing*. **HH** groups are common in forests, woodlands and mature gardens from the coast up to 1650m (rarely to 2200m), and often flock with Silvery-cheeked Hornbills. **Vo** a loud far-carrying, distressed braying (recalls a crying baby) *naaay-naaaaaay-naaaaay-naaaay* which often weakens and dies away as if the bird has lost interest in calling.

Silvery-cheeked Hornbill *Bycanistes brevis* 74cm, 29"

Larger than Trumpeter Hornbill with *white underparts confined to lower belly and vent*. Face and ear-coverts are tipped silvery in ads, but often hard to see at a distance. Ad ♂ has a massive bill and pale cream casque which may extend beyond the bill tip and a blue-grey eye-ring, while ad ♀ has a duller low casque confined to back half of bill, and a pinkish eye-ring. Imm is duller with a smaller bill, brownish face and dull not brownish-red eyes. *In flight, reveals entirely black upperwings* and a white carpal patch in the underwing. **HH** family parties are widespread and locally common in highland forests, woodlands and mature gardens from sea-level to 2600m. **Vo** strident and loud goat-like braying *wa-wa-wa-wa-wa* and a longer rising and falling *aah-aaaah-aaaah-aaah-aah-ah* which lacks the pathetic crying edge and die-away effect of Trumpeter Hornbill.

Black-and-white-casqued Hornbill *Bycanistes subcylindricus* 74cm, 29"

Similar size to Silvery-cheeked Hornbill but with much more extensive white in the wings. Ad ♂ has a shorter bicoloured casque (blackish at front and pale behind); ad ♀ has a smaller darker casque. Both sexes have greyish eye-rings which tend to be more pinkish-red in ♀. Duller imm has a small black bill lacking the casque and dull eyes. *In flight, reveals broad white band along back of wing* (primaries and secondaries), *and a black tail with white corners*. **HH** groups may be common in mature woodland and forests including riverine areas, and in cultivated land with large trees from 700–2600m in most of Ug, Rw and Bu, as well as in WKe and NWTz. **Vo** spectacular and musical bugled *waah* or *waaaah* developing into a cacophonous din when birds call together.

White-thighed Hornbill *Bycanistes cylindricus* 71cm, 28"

In our area, race *albotibialis* occurs: ad ♂ has a large cream casque and yellowish bare skin round the eye, white belly and thighs (not unique!), and an *all-white tail with a black band*. Ad ♀ is similar, but has a smaller bill and casque. Imm is duller than ads with no casque on bill. Has broad white band along back of wing like Black-and-white-casqued Hornbill, but all-white tail with black central band is obvious in flight. **HH** pairs and small groups are rather local residents of primary forest from 900–1400m in extreme WUg. **Vo** calls a very dry and rasping long sequence of identical upslurs *rrah-rrah-rrah...* which sometimes accelerate.

Plate 124

Trumpeter
Hornbill

Silvery-cheeked
Hornbill

Black-and-
white-casqued
Hornbill

White-thighed
Hornbill

Black-casqued Wattled Hornbill *Ceratogymna atrata* 80cm, 31"

Stonking great forest hornbill which is *all-black with white tips to the tail*. Ad ♂ has a large bill and a very large blackish casque, rough feathering on the back of the head, and bare blue skin around the eye with blue wattles (which dangle in flight). Smaller ad ♀ is similar, but with a reduced casque and rusty-brown head. Imm is similar to ♀, but has a dark brown head, lacks the wattles, and has a pale casque-less bill. Flight is direct and strong, revealing all-black plumage (except for white tail tips), and making a striking loud whooshing which is audible over long distances. **HH** pairs and small family groups are not uncommon in the canopy of dense primary forest in the Semliki lowlands in WUg at 700m. **Vo** a very loud high-toned musical barking sequence which concludes with a rising and falling *kwaa-a-wah* which is audible over long distances.

GROUND-HORNBILLS

An endemic family of atypical pedestrian hornbills adapted to ground dwelling (hence name), and some of Africa's most engaging birds. Live in closely knit co-operative family groups and do not seal their nests. Walk over large distances to feed, only taking to trees in defence, and to roost or breed. Capture a catholic diet from termites to hares (even young eaglets from nests!), and indulge in wide range of social chasing, preening and sunbathing.

Southern Ground-hornbill *Bucorvus leadbeateri* 102cm, 40"
[Ground Hornbill]

Very large shaggy-looking black bird with bare bright red eye and throat wattles, a long heavy decurved bill (with a small casque), and stout black legs. Ad ♂ has eye and throat wattles all red, and ad ♀ is similar but has a small patch of violet-blue in the centre of the throat. Both have pale yellow eyes. Imm is duller and brown-tinged, with a smaller bill, rather yellowish-brown bare facial and throat patches, and brown eyes. Birds prefer to lope off when disturbed, but in flight they reveal striking white primary feathers, which are hard to see when the wings are folded. **HH** small groups are widespread, but often local, in moister bushed and wooded grassland to 3000m, from CKe southwards into Tz, Rw and Bu. **Vo** often calls at dawn when the air is cool and still and calls can carry over long distances, a very deep reverberant booming *gump-rump-rumrumrump*.

Abyssinian Ground-hornbill *Bucorvus abyssinicus* 110cm, 43"

Very similar though slightly larger than Southern Ground-hornbill, ad ♂ has a larger bill topped with an open casque, a pale yellowish patch at base of upper mandible, and blue skin around the eye and on the throat. Slightly smaller ad ♀ has a reduced casque, and entirely blue eye skin and wattles. Imm is brownish-black, has a poorly formed casque and smaller greyish wattles. In flight, reveals striking white primary feathers. **HH** pairs and family groups are local and uncommon in much drier semi-arid bush and woodland than Southern, occurring widely to 2500m in NUg and NWKe (as far south as Lake Baringo). **Vo** similar deep and reverberant quality to Southern Ground-hornbill, a rather more bouncy *w'rump-rah-rah-rah* given at well-spaced intervals.

Plate 125

**Black-casqued
Wattled Hornbill**

♀

♂

Imm

♀

**Southern
Ground-hornbill**

♂

**Abyssinian
Ground-hornbill**

♂

♀

FOREST TINKERBIRDS

Six closely related tinkerbirds, all are dark above and paler below, with yellow bars and feather edges in wings (except one atypical species: Speckled). All can be identified by a combination of head pattern and rump colour. They also make repetitive tink-tink calls from which the group name is derived. Sexes alike.

Yellow-rumped Tinkerbird   *Pogoniulus bilineatus*   10cm, 4"
[Golden-rumped Tinker Barbet]

Ad has a black head with two white stripes above and below the eye, a white throat, two short bright yellow wing bars and yellow wing feather edges. Birds either have gold rumps (three races: *jacksoni* and nominate in the highlands, and coastal *fischeri*), or lemon rumps (two races *mfumbiri* and *leucolaima* in mid-altitude areas from Rw to WKe). Belly is variably washed yellow, brighter in golden-rumped races. Imms resemble ads, but are duller with a pale base to the bill. **HH** singles and pairs are widespread and common in forests, dense woodlands, thickets and gardens from sea-level to 3000m. **Vo** highland birds call a long series of random 3 or 4 note sets of metallic *ponk-ponk-ponk-ponk*; western races are similar, but higher pitched and faster. The coastal race is very different, giving an introductory note followed by a very rapid series of over 20 *ponk* notes, almost trilled.

Yellow-throated Tinkerbird   *Pogoniulus subsulphureus*   10cm, 4"

Very similar to Yellow-rumped Tinkerbird, but the head stripes and throat are lightly washed yellow contrasting slightly with the greyish underparts. Yellow wing bars and feather edgings are slightly less well defined. Imm is similar to ad, but duller with a scaly back, and paler yellow throat. **HH** singles and pairs may be locally common in forest, notably at edges and in clearings, in W and SUg from 700–2100m. **Vo** similar to Yellow-rumped, but calls are faster and higher pitched.

Red-rumped Tinkerbird   *Pogoniulus atroflavus*   13cm, 5"

Only tinkerbird with a *bright red rump*. Glossed black above and strongly washed yellow below, with three fine yellow stripes on the side of the head. Imm is similar, but has a duller red rump, and is greyer below with a paler bill. **HH** scarce resident of Semliki Forest, WUg, at 700m. **Vo** slow hollow sounding *ponk-ponk...* given in a long series, and also a rapid musical *purrrrrt...* when excited.

Western Green Tinkerbird   *Pogoniulus coryphaeus*   9cm, 3.5"

A small distinctive tinkerbird which is black above with a golden-yellow crown, nape, back and rump, forming a *yellow stripe from head to rump*, and grey-olive below with a pale moustachial stripe. Imm is duller than ad with a pale base to the bill. **HH** singles and pairs are uncommon in highland forest from 1550–2500m in SWUg, Rw and Bu. Often close to streams and much more rarely into secondary forest and woodland. **Vo** common call is a series of rapid five note dry chips repeated for long periods, and also a musical downslurred trill similar to Eastern Green Tinkerbird.

Speckled Tinkerbird   *Pogoniulus scolopaceus*   11cm, 4.5"

Large rather *atypical dull olive tinkerbird with a pale eye*: dark olive above with light feather scaling, a whitish throat, and pale olive below with much dusky mottling and streaking. Imm is similar to ad, but has a pale yellow base to the lower mandible, and some barring on the throat. **HH** singles and pairs are often common in forest, forest edge and clearings with large trees, from 700–1800m from WUg across to Mt Elgon, and formerly also in WKe. **Vo** monotonously calls a quail-like nasal 3 or 4 note *chititit...* more than once per second.

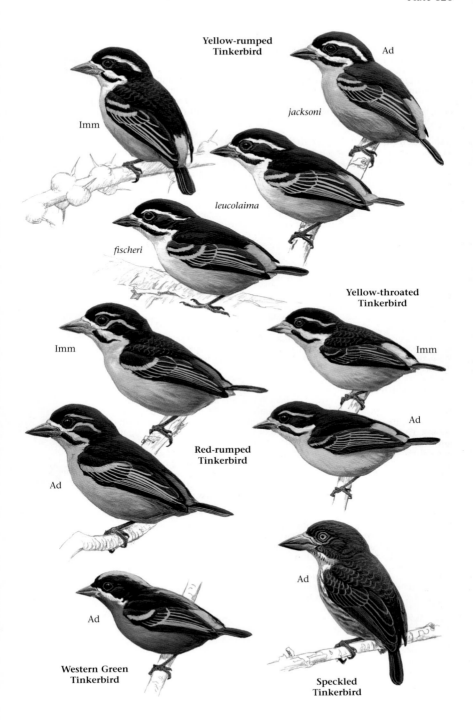

Plate 126

Yellow-rumped
Tinkerbird

Ad

Imm

jacksoni

leucolaima

fischeri

Yellow-throated
Tinkerbird

Imm

Imm

Ad

Red-rumped
Tinkerbird

Ad

Ad

Western Green
Tinkerbird

Ad

Speckled
Tinkerbird

Eastern Green Tinkerbird *Pogoniulus simplex* 9cm, 3.5"
[Green Tinker Barbet]
Small dull olive-green tinkerbird with *no moustachial stripe* and a pinkish base to the black bill. Greenish-yellow above, with yellow wing bars, a lemon-yellow rump, and pale grey-green below. Imm is very similar, but with a more extensive pale base to the bill. **HH** singles and pairs are rather uncommon mainly in coastal forests and woodland, but up to 900m (in the Usambara Mts, NETz). **Vo** usual call is a rapid tinny trill often followed by similar trills that drop in tone, and a fast musical *poo-poo-poo-poo-poo-poo-poo* of up to seven identical bell-like notes, similar to the coastal race of Yellow-rumped Tinkerbird but even more rapid.

Moustached Green Tinkerbird *Pogoniulus leucomystax* 9cm, 3.5"
Very similar to Eastern Green Tinkerbird, *but has a pale greyish moustachial stripe*, and an obvious pale pink base to the bill. Greenish above with yellow wing bars, a golden-yellow rump, and grey-green below. Imm may be yellower below. **HH** singles and pairs are common in highland forest from 1400–3000m in CKe to STz (ranging down to 900m in the Usambara Mts, NETz, where it overlaps with Eastern Green Tinkerbird). **Vo** coastal birds give a rapid series of up to six dry chipping notes *tipipipipip...*, while inland birds call a similar series which is higher pitched and more metallic.

DULLER BARBETS
A varied group of dull green or dark brown barbets of woodland and forest which can be identified on colour and head pattern. Sexes are alike.

Green Barbet *Stactolaema olivacea* 15cm, 6"
Stocky upright dark-headed barbet: ad is *dull olive-green above and yellowish olive-green below*. On the Rondo Plateau, SETz, distinctive race *woodwardi* has a pale yellow area behind the eye. Imm is similar, but duller. **HH** singles and pairs may be common in forest and woodland in coastal Ke, but are more widespread up to 1800m in Tz. **Vo** calls a sad repeated *kwop-kwop-kwop-kwop-...* often in the heat of the day (like the distant sound of an axe within a wood).

Whyte's Barbet *Stactolaema whytii* 17cm, 6.5"
Dark dusky brown barbet with a yellow forehead, *white line under the eye and white wing patches*, with some pale scaling on the belly and flanks. Imm is similar, but yellow reduced to spotting on forehead, and limited body scaling. Nominate ad in STz may lack yellow on the forecrown. **HH** small groups are local and rather uncommon in miombo woodland in SW and STz below 1700m. **Vo** call is a *pooh-pooh-pooh-...* in a slightly descending series similar to Red-fronted Barbet but more wheezy. Also a sharp, pinched and repeated *kweech*.

White-eared Barbet *Stactolaema leucotis* 17cm, 6.5"
Dark barbet with a white rump and belly. Two races occur: from CKe to NTz race *kilimense* has a *curved white stripe behind the eye*, while in C and STz *leucogrammica* has a swollen stripe which almost encircles the eye. Imms are similar, but have a less defined face pattern, and a pale base to the bill. **HH** pairs are common but patchily distributed in forest and forest edge from sea-level to 2000m. **Vo** calls a loud *kwi-kwi-kwi-...*, either singly or in a rapid series.

Grey-throated Barbet *Gymnobucco bonapartei* 18cm, 7"
Distinctive grey-headed brown barbet with yellow-white eyes and *erect yellow-brown bristle-tufts* on each side of base of bill. Imm is similar, but more uniform with reduced bristles, dark brown eyes, and a pale yellow base to the bill. **HH** singles and groups are often common and widespread in forest, woodland and forest edge from 900–2100m in the west. Often perch high in dead trees. **Vo** noisy, calling a frequent very pinched downslurred nasal *kweee*.

Plate 127

Eastern Green
Tinkerbird

Ad

Ad

Ad

woodwardi

Moustached Green
Tinkerbird

Green
Barbet

Imm

Whyte's
Barbet

Imm

kilimense

Ad

Ad

Imm

White-eared
Barbet

Ad

Ad

Grey-throated
Barbet

leucogrammica

BUSH BARBETS AND TINKERBIRDS

A similar-looking group of bush and woodland barbets with boldly striped heads, and blackish upperparts spotted or streaked with yellow. They are best identified by the presence or absence of red on the forecrown and markings on the underparts. Smaller tinkerbirds have different coloured forecrowns. Sexes similar.

Red-fronted Tinkerbird *Pogoniulus pusillus* 10cm, 4"
[Red-fronted Tinker Barbet]
A small confiding tinkerbird with a *red forehead*. Streaked whitish on black above, with a yellowish rump, and buffy-yellow underparts. It is much smaller than Red-fronted Barbet and has a short malar stripe. Imm is similar, but lacks red forehead. **HH** singles and pairs are common and widespread in dry bush and woodland from sea-level to 2200m. **Vo** common call is a fairly rapid continuous series of metallic *ponk-ponk-ponk...* notes, also gives a repeated double *po-ponk,* and a fast rather nasal trill when excited.

Yellow-fronted Tinkerbird *Pogoniulus chrysoconus* 10cm, 4"
[Yellow-fronted Tinker Barbet]
Very similar to Red-fronted Tinkerbird, but with a *yellow-orange forecrown spot and much stronger yellow wash on the underparts*. Imm is similar, but lacks yellow forehead. **HH** singles and pairs are widespread and locally common in moister habitats than Red-fronted including forest edge, riverine woodland, thickets and mature gardens, from sea-level to 1500m. **Vo** some calls are doubtfully distinguishable from Red-fronted Tinkerbird, but possibly faster and lower-pitched. Also utters a very fast trill when excited.

Red-fronted Barbet *Tricholaema diademata* 17cm, 6.5"
Stocky, robust barbet with a *long yellow-white supercilium and red forecrown spot*. From NEUg to NKe the nominate race is white below with spots on lower flanks, while from CKe to CTz *massaica* is buff below, with heavier spots on the breast, belly and flanks. Imms are duller with just a little red over a paler bill. **HH** widespread in dry bush and woodland from 600–2100m. **Vo** wide vocabulary, usually calls a rapid descending and hollow *pooh-pooh-pooh-pooh,* and a slow, nasal and pinched *wah wah wah...*

Miombo Pied Barbet *Tricholaema frontata* 17cm, 6.5"
Very similar to Red-fronted Barbet (but ranges do not overlap); differs in having a *browner eye patch, scaly moustachial streak, brownish-grey bill, and more spotting on a yellow-washed breast*. Imm is similar, but lacks red over the bill. **HH** singles and pairs are local to miombo woodland in SWTz. **Vo** song is a long series of hollow *pooh* notes, falling terminally, somewhat like a wood-dove.

Spot-flanked Barbet *Tricholaema lacrymosa* 14cm, 5.5"
Ad has a broad black bib tapering to the centre of the breast, boldly spotted buff-white flanks and a pale yellow-orange eye (darker in ♀). Imm is greyer above and has brown eyes. **HH** widespread and sometimes common in wooded and bushed grassland, as well as riverine forest below 2000m. Prefers rather moister habitat to similar Black-throated Barbet. **Vo** call is a long series of sharp *kwek* notes, commencing slowly and accelerating with a strange whiplash effect. Also a series of nasal *weh weh weh..*and *poop-poop...*notes similar to Red-fronted Barbet.

Black-throated Barbet *Tricholaema melanocephala* 14cm, 5.5"
Widespread race *stigmatothorax* has a boldly striped head and long blackish-brown bib which tapers to a sharp point in the centre of a whitish belly (no spots on flanks). In the Wembere area of NTz, race *flavibuccalis* has the head stripes washed yellow, and a short bib terminating mid-breast. Imms are rather duller with a pale bill. **HH** singles and pairs inhabit semi-arid bush and thorn-scrub country from near the coast to 1500m. **Vo** calls a throaty *hiau-hiau-hiau...,* sometimes breaking into descending musical churrs and often in duet.

Plate 128

Yellow-fronted
Tinkerbird

Ad

Imm

Ad

Imm

Red-fronted
Tinkerbird

Ad

Imm

nominate

Red-fronted
Barbet

Imm

Ad

massaica

Ad

Miombo Pied
Barbet

Spot-flanked
Barbet

Ad

Ad

Ad

Ad

Black-throated
Barbet

flavibuccalis

stigmatothorax

WOODLAND AND FOREST BARBETS

A varied group of medium-sized and large barbets found mainly in woodland and forest, several have extensive areas of black in the plumage and red on the head, one is boldly patterned black and white, some, including Yellow-billed Barbet (on plate 131) have yellow bellies. Sexes alike.

Hairy-breasted Barbet *Tricholaema hirsuta* 18cm, 7"
Ad has a black head with two white stripes on each side suggesting a giant tinkerbird. *Greenish-yellow below, with black streaks becoming heavily spotted from mid-breast to vent* (close views reveal long separated hair-like breast feathers). Imm is very similar, but more barred on flanks. **HH** singles and pairs are locally common in forest, riverine forest and woodland from 700–1800m in S and WUg, NWTz, and WKe (Kakamega only). **Vo** calls repeated low hollow identical paced notes *pooh pooh pooh...*

Yellow-spotted Barbet *Buccanodon duchaillui* 17cm, 6.5"
Ad is a boldly marked blue-black forest barbet, extensively spotted and barred with yellow, with a *scarlet forehead patch, and a long curving yellow line from eye to hindneck.* Imm is similar to ad, but less well marked, lacks the red forehead, and black bill has a pale yellow base. **HH** singles and small groups are common residents of western forests, being very active in the canopy and around fruiting trees, often in mixed species flocks, from 1150–2400m. **Vo** typically gives a low purred snoring trill delivered from high in the canopy *prrrrrrrrrr...*, also gives a hooting *boo-boo-boo.*

Black-backed Barbet *Lybius minor* 19cm, 7.5"
In our area, race *macclounii* is a bold black and white barbet with a red forecrown, a distinct white 'V' on the back, and an apricot-pink flush over the belly. Bill is large and cream-coloured. Imm resembles ad, but is browner, and lacks an obvious red forecrown. **HH** uncommon residents of riverine forest, forest edge and thickets, in Bu and WTz, often near termite mounds. **Vo** short rasping calls which resemble but are more rapid and rhythmical than those of Broad-billed Roller.

Black-collared Barbet *Lybius torquatus* 19cm, 7.5"
Western race *pumilio* and eastern *irroratus* are a striking pattern of a *red face and breast and a yellow belly divided by a black collar*, with a black-brown back, and heavy black bill. Imm has a black face with red-brown flecking, no yellow below, and a pale base to the bill. In SETz, distinctive race *zombae* has a black head, variably speckled with white, and is pale buff-yellow below. **HH** pairs are local in a range of woodland and forest edge, as well as gardens, from sea-level to 1600m. **Vo** calls start with growled churrs and develop into a characterful bounding *twi-popopop twi-popopop...* (first note of each series is higher, last note rapid and identical, the whole effect being like a rolling wave).

Brown-breasted Barbet *Lybius melanopterus* 19cm, 7.5"
Large eastern barbet with a red head (streaked black on the nape), *a broad brown breast band*, white from mid-breast to vent, and a pale bill. Imm is similar, but has much less red in the face, a grey-brown breast, and a darker bill. **HH** singles and pairs may be common in woodland and forest edge, as well as in gardens and abandoned farms, along the coastal strip and inland, from sea-level to 1700m. **Vo** call is a repeated nasal and very pinched *wek.*

Plate 129

Yellow-spotted Barbet

Imm

Ad

Hairy-breasted Barbet

Ad

irroratus

Imm

Black-backed Barbet

Ad

Ad

Imm

Ad

Black-collared Barbet

Ad

zombae

Imm

Brown-breasted Barbet

White-headed Barbet *Lybius leucocephalus* 19cm, 7.5"

Complex species with four races (some of which interbreed): all ads have *white heads and rumps*, but vary as follows: nominate in all Ug, NWTz and WKe has extensive white in the wings, is blackish below with pale streaked flanks, and has a black tail; race *senex* in CKe is white except for its black-brown wings and mantle; *albicauda* in SKe and NTz is dark brown mottled white below, with some white in the wings, and a white tail; and *lynesi* in CTz is similar, but has a variable blackish base to the tail. All imms have brown-mottled heads and brown tails, but otherwise resemble dull ads. **HH** social: pairs and family parties are common and widespread in bushed and wooded grassland, as well as gardens, often near fruiting fig trees, from sea-level to 2200m. **Vo** impressive range of loud growling, harsh gurgling and sharp very babbler-like chattering calls, often with exaggerated displays of bowing and gaping.

Black-billed Barbet *Lybius guifsobalito* 17cm, 6.5"

Very similar to Red-faced Barbet: ad has a *bright red face, throat and upper breast*, and a black bill. Flight feathers are edged pale yellow, and the upper-wing-coverts are edged whitish. Imm is duller with a brownish-black head and mottled red on the face and throat. **HH** pairs and small parties are widespread at low densities in drier bush and woodland through most of Ug to extreme WKe from 600–2000m. **Vo** calls is a mechanical rolling *ki-twop ki-twop ki-twop...*, first note of each series higher.

Red-faced Barbet *Lybius rubrifacies* 17cm, 6.5"   ●

Very similar to Black-billed Barbet, but has a paler bill with *red confined to the face and plain black wing-coverts*. Imm is similar to ad, but duller with a black and red mottled face. **HH** EA endemic: pairs and small parties are widespread but local in woodland, wooded grassland and cultivation with mature trees from 1200–1500m. It is restricted to a small area of SWUg, Rw, Bu and NWTz (where there is no overlap with Black-billed). **Vo** voice is very similar to closely related Black-billed Barbet.

Double-toothed Barbet *Lybius bidentatus* 23cm, 9"

Impressive ivory-billed barbet which is black above (with a white centre to the back), and *bright red below with white crescent patches on the lower flanks*; creamy-white eyes are surrounded by bare yellow skin. ♀ is like ♂, but has a few black streaks in red flanks. Imm is duller, showing much less red below, and greyish skin round dull brown eyes. **HH** pairs and family groups are widespread and common in a range of woodland, wooded grassland, gardens and cultivation with scattered fig trees from 900–2300m. **Vo** loud song is a nightjar-like churring, but much raspier, and the call is a dry frog-like rasp *erk*.

Black-breasted Barbet *Lybius rolleti* 28cm, 11"

Spectacular huge black barbet with a massive ivory bill, white on the back, *white flank patches, and a bright red lower breast and belly*. Eyes are brown sur-rounded by blue-grey orbital skin. ♀ is very similar to ♂, but white flank patches are finely spotted black. Imm is browner above and below, with a duller orange-red belly. **HH** pairs and family groups are widespread and uncommon in riverine woodland, drier wooded grassland and cultivation with scattered fig trees across NUg, from 900–1200m. **Vo** reported to utter low rasping or harsh scraping notes and whistles.

Plate 130

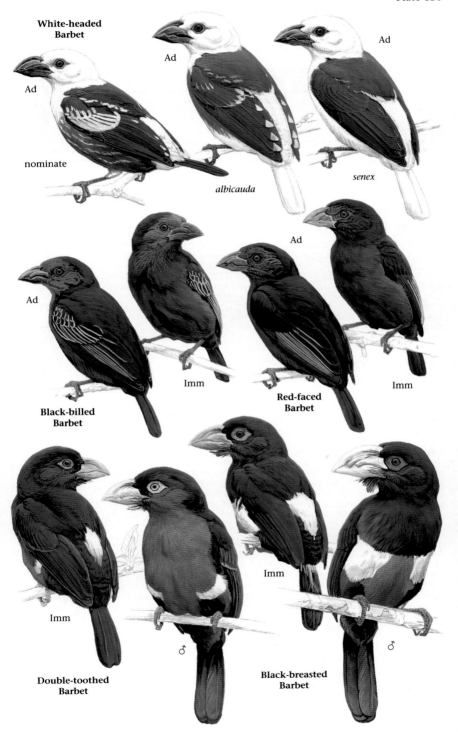

White-headed Barbet

Ad

Ad

Ad

Ad

nominate

albicauda

senex

Black-billed Barbet

Ad

Ad

Imm

Imm

Red-faced Barbet

Imm

♂

Double-toothed Barbet

Imm

♂

Black-breasted Barbet

GROUND BARBETS

Colourful largely ground-dwelling barbets with narrow tails, and brightly patterned black, yellow, white and red plumage. All have rather mechanical songs, and some duet. Easily identified by head and breast patterns. Sexes are similar.

d'Arnaud's Barbet *Trachyphonus darnaudii* 18cm, 7"

Three races occur, varying in the extent of black on the crown and throat. All ads have *pinkish bills, pale yellowish-orange heads,* a broken black breast band, and an *orange-red vent.* Nominate race (NUg to NKe) has the crown speckled black and a variable but small black bib, *boehmi* (EKe to NETz) has a similar small bib, but the crown is black, and *emini* (elsewhere) has a black cap and larger black bib. Imms are similar but rather duller, with browner crowns. **HH** pairs and family groups are widespread and common in semi-arid bushed and wooded grassland from sea level to 2000m. They are frequently seen on the ground near termite hills, or moving through the bush with rather weak low flight. **Vo** song is a mechanical duetting accompanied by cocked and frantically waving tails: it is a set of two rising and two falling notes repeated for long periods *kee-ta-ti-tootle kee-ta-ti-tootle...*

Usambiro Barbet *Trachyphonus usambiro* 19cm, 7.5" ●

Very similar to d'Arnaud's Barbet (and may be treated as conspecific), but is a little larger, with a *darker grey bill, a suffused greenish tone to the head* and a heavier blackish spotted breast band. Imm is similar to ad, but rather duller. **HH** EA endemic: pairs and family groups are widespread and common in the bushed and wooded grassland of SWKe and NTz (centred on the Mara-Serengeti ecosystem) from 1100–2100m. **Vo** displays like d'Arnaud's Barbet with a rattled duet, but one bird calls a short rising series of clicks, while the other accompanies with a croaking *wi-tuk.*

Red-and-yellow Barbet *Trachyphonus erythrocephalus* 23cm, 9"

Stunning red, black and yellow spotted barbet, with a *bright red-bill, red-face and striking white comma behind the eye.* From NEUg to NKe ad ♂ versicolor has red confined around the white comma, and a much plainer yellow breast; while from SKe to NETz nominate birds have a red-face and dark crown, with a red-orange upper breast. ♀ is similar to ♂ in both races, but has the orange crown speckled with black, and a browner back. Imms similar to ads, but with less orange. **HH** pairs and family parties are widespread and locally common in dry bush and woodland with termite mounds below 2100m. **Vo** perform spectacular loud rolling duets, with a musical and reverberant series of three descending notes repeated endlessly as a wave *teedle-kwau teedle-kwau teedle-kwau...*

Crested Barbet *Trachyphonus vaillantii* 23cm, 9"

Ad has a red speckled yellow face, *a small but conspicuous black crest, and a black breast band speckled with white.* ♀ is like ♂ but may be slightly duller. Imm is like ad, but is browner above, with a smaller crest. **HH** pairs and family groups are rather local and seldom common in bush and woodland, including miombo, from sea-level to 1300m. They may be found in thickets near termite mounds. **Vo** song is a long rather high-pitched musical rattle *trrrrrrrrrrrrrrrrrrrr...*

Yellow-billed Barbet *Trachylaemus purpuratus* 25cm, 10"

Striking long-tailed forest barbet with a *yellow bill and large patch of bare yellow skin around the eyes;* remainder of upperparts black, breast very dark maroon (but often looks blackish in the field), lower breast to vent largely yellow more spotted yellow on black towards the vent. Sexes are alike. Imm is duller without maroon on breast and more extensive yellow below. **HH** singles and pairs are common and widespread in primary and secondary forest, including clearings, from 700–2800m. **Vo** song is a monotonous series of identical musical hollow *poop poop poop* given at about one per second, and less often a paired *cu-coop.*

Plate 131

nominate

emini

Usambiro
Barbet

Ad

Ad

Ad

d'Arnaud's
Barbet

♂

♂

♀

nominate

Red-and-yellow
Barbet

versicolor

Imm

Ad

Crested
Barbet

Ad

Imm

Yellow-billed
Barbet

HONEYGUIDES

Medium and small dull plumaged birds with conspicuous white outer-tails. They form three distinct groups, large with stout bills, small with stubby bills, and small with slender bills. Sexes alike, unless otherwise described. All are brood parasites: *Indicator* lay their eggs in the nests of hole-nesting species like bee-eaters, barbets and woodpeckers; while *Prodotiscus* parasitise species with globular nests, like cisticolas, white-eyes and sunbirds. All *Indicator* species feed on both bees' wax and insects.

LARGE HONEYGUIDES

With reasonable views these four distinctive species can easily be identified. All are usually solitary and rather sluggish.

Greater Honeyguide   *Indicator indicator*   19cm, 7.5"
[Black-throated Honeyguide]

Ad ♂ has a *pale-pinkish bill, black throat and white ear patch*. Remainder of plumage is dull brown with small yellowish shoulders (usually concealed); in worn plumage they may show a small whitish area on the rump. White outer-tail noticeable in undulating flight or when landing. ♀ mostly dull brown above with paler and greyer underparts and a grey-brown bill. Imm is more olive-brown above than ads, with a *creamy-yellow throat and breast*, and a small white area on the lower rump. **HH** common and widespread in riverine and open woodland, bush country, and farmland with scattered large trees, from sea-level to 3000m. It sits upright in the canopy, calling repeatedly, often from well-established song posts. Known to lead people and ratels to bees' nests. **Vo** song is a far-carrying repeated and explosive *wi-chew wi-chew wi-chew...*, first note high, second lower, and also a rather complaining nasal chattering (which is used to attract honey hunters).

Scaly-throated Honeyguide   *Indicator variegatus*   19cm, 7.5"

Mostly dull olive-green above with a browner wash to the head, *forecrown, throat, and breast are mixed dark grey and white, giving a scaly or mottled appearance*. Mid-breast to vent plain dirty white, sometimes tinged yellowish. Imm is similar but washed greenish on the upperparts and more heavily marked below. **HH** locally common, but never numerous in a wide variety of habitats including forest, woodland, thickets and bush country from sea-level to 3350m. Rather shy and presence is often first noticed by hearing distinctive call. **Vo** call is a long rather purred and rising trill *trrrreeeeeeeeeeeeee*, and also gives a complaining *tew-tew-tew...*

Spotted Honeyguide   *Indicator maculatus*   19cm, 7.5"

Mostly plain olive-green above including the forecrown, brighter on back and wings. Throat is yellowish-white narrowly streaked grey, *breast olive with distinctive creamy spots extending on to the flanks*, and becoming more streaked on the lower breast and belly. Imm is similar but with small greenish spots on the forecrown, and more extensive streaking (rather than spots) below. **HH** in our area only known from the Semliki Valley, WUg, where it is rare in the forest interior between 700–900m. **Vo** extremely similar to Scaly-throated Honeyguide, a rising trilled whistle that may end with a mournful downslur.

Lyre-tailed Honeyguide   *Melichneutes robustus*   19cm, 7.5"

Combination of brown upperparts, pale yellowish-buff underparts and *unique lyre-shaped tail* make this species unmistakable. Imm is dark blackish-brown above and on the throat, with an olive-brown breast and creamy-white lower breast to vent. **HH** in our area known only from Semliki Valley, WUg, at 700m where it is a very rare bird. Makes amazing display flights high over the canopy and invariably out of sight, when air passing through the stiff tail produces a loud and accelerating *farr-ah, farr-ah, farr-ah*, perhaps repeated 30 times. **Vo** utters a slow chattering and an occasional *prrr...* in flight.

Plate 132

Greater Honeyguide
♂
Imm
♀

Scaly-throated Honeyguide
Ad
Imm
Imm

Lyre-tailed Honeyguide
Ad
Imm
Ad

Spotted Honeyguide

SMALLER STUBBY-BILLED HONEYGUIDES

Very similar looking and confusing grey and olive honeyguides with short stout bills. Presence or lack of loral spots, malar stripes, and the exact colour of underparts aid identification. The variable flank streaking on several species does not help identify them in the field.

Lesser Honeyguide *Indicator minor* 14cm, 5.5"
Classic common honeyguide: medium-sized, with a grey head and underparts, and an indistinctly streaked olive-green back and wings. Ad has *medium grey underparts, a small pale loral spot, and dark grey malar stripes.* Imm has the head uniform grey, lacking both the loral spots and malar stripes. **HH** a rather active, common and widespread species, inhabiting forest edge, open woodland, bush country and trees within cultivated areas, from sea-level to 3000m. It does not usually enter forest interiors. **Vo** song starts with a short downslur and then, after a brief pause, continues as a series of dry chips at about two per second *tew chet-chet-chet-chet-chet-chet...*, and also utters a nasal chittering

Thick-billed Honeyguide *Indicator conirostris* 14cm, 5.5"
Very similar to Lesser Honeyguide (and sometimes considered conspecific with it), but the *head and underparts are darker grey*, back streaking is usually more distinct, and there are no visible loral spots or malar stripes. Imm is similar, but greener above with some streaking on the throat. **HH** rather local and uncommon in forest interiors from 700–2300m. **Vo** call is very similar to Lesser Honeyguide, but appears to lack the introductory note, at least at times, and the series is a drier more strident *chit-chit-chit...*

Pallid Honeyguide *Indicator meliphilus* 12cm, 5"
[Eastern Honeyguide]
Slightly smaller than Lesser Honeyguide with light grey underparts, a plainer back, and smaller bill. Head is pale grey accentuating the small dark eyes and giving the bird a beady-eyed look. White loral spot usually present but often hard to see, and there are *no dark malar stripes.* Imm is more yellowish-green above and slightly darker below. **HH** unobtrusive and uncommon, inhabiting woodland and clearings within forest from sea-level-2000m. **Vo** call is a rising series of lispy upslurred notes starting with *fwo* and then continuing *fwee-tk fwee-tk fwee-tk...*

Willcock's Honeyguide *Indicator willcocksi* 12cm, 5"
Very similar to several other honeyguides but smaller than Lesser and larger than Dwarf. It *lacks both loral spots and malar stripes* (similar-sized Least has distinct loral spots and malar stripes). Throat and belly pale olive-grey, with a *broad band of darker olive-grey across the breast.* Imm is washed greenish both above and on the breast. **HH** in our area an uncommon forest bird restricted to WUg and Rw from 1200–1800m. **Vo** call is a wheezy series of repeated upslurs *h'whi't-h'whi't-h'whi-t...*

Least Honeyguide *Indicator exilis* 12cm, 5"
A *small dark species with distinct whitish loral spots and dark malar stripes.* It may show quite heavy streaking on both the upperparts and the flanks. Underparts plain grey-olive with slightly pale throat. Imm similar but darker and often lacks loral spots and malar stripes. **HH** a restless and uncommon species of the forest interior from 700–2300m. **Vo** call is very similar to Lesser Honeyguide, but lacks the introductory note, and is a slower and fuller series *chiet-chiet-chiet...*

Dwarf Honeyguide *Indicator pumilio* 10cm, 4" ●
A *very small dark honeyguide with white loral spots, but no malar stripes.* In good light may show narrow streaking across the breast. Imm lacks loral spots and is greyer above. **HH** a little known bird of forest and forest edge, virtually endemic to high country around the Albertine Rift, from 1500–2400m. **Vo** call is a repeated whistled downslur *seeu-seeu-seeu-...*

Plate 133

Lesser
Honeyguide

Thick-billed
Honeyguide

Ad

Ad

Ad

Ad

Ad

Willcock's
Honeyguide

Pallid
Honeyguide

Ad

Ad

Least
Honeyguide

Dwarf
Honeyguide

SLIM-BILLED HONEYBIRDS

Three small species with slender bills (also known as honeyguides). Basic colour and white outer-tails resemble *Indicator* honeyguides, but their slender bills and active warbler-like behaviour make them separable. All frequently spread their tails, both in display and while foraging, as they glean leaves for insects. Best identified by back colour and tail pattern, white erectile feathers on the sides of their rumps are usually concealed.

Wahlberg's Honeybird *Prodotiscus regulus* 12cm, 5"
[Sharp-billed Honeyguide]
A brown and white honeybird with a *dull brown head, back and wings: tail of ad has a black centre and tips.* Breast brownish-grey, throat and belly paler dirty white. Imm is similar, but slightly paler above washed yellowish below, with an all-white outer-tail. **HH** local and uncommon in open wooded areas and bush country from sea-level to 2000m. **Vo** song is a long very dry rattle.

Eastern Honeybird *Prodotiscus zambesiae* 10cm, 4"
[Slender-billed Honeyguide]
In areas of overlap with Wahlberg's Honeybird easily separated by olive-green back and wings (not brown). Outer-tail plain white on ad, underparts greyish with a paler belly. Imm is similar, but paler and more buffy with small dark tips to the outer-tail feathers. Nominate birds in SWTz are paler than race *ellenbecki* elsewhere. **HH** rather local at forest edge and in mixed woodlands, from near sea-level to 1850m. Often joins mixed-species flocks. **Vo** displaying birds fly low over the treetops calling a chittering high-pitched rattle.

Cassin's Honeybird *Prodotiscus insignis* 11cm, 4.5"
Similar to Eastern Honeybird but darker olive-grey on the underparts (except for a pale belly). Range completely different. Imm is like ad but duller above. **HH** local and rather uncommon in western forests from 700–2200m. **Vo** calls reported to include a chatter and a weak *whi-hi-hi* or *ski-a*.

Zenker's Honeyguide *Melignomon zenkeri* 14cm, 5.5"
A medium-sized dull olive rather sluggish honeyguide with a brown-olive back and a fairly slender bill (recalling a small greenbul or cuckoo). White outer-tail is usually only visible in flight, but most of the undertail is greyish-white if seen from below. Legs yellowish. Imm is brighter and more olive-green above. **HH** a rare bird in our area, known only from the Semliki Valley, WUg, at 700m. **Vo** calls a long series of loud similar chips at about two per second, much like a softer and muffled Thick-billed Honeyguide, but the notes accelerate, are more whistled and drop in tone to fade at the end.

PICULET

Small almost crombec-like bird related to the woodpeckers. Unique in the region, it should not be mistaken for any other species.

African Piculet *Sasia africana* 8cm, 3"
A tiny green and grey bird with a tail-less appearance. Ad ♂ has a bright red forecrown and narrow white lines above and behind the eyes. ♀ lacks the red. Imm is similar to ♀, but with rufous on the throat and belly. **HH** in our area restricted to the Semliki Valley, WUg, where it is reasonably common in forest and secondary growth at 700m. **Vo** call is a high-pitched tinkling trill like breaking glass.

Plate 134

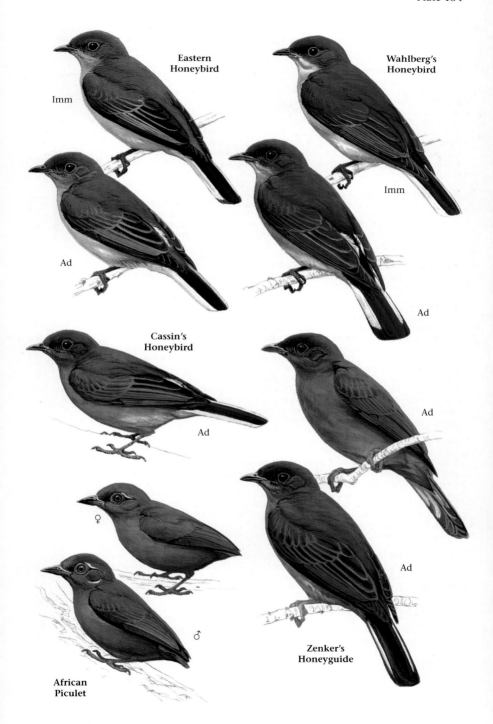

Eastern
Honeybird

Imm

Ad

Wahlberg's
Honeybird

Imm

Ad

Cassin's
Honeybird

Ad

Ad

♀

♂

Ad

African
Piculet

Zenker's
Honeyguide

WRYNECKS

Curious cryptically patterned woodpecker relatives, although their appearance and behaviour is quite different, often suggesting a large warbler or thrush at first glance. They are frequently seen on the ground where they feed on ants, but fly in to trees if disturbed. Sexes are alike.

Red-throated Wryneck *Jynx ruficollis* 19 cm, 7.5"

Ad has the upperparts all finely mottled, barred and speckled with brown, grey and black, with a series of darker spots forming a streak on the nape and back. *Throat and upper breast rufous*, remainder of underparts buffy, with fine brown streaks and bars and a rufous wash to the vent. Imm is darker than ad with more barred upperparts: rufous on the throat and breast is less extensive and also finely barred. **HH** widespread, but only locally common resident in open woodland, remnant forest edges and cultivated area with scattered trees, from 600–3000m. **Vo** call is a raptor-like and piercing *cor-quee-quee-quee-quee-quee* and also a chittering when excited.

Eurasian Wryneck *Jynx torquilla* 18 cm, 7"

Similar to Red-throated Wryneck being mottled, barred and speckled grey-brown with a blackish stripe down nape and back, but differs in having a dark streak through the eye and *no rufous on the throat and breast*. **HH** very scarce Palearctic visitor to open woodland and bush country from Oct–Apr. **Vo** silent in region.

THREE FOREST WOODPECKERS

These three woodpeckers are found only in forest. They all have plain green or olive backs and barred or spotted underparts.

Tullberg's Woodpecker *Campethera tullbergi* 19 cm, 7.5"
[Fine-banded Woodpecker]

Ad ♂ is plain olive-green above with a red cap variably mottled blackish on the forecrown. Sides of face and throat grey with very fine dark barring, remainder of underparts *yellowish-green entirely barred with dark olive*. Ad ♀ is similar but crown is black with small white spots. Imm is duller above and more heavily barred below. In our area two similar races occur: widespread *taeniolaema* and slightly more yellow *hausbergi* east of the Great Rift Valley. **HH** singles and pairs are locally common in montane forest from 1600–3000m. Frequently seen in mixed-species flocks. **Vo** a remarkably silent species: call not recorded, but is said to give a loud *kweek-kweek-kweek...*

Buff-spotted Woodpecker *Campethera nivosa* 15cm, 6"

Small woodpecker with a small bill: ad ♂ is olive-green above with an olive-brown cap and red restricted to the nape. Sides of face and throat are pale yellow or greyish with fine dark streaks: remainder of *underparts dark olive spotted across the breast and barred on the flanks with pale yellow*. Ad ♀ is similar but cap is entirely dark olive-brown. Imm is similar to ♀. **HH** singles and pairs are locally common in forest and thick secondary growth below 1800m. Often joins mixed-species flocks, particularly in the lower levels of tangled vines and undergrowth. **Vo** normal call is a well-spaced *weeeooooooo* rising towards the end, but also gives a burry downslurred *pheeu*.

Brown-eared Woodpecker *Campethera caroli* 19 cm, 7.5"

Ad ♂ is dark olive above with a brown and red cap and a conspicuous *large rufous-brown ear-patch*. Underparts are entirely spotted pale buffy-yellow on olive. Ad ♀ is similar but crown is entirely brown. Imm similar to ♀ but greener above, with paler spots on underparts and some barring on the belly. **HH** single birds or pairs are locally common in forest and good secondary growth from 700–1800m. Joins mixed-species flocks and usually feeds in the middle and higher levels. **Vo** calls an upslurred and then descending *weeeeeeeyu* with a slight ascent in the middle.

Plate 135

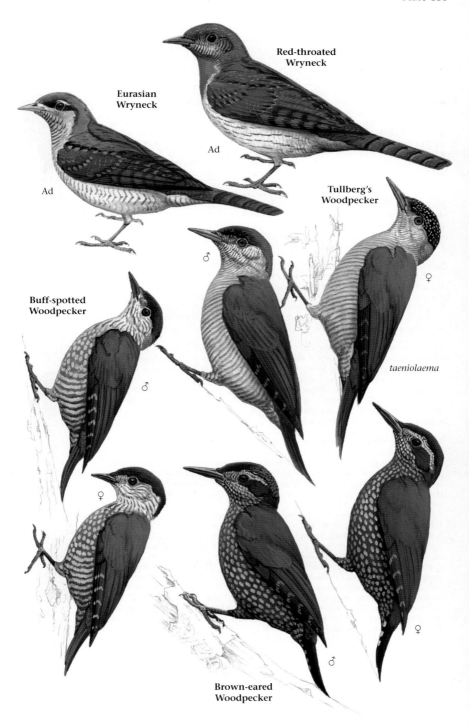

Eurasian Wryneck

Red-throated Wryneck

Ad

Ad

Tullberg's Woodpecker

♀

Buff-spotted Woodpecker

♂

♂

taeniolaema

♀

♀

♂

Brown-eared Woodpecker

WOODLAND WOODPECKERS

A group of five very similar woodland and bush country woodpeckers which are hard to identify: careful attention to face markings and range aid identification. Males all have a red cap and malar stripe and females have a black forecrown peppered with white and red on the hindcrown only. All have golden-yellow tail shafts. Immatures tend to be similar to females but darker and more boldly marked.

Nubian Woodpecker *Campethera nubica* 20cm, 8"

Ad ♂ has the *ear-coverts narrowly streaked black and white and a white throat*. Ad ♀ has similar *streaked ear-coverts and white throat* but the malar stripe is black speckled with white. Both sexes are spotted below. Highland birds tend to be darker than those near the coast. Beware, some juvs can be quite streaky below. **HH** common and widespread in dry bush, acacia and wooded grasslands from sea-level to 2300m. **Vo** calls a long series of repeated hardly varying metallic *tinkh-tinkh-tinkh-tinkh-tinkh...* notes, which speed up and slow down with levels of excitement and are frequently given in duet.

Bennett's Woodpecker *Campethera bennettii* 20cm, 8"

Ad ♂ has the *ear-coverts and throat white*. Ad ♀ has the *ear-coverts and throat chocolate-brown*. Both sexes are spotted below. **HH** in our area it is rather local and uncommon and restricted to open woodland and miombo from ERw to SWTz. **Vo** calls a loud rather wader-like and musical trill.

Speckle-throated Woodpecker *Campethera scriptoricauda* 20cm, 8"

Ad ♂ has the *ear-coverts streaked black and white, and the throat finely speckled with black*. Ad ♀ has similar *streaked ear-coverts and speckled throat*, but the malar stripe is black speckled with white. Both sexes have a *yellowish base to the lower mandible* and are spotted below. **HH** locally common in miombo and other open woodland throughout much of eastern Tz. **Vo** call unrecorded.

Golden-tailed Woodpecker *Campethera abingoni* 20cm, 8"

Golden-tail is not distinctive! Both sexes differ from all preceding woodpeckers by streaked (not spotted) underparts, and from the very similar Mombasa Woodpecker by having *black throats speckled with white*. Imm is similar but has some barring on the flanks and belly. **HH** locally common in forest, riverine woodland and dense thickets below 2000m. **Vo** call is a rising and falling slurred *tch'waaye*, the first note harsh and grating and the remainder nasal and complaining.

Mombasa Woodpecker *Campethera mombassica* 20cm, 8"

Very similar to Golden-tailed Woodpecker with streaked underparts, both sexes differ in having *plain whitish throats* and very lightly speckled upperparts (may appear plain in the field). **HH** locally common in forest and woodland in coastal Ke and inland along the Tana River, and in NETz to the Usambara Mts. **Vo** call is a rising and burry dry trill *whirrrrrr-whirrrrrr-whirrrrrr-whirrrrrr*.

Green-backed Woodpecker *Campethera cailliautii* 17cm, 6.5"

A small woodpecker with four races divided into two distinct forms: those with spotted underparts were formerly called **Little Spotted Woodpecker**. In SWUg, WTz and SWKe race *nyansae* has fine streaks above, and the spotted underparts have barring on the flanks; in coastal Ke and NETz nominate birds are spotted above and below; and in E and STz *loveridgei* is similar but more barred above. In Semliki Forest, WUg, distinctive race *permista* is plain green above, and entirely barred below. In all races ♂♂ lack red malar stripe. **HH** locally common but with a patchy distribution in forest and woodland, from sea-level to 2100m. Joins mixed-species feeding flocks. **Vo** races in spotted group call an irregular, rather lazy upslurred *kewiu* or *kiu-week*, while *permista* calls a series of six or so piercing high-pitched upslurred *ke-wii*.

Plate 136

Bennett's Woodpecker

Nubian Woodpecker

♂

♀

♂

♀

Speckle-throated Woodpecker

♂

♀

Golden-tailed Woodpecker

♂

♀

nominate

Green-backed Woodpecker

♂

permista

♂

♂

Mombasa Woodpecker

♀

SMALL WOODPECKERS

A mixed group of small woodpeckers (including Green-backed on plate 136). They inhabit an equally varied range of habitats, from forest to dry bush. All are reasonably easily identified if seen well. In *Dendropicos* and *Picoides* immatures of both sexes have a small amount of red on the crown, usually slightly more in males.

Cardinal Woodpecker *Dendropicos fuscescens* 14cm, 5.5"
Small woodpecker with *lightly streaked sides to the face, well streaked underparts, and spotted wings*. Three races also have distinctly *barred backs*: *hemprichii* in N and EKe, *massaicus* in NEUg through CKe to NTz, and *hartlaubii* in SEKe and most of Tz (*hartlaubii* is also more yellow below). In the highlands of Ug, Rw and Bu east to WKe, race *lepidus* has an olive back with darker olive barring (it can look plain in the field). In all races the ad ♂ has a largely red and ad ♀ a blackish-brown cap: the tail has golden-yellow shafts. **HH** East Africa's most common and widespread woodpecker, inhabiting forest edge and clearings, open woodland, dry bush and cultivation, from sea-level to 3000m. **Vo** calls a very cross-sounding series of dry high-pitched and tuneless rattled churrs that change slightly in pitch.

Brown-backed Woodpecker *Picoides obsoletus* 14cm, 5.5"
Similar to Cardinal Woodpecker, but easily identified by a *large dark brown patch on the ear-coverts encircled with white, and a brown tail with small white spots*. Ad ♂ has red restricted to rear of crown and ad ♀ has the crown and nape entirely brown. Three distinct races occur: in Ug nominate birds are brown above and faintly streaked below; in NEUg, CKe, and NTz *ingens* is darker above and more streaked below; and in the Crater Highlands, Tz, race *crateri* is blackish-brown above with heavy streaks below almost forming a band across the breast. **HH** singles and pairs are local and rather uncommon in a variety of woodland, forest edge and cultivated areas with large scattered trees, from sea-level to 2300m. **Vo** usual call is a rattled musical *chreetchee-chree-chee* or variants, and also a series of upslurred squeals, rather like a small raptor.

Elliot's Woodpecker *Dendropicos elliotii* 18cm, 7"
The only woodpecker with a *plain dark olive back, wings and tail and well-streaked yellowish underparts*. Closer views reveal rather plain sides to the face, a black forecrown with red on the hindcrown and nape in ad ♂, or an all-black crown and nape in ad ♀. **HH** rather uncommon residents in highland forests of WUg, Rw and Bu, with rare isolated records from west Mt. Elgon, Ug. **Vo** call is a cross-sounding rattled rising and falling buzzy churr, and also gives a nasal complaining *weeeyu*.

Speckle-breasted Woodpecker *Dendropicos poecilolaemus* 14cm, 5.5"
[Uganda Spotted Woodpecker]
Combination of lightly barred back, spotted wings and *pale yellow underparts with fine black speckling across the breast* is distinctive. Ad ♂ has red restricted to the hindcrown and nape, while ad ♀ has the crown and nape blackish-brown. Both sexes show a small area of red on the rump in fresh plumage but this is quickly worn off: tail has golden-yellow shafts. **HH** locally common in open woodland, at forest edge, and along wooded streams within farmland, from 700–2100m. **Vo** calls a hurried series of harsh metallic churrs *chrrr'chrrr'chrrr...* and also a repeated *ch-rit*.

Gabon Woodpecker *Dendropicos gabonensis* 14cm, 5.5"
Small dark woodpecker with a plain olive-green back, wings and tail, narrowly streaked sides to the face, and *yellowish underparts broadly and heavily streaked, spotted and barred blackish*. Ad ♂ has a red hindcrown and nape, while ad ♀ has entire crown dark brown. **HH** in our area only known from Semliki Forest, WUg, where it is probably very uncommon. **Vo** calls a musical trilled rattle and a harsh *tree-trree-trree*.

Plate 137

Cardinal
Woodpecker

♂

hemprichii

♀

♂

lepidus

Brown-backed
Woodpecker

♂

♀

nominate

♂

♀

Elliot's
Woodpecker

Speckle-breasted
Woodpecker

♀

♂

Gabon Woodpecker

♂

♀

STRIPE-FACED WOODPECKERS
Three forest or woodland woodpeckers with distinct strong face patterns.

Bearded Woodpecker *Dendropicos namaquus* 23cm, 9"

A large woodpecker with a *bold black and white face pattern,* finely barred dark olive back and wings, and paler *tightly barred olive-brown and buff underparts.* Ad ♂ has a black forecrown (with tiny white speckles) and a red hindcrown. Ad ♀ has the entire crown blackish. Imm has speckled red, black and white on the crown in both sexes. **HH** widespread, but rather local in variety of woodland and bush country with large trees, from sea-level to 3000m. **Vo** call is a long descending series of yelps *kree-kree-kree-kreekreekree...* that accelerate towards the end.

Stierling's Woodpecker *Dendropicos stierlingi* 17cm, 6.5"

Similar to Bearded Woodpecker, but much smaller with a *plain dark olive-brown back, wings and tail, and whitish underparts distinctly cross-barred and streaked with brown.* Ad ♂ has a mostly red crown with a brown forecrown. Ad ♀ has crown entirely blackish-brown. Imm has red on the crown in both sexes. **HH** very local and poorly known in miombo woodland across STz. **Vo** call is a low wavering rattle.

Yellow-crested Woodpecker *Dendropicos xantholophus* 23cm, 9"

A large dark woodpecker with a bold black and white face pattern, a virtu-ally plain dark olive back, wings and tail, and *olive-brown underparts well spotted with pale yellowish-buff,* becoming barred on the lower flanks and vent. Ad ♂ has a *small area of yellow on the hindcrown* (which is often hard to see), ad ♀ has an entirely blackish crown and nape. Imm has yellow on the crown in both sexes. **HH** locally common in good forest and dense sec-ondary growth from 700–2150m. **Vo** calls an excited *kwikwikwi...* and a repeated slurred and burry descending *kree.*

GREY WOODPECKERS
Plain olive-green and grey woodpeckers with varying amount of red on the head, rump and belly. Variously considered as two or three species.

Grey Woodpecker *Dendropicos goertae* 19cm, 7.5"

Two distinct races occur in our area. In Ug south to NWTz and east to CKe (north of the equator) nominate ad ♂ has a red crown and rump, and *no or very little red, yellow, or orange on the belly.* Ad ♀ is similar but lacks red on the head. In the CKe highlands south to NTz, ad ♂ of race *rhodeogaster* has similar red on the crown and rump, but has a *large patch of red on the belly.* Ad ♀ is similar but with no red on the crown. This race is sometimes con-sidered conspecific with the Ethiopian form *spodocephalus* and known as **Grey-headed Woodpecker.** Imms are duller than ads, with slightly barred underparts and less intense red areas. **HH** common in a wide range of woodland, forest edge, bush country and farmland with trees, from 700–3000m. **Vo** common call is a descending series of squealed *kwikwik-wi...,* but also gives an upslurred musical and churred *trrree't'ri'tree.*

Olive Woodpecker *Dendropicos griseocephalus* 18cm, 7"

Similar to Grey Woodpecker but darker overall with *largely olive, not grey, underparts.* Ad ♂ has a red crown and rump, and in race *ruwenzori* (WUg south to STz) also has red on the belly. In N and NETz *kilimensis* is greyer below and lacks red on the belly. ♀♀ of both races lack red on the head. Imms have some red on the crown in both sexes, and greyer underparts than ads. **HH** locally common in montane forest from 900–3700m, where it frequently joins mixed-species flocks. Where occurring with Grey Woodpecker, it prefers higher altitudes and forest interior. Hybrids are known from Rw. **Vo** commonly calls a repeated upslurred *krrrrreee,* while other calls are similar to Grey, but burrier, and less piercing.

Plate 138

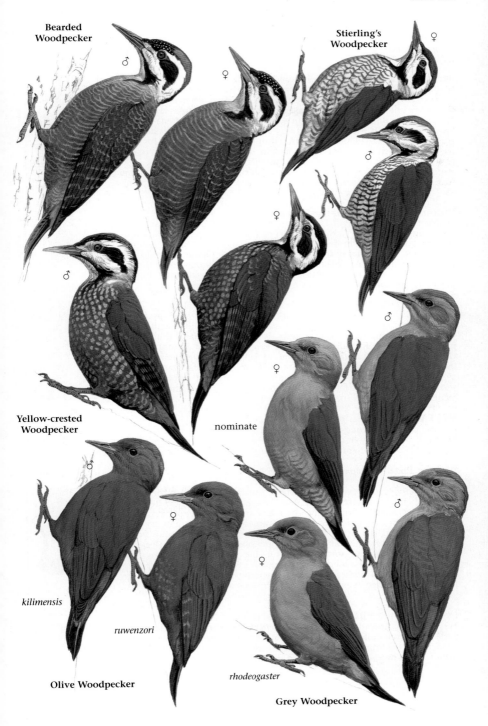

Bearded Woodpecker ♂ ♀

Stierling's Woodpecker ♀ ♂

♀

Yellow-crested Woodpecker ♂

nominate ♀ ♂

kilimensis ♂ ♀ *ruwenzori*

Olive Woodpecker

rhodeogaster ♀ ♂

Grey Woodpecker

BROADBILLS

Small thickset birds with flat wide bills that inhabit forest interiors. During a tight circular display flight, African and Rufous-sided broadbills make a remarkable mechanical sound with their wings (produced by the air moving through their stiff primaries). Immatures are like adults, but duller.

African Broadbill   *Smithornis capensis*   13cm, 5"
Small and chunky: ad ♂ is dark brown above with a black cap, grey-brown ear-coverts, a white back (which is difficult to see when perched), and buffy or whitish underparts heavily streaked throughout with black. Ad ♀ is similar, but has a duller grey-crown. In coastal Ke and SETz birds have grey-brown crowns. **HH** widespread, but very shy, local and solitary residents of good forest from sea-level to 1800m. Sit upright and motionless for long periods, but then fly fast and direct, and are difficult to relocate. **Vo** in display the wings make a loud far-carrying, mechanical and vibrating *br-er-errrrrrrr* slightly falling then rising, before falling to fade. At close quarters high whistled introductory notes can be heard, a quiet mewing *huiii, huiii*. **SS** ♀ African Shrike-flycatcher.

Rufous-sided Broadbill   *Smithornis rufolateralis*   11cm, 4.5"
Similar to African Broadbill, but black cap extends well below eye and over ear-coverts, and has *bright rufous patches on sides of breast*. White back usually concealed except in display flight. ♀ similar, but cap dark grey. **HH** restricted to the interior of forests in WUg from 700–1300m. **Vo** in display wings create higher pitched sound than African Broadbill, without the rising and falling effect. High introductory notes audible at close range, a quiet *huiii*, sometimes followed by a long drawn out *wheeeee*.

African Green Broadbill   *Pseudocalyptomena graueri*   11cm, 4.5"   ● ●
Beautiful *leaf-green broadbill with a pale blue throat, upper breast and vent*. Crown is buff-green with small dark streaks. Imm is duller with green vent. **HH** endemic to montane forests along the Albertine Rift and very uncommon in the Bwindi-Impenetrable Forest, SWUg, at around 2200m. Groups of 2–4 occur in the upper levels of forest undergrowth and in the lower canopy. May join mixed-species flocks, moving along branches and gleaning for insects. **Vo** call is a high pitched hissing rhythmical series *sii-sii-sii-siiiii*, the last note falling slightly then rising, given perched or while feeding in a group as a contact call.

PITTAS

Ground-dwelling colourful birds with strong straight bills, long legs and short tails. Breeding birds call and display in the canopy, but otherwise are usually found in leaf litter on the forest floor. Despite their bright colours can be very hard to see. Flight is fast and direct. Sexes alike.

African Pitta   *Pitta angolensis*   18cm, 7"
[Angola Pitta]
Very attractive and distinctive with a boldly marked head, green back, blue shoulders and a red belly. In flight, black wings show obvious white patch at base of primaries: bright blue shoulders and rump conspicuous. Best identified from Green-breasted Pitta by *tawny-buff breast*. Imm duller with buffy-pink vent. **HH** extremely shy, often on the ground within dense cover, and standing motionless for long periods. Breeds in SETz Dec–Apr, elsewhere migratory, occurring in small numbers north to WUg and coastal Ke, May–Sep. **Vo** calls a loud far-carrying and explosive *quoip* (given from a lateral branch in mid-canopy and coinciding with a jump). Notes are identical and spaced every few seconds. On migration makes a low croaking sound.

Green-breasted Pitta   *Pitta reichenowi*   18cm, 7"
Very similar to African Pitta, but *breast green*, whitish throat bordered below with black. Imm duller and darker then ad with an olive-brown breast. **HH** restricted to the interior of forests in W and SUg from 1100–1400m. Rarely recorded and must be considered very uncommon. **Vo** unknown.

Plate 139

display flight

Rufous-sided
Broadbill

♀   ♂

♂

♀

African
Broadbill

African Green
Broadbill

Ad

Imm

Ad

Ad

Green-breasted
Pitta

African
Pitta

LARKS

A difficult group to identify without comparative experience of the more common species; further complicated by different populations of several having different colour morphs, often matching the soil type they live on. Pay careful attention to presence or lack of rufous in wings, colour of outer-tail, face pattern and habitat. Sexes alike. Immatures similar to adults unless otherwise described.

GRASSLAND AND BUSHED GRASSLAND LARKS

Rufous-naped Lark *Mirafra africana* 18cm, 7"

Quite large and short-tailed, with conspicuous rufous wings in flight. No (or very little) rufous on the nape in our area. Bill long, obvious pale buffy supercilium, crown feathers often raised giving a shaggy headed appearance, outer-tail buffy. Seven races occur: *athi* is typical of most forms; *nyikae* and *nigrescens* (from above 2000m around Njombe SWTz) are much darker above and the breast streaking on *nigrescens* extends over the flanks; *tropicalis* (CUg–CTz) is strongly washed rufous below. **HH** most common and widespread lark, occurs in grasslands with or without bush cover, and in open farmland from 1000–3000m. Sings from the tops of prominent perches including bushes, termite hills and fence posts. **Vo** normal song *sii-su-eeeee* with middle falling and the last part gently rising to fade. Many local variations based on this, also a monotonous piping. Often the most characteristic wet-season call of upland grasslands.

Red-winged Lark *Mirafra hypermetra* 23cm, 9"

A large version of Rufous-naped Lark with a longer tail and *black spots at sides of breast usually forming two small blackish patches* (may not be visible on worn birds or imms). Long bill, rufous wings, buffy supercilium, slight shaggy appearance to crown and brown tail all generally similar to Rufous-naped. **HH** occurs mainly to N and E of Rufous-naped from near sea-level to 1350m, preferring drier areas with more bush cover. Often perches and sings from the tops of small bushes. **Vo** very fluty, rather chat-like song, with short varied phrases repeated monotonously. Usually given from a perch, but also in heavy laboured flight.

Angola Lark *Mirafra angolensis* 17cm, 6.5"

Similar to dark forms of Rufous-naped Lark, but with a thinly streaked breast, less rufous in the wings and a *conspicuous buff-white outer-tail* obvious in flight. **HH** in our area known only from near Mumba, SWTz. **Vo** unmistakable, loud, mournful rising and falling series of burry notes. Usually from ground, but has a distinctive display flight climbing to about 20m and then gliding down. Also chips and squeaks.

Flappet Lark *Mirafra rufocinnamomea* 14cm, 5.5"

Fairly small with four races in our area. Generally *very brown (or rufous brown) both above and below,* with a buffy-rufous outer-tail. Races *tigriana* and *kawirondensis* (in the west) are heavily spotted blackish above, *torrida* (NEUg-ETz) is much more rufous, and *fischeri* (SEKe-STz) is warm earthy-brown above without bold markings. **HH** often first encountered in display flight when it makes loud far-carrying *prrrrrrrr-rrrp* sound with its wings. On the ground rather shy, often crouching and keeping near to cover. Inhabits grasslands with or without scattered trees and bush from sea-level to 1800m. **Vo** rarely heard song from top of bush is a loud, piercing serin-like rising and falling *si-uu-si-si-uu* similar to Southern Grosbeak-Canary.

Sun Lark *Galerida modesta* 15cm, 6"

Fairly small, rather dark above with buffy-white supercilium, and dull rufous on wings visible in flight. Can raise crown feathers giving a crested appearance. Below white throat contrasts with pale brown underparts and a heavily streaked breast. Similar Flappet Lark never raises crest and is browner below with indistinct breast streaking. Fawn-coloured Lark is larger, whiter below and occurs to the east. **HH** restricted to bare ground and short grass in extreme NWUg. Found in pairs or small flocks, but very uncommon. **Vo** song is similar to Fawn-coloured Lark, but more rapid with fuller notes, and less scratchy.

Plate 140

nigrescens

tropicalis

Rufous-naped Lark

athi

Angola Lark

Red-winged Lark

fischeri

kawirondensis

Sun Lark

Flappet Lark

Somali Short-toed Lark *Calandrella somalica* 14cm, 5.5"

Smallish, size similar to Singing Bush and Flappet larks. Two races occur: *athensis* (**Athi Short-toed Lark**) from SKe to NTz is grey-brown above with heavy blackish streaks and buffy fringes: *pale supercilium and eye-ring and a pale pinkish bill* are distinctive at close range. *Wings without rufous patches*, tail dark with buffy-white edges. Breast to vent washed pale brown with short heavy dark streaks across breast, throat whitish. Race *megaensis* in NKe is similar, but general tone more sandy-buff. Flappet is much browner below, while Singing Bush has an obvious white outer-tail and rufous wing patches. **HH** occurs in flocks on open ground with short grass cover from 1200–1850m. Generally uncommon away from the Athi Plains, Ke and Arusha area, NTz. **Vo** song complex, rising and falling notes incorporating mimicry, vaguely like a smoother version of an *Acrocephalus* warbler.

White-tailed Lark *Mirafra albicauda* 13cm, 5"

Similar to Flappet and Singing Bush larks but *upperparts very heavily streaked blackish* giving a much darker impression. Rufous patches on wings and *white outer-tail obvious in flight.* Underparts buffy with short blackish breast streaks, throat white. **HH** generally uncommon in grasslands with or without open woodland from 600–2000m; particularly attracted to black cotton soil. **Vo** songs differ: west of the Rift Valley sings a complex rambling of harsh and sweet notes, plus much mimicry, either from a perch or in a fluttering hesitant song-flight. In the east, a scratchy short-spaced repeated series is sung in flight.

DRY COUNTRY LARKS

Fawn-coloured Lark *Mirafra africanoides* 16cm, 6"

Medium-sized with variable colour morphs which are generally paler in arid areas, more rufous on red soils and darker in the highlands. All are quite heavily streaked above with a *bold white supercilium* and rufous wing patches which are visible in flight. Underparts whitish with short blackish streaks across the breast. Slightly smaller Flappet Lark has an indistinct supercilium and is much browner below. **HH** solitary birds and pairs are common from 500–1800m, inhabiting semi-arid and bush country with or without some grass cover. **Vo** scratchy serin-like song is usually a short and hurried series given from a bush top or in flight.

Gillett's Lark *Mirafra gilletti* 17cm, 6.5"

Similar to Fawn-coloured Lark with a long whitish supercilium, but differs in having a pinkish-rufous crown and ear-coverts, a *greyish rump and rufous-brown streaking across the breast* (blackish on Fawn-coloured). **HH** in our area known only from birds collected near the Somali border in 1901. Prefers open arid bush country on sandy or stony soils. **Vo** usual song from a low shrub is a monotonous *sii-sii-sii-seeu-seu* the first three notes identical, the last two lower, falling and more hurried and ending rather abruptly. It is soft, lacking all the scratchiness of Fawn-coloured Lark.

Singing Bush Lark *Mirafra cantillans* 13cm, 5"

Fairly small, grey-brown above with dark streaking, *buffy supercilium accentuates dark ear-coverts*, bill dark above, pinkish below. Underparts buffy with small streaks on sides of breast, throat white. In often rather hesitant flight shows rufous wing patches and an obvious *pure white outer-tail*. **HH** locally common in bush country with sparse grass cover from sea-level to 1800m. Also appears in flocks in seasonal grasslands during the rains. Flies and then dives into cover when flushed. **Vo** sings from a high circling flight or from bushes, a continuous rather monotonous series of repeated notes preceded by slower slightly lower notes resulting in a distinctive pattern.

Friedmann's Lark *Mirafra pulpa* 13cm, 5"

Very similar to Singing Bush Lark, but overall tones *more rufous* and the bill is slightly larger. Best identified by voice and has a white-throated look when calling. **HH** little known: most records are after the rains in the Tsavo region of Ke. Likes open bush country with short grass cover from 600–900m. **Vo** calls from the tops of bushes and in flight, a rising and falling reedy whistled *whooyu*, repeated at about 2 second intervals.

Plate 141

athensis

Somali Short-toed Lark

megaensis

White-tailed

White-tailed Lark

Fawn-coloured Lark

Gillett's Lark

Gillett's

Singing

Friedmann's Lark

Singing Bush Lark

Pink-breasted Lark *Mirafra poecilosterna* 16cm, 6"
Slim appearance and bill give a rather pipit-like impression. Upperparts lightly mottled grey-brown with a greyer crown, *sides of face, throat and breast mottled pinkish-brown* like no other lark or pipit. **HH** common in bush country with little ground cover from 150–1800m, where frequently perches on bush tops. **Vo** monotonous descending hissed song is given from small trees (similar to song of overlapping Ashy Cisticola). Also utters an occasional single squeaked *tseet* from the ground.

Crested Lark *Galerida cristata* 17cm, 6.5"
A sandy grey-brown lark with a *long pointed crest* which is often raised (or can be blown up by the wind), but is not always immediately obvious. Underparts very pale sandy with dark brown streaks across the breast. Very similar Thekla Lark is darker above with heavier short spots across the breast. **HH** common within range particularly in sandy desert with sparse cover from 400–900m. Usually in pairs, but more may gather at water holes. **Vo** long rambling song usually from ground or a low perch consists of many randomly introduced rather scratchy notes (some sound like a high-pitched more hurried version of Rufous-naped Lark).

Thekla Lark *Galerida theklae* 17cm, 6.5"
Very similar to Crested Lark but darker above with shorter heavier spots across the breast. Combination of dark toned upperparts and breast spotting accentuates whiteness of the throat. **HH** occurs in pairs and loose flocks in rockier areas than Crested Lark. Very common in the lava deserts east of Lake Turkana, Ke, from 400–1300m. **Vo** sings from rocky ground, a short series of sweet notes recalling a bunting. More complex series with mimicry in flight.

Collared Lark *Mirafra collaris* 15cm, 6"
An attractive and distinctive species. Mostly *bright cinnamon-rufous above,* with a lightly streaked black and white hindneck. *Black band across base of neck separates white throat from red mottling across upper breast.* In flight, rufous upperparts and wing-coverts contrast with *blackish flight feathers and tail.* **HH** little known within our area, but occurs in arid bush country on red soils from 100–1350m. **Vo** song is poorly known, but reported as a plaintive rising whistle.

Williams's Lark *Mirafra williamsi* 14cm, 5.5" ●
Similar to Singing Bush and White-tailed larks but not so heavily streaked above. Two colour morphs occur: both are comparatively plain above (apart from some crown streaking). The dark morph is blackish-brown above, with *dark chestnut and black mottling and streaking on the breast and flanks*; rufous morph is rufous-brown above with dark rufous-brown streaking across the breast. In rather strong and direct flight both show rufous wing patches and white outer-tail feathers. *Bill pale greyish or pinkish above and white below.* **HH** Ke endemic known only from the Dida-Galgalu desert area and between Isiolo and Garba Tula. It inhabits rocky lava desert with short grass cover from 600–1350m. **Vo** song is described as being thin and rather scratchy, with random loud sharper notes towards the end.

Plate 142

Pink-breasted Lark

Crested Lark

Thekla Lark

Collared Lark

Williams's Lark

rufous

dark

OTHER LARKS

These larks do not fit easily into the previously mentioned groups. They are not specifically related or similar looking and are included here purely for convenience.

Red-capped Lark *Calandrella cinerea* 15cm, 6″

Scattered but widespread race *saturatior* is a distinctive lark with a *bright rufous cap* (which is sometimes raised) and *rufous patches on either side of the breast*. It has a bold white supercilium, unstreaked underparts, and shows a very dark white-edged tail when flushed. CKe highland race *williamsi* is greyer and more streaked above. Imm is very different with dark brown upperparts, finely spotted white on the crown, and with white fringes to the mantle; underparts with some brown spots. **HH** widespread and common but with a patchy distribution, sometimes gathering in large flocks on short grasslands from 950–3000m. **Vo** in circular flight utters a continuous rhythmical and monotonous song based on one note. Single liquid chirrups given when flushed.

Greater Short-toed Lark *Calandrella brachydactyla* 14cm, 5.5″

Eastern race *longipennis* has occurred as a vagrant. Best identified by *pale overall coloration* with a *small pale yellowish bill*, and dark tail with white on the outermost feathers. Also shows a creamy-buff supercilium, and small light streaks at sides of upper breast sometimes appearing as a distinctive small dark patch. **HH** in our area, known from only two Ke records: Athi River in Nov 1899 and Ukunda in Dec 1964. **Vo** song not heard in region.

Short-tailed Lark *Pseudalaemon fremantlii* 14cm, 5.5″

A boldly marked, rather long-billed and short-tailed lark, with a distinctive *black crescent below the eye and vertical bar down the cheek*. Northern race *megaensis* is more rufous than the southern grey toned *delamerei*, although this race also has a rufous morph. **HH** resident and erratic wanderer usually found in small flocks on dry soils with short grass, and on burnt grassland, from 1000–1700m. **Vo** distinctive song is an attractive jumble of rising and falling notes with minor-key intrusions. On the ground, it calls with chips and explosive downslurs.

Spike-heeled Lark *Chersomanes albofasciata* 12cm, 5″

Dark brown above with pale edgings giving a scaly appearance. *Bill long and decurved, throat very white contrasting with remainder of underparts which are entirely rufous with some streaking across the breast*. In flight, shows distinctive *white band across end of tail*. **HH** strikingly upright lark only known in our area from white soils in semi-arid country about 45km north of Arusha, Tz. Found in pairs or small groups on bare ground from 1350–1550m. **Vo** un-lark-like calls more likely to be confused with a shorebird.

Rufous-rumped Lark *Pinarocorys erythropygia* 20cm, 8″

A large dark brown lark with a bold face pattern and heavily spotted underparts. From similar Dusky Lark by *rufous rump and sides to tail*, flanks and vent washed russet. **HH** in our area uncommon and largely a migrant from the north-west favouring burnt grasslands and open woodland. **Vo** song and calls are long, mournful, whistled downslurs with occasional intrusive scratchy burrs.

Dusky Lark *Pinarocorys nigricans* 20cm, 8″

Uniform dark blackish-brown above without rufous on the rump, tail or flanks. Within range could possibly be confused with Groundscraper Thrush (see plate 171). **HH** mainly found in small flocks in miombo woodland, but also on burnt and open grassland with some tree cover. Birds actively forage on the ground and frequently flick their wings. **Vo** usually silent in region, but a repeated monotonous *scree-scree-scree-...*, is recorded elsewhere.

Plate 143

Imm

Red-capped Lark

saturatior

Greater Short-toed
Lark

Ad

megaensis

Short-tailed Lark

Spike-heeled
Lark

Dusky Lark

Rufous-rumped Lark

Masked Lark *Spizocorys personata* 15cm, 6"
A distinctive lark with grey-brown or warm brown upperparts, a *black face mask and a pale pinkish or horn coloured bill.* Underparts unstreaked with the small whitish throat blending to greyish breast and rufous belly. **HH** common within restricted range, inhabiting black lava desert with sparse grass cover, from 400–1600m. **Vo** various calls described in flight and on the ground include a rolling *tew-tew-tutew-tew,* and a high-pitched *treeeeeeee.*

SPARROW-LARKS
Small chunky sparrow-like larks with heavy bills, usually found in flocks. Sexually dimorphic: males are boldly marked on the head and underparts; females and immatures are much more drab.

Fischer's Sparrow-Lark *Eremopterix leucopareia* 11cm, 4.5"
Ad ♂ has blackish-brown facial markings adjoining a *paler brown (or chestnut-brown) crown and nape; no white on crown.* Blackish-brown stripe from chin to vent forms a *neat line down centre of breast,* sides of breast and flanks buffy. Back and wings dull grey-brown, and no white on tail. Ad ♀ has *upperparts medium brown and a dark blackish-brown stripe on belly.* Imm is like a dull ♀ with more mottled upperparts; small dark mark on belly very hard to see. **HH** common and widespread occurring up to 2000m in dry grasslands, on airstrips and in semi-arid areas. Mainly to the west of other sparrow-larks. **Vo** usual call heard from perched or flying birds is a double, and quite explosive *tsi-sit,* the song being an embellishment of these notes and rather sparrow-like.

Chestnut-headed Sparrow-Lark *Eremopterix signata* 11cm, 4.5"
In nominate race, ad ♂ is similar to Fischer's Sparrow-Lark, but cleaner looking. *Black or dark chestnut facial markings encircle white patch on crown.* Cheek patch very white. Facial pattern extends as a *broad black vertical stripe from chin to vent* (broader than on Fischer's), sides of breast and flanks white. Back and wings pale grey-brown, narrow white tail edges. Ad ♀ has indication of ♂-like facial pattern but crown brown, *supercilium pale-rufous,* cheeks buffy-white, and upperparts greyer than ♀ Fischer's. Imm is like a poorly marked ♀. Race *harrisoni* in north-west of range is greyer above. **HH** common in a variety of arid and semi-arid habitats including lava rock and sandy desert, open stony areas with some bush cover, and short dry grasslands from sea-level to 1500m. **Vo** call consists of spaced piping notes, some similar to Lesser Striped Swallow. Song is a series of repeated and rising mournful notes.

Chestnut-backed Sparrow-Lark *Eremopterix leucotis* 13cm, 5"
[Chestnut-backed Finchlark]
Ad ♂ is a distinctive sparrow-lark, with a *rich chestnut back and wings,* a bold black and white head pattern and mostly black underparts. White on ear-coverts and nape, not on crown. Shows white on outer-tail in flight. Ad ♀ duller than ♂ with variable (but usually extensive) black mottling on the head and underparts, and *chestnut wing-coverts.* Imm is like a pale ♀. **HH** rather local within range and subject to erratic wanderings. Can occur in large numbers, particularly liking black soils and recently burnt grasslands, between sea-level and 1800m. **Vo** song is more complex than that of the other sparrow-larks, a mournful series of slurs and chips delivered both in flight and from the ground.

Plate 144

Fischer's
Sparrow-Lark

Masked Lark

nominate

Chestnut-headed
Sparrow-Lark

Chestnut-backed Sparrow-Lark

MARTINS AND SWALLOWS

Highly aerial birds that prefer open areas and often occur together in mixed-species flocks. Most martins are brown and white with short only slightly forked tails. Swallows of the genus *Hirundo* are mostly blue-black above, although some have red rumps, with deeply forked and white spotted tails. Saw-wings also have deeply forked tails, but these are broader (particularly at the base) and lack the white spots. Sexes alike; immatures similar to ads, but duller with pale fringed upperparts, and shorter tails in the *Hirundo* swallows. Some species migrate in large numbers.

BROWN AND WHITE MARTINS

Rock Martin   *Hirundo fuligula*   12cm, 5"
Brown martin showing a slightly contrasting rufous throat if seen well. In flight, fanned tail shows small white spots near the end of each feather. **HH** common and widespread occurring in pairs and small loose flocks wherever there are cliffs, but also breeds on buildings in towns. Most numerous in the highlands above 1500m, but occasionally occurs down to sea-level. **Vo** utters short monotonous phrases, each terminating in a buzzy *churr*.

Plain Martin   *Riparia paludicola*   12cm, 5"
[Brown-throated Sand Martin]
Entire upperparts, throat and breast are brown: *belly is white*. **HH** common and widespread species which often occurs in large flocks over water in the highlands, but which is not restricted to specific altitudes. **Vo** calls a harsh rasping *churr* from perches and in flight.

Sand Martin   *Riparia riparia*   12cm, 5"
[Bank Swallow]
Plain brown above and white below with a brown breast band, uniform brown underwing, and slightly forked tail. Similar Banded Martin is much larger with white underwing-coverts. **HH** common Palearctic visitor occurring from Sep to early-May between sea level and 1800m. Sometimes appears in flocks of thousands which move fast and direct on migration. **Vo** series of churrs on different notes resulting in a formless song which is twittering and rather lark-like in quality.

Banded Martin   *Riparia cincta*   15cm, 6"
Similar to Sand Martin but much larger, with a *short white stripe in front of the eyes*, *white underwing-coverts* and a square-ended tail. **HH** single birds or small flocks occur over grasslands from sea-level to 2500m. Flight is low and slow with frequent glides. **Vo** musical notes are given in descending series, with a twangy, nasal, rather lark-like quality. Calls in flight, but the song is usually delivered from top of low vegetation.

Mascarene Martin   *Phedina borbonica*   14cm, 5.5"
Above brown with darker wings and tail. Underparts white with *extensive brown streaking* and grey-brown flanks. In flight, breast streaking can be difficult to see against a bright sky. **HH** very rare visitor from Madagascar to coastal Ke and Tz in Jun–Aug. **Vo** call is a double nasal buzz.

Common House Martin   *Delichon urbica*   14cm, 5.5 "
[Northern House Martin]
Rather stocky blue-black martin with a *white rump and underparts*: tail forked, but not elongated as with some pale-rumped swallows. Imm duller and browner. **HH** common Palearctic visitor from Sep–Apr. **Vo** in flight gives a pleasant, short, buzzy chirp, often with many calling at the same time. **SS** Grey-rumped Swallow and white-rumped swifts.

Plate 145

Rock Martin

Sand Martin

Plain Martin

Banded Martin

Mascarene Martin

Ad

Common House Martin

SWALLOWS WITH RUFOUS RUMPS

Colour of ear-coverts, underwing-coverts and underparts aid identification. Sexes are similar, but female may have shorter outer-tail streamers. Immatures are even shorter-tailed, with duller (sometimes brownish) upperparts and paler underparts.

Red-rumped Swallow *Hirundo daurica* 18cm, 7″
Blue-black cap descends to eye and down nape: *ear-coverts rufous*. All pale rufous below with *black undertail-coverts*, pale rufous underwing-coverts, and a dark tail. **HH** common and widespread within range although more numerous above 1000m. **Vo** flight call consists of a pinched, nasal and rather trumpeted *zwink-zwink*. Song is a quiet rambling of soft nasal squeaks, each phrase ending in a louder *schwee-eenk*.

Mosque Swallow *Hirundo senegalensis* 21cm, 8″
Larger and bulkier than Red-rumped Swallow, but similar with a blue-black cap also descending to the eye and rufous ear-coverts. *Pale throat contrasts with richer rufous breast* and rufous (not black) undertail-coverts. Easily identified in flight by *white underwing-coverts* contrasting with blackish flight feathers. Race *monteiri* (Tz and EKe) has white spots on the tail, while *saturatior* (elsewhere) has an all-dark tail. **HH** pairs or small loose flocks are widespread from sea-level to 2600m, occurring in all but the most arid areas. **Vo** song is loud and rambling, given either perched or in flight. Notes are drawn-out nasal slurs, very similar in quality to Grey-backed Fiscal.

Rufous-chested Swallow *Hirundo semirufa* 19cm, 7.5″
[Red-breasted Swallow]
Blue-black cap extends below eye and over ear-coverts. Chin to undertail-coverts rufous, with pale rufous underwing-coverts. Ad in fresh plumage has very long tail streamers giving a rather slim appearance. **HH** single birds and pairs are generally uncommon, occurring in wooded grasslands and cultivated areas from 700–1700m in the west. **Vo** song is a hurried nasal jumble, ending with a high-pitched drawn-out descending *seeeeuuu*. This can be given frequently, usually from the vicinity of a termite mound, but is also given in flight.

Lesser Striped Swallow *Hirundo abyssinica* 17cm, 6.5″
A strongly marked and richly coloured swallow with an extensive *bright rufous cap and heavy black streaking on white underparts*. **HH** pairs and small groups are widespread and common from sea-level to 2200m, occurring in a wide range of habitats apart from very arid country. **Vo** cheerful ramble of rising and falling nasal chips and twitters, terminating in a louder and deliberate well-spaced series of descending nasal notes. Usually given from a perch, but will sing in flight.

Greater Striped Swallow *Hirundo cucullata* 18cm, 7″
Much paler and less well-marked than Lesser Striped Swallow. Underparts buffy (not white) with *indistinct streaking* only visible at close range. May suggest Red-rumped Swallow, but lacks the black undertail-coverts. **HH** an intra-African migrant from the south which is rare in our area, and only recorded from S and CTz. **Vo** song is unlikely to be heard, but calls resemble those of Red-rumped Swallow.

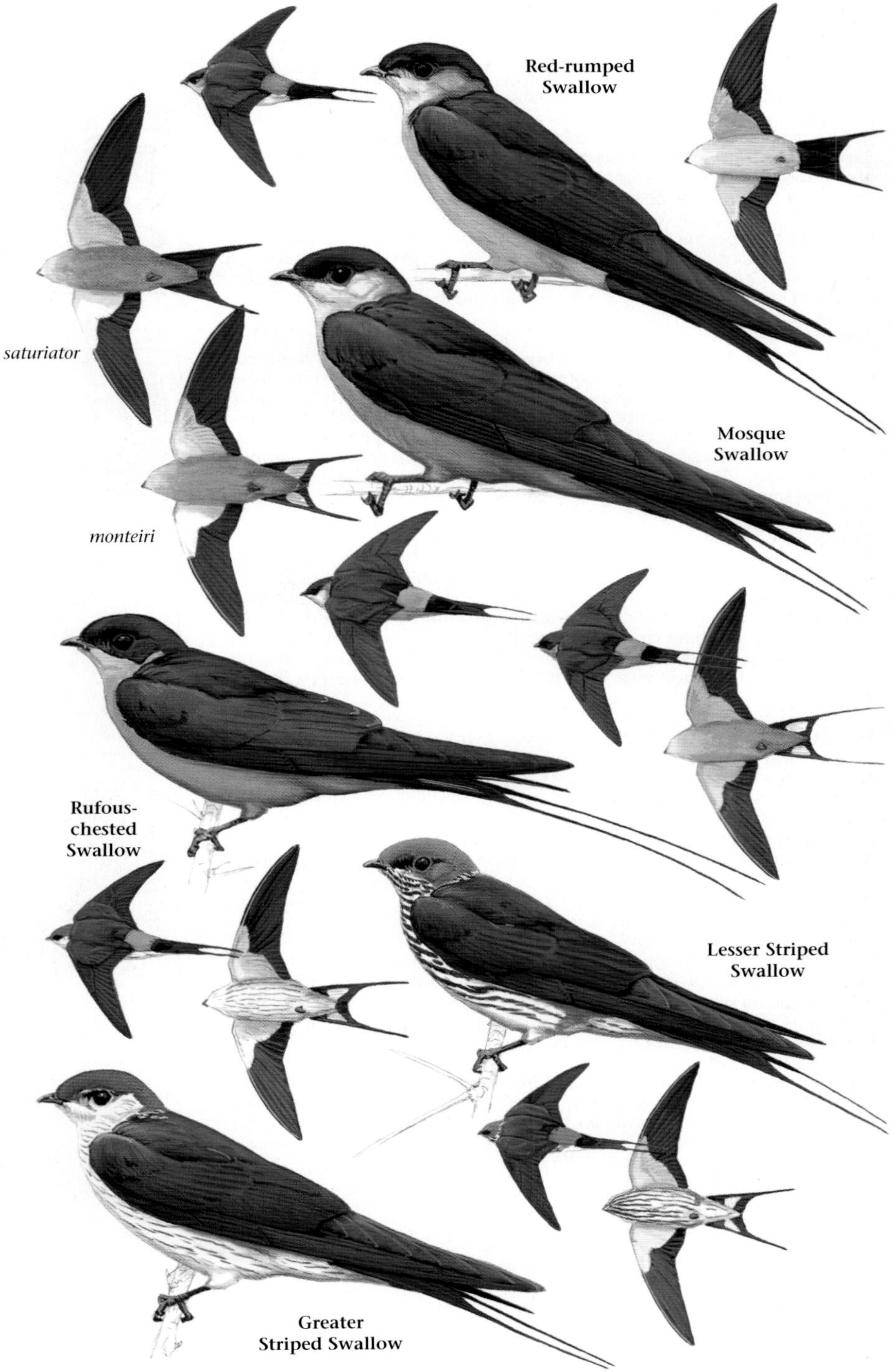

Plate 146

Red-rumped
Swallow

saturiator

monteiri

Mosque
Swallow

Rufous-
chested
Swallow

Lesser Striped
Swallow

Greater
Striped Swallow

BLUE-BLACK AND WHITE SWALLOWS
Chestnut head and throat markings, and the presence or absence of breast bands aid identification.

Barn Swallow   *Hirundo rustica*   19cm, 7.5"
[European Swallow]
Ad ♂ has upperparts and breast band blue-black, a *chestnut forecrown and throat*, and white or pinkish underparts (grey in Angola Swallow). Tail is deeply forked with white spots on shorter central feathers. Imm is variable, duller and browner above, with less chestnut on the head and throat, and a shorter tail. **HH** very common Palearctic visitor from Aug–Apr occurring throughout the region from sea-level to 3000m. Sometimes migrates and roosts in huge flocks. A few birds stay all year round. **Vo** usually fairly silent in the region, but song delivered in flight or perched is a continuous rambling and cheerful twitter, with a finch-like quality.

Angola Swallow   *Hirundo angolensis*   15cm, 6"
Very similar to Barn Swallow, but *upperparts brighter blue* in good light, and tail forked but short with obvious large white spots. Chestnut throat extends through a broken breast band and the *remainder of the underparts are grey*. **HH** common mainly to the west of the Great Rift Valley, but also locally in ETz. Occurs in villages and a wide variety of open country from about 700–2600m, often nesting under bridges. **Vo** song given from a perch consists of loud squeaky, rather unpleasant notes. Flight calls have the same squeaky quality.

Ethiopian Swallow   *Hirundo aethiopica*   13cm, 5"
Similar to Barn Swallow with a chestnut forecrown, but has a *white or very pale buff throat, and an incomplete blackish breast band*. In good light looks blue above and very white below. Forked tail has large white spots and is shorter than ad Barn Swallow. **HH** although found in a wide variety of open country, it is only common along the Ke coast, occurring elsewhere in scattered pockets to 1900m. **Vo** most calls are nasal and harsh, but the infrequently heard song given in flight consists of many sweet cadences and trills.

Wire-tailed Swallow   *Hirundo smithii*   18cm, 7"
Ad ♂ is shiny blue above and very white below with a *neat chestnut cap*. In good plumage the white spotted tail has *long very thin wires,* but these can be hard to see at any distance. Imm has a dull brown crown and no tail wires. **HH** a fast-flying common and widespread swallow, usually in pairs and often near water, from sea-level to 2400m. **Vo** rather quiet, the song is a subdued twittering similar to Barn Swallow, but of a shorter duration.

White-throated Swallow   *Hirundo albigularis*   17cm, 6.5"
Similar to Ethiopian Swallow with a chestnut forecrown and white throat, but has a *complete breast band*. Stockier than Ethiopian, with proportions more like Barn Swallow: strongly forked white-spotted tail does not have very long outer-tail feathers. **HH** only one EA record at Lake Jipe, NETz, July 1957. **Vo** unlikely to be heard in the region.

Pearl-breasted Swallow   *Hirundo dimidiata*   14cm, 5.5"
Like a very dull Wire-tailed Swallow *without any chestnut on the crown or tail wires*. Underparts including the underwing-coverts are white. Tail is forked, but without white spots or long outer streamers. **HH** very uncommon in our area with the few records all from SWTz. **Vo** most notes are harsh, unattractive and nasal.

Plate 147

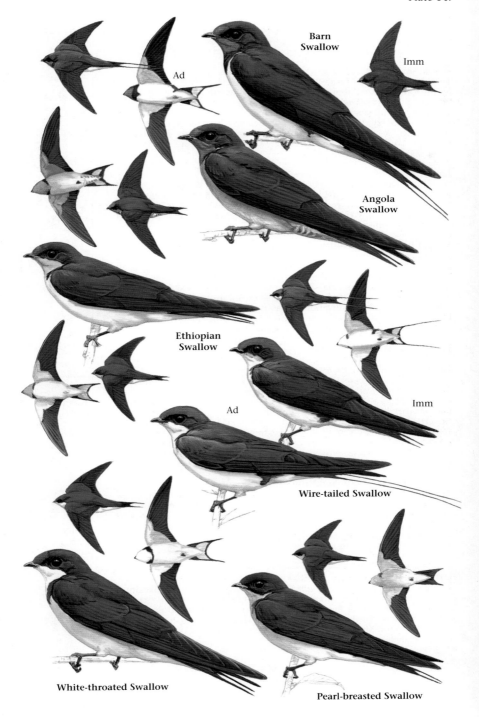

Barn Swallow

Ad

Imm

Angola Swallow

Ethiopian Swallow

Ad

Imm

Wire-tailed Swallow

White-throated Swallow

Pearl-breasted Swallow

SAW-WINGS

Black or black and white swallows with a variable dark green gloss which is difficult to see in the field. Male has a broad-based deeply forked tail that is shorter in female and immatures. Rather sedentary, often flying repeatedly around trees or small clearings.

Black Saw-wing *Psalidoprocne holomelas* 15cm, 6"
Three races occur: ad of widespread *massaica* is *all black* with a broad-based deeply forked tail, western *ruwenzori* is similar but shorter tailed, while the nominate race in coastal Ke is smaller overall. If seen well all show silvery grey-brown underwing-coverts. **HH** pairs and small flocks are common, mainly in the highlands, but range from sea-level to 3500m. Often occur in clearings in forest or over riverine woodland, frequently perching on tree tops. **Vo** frequently utters seemingly random soft nasal squeaks *weeu, see* in flight and also when perched.

Eastern Saw-wing *Psalidoprocne orientalis* 15cm, 6"
Sometimes considered a race of Black Saw-wing. Ad is easily identified by *pure white underwing-coverts*. Imm duller, browner and shorter tailed with greyish underwing-coverts. **HH** widespread, but localised in S and ETz from sea-level to 1800m. **Vo** similar to Black Saw-wing, but all calls are harsh and lack the nasal effect.

White-headed Saw-wing *Psalidoprocne albiceps* 14cm, 5.5"
Ad ♂ is very distinctive with a *pure white head and narrow black eye-lines*. Ad ♀ has dark ashy grey-brown head and is whiter on the throat. Imm is all dull dark brown with a slightly paler throat (which is difficult to see in the field). **HH** common from 700–2400m, occurring in a wider variety of habitats than other saw-wings, including forest clearings, open woodland, bushed grassland and cultivation. **Vo** similar to Black Saw-wing but is more hissing and breaks into a quiet chatter. Calls less frequently than most swallows, but will do so especially during aerial chases.

DARK BLUE SWALLOWS

Blue Swallow *Hirundo atrocaerulea* 23cm, 9" ●
Ad ♂ is glossy dark blue, sometimes showing a few white streaks along the flanks, *outer-tail feathers very long and narrow* (can be hard to see in the field). Ad ♀ has a shorter tail. Imm and non-br ads are dull blackish with random dark blue patches and short tails, resembling large blackish martins. **HH** breeds in the high grasslands of STz (and further south) between Sep–Apr, migrating north into Ug and extreme WKe from May–Sep, where it is uncommon and often at lower altitudes. It occurs over wet grasslands, rank cultivation and swamp edge. **Vo** perched and flight calls are harsh and obtrusive, but they will also utter a pleasant subdued twittering.

White-throated Blue Swallow *Hirundo nigrita* 14cm, 5.5"
Ad is all glossy dark blue swallow, with a *white bar across the throat,* and a slightly forked tail which shows white spots when spread. Imm is duller and browner. **HH** in our area known only from along the Semliki River in WUg, where it sits on partially submerged rocks and overhanging branches in primary forest. **Vo** generally quiet, but utters single sharp notes in flight and occasional musical twitters.

Grey-rumped Swallow *Pseudhirundo griseopyga* 15cm, 6"
A slim swallow with a *pale grey rump and grey-brown crown*. Sexes alike. Imm is duller with a browner rump and shorter tail. **HH** commonly seen in flocks, but rather local from 900–2200m over open grassland and burnt areas. Uniquely breeds in rodent burrows. **Vo** calls are harsh and burry, more like a Sand Martin than other *Hirundo* swallows, and flocks utter low churrs while feeding. **SS** House Martin.

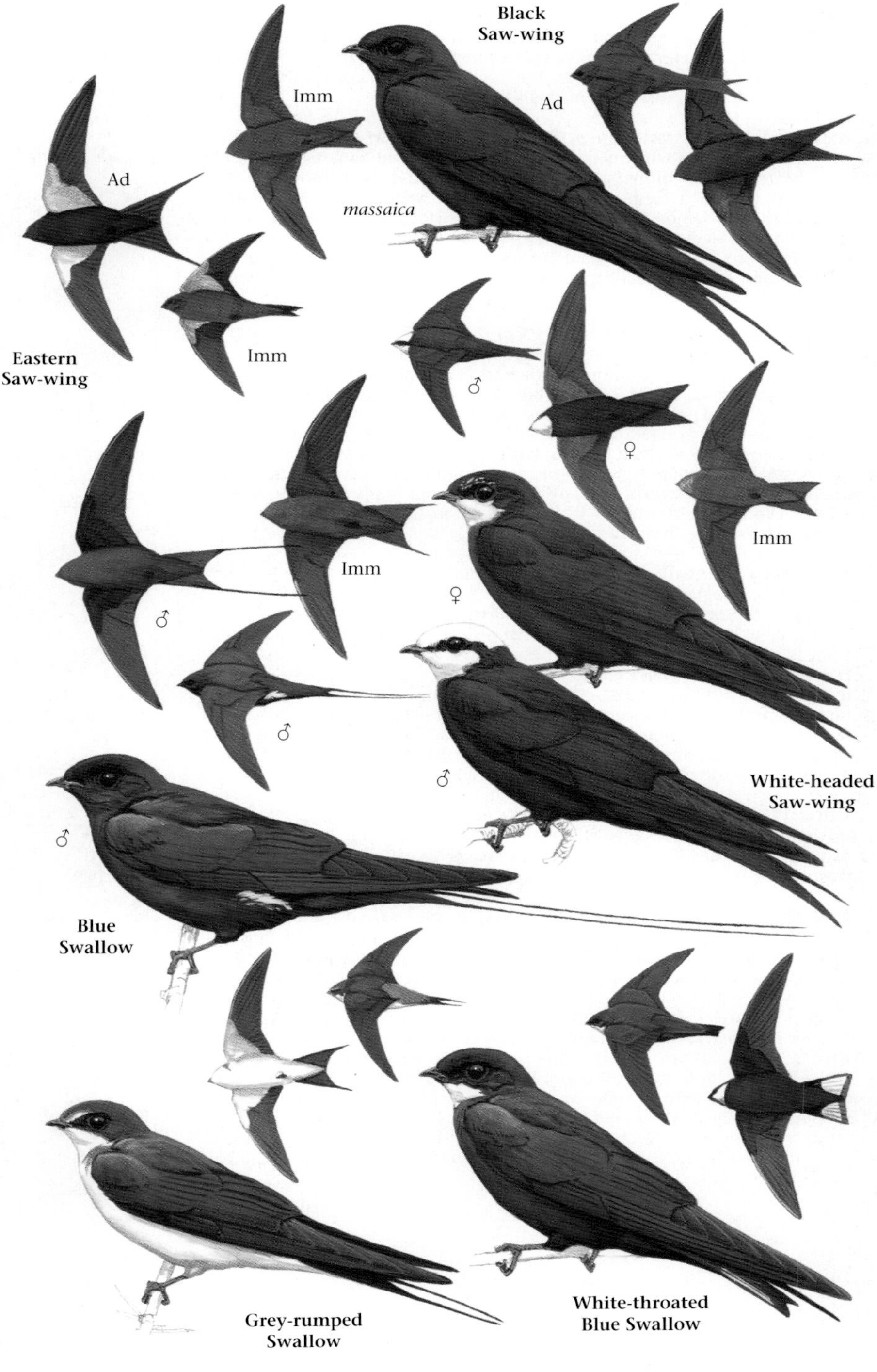

Plate 148

Black
Saw-wing

Imm

Ad

massaica

Eastern
Saw-wing

Ad

Imm

♂

♀

Imm

Imm

♂

♀

♂

♂

White-headed
Saw-wing

Blue
Swallow

♂

Grey-rumped
Swallow

White-throated
Blue Swallow

WAGTAILS

Slim birds with long tails and legs, often seen walking on the ground constantly bobbing their tails. The three Palearctic migrant species begin arriving during Sep–Oct. They are mostly drab non-breeding and first year birds, but breeding adult males can be seen from Feb until they migrate north again mainly from Mar–May.

African Pied Wagtail *Motacilla aguimp*   20cm, 8"

Only very black and white wagtail in the region: *ad without grey or brown in the plumage*, and a comparatively broad breast band. Imm brownish-grey above. All ages identified from Cape and White wagtails by *extensive white wing patches*. **HH** most common and widespread resident wagtail, occurring from sea-level to 3000m along river banks, lakeshores, in cultivated areas and forest glades, as well as in towns. **Vo** sweet calls are frequently paired notes, which break into an attractive complex and warbled song.

White Wagtail *Motacilla alba*   19cm, 7.5"

Non-br ♂ has the crown, nape and breast band black, giving a *white-faced appearance* which is even more obvious in br plumage when the throat is also black. Non-br ♀ and 1st year are rather dingy, with crown to rump grey, face washed pale olivaceous, and a dark narrow breast band. Very similar to imm Cape Wagtail, but greyer above, not brown. Br ♀ similar to br ♂, but is not quite so clean looking with some grey on the crown. **HH** singles or small groups are scarce Palearctic migrants from Nov–Mar, occurring mainly around the northern lakes and on isolated pools from sea-level to 1600m. **Vo** does not sing in region, but often calls with an urgent dry paired *chh-tit* in flight or on the ground.

Mountain Wagtail *Motacilla clara*   19cm, 7.5"
[Long-tailed Wagtail]

Elegant and proportionately longer tailed than other wagtails. Ad is largely clear grey above and white below with a neat narrow black breast band. Imm is similar, but washed brown above, with an indistinct breast band. **HH** pairs are widespread residents along rocky fast-flowing rivers and at forest edges: although most common in the highlands, they may occur down to 500m. **Vo** very vocal: one simple song is usually three notes *siiii seee-uu* (first rising then last notes falling to fade); the alarm and contact calls are a strange metallic and explosive *chit*, which can break into complex whistles and descending trills with a buzzing quality.

Cape Wagtail *Motacilla capensis*   20cm, 8"

Ad is olive-brown above with *no white panel in the wing* (although may show pale feather edges), and washed creamy-buff below with a narrow dark breast band. Similar imm African Pied Wagtail has large white wing patch. Imm Cape Wagtail has buffy fringes to the wing-coverts and is washed yellowish-buff on the belly. **HH** pairs are resident but rather local near lakes and ponds from 900–3000m. **Vo** calls an upslurred interrogatory *siuweeee* and *chweet-chweet* mainly in flight, but may also mix these calls into a simple song.

Grey Wagtail *Motacilla cinerea*   20cm, 8"

Non-br plumage variable but identified by combination of grey upperparts with a yellow rump, yellow underparts (may be restricted to vent), a whitish throat, and no breast band. Br ♂ has yellow underparts and a black throat. ♀ has a white throat and yellow breast to vent. **HH** Palearctic migrant which mainly occurs in small numbers along streams in the highlands from late-Sep–Mar, but ranges down to sea-level on passage. **Vo** call is a loud, harsh and explosive *ti-titt*. Infrequently heard song is the call interspersed with a loud *siiii*.

Plate 149

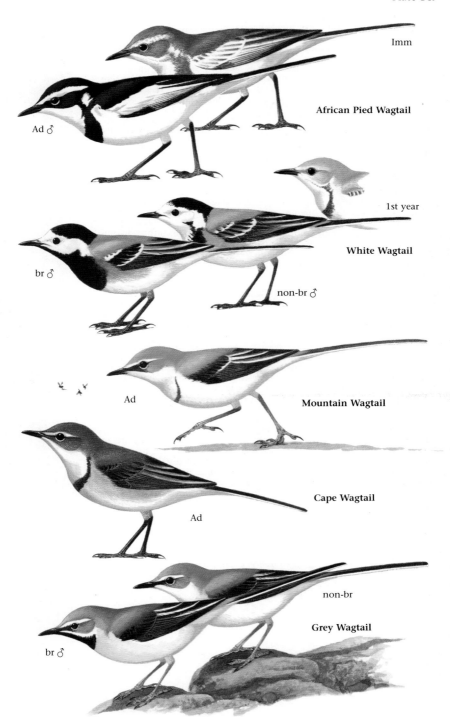

Imm

African Pied Wagtail

Ad ♂

1st year

White Wagtail

br ♂

non-br ♂

Ad

Mountain Wagtail

Cape Wagtail

Ad

non-br

Grey Wagtail

br ♂

Yellow Wagtail   *Motacilla flava*   19cm, 7.5"

On arrival in EA the plumage is highly varied and for many birds racial separation is not possible. Typical individuals are brownish above with variable yellow below, often strongest on the belly and flanks. Ad ♂♂ have the most extensive yellow underparts, but do not have their distinctive br head patterns. ♀ and 1st year birds have olive-brown or plain brown upperparts and usually show some yellow on the belly, but may have entirely white underparts. From Jan, ♂♂ (and some ♀♀) acquire distinctive head patterns and become greener above and entirely yellow below (except for whitish throats on ♀♀). Six races occur and are described below: *feldegg* has a completely black top to the head; *thunbergi* has a dark grey crown blending into a blackish face; *flava* has a blue-grey crown and darker cheeks separated by a distinct white supercilium; *beema* has a pale grey crown and cheek separated by a white supercilium; *lutea* has the head mostly yellow, variably washed with green on the crown and ear-coverts; and *leucocephala* has an almost entirely white head. The race '*superciliaris*' recorded from Ke is now considered to be a hybrid between *feldegg* and *flava*. Since hybrids are not uncommon, some individuals can never be racially assigned. Differs from larger Grey Wagtail in all plumages by never having a grey mantle. **HH** a very common Palearctic migrant from Sep–May, with several different races often occurring together sometimes in flocks of thousands. Birds favour lakeshores, swampy land, short grasslands and open cultivation, frequently associating with cattle and plains game, from sea-level to 3000m. **Vo** very vocal: call given in flight and on the ground is a rising *sweeep*, softer than other wagtails in the region. The race *feldegg* sounds considerably harsher.

GOLDEN PIPIT AND LONGCLAWS

Longclaws (on plate 151) are ground-dwelling birds which are streaky brown above, with variable amounts of yellow, orange or red below, and a black band or streaking across the breast. Golden Pipit resembles some of these, but is particularly distinctive in flight when the male suddenly reveals bright yellow in the wings

Golden Pipit   *Tmetothylacus tenellus*   16cm, 6"

Ad ♂ is streaked and mottled dark brown, olive-yellow and buff above, and brilliant yellow with a neat black breast band below. In flight, *bright yellow wings with black tips and a bright yellow outer-tail* are obvious. Ad ♀ is more like a typical pipit, but has dull yellow edges to the primaries and outer-tail, and is mainly plain buff below with pale yellow restricted to the belly. Underwing-coverts are also pale yellow. Imm is browner and even more pipit-like with streaking across the breast, but may show yellowish wing edgings. **HH** pairs and small groups are sometimes common residents of bushed and wooded grassland in dry country from sea-level to 1800m. Local movements occur, often in response to rains. **Vo** usually silent, but can be very vocal after rains when the complex whistled song has a weaver-like quality.

Plate 150

flava

lutea

thunbergi

feldegg

beema

leucocephala

'*superciliaris*'

flava
Juv

flava

br ♂

Yellow Wagtail

flava

♀

1st year

♂

♀

♂

♀

Golden Pipit

Yellow-throated Longclaw *Macronyx croceus* 22cm, 9"

Ad is brown above with darker brown centres to the feathers giving a heavy mottled appearance. Bright yellow below with a broad black breast band and *short black streaks on sides of breast*. In gliding flight, shows conspicuous white corners to the tail. Imm is paler and browner, throat to breast buffy, blackish streaks across breast, and pale yellow restricted to flanks and belly. **HH** the most common and widespread longclaw inhabiting grasslands, open bush country and cultivated areas from sea-level to 2300m. Feeds on the ground, but frequently perches on the tops of bushes and fence posts. **Vo** quite a varied repertoire, commonest calls consist of whistled drawn out *seeueeeee*, or a rapid *wi-pi-pi-pi-pi-pi* usually given in laboured flight.

Fülleborn's Longclaw *Macronyx fuellebornii* 22cm, 9"

Very similar to Yellow-throated Longclaw, but *flanks and vent buff-brown. Black breast band does not have streaking extending on to sides of breast*. In flight, shows slightly less white on corners of the tail. Imm is buff-brown below with an indistinct brownish breast band that is not streaked as in imm Yellow-throated. **HH** locally common in the highlands of S and SWTz, where it frequents grasslands and fringes of marshy areas from 1900–2600m. **Vo** call is a short mournful descending *peeu*, and the song is an energetic warble *tu-wii-ti-choo wee-ti-choo*.

Sharpe's Longclaw *Macronyx sharpei* 17cm, 6.5" ● ●

The smallest longclaw: ad ♂ is boldly marked above, yellow below with black streaks across the breast and down the flanks, and *no solid black breast band*. Ad ♀ is similar but slightly duller. In flight, shows white outer-tail feathers (not just corners). Imm is paler above, buffy below with brown breast streaking, and pale yellow from breast to vent. **HH** globally threatened EA montane endemic which is a generally uncommon and localised resident from Mt Elgon to Mt Kenya, inhabiting grazed open grasslands and short moist tussock grass from 1850–3400m. **Vo** usually silent, but has a varied repertoire. In flight, gives a rhythmical warble and also calls *wi-wi-wi-wi-wi-wi-...* accelerating in tempo as the bird descends earthwards. Sometimes gives a harsh repeated pipit-like *sit*.

Pangani Longclaw *Macronyx aurantiigula* 20cm, 8"

Ad is similar to Yellow-throated Longclaw, but throat is usually orange or orange-yellow (beware ♀ and older imms may have yellow throats). Centre of breast to vent bright yellow, *narrow black breast band has extensive black streaking extending down over tawny-buff flanks*. Imm has an ill-defined breast band and mainly buff underparts with some yellow on the breast. **HH** locally common in generally dry bushed grasslands to the east from sea-level to 1800m. **Vo** not so vocal, the call is a varied drawn out and whistled *siuuweeeee* rising then falling and rising to fade.

Rosy-breasted Longclaw *Macronyx ameliae* 20cm, 8"
[Pink-throated Longclaw]

Ad is boldly scalloped above blackish and creamy-buff. ♂ is *bright rosy-red below* with a black breast band and ♀ is similar but much paler. In distinctive fluttery flight, slender tail shows white edges, not just corners. Imm is boldly marked above like ad, but buffy brown below with blackish streaks across the breast (very pipit-like), and red confined to centre of belly (difficult to see). **HH** locally common in open damp grasslands from 600–2200m. Shyer than other longclaws, often running on the ground within cover. **Vo** song varies slightly from place to place, but most commonly heard phrase is a *su-su-su-su-su-su-su-su-su-seeeeeeeee* with the last note higher.

Plate 151

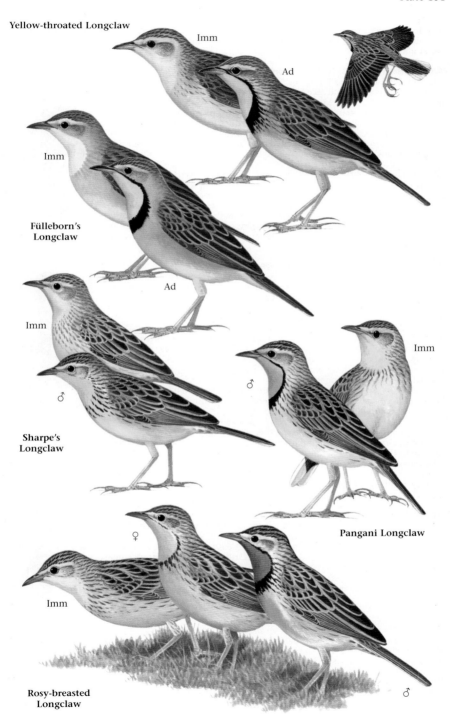

Yellow-throated Longclaw

Imm

Ad

Imm

Fülleborn's
Longclaw

Ad

Imm

Imm

♂

♂

Sharpe's
Longclaw

Pangani Longclaw

♀

Imm

Rosy-breasted
Longclaw

♂

PIPITS

A difficult group of slim brown birds with slender bills and longish tails. Density of streaking on mantle and breast, presence or lack of white in the tail, habitat and calls all aid identification. Sexes and immatures are generally similar.

Grassland Pipit   *Anthus cinnamomeus*   17cm, 6.5"
[African Pipit, Grassveld Pipit]

Common and widespread race *lacuum* is medium brown above with darker streaks on the crown and mantle. Facial pattern is strong, with an obvious buffy supercilium, narrow dark eye line, and dark malar stripe. Lower mandible yellowish, legs pinkish. Buffy-white below with short dark streaks across the breast, flanks are usually plain. In flight, shows extensive white in the outer-tail. The much darker race *latistriatus* is commonly known as **Jackson's Pipit**. It is blackish-brown above and rich buff below, with a contrasting whitish throat, and black streaks which extend across the breast and flanks. Lower mandible and legs pinkish. **HH** very common in open country from sea-level up to 3400m, except for desert areas – although it occurs in coastal dunes. Race *latistriatus* is found in montane and other grassland areas in SUg and WTz, and very rarely in WKe. **Vo** voice varies regionally: typical song is a repeated *trrlit-trrlit-trrlit*, and the flight-call a repeated *trit*. Race *latistriatus* sings a rapid-fire *tit-it-it-it-it-it-it*, followed by a sweeter *trit-rit-rit-rit-rit* ending in a similar but longer descending series. It calls *chrit*.

Long-billed Pipit   *Anthus similis*   18cm, 7"

Race *hararensis* is a large comparatively uniform pipit, similar to Grassland Pipit, but with streaking generally less well pronounced. Birds often appear dark in worn plumage. Bill is long, but not really obviously so. In flight, tail looks long with buffy-white outer-tail feathers. It occurs in rocky country with light grass cover. Race *nyassae* is restricted to miombo woodland in W and SWTz (south of dotted line on map). It is a warmer buff bird, with heavier streaking above and below, buffy flanks, and a slightly whiter outer-tail. Race *chyuluensis* in the Chyulu Hills and Nairobi NP, Ke, is very similar, but has an all-buff outer-tail. When flushed, both these races fly up into trees and walk along branches, and may be a separate species, **Wood Pipit**. **HH** widespread but never numerous, they are usually solitary or in pairs. **Vo** song is a lazy series of four notes repeated randomly *chrit...swit...chweep chreer...*, and the flight-call is a muffled *trrit-tip*. Wood Pipit song is similar, but higher pitched.

Malindi Pipit   *Anthus melindae*   16cm, 6"

Similar to Grassland Pipit, but darker and more mottled above, rather than streaked. Streaking on the underparts is bolder and more extensive. *Obvious yellow base to lower mandible and rich orange-yellow legs.* Shows white outer-tail in flight. **HH** in our area restricted to coastal grasslands and salt pans mainly north of Malindi, Ke. **Vo** song is a rapidly delivered continuous series that is softer than other large pipits; flight-call is *shreep*.

Striped Pipit   *Anthus lineiventris*   18cm, 7"

A large boldly marked pipit with a long buff supercilium. Streaks on the underparts are dark and long, extending well on to flanks and belly. *Green-tinged primary edges* distinctive, but not always easy to see. In flight, shows a white outer-tail. **HH** pairs and single birds inhabit rocky hills with some woodland below 2000m. Feeds on the ground flying to bushes if disturbed. **Vo** most attractive pipit song with rapid varied and bunting-like sweet descending notes, carrying a considerable distance.

Bush Pipit   *Anthus caffer*   13cm, 5"
[Bushveld Pipit]

A small rather *plain-faced pipit with an indistinct supercilium and no malar stripe*. Warm brown above with darker streaking, and whitish below finely streaked with dark brown across the breast and flanks. White outer-tail. Tree Pipit is larger with a dark malar stripe and heavier streaking below. **HH** local and uncommon in bushed and wooded grassland, where it feeds on the ground, and flies into trees when disturbed. **Vo** quite silent for a pipit, the song is a nasal and monotonous *wii-zhweep* given from the top of a small bush, the effect being rather see-saw-like.

Plate 152

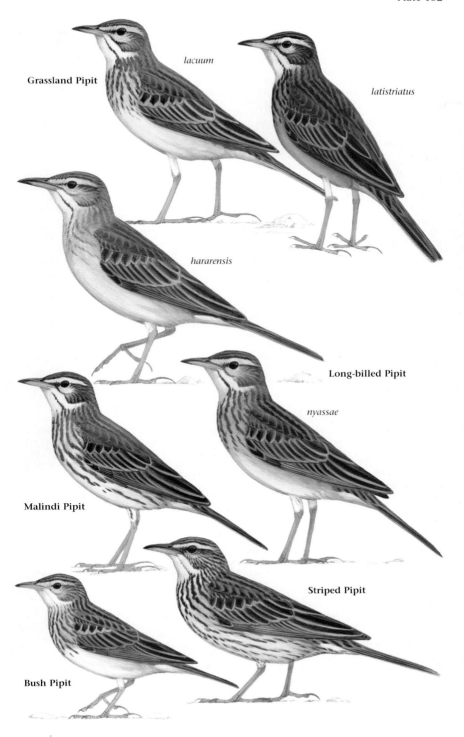

Grassland Pipit

lacuum

latistriatus

hararensis

Long-billed Pipit

nyassae

Malindi Pipit

Striped Pipit

Bush Pipit

Plain-backed Pipit *Anthus leucophrys* 17cm, 6.5"

Paler than Grassland Pipit with a *plain or only lightly marked back;* pale buffy or cinnamon-buff below with indistinct streaks on the breast. Lower mandible is yellowish-pink. In flight, *tail looks uniform dark brown with buff edges.* Four races occur, making up two distinct groups: *zenkeri* is typical of the three widespread darker races, while paler and sandier *goodsoni* (in CKe, SKe and NTz) is sometimes considered a race of Buffy Pipit. **HH** patchily distributed and locally common, it prefers short grass with or without trees from 700–2200m. **Vo** widespread races have a rather monotonous Long-billed Pipit-like song, but the notes are scratchier and less distinct. Race *goodsoni* is not distinguishable from Buffy Pipit.

Buffy Pipit *Anthus vaalensis* 17cm, 6.5"

Extremely similar to Plain-backed Pipit and best told apart where ranges overlap by pink base to the lower mandible (yellowish-pink in Plain-backed). **HH** in our area, known only from dry grasslands in SWTz between 1000–2500m. **Vo** song is very sparrow-like, a monotonous series of dry chirps, virtually unvarying.

Tawny Pipit *Anthus campestris* 17cm, 6.5"

Ad is pale and plain-looking except for *pale fringed very dark median coverts* which form a band across the wing. Outer-tail white. Imm is streaked both above and across the breast. Rather wagtail-like: running around and frequently bobbing its tail. **HH** very uncommon Palearctic migrant recorded from short grass and lake shores. **Vo** calls given in flight and on the ground are a softer *seeep* than that of other large pipits and a chirpy *tsuc*.

Tree Pipit *Anthus trivialis* 15cm, 6"

Olive-brown and heavily streaked above with a plain rump, buff supercilium, and narrow dark malar stripes. Buff-white below with long dark streaks across the breast (less distinct on flanks). White on outer-tail feathers. **HH** common Palearctic visitor and passage migrant Oct–May mainly from 700–3000m, favouring a wide variety of open wooded areas. **Vo** commonly calls a distinctive nasal *eeez.*

Red-throated Pipit *Anthus cervinus* 15cm, 6"

Heavily streaked both above and below including the rump and flanks, with a white outer-tail. Br ad has brick-red on the face and upper breast, but extent and intensity varies, and non-br birds show little or no red. **HH** common Palearctic passage migrant and visitor to marshy grasslands and lakeshores from Oct–Apr from sea-level to 3300m. **Vo** invariably calls a single sharp *zeez* in flight.

Short-tailed Pipit *Anthus brachyurus* 12cm, 5"

Small and very dark above with only an indistinct supercilium, heavily and extensively streaked below. Looks very small and very dark with a short white-edged tail. **HH** solitary or in loose flocks on burnt or short grasslands from 1000–2000m. Difficult to observe, runs on ground, and stays close to cover. **Vo** aerial song in STz has a slurred burry quality, similar to Rufous-chested Swallow. Flight-call is a soft *tip-tiptiptiptiptip*, given immediately before plunging into cover.

Sokoke Pipit *Anthus sokokensis* 12cm, 5" ● ●

Small and richly marked: reddish-buff and black streaked above, white below with bold black streaks across the breast. Two whitish wing bars are often prominent. Outer-tail edged white. **HH** East African endemic confined to largely undisturbed Ke and Tz coastal forests. Pairs or single birds feed in the leaf litter, but fly into trees if disturbed. **Vo** calls from the ground or tree perches a strong repeated, high-pitched and rising *tseeeee.* Song given in a high undulating aerial display above the canopy is a repeated *seueeeee* falling then rising to fade.

Plate 153

Plain-backed
Pipit

zenkeri

goodsoni

Buffy Pipit

Tawny Pipit

br

Tree Pipit

Red-throated
Pipit

non-br

Short-tailed Pipit

Sokoke Pipit

CUCKOO-SHRIKES

Found alone, in pairs, or as members of mixed-species flocks, cuckoo-shrikes are medium-sized rather quiet birds which tend to keep a horizontal posture as they move actively, but slowly through cover. Male *Campephaga* are all a similar blue-black with orange-yellow gapes, and could be confused with several other species like drongos or black flycatchers (but those species sit upright). Black boubous lack the blue-black gloss and have heavy bush-shrike bills. Females are distinctively marked with yellow, grey, white and black. The grey *Coracina* cuckoo-shrikes behave similarly.

Black Cuckoo-shrike   *Campephaga flava*   20cm, 8"

Ad ♂ is wholly glossy blue-black with a *small orange-yellow gape*: some have yellow shoulder patches. Ad ♀ is olive-brown above with blackish barring, and obviously yellow-edged wings and tail. White below washed with yellow on sides of breast and barred throughout with small black crescents. Much yellow on undertail. Imm is similar to ♀, but with very heavy barring. Occasionally hybridises with Red-shouldered Cuckoo-shrike. **HH** widespread and common in woodlands, forest edges and scrub, from sea-level to 3000m. Numbers increase greatly Apr–Sep when birds from the southern tropics arrive. **Vo** unless breeding, it is rather quiet: the commonest call being a repeated insect-like trill lasting 2 seconds; a louder descending *shree-shree-shree*, is given less frequently.

Red-shouldered Cuckoo-shrike   *Campephaga phoenicea*   20cm, 8"

Ad ♂ is glossy blue-black with *brilliant red shoulders* (on worn birds appearing more orange-yellow). Ad ♀ is very similar to ♀ Black Cuckoo-shrike, but more *grey-brown above*, with a mostly black undertail (except for yellow tips). Imm is like ♀, but more densely barred and spotted. **HH** locally common in the west, occurring in forest edge, open woodlands and overgrown cultivation. **Vo** quiet, only occasionally giving a high-pitched sibilant hissing, and a soft *tit-tit-tit-tit-tit…*

Purple-throated Cuckoo-shrike   *Campephaga quiscalina*   20cm, 8"

Ad ♂ very similar to Black Cuckoo-shrike, but slightly stockier with a *smaller orange-yellow gape*. In good light *purple throat and breast* contrast with otherwise glossy blue-black plumage. Ad ♀ has a greyish head contrasting with quite uniform olive-green upperparts and *dull green wings*. Bright yellow below, with indistinct dusky bars, and a dirty white throat. Imm is like ♀, but heavily barred both above and below, and has a brownish washed head. ♂ of scarce race *munzneri* in ETz has a steel-blue throat. **HH** rather uncommon in the mid and upper canopy of highland forest and forest edge from 1700–2500m. **Vo** calls are varied, but based on a short sharp downslurred *siu*, given in series or repeated emphatically.

Petit's Cuckoo-shrike   *Campephaga petiti*   20cm, 8"

Ad ♂ has *large and conspicuous orange-yellow gape wattles*. Ad ♀ can be confused with ♀ Purple-throated Cuckoo-shrike, but upperparts are strongly barred blackish on yellow and olive-green, and the *wings are blackish with bright yellow edgings*. Underparts *bright yellow with variable amount of black barring*. Imm is similar to ♀, but may be virtually unbarred above. **HH** locally common western cuckoo-shrike inhabiting the middle levels and canopy of good forest from 1400–1800m. **Vo** song is a strong, rhythmical whistled series *sisisi-seeuu* the first notes identical, the last note falling in tone.

Plate 154

Black Cuckoo-shrike

Red-shouldered Cuckoo-shrike

**Purple-throated
Cuckoo-shrike**

Petit's Cuckoo-shrike

Grey Cuckoo-shrike *Coracina caesia* 22cm, 8.5"
Ad ♂ is an almost uniform medium grey (although wings are slightly darker), with blackish lores and chin, and conspicuous large dark eyes with pale eye-rings. Ad ♀ is similar but lacks dark lores and chin. Imm finely barred greyish-brown and white with a darker tail. **HH** widespread and common in the canopy of highland forest typically above 1500m. Also on mountain and hill forests nearer the coast where it is recorded down to near sea-level. **Vo** contact call is a high-pitched hissing, and the song a high-pitched and complex jumble of twitters and squeaks.

White-breasted Cuckoo-shrike *Coracina pectoralis* 25cm, 10"
Ad ♂ distinctive: grey above with darker wings and tail, throat to upper breast grey with remainder of underparts snowy white. Ad ♀ is similar to ♂ but all white below or with a pale grey wash across the breast. Imm finely barred grey, brown and white above, with dark spotting on white below. **HH** mainly an uncommon resident of miombo and other woodlands from sea-level to 1700m. **Vo** usual call is a high-pitched upslurred burry *swit*, and the song is a rather rhythmical mixture of similar burry upslurs and downslurs interspersed with chattering.

NICATORS
Fairly large olive-green birds with large shrike-like bills and loud bubbling songs. Their affinities are uncertain and they are placed by various authors with either greenbuls or bush-shrikes. Solitary unless breeding, they are shy birds of the forest interior, active but slow, skulking around within cover. Their vibrant song and harsh contact calls can be heard throughout the day. Sexes and immatures look alike, but males are larger than females.

Eastern Nicator *Nicator gularis* 23cm, 9"
[Yellow-spotted Nicator]
Ad is olive-green above with obvious creamy-yellow spots on the wing-coverts and secondaries, and a *grey-brown wash to the crown and ear-coverts*. Washed grey-brown below, and whiter on the belly with a yellow vent. **HH** common but very difficult to see, inhabiting forest, patches of woodland and other dense cover in the east from sea-level to 1900m. **Vo** extremely vocal, invariably from dense cover, with a loud song, that starts hesitantly with a *yu-ik-wit-wer-trrr* and bubbles into a jumbled *cho-chou-choou-chueeee*. Also calls a repeated sharp *tuk*.

Western Nicator *Nicator chloris* 23cm, 9"
Very similar to Eastern Nicator, but *sides of face and crown olive-green*. Best identified by range and some vocalisations. **HH** similar habits as Eastern, but restricted to the west where it is a bird of good forest and well established secondary growth from about 700–1850m. **Vo** frequently calls a loud raptor-like *quek-quek-quek-...*, other vocalisations are similar to Eastern Nicator, but slightly more muffled.

Yellow-throated Nicator *Nicator vireo* 17cm, 6.5"
Similar to but smaller than other nicators with an obvious *yellow throat*. **HH** in our area restricted to forest in the Semliki Valley, Ug, from 700–900m, where it is extremely difficult to see. **Vo** calls a distinctive whistled and very rhythmical *fwee fwee-fwee-fwee-fwee-wee-wee-we-weep* (third and fourth notes higher pitched, and final note is upslurred).

Plate 155

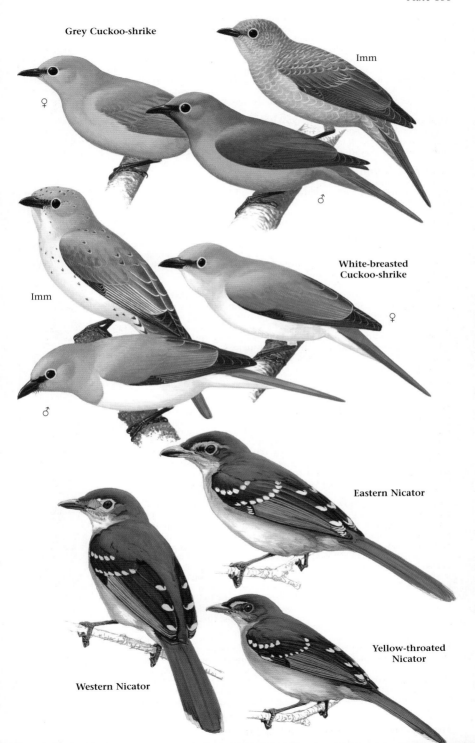

Grey Cuckoo-shrike

Imm

♀

♂

Imm

White-breasted
Cuckoo-shrike

♀

♂

Eastern Nicator

Western Nicator

Yellow-throated
Nicator

BULBULS, GREENBULS AND BROWNBULS

With only a few exceptions, an extremely difficult group to identify. Plate 156 introduces some of the more common and widespread species. Plates 157–162 are groupings arranged purely to aid field identification. Species restricted to geographical areas may be together even though they represent different genera. They may be arranged on the basis of plumage similarities, behaviour, or for some other reason – the text should explain. Consider the characteristics of different genera, preference for any particular forest level, range and voice. Carefully check for small eye-rings, the exact colour of head, breast, flanks and tails (and beware yellow early morning light). Sexes are alike or very similar. Immatures are only described if noticeably different from adults.

Common Bulbul (in genus *Pycnonotus*) is one of East Africa's most common and widespread birds: it will soon become familiar. The ten **ANDROPADUS** greenbuls are a very difficult group, however: they are mostly dull plumaged slightly stocky birds, with short or medium length bills. Solitary or in pairs (unless at fruiting trees), they mostly occur in the mid-stratum and canopy of forests.

Common Bulbul *Pycnonotus barbatus* 18cm, 7"
[Black-eyed Bulbul]

Slim, brownish bird with an almost black head (which may show a slight crest), pale belly and a *bright yellow vent*. Race *tricolor* has the head and breast plain dark blackish-brown, while *dodsoni* (**Dodson's Bulbul**) has a white ear mark and pale feather edgings to the side of its neck. **HH** extremely common and widespread in virtually all habitats throughout the region from sea-level to 3000m. Race *dodsoni* occurs in dry N and NEKe. **Vo** sings a fairly slow deliberate set of descending notes, accelerating as the birds become excitable. Also a variety of chatters given at all times. Race *dodsoni* is similar, but faster and more shrill.

Yellow-whiskered Greenbul *Andropadus latirostris* 18cm, 7"

Dull olive-green with distinctive *bright yellow whiskers down sides of throat* and a reddish-brown tail. Imm is all dull olive-brown and similar to Little Greenbul, but its bill has an orange-yellow base. **HH** very common within its range, inhabiting highland forest, forest strips and wooded gardens from 700–3000m. **Vo** calls and sings throughout the day a dull ramble of *chirrup*, *chup* and *chop* notes, with an occasional burst of higher pitched chatterring.

Little Greenbul *Andropadus virens* 17cm, 6.5 "

Small totally dull olive greenbul with a short rather stout dark bill, dull yellowish-brown legs, and a reddish-brown tail. Imm is like ad, but washed brown above. **HH** patchily distributed, but common within range from sea-level to 1800m (mainly below 1500m), where it prefers thick secondary growth and forest edge. Solitary and shy, but very noisy. **Vo** persistent songster throughout day and most musical of the genus, call notes being sweet and pure. After identical introductory *chups*, the song is a fast run of numerous bubbling notes, ending in a complex flourish of chatters and whistles.

Mountain Greenbul *Andropadus nigriceps* 18cm, 7"

Six races occur, forming three distinct groupings (different species may be involved): from the west to CKe race *kikuyuensis* has a grey crown, throat and breast, contrasting with yellowish underparts; in N and NETz the nominate race has a blackish crown, throat and most of underparts greyish; while in C and SWTz *chlorigula* (**Green-throated Greenbul ●**: encircled by dotted line on map) is pale grey below with a band of olive-green across the lower throat and upper breast. All races are mainly green above and have whitish broken or unbroken eye-rings. **HH** common and easy to observe in many highland forests throughout the region from 1350–3300m. **Vo** geographically variable, the basic song a deep throaty delivery with clear notes, most phrases rising, some with cat-like calls. Green-throated is similar with short rising interrogatory phrases.

Slender-billed Greenbul *Andropadus gracilirostris* 18cm, 7"

Distinctive, being plain olive-brown or olive-green above and *all plain grey below*, with a comparatively slender bill for the genus. **HH** common in forest and forest edge canopy, often in fruiting trees, from 700–2500m. **Vo** very noisy: commonest call is an upslur followed by a more tremulous downslur *sweeyu*. The rarely heard song is a subdued and varied chattering.

Plate 156

Common Bulbul

tricolor

Yellow-whiskered Greenbul

Ad

dodsoni

Imm

Little Greenbul

kikuyuensis

chlorigula

nominate

Slender-billed Greenbul

Mountain Greenbul

Reasonably widespread greenbuls which include both *Andropadus* and *Phyllastrephus* (which are the most diverse genera and pose the biggest identification problems). **PHYLLASTREPHUS** are slim-looking greenbuls with slender bills; many are brown above with red-brown tails. They are mostly in the undergrowth or middle levels of forest interiors, so a slender-billed bird in undergrowth may well be a *Phyllastrephus*, greenbul, while a shorter-billed bird in mid-stratum vines is more likely to be an *Andropadus*.

Grey-olive Greenbul   *Phyllastrephus cerviniventris*   17cm, 6.5"

A typical *Phyllastrephus* which is dull brown above with a reddish-brown tail, a buff-white throat which contrasts slightly with a greyish-olive wash across the breast and flanks, and a pale tawny-brown vent. *Long pinkish-horn lower mandible and pale pinkish legs* are the most noticeable features. Eyes yellowish-white or orange-brown. Best identified from Fischer's and Cabanis's greenbuls and Terrestrial Brownbul by having pale pink (not dark) legs. **HH** pairs or small flocks are generally uncommon in undergrowth and thick tangles in remnant forest patches, ground-water forest, and along streams below 1500m. Frequently flicks wings and tail. **Vo** song is a short sequence of rising then falling notes, followed by a longer series of nasal upslurs which sometimes break into a chatter. Vocally distinct locally, but the pattern and the nasal quality are always recognisable.

Shelley's Greenbul   *Andropadus masukuensis*   17cm, 6.5"

Two distinct forms occur: in the west races *kakamegae* (WKe) and *kungwensis* (WTz) have *grey heads*, are bright olive-green above, and duller paler olive-green or yellowish-olive below. In Tz, the nominate race and *roehli* have *dull olive heads, with grey restricted to sides of face and throat*, and the remaining underparts are dull olive, paler than upperparts. All races have small white eye-rings. If treated as a good species, western races become **Kakamega Greenbul** *Andropadus kakamegae,* while eastern races remain as Shelley's Greenbul. **HH** single birds and pairs are local but not uncommon in the middle levels of forest interior from 500–2300m. Western birds climb along tree trunks like woodpeckers. **Vo** race *kakamegae* is virtually silent (no song has been recorded), but nominate birds frequently call a diagnostic high upslurred *qui-qui-qui-qui-...*, similar to a slowed-up version of Red-throated Wryneck.

Stripe-cheeked Greenbul   *Andropadus milanjensis*   19cm, 7.5"
[Stripe-cheeked Bulbul]

Two races occur: northerly *striifacies* is olive-green above, bright olive-yellow below, with dark ear-coverts which show narrow white streaks at close range, and pale eyes. Race *olivaceiceps* in STz is darker above and greener below, and has dark eyes. Imms are much duller with virtually no streaking on sides of face. **HH** common in highland forest from 150–1850m throughout Tz north to SEKe, and most frequent in middle levels and canopy. **Vo** song has the same deep throaty quality of Mountain Greenbul, but a slow and deliberate delivery that varies locally. Common call is a rapid monotonous *wikawikawikawika.....wik!*

Yellow-streaked Greenbul   *Phyllastrephus flavostriatus*   20cm, 8"
[Yellow-streaked Bulbul]

A slender greenbul with *whitish underparts (variably streaked with pale yellow) which invariably moves around in the mid-canopy flicking one wing*. Three races differ mainly in their crown, back and wing colour: in SWUg-Bu *olivaceogriseus* has a clear grey crown and back and green wings; in WTz *kungwensis* is darker, while in ETz *tenuirostris* has an olive-grey crown and browner wings. Race *alfredi* on the Ufipa Plateau, SWTz is much browner above including the crown (and is sometimes split as **Sharpe's Greenbul ●**). **HH** singles or small flocks, often in mixed bird parties, are patchily distributed in forest from sea-level to 2400m (mainly in highland forest). **Vo** song commences with a series of chips followed by a slow delivery of louder descending notes. Alarm is a rapid bubbling chatter.

Plate 157

Grey-olive
Greenbul

Shelley's
Greenbul

kakamegae

roehli

striifacies

olivaceiceps

Stripe-cheeked
Greenbul

tenuirostris

alfredi

Yellow-streaked
Greenbul

Mainly eastern greenbuls including a single *Chlorocichla* species. **CHLOROCICHLA** are rather bulky, strong-billed, noisy greenbuls, which prefer forest edge and clearings, secondary growth, thickets, and overgrown cultivation.

Fischer's Greenbul   *Phyllastrephus fischeri*   18cm, 7"
Plain olive-brown above with a dull reddish tail. Only member of its genus in coastal forests with *creamy-white eyes*. Below very white throat contrasts with olive-brown breast and flanks. **HH** small flocks are common in forest undergrowth and thick bush in the coastal lowlands and up to 600m in the East Usambara Mts, NETz. Shy and difficult to observe but presence announced by frequent noisy contact calls. **Vo** foraging groups utter a constant deep, throaty, descending and chattering *cheee-cha-cha-cha-cha-cha* that accelerates and fades.

Northern Brownbul   *Phyllastrephus strepitans*   17cm, 6.5"
Very similar to Terrestrial Brownbul, but more russet above, with a *russet-brown rump and tail,* and greyish-brown below with a less contrasting whiter throat. Eyes are brown or slightly red-brown: Fischer's Greenbul has pale eyes. **HH** small flocks are common in thickets in coastal lowlands and in thicker cover within semi-arid areas to the north and east, mainly below 1000m. **Vo** parties maintain a continuous rather nasal and pinched chatter from mid-canopy (which recalls the larger babblers).

Terrestrial Brownbul   *Phyllastrephus terrestris*   19cm, 7.5"
[Terrestrial Bulbul]
Very similar to Fisher's Greenbul but with *wine-red eyes* (not creamy-white). Told from Northern Brownbul by being *more earth-brown above* without the russet overtones to rump and tail. White throat also contrasts more with the greyish-brown breast and flanks. **HH** small flocks are rather uncommon in the undergrowth of coastal forest, along wooded streams, and in thickets and dense bush. **Vo** from near the ground it delivers a babbler-like chattering, which is lower pitched than Northern Brownbul, and lacks the harshness and laughing quality of Fischer's Greenbul.

Tiny Greenbul   *Phyllastrephus debilis*   13cm, 5"
[Slender Bulbul]
Small and warbler-like: in race *rabai*, grey crown and sides of head contrast with greenish back, wings and tail. Light greyish below, whiter on the throat, with variable yellow streaking which can be difficult to see in the field. Eye creamy-white or yellowish. Race *albigula* from the Nguru and Usambara Mts, NETz, is olive on the crown and nape. **HH** pairs and small flocks are local and uncommon in the undergrowth and middle-canopy of most types of coastal forest and woodland from sea-level to 1500m. Often joins mixed-species flocks. **Vo** a remarkably loud low-pitched nasal and rhythmic song, includes a bubbling trill and urgent *na'na'na' nya-na...*

Zanzibar Sombre Greenbul   *Andropadus importunus*   18cm, 7"
[Sombre Bulbul]
Race *insularis* is olive-brown above and yellowish-olive below with noticeable *creamy-white eyes*. In SETz, race *hypozanthus* is greener above and brighter yellower below. Imm similar, but with a dark eye and small yellowish eye-ring. **HH** very common throughout the coastal region, and rather less common in the CKe highlands up to 2000m. **Vo** calls from bush tops or telephone wires, a fast rising and falling series of cheerful notes with the quality of Common Bulbul. Sings throughout the heat of the day.

Yellow-bellied Greenbul   *Chlorocichla flaviventris*   22cm 8.5"
[Yellow-bellied Bulbul]
Large and quite thickset. Eastern race *centralis* is dark olive-green above, with ruffled crown feathers often raised as shaggy crest, an obvious *white crescent above the red-brown eye, and sulphur yellow underparts*. In W and STz, race *occidentalis* is lighter olive-green above. **HH** within range singles and pairs are common in all types of thick cover, from sea-level to 2100m on Mt. Kilimanjaro, NTz. **Vo** basic song is five slow rather halting nasal notes *eh...eh...uh...eeh...eh* (first two and final note identical, third lower, fourth higher than first), often initiated with rather angry slurred churrs.

Plate 158

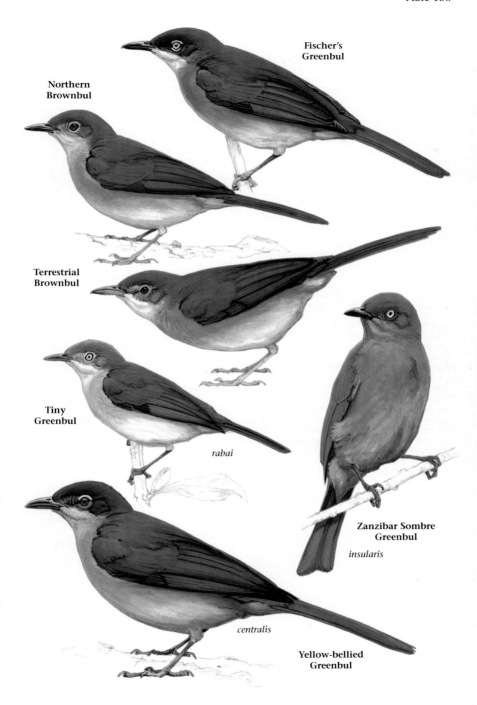

Fischer's
Greenbul

Northern
Brownbul

Terrestrial
Brownbul

Tiny
Greenbul

rabai

Zanzibar Sombre
Greenbul

insularis

centralis

Yellow-bellied
Greenbul

Mainly western greenbuls: both *Phyllastrephus* and *Andropadus* species are included (see also headings on plates 156 and 157).

Cabanis's Greenbul   *Phyllastrephus cabanisi*   19cm, 7.5"

Two distinct forms occur: westerly races nominate and *sucosus* are greenish-olive above, with a rufous tail, and yellowish below, washed dark olive across the breast and flanks, with a *creamy-yellow throat* which is often conspicuous. East of the Great Rift Valley race *placidus* (formerly known as Placid Greenbul) is dull brownish-olive above with a warm russet-brown tail and a *creamy-white throat* contrasting with a greyish-olive breast and flanks. Blue-grey legs distinguish this species from pale-legged Grey-olive Greenbul. **HH** noisy small flocks in a variety of thick undergrowth, mainly in highland forests, but down to 600m in NETz. **Vo** song starts as low-pitched chattering and breaks into a higher see-sawing *wii-werr...*, a second bird accompanying with regularly spaced growls. Race *placidus* is similar but grating.

Little Grey Greenbul   *Andropadus gracilis*   15cm, 6"

A small species: mostly olive above with a grey wash to the crown and sides of face, a small narrow white eye-ring, greyish underparts with a *pale-yellow belly and gingery flanks,* and a slightly russet-brown tail. **HH** occurs singly and in pairs in primary and secondary forest from 700–1700m, with a preference for the mid-canopy and forest edge. It is locally common in Ug, and uncommon in Kakamega Forest, WKe. **Vo** the only definitely known call is a series of rapid spitted notes *tt-tt-tt-tt-tt-tt.*

Ansorge's Greenbul   *Andropadus ansorgei*   15cm, 6"

Extremely similar to Little Grey Greenbul, including the small white eye-ring and gingerish wash to belly and flanks. Slightly browner above and on crown, but hard to assess accurately in forest light. Best separated by *lack of yellow in plumage*, including the belly. **HH** in our area known only from Kakamega Forest, WKe, where single birds and pairs are common and unobtrusive, and often seen foraging in the middle levels and on open branches in the lower canopy. **Vo** a three-note querulous *wee-wer-weet* (middle note slightly lower than other two).

Toro Olive Greenbul   *Phyllastrephus hypochloris*   18cm, 7"

Similar to several other greenbuls being dull olive above with a reddish-brown tail. Mostly pale olive-grey below with slightly browner flanks, and *yellow streaks on the lower breast and belly* which are distinctive but hard to see in the field. Similar Cabanis's Greenbul has a creamy-yellowish throat and darker olive breast. The slender bill eliminates all *Andropadus* species. **HH** pairs and small parties are shy and uncommon, keeping to thick cover within primary forest from 700–1800m. **Vo** song starts with descending often paired burry notes, followed by a loud descending *shreee-shreee-shreee-shreee-shreee* like a scold in response to the first notes.

Cameroon Sombre Greenbul   *Andropadus curvirostris*   18cm, 7"

[Plain Greenbul]
Drab and nondescript, with a small greyish-white eye-ring, reddish-brown tail and yellowish belly all adding to confusion with other species. In good light best identified by *grey throat contrasting slightly with darker olive head and breast*. Most similar to Little Greenbul, but that species has plain olive underparts. **HH** common in both primary and secondary forests from 700–2300m. It prefers undergrowth and the lower mid-levels, but is not shy, sometimes feeding at forest edge in open leafy shrubs. **Vo** calls a three-note *wit-woo-werrrr*, the last slightly falling and tremulous.

Plate 159

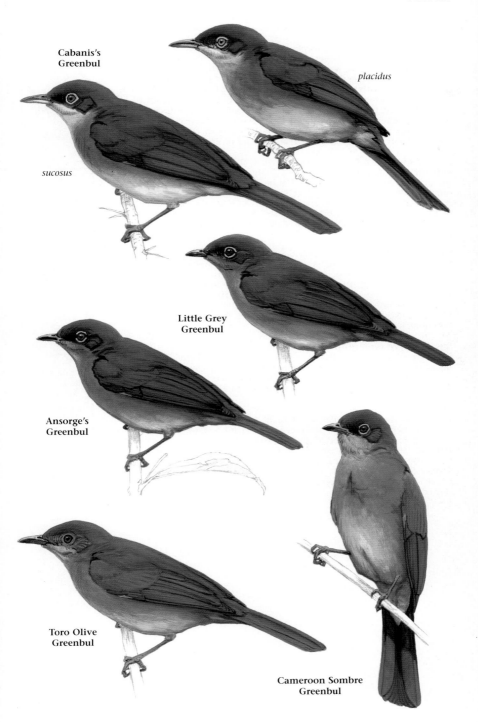

Cabanis's
Greenbul

placidus

sucosus

Little Grey
Greenbul

Ansorge's
Greenbul

Toro Olive
Greenbul

Cameroon Sombre
Greenbul

More greenbuls restricted to the west. In addition to the genera included earlier we have the monotypic *Pyrrhurus*, a stout-billed species with a large broad tail.

Icterine Greenbul *Phyllastrephus icterinus* 17cm, 6.5"

Very similar to slightly larger Xavier's Greenbul: both species are green above and yellow below with a reddish-brown tail, which is *slightly brighter in Icterine*. ♂♂ are larger than ♀♀, with an overlap in size between ♂ Icterine and ♀ Xavier's. With familiarity small ♀ Icterine, or large ♂ Xavier's can be separated on size alone, but otherwise can only safely distinguished by voice. **HH** noisy flocks of 3–8 birds are locally common in the undergrowth of primary forest from 700–1250m, often with mixed-species flocks. **Vo** calls of this and Xavier's Greenbul have often been confused. Icterine makes a harsh churring similar to many species of tits.

Xavier's Greenbul *Phyllastrephus xavieri* 18cm, 7"

Very similar to Icterine Greenbul, but ♂ larger and tail not quite so bright rufous (comments under Icterine). **HH** more widespread than Icterine, but only locally common from 700–1500m. It also occurs in pairs and small groups with mixed-species flocks, but usually in tangled vines and creepers of the middle-storey. **Vo** often confused with Icterine Greenbul, but it makes a long agitated series of low, nasal *aahnk-aahnk* or a rising series of *aaahnk-a-aah...* notes.

Simple Greenbul *Chlorocichla simplex* 21cm, 8"

Large and somewhat stout, a typical *Chlorocichla* greenbul. Plain dark brown above with an *obvious white crescent over the eye*. Below a very white throat contrasts with the pale grey-brown breast and flanks. It shows distinctive pale orange underwing-coverts in flight. **HH** very rare in our area and only recorded from Semliki Forest, WUg, at 700m. **Vo** calls a low scratchy and rather rapid series of notes, which is similar to Yellow-throated Greenbul, but lacks all the exuberance.

Sassi's Olive Greenbul *Phyllastrephus lorenzi* 15cm, 6" ●

Small greenbul which is olive-brown above, with a *mottled black crown and rufous-brown nape patch*. Olive-yellow below washed greenish across the breast and flanks, with reddish-brown tail. **HH** the only record is of a single bird at 700m in Semliki Forest, WUg, in Jun 1967. **Vo** song and calls unknown.

Leaf-love *Pyrrhurus scandens* 21cm, 8"

Mostly brown above, with a pale greyish crown and a *rather conspicuous russet tail*. Below, its white throat grades into a buffy breast, flanks and vent. **HH** small noisy flocks occur within forest and other well-wooded areas from 700–1200m, foraging at all levels and frequently joining mixed-species flocks. **Vo** typically duets, with one bird giving a low but loud *chuck-a-chonk,* and the second following with a higher series of sweeter slurred notes.

Plate 160

Icterine
Greenbul

Xavier's
Greenbul

Simple
Greenbul

Sassi's Olive
Greenbul

Leaf-love

More greenbuls restricted to the west. Genus **BLEDA** the Bristlebills are stocky undergrowth species with rather stout bills, and genus **CRINIGER** are greenbuls with distinctive fluffy white throats which tend to inhabit the mid-strata of forest interiors.

Joyful Greenbul   *Chlorocichla laetissima*   23cm, 9"

Large greenbul which is bright yellowish-green above and largely bright yellow below, washed greenish on the flanks. **HH** locally common within a rather patchy range, it occurs in noisy active flocks moving through the middle levels and lower canopy of primary and secondary forest from 1400–2300m. **Vo** very vocal with a striking and memorable song: proclaims a cheerful and explosive *fwit-fwit-fwit...* before a rapid and exuberant (joyful!) sequence, which ends with a set of squeaky *wi-wi-wi-wi-wi-wi-wi...* notes.

Red-tailed Bristlebill   *Bleda syndactyla*   22cm, 8.5"

Dark greenish-olive above, with a small patch of pale blue-grey skin around the eye (mainly above it), and a contrasting plain red-brown tail. Below, yellow with the *yellow throat contrasting with an olive wash across the breast.* Imm is russet-brown above with yellowish-green skin around the eye, and variably washed russet below. **HH** locally common but shy in thick forest undergrowth from 700–2150m. Usually solitary or in pairs, it forages along quiet trails at dusk, and often attends ant-swarms. **Vo** vocal throughout the day, the song typically involves long, low tremulous whistles that run together, either descending or ascending. Alarm is a loud rapid and continuous *tip-tip-tip-tip*.

Green-tailed Bristlebill   *Bleda eximia*   22cm, 8.5"

Almost entirely olive-green above with pale yellow eyes and *broad bright yellow tips to the outer-tail feathers.* Below bright yellow washed green on sides of breast and flanks. Imm is dark rusty-brown and slightly paler below. **HH** uncommon away from Semliki Forest, WUg, from 700–1250m. Secretive, keeping to undergrowth and thick tangled vines within primary forest. **Vo** sings very loudly, typically a slow *tak-tak-tak...* and then a series of whistled notes which descend and become burry. Alarm is a loud continuous churring.

Red-tailed Greenbul   *Criniger calurus*   21cm, 8"

A distinctive and rather beautiful greenbul which is olive above, with a darker olive head, and a reddish uppertail. Conspicuous *white throat is often puffed out* and contrasts strongly both with the dark head and the yellow-green breast to vent. **HH** locally common in forest undergrowth and mid-storey, often in mixed-species flocks, from 700–1500m. **Vo** sings a loud song consisting of a short burry series of three or four notes, typically rising then falling. Call is a double upslurred *cher-wee cher-weee.*

Eastern Bearded Greenbul   *Criniger chloronotus*   22cm, 8.5"

Similar to Red-tailed Greenbul, but larger and greyer on the head with a much brighter rufous tail. Reveals a similar puffed-out white throat, but the *breast to belly is mostly greyish-brown* not yellow-green. **HH** in our area, very rare and only recorded once from Semliki Forest, WUg, at 700m. **Vo** calls a loud reedy two-note whistle *fwee-fweeee* (the second longer note five tones higher than the first),

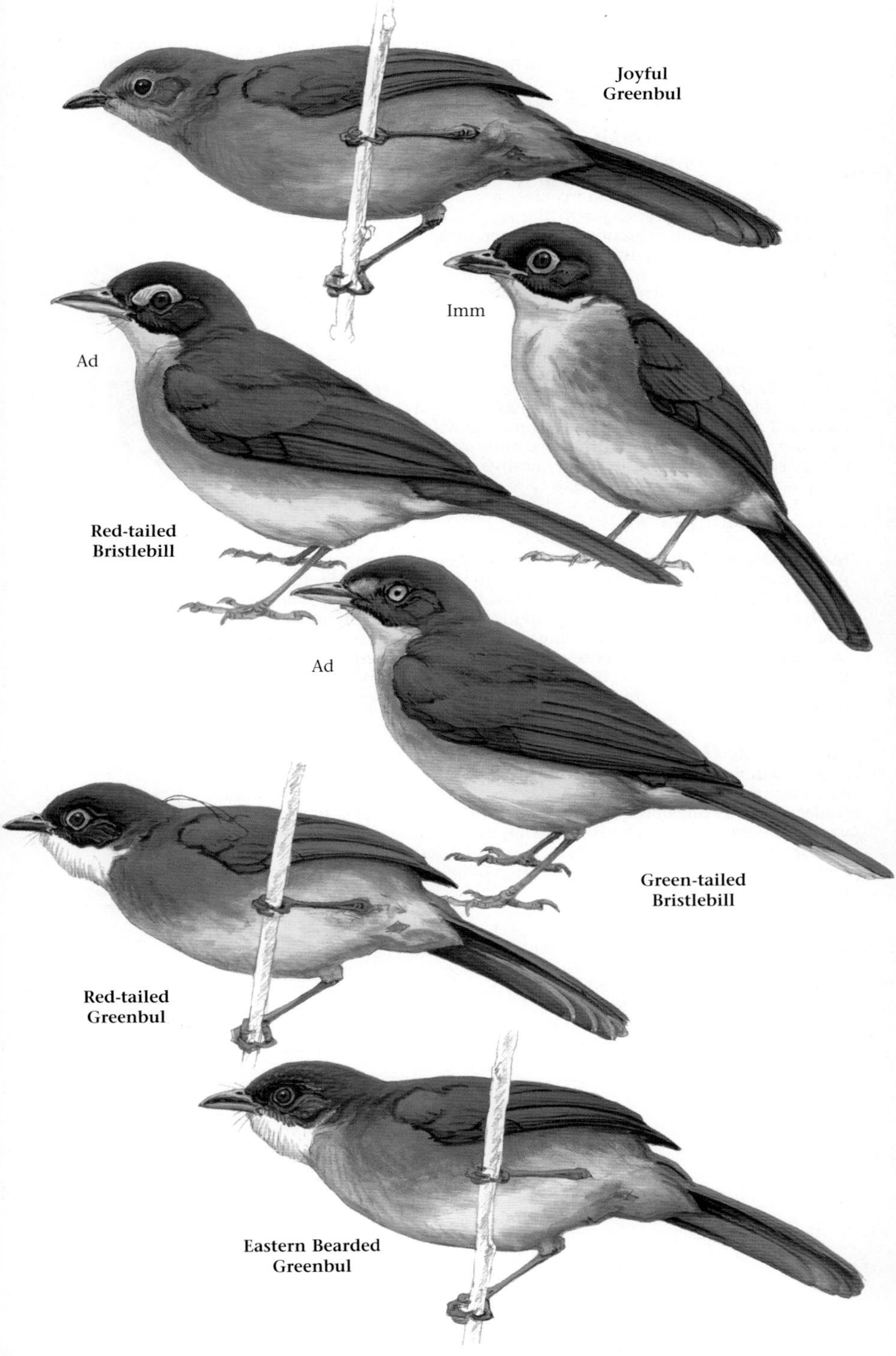

Plate 161

Joyful
Greenbul

Imm

Ad

Red-tailed
Bristlebill

Ad

Green-tailed
Bristlebill

Red-tailed
Greenbul

Eastern Bearded
Greenbul

More western greenbuls, including two monotypic genera *Thescelocichla* which is a large, stout-billed greenbul occurring in noisy flocks throughout all levels of the forest, and *Ixonotus*, also a flocking species, but much more slender and restricted to the canopy. *Baeopogon* is the only honeyguide greenbul in our area. It is very different from other greenbuls, but remarkably similar to a large slender-billed honeyguide. Usually seen singly or in pairs, they are also canopy birds.

White-throated Greenbul   *Phyllastrephus albigularis*   17cm, 6.5"

A typical *Phyllastrephus*, which is grey-brown on the head with an olive back and wings, and a reddish-brown tail. Below, a white throat contrasts with an olive washed breast and yellowish vent. Most similar to Cabanis's Greenbul, but only overlaps with the race *sucosus* which has a creamy-yellow throat. **HH** small groups are common in the undergrowth and lower middle-levels of primary and secondary forest from 900–1850m, and often join mixed-species flocks. **Vo** very noisy, calling an ascending harsh *shree-shree...* ending with a series of identical nasal notes, and a very harsh chattering and churring.

Yellow-throated Greenbul   *Chlorocichla flavicollis*   22cm, 8.5"

[Yellow-throated Leaflove]
Large, dull and olive-grey-brown above with a *contrasting pale creamy-yellow throat*. Often looks rather dishevelled. **HH** pairs and small groups are common and noisy in a variety of thick undergrowth away from good forest, including wooded streams, thickets and overgrown cultivation, from 900–2300m. **Vo** varies locally, but typically sings a rather excitable babbler-like chattering, commonly in flight.

Swamp Palm Bulbul   *Thescelocichla leucopleura*   23cm, 9"

A large species which is dark olive-brown above, with grey and white streaked ear-coverts, and *conspicuous broad white tips to the outer-tail feathers*. It is whitish below, with grey streaking on the throat and upper breast, and a pale creamy-yellow lower breast to vent. **HH** noisy flocks inhabit swampy areas within forest, forest edge and cultivation especially with oil palms. Fairly common at 700m around Semliki Forest, WUg. **Vo** calls are similar to Leaf-love, but unbroken, a cheerful low babbling which rises and falls.

Honeyguide Greenbul   *Baeopogon indicator*   19cm, 7.5"

Ad ♂ resembles a large honeyguide with a slender bill and a white eye. ♀ and imm are similar, but have dark eyes. In flight, the white outer-tail feathers are conspicuous. **HH** single birds are not uncommon in the canopy of good forest from 700–2000m, but are difficult to locate unless calling or seen in flight. **Vo** calls a mournful, descending whistled *wi-yu-t'widdly-t'wi-yu* from high in canopy, often followed by a long rising querulous *pweeeeeee*.

Spotted Greenbul   *Ixonotus guttatus*   17cm, 6.5"

Distinctive rather slim greenbul which is blackish olive-brown above (slightly greyer on the head) with *large white spots on the wings and rump*. Centre of tail black, outer-tail feathers pure white. Below white with a creamy wash to the belly and flanks. **HH** small chattering flocks are very active in forest from 900–1250m and usually seen as they move through the canopy at the forest edge. **Vo** birds persistently call, often in flight, giving a smooth rhythmical chittering of spitted notes.

Plate 162

White-throated
Greenbul

Yellow-throated
Greenbul

Swamp Palm
Bulbul

♂

Honeyguide
Greenbul

Spotted
Greenbul

SMALL ROBINS AND AKALATS

Small, shy thrushes of dense forest undergrowth which often forage along trails at dawn and dusk. Difficult to observe in the gloomy forest interior, but some similar species can be identified on a combination of voice, range and altitude. Sexes alike.

White-starred Robin *Pogonocichla stellata*   15cm, 6"
[Starred Robin]

Seven races occur, but all are variations on a similar theme. Only *elgonensis* differs markedly by having an almost plain black tail. Typically ads have a slate-blue head, green back and bright yellow underparts. Tail yellow with black central feathers and terminal band. White spots in front of eyes and on breast often concealed. Imm olive-green above, dull yellow below, tail pattern as ad, but duller. Juv darker with pale spotting above, underparts yellow with scaly black markings. **HH** common but rather shy, inhabiting undergrowth of highland forest and bamboo usually above 1600m, but down to 300m in NETz. Race *elgonensis* occurs only on Mt Elgon in Ug and Ke. **Vo** varies racially and often mimics, but strong song is typically six whistled rising then falling notes (more frequently heard sub-song is similar but muffled). Call is a see-saw piping *pi-pi pi-pi...*

Swynnerton's Robin *Swynnertonia swynnertoni*   13cm, 5"   ●●

Rather similar to White-starred Robin, but distinctive with a *white breast bar edged in black*, and a *plain dark grey tail*. Muted grey and olive above, not bright and bold. Breast yellow blending to white on belly. ♀ is slightly paler and duller. Juv browner above than ♀ with some buffy spotting, paler below with light brown scaling across the breast. **HH** in our area rare and restricted to forest from 200–1700m in ETz, where it prefers undergrowth with ample leaf litter. **Vo** usual song is a four-note refrain, first two notes descending, then a brief pause followed by two repeated lower notes *peee-eeee......pur pur.*

Equatorial Akalat *Sheppardia aequatorialis*   13cm, 5"

Olive-brown above with a slightly more rufous tail. Small area of grey around the eyes is difficult to see in shady forest undergrowth. Pale orange-brown below except for a white belly. Juv is dark brown above with pale rufous spotting, mottled black and tawny below. **HH** not uncommon, but a shy resident of undergrowth and middle levels within highland forest from 1600–2500m. **Vo** quiet for a forest-chat, song is rather like the repeated call of African Scops-Owl, a burry *prrru-prrru* on the same note.

Lowland Akalat *Sheppardia cyornithopsis*   13cm, 5"

Extremely similar to Equatorial Akalat, but with brown washed flanks, and slightly more white on the belly. Best identified on range and altitude. **HH** in our area it is very local in forest from 700–1200m, replacing Equatorial Akalat in Semliki and Malabigambo in SWUg, and at Minziro in NWTz. **Vo** unknown.

Forest Robin *Stiphrornis erythrothorax*   11cm, 4.5"

Like a very bright version of Equatorial Akalat with an *obvious white spot in front of each eye and blackish cheeks*. Dark grey-brown washed with olive above, throat and breast bright orange-yellow, lower breast to vent white. Juv spotted with rufous above, dull rufous and grey-brown below with a pale throat and belly. **HH** solitary or in pairs, inhabiting primary forest undergrowth from 700–1800m. There is one old record from 2500m at Kipkabus, WKe. **Vo** persistent loud songster with local variation, which sings obvious repeated scratchy thrush-like phrases (a faster version could be mistaken for Grey Longbill).

Plate 163

White-starred
Robin

Imm

Ad

Juv

Juv

Ad

Juv

Ad

Equatorial
Akalat

Swynnerton's
Robin

Ad

Juv

Juv

Ad

Forest
Robin

Ad

Lowland
Akalat

East Coast Akalat *Sheppardia gunningi* 12cm, 5" ●
[Gunning's Robin]
Mostly olive-brown above with blue-grey wing-coverts and edges to the primaries. Supercilium and lores blue-grey; throat, breast and flanks strong (but pale) orange-yellow, belly and vent white. Juv olive-brown above with pale spots, underparts buff-brown with darker brown scalloping across breast. **HH** very local and shy akalat of dense coastal forest undergrowth below 300m. **Vo** seasonally vocal. Song can be strong or muffled and is difficult to pin-point. After a few piping notes, it gives a variable liquid rising and falling *werwiderly-widerly...*, with all the notes running into each other. This is often repeated for long periods.

Sharpe's Akalat *Sheppardia sharpei* 12cm, 5" ●
Similar but duller than East Coast Akalat: *wings olive-brown and uniform with rest of upperparts*. Short supercilium is white on nominate southern birds, grey on *usambarae* in the Nguru and Usambara Mts, NETz. Throat, breast and flanks buffy-orange. Juv is dark above with buffy spotting, pale warm buff below with black scalloping across the breast. **HH** shy and secretive in the undergrowth of highland forest and bamboo from 600–2600m. **Vo** song is a repeated slightly varying and simple *ti-tu-ti'wi-tu-tu* (which is similar to Uganda Woodland Warbler).

Usambara Akalat *Sheppardia montana* 14cm, 5.5" ● ●
[Usambara Ground Robin]
All olive-brown above, with a short rusty stripe and whitish spot in front of the eye (concealed unless the bird is excited). Washed olive-grey below, with a paler throat and whitish belly. Juv is dark above with buffy spotting, and heavily mottled dark brown and pale buff below. **HH** rather uncommon and shy Tz endemic only known from 1600–2300m in the West Usambara Mts where it inhabits undergrowth. **Vo** a continuous rising and falling series of lispy notes interspersed frequently with a very harsh *chahh*. Call and alarm is a similar harsh *chah*, usually given in a rhythmical rising series.

Bocage's Akalat *Sheppardia bocagei* 15cm, 6"
[Bocage's Ground Robin]
In some ways resembles a small robin-chat, but lack of white supercilium and plain tail suggests otherwise. Upperparts are generally tawny-brown with the crown being either a greyish-olive in race *chapini*, or olive-brown with a narrow black line under the eye in *kungwensis*. Both have extensive orange underparts and whitish bellies. Juv is dark above with rufous spots, heavily mottled rufous-buff and black below. **HH** race *kungwensis* is found in WTz where it inhabits forest understorey and bamboo on the Mahari Mts from 1800–2400m; while *chapini* is known from near Kitungulu, SWTz, where it occupies miombo and riverine woodland at 1400m. **Vo** a loud and emphatic rising and falling chat-like song with short phrases which is rather forced and not very musical.

Iringa Akalat *Sheppardia lowei* 14cm, 5.5" ● ●
[Iringa Ground Robin]
Dingy brown above with a short dull yellowish-olive stripe from base of bill to top of eye (can be concealed). Underparts are mostly pale olive-brown with a yellowish-buff throat, and whitish belly. **HH** Tz endemic restricted to highland forests to the south of Iringa. It is another undergrowth species with a preference for drier type forest from 1450–2500m. **Vo** song is a slowly rising and falling series of simple loud piping notes and downslurs, often interspersed with snatches of Spot-throat imitations. Sings from vines 5–6m above the ground.

Plate 164

Sharpe's Akalat

Juv

Juv

Ad

usambarae

Ad

East Coast Akalat

Ad

Juv

Usambara Akalat

Ad

Juv

Ad

chapini

Ad

Ad

Bocage's Akalat

Iringa Akalat

kungwensis

ALETHES
Medium-sized forest thrushes which are generally brown above and pale grey or white below. All inhabit dense undergrowth, but come on to quiet trails at dawn and dusk, or after rain. Shy and usually solitary, they are all fond of following ant-swarms and sometimes small groups forage together. Sexes alike.

Brown-chested Alethe   *Alethe poliocephala*   15cm, 6"

Dark grey-brown head contrasts slightly with the dark chestnut-brown (or dull brown) back and wings. Dull white stripe from base of bill to just behind the eye (only obvious in front view). Underparts, white on throat, otherwise dingy white, washed grey-brown on breast and flanks. Juv dark brown above with orange spotting, buff and grey below with black fringes to the breast feathers. **HH** common and widespread in forest from 700–2800m, but more typically at higher altitudes. **Vo** quiet for an alethe, song is an infrequently heard series of whistled downslurs. Utters harsh notes at ant-swarms and a nasal alarm similar to Grey-chested Illadopsis.

White-chested Alethe   *Alethe fuelleborni*   20cm, 8"

[White-breasted Alethe]
Larger than Brown-chested Alethe with a bright chestnut-brown mantle, rump and tail, no white supercilium, and very dark sides to the face. Bright white below with a strong grey-brown wash to sides of breast and flanks. Juv dark brown above with some pale orange spots, mottled grey, buff and orange below with extensive dark scaly fringes. **HH** not uncommon within its restricted range but exceptionally shy and hard to see. Inhabits the lower levels of mature highland forest from 900–2600m. **Vo** calls a loud lazy piping at dawn and dusk. Slightly variable song is usually a repeated rising series of three very burry notes *wer-ter-wii* followed by a pause, and then a rising *weii wer-ee*.

Red-throated Alethe   *Alethe poliophrys*   15cm, 6"   ●

Head is black with a long broad grey supercilium extending to the nape and a distinctive *brick-red throat*. Otherwise chestnut-brown above and dull greyish-white below. Juv is dark above and on the breast with many rufous spots and streaks. **HH** endemic to the highland forests along the Albertine Rift from 1500–3000m. **Vo** a noisy, monotonous songster. Most calls are repeated piping notes, or rising and falling slurs, apparently delivered randomly.

Fire-crested Alethe   *Alethe diademata*   18cm, 7"

Mainly chestnut-brown above with a blackish tail. Top of head often appears plain brown, as orange crown stripe can be hard to see (unless raised in alarm). Sides of face grey, underparts white washed grey on sides of breast and flanks. Juv dark brown with orange spots above, white and orange below with dark scaly feather fringes. **HH** common in mature forest and nearby secondary growth from 700–1500m. Feeds mainly on the ground, but ascends and calls from tangled vines in mid-storey. **Vo** song is a complex rather subdued delivery of chatters and squeaks. Commonly heard call is a loud repeated, but rather hesitant *foo feeeu* with the second note downslurred.

Plate 165

Juv

Ad

Juv

**Brown-chested
Alethe**

Ad

**White-chested
Alethe**

Juv

Juv

Ad

**Red-throated
Alethe**

Ad

**Fire-crested
Alethe**

ROBIN-CHATS

Small or medium-sized thrushes, mostly with orange underparts, a white supercilium and a dark centre to the rufous tail. Sexes alike: spotted and scaly juvenile or immature plumage is quickly lost and not often seen in the field (as with many other juvenile thrushes). All are usually solitary or in pairs. Fabulous songsters with much variation and mimicry.

Cape Robin-Chat   *Cossypha caffra*   17cm, 6.5"
[Cape Robin]

Paler than most other robin-chats: *orange on underparts is restricted to the throat, breast, and vent; belly and flanks grey.* White supercilium and blackish face, but much of the head is olive-grey (not as black and white as most other robin-chats). Juv brown above with buffy spots, pale-brown below with scaly dark feather edgings. **HH** common in a wide variety of habitats including moorland, forest edge, cultivation and gardens from 1600–3400m (occasionally as low as 500m in Tz). **Vo** a very thrush-like songster, with short varied phrases repeated after short pauses.

White-browed Robin-Chat   *Cossypha heuglini*   20cm, 8"
[Heuglin's Robin]

Boldly marked and entirely bright rufous-orange below. Crown and sides of face black with a long white supercilium. *Tail rufous-orange usually with olive-brown central feathers.* Juv heavily spotted, with less pronounced supercilium, and rufous-brown below with dark scaling. Coastal race *intermedia* is slightly smaller. **HH** most widespread robin-chat in our area, common in many habitats from sea-level to 2200m, but avoids forest interiors and desert-like country. White-browed prefers lower altitudes and more open habitats than Rüppell's Robin-Chat. **Vo** song is a simple refrain of three high notes, followed by two lower notes, with each sequence increasing in volume and becoming more rapid and urgent. Alarm call is a loud but wooden *takata-kata-kata.*

Rüppell's Robin-Chat   *Cossypha semirufa*   18cm, 7"

Very similar to White-browed Robin-Chat, but *tail is rufous-orange with blackish central tail feathers.* Juv is similar to juv White-browed. **HH** much more of a highland forest bird than White-browed Robin-Chat, but also in overgrown gardens, from 1400–2300m. **Vo** the most accomplished songster, the basic song is a musical warbled, thrush-like refrain given both continuously and in short bursts. Often mimics birds in its neighbourhood, plus other small animal noises and human whistles. Sings continuously from cover, particularly before dawn and at dusk.

Blue-shouldered Robin-Chat   *Cossypha cyanocampter*   15cm, 6"

Smaller than White-browed Robin-Chat with blacker wings, a *small bright steel-blue shoulder patch*, and paler yellow-orange underparts. Tail rufous with a black centre. Imm resembles other imm robin-chats, but quickly gains blue shoulder patch. **HH** generally uncommmon in thick forest undergrowth from 700–2000m, where it is very shy and difficult to observe. **Vo** a most accomplished mimic incorporating human whistles and the sounds of many other forest inhabitants into its song. Picks up refrains very quickly, but lacks the sweetness of Rüppell's Robin-Chat, and tends to ramble.

Snowy-headed Robin-Chat   *Cossypha niveicapilla*   22cm, 8.5"
[Snowy-crowned Robin-Chat]

A large robin-chat with a white stripe over top of crown (which can be difficult to see): large black patches on sides of head and the rufous collar are often more obvious. Mantle and wings are slaty, and the centre-tail is black. Juv similar to other juv robin-chats but larger. **HH** not uncommon but shy in forest, remnant woodland and thickets from 900–2400m. **Vo** usually heard at dusk, the rapidly delivered strong and varied song has a fluty quality. Birds incorporate much mimicry, but most of the song is their own. Common call is a repeated mournful piping *fweeeeo…*

Plate 166

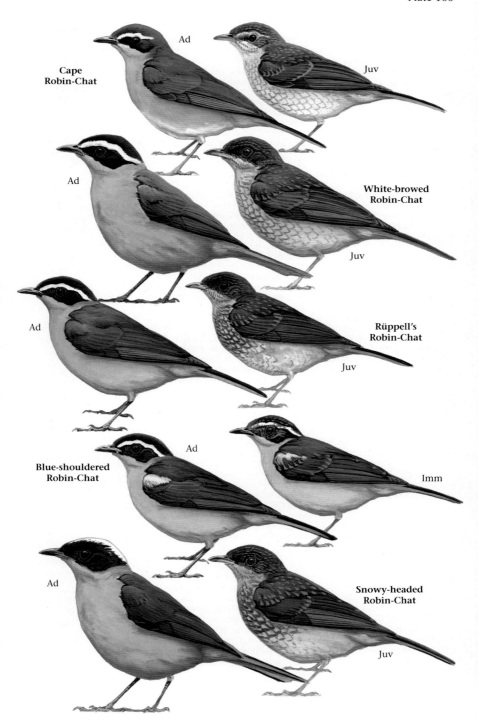

Cape
Robin-Chat

Ad

Juv

White-browed
Robin-Chat

Ad

Juv

Rüppell's
Robin-Chat

Ad

Juv

Blue-shouldered
Robin-Chat

Ad

Imm

Snowy-headed
Robin-Chat

Ad

Juv

Red-capped Robin-Chat *Cossypha natalensis* 17cm, 6.5"
[Natal Robin]

Only robin-chat with a *rufous-orange head;* if seen well beady black eyes are conspicuous. Mantle and wings blue-grey, tail rufous with a black centre. Juv mottled black and rufous above, paler below with dark scaling. **HH** a shy but common bird of forest undergrowth and thicket from sea-level to 2200m. Resident and intra-African migrant populations occur, but movements are poorly understood. Birds are numerous in the west and in coastal regions from May to Nov, while smaller numbers of resident birds occur all year round and are scattered throughout the region. **Vo** an accomplished mimic, bouts of singing can last many minutes. Quality is drunken or lazy compared with other robin-chats, notes are slurred and not too pure. Commonest call is monotonous, distinct and endless repeated *preeep-prooop.*

Grey-winged Robin-Chat *Cossypha polioptera* 15cm, 6"
[Grey-winged Robin]

A small species sometimes considered to be an akalat, but voice (including mimicry) is much more robin-chat-like. Upperparts show a dark grey crown, white supercilium with fine black streaks, and a narrow black eye-line. Wings are olive-brown with blue-grey shoulders; *tail is plain rufous-brown.* Mainly rufous-orange below with a whitish belly. Juv is brown above with rufous spotting and a short rufous supercilium, a blue-grey patch on the wing-coverts, and plain pale rufous underparts. **HH** rather local in forest undergrowth and thickets along streams from 1100–2150m. Often on the ground in leaf litter, shy and difficult to observe. **Vo** some local variation and mimicry. Songs can be slow sweet refrains or rapid high-pitched and regular musical phrases.

Archer's Robin-Chat *Cossypha archeri* 15cm, 6" ●

Rather dull robin-chat: mostly orange-brown with a narrow white supercilium and a small dark face. Comparatively pale orange-rufous head and underparts contrast with browner wings, and an *all rufous tail.* Juv is similar to ad, but is darkly mottled olive-brown below. **HH** endemic to mountains along the Albertine Rift from 1600–4000m where it is common in forest undergrowth and nearby thickly vegetated stream-sides. **Vo** a strongly delivered rising and falling song, in which individual notes are difficult to distinguish, but the overall feel is uniquely tinny and metallic.

Olive-flanked Robin-Chat *Cossypha anomala* 15cm, 6"

A dark robin-chat with a *distinctive white forecrown, supercilium and throat.* Varies from pale to very dark grey below, but always with some rufous on the flanks. Three races occur: *mbuluensis* in NTz is very dark including the underparts, *grotei* of E and STz has a pale grey breast blending into a white belly: both these races have rufous tails with black central feathers. Also in STz race *macclounii* has the underparts similar to *grotei*, but the tail is uniform red-brown. Juvs are very dark brown above with some pale speckling, and extensively scaled below. **HH** uncommon in and around highland forest and along nearby wooded streams from 1500–2600m, usually in undergrowth but sings from tops of small trees. **Vo** song varies geographically: it suggests Cape Robin-Chat but is louder with more deliberate short phrases.

White-bellied Robin-Chat *Cossyphicula roberti* 13cm, 5"

A small species which superficially resembles an akalat, but black centre to rufous tail immediately suggests a robin-chat. In our area, race *rufescentior* is plain olive-brown above with a narrow pale line above lores, and rufous-orange below (with a white belly). Juv is like ad, but streaked and spotted black and rufous above, scaly black on rufous below. **HH** not uncommon but difficult to observe in thick undergrowth particularly along streams in montane forest from 1600–2000m. **Vo** a formless, high-pitched rising and falling song which is rather muffled, though similar to the stronger refrains of Forest Robin.

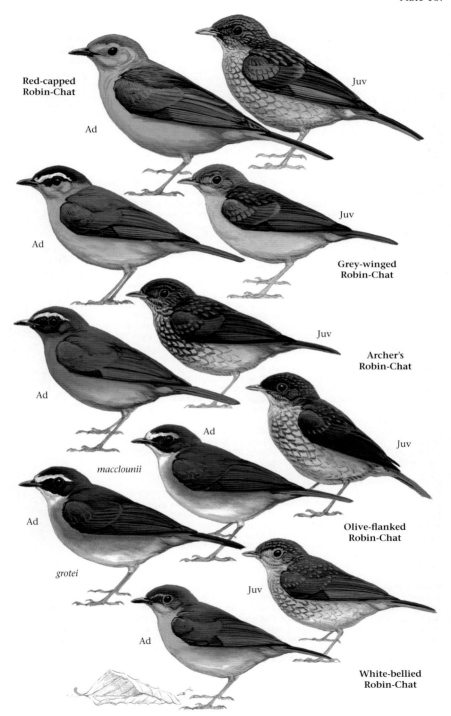

Plate 167

Red-capped
Robin-Chat

Ad

Juv

Ad

Juv

Grey-winged
Robin-Chat

Juv

Archer's
Robin-Chat

Ad

maclounii

Ad

Ad

grotei

Juv

Olive-flanked
Robin-Chat

Juv

Ad

White-bellied
Robin-Chat

TURDUS THRUSHES

Well-known genus of larger thrushes: several are similar, but in the main have different ranges, habitat preference and altitudinal limits. Sexes alike. Juveniles are rather like adults, but have small spots on the wing-coverts and heavy spotting over the breast.

Olive Thrush *Turdus olivaceus* 22cm, 8.5"

Eight races occur, differing mainly in tone with those at higher altitudes (particularly on isolated mountains) generally darker than forms lower down. Typical ads are dark grey-brown above with an *orange bill* and small orange eye-ring; whitish or grey-brown throat is streaked faintly or strongly with black. Breast grey-brown, belly and flanks rich rufous-orange extending right across the lower breast. Juv is generally darker than ad with small buffy spots on the wings, and the breast is heavily spotted dark brown. In the Pare and Usambara Mts, NETz, distinctive race *roehli* has a much darker crown, a speckled throat and is buffy across the breast. **HH** pairs are the most common and widespread *Turdus* thrushes in the highlands, occupying a wide range of habitats including heath, forest edge, gardens and cultivation, mainly above 1600m (but down to 900m in the Usambara Mts, NETz). **Vo** song consists of short typical thrush-like phra-ses followed by a pause, each phrase ends with a short series of repeated subdued notes like an echo.

African Thrush *Turdus pelios* 22cm, 8.5"

Very similar to Olive Thrush, but *paler with a pale yellow-orange bill* and lightly and evenly streaked brown on buff throat. Breast is pale grey-brown with pale buff-orange flanks *which do not usually extend over the lower breast* (rarely as a faint wash). **HH** largely replaces Olive Thrush in the west, being common and widespread in forest edge, thickets, gardens and cultivation. In areas where Olive also occurs African is at lower altitudes, but African reaches 2000m if Olive Thrush is not present. **Vo** more varied than Olive Thrush, with a completely different structure of various repeated phrases given for long periods without pause, and no softer terminal calls. May mimic other birds.

Taita Thrush *Turdus helleri* 22cm, 8.5" ● ●

Very dark above with a completely black head, a bright red-orange bill and eye-ring, a dark blackish-grey breast: lower breast to vent white and bright chestnut flanks. It is sometimes considered a race of Olive Thrush. **HH** Ke endemic: confined to tiny remnant forests in Taita Hills (where rare and endangered). Shy, staying within forest interior where it feeds on the ground. **Vo** sings from concealed middle levels. Much richer and slower than Olive Thrush, with similar very quiet hissed notes ending each phrase. In the Taita Hills, Orange Ground-Thrush has a very similar varied song which may be indistinguishable.

African Bare-eyed Thrush *Turdus tephronotus* 22cm, 8.5"

Grey above with a yellow bill and a *diamond-shaped patch of bare orange-yellow skin around the eye*, and a white throat strongly streaked with black: breast grey, lower breast and flanks rufous. **HH** common but retiring resident of generally drier areas including coastal scrub, riverine vegetation and wooded bushland from sea-level to 1750m. **Vo** song is similar, but louder and slower than Olive Thrush, incorporating a diagnostic rapid bubbly *pi-pu pi-pu pi-pu* which has a peculiar nasal quality, and is also given as alarm.

Kurrichane Thrush *Turdus libonyanus* 22cm, 8.5"

Similar to African Thrush with a narrow yellow eye-ring, a *more orange bill, and a white throat, with short dark streaks at the sides forming heavy malar stripes*. Breast and flanks are pale brownish or orange-buff. Bare-eyed Thrush has large yellow eye-rings and a more evenly streaked throat. **HH** mainly resident in miombo woodland, although also in acacia bush country, from sea-level to 1900m. In NWTz it overlaps with African, but that species is in riverine woodland not miombo. **Vo** similar to Olive Thrush, but some notes are more shrill and phrases are usually shorter.

Plate 168

Olive Thrush

Juv

Ad

roehli

African Thrush

Taita Thrush

African
Bare-eyed Thrush

Kurrichane Thrush

GROUND-THRUSHES

Shy and difficult group to identify, ground-thrushes keep to thick cover within forest under-growth. Several differ only in head colour, eye-rings, and facial markings. All are sedentary, so range and altitude are important. Sexes alike. Juveniles generally have small buffy spots above and heavily mottled breasts. Songs are rich and highly varied, but of limited use for identification, since ground-thrushes readily respond to one another's songs.

Abyssinian Ground-Thrush *Zoothera piaggiae* 19cm, 7.5"

Very similar to Orange Ground-Thrush, but has a *large white eye-ring and orange-brown forecrown* (and crown in the west), with overall tones to upperparts warmer russet-brown. **HH** widespread in forested highlands across W, C, and NKe, and in the Nguruman Forest in SKe. Overlaps with Orange Ground-Thrush on Mt Kenya, but occurs above 2300m, Orange below 2000m (together at Kieni Forest, Ke, between 2100–2300m, but Orange is rare there). In Tz only on Kilimanjaro, Loliondo and Magaidu, while in Ug there are separate populations on Mt Moroto in the north-east and the Rwenzori Mts in the south-west. **Vo** song similar to Olive Thrush, but richer and flutier, although not usually as rich and varied as Orange Ground-Thrush.

Orange Ground-Thrush *Zoothera gurneyi* 19cm, 7.5"

Very similar to Abyssinian Ground-Thrush, but has a *narrower broken white eye-ring, an olive grey-brown crown and forecrown*, an indication of a dark mark below the eye and a greyish patch on the ear-coverts. **HH** only ground-thrush in much of Tz, from 450m in the East Usambaras, to 2400m on Mt Meru. In Ke it occurs on Mrima Hill in the SE (at only 300m), in the Chyulu and Taita Hills, and on the wetter N, E and S, slopes of Mt Kenya below 2000m. (It overlaps with Abyssinian Ground-Thrush at Kieni Forest, but is rare there.) **Vo** musical fluty song is slower than that of Abyssinian Ground-Thrush, and some phrases are identical to those of Taita Thrush.

Kivu Ground-Thrush *Zoothera tanganjicae* 19cm, 7.5" ●

Very similar to Abyssinian Ground-Thrush, but brighter with *an entirely orange-brown forecrown to nape*. **HH** common in parts of Nyungwe Forest, Rw, and Kibira Forest, Bu, between 1750–2700m. In SWUg it is less common, occurring in Bwindi-Impenetrable Forest from 1500–1850m, and on Mt Muhavura to 2900m. **Vo** sings melodic slow loud and deliberate notes, with a fluty delivery which is more like Orange than Abyssinian Ground-Thrush.

Black-eared Ground-Thrush *Zoothera cameronensis* 18cm, 7"

Race *graueri* is grey-brown above with a pale face, a vertical black bar through the eye, and a blackish spot on the ear-coverts. *Pale rufous-brown below, faintly streaked across the breast*. Race *kibalensis* was collected in Kibale Forest, Ug, in 1966, but has never been found again: it is more rufous. **HH** in our area known only from the Budongo and Bugoma forests of WUg. **Vo** unknown.

Oberlaender's Ground-Thrush *Zoothera oberlaenderi* 19cm, 7.5" ●
[Forest Ground-Thrush]

Similar to Kivu Ground-Thrush, but has a vertical black line through the eye. **HH** rare in our area, it is only known from forest in Semliki at 700m, and Bwindi and Mgahinga from 1500–1850m, in WUg. **Vo** a sweet, fluty and slowly delivered song which is more complex, varied and rambling than those of the other ground-thrushes.

Grey Ground-Thrush *Zoothera princei* 19cm, 7.5"

Very similar to slightly smaller Black-eared Ground-Thrush, but has a whiter face, and a vertical black bar from below the eye. **HH** in our area only known from Budongo, Bugoma and Semliki forests in WUg where it is rare. **Vo** unknown.

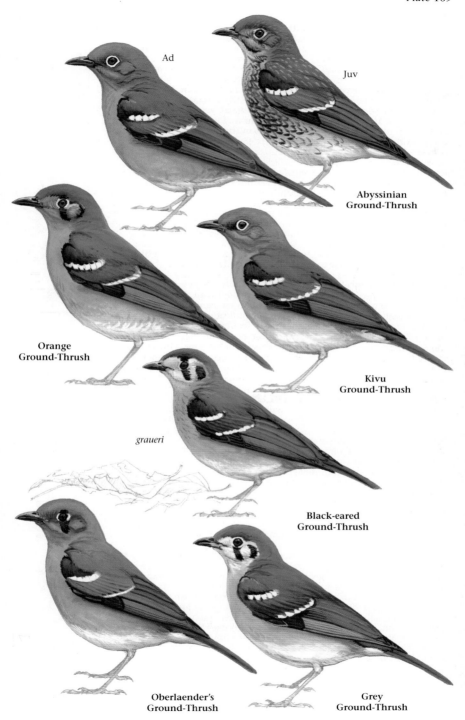

Plate 169

Ad

Juv

**Abyssinian
Ground-Thrush**

**Orange
Ground-Thrush**

**Kivu
Ground-Thrush**

graueri

**Black-eared
Ground-Thrush**

**Oberlaender's
Ground-Thrush**

**Grey
Ground-Thrush**

ANT-THRUSHES

Rufous-brown thrush-like birds with rather small heads and long tails. Rufous Flycatcher-Thrush is slightly smaller and more rounded with an upright posture. Sexes alike.

White-tailed Ant-Thrush *Neocossyphus poensis* 20cm, 8"

Dark brown above with a *blackish tail broadly tipped white on outer corners* (not obvious when perched or standing). In flight, shows a rufous wing bar. Race *praepectoralis* in Ug, Rw and Bu is bright rufous below and thus very similar to Red-tailed Ant-Thrush if the white tail corners are not seen. In WKe, races *kakamegoes* and *nigridorsalis* are variably washed duller olive-brown below. **HH** shy, but locally common in forest undergrowth from 700–2520m (often on the ground near ant-swarms). **Vo** commonest call is a loud spitted tuneless *trtttt* often given in flight and followed by a single rising or falling downslur.

Red-tailed Ant-Thrush *Neocossyphus rufus* 22cm, 8.5"

Mostly bright rufous with a slightly duller brown head and mantle, and a rufous-brown tail (which is slightly darker in centre). Very similar to Rufous Flycatcher-Thrush, but has a more typical thrush-like horizontal stance, a smaller rounded head, and longer bill. Imm like ad but duller. **HH** two widely separated populations in forest undergrowth from sea-level to 900m in the east and 700–1400 in the west. **Vo** western and coastal birds differ: in the west, the call is a sharp crack followed by several rising and falling whistles, ending in a chatter; coastal birds give a ratchet-like *trrrt*, and this is often followed by a long falling whistle *fweeeeeee*.

Rufous Flycatcher-Thrush *Stizorhina fraseri* 19cm, 7.5"

Very similar to Red-tailed Ant-Thrush, but smaller with a shorter bill and tail, and often a more upright flycatcher-like stance. Rufous band across wing (particularly underwing) good for identification, but hard to see as the bird moves quickly. Sometimes raises feathers on hindcrown giving head a slightly angular and crested appearance. Imm duller than ad. **HH** inhabits both middle levels and undergrowth of forest interior from 700–1500m. **Vo** a distinctive sound of western forests; call is a rising series of four slow whistled upslurs, the last longest *fwee fwee fwee fweeeep*. Also calls a loud and aggressive *fwifwifwifwifwifwifwii*.

THRUSH-LIKE FOREST BABBLERS

Two very shy and difficult to observe species of uncertain affinities, most recently placed in the genus *Modulatrix* in the family Timaliidae, babblers. Sexes alike.

Spot-throat *Modulatrix stictigula* 19cm, 7.5" ●

A smallish thrush-like bird which is dark olive-brown above and brighter tawny-brown below. Throat is paler with small blackish spots (but these are difficult to see in the field). A pale greyish eye-ring is conspicuous against the darker head. Imm is like ad but duller. **HH** localised, but sometimes common in the West Usambara Mts and Iringa highlands of Tz from 900–2200m. Shy inhabitant of dense undergrowth and dark areas of the forest floor. **Vo** draws attention with a long drawn out high-pitched and descending whistled *seeeeeeu*. Song is a very loud and piercing rather thrush-like series of strong notes ending in a burry flourish.

Dappled Mountain-Robin *Modulatrix orostruthus* 19cm, 7.5" ● ●
[Dapple-throat]

Olive-brown above with a greenish wash to the mantle and wing-coverts, a darker and browner tail, and *pale yellowish below broadly streaked olive*. Imm plain dull olive below. **HH** keeps to dense undergrowth within undisturbed forest from 900–1700m, where it is very shy and localised. **Vo** song is a rising and falling fluty *wi-lu-wi-lu-wil'li-lu* (remarkably like Grey-chested Illadopsis) and it also makes a Common Bulbul-like chattering.

Plate 170

White-tailed
Ant-Thrush

Red-tailed
Ant-Thrush

Rufous
Flycatcher-
Thrush

Spot-throat

Ad

Dappled Mountain-Robin

TWO THRUSHES WITH HEAVILY SPOTTED UNDERPARTS

Spotted Ground-Thrush *Zoothera guttata* 21cm, 8" ●

Olive-brown above with black bands through the eyes and on the ear-coverts, with *white spots on the wing-coverts forming two bars*, and white below with heavy black spotting. Sexes are alike. **HH** uncommon intra-African migrant from the south (breeds on the Rondo Plateau, STz), to forests on Ke coast, but only regular at Gedi and Arabuko-Sokoke between Mar–Oct. Solitary, feeds in leaf litter, and very hard to see in dappled forest light. **Vo** loud, melodic and varied song, but migrants are usually silent, possibly uttering a thin whistle.

Groundscraper Thrush *Psophocichla litsipsirupa* 22cm, 8.5"

Similar to Spotted Ground-Thrush, but greyer above and *lacking white spots on the wings*. In flight, rufous bases to primaries appear as two pale-buffy patches. Yellow-buff under wing-coverts are also conspicuous. Imm is finely spotted with buffy-white above. **HH** pairs and small groups are localised, but not uncommon in wooded grasslands from 900–1900m. **Vo** song is loud, slow and very burry, but quite melodic. Diagnostic call is a rapid clicking of hollow-sounding notes. **SS** Dusky Lark.

ROCK-THRUSHES
Three small or medium-sized thrushes, males (and one female) are blue-grey and rufous, best identified by colour of crown, backs, and tail pattern. Scaly looking female-type plumage is more difficult: look for markings on the breast and the tail pattern.

Common Rock-Thrush *Monticola saxatilis* 20cm, 8"
[European Rock-Thrush]

Br ♂ has the head, throat and upper mantle blue-grey, *back white*, remainder of underparts and *all except centre-tail feathers orange-red*. Non-br ♂ *mottled and scaly all over with a rufous tail*, and shows some rusty feathers amongst barring below. ♀ and 1st year similar to non-br ♂, but generally browner, rufous mainly on tail but also washed pale-rufous on lower underparts. Often stands upright, longer-billed and shorter-tailed than other rock-thrushes. **HH** common and widespread Palearctic passage and winter visitor from Oct–Apr, which favours open wood and bushland. **Vo** silent and unlikely to sing in the region, but may utter a soft *tak*.

Miombo Rock-Thrush *Monticola angolensis* 19cm, 7.5"

Ad ♂ similar to Common Rock-Thrush, but lacks white back and if seen well some show *blackish mottling from crown to mantle*. ♀ similar to ♀ Common, but has less and fainter scalloping across orange washed breast, and usually shows distinct dark malar stripes. Imm like ♀ but more heavily mottled below. **HH** pairs are local and resident in miombo woodland. **Vo** utters a fluty, melodic and thrush-like rolling song, varied phrases starting with *wheeoo wheeoo wheeoo*.

Little Rock-Thrush *Monticola rufocinereus* 15cm, 6"

Slimmer and longer-tailed than Common Rock-Thrush, like a small robin-chat: ad ♂ is brownish-grey above, without white back of Common, and with a bold blackish *centre-tail and tips forming a distinctive inverted 'T' shape*. Miombo Rock-Thrush has less black on the tail and a different range. ♀ duller and paler than ♂. Imm spotted buff above, scaly blackish on buff below: tail like ad. **HH** pairs occur patchily within range, on rocky escarpments and in broken hill country with some tree cover. **Vo** sings from tops of small trees a simple, but sweet thrush-like refrain, ending each phrases with a double *zi-zit*, rather like is-it at the end of a sentence.

Plate 171

Spotted
Ground-Thrush

Groundscraper
Thrush

Ad

br ♂

♀

Common
Rock-Thrush

♀

Little
Rock-Thrush

♀

♂

♂

Miombo
Rock-Thrush

WHITE-WINGED CHATS
Medium-sized chats with variable white patches on crown, throat, or wings. Frequently on the ground or singing from prominent perches. Usually in pairs or small groups.

Northern Anteater Chat *Myrmecocichla aethiops* 18cm, 7"
Appears all dark brown when perched, but *large whitish patches in primaries* are obvious in flight. Sexes are alike. Imm is slightly scaly on the throat and breast. **HH** pairs and family groups are common residents of open country and farmland mainly above 1500m, often on ground or perching on low bushes, fences and termite hills. **Vo** loud, rolling and musical, but rather monotonous song repeated at length with little variation (several birds may sing together).

Sooty Chat *Myrmecocichla nigra* 18cm, 7"
Ad ♂ is similar to Northern Anteater Chat, but is much blacker and the *white wing patch is confined to the coverts* (not the primaries). Imm ♂ is like a dull ad ♂. Ad ♀ and imm ♀ are all sooty brown without white in the wings. **HH** pairs are common in lightly wooded grasslands from sea-level to 1700m, mainly to the west and south of Northern Anteater Chat. **Vo** much more melodic and varied than Northern Anteater Chat, often with mimicry in the long refrains, and regularly given in a parachuting song flight.

Cliff Chat *Myrmecocichla cinnamomeiventris* 21cm, 8"
[Mocking Chat]
Ad ♂ is an attractive black and rufous chat with a white shoulder patch and narrow whitish band across the breast. Ad ♀ has a similar basic pattern, but is more grey and rufous without any white. Imm ♂ and imm ♀ like dull versions of ads. **HH** pairs are widespread, but patchily distributed, frequenting rocky gorges and hill sides from 600–2200m. **Vo** complex song with lots of local variation. It is long rambling and rather thrush-like, but notes are more spitted, and interspersed with sweet warblings and flourishes which can be very like the song of Irania. Frequently amplified by the rocky gorge habitat.

White-headed Black Chat *Myrmecocichla arnoti* 18cm, 7"
[Arnot's Chat]
Ad ♂ has a *white crown and shoulder patch.* Ad ♀ has a black crown and the *throat to upper breast and shoulder patch are white.* Imm is mostly blackish except for white on the shoulder and may show an indication of white on the crown or throat according to sex. **HH** pairs occur in a variety of habitat from 150–1600m, favouring miombo woodland in Tz, but open bushy hillsides and the vicinity of buildings in Rw and Bu. **Vo** song is a mixture of harsh sparrow-like chipping and sweet fluty musical refrains.

White-fronted Black Chat *Myrmecocichla albifrons* 16cm, 6"
Ad ♂ is similar to Sooty Chat, but smaller with a *white forecrown and shoulder.* Ad ♀ is all blackish. Imm is like dull ad, but with some tawny mottling on the wings and below. **HH** restricted range, found in open bush and semi-arid country from 800–2500m, often on small trees. Drops to ground to feed. **Vo** call consists of repeated whistled downslurred *siuu,* while the song is a repeated rambling warble.

Plate 172

Northern

Ad

**Northern
Anteater Chat**

Sooty

♀

Sooty Chat

♂

Cliff Chat

♂

♀

♂

Imm

**White-headed
Black Chat**

♀

♂

♀

**White-fronted
Black Chat**

TWO SMALL OPEN COUNTRY CHATS

Common Stonechat *Saxicola torquata* 13cm, 5"

Races and individuals highly variable: typical ad ♂ has a *black head and throat,* chestnut or black on the breast (varies in size), white patches on sides of the neck, wings and rump, and a blackish tail. Ad ♀ is streaked brown and buff with *only a very indistinct supercilium,* white wing stripe, and a brown throat which contrasts slightly with the pale rufous-brown breast. Imm is like ♀ but duller. Distinctive race *albofasciata* occurs in extreme NEUg. Recent work suggests that all African races may be a good species: **African Stonechat**. **HH** widespread and common from 500–2500m, generally in highlands, but at lower altitudes and in marshes in Tz. Sits in the open on fence posts, tree stumps and small bushes. **Vo** attractive repeated short scratchy warbling song which may be sung for long periods without much variation.

Whinchat *Saxicola rubetra* 13cm, 5"

Br ♂ has a distinctive *long white supercilium and blackish ear-coverts.* Washed buffy-orange below, with white patches on wing-coverts and at either side of tail base. Non-br ♂, ♀ and 1st winter resemble ♀ Common Stonechat: best distinguished by a *well-defined buffy supercilium and white base to the outer-tail.* **HH** winter visitor and Palearctic passage migrant from Oct–Apr which can be common in the west. Sits on small bushes and trees within grasslands and cultivated areas. **Vo** usually silent, but may sing a similar song to Common Stonechat.

AFRICAN WHEATEARS
Medium-sized chat-like birds mostly with white or buffy rumps and an inverted black 'T' on the tail. Mainly ground-dwelling in open country.

Capped Wheatear *Oenanthe pileata* 17cm, 6.5"

Ad has a narrow white band across the forecrown, a white supercilium, *white throat, and a broad black breast band.* Imm similar to ♀ Northern Wheatear but spotted above with buff, and washed yellow-brown with darker brown mottling below. **HH** common and widespread on short grassy plains above 1400m, migrants may be lower. Stands very upright, often on fence posts and other small perches. **Vo** sings a mixture of harsh and sweet notes in short bursts, often with mimicry, and sometimes performs a low song flight. Alarm call is a muffled *tik.*

Schalow's Wheatear *Oenanthe schalowi* 15cm, 6"

[Mourning Wheatear]
Ad ♂ blackish with a dingy brown crown, white belly and unique *cinnamon-buff rump and undertail.* Tail orange-buff with black T. ♀ rump and tail similar to ♂, remainder of plumage mostly dark brown, with a whitish lower breast to belly. Imm like dull ♀ with buff speckles. **HH** endemic to the Rift Valley area of CKe and NTz. Particularly fond of rocky hillsides with some grass and scattered bushes. **Vo** sings short bursts of identical muffled but sweet refrains.

Heuglin's Wheatear *Oenanthe heuglini* 14cm, 5.5"

Overall appearance is like ♀ Northern Wheatear, but much darker and more uniform brown-olive above with a dark line through the eye, a narrow whitish supercilium, and less white at base of outertail. Often *warm brown-olive below,* but richer rufous-brown when fresh, and paler on the throat and belly. Br ad has a dark ear-patch reminiscent of Northern, but crown and mantle are never grey. Sexes are alike. **HH** rather local, but makes erratic movements and is sometimes common in NEUg. Perches in bushes within burnt grassland, dropping to feed on the ground: frequently waves its tail. **Vo** song is not recorded from the region.

Plate 173

albofasciata

♂

♀

Common Stonechat

♂

Imm

br ♂

br ♀

Capped Wheatear

Ad

Whinchat

Capped

Schalow's

Whinchat

Heuglin's

♀

Schalow's Wheatear

♂

Heuglin's Wheatear

PALEARCTIC WHEATEARS

Several similar looking wheatears occurring in East Africa from Sep–Apr. All (except Desert) have typical wheatear tail pattern: white with a black inverted 'T'. Width of terminal tail band, colour of wings and exact shape of black on head (if present) aid identification. All prefer open country, often on the ground but also in low bushes.

Northern Wheatear   *Oenanthe oenanthe*   15cm, 6"
[European Wheatear]

Br ♂ is distinctive with a grey crown, nape and mantle, a broad black mask and black wings, and a buffy throat and breast. Terminal tail band broader than Pied and Black-eared wheatears. ♀ and non-br ♂ are earthy brown above, with a pale supercilium, variable dark line through the eye, dark brown wings, and buffy underparts. In flight, *dark wings contrast strongly with a paler brown mantle*. 1st year has buffy wing edges and can be confused with Isabelline Wheatear but the tail band is always narrower. **HH** common and widespread passage migrant and winter visitor to a very wide range of more open habitats from Sep–Apr. **Vo** usually silent, but may sing before departing a mixture of rapid scratchy and sweet notes. Alarm call is an oft-repeated *tak...*

Isabelline Wheatear   *Oenanthe isabellina*   17cm, 6.5"

Very similar to ♀ Northern Wheatear, but often stands very upright and is generally paler, slightly larger and stronger-billed. *Wings have broad buffy feather edgings and in flight appear more or less uniform with the mantle.* Terminal tail band is broader than in Northern. **HH** a common passage and winter visitor from Oct–Mar, generally preferring dry country, but can turn up in any open area within wintering range. **Vo** usually silent, but song consists of a complex warble of scratchy and nasal twanging. Call is a harsh *tchak...*

Pied Wheatear   *Oenanthe pleschanka*   15cm, 6"

Only white-rumped black and white wheatear likely to be encountered. Br ♂ has *black on the face and upper breast extending back over the mantle and wings*, with crown and nape white or silvery-grey in fresh plumage, and a narrow terminal tail band. In Oct, new arrivals (including ♂, ♀ and 1st year) are variable, but basically dull brown on the crown with a buffy supercilium, and with sides of neck, throat, *mantle and wings dark brown or blackish* often variably mottled. An uncommon white-throated form '*vittata*' also occurs. **HH** common winter visitor with a preference for dry country; often perches on small bushes. **Vo** usually silent in EA, but song is a short sweet refrain interspersed with harsh *chak* notes. Call is a soft, muffled *chat* repeated frequently.

Black-eared Wheatear   *Oenanthe hispanica*   15cm, 6"

Ad ♂ has both pale and black-throated forms (the latter not recorded in EA). Pale-throated birds differ from white-throated Pied Wheatear in having a *buffy-grey or whitish mantle* uniform with crown and nape. On the black-throated form the *black face mask does not join with black wings*. More white in tail than any other wheatear in region. ♀ is virtually identical to ♀ Pied. **HH** rare vagrant with only two Ke records: near Nairobi, Mar–Apr 1984 and Lake Baringo, Dec 1994. **Vo** usually silent in EA, but song consists of short warbled refrains, lacking the harsh scratchiness of other wheatears (and recalling Rufous-chested Swallow).

Desert Wheatear   *Oenanthe deserti*   15cm, 6"

Differs from the other wheatears in having a *virtually all-black tail* only showing white at the very base. Ad ♂ can be further identified from Pied Wheatear by its sandy mantle, and from the black-throated form of Black-eared Wheatear by the black of face mask being joined to the wings. **HH** rare vagrant with only two Ke records: Kiunga Feb 1984 and Kerio Valley Oct 1996. **Vo** song not recorded in region.

Plate 174

Northern
Wheatear

♂

♀

'vittata'
♂

Isabelline
Wheatear

♀

non-br
♂

♂

Pied
Wheatear

non-br ♂

♀

Black-eared
Wheatear

♂

♂

♀

Desert
Wheatear

MIGRANT NIGHTINGALES AND CHATS

Thrush Nightingale   *Luscinia luscinia*   17cm, 6.5"
[Sprosser]

Very similar to Nightingale being a medium-sized brown chat-like bird with a *slightly contrasting dull rufous-brown tail* and a dark eye with a narrow whitish eye-ring. Dingy pale grey-brown below with *indistinct mottling across the breast* and a whiter throat. Sexes are alike. **HH** common Palearctic migrant from Oct–Dec and Mar–Apr, preferring thickets and leafy bush country below 1500m, mainly east of the Rift Valley (but more widespread in STz). Small numbers winter in E and CKe and SWTz. **Vo** two common calls (similar in Nightingale), are a strident whistled *weeep* and a harsh *takk*. Often sings with a loud rather strident musical refrain of sweet and harsh notes, which continues for long periods without pause (not as pure or disjointed as Nightingale).

Nightingale   *Luscinia megarhynchos*   17cm, 6.5"

Three races occur and are very similar to Thrush Nightingale. All can be distinguished by *plain underparts* (not mottled) and warmer rufous rumps and tails. They vary mainly in the colour of the upperparts; nominate (mainly western) is mostly warm rufous-brown above; *africana* (mainly central) is duller brown on the back and wings, and *hafizi* (mainly coastal) is colder brown-grey above, with rufous restricted to the rump and tail. All have dark eyes with a narrow whitish eye-ring. Sexes alike. **HH** common Palearctic migrant and winter visitor mainly across Ug and Ke. Wintering birds (Oct–Apr) occur in similar habitat to Thrush Nightingale. **Vo** call is a loud and harsh *tk-tk-trrrrrrk* (like running a stick along a fence), but also utters a muffled *tuk tuk* in alarm, and a strong whistled *wheet* at dawn or as a prelude to song. Song is a loud complex warble of mainly sweet notes, with a pause between each sequence.

Rufous Bush Chat   *Cercotrichas galactotes*   17cm, 6.5"
[Rufous-tailed Scrub-Robin]

Grey-brown above with a dark eye line and long off-white supercilium, a rufous rump and tail which is tipped black and white and often cocked and waved. Sexes alike. **HH** common Palearctic winter visitor from Nov–Apr, mainly below 1000m in dry bush country in the north and east. **Vo** usually silent, but may call a quiet and hesitant *seeep.*

Irania   *Irania gutturalis*   18cm, 7"
[White-throated Robin]

Ad ♂ is boldly marked: blue-grey above with an *all-black tail* contrasting with a black and white head pattern and a rich rufous-orange breast. ♀ is rather plain grey-brown above with a blackish tail, a whitish throat, scaly buff and grey breast, and pale rufous-orange washed flanks. 1st year is like ♀, but has browner wings and lightly spotted greater coverts. **HH** rather scarce and local Palearctic migrant to thickets, dense bush and gullies from 500–1400m in EKe and Tz where it is easily overlooked. **Vo** sings regularly from Feb until departure, a loud musical warble, not unlike a speeded-up version of Thrush Nightingale. Alarm is a throaty *trrrr* (similar to but quieter than Nightingale).

Common Redstart   *Phoenicurus phoenicurus*   14cm, 5.5"

From Oct–Dec non-br ♂ has pale fringes to plumage giving a frosty and mottled appearance. In Jan–Apr, ♂ is grey above with a white forehead, black face, bright orange-red underparts, and a bright rufous tail with a dark brown centre. ♀ is grey-brown above with a narrow pale eye-ring and buffy below with a paler throat and buffy-orange breast; tail as ♂. **HH** reasonably regular Palearctic visitor to NUg and NWKe from Oct–Apr, favouring wooded areas and thickets. Slim with quick movements and often first noticed when it shows a flash of rufous tail. **Vo** usually silent, but occasionally calls a soft *tik.*

Plate 175

nominate

Thrush
Nightingale

Nightingale

hafizi

Rufous Bush
Chat

♀

♂

Irania

♀

Common
Redstart

♂

SCRUB-ROBINS
Similar looking chat-like birds with mostly rufous or black tails, tipped white on all except central feathers. Tails are frequently cocked, waved and spread. Colour of underparts, the presence or absence of streaking and tail markings aid identification. Sexes alike. Juveniles are mottled with buff and dark brown.

White-browed Scrub-Robin *Cercotrichas leucophrys* 15cm, 6"
[White-browed Robin]
Six races occur in two distinct groups: white-winged forms inhabit drier areas mainly to the north and east, red-backed birds in higher country and wetter coastal Ke. White-winged forms are typically paler-backed with lighter streaking on the breast. They have a greyer crown and nape, earth-brown mantle and *broad white edges to the wing-coverts and inner secondaries forming a large single patch.* Red-backed forms are darker crowned and *heavily streaked with dark blackish-brown underparts,* white edges to wing-coverts are less extensive often forming two bars. All races have a rufous rump and mainly rufous tail *ending with blackish* sub-terminal spots and white tips. **HH** common in a wide variety of habitats (apart from forest and barren desert) from sea-level to 2200m. Often keeps to cover unless singing, when displays repeatedly from bush tops. **Vo** an accomplished and persistent songster which varies locally and individually: the usual song consists of loud phrases repeated over and over again with or without modification.

Brown-backed Scrub-Robin *Cercotrichas hartlaubi* 15cm, 6"
Similar to White-browed Scrub-Robin, but has a *darker brown crown and back, very dark brown wings edged white on greater and lesser coverts – forming two bars.* Whitish underparts are lightly streaked grey. Lower rump and base of tail rufous, with a broad blackish sub-terminal band and white tips. **HH** pairs are patchily distributed, being more common in the west, inhabiting forest edge, open wooded or bush country with long grass and edges of cultivation, from 900–2200m. Sings from bush tops, but otherwise shy and retiring. **Vo** song is sweeter than that of White-browed Scrub-Robin, but lacks the variety of phrases.

Eastern Bearded Scrub-Robin *Cercotrichas quadrivirgata* 15cm, 6"
[Eastern Bearded Robin]
Rather plain olive-brown above with a bold face pattern, *pale buffy-orange on the breast and flanks,* a warm rufous rump, and blackish-brown tail with white tips. On Mafia and Zanzibar, Tz, the race *greenwayi* is greyer above and very pale below. **HH** often shy and difficult to observe, keeping to thick cover in forest, wooded valleys and thick scrub from sea-level to 1000m (and occasionally 1800m). **Vo** a persistent singer, particularly at dawn and dusk with pleasant and varied whistles, with individuals often repeating favoured phrases. Alarm is a harsh *chrrrt.*

Miombo Bearded Scrub-Robin *Cercotrichas barbata* 15cm, 6"
Very similar to Eastern Bearded Scrub-Robin, but slightly paler above with rufous washed ear-coverts and with more *extensive and stronger rufous washed underparts.* **HH** patchily distributed within a restricted range, keeping to thick cover in miombo woodland from 1000–1500m. **Vo** similar song to Eastern Bearded Scrub-Robin, but louder with much purer notes.

Northern Bearded Scrub-Robin *Cercotrichas leucosticta* 15cm, 6"
[Forest Scrub-Robin]
Darker above than other scrub-robins, with a *plain grey breast and flanks,* white throat and belly, and a black tail with white tips. **HH** in our area, known only from Semliki Forest, WUg. **Vo** very different to other scrub-robins, the song is a rising and falling repeated series of whistled minor key notes.

Plate 176

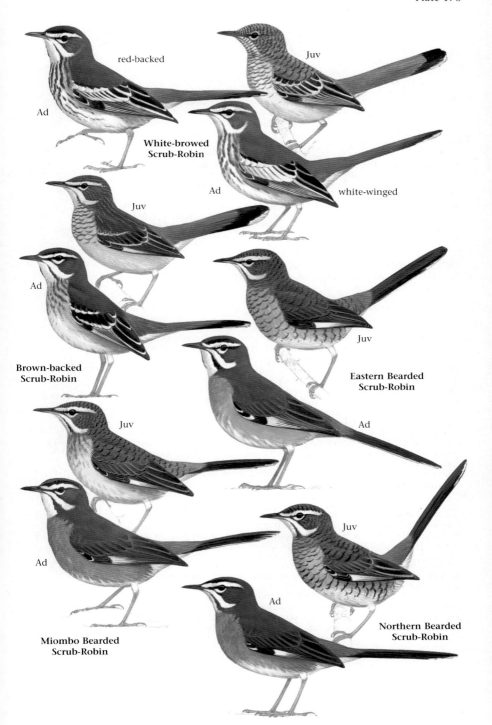

red-backed

White-browed
Scrub-Robin

Ad

Juv

Ad

white-winged

Juv

Ad

Brown-backed
Scrub-Robin

Eastern Bearded
Scrub-Robin

Juv

Juv

Ad

Miombo Bearded
Scrub-Robin

Ad

Juv

Ad

Northern Bearded
Scrub-Robin

MORNING-THRUSHES

Two vociferous thrushes with powerful songs which include some mimicry. Sexes alike.

Spotted Morning-Thrush *Cichladusa guttata* 17cm, 6.5"

[Spotted Palm-Thrush]

Uniform brown or rich brown above with a white supercilium, rufous-brown rump and tail. Whitish below with black malar stripes extending as spots across the breast and as elongated streaks on the flanks. Imm is duller. **HH** occurs in coastal thickets, wooded grasslands and semi-arid bush, feeding on ground in the vicinity of cover. **Vo** characteristic voice of dry scrub: sings throughout the day and on moonlit nights. Flutier than scrub-robins, almost thrush-like, song usually consists of short repeated or alternating phrases, with some mimicry.

Collared Palm-Thrush *Cichladusa arquata* 18cm, 7"

Mostly warm russet-brown above, with a pale cream eye, a *creamy-white throat with a narrow black bib,* and grey sides to head, breast and flanks. Imm is variably streaked below with brown. **HH** pairs are rather shy and associated with palms and nearby undergrowth, being common in some coastal areas, and patchily distributed in suitable habitat in the west. **Vo** may sing for long periods: song is similar to that of Spotted Morning-Thrush, but more varied and scratchy.

DULL RESIDENT CHATS

Tame, subdued, dull plumaged chats, which frequently flick their wings while foraging or after landing. Sexes alike.

Familiar Chat *Cercomela familiaris* 15cm, 6"

[Red-tailed Chat]

Rather uniform drab brown chat with a *rufous rump and outer-tail; centre of tail and terminal band blackish making an inverted 'T'.* Imm is spotted buff above, mottled buff and dark brown below. **HH** pairs are local away from the southern part of their range inhabiting open woods and bush country often in rocky areas, and frequently in small trees (but also on ground when feeding). **Vo** sings from bush tops a tuneless scratchy warble incorporating its call, a repeated *wii cha-cha.*

Brown-tailed Rock Chat *Cercomela scotocerca* 14cm, 5.5"

Similar to Familiar Chat, but *no rufous in plumage.* Ear-coverts slightly warm brown, but otherwise all drab dark brown. Imm is like ad. **HH** localised in rocky semi-arid bushland where it sits on bushes and drops to ground to feed, particularly in broken rocky areas. **Vo** repeated wispy song begins *wip* followed immediately by a burry rolling liquid *shrererererereep.*

Alpine Chat *Cercomela sordida* 14cm, 5.5"

[Moorland Chat]

A dumpy short-tailed chat with a wheatear-like tail pattern: white outer bases, a black centre and terminal band. Three races occur: in Ug and Ke, *ernesti* is dark brown above and buffy-brown below, while on Mt Kilimanjaro, Tz, *hypospodia* has a darker crown and greyer underparts, and in the Crater Highlands *olimotienis* is intermediate. Imms are lightly scaled above, and speckled below. **HH** common in giant heather and on moorlands above the tree line, occasionally occurring lower along vehicle tracks, or in forest clearings. Tame and inquisitive, hopping around on ground, and perching on low vegetation. **Vo** song is formless and unattractive series of various sparrow-like chirps, interspersed with squeaks.

Plate 177

Spotted Morning-Thrush

Ad

Collared Palm-Thrush

Ad

Familiar Chat

Ad

Imm

Brown-tailed Rock Chat

ernesti

Ad

Ad

hypospodia

Alpine Chat

CHLOROPETA WARBLERS

Three warblers (formerly known as flycatcher-warblers). Often skulk in thick vegetation, but also perch prominently and hawk flycatcher-like after insects. All may show bright orange-red mouth linings when singing. Sexes alike.

Dark-capped Yellow Warbler *Chloropeta natalensis* 14cm, 5.5"
[Yellow Warbler]

Two races occur: widespread *massaica* is olive-brown above with a darker *blackish-brown crown* (rear may be slightly raised giving a crested appearance) and entirely yellow below; while the nominate race in STz has crown only a little darker than mantle. Imms are tawny-brown above and yellow washed with tawny below. **HH** pairs are widespread, inhabiting undergrowth and dense vegetation, often near water, from 800–2300m. Sings frequently from within cover, but also from exposed perches at dawn. **Vo** varied song commonly begins with a few chips and continues with either a rather urgent *tp...wi-chi-wi-chi-wi-chi-wi-chi* or a nasal *weeeez*.

Mountain Yellow Warbler *Chloropeta similis* 14cm, 5.5"

Similar to Dark-capped Yellow Warbler, *but uniform dull olive-green above including the head*. Imm is slightly darker above and more buffy below. **HH** common in forest and bamboo at higher altitudes from 1800–3400m. Rather active, climbing around within the middle and lower levels of any forest vegetation, singing from within cover and while on the move. **Vo** beautiful songster, with a long, varied, sweet and repeated refrain which is characteristic of the bamboo zone. Phrases begin *wee-weeu* before breaking into a medley of chips and flourishes with twanging notes.

Papyrus Yellow Warbler *Chloropeta gracilirostris* 14cm, 5.5" ●

In our area, the nominate race is very similar to Mountain Yellow Warbler, but the mantle, wings and tail are tawny-brown, and the yellow underparts are tinged tawny on the flanks and vent. Imm is also washed tawny below. **HH** localised little known and uncommon resident of dense papyrus beds from 900–2050m. Gives the impression of a very yellow *Acrocephalus* warbler. **Vo** sings infrequently, with varied chips and churrs that recall a starling more than a warbler.

ACROCEPHALUS WARBLERS

Acrocephalus are similar-looking plain warblers, with rather flat heads, pointed bills, and rounded tails, that are invariably brown above and paler below. Size, overall tone, leg colour and range aid identification. Sexes alike. The date can also give a useful clue, since five are Palearctic migrants.

Lesser Swamp Warbler *Acrocephalus gracilirostris* 15cm, 6"
[Cape Reed Warbler]

Smaller than Greater Swamp Warbler and larger than African Reed Warbler. Three races occur: all have a whitish throat contrasting with a darker breast and flanks, and longish thin bills. Race *jacksoni* (Ug to WKe) is greyish-brown above and below, with a whiter belly; *parvus* (CKe to NTz highlands) is tawny-brown above with a slightly rufous rump and greyish-brown on the breast and flanks; and *leptorhynchus* (EKe and ETz lowlands) is tawny above with a brighter rufous rump, and a paler tawny-buff breast and flanks. All have a short pale supercilium and dark grey legs. **HH** common, widespread resident of waterside vegetation, reed beds and papyrus. **Vo** loud, frequent and fluid songster mixing melodious phrases with subdued chattering. Commonest calls include a see-sawing and rapidly delivered interrogatory *wee-ter-ree-ter-ree-ter-reet*.

Greater Swamp Warbler *Acrocephalus rufescens* 18cm, 7"

Larger than Lesser Swamp Warbler and more uniform darker earth-brown above (although slightly tinged rufous on the rump). *White throat blends gradually into grey-brown underparts*. Bill noticeably big and strong, a short indistinct supercilium, and greyish legs. **HH** common resident within range, inhabiting papyrus swamps, and occurring from 600–2000m. **Vo** unlike any other *Acrocephalus*, the slow deliberate song is a deep, gravelly and rhythmic *wer-ker-chi-chuk-chuk-chuk-chuk-chuk*, regularly interrupted by *erk* and a liquid *donk* or variations.

Plate 178

Dark-capped
Yellow Warbler

massaica   Ad   Imm

Mountain
Yellow Warbler

Papyrus Yellow
Warbler

leptorhynchus   *parvus*

Lesser Swamp
Warbler

Greater Swamp
Warbler

African Reed Warbler   *Acrocephalus baeticatus*   13cm, 5"
[African Marsh Warbler]
Much smaller than Lesser Swamp Warbler, and shorter-winged and much warmer buffy-brown than similar-looking Palearctic species. Two races occur: widespread *cinnamomeus* is *pale warm-brown above* with a short buffy supercilium, a whitish throat and *warm buffy breast and flanks;* in ETz *suahelicus* is slightly larger and duller above. Legs grey-brown. **HH** widespread, but seldom common resident of marshes, reedbeds and rank vegetation from sea-level to 1900m. **Vo** has a typical *Acrocephalus* song, sounding much like Eurasian Reed Warbler, but notes are slower, clearer and smoother.

Marsh Warbler   *Acrocephalus palustris*   13cm, 5"
[European Marsh Warbler]
Extremely similar to Eurasian Reed Warbler, but uniform cold olive-brown above and whitish below with a buffy-yellow tinge. Legs pale pinkish-brown (but can be dark on 1st year birds). In addition to colder tones, Marsh is plumper than Eurasian Reed with a more rounded head and shorter bill. Both species have short pale supercilia and small eye-rings. **HH** very common Palearctic migrant from Oct–Apr to a variety of bush country and overgrown cultivation, mainly east of the Great Rift Valley, and uncommon elsewhere. **Vo** not particularly vocal in East Africa (but heard from Feb to departure). Full song includes mimicry and is rich and melodic for an *Acrocephalus,* but still scratchy.

Eurasian Reed Warbler   *Acrocephalus scirpaceus*   14cm, 5.5"
In our area, the race *fuscus* is brown above, with grey-olive tones to the head and nape, and whitish underparts. It is extremely similar to Marsh Warbler but has a very slightly rufous washed rump, and whiter underparts. Some individuals are warmer brown above with *more russet tones to the rump,* and whitish below with buffy brown sides to the breast and flanks. In all birds the *head appears flat topped, not rounded.* Legs usually dark brownish. **HH** Palearctic winter visitor from Oct–Apr which is widespread (but only common west of the Rift Valley), and inhabits thickets, bush, rank vegetation and cultivation. **Vo** sings a classic *Acrocephalus* song for long periods without pause: most notes are rather scratchy, twangy and unmusical. Alarm is a frequently repeated harsh burry *cherrr.*

Great Reed Warbler   *Acrocephalus arundinaceus*   19cm, 7.5"
Very large and warm brown above with a distinct buffy supercilium and strong bill. Below whitish with a strong tawny-buff wash on sides of the breast and flanks. *Legs are usually pale brownish.* **HH** a rather local Palearctic winter visitor from Oct to early May, but more numerous in Apr east of the Great Rift Valley. Inhabits rank vegetation and thickets. **Vo** song is much slower than the smaller *Acrocephalus* warblers, though still typical, a loud, deep scratchy and croaking medley. Call is a single *chakk.*

Basra Reed Warbler   *Acrocephalus griseldis*   17cm, 6.5"
Larger than Eurasian Reed Warbler but smaller and slimmer than Great Reed Warbler. Cold olive-brown above with an obvious whitish supercilium above a broad dark loral line, a long, slim bill and a dark tail. White below, faintly washed buff on sides of the breast and flanks. Legs grey. **HH** Palearctic visitor from Nov–Apr mainly in the east, but occasionally in the Great Rift Valley, occurring in marshy areas and damp thickets. **Vo** may be heard prior to departure and, while obviously an *Acrocephalus* song, it is coarse and tuneless with rather similar notes that sound like a protracted scolding.

Plate 179

African Reed Warbler *suahelicus*

cinnamomeus

Marsh Warbler

Ad

fuscus

Ad

Eurasian Reed Warbler

'warm brown'

Great Reed Warbler

Basra Reed Warbler

Sedge Warbler *Acrocephalus schoenobaenus*   13cm, 5"
Streaked above with a *distinctive bold creamy supercilium,* and whitish below with buffy-rufous flanks. In flight, shows a contrasting *plain rufous rump* and a dark tail. 1st year birds may show an indication of a pale crown stripe. **HH** common Palearctic visitor to reedbeds, marshes and lakeside vegetation from Nov–Apr. Wintering birds are most numerous in the west, but there is also a strong and widespread northerly passage in Apr. **Vo** often heard, but its typical song is subdued, sweeter and far less scratchy than the other small *Acrocephalus.*

LOCUSTELLA WARBLERS
Shy brown warblers with rather weak bills, indistinct superciliary stripes, strongly graduated tails and very long undertail coverts (which may be mottled or streaked). Sexes are alike. Palearctic migrants, two of which are extremely rare.

River Warbler *Locustella fluviatilis*   14cm, 5.5"
Cold olive-brown above, with a narrow supercilium, and *mottle-streaked breast: undertail-coverts are long and conspicuously pale-tipped.* Legs are pink. **HH** not uncommon Palearctic passage migrant from Nov–Apr in EKe, but shy and difficult to observe. Inhabits thick scrub and undergrowth. **Vo** rarely heard song is a protracted rattling *zri-zri-zri-zri-zri…*(like a Yellow Bishop), and the call is a soft irregularly repeated *tak.*

Savi's Warbler *Locustella luscinioides*   14cm, 5.5"
Warm plain olive-brown above, with an indistinct supercilium, a whitish throat and belly which contrast with a deep buff breast and flanks: *long buff undertail-coverts are plain or only lightly mottled.* Some birds show a faint gorget of small spots around base of neck. **HH** Palearctic vagrant: two records, both from Ngulia in Tsavo West NP, Ke, Dec 1975 and 1987. **Vo** not recorded in the region.

Grasshopper Warbler *Locustella naevia*   13cm, 5"
Olive-brown above finely streaked dark brown on crown and more boldly on the mantle, with a weak supercilium, and whitish below with a fine streaked gorget: both the olive-brown upper and *long pale undertail-coverts are darkly mottled.* **HH** Palearctic vagrant: with two Ke records, one from the Nguruman Hills in Jun 1977, and one at Marsabit, Mar 2000. **Vo** not recorded in the region.

BRADYPTERUS WARBLERS
Rather plain skulking brown warblers of marshes and dense forest undergrowth, some with streaking across the breast. Often first draw attention to themselves with their powerful songs, but remain hard to see. Sexes alike.

White-winged Warbler *Bradypterus carpalis*   17cm, 6.5"
Large and plain dark brown above, whitish below with bold short blackish streaks across the throat and upper breast. A *small white patch at shoulder of wing* is often most obvious in display flight. Imm has less distinct throat streaks, and is washed brownish from breast to vent. **HH** common in dense papyrus beds from 1100–2050m, but secretive and very difficult to see. Responds to pishing, often announcing its arrival with a loud burring of wings. **Vo** song varies locally, but is based on a loud accelerating *teek teek teek teek chup chup chup chup chup tut tut tt tt'woo* which either rises or falls at the end.

Plate 180

Sedge Warbler

River Warbler

Savi's Warbler

Grasshopper Warbler

White-winged Warbler

Ad

Cinnamon Bracken Warbler *Bradypterus cinnamomeus*   15cm, 6"

Widespread nominate and very similar western race *mildbreadi* are uniform rufous-brown or dark brown above, with a long buffy supercilium, white throat and centre of belly, and a *bright warm rufous band across the breast and flanks*. Race *nyassae* in E and STz is duller and paler with a buffy throat and buff-brown breast. **HH** common in undergrowth, at forest edge and in bracken, mainly over 1000m (often above 2000m). Creeps around in thick cover and is usually located by its loud song, or by a flash of rufous as it flies. When they occur together, Evergreen Forest Warbler is in the forest interior and Cinnamon Bracken is at the edge. **Vo** varies a little locally, but typical loud song is an introductory *wii* followed by 3–6 identical explosive spitted notes. Call is a nasal *pink*.

Evergreen Forest Warbler *Bradypterus lopezi*   15cm, 6"

Similar to Cinnamon Bracken Warbler, but much dingier brown above and below, with a pale supercilium, and a narrow dishevelled spiky tail. If seen well may show an indistinctly streaked gorget. Three similar races occur: *mariae* is typical. Distinctive race *barakae* in W and SWUg has a rufous head and breast contrasting with dull rufous-brown back, wings and tail, a faint dark line through the eye and a whitish belly. **HH** widespread, but patchily distributed in forest undergrowth above 1500m (but down to 900m in NETz). Very difficult to observe, staying in the thickest cover, often very low, even on the ground. **Vo** song varies locally, but typically increases in volume through each refrain. A rising *weep* precedes identical notes that are rapid or slow, single or paired, producing a rattling effect. Call is a deep throaty *churrr*.

Bamboo Warbler *Bradypterus alfredi*   15cm, 6"

Dark brown above with a short light supercilium (similar to most races of Evergreen Forest Warbler). White on throat blurs into olive-brown breast, lower breast to vent white with a *strong grey wash over sides of breast and flanks*. In Ug, birds are slightly more rufous above with paler grey flanks. **HH** rare warbler of forest undergrowth, long grass and bamboo, known only from WUg at 1200–1600m, and the Mahari Mts, WTz, from 1800–2300m. **Vo** simple song is a hollow sounding and repeated series of 10 or so paired notes *tik-er-tik-er-tik-er...*

Little Rush Warbler *Bradypterus baboecala*   15cm, 6"

[African Sedge Warbler]
Three races occur within two distinct groups that may be specifically distinct. The northern group consists of the race *elgonensis* (in EUg, and W and CKe) and *centralis* (in SWUg, Rw, Bu and NTz): they are very similar with short heavy streaks across the breast, *elgonensis* differs in having more rufous-brown upperparts. The southern group consists of *moreaui* (together with other races outside our area), it has dark brown upperparts and only very light streaking across the breast (may look plain in the field). All races have well-rounded tails. **HH** common and widespread in swamps and marshes from sea-level to 2300m. Displays over reed tops with loud burring wings. **Vo** northern group sing a high-pitched almost hissing series of descending notes that accelerate to end in a dying rattle, and the call is a nasal *pink-pink*. The southern group has a similar pattern but the notes are much slower, louder and deeper, similar to White-winged Warbler. All follow their song with a low aerial display of wing burring.

Grauer's Rush Warbler *Bradypterus graueri*   17cm, 6.5"   ● ●

Like a large version of Little Rush Warbler, but with a more distinct white supercilium, and *heavier blackish streaking across the upper breast*. **HH** endemic to swamps in high country from 1950–2600m in the Albertine Rift. Not uncommon in its restricted range but shy and difficult to observe. **Vo** some local variation, but the typical song is a dry rattling and trilled *chip chip chip-chip-chip chweeeeer*, with the last note upslurred.

Plate 181

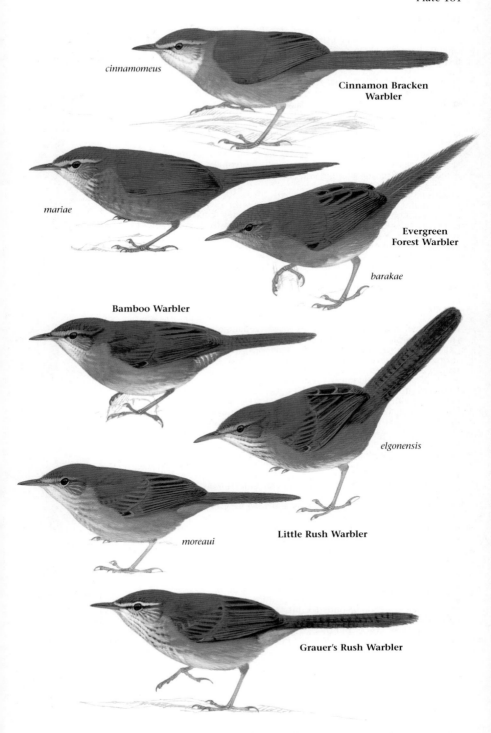

cinnamomeus

Cinnamon Bracken Warbler

mariae

Evergreen Forest Warbler

barakae

Bamboo Warbler

elgonensis

Little Rush Warbler

moreaui

Grauer's Rush Warbler

HIPPOLAIS WARBLERS

A difficult group of Palearctic warblers mostly with fairly uniform coloration, flat-looking heads, short superciliary stripes and strong bills. Tails are square-ended with short undertail-coverts. Pay careful attention to size, overall tone, wing panels and wing length, as well as behaviour like tail flicking and waving. Sexes alike.

Olivaceous Warbler *Hippolais pallida* 13cm, 5"

Fairly uniform grey-brown above (no wing panel), with a pale supercilium, and paler creamy-buff below. Outer-tail feathers narrowly edged whitish (but not easy to see in the field). Lower mandible pale yellowish-horn, easily noticeable as the bird is usually seen from below. Legs pinkish or brownish-grey. **HH** common and widespread passage migrant and winter visitor from sea-level to 1900m from Oct–Apr. Always on the move, often bobbing its tail downwards while calling, it is particularly fond of the canopy of large acacia trees. **Vo** regularly calls a fairly harsh *chk*, and also often sings a soft *Acrocephalus*-like refrain.

Upcher's Warbler *Hippolais languida* 14cm, 5.5"

Larger than Olivaceous Warbler: greyer above with a whitish supercilium, and duller white below with pale buffy or buffy-grey flanks. Narrow white edges to the *longer and much darker tail* are more easily seen (as it is constantly waved or even slightly fanned). Wings are also darker with a pale panel on secondaries when fresh, but less distinct than wing panel on Olive-tree Warbler. Lower mandible pinkish; legs pinkish-grey. **HH** fairly uncommon winter visitor in the east from Nov to early Apr, and occasional in the Great Rift Valley on passage. It inhabits dry bush country from sea-level to 1200m, tending to keep to cover and occasionally feeding on the ground. **Vo** call is unlike Olivaceous Warbler, a soft nasal *chah-chah-chah...*, repeated rapidly and for long periods if agitated.

Olive-tree Warbler *Hippolais olivetorum* 15cm, 6"

Largest *Hippolais*: grey-brown above with a narrow whitish supercilium and whitish below with a variable pale-grey wash. It has a noticeably long strong bill with a *yellowish-horn base to lower mandible*. Long wings are darker than mantle and in fresh plumage pale-edged secondaries form a noticeable pale wing panel. Tail is very dark with narrow white edges to outer feathers. Strong blue-grey legs. **HH** much less common than Upcher's Warbler, occurring mostly on passage in Oct–Dec and Mar–Apr, but a few winter in STz. **Vo** call is a harsh *tak;* its rarely heard song is *Acrocephalus*-like but deeper and more musical, not scratchy.

Icterine Warbler *Hippolais icterina* 13cm, 5"

Greenish-olive above and yellow below, with a prominent yellow supercilium. Long, pointed wings show a long primary projection (equal in length to tertials). Before departure, freshly plumaged birds have yellow-edged secondaries forming an *obvious wing panel*, but 1st year birds arriving in Oct–Dec are much more washed out, often appearing dull greyish-green above and very pale yellow or mostly white below. Can be similar to other *Hippolais* or even dull Willow Warbler, but the long primary projection and lack of a dark eye line are distinctive. Lower mandible pinkish. *Legs blue-grey.* **HH** most common in the west, both on passage and as a winter visitor, but uncommon east of the Great Rift Valley. **Vo** regularly heard in region: song is an *Acrocephalus*-like, but constant more musical rambling interspersed with sweeter squeaks and chips. Call is a simple *tak*.

Melodious Warbler *Hippolais polyglotta* 13cm, 5"

Very similar to Icterine Warbler, but with a shorter wing which never shows a pale panel on secondaries (primary projection is half length of tertials). Pinkish lower mandible. *Legs brownish-grey.* **HH** vagrant: normally winters in West Africa, and there is only one record: a presumed 1st year bird caught at Ngulia, Tsavo West NP, Ke, in Nov 1995. **Vo** not heard in the region.

Plate 182

Olivaceous
Warbler

Upcher's Warbler

Olive-tree Warbler

1st year

Icterine Warbler

Melodious Warbler

SYLVIA WARBLERS
A group of variable warblers with well-rounded heads, short strong bills and narrow square-ended tails. Some are sexually dimorphic.

Garden Warbler *Sylvia borin* 14cm, 5.5"

Rather uniform greyish-brown warbler with an indistinct short buffy super-cilium, narrow pale eye-ring, and a noticeable dark eye. Buffy-brown below with grey-brown legs. *Well-rounded head and short bill* distinguish it from similar *Hippolais* warblers. **HH** common and widespread Palearctic visitor from Oct–Apr (wintering from CUg southwards). Occurs in a variety of woodland, from forest edge to lush bush country and gardens, from 800–2000m. **Vo** vocal in EA, song is a varied continuous warble which is similar to Blackcap, but lacks the scratchiness and is more muffled and sweeter. Calls an abrupt and repeated *teck*.

Barred Warbler *Sylvia nisoria* 17cm, 6.5"

Large and rather long-tailed, grey or grey-brown above with narrow whitish wing bars and variable degrees of barring below. Ad ♂ is well barred on the underparts with distinctive pale yellow eyes. Ad ♀ is browner above and less barred below. 1st years show only the slightest indication of bar-ring (often restricted to flanks and vent), and eyes are dark resembling a Garden Warbler, but Barred can be identified by larger size, longer tail and pale-tipped wing-coverts. **HH** common Palearctic migrant from Oct to Apr which is numerous in thick cover in bush country from sea-level to 1200m, mainly in the north and east. **Vo** call is a repeated dry *chek-chek-chek*, and its seldom heard song is a rich and varied sweet warbling.

Common Whitethroat *Sylvia communis* 14cm, 5.5"

Ad ♂ has a greyish hood, a narrow white eye-ring, a *white throat, rusty edged wings*, a pinkish breast, and a fairly long tail with narrow white edges. ♀ has a brownish hood and is paler below. Legs pale pinky-brown. 1st year like ♀ but dingier. **HH** common Palearctic passage migrant and winter visitor from Oct–May. It is most numerous in the east, occurring in a wide variety of habitats, including woodland and dry scrub, from sea-level to 3000m. **Vo** commonly calls a dry *tek tek*, and its song in EA is similar to Garden Warbler but more rambling.

Blackcap *Sylvia atricapilla* 14cm, 5.5"

Ad ♂ is grey-brown above and paler grey below with a striking *black skull cap*. Similar ad ♀ is slightly browner above, and buffier below with a *bright rusty reddish-brown cap*. 1st year similar to ♀ but duller. **HH** common Palearctic winter visitor occurring in a wide variety of habitats from Oct–Apr, including scrub and forest edge, but mainly in the highlands above 1600m (from 1000m in NETz). **Vo** call is a hard, sometimes rapid *tak tak tak*, and song is a scratchy but not unpleasant warble often heard from January until departure.

Buff-bellied Warbler *Phyllolais pulchella* 10cm, 4"

A small, slim pale warbler which is uniform olive-grey above and pale creamy-yellow below, with a very narrow white-edged tail. Pink lower mandible and legs obvious in the field. **HH** small groups of 2–6 are com-mon within range from 600–2000m; usually in acacias where they busily forage in the tree canopy. **Vo** a noisy species, parties frequently call a spit-ted chittering *tit-tit-tit-tit-tit...*, which often breaks into a dry trill.

Plate 183

Garden Warbler

1st year

Barred Warbler

Ad ♂

1st year

Common Whitethroat

Ad ♂

♀

Blackcap

Ad ♂

Buff-bellied Warbler

PHYLLOSCOPUS WARBLERS

Phylloscopus or leaf warblers are small greenish arboreal birds, with rather rounded heads, slim bills and thin slender legs. They are very active flitting through the upper storeys and canopy of trees. Some have yellow on the face or underparts. Sexes alike.

Willow Warbler *Phylloscopus trochilus* 11cm, 4.5"
Two races occur: widespread and typical *acredula* is dull olive above and pale yellow below, although 1st year birds have much more yellow on the underparts. Less common eastern *yakutensis* (from Siberia) is olive-brown above and whitish below. Both show an indistinct dark line through the eye and long, pale yellow or whitish superciliary stripes. Legs usually pale yellowish-brown, but dark on some birds. Song is the best distinction from Common Chiffchaff. **HH** very common Palearctic visitor from late Sep to early May in a wide variety of bush and woodland from sea-level to 3000m, usually at lower altitudes than Chiffchaff. **Vo** song is a silvery descending cadence terminating in a flourish, and the call is a short interrogatory rising *wheep* which ends abruptly.

Common Chiffchaff *Phylloscopus collybita* 11cm, 4.5"
Extremely similar to Willow Warbler, but usually has *very dark legs*. Grey-olive or olive-brown above; white or buffy below. Other subtle differences from Willow are a more rounded crown, supercilium generally not so well marked, bill shorter and darker, but only safely told from Willow Warbler by song. **HH** generally uncommon Palearctic visitor, mainly to highland forest above 2000m, from Oct–Apr. **Vo** usually located by song, its ono-matopoeic *chiff-chiff-chaff-chiff-chaff...* is very distinctive, and it sings from January up to departure. Call is also an upslurred *wheep*, a little longer and higher pitched than Willow Warbler.

Wood Warbler *Phylloscopus sibilatrix* 12cm, 5"
Larger than Willow Warbler or Common Chiffchaff and greener above, with longer wings, and a brighter yellow supercilium, face and upper breast. Very white below with a rather short tail making the undertail-coverts look long and giving the bird a drawn out look towards its rear end. Legs yellowish-brown. **HH** a Palearctic visitor from Nov–Apr which is reasonably common in the west, but scarce elsewhere. It inhabits forest and woodland, feeding in the middle and higher level of tall trees. **Vo** usually silent, but song is an attractive descending silvery cadence that breaks into a dry trill, ending with or without a descending series of mournful pipings. Call is a monotone *hweeet*.

Yellow-throated Woodland Warbler *Phylloscopus ruficapillus* 11cm, 4.5"
[Yellow-throated Warbler]
Typical leaf warbler with variably coloured crown and nape: olive-brown in race *minullus* (Taita Hills, SEKe south to the Ulugurus Mts, ETz), orange-brown in *johnstoni* (Mt Rungwe, STz), while *ochrogularis* (Mahari Mts, WTz) has the face and throat washed orange-yellow. Overall appearance is olive-green above, with a *yellow supercilium, sides of face, throat and vent;* otherwise whitish or very pale grey below. **HH** common within its range, inhabiting canopy and middle levels of highland forest from 800–2300m. **Vo** some local variation in song which is generally a strong, but not particularly sweet, descending and see-sawing *ter-twi-ter-twi-ter-twi-te-twi-twi...*

Laura's Warbler *Phylloscopus laurae* 11cm, 4.5"
Similar to Yellow-throated Woodland Warbler, but is *uniform bright green above including the crown and nape,* with a yellow supercilium. Throat to upper breast and vent bright lemon-yellow, belly and flanks greyish. **HH** restricted range, in EA known only from Kitungulu, in extreme SWTz, at 1400m. **Vo** loud song from mid-canopy is a sweet descending *twi-li-twi-li-twi-li-twi-li-twi-li* repeated every couple of seconds with slight variation.

Plate 184

1st year

acredula

Willow Warbler

yakutensis

Common Chiffchaff

Wood Warbler

Yellow-throated Woodland Warbler

ochrogularis

minullus

Laura's Warbler

Uganda Woodland Warbler *Phylloscopus budongoensis* 10cm, 4"

Rather like a small Willow Warbler, but with a more distinct *white supercilium and a narrow black line through the eye*. Whitish below with grey-washed flanks. Imm is washed pale olive on the breast and flanks. **HH** single birds inhabit the canopy and middle levels of primary forest from 1200–1900m, where they are constantly on the move calling frequently while feeding. **Vo** a short rising and falling series of 4–7 distinct silvery notes *si-wi-si-wi-wi-si.*

Brown Woodland Warbler *Phylloscopus umbrovirens* 11cm, 4.5"

Much *browner than other leaf warblers* in our area with the *wings and tail edged green*. Three races occur: widespread *mackensianus* is warm brown above, with a long buffy supercilium, and dark eye line; *alpinus* (WUg) is similar, but more grey-brown above and greyer on the flanks; while *fugglescouchmani* (Uluguru Mts, ETz) is entirely rich brown below. **HH** common in many highland forests above 1500m. **Vo** variable and complex song of sweet see-sawing notes followed by trills and flourishes, with very brief pause between each phrase.

Red-faced Woodland Warbler *Phylloscopus laetus* 10cm, 4" ●

A typical leaf warbler, but with a *brick-red wash to the supercilium, face and throat*, remainder of underparts pale buffy-white washed pale grey on the flanks. Imm has an indistinct rusty or yellowish face. **HH** endemic to mountains along the Albertine Rift where it is common in forest above 1550m. **Vo** song is a loud, strong, and short monotonous series with two different tones given in different orders and rhythms, for long periods.

Green Hylia *Hylia prasina* 12cm, 5"

Presently thought to be a warbler, but Green Hylia often looks like a short-tailed and stocky female sunbird. Overall dull olive-green, although paler grey-olive below. *Fairly broad buffy supercilium curves over eye and bill is short, black and slightly decurved*. Imm darker olive below than ad with a yellowish bill. **HH** an active bird usually found in the middle and higher levels of primary forest from 700–1800m. It may join bird parties and is often first located by its call. **Vo** the extraordinary song is a strong obtrusive ratchet like *tr-rr-rt*, followed by a long pause of up to four seconds, then two whistled downslurs *feeew-feeew*, the second slightly lower than the first

Short-tailed Warbler *Hemitesia neumanni* 10cm, 4" ●

Poorly known species with no close relatives in Africa. Uniform dull olive-green above, with a darker and browner short tail, an olive crown, and broad long off-white superciliary stripes bordered above and below with black. Underparts are variable on the throat and breast, yellow (Ug) or pale olive-green (Rw and Bu): both forms have olive flanks and are white on the belly. **HH** endemic to mountains along the Albertine Rift from 1500–2350m. Single birds or pairs live in dense forest undergrowth, particularly along streams, and rarely leave thick cover. **Vo** a loud and far-carrying three-note song, the first note separated from the second two *su…siu-soo* or *si…si-su*. At close range soft lispy notes can be heard between each call.

Plate 185

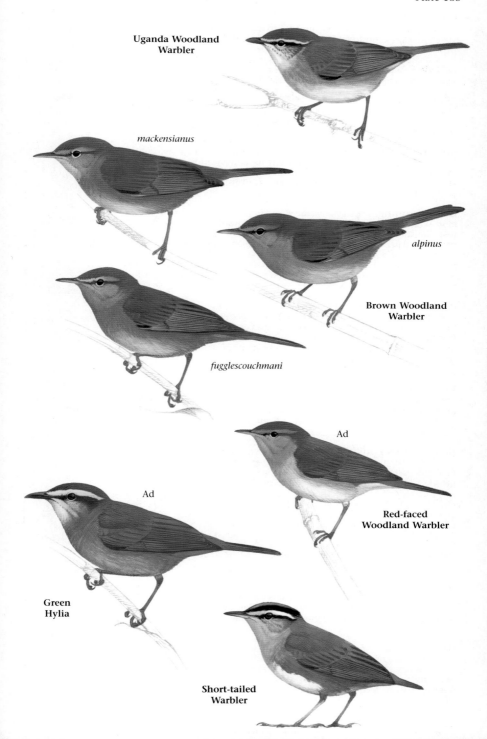

Uganda Woodland Warbler

mackensianus

alpinus

Brown Woodland Warbler

fugglescouchmani

Ad

Ad

Red-faced Woodland Warbler

Green Hylia

Short-tailed Warbler

FOREST CROMBECS

Crombecs are small active very short-tailed warblers, often in pairs or mixed-species flocks. These three are mainly forest dwellers (although Green Crombec also tolerates nearby disturbed habitats and riverine strip woodland). Sexes alike.

White-browed Crombec *Sylvietta leucophrys* 9cm, 3.5"
Two distinct races occur: both have a *curving white supercilium, a chestnut line through the eye,* and are pale grey or olive below with yellow undertail-coverts. In WUg and Ke the nominate race has the crown and nape chestnut-brown, a very white supercilium and pale grey underparts; while in SWUg to WTz race *chloronota* is more rusty-brown on the ear-coverts and is washed olive across the breast. Nominate imm has an indistinct supercilium and brownish breast, while imm *chloronota* is similar, but rusty above. **HH** inhabits highland forest above 1550m, including canopy, tangled vines and undergrowth. **Vo** varies locally, but always reminiscent of the woodland-warblers: typically nominate song is a rolling, distinct sequence of clear notes with no embellishments *si-si-si-su-si-si-si-su-si-si-su-su-si,* while *chloronota* tends to sing a silvery rising and falling series.

Green Crombec *Sylvietta virens* 9cm, 3.5"
Mostly dull olive-green above with a brownish wash to the crown and a very indistinct buff supercilium. Throat to breast is dingy grey-brown becoming paler on the belly: legs pink. Can be confused with a tail-less Olive-green Camaroptera. Imm is washed yellowish below. **HH** locally common in the middle and lower levels of primary forest, secondary growth and woodland along streams from 700–1400m. **Vo** song is a hurried, rising and falling *si-sit-si-sitsi-si-sisi-su.*

Lemon-bellied Crombec *Sylvietta denti* 8cm, 3"
Smaller than Green Crombec with indistinct speckling on the cheeks and throat, an olive wash across the breast and a pale yellow belly: legs brown. Imm more yellow above. **HH** in our area it is uncommon and restricted to the canopy of Semliki and Budongo forests in WUg. **Vo** sings a loud *sisisi-sisisisisisisiu* with the last note falling

LONGBILLS

Three warblers with long straight bills. Kretschmer's is very greenbul-like, while Yellow and Grey have noticeably short wings and tails. Sexes are alike, immatures are generally paler than adults. All are often illustrated with fluffed out long rump and flank feathers, but this is not usually obvious in the field.

Kretschmer's Longbill *Macrosphenus kretschmeri* 15cm, 6"
Very greenbul-like, with obvious whitish eyes and a long pinkish lower mandible. Greyish crown, nape and ear-coverts contrast with the olive-green mantle, wings and tail. Below, largely yellowish-olive with a paler grey throat and variable yellow wash to the belly. Imm is like ad, but the crown is olive. **HH** uncommon in forest and along well-wooded streams in ETz from 500–1800m. It inhabits both undergrowth and lower canopy where it is rather vocal but shy, often singing from within deep cover. **Vo** bulbul-like song has some local variation but is typically a loud *wi-k'chk k'chk k'chk.*

Yellow Longbill *Macrosphenus flavicans* 13cm, 5"
In the field, appears wholly olive-green above (although washed grey-brown on the head), with a noticeable long slender bill and yellow eyes. Yellow underparts are richer on the flanks and vent, paler and greyer on the throat: legs greyish. **HH** found at all levels within good forest in S and WUg from 700–1400m, but typically shy and difficult to observe. **Vo** song is a distinctive and far-carrying sequence of notes descending in half-tones *pi pi pi pi pi pi pi pi pi pi pi...*

Grey Longbill *Macrosphenus concolor* 13cm, 5"
Entirely olive-green above and paler greyish-olive below with a variable yellow wash. Eyes grey-brown, bill long, but not so obvious as the other longbills: legs pale pinkish-brown. **HH** a local and shy resident of forest undergrowth in S and WUg from 1000–1400m. **Vo** sings a continuous rolling *widderuly-widderuly-widderuly-widderuly...*

Plate 186

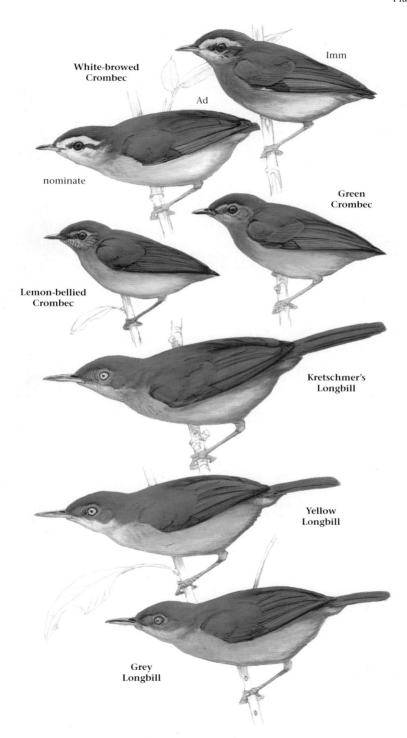

White-browed
Crombec

Imm

Ad

nominate

Green
Crombec

Lemon-bellied
Crombec

Kretschmer's
Longbill

Yellow
Longbill

Grey
Longbill

BUSH AND WOODLAND CROMBECS

Very small warblers of bush and woodland with a tail-less appearance. All are very active, constantly foraging as they move from tree to tree. Solitary or in pairs, they often join mixed-species flocks. Sexes are alike.

Northern Crombec *Sylvietta brachyura* 8cm, 3"

Uniform grey above, with a *whitish face and throat* giving a pale-faced appearance, a dark eye-line, and buffy-cinnamon underparts. Two distinct races occur: *carnapi* (Ug-WKe) has the supercilium and throat tawny-buff, while *leucopsis* (NKe-NETz) has the supercilium and throat whitish. Imms have buffy tips to the wing-coverts. **HH** a common resident of woodland, gardens and dry bush country from sea-level to 2000m. **Vo** usually a simple repeated phrase, but western birds sound like a lispy version of Green Crombec. Eastern birds have a long sweet complex song like a *Sylvia* warbler with serin-like phrases interjected.

Red-faced Crombec *Sylvietta whytii* 9cm, 3.5"

Slightly larger than Northern Crombec with similar grey or grey-brown upperparts, but *lacks pale-faced appearance with sides of face, throat and most of underparts plain cinnamon*. Three races occur and intergrade, but generally birds in Ug, WKe and WTz are more richly coloured, while northern and eastern birds are paler. Imms have buffy tips to the wing-coverts. **HH** common and widespread resident of a wide variety of woodland and bush country from sea-level to 2000m. **Vo** differs locally, but usually sings a variation of a loud, repeated rolling *si-si-siu si-si-siu si-si-siu si-si-siu*.

Red-capped Crombec *Sylvietta ruficapilla* 10cm, 4"

A greyish-brown crombec with *chestnut ear-coverts and a large chestnut spot on the breast*. Birds recorded in our area are the race *chubbi* which lacks a red cap! Imm has a buffy wash to the crown and mantle. **HH** known from miombo woodland near Tatanda and Tukuyu in SWTz. **Vo** a typical crombec-song, but burry, with a simple repeated rising and then falling phrase *sh-shre-shri-shri-shrer*.

Somali Long-billed Crombec *Sylvietta isabellina* 10cm, 4"

Pale buffy-grey crombec with a long bill and whitish superciliary stripes. Very pale buffy-white below, palest on the throat. Imm similar, but lightly mottled on throat. **HH** generally uncommon in dry bush country of NE and EKe below 1000m. **Vo** song is a typical crombec-like *tichi tichi tichi ri-ti-chu*, the last note lower. In flight calls a sharp *chik*.

Long-billed Crombec *Sylvietta rufescens* 9cm, 3.5"

Birds in our area are not particularly long-billed and thus very similar to Northern Crombec, but ranges do not overlap. Buffy-cinnamon below merging gradually into a paler face. Grey line through eye and buffy supercilium further distinguish Long-billed from Red-faced Crombec with which it does overlap. Imm is paler than ad. **HH** in our area, it is local but fairly common in both Rusizi NP, Bu, and near Tatanda and Tunduma, SWTz. **Vo** song is a simple typically crombec-like see-sawing series of 5–6 *chi-choyi* notes.

Plate 187

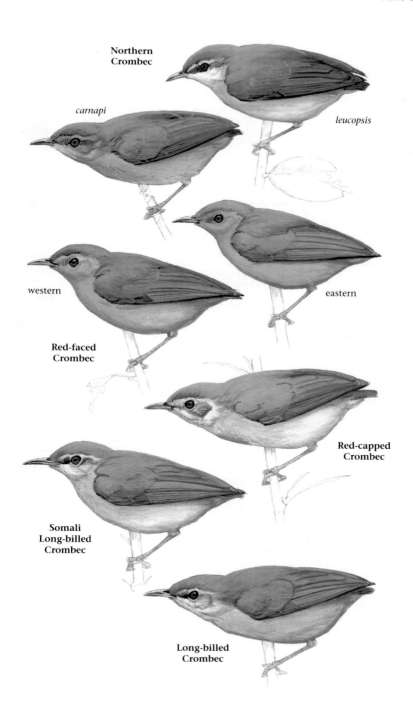

Northern
Crombec

carnapi

leucopsis

western

eastern

Red-faced
Crombec

Red-capped
Crombec

Somali
Long-billed
Crombec

Long-billed
Crombec

EREMOMELAS

Active small warblers of the canopy and middle levels in a variety of forest, woodland and bush country. Usually found as pairs or small flocks, and often join mixed-bird parties. Sexes alike.

Yellow-bellied Eremomela *Eremomela icteropygialis* 10 cm, 4"
A short-tailed species: ad is grey above, whitish on the throat and breast, and *bright yellow from the breast or lower breast to vent*. Imm is variably washed olive above, yellow on the underparts paler and often restricted to the ventral area (very similar to Yellow-vented Eremomela). **HH** pairs are widespread in open woodland and bush country up to 1900m. Often found in mixed-species flocks with white-eyes, penduline-tits and crombecs. **Vo** rather crombec-like, but more penetrating, song is a variable rising and falling or rolling series of distinct notes, typically *t'tri-t'ri-t'tri*. Also a nasal contact note used also in display.

Yellow-vented Eremomela *Eremomela flavicrissalis* 9 cm, 3.5"
Slightly smaller than Yellow-bellied Eremomela, with a very short tail and *pale yellow restricted to the vent*. Imm has almost no yellow or just the faintest wash. **HH** restricted to the N and E in dry bush and semi-desert country below 1200m. **Vo** differs from Yellow-bellied in the scratchiness of its song, a loud and burry *ser-si-ser'si-sit*. **SS** Mouse-coloured Penduline-tit.

Green-capped Eremomela *Eremomela scotops* 11cm, 4.5"
Greyish above with olive-green or yellowish-green crown and sides to the head, and a narrow black line from bill to pale eye. Three races occur and differ mainly in underpart colour: widespread western *citriniceps* is basically yellow on the throat and breast with a greyish-white belly; similar *kikuyuensis* in CKe has a very pale yellow belly; and eastern *occipitalis* is entirely yellow below. All imms are paler than ads and olive washed above. **HH** rather local with a patchy distribution from sea-level to 1800m. More common in the west and southern part of range where small flocks are common, particularly in *Brachystegia* or miombo woodland. **Vo** contact and alarm calls consist of very guttural continuous short churrs and a chattering *srrrrr-srrrr-srrrrr...*

Green-backed Eremomela *Eremomela pusilla* 11 cm, 4.5"
A bright and attractive warbler. In our area, race *canescens* is olive-green above, with a well-defined grey crown and nape and broad dark line through the eye. Below, a *very white throat and upper breast* contrast with the bright yellow breast to vent. Eyes yellowish, legs bright orange-pink. Imm like ad but duller and paler. **HH** a localised species found in small flocks in open bush and woodlands from 600–2200m. **Vo** an effervescent rambling of excitable musical chips and churrs and louder *wi-chi-chit* phrases.

Rufous-crowned Eremomela *Eremomela badiceps* 10cm, 4"
[Brown-crowned Eremomela]
A greyish eremomela (paler and creamier below) with a *wholly chestnut crown*, a black streak through the eye and a narrow black band across the upper breast. Imm washed greenish above with only a faint indication of a rufous crown, and entirely creamy-yellow below. **HH** small flocks are uncommon in the forest canopy (particularly at the edge) in WUg from 700–1400m. **Vo** frequently given call is a series of machine-gun-like spitted notes *t't't't't't'...* heard from feeding parties or during aerial chases.

Turner's Eremomela *Eremomela turneri* 10cm, 4"
Similar to Rufous-crowned Eremomela, but *chestnut is restricted to forecrown*. Imm is very plain, washed olive above and creamy-yellow below. **HH** an uncommon and globally threatened species in our area known from forests around Kakamega, WKe, and near Kigezi in SWUg, from 1500–1700m. **Vo** highly vocal giving repeated *chichichichichichi...*, notes often interspersed with soft chipping resembling a rattle.

Plate 188

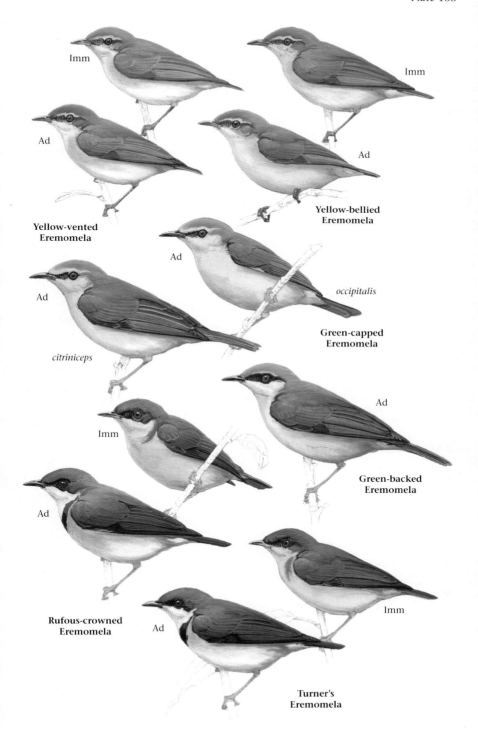

Imm

Imm

Ad

Ad

Yellow-bellied Eremomela

Yellow-vented Eremomela

Ad

Ad

occipitalis

Green-capped Eremomela

citriniceps

Imm

Ad

Green-backed Eremomela

Ad

Rufous-crowned Eremomela

Ad

Imm

Turner's Eremomela

HYLIOTAS
Small active warblers of the canopy, which constantly move around with a rather horizontal posture. Difficult to identify, but they occupy different habitats within their ranges: look for exact colour of upperparts, extent of tawny on the underparts and white in the wing. Usually in pairs, but they also join mixed species flocks. Immatures are duller than adults with buffy fringed upperparts.

Yellow-bellied Hyliota *Hyliota flavigaster* 11cm, 4.5"
[Yellow-breasted Hyliota]

Two distinct races occur: ad ♂ nominate (mainly in Ug to WKe) is *glossy blue-black above* with white in the wing (like race *slatini* of Southern Hyliota), but the *underparts are extensively washed with rich tawny-yellow*, paler on the belly. Ad ♀ is similar but dark-grey above. Southern race *barbozae* (W and SETz) differs in having variable white edges to the secondaries, which sometimes appear as a white bar. **HH** rather localised, but not uncommon in the west and south from 100–1800m, where they like leafy trees within open woodland, particularly miombo. **Vo** usual call is an explosive two-note *swit-itt*, the second note slightly lower than the first, and the song is a rapid twittering, incorporating the same notes.

Southern Hyliota *Hyliota australis* 11cm, 4.5"
[Mashona Hyliota]

Ad ♂ of race *slatini* is similar to Yellow-bellied Hyliota, but *duller black above and paler below* (especially on the belly). Ad ♀ is duller grey-brown above. Poorly known race *usambarae* (**Usambara Hyliota ●**) has a richer orange breast and white edges to the secondaries. **HH** in our area *slatini* is known only from forest at Semliki, WUg, and Kakamega, WKe, at 700–1700m. Race *usambarae* is endemic to the Usambara Mts, NETz, particularly at 300–400m, but rarely up to 1000m. **Vo** song of *slatini* begins with a introductory chipping and continues as a strong metallic twittering rattle, this may be either nearly monotone, or gently rising and falling and more musical. The voice of *usambarae* is not known.

Violet-backed Hyliota *Hyliota violacea* 12cm, 5"

Ads are *glossy violet-blue-black above*, with a small area of white on two inner greater upperwing-coverts (can be very hard to see in the field). Ad ♂ has the underparts very pale buff-white, while the ad ♀ is strongly washed with rusty-orange. **HH** in our area pairs are uncommon and only known from Nyungwe Forest, SWRw, at 1700–2000m. **Vo** calls a sharp *ti-tit* which can break into a hurried and complex swizzle.

BATHMOCERCUS WARBLERS
Two distinctive warblers of thick forest undergrowth. They occur in pairs or family groups and are most often located by their far-carrying penetrating whistles and duets.

Black-faced Rufous Warbler *Bathmocercus rufus* 13cm, 5"

Ad ♂ is unlike any other bird being *bright chestnut with a broad black vertical stripe down the face, throat and breast*. Ad ♀ has a similar black facial stripe but is olive-grey above. Imm is plainer dull olive-grey with random patches of rufous in the imm ♂. **HH** common, but very shy and restricted to the undergrowth within primary forest of the west, from 700–2800m. **Vo** often duets: the ♂ sings a monotone piercing piping, while the ♀ accompanies with a rattling doubled or tripled *chlt-chlt*. The feeding or alarm call is also this note repeated by the group.

Mrs Moreau's Warbler *Bathmocercus winifredae* 13cm, 5" ●●

Ad ♂ is a rather dull olivaceous-brown warbler with a *bright chestnut head, throat and upper breast*. Ad ♀ is similar but paler on the head and breast. Imm has the upperparts olive with a pale-chestnut face and breast. **HH** shy Tz endemic known only from dense forest undergrowth in the Uluguru, Ukaguru, and Udzungwa mountains from 1300–2350m. **Vo** often duets: the ♂ sings a loud piercing but musical piping *wii wi-ch'wi*, while the ♀ accompanies with a repeated piping on one note.

Plate 189

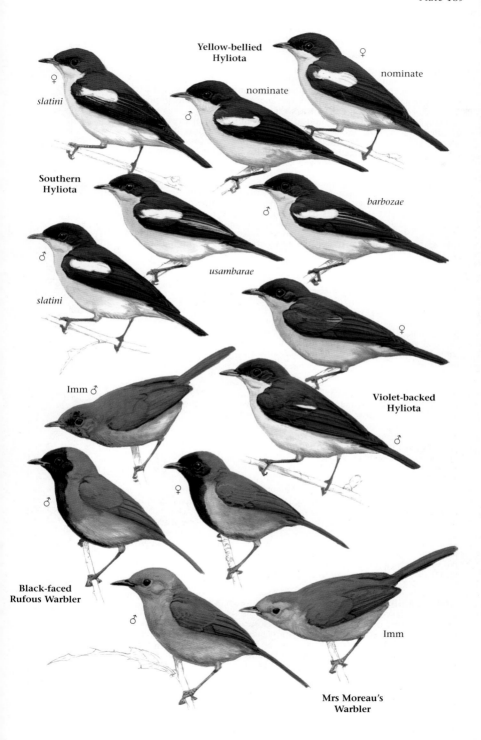

Yellow-bellied
Hyliota

nominate

nominate

♀

slatini

♂

♀

Southern
Hyliota

barbozae

♂

♂

slatini

usambarae

♀

Imm ♂

Violet-backed
Hyliota

♂

♂

♀

Black-faced
Rufous Warbler

Imm

♂

Mrs Moreau's
Warbler

PARISOMAS

Active warblers which are constantly on the move in the canopy of acacia woodland. Formerly known as tit-flycatchers, they are treated by some recent authors as *Sylvia* warblers. Sexes are alike.

Banded Parisoma   *Parisoma boehmi*   13cm, 5"

Widespread nominate birds are greyish above with pale eyes, white wing-bars, a distinct black breast band, tawny-buff flanks and vent, and a fairly long white-edged dark tail. Northern race *marsabit* is much paler. Imms are washed brownish above, with buffy wing bars, and no black breast band. **HH** single birds or pairs are found in acacia country and open woodlands usually below 1700m. **Vo** attractive loud rolling and rattling song begins with a reeling fluid trill and continues *chip-chit-wurr-chewy-chewy-chewy*. Often pairs will call together and may be answered by other parisomas nearby.

Brown Parisoma   *Parisoma lugens*   13cm, 5"

Rather uniform dull dark brown warbler with slightly paler grey-brown throat to breast, a dingy white belly, and *narrow white edges to the tail*. Imm resembles ad. **HH** single birds or pairs inhabit open highland woodland and forest edge from 1400–2500m, where they are particularly fond of large acacia trees. **Vo** not as vocal as Banded Parisoma, a complex, rambling slow and lazy warbling *swee-seet-s-swee-wee*, and a monotonous loud *ch-wee ch'wee*.

Broad-tailed Warbler   *Schoenicola brevirostris*   15cm, 6"

Resembles a dark-coloured, short-billed Eurasian Reed Warbler with a *long broad black tail* (which is obvious in flight). Imm washed pale-yellow below. **HH** resident of dense grassland, moist bush and cultivation from 800–2150m. Hard to see unless flushed from wet grass, but will sit on exposed grass stems, and performs a flight display. **Vo** song is a simple short, metallic piping *ping ping ping...* Alarm and contact notes are a sharp *tak-tak-tak...*

African Moustached Warbler   *Melocichla mentalis*   19cm, 7.5"

Bulbul-sized warbler which is plain brown above with a chestnut washed forecrown, pale yellow eyes, and medium brown below with a blackish-brown tail. When seen well facial pattern distinct, with a white supercilium, *white throat and narrow black malar streak*. Imm is like dull a dark-eyed ad. **HH** often in pairs in thick cover along streams from sea-level to 2500m, where shy but vocal singing frequently from concealed perches. **Vo** one of the best songsters of rank herbage. Basic song begins with a series of *tip tip tip...* breaking into a varied and complex falling flourish, ending *tweedle-iddle-ee*. Also utters a nasal scolding *chahhchahhchahh...* and is a capable mimic.

Grauer's Warbler   *Graueria vittata*   14cm, 5.5"   ●

A dingy dark-olive warbler suggesting a camaroptera. Face, throat and breast are buffy-olive with blackish fringes, appearing *as fine scaly bars at close range*. **HH** a very localised endemic of montane forest along the Albertine Rift which is not uncommon in the undergrowth and middle level tangled creepers of thick forest from 1600–2500m. **Vo** an unobtrusive, reverberant, and gently rising *hrrrrrrrrrrrrr* (like a muffled Scaly-throated Honeyguide).

African Tailorbird   *Orthotomus metopias*   10cm, 4"   ●

[Red-capped Forest Warbler]

An unusual bird now thought to be most closely related to the Asian tailor-birds. Overall appearance suggests a short-tailed apalis: olive-brown above with a rich chestnut crown, ear-coverts and sides of neck. Centre of throat to vent whitish, washed grey on the flanks. Imm washed pale yellow below. **HH** almost endemic to Tz (but also in NW Mozambique). Pairs or small groups inhabit thick forest undergrowth from 1000–2500m. Not uncommon, but shy and difficult to observe. **Vo** highly varied, loud and penetrating: typical calls are repeated falling *cheeah*, a rapid *chierp*, and duetted *wiier* (♂ upslur) *p'chu* (♀ twangy).

Plate 190

Banded Parisoma

Ad

Imm

marsabit

nominate

Ad

Brown Parisoma

Broad-tailed Warbler

Ad

African Moustached Warbler

Ad

Grauer's Warbler

African Tailorbird

Ad

CISTICOLAS

A large genus of streaked or plain brown warblers which are one of Africa's most challenging groups of birds to identify. Points to look for are dealt with separately in the relevant sections below.

SMALL STREAKED CISTICOLAS

Rump and tail colour, song and habitat aid identification. Immatures of all are rustier above and yellowish below (except Desert Cisticola). All are found singly or in pairs, but may be numerous within suitable habitat.

Pectoral-patch Cisticola   *Cisticola brunnescens*   9cm, 3.5"

Small with a very short blackish white-tipped tail and *no obviously contrasting coloured rump*. Br ♂ has an *unstreaked crown and blackish lores*, and often shows dark patches at sides of the breast. Non-br ♂ and ♀ have the forecrown to tail evenly streaked, no loral spot and no breast patches. Br ♂ of race *cinnamomeus* (**Pale-crowned Cisticola**) in SWTz is darker and more rufous with a mottled yellow-brown crown, plain rufous rump and a rufous-tipped tail. **HH** common in grassland from 1400–2000m in Ke, 1400–2500m in Tz (and *cinnamomeus* in wetter grass above 1800m). **Vo** in high level display repeats a soft *chht...chht...chht...*, often preceded by a wing-click, before plummeting earthwards with accelerating *chht* notes ending abruptly on apparent impact, or continuing in a low wavering flight over the grass. Neither calls nor wing-snaps relate to changes of direction. Also utters a soft *tic*.

Zitting Cisticola   *Cisticola juncidis*   10cm, 4"

[Fan-tailed Cisticola]
Widespread race *uropygialis* is fairly evenly streaked above, but shows a paler nape collar and in flight a *plain rufous-buff rump*, and a medium brown tail with dark sub-terminal spots and pale tips (longer than most others in this group). Race *terrestris* in Bu and STz is darker. **HH** common and widespread in both damp and dry grasslands from sea-level to 3000m. **Vo** cruises in a display-flight calling *zit...zit...zit...* (hence name) at the top of each of a series of undulations, never wing-snaps.

Desert Cisticola   *Cisticola aridulus*   10cm, 4"

Like Zitting Cisticola with a *plain rufous-buff rump,* but tail (which is also longish) is much *blacker* with white tips. Pectoral-patch Cisticola has a similar but shorter tail and lacks the rufous rump. Imm has white underparts. **HH** common and widespread in short dry open grasslands (not restricted to desert areas) from sea-level to 1800m. **Vo** calls a high-pitched plaintive *p'ink... p'ink... p'ink...*, at half-second intervals either from a perch or in a low display flight, usually a wing-snap accompanies each note.

Wing-snapping Cisticola   *Cisticola ayresii*   9cm, 3.5"

[Ayres's Cisticola]
Br ♂ is *very small and short-tailed,* heavily streaked above with a dark crown, contrasting rufous rump and blackish white-tipped tail. Non-br ♂ and ♀ are slightly longer-tailed. Pectoral-patch Cisticola lacks the rufous rump. Zitting Cisticola has a longer and browner tail. **HH** inhabits open grass and moorlands, common down to 1200m in the west, but mainly above 1800m in Ke and SWTz. **Vo** display flight includes spates of wing-snapping and erratic manoeuvres, often very high and out of sight, while singing varied sweet short phrases.

Black-backed Cisticola   *Cisticola eximius*   10cm, 4"

Br ♂ has a *plain rich rufous crown and nape*, a very heavily streaked back, rich rufous rump and a short very dark pale-tipped tail: flanks washed rufous. Non-br ♂ has a heavily streaked crown separated from the back by a *rufous nape collar*: tail longer. ♀ is similar but shorter-tailed. **HH** uncommon in both short and seasonally flooded grasslands from 900–1500m. **Vo** displays like a Pectoral-patch Cisticola including wing-snapping, but the song is a burry repeated phrase, *tlii-tlii-tlii tlu-tlu-tlu...* with some variation.

Plate 191

**Pectoral-patch
Cisticola**

br ♂

Imm

♀

**Zitting
Cisticola**

uropygialis

br ♂

**Desert
Cisticola**

**Wing-snapping
Cisticola**

br ♂

♀

**Black-backed
Cisticola**

SMALL RUFOUS-CROWNED CISTICOLAS

Tiny Cisticola   *Cisticola nanus*   9cm, 3.5"

A small short-tailed cisticola with a *bright rufous crown, plain greyish-brown back* (may look very lightly streaked at close range), and buffy-white underparts: can show a short pale line in front of the eye. Imm is mostly rufous above and buffy-yellow below. **HH** pairs are rather local in dry woodland and acacia, often in mixed bird parties, from near sea-level to 1500m. **Vo** sings a rather prinia-like monotonous series of see-sawing notes or a musical chittering from the tops of bushes and trees. Also a rapidly delivered set of *cht* notes as an alarm.

Red-pate Cisticola   *Cisticola ruficeps*   10cm, 4"

In our area, the race *mongalla* occurs: br ad is similar to Tiny Cisticola, but slightly larger and longer-tailed, with a *dull chestnut crown and nape, and a plain slightly browner back*. Non-br is a very different looking bird, with a bright rufous crown and nape, and a heavily streaked back: tail is longer in non-br. Br-ad may also show a narrow white supercilium which is more obvious in non-br. Imm is like non-br ad but duller and yellowish below. **HH** uncommon resident of dry bush country and wooded grasslands in NEUg (to extreme NWKe). **Vo** song is a ringing, penetrating and continuous piping *pi-pi-pi-pi...*

STOUT CISTICOLAS

Rather stocky cisticolas without distinctive wing panels. Males are noticeably larger then females. Immatures are washed yellowish below.

Stout Cisticola   *Cisticola robustus*   ♂ 14cm, 5.5"

A distinctive large cisticola: two races occur (sometimes considered good species). Widespread race *nuchalis* has the rufous crown thinly streaked with black, an *unstreaked bright rufous nape, and heavily streaked back*: tail blackish with obvious white tips. Similar race *awemba* (**Angola Cisticola**) is more red-brown above with a different dialect and occurs on the Ufipa Plateau in SWTz. In both races, imms are yellow below with some streaking on the nape. **HH** pairs and groups, often lots of birds together, are common in long open grasslands, or grasslands with scattered bushes from 1200–2700m. **Vo** song is a dry, rattling monotone wind, with introductory notes (lacking in Winding Cisticola) *trt-trt-trrrrrrt*. Also a drawn-out nasal upslurred *zweeenk* is given singly, and a loud repeated *pip-pip-pip-pip...*

Aberdare Cisticola   *Cisticola aberdare*   ♂ 14cm, 5.5"   ●●

Very similar to Stout Cisticola, but *black streaking on crown extends down over nape* (therefore nape does not contrast so strongly with the back), and the tail appears longer and blacker with buff tips. **HH** Ke endemic: found only in the high grasslands on either side of the Great Rift Valley from 2300–3700m. **Vo** calls *chwichwichwichwi* followed by varying bubbly throaty churrs, which are very different from Stout Cisticola.

Croaking Cisticola   *Cisticola natalensis*   ♂ 14cm, 5.5"

Five races occur, but differ only as variations on a theme. Generally a large bulky cisticola with a thick slightly decurved bill. Darkly streaked above on paler brown, *without bright rufous in plumage* although some races are more rufous toned in non-br and some have an indistinct warm brown wing panel. Tail brown with sub-terminal dark spots and white tips. **HH** pairs are locally common and widespread in tall grasslands with scattered bushes from sea-level to 2200m. **Vo** unique among cisticolas: a drawn-out nasal call terminating in a short explosive note, *tk'weeeeeeee-chunk* and a repeated see-sawing metallic *tink-tonk...*, first note higher.

Plate 192

Tiny
Cisticola

Ad

non-br

Red-pate Cisticola

br

Imm

♂
awemba

♂

♀
nuchalis

Stout Cisticola

♀

♂

Aberdare Cisticola

♀

♂

Croaking Cisticola

STREAK-BACKED CISTICOLAS

A group of streak-backed cisticolas: note amount of rufous on head, density of streaking on back, rufous in wing panels (if present), tail pattern, habitat and call. Immatures are yellowish below.

Rattling Cisticola   *Cisticola chiniana*   14cm, 5.5"

Ten races occur, presenting slight variations on a basic theme: crown and nape only lightly washed with dull rufous which is usually (but not always) streaked, with a medium-dense streaked back, and *no obvious rufous wing panel*: tail brown with dark sub-terminal spots and whitish tips. Coastal races *heterophrys* and *emendatus* are almost plain-backed with a dull rufous wing panel. **HH** most common and widespread cisticola, of acacia country, open woodlands and cultivation from sea-level to 2100m. Usually in cover near the ground, but scolds and calls from bush tops, and virtually always responds to pishing. **Vo** varies locally, but distinct rattling always present: it can be musical or dry. Song is 3–5 squeaky downslurs followed by a lower scolding rattle *wiu-wiu-wiu-chuchuchuchuch*. Call note is a rather nasal tit-like *chht*.

Boran Cisticola   *Cisticola bodessa*   14cm, 5.5"

Extremely similar to Rattling Cisticola, but crown plain dull brown, and back is not as heavily streaked as most races of Rattling. Best identified by voice. **HH** pairs are very localised within range, occurring on rocky hill-sides with some bush and cover from 850–2100m. **Vo** song is distinctive, fast and clear, commencing with *chik-chik-chik* followed by a liquid descending *chewewewewewewe*.

Churring Cisticola   *Cisticola njombe*   14cm, 5.5"   ●

Bright plain rufous crown and nape (extending on to cheeks), with a medium-dense dark streaked grey back, and buffy-white below with *extensive grey on the flanks*: tail brown with dark sub-terminal spots and pale tips. No obvious rufous wing panel. **HH** locally common in montane grassland and rank grass, bracken-fern and the fringes of wetlands from 1800–3000m in the highlands of STz. **Vo** call is a rolling, descending and liquid *churr-t, churr-t*, given in series of 6–8 separated by short pauses.

Wailing Cisticola   *Cisticola lais*   14cm, 5.5"

Two races occur (which may be distinct species): northern race *distinctus* (**Lynes's Cisticola**) is a rather *dark-toned* streak-backed cisticola with an *extensive wash of dull rusty-brown to the head and ear-coverts*, and buffy-brown underparts which add to overall dingy appearance. Southern race *semifasciatus* (south of dotted line on map) is a paler looking bird with a streaked rufous-brown crown, a pale buffy supercilium and sides to the face. **HH** common and localised on rocky hills with bush cover from 1500–2750m, where they creep about unobtrusively close to the ground. **Vo** Race *distinctus* sings a varied, enthusiastic buzzy but somewhat discordant refrain, incorporating nasal upslurs, throaty churrs and loud chips. Call is a loud nasal repeated *zweenk*. Race *semifasciatus* is slower, smoother and less varied.

Ashy Cisticola   *Cisticola cinereolus*   13cm, 5"

A slim ashy-grey or grey-brown cisticola which is uniformly streaked above and *lacks any rufous* in the plumage: brownish tail with dark sub-terminal spots and white tips. **HH** pairs are common in dry bush country from 300–1300m, perching openly on low bushes to sing. **Vo** song is a pretty, liquid descending, whistled refrain *si-swi-si-swi-siwoo*. Calls are a pinched nasal *tsit* and *tseent*.

Tana River Cisticola   *Cisticola restrictus*   13cm, 5"   ●

Very like Ashy Cisticola, but browner toned, with a *light rufous washed crown and nape* contrasting slightly with the back, and *flanks and sides of breast washed grey*: tail brown with dark sub-terminal spots and buffy tips. **HH** Ke endemic which is rare and virtually unknown. Collected in the lower Tana River basin in semi-arid bush. **Vo** song is unknown.

Plate 193

heterophrys

Rattling
Cisticola

Boran Cisticola

Churring
Cisticola

Wailing
Cisticola

semifasciatus

distinctus

Ashy
Cisticola

Tana River
Cisticola

WETLAND STREAK-BACKED CISTICOLAS

Cisticolas characteristic of wetland habitats: note amount of rufous on head, density of streaking on back, intensity of rufous in wing panels, tail pattern, habitat, range and call. Immatures are yellowish below.

Winding Cisticola   *Cisticola galactotes*   13cm, 5"
[Black-backed Cisticola in southern Africa]

Four races occur: typically boldly streaked with a *rufous crown and obvious rufous wing panels:* tail is grey or brown with dark sub-terminal spots and white tips. Race *haematocephalus* in coastal Ke and ETz is much duller on the crown, with a pale face, less distinct back streaking, and only a dull rufous wing panel. **HH** very common in reeds, sedges and rank vegetation from sea-level to 2300m, most races near water, but *haematocephalus* also occurs in drier scrubby bush. **Vo** most races call like a ratcheting fishing-reel *rrrrrrrrrrrrrr,* but voices vary locally from complex and musical winds to much more simple trills, often with a set of squeaky upslurs *wiii wiii wiii...* Race *haematocephalus* has a short monotonous raspy trill, similar to a prinia.

Carruther's Cisticola   *Cisticola carruthersi*   13cm, 5"

Very similar to Winding Cisticola, but crown chestnut-brown, *wing panel dull brown* (not bright rufous) and *upperside of tail mostly blackish* apart from white tips. **HH** locally common and restricted to papyrus swamps around Lake Victoria, but in other wetland vegetation in SWUg, Rw and Bu, from 700–2200m. **Vo** an explosive machine-gun burst of identical notes lasting 2–3 seconds, with long breaks between each series.

Levaillant's Cisticola   *Cisticola tinniens*   13cm, 5"

Similar to Winding Cisticola, but brighter, bolder and blacker. *Crown and nape very bright rufous, back very heavily streaked black, and wing panel very bright rufous: tail rufous with blackish centre and white tips.* **HH** pairs are common in tall grasses and reed beds within highland swamps from 2000–3200m. **Vo** song is a hurried, musical refrain given at intervals of 2–3 seconds, a descending *wit-chup* followed by an ascending *chererrerrerrit.*

White-tailed Cisticola   *Cisticola* (species undescribed)

Similar to Carruther's Cisticola with a warm brown crown and dull brown wing panel. It differs in having an obvious *pale supercilium,* a grey back with blackish streaks, and pale underparts washed grey on sides of neck and flanks. Tail very distinct being brown with white outer-tail feather webs and broad white tips forming an *obvious white 'U' right around the tail,* underside of tail plain silver-grey. Br birds are shorter-tailed. **HH** Tz endemic, discovered in 1986 and restricted to the Kilombero swamp at 250m near Ifakara in ETz. Common in sedges and long grass on dry ground around the swamp. **Vo** common call is a unique descending series of 5–6 nasal squeaks, but also winds like a Winding Cisticola, and sings a long refrain incorporating random squeaks and chattering.

Chirping Cisticola   *Cisticola pipiens*   14cm, 5.5"

Very similar to some races of Winding Cisticola (and best identified by voice), but duller with a darker reddish-brown crown, greyer-brown back, a dull brown wing panel, and a brown tail with black sub-terminal spots and pale tips (often spread). **HH** In our area, pairs and family parties are restricted to fairly dense swamp vegetation along the Mumba stream in SWTz and in lakeside vegetation near Bujumbura, Bu. ♂ sings from reed tops and during display flights when fanned tail is noticeable. **Vo** two main calls are given: an explosive *chip* followed by up to seven identical upslurs *twee-twee-twee...,* and also a *chip-chip,* followed by a drawn-out buzzy wind, and then a series of up to six staccato chips.

Plate 194

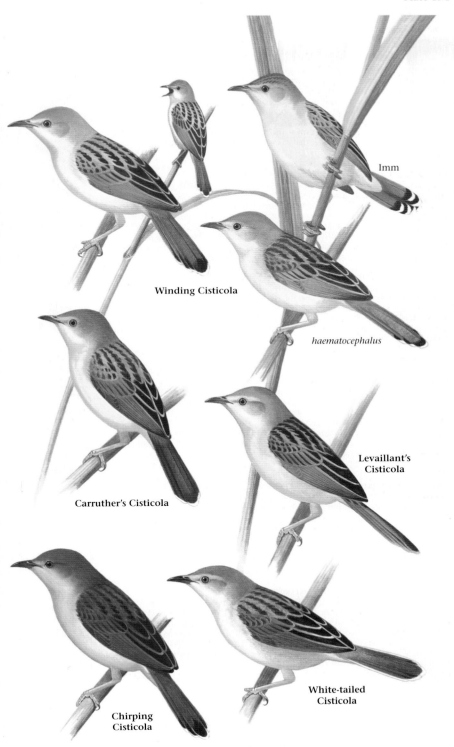

Winding Cisticola

Imm

haematocephalus

Carruther's Cisticola

Levaillant's Cisticola

Chirping Cisticola

White-tailed Cisticola

PLAIN-BACKED CISTICOLAS

A group of similar cisticolas with plain backs. Extent of rufous on head, presence or absence of rufous wing panels and indistinct back streaking, range and calls all aid identification. Sexes similar.

Singing Cisticola   *Cisticola cantans*   14cm, 5.5"

Ad has a *rufous crown and wing panel* contrasting with a plain grey-brown back, and is whitish below washed buffy on sides of breast. Imm is slightly more rufous above. **HH** pairs are common and widespread in fairly dense vegetation at forest edge, around cultivation, in rank undergrowth and gardens, from sea-level to 2500m. **Vo** despite name, song is very simple: typically ♂ first delivers loud chips and then an explosive paired *whi-chip whi-chip...*, and ♀ joins in with dry raspy churrs or the same.

Red-faced Cisticola   *Cisticola erythrops*   14cm, 5.5"

Similar to Singing Cisticola, but ad has a *variable rusty wash extending over face and ear-coverts,* a more grey-brown crown uniform with the nape and back, and *no contrasting rufous wing panel*: variable below but often buffy-brown. Imm is more rufous-brown above. **HH** pairs are common in luxuriant vegetation, often near streams or lakes, from sea-level to 2300m, although they occupy cultivated land in Rw and Bu. **Vo** sings a complex rather rhythmic duet: generally ♂ gives a nasal *zwink* and *chip-wee* notes, whilst ♀ utters rising piping squeaks *hoo-hoo-hoo-wiwiwi*.

Hunter's Cisticola   *Cisticola hunteri*   14cm, 5.5"   ●

Ad is dull brown with a slightly contrasting chestnut-brown crown, dark lores, a brown back (showing variable darker streaking only visible in good light), and greyish underparts with a whiter throat. Imm is warmer brown above. **HH** EA endemic: small parties inhabit overgrown cultivation, remnant valley herbage, forest edge and giant heather in the highlands from 1550–4400m. **Vo** sings a loud far-carrying, excited and highly distinctive musical duet from bush tops. One bird calls a rising and falling rolling trill *tweetrrrrrr tweetrrrrrr...* while another (or more) joins in with *see-tuit...*

Chubb's Cisticola   *Cisticola chubbi*   14cm, 5.5"

Very similar to Hunter's Cisticola, but ad has *black lores, a brighter rufous crown* contrasting with a totally unstreaked grey-brown back, and creamy-buff underparts with a whiter throat. Imm is duller than ad. **HH** pairs and small groups have a mainly western distribution from 1600–2500m, overlapping with Hunter's on Mt Elgon where Chubb's is below and Hunter's above 2500m. **Vo** duetted song is a repeated descending and explosive series of three notes: *wi-ti-chiow wi-ti-chiow wi-ti-chiow...*

Black-lored Cisticola   *Cisticola nigriloris*   15cm, 6"   ●

Similar to Chubb's Cisticola, but ad is larger with a very bright rufous crown, slightly paler nape, and a *large area of black on the lores and around the eyes*. Underparts are pale grey with a creamy-white throat. Imm is washed rusty above and yellowish below. **HH** southerly counterpart of Chubb's and Hunter's cisticolas, in our area restricted to thick cover on hillsides in the highlands of STz. **Vo** song is a duet of three unique penetrating squeaky-hinge notes *eek-zheek-pheuwww eek-zheek-pheuwww...*

Kilombero Cisticola   *Cisticola* (species undescribed)

Ad is similar to other rufous-crowned duetting cisticolas, but has a *short bold white supercilium,* just a hint of a dark loral line (not black lores), a warm brown tail with greyish-white tips (which appear as obvious white band when fanned during excited duetting), and buff underparts. **HH** Tz endemic, discovered in 1986 and restricted to the Kilombero swamp at 250m near Ifakara, ETz, where it prefers flooded reedbeds. **Vo** sounds rather similar to a gate in need of oiling, with pattern and quality very like Black-lored Cisticola, but greater individual variation in songs (and no overlap in range or habitat).

Plate 195

Red-faced
Cisticola

Singing Cisticola

Hunter's Cisticola

Chubb's Cisticola

Kilombero Cisticola

Black-lored Cisticola

Trilling Cisticola   *Cisticola woosnami*   14cm, 5.5"
Ad is rather plain with a *dull chestnut-brown crown contrasting only slightly with a brown back*, no obvious wing panel, and whitish below with pale grey flanks. Tail has dark sub-terminal spots and pale tips. ♀ is smaller and slightly brighter on the crown. Imm is much more rufous above and yellow below. Race *lufira* in SWTz is warmer brown above and very buffy brown below. **HH** pairs are common in a wide variety of grassland with scattered bush and trees from 900–2000m, and also in miombo in Tz. **Vo** unique song is a musical trill rising to a crescendo and lasting 3–4 seconds *trrrrrrrrrrrrrrrrr* with long pauses. Call is a series of hollow scolds *tyap-ayap...*

Whistling Cisticola   *Cisticola lateralis*   14cm, 5.5"
Very similar to Trilling Cisticola, but ad is even more uniform above, with a *dull brown crown not contrasting with the back*, a white throat (often looks very white on singing birds), and grey sides to the neck. Tail with dark sub-terminal spots and pale tips. ♀ is smaller. Imm is rusty above and yellow below. **HH** pairs and family parties are locally common in scrub around cultivation, moist bush country, and at the forest edge, from 900–1900m in Ug. **Vo** a distinctive descending, rising or rising and falling muffled song repeated with a short pause between each series. Typically *cha....chah-chah-chahchahchahchah.*

Rock-loving Cisticola   *Cisticola aberrans*   14cm, 5.5"
Four races occur: all ads have a *rufous crown and long pale supercilium*, but differ mainly in overall tone and the extent of spotting in the tail. Race *petrophilus* (NUg) has a rufous-brown crown contrasting with a dull brown back, and is buff to rich buff below, with black sub-terminal spots on most of the tail; race *emini* (SWKe to NWTz) is similar, but is paler buff below; and race *teitensis* (SEKe to NETz) has the back rufous-brown uniform with the crown; race *nyika* (**Lazy Cisticola**) (SWTz) is also more uniform rufous above, but has a longer tail with less obvious sub-terminal spots. Some seasonal plumage variation also occurs (usually richer rufous above when non-br). Imms are generally more rufous than ads. **HH** pairs are rather shy and local, scuttling mouse-like over rocks and in nearby low bushes, on kopjes and rocky hillsides from 600–2150m. Occasionally cocks its tail upright. **Vo** common call is a very nasal and pinched upslur, usually a seesawing *eeyh aayh...*, but also gives a short, paired rattled trill. Song incorporates upslurs with chattering and bubbling. Race *nyika* calls are similar but more complaining.

CISTICOLAS WITHOUT OBVIOUS CLOSE AFFINITIES

Siffling Cisticola   *Cisticola brachypterus*   11cm, 4.5"
[Short-winged Cisticola]
A rather drab and variable species (with a beady-eyed look) best identified by song. Six races vary slightly in density of streaking above, which also varies seasonally, being indistinct in br birds (especially western), and usually heavier in non-br. Buffy below with a whiter throat. No rufous on crown or wing. Tail is dull brown with dark sub-terminal spots and white tips. Imm is yellow below. **HH** common and widespread but inconspicuous frequenting bushed grasslands and open forest edge from sea-level to 2200m, often singing from the tops of small trees. **Vo** quiet and high-pitched song varies locally, but it is usually a repeated series of three or more sibilant descending notes *si-si-siu si-si-siu...*

Foxy Cisticola   *Cisticola troglodytes*   10cm, 4"
Ad is a small distinctive cisticola which is entirely *plain bright rufous above, and rich buff below* with a paler throat. Imm is duller above and yellow below. **HH** localised and generally uncommon in wooded grasslands from 650–2200m where it creeps around in low bushes, but then flies to tree tops when flushed. **Vo** common call is a rapid series of harsh chat-like *tat-tat-tat-tat-...* and a *tiptiptiptip....* Rarely heard song is a long series of nasal chips and slurs.

Plate 196

Whistling Cisticola

Trilling Cisticola

emini

Rock-loving
Cisticola

nyika

non-br

br

Foxy Cisticola

Ad

Siffling
Cisticola

Long-tailed Cisticola *Cisticola angusticaudus* 11cm, 4.5"
[Tabora Cisticola]
A uniquely long-tailed cisticola: br ad has a bright rufous crown contrasting with a plain grey-brown back, and a *long dark narrow tail with white tips* (shorter in non-br plumage). Imm is duller and browner above, washed pale yellow below. **HH** single birds or small parties occur in acacia grasslands below 1400m; they are constantly on the move working through low bushes and on the ground. **Vo** song is a repeated soft piping delivered from a perch or in a display flight; call is a harsh repeated chipping.

Piping Cisticola *Cisticola fulvicapillus* 10cm, 4"
[Neddicky]
Sometimes considered conspecific with Long-tailed Cisticola, but in our area the race *muelleri* differs in having more extensive rufous on the crown and nape, a browner back and shorter tail. Imm is more rufous-brown above and whiter below. **HH** pairs and small parties are in open grasslands and scrub from sea-level to 1400m, often within miombo woodland. **Vo** song is a rapid piping on one note, similar to Long-tailed Cisticola, but perhaps a little faster; call is a harsh chittering.

Red-fronted Warbler *Spiloptila rufifrons* 11cm, 4.5"
A small warbler with a *variable amount of rufous on the forecrown and crown*, an ashy-brown back, and whitish underparts. Long narrow white-tipped blackish tail is habitually cocked and waved from side to side. Imm lacks rufous on the forecrown. Race *rufidorsalis* in SEKe has the back washed rufous and may show an indication of a blackish breast band. **HH** pairs and small family parties are common in dry bush from 400–1300m, endlessly searching for insects in low dry vegetation, rarely far above the ground. **Vo** lively song is a long and varied medley of nasal buzzes and chips (each note repeated many times before the next). Call is a harsh repeated nasal slur.

Red-winged Warbler *Heliolais erythroptera* 12cm, 5"
Rather similar to Tawny-flanked Prinia, but lacks the broad supercilium. Br ad has *rufous wings* which contrast with paler olive-brown upperparts, greyish sides to the face, and white underparts (washed buff on the flanks and belly). Tail is long with blackish sub-terminal spots and white tips. Non-br ad has a browner back. Sexes alike. **HH** pairs and small family parties are generally uncommon in long grass within open woodland, including miombo, from sea-level to 1500m. They are often in the undergrowth (but fly to prominent tree tops if disturbed or displaying). **Vo** varies locally, but the song is always strident and based around a repeated sharp *chip*, or a nasal downslur; a prinia-like *chtchtchtcht..., siusiusiusiu...* or *tsitsitsitsitsi...*

Red-winged Grey Warbler *Drymocichla incana* 12cm, 5"
In our area, nominate race is a cold grey warbler which is paler below and has *orange-red bases to the primaries forming a patch on the closed wing*. Bill is slender and black, eyes are dark, and legs are orange-red. Sexes alike. Imm is paler with a buffy wash to flanks and belly. **HH** in our area small groups of 3–6 birds are uncommon in NWUg from 600–1200m, usually in trees in swampy rank grassland, or in riverine woodland. **Vo** parties often excitedly break into a musical and lively duetted song which incorporates chips and squealing notes based around *wi-chip-wi-chip-wi-chip...*

Plate 197

Long-tailed Cisticola

br

Piping Cisticola

Ad

Ad

nominate

Imm

Red-fronted
Warbler

br

Red-winged
Warbler

Ad

Red-winged Grey
Warbler

PRINIAS

Small active warblers mainly found in the undergrowth, which frequently cock and wave their long tails from side to side. Sexes alike.

Tawny-flanked Prinia *Prinia subflava* 11cm, 4.5"

Most common and widespread prinia: seasonal and racial differences centre mainly on the amount of grey or brown above. Typical birds are pale-brown or grey-brown, with an obvious pale supercilium, narrow dark eye-line, off-white throat and breast, and *pale tawny-buff washed belly and flanks*. Imm is washed yellowish below. **HH** pairs are very common, usually active low down in all habitats except forest interior and arid areas, including gardens, bushed grasslands, overgrown cultivation and clearings within forest from sea-level to 2300m. **Vo** simple unmusical song consists of a rapid-fire *titititititititit*... or a rasping *zhertzhertzhert*... Also a buzzy scolding call *jeee jeee*...

Pale Prinia *Prinia somalica* 11cm, 4.5"

Very similar to Tawny-flanked Prinia, but is generally paler with *whiter underparts* lacking a tawny wash on the flanks. Imm is washed very pale-buff on the breast and flanks. **HH** single birds and pairs inhabit dry bush country with or without grass cover, preferring drier situations to Tawny-flanked where ranges overlap. **Vo** song differs from Tawny-flanked Prinia in being a rattle of dry, cricket-like notes lasting 4–5 seconds *zherzherzherzherzher*...

White-chinned Prinia *Prinia leucopogon* 13cm, 5"

Mostly grey warbler with a *creamy-white throat*, darker grey ear-coverts, a red-brown eye and pink legs. Tail is broader than typical prinias. **HH** small groups are common in secondary forest growth, forest edge, and in thick cover along streams, from 1100 to 2400m. **Vo** duetting, energetic and excitable singing of rapid chips and squeaks, variously *chippity-chu-chu chi-chu-chi-chi*...

Banded Prinia *Prinia bairdii* 11cm, 4.5"

Three races (which are sometimes considered two species) occur. If split, highland races *melanops* and *obscura* become **Black-faced Prinia** *Prinia melanops* (found in the west from 1550–3000m), while the nominate race remains **Banded Prinia** (Semliki Forest, WUg at 700m). Highland birds have a blackish face and throat; lowland birds have the breast banding extending up on to the throat. Both are blackish-brown above, with white spotted wing-coverts, a long white-tipped tail, and are heavily banded below making either form unmistakable. Imm is browner above with indistinct barring below. **HH** common in parts of its range, but shy and difficult to see in thick forest undergrowth. **Vo** song is usually given as a duet: ♂ repeats series of high nasal rhythmical notes *ch'zi-ch'zi-ch'zi-ch'zi-ch'zi*... while ♀ peeps plaintively *piu piu*....

Grey-capped Warbler *Eminia lepida* 15cm, 6"

A large stocky, distinctive warbler which should not be confused if seen well. Basic grey and green plumage with a *black band running around the crown and a chestnut throat patch* is unique. Imm is duller with less chestnut on the throat. **HH** shy but very vocal, with pairs inhabiting a wide variety of thick undergrowth, including gardens, forest edge and river courses from 800–2500m. **Vo** often duetted loud song is variable, but easily recognised, since notes are slow, strong and fluty typically *wer-wi-wi*... *whii-chutchutchutchutchutchutchutchut*... (with the ♂ trilling and ♀ adding rising nasal upslurs).

Plate 198

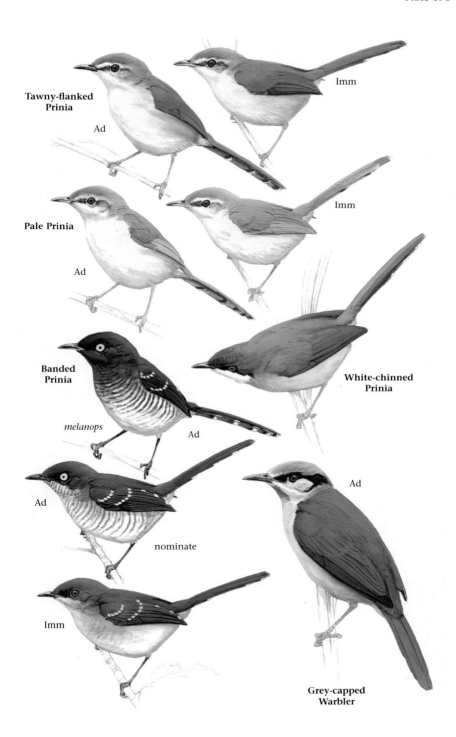

Tawny-flanked Prinia

Imm

Ad

Pale Prinia

Imm

Ad

Banded Prinia

melanops

Ad

White-chinned Prinia

Ad

nominate

Imm

Ad

Grey-capped Warbler

CAMAROPTERAS AND WREN-WARBLERS

A closely related and taxonomically confusing group of small warblers which are variously lumped and split across the continent. Camaropteras inhabit forest and more verdant habitats, while the wren-warblers (which are barred below) prefer miombo woodland and dry bush country. Both genera cock their tails, which are also frequently fanned in the wren-warblers. Sexes are alike.

Grey-backed Camaroptera *Camaroptera brachyura* 10cm, 4"
[Grey-backed Bleating Warbler, Green-backed Bleating Warbler]
Eight races occur in two distinct groups. Grey-backed birds are mainly in the west and central regions, although they reach the Ke coast north of Mombasa. Green-backed birds occur in coastal SEKe southwards in E and STz. Several races are known to hybridise. If considered specifically distinct green-backed races are *Camaroptera brachyura* (**Green-backed Camaroptera**) and grey-backed *Camaroptera brevicaudata*. Both are grey with green wings, but *brachyura* races also have a green mantle. Some races are browner above when breeding, and they vary from grey to pale greyish-white below. Imms are variably washed yellow on the underparts. **HH** very common in the undergrowth and the lower levels of forest, thick bush, gardens and cultivation, from sea-level to 2200m. **Vo** musically versatile although all calls are simple. Frequently heard is a very nasal pinched wheeze *bzeeee* (often described as a bleat). Song is a loud whip-cracked *t'chk t'chk t'chk*, and also a nasal *wiwiwiwiwiwi...*

Olive-green Camaroptera *Camaroptera chloronota* 10cm, 4"
A dull drab camaroptera of the forest interior. Ad has olive-brown upperparts with slightly greener wings: the face and breast are dull tawny-brown contrasting with a whiter belly and vent. Imm is generally greener and variably washed yellowish below. **HH** solitary birds or pairs are common in tangled vines and undergrowth within primary forest from 700–2000m. **Vo** calls a soft *weep weep...* which often leads into an unusual high-pitched and insect-like piping on one note *ee-ee-ee-ee-ee-ee-ee-ee-ee-ee...*

Yellow-browed Camaroptera *Camaroptera superciliaris* 10cm, 4"
Yellowish-green above with a bright yellow supercilium and sides to the face: lores are black and bill is fairly long. The underparts are mainly white with a bright yellow vent, although calling birds inflate and expose pale-blue pouches on either side of the neck. Imm duller than ad with a yellowish wash to the throat and breast. **HH** quite common in lowland forest and secondary growth in WUg from 700–1550m. **Vo** song consists of two paired rhythmical upslurs with a muffled quality *tuu'it tuu'it tuu'it...*, while the call is a pair of musical downslurs preceded by a soft click *t-ku'wiu t-ku'wiu...*

Grey Wren-Warbler *Calamonastes simplex* 13cm, 5"
All dark grey-brown with a broad tail which is often cocked and waved. At close range may show a slightly speckled throat and some indistinct barring on the belly. **HH** common in acacia scrub and bushed savanna from 100–1300m. Usually seen slowly moving around low down in bushes, or even on the ground below them, but will move to the tops of small trees when calling. **Vo** song is an explosive repeated *chup, chup, chup* called for long periods at about once per second.

Miombo Wren-Warbler *Calamonastes undosus* 13cm, 5"
[Stierling's Barred Warbler]
Two races occur (which may be specifically distinct, although they hybridise in a small area in Zambia). The more westerly nominate race (**Pale Wren-Warbler**) is grey-brown above (paler than Grey Wren-Warbler) and dingy greyish-white below with narrow darker grey-brown barring, particularly on the throat and breast and variably onto the flanks. In E and STz *stierlingi* (**Barred Wren-Warbler**) is rufous olive-brown above with small white tips to the wing-coverts and distinct blackish and white barred underparts. Imm is washed tawny on the vent. **HH** both races favour open grassy hills with scattered bush and trees (particularly miombo) from near sea-level to 1700m. **Vo** nominate birds sound like a musical sparrow, calling for long periods about once every second *cherp cherp cherp....* Race *stierlingi* calls a totally different insect-like short tinny trill *tlllllng tlllllng tlllllng...*

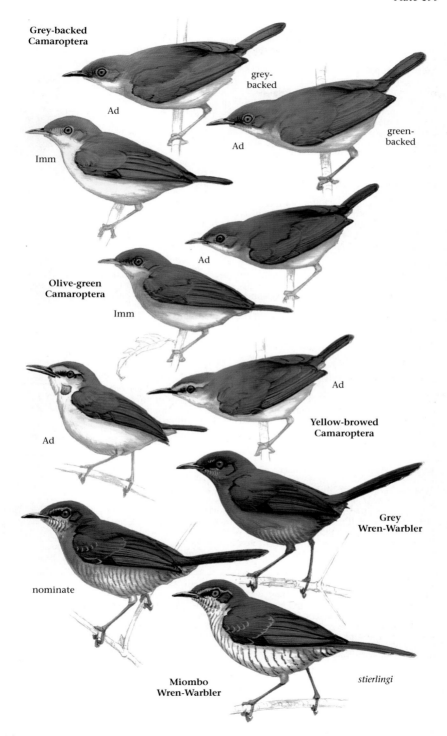

Plate 199

Grey-backed
Camaroptera

grey-
backed

Ad

Ad

green-
backed

Ad

Imm

Olive-green
Camaroptera

Imm

Ad

Ad

Yellow-browed
Camaroptera

Grey
Wren-Warbler

nominate

Miombo
Wren-Warbler

stierlingi

APALIS WARBLERS

Small fairly long-tailed warblers usually found in pairs or small groups, actively moving through the foliage as they search for food. Most inhabit canopy and middle levels of forest where they draw attention to themselves with frequent, repetitive calls and songs.

Yellow-breasted Apalis *Apalis flavida* 13cm, 5"

A complex species with several races which have been variously placed in two groups based on tail colour. All forms are greenish above with yellow across the breast, and have varying amounts of grey on the crown. Many have a small black breast spot. In NEUg, N and EKe, race *flavocincta* (**Brown-tailed Apalis**) lacks the black breast smudge, has grey on the fore-crown only, and a brown uppertail (which can be hard to see in the field). Elsewhere, they have green uppertails, and further vary as follows: western birds have grey crowns and little or no black on the breast; southern birds have similar crown colour, but show a distinctive black breast smudge; and those in CKe and NTz have grey restricted to the forecrown, and a black breast spot is distinctive in the ♂ only. **HH** pairs are common and widespread in a variety of woodland, riverine forest, bush, gardens and cultivation from sea-level to 2200m. **Vo** race *flavocincta* sings a monotonous dry rasping duet, with the ♂ calling *krik-krik-krik...* whilst the ♀ accompanies with very quiet throaty growls. Green-tailed birds have a slower more distinctive rhythm like a galloping horse, with the ♂ calling *chirrit-chirrit-chirrit-...*, while the ♀ accompanies with rising nasal *eek eek eek eek...*

Grey Apalis *Apalis cinerea* 13cm, 5"

Brown washed crown contrasts slightly with greyer mantle and wings (less so in ♀), and *white outer-tail feathers* easily distinguish this species from Brown-headed Apalis. Very similar Kungwe Apalis is colder grey above without any hint of brown on the crown. Imm is washed olive above and very pale yellow below. **HH** common in the highland forests of Ke, but at lower altitudes in the west over a range of from 1200–3000m. Primarily a canopy species but it will forage at lower levels, particularly along the forest edge. **Vo** ♂ calls a monotonous *chip-chip-chip...*, often accompanied with wing-snapping, while the ♀ gives a frequent high-pitched rattle.

Brown-headed Apalis *Apalis alticola* 13cm, 5"

Very similar to Grey Apalis, but the crown is darker brown and the *outer-tail grey with white tips*. **HH** common, replacing Grey Apalis in most of the highland forests of Tz from 1200–2200m, only overlapping in the Nguruman Hills, Ke and Loliondo, Tz. **Vo** displays with wing-snapping, and the song is also similar in quality and tone to Grey Apalis, although it calls with a paired note almost saying *ri-kit ri-kit...*

Kungwe Apalis *Apalis argentea* 13cm, 5" ● ●

Ad ♂ is similar to Grey Apalis but the *crown and mantle are a clear cool grey* (with no brown wash to the crown) and the whitish forecrown and lores give a *pale-faced appearance*. Ad ♀ is washed pale olive-green on the mantle and wings. Sometimes considered conspecific with Buff-throated Apalis. **HH** pairs and small flocks are uncommon residents of the forest canopy in Nyungwe Forest, Rw, Kibira and Bururi forests, Bu, and the Mahale Mts, WTz, from 1200–2350m. Often also joins mixed-species flocks. **Vo** ♂ is reported to call *prui-tju, prui-tju, prui-tju* and ♀ may join in with occasional *tjup* notes.

Long-billed Tailorbird *Orthotomus moreaui* 13cm, 5" ● ●

An atypical grey and white warbler with the forehead to top of crown warm dull brown and a *long thin black bill*. Sexes alike. This curious species is sometimes called the Long-billed Apalis *Apalis moreaui*. **HH** rare and restricted to the undergrowth and middle levels of forest, particularly along streams, in the Amani area of the East Usambara Mts, NETz, at 900m. **Vo** several different songs: all consist of simple repeated notes and are typically apalis-like including *chep-chep-chep...*, an upslurred *weeh-weeh-weeh...*, or *t'yau-t'yau-t'yau...*

Plate 200

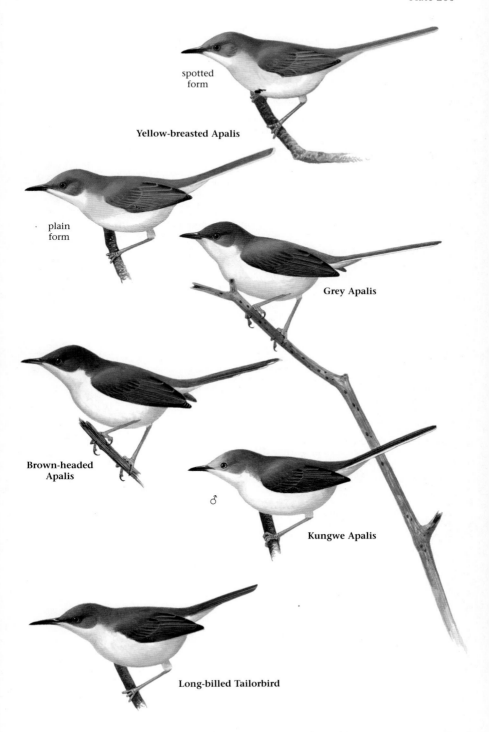

spotted
form

Yellow-breasted Apalis

plain
form

Grey Apalis

**Brown-headed
Apalis**

♂

Kungwe Apalis

Long-billed Tailorbird

Karamoja Apalis *Apalis karamojae* 11cm, 4.5" ●●
Nominate race in Ug is ash-grey above with a short whitish supercilium, an obvious· *white patch in the inner secondaries*, and creamy-white underparts with a white outer-tail. Sexes are alike. In Tz race *stronachi*, the ♂ is more brownish-grey above with greyer flanks, and the ♀ is paler. **HH** very localised and uncommon EA endemic with two populations, one centred on the Mt Moroto to Kidepo NP area in NEUg; the other on the Wembere floodplain in CTz. Particularly fond of *Acacia drepanolobium* where up to six birds have been seen together. **Vo** unknown.

Black-headed Apalis *Apalis melanocephala* 13cm, 5"
A black and white apalis with a *largely black tail with white tips*. Four races occur: ♂♂ of the nominate race (from coastal Ke to the East Usambara Mts, NETz) and of race *muhuluensis* (in STz) are very black above; while in the SEKe and NETz highlands *moschi* has a dark grey crown and upperparts with black restricted to sides of the face; and in the CKe highlands *nigrodorsalis* is blackish-brown above. All ♀♀ are typically paler and more olivaceous grey above. **HH** usually in pairs in the canopy and middle levels of eastern forests, frequently in mixed bird parties from sea-level to 2150m. **Vo** song is a typical monotonous apalis-like chipping, but with some geographic variation: a sibilant *tiree-tiree-tiree-tiree...* repeated 4–5 times and then again after a pause of varying length.

Chestnut-throated Apalis *Apalis porphyrolaema* 11cm, 4.5"
Predominantly grey apalis with paler underparts and a *small clear-cut chestnut throat*. Tail grey with inconspicuous grey tips. Imm is washed pale yellow on the throat, sides of face and belly. **HH** pairs and single birds are common in the canopy of highland forests from 1700–3400m. **Vo** a unique sounding apalis: ♂ sings a set of two ringing dry trills on one level, similar to a modern telephone, *t-t-trrriiii trrrriiii* and the ♀ accompanies this with rapid seeping notes.

Chapin's Apalis *Apalis chapini* 11cm, 4.5" ●
A grey pale-bellied apalis with a *strong wash of rufous-chestnut to the face and breast*. Two races occur: more northerly nominate birds have a whitish chin, while in the STz highlands *strausae* is rufous over the whole face, throat and breast. Imms are mostly grey with a buffy wash to the throat and breast. **HH** inhabits canopy and middle levels in the highland forests of E and STz, from 1500–2000m. **Vo** there is some local variation, but most calls are insect-like and higher-pitched than other apalises. Nominate birds utter chipping notes and sing a repeated *tsitsitsitsitsitsitsitsi...*, while *strausae* tends to have more form and duets, the ♂ singing a high-pitched galloping *ch'lit-ch'lit-ch'lit-ch'lit...*, while the ♀ calls a rapid *pi-pi-pi-pi-pi...*

Plate 201

Karamoja Apalis

nominate

♀

Black-headed
Apalis

♂

nominate

Imm

Chestnut-throated Apalis

Ad

nominate

Imm

Ad

Chapin's Apalis

Buff-throated Apalis *Apalis rufogularis* 11cm, 4.5"
In race *nigrescens* ad ♂ is blackish-brown above, pale creamy-white below, and has a *dark tail with four pairs of white outer-tail feathers* which are very obvious in flight. Ad ♀ is similar, but the *throat to upper breast is tawny-buff*. Imm is olive-grey above with a yellow wash to the throat and breast. In SWUg, race *kigezi* is greyer above in both sexes. **HH** pairs are common in the forest canopy across W and SUg from 700–1800m, and less numerous in NWTz and WKe between 1200 and 2400m. **Vo** similar to Grey Apalis, but notes are softer, more whistled than harsh. Western birds tend to be louder and sharper than those further east. Song is a monotonous repeated two-toned chipping *ch'rip-ch'rip-ch'rip-...*, often accompanied by wing-snapping.

Black-collared Apalis *Apalis pulchra* 11cm, 4.5"
A boldly marked and attractive apalis which is wholly dark grey above, with white outer-tail feathers, and white below with a distinct *black collar and bright chestnut flanks*. Sexes are alike. Imm is paler with a dark grey breast band. **HH** pairs and small groups are common in forest undergrowth and tangled vines from 1550–2400m, being most numerous in WKe, less so in the central Ke highlands. **Vo** song consists of repeated sets of paired, pinched nasal notes on alternating see-sawing tones *zeeu-zeeu-zeeu...* usually 4–7 paired notes per series.

Collared Apalis *Apalis ruwenzorii* 11cm, 4.5" ●
Like a washed-out version of Black-collared Apalis without any white in the tail. Below chestnut is more extensive and much paler, covering the chin, throat, sides of breast, flanks and vent. Breast band is dark grey, paler and less distinct on the ♀ and imm. **HH** Albertine Rift endemic: common in pairs and family groups in the undergrowth of highland forests in WUg, Rw and Bu, from 1550–3100m. **Vo** very similar to Black-collared Apalis and songs are virtually indistinguishable but possibly less nasal.

Bar-throated Apalis *Apalis thoracica* 11cm, 4.5"
Several distinct races occur differing chiefly in the colour of the crown, back and underparts. In the Chyulu Hills, Ke, in NTz and in the Udzungwa Mts, ETz, the race *griseiceps* has a brownish cap, yellowish-green back, a white throat and breast cut by a narrow black band, and the lower breast to vent is bright yellow; from NE to SWTz (where not occupied by any other races) *murina* is similar, but has a grey back, greenish flanks and a yellow lower belly; in the South Pare Mts, NTz, very similar *pareensis* has yellow restricted to the vent; and in the Uluguru Mts, ETz, the race *uluguru* is like *griseiceps* but with the yellow extending from the breast band to the vent; while in Songea, STz, *arnoldi* is also similar to *griseiceps*, but has a duller crown and back. In the Taita Hills, SEKe, distinctive race *fuscigularis* (**Taita Apalis** ●●) has totally dark brownish-grey upperparts, a blackish-brown throat and upper breast, and the lower breast to vent washed very pale yellow. Taita Apalis is globally threatened. **HH** common in undergrowth and middle levels of forests within range from 1300–3200m. **Vo** a complicated picture, with songs varying almost as much as the birds do in plumage: race *murina* has a descending dry trill, *uluguru* has a two-tone repeated chipping, *griseiceps* and *arnoldi* are similar to *uluguru* but more rapid, and the ♀ accompanies with a dry rattle, and *fuscigularis* calls a fast chipping while the ♀ accompanies with metallic tinks. Clearly there is much work to be done!

Plate 202

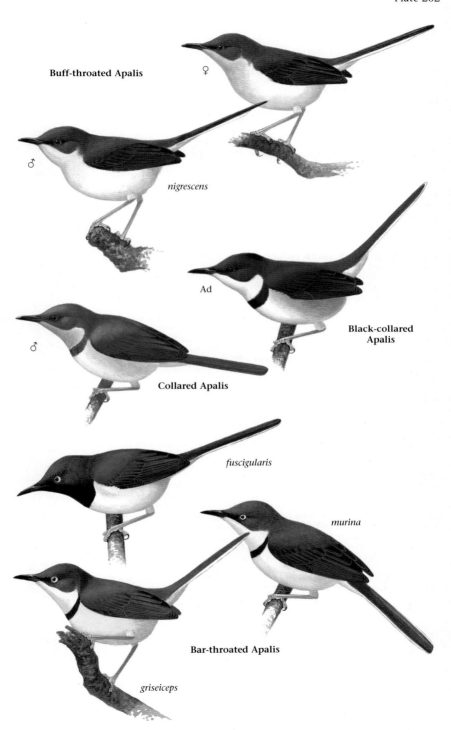

Buff-throated Apalis

♀

♂

nigrescens

Ad

Black-collared Apalis

♂

Collared Apalis

fuscigularis

murina

Bar-throated Apalis

griseiceps

Black-throated Apalis *Apalis jacksoni* 11cm, 4.5″

A bright and attractive apalis: ad ♂ has a black throat and sides to face separated by a broad white malar stripe, a grey crown, green back, and dark grey wings with variable whitish edges to the inner secondaries. Bright yellow below washed greenish on the flanks. Ad ♀ is similar, but with a grey crown and throat. Imm ♂ is duller with a greenish crown and greyish throat, while the imm ♀ has a yellowish throat. **HH** pairs are common in the canopy of highland forest from 1200–2400m. **Vo** song differs from all other apalises, in sounding musical hollow and metallic: a see-sawing two-tone call repeated for long periods *t'link-t'link-t'link-...*

Masked Apalis *Apalis binotata* 11cm, 4.5″

Ad ♂ has a grey crown and sides to the head separated from a black throat and upper breast by a narrow white stripe. Otherwise fairly uniform green above, with sides of breast and flanks paler green blending to a whitish belly. Ad ♀ has the black restricted to the throat and a broader white stripe. Imm is entirely green above and yellowish on the throat and breast. **HH** local and generally uncommon, occurring in forest undergrowth and dense tangled vines from 1200–1500m. **Vo** call is a harsh ratchet-like rasping quite unlike other apalises (except for Mountain Masked), it is followed by a hollow two-tone repeated see-sawing with a galloping-horse rhythm *k'jit-k'jit-k'jit-k'jit-...*

Mountain Masked Apalis *Apalis personata* 11cm, 4.5″   ●

Ad has a broad black vertical stripe extending from crown, over sides of face, throat and down to the lower breast, which contrasts with a conspicuous small white patch beside the ear-coverts. Otherwise dull green above with a greyish-olive lower body. Sexes are alike. Imm is plain dull green above, pale greyish-olive below with a creamy throat. **HH** endemic to forests along the Albertine Rift from 1500–2800m, where it prefers the canopy and middle levels but is also occasionally in the undergrowth. **Vo** calls virtually identical to Masked Apalis, possibly a little higher pitched.

Black-capped Apalis *Apalis nigriceps* 11cm, 4.5″

Ad ♂ has a black cap, a golden yellow-green back, white underparts with a conspicuous black band across the lower neck, and white outer-tail feathers. Ad ♀ is similar, but the crown and neck band are greyer. Imm is uniform olive-green above, lacks the black neck band, and is pale yellowish below. **HH** pairs are rather sparsely distributed in forest from 1000–1400m in W and SUg, but they are not uncommon at Budongo Forest, preferring the canopy and often joining mixed-species flocks. **Vo** unlike most apalises it calls an irregularly repeated triple *wi'chi-chit wi'chi-chit...* which may end with a monotone trill.

White-winged Apalis *Apalis chariessa* 13cm, 5″   ● ●

A bright and beautiful apalis: ad ♂ is glossy blue-black above with a conspicuous white wing patch, and a blue-black band separating its white throat from an orange upper breast and bright yellow belly. Ad ♀ has a grey crown contrasting with a green mantle, grey wings with a whitish patch, and is pale orange-yellow below with a grey neck band. Imm is like a dull ♀ with a yellowish patch on the throat. **HH** pairs or small groups are very local in the canopy of forests and sometimes join mixed-species flocks. Known from the Udzungwa and Uluguru Mts in ETz, from 1000–2000m, and formerly on the lower Tana River, Ke, at 100m. **Vo** a high penetrating two-tone see-sawing call, with an irregular rhythm and very short breaks between each series *witi-witi-witi-witi witi-witi witi-witi-witi...*

Plate 203

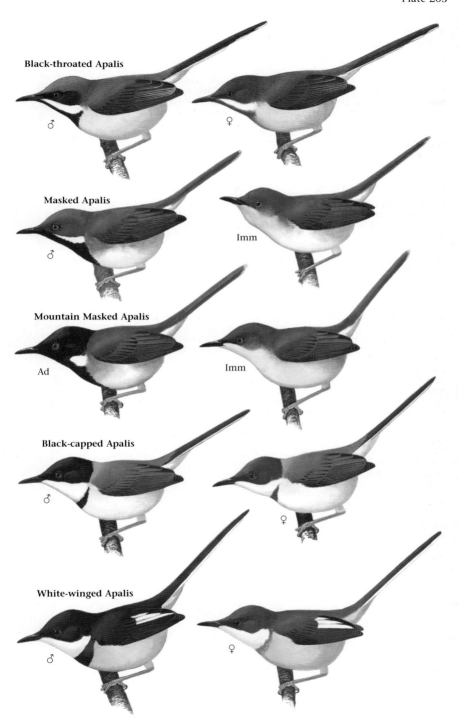

Black-throated Apalis
♂
♀

Masked Apalis
♂
Imm

Mountain Masked Apalis
Ad
Imm

Black-capped Apalis
♂
♀

White-winged Apalis
♂
♀

SLATY FLYCATCHER
A familiar highland bird which can be used as a good comparative species once well known. Larger than most *Muscicapa* species. Sexes are alike.

White-eyed Slaty Flycatcher   *Melaenornis fischeri*   17cm, 6.5"
[Slaty Flycatcher]
Three races occur: in NEUg, Ke and NETz nominate birds are distinctive, being dark blue-grey above and paler below (blending to whitish on the belly), with a *conspicuous broad white eye-ring*, and blue-grey bill with a black tip; in the highlands of Tz *nyikensis* is more slate-grey with a small eye-ring; and in WUg, Rw and Bu *toruensis* is blue-grey like the nominate race, but has an inconspicuous eye-ring. Imms are spotted with buffy-white above, mottled and scalloped blackish across the breast and flanks. **HH** common and widespread at forest edge, in wooded glades and gardens from 1350–3000m. **Vo** rarely heard song consists of a sibilant hissing and clicking interspersed with very loud and explosive *swee-wi-yu* calls. More common call is a complaining *trrr-trrr*.

BLACK FLYCATCHERS
Three similar-looking flycatchers best identified by overall colour, eye colour, song and range. These are typical flycatchers sitting quietly with an upright posture for long periods. Sexes alike. Also consider other black birds like cuckoo-shrikes (plate 154), boubous (plate 235), and drongos (plate 241).

Southern Black Flycatcher   *Melaenornis pammelaina*   18cm, 7"
Ad is very similar to Northern Black Flycatcher, but differs in being *glossy blue-black* (not dull black): eye dark brown. Similar drongos have red eyes, black boubous have a horizontal posture, cuckoo-shrikes are restless and have an obvious yellow gape. Imm is dull black, spotted above with buff and scalloped below. **HH** locally common in a wide variety of drier woodland, bush and cultivation from sea-level to 1800m. In Ke occurs mainly east of Great Rift Valley, but they are widespread in Tz and extend west to Bu and Rw. **Vo** song is very complex, sweet and warbler-like.

Northern Black Flycatcher   *Melaenornis edolioides*   18cm, 7"
Two races occur: in Ug, WKe and NWTz the more widespread *lugubris* is totally *dull slate-black* with dark brown eyes, while at Moyale in NKe *schistacea* is dull grey-black. Imms are streaked with tawny on the crown, more heavily spotted with tawny elsewhere. For differences from Southern Black Flycatcher and other similar black birds see that species. **HH** widespread to the north and west of the Southern Black, occupying woodland, dry bush country and cultivated areas. In Ke common mainly west of the Great Rift Valley from 400–800m. **Vo** song is very different from Southern Black Flycatcher, being rather slow and sibilant, with many long drawn-out burry slurs and occasional soft nasal chips.

Yellow-eyed Black Flycatcher   *Melaenornis ardesiacus*   18cm, 7"   ●
Ad is very dark slaty-grey with *creamy-yellow eyes*. Imm is spotted off-white below and eyes may be dark. **HH** endemic to montane forest along the Albertine Rift, where it can be locally common in clearings and along the forest edge from 1550–2450m. **Vo** typically utters a whispery, rapid *zweeink- zweeink- zweeink…*, repeated with slight variations, but also has a loud, rich and melodic song with many thrush-like phrases.

Plate 204

White-eyed Slaty Flycatcher

nyikensis

Ad

Imm

nominate

Ad

Imm

Southern Black Flycatcher

Imm

Ad

Yellow-eyed Black Flycatcher

Ad

Imm

Northern Black Flycatcher

Ad

lugubris

FICEDULA FLYCATCHERS

Three similar Palearctic migrant flycatchers. In Feb–Apr (spring) the distinctive black and white males have different amounts of white on the hindneck, forecrown and wings. However, most records are of similar looking grey-brown non-breeding males, females and 1st year birds, which can be extremely difficult to identify. Non-breeding adults of both sexes have typical female-like plumage, but are generally browner than breeding females. Most can be identified by the extent of white in the wing, particularly on the median coverts and the primary bases. Many 1st year birds cannot be identified with certainty, unless showing some of the distinctive adult features. Particularly beware of 1st year birds with white tips to the median coverts: birds with extensive broad white tips are Semi-collared, but both Collared and Pied can show some scattered white tips in this plumage. In all three species birds can be aged by the extent of white on the tertials; in adults this extends smoothly around the end of the feathers, in 1st year birds it stops abruptly near the tip.

Semi-collared Flycatcher   *Ficedula semitorquata*   13cm, 5"

Br ♂ has one or two small white patches on the forecrown, a *half-collar on the hindneck*, a small white patch at base of primaries and white-tipped median coverts forming a second wing bar. *Open tail shows a wheatear-like pattern, with much white in outer-tail bases.* Br ♀ is grey-brown above, with a variable but often paler rump: *white tips to the median coverts form a second wing bar*, and white patch at base of primaries is intermediate in size between Collared and Pied flycatchers. Non-br ♂ is like ♀ but much blacker on the wings and tail. It differs from non-br ♂ Collared in having distinct white tips to the median coverts. **HH** owing to confusion with Collared Flycatcher the exact status is unclear, but it is locally common in the west from Sep–Apr, with some birds wintering in C and STz. It is uncommon but regular in WKe. **Vo** variously reported as an occasional sharp *eeet, eeep,* or *tec.*

Collared Flycatcher   *Ficedula albicollis*   13cm, 5"

Br ♂ has a *large patch of white on the forecrown, a complete white collar on the hindneck, a large white patch at base of primaries*, usually some white on rump and usually an all black tail. Br ♀ is grey-brown above with a paler rump, a comparatively *large white primary patch*, and often pale sides to the neck. Note, rarely they have pale tips to the median coverts, but these are not as well defined as on Semi-collared Flycatcher. Non-br ♂ is like ♀ but has much black in the wings and tail: lack of white on the median coverts separates it from non-br ♂ Semi-collared. **HH** status uncertain, but it appears to be most frequent in the far west, certainly occurring in Rw and Bu, with other reports from WTz and once in WKe. **Vo** reported as similar to Semi-collared Flycatcher, but higher-pitched.

Pied Flycatcher   *Ficedula hypoleuca*   13cm, 5"

Br ♂ is usually black and white, but also has a grey-brown form. Both have the same identification features: a variable sized patch of white on the forecrown (sometimes divided), *white does not extend far on to sides of neck, white at base of primaries is hardly visible*, tail may be all black or with some white in sides. Br ♀ is rather uniform brownish above, with the rump barely contrasting with the remainder of the upperparts, the *white primary patch is minute or barely visible*. Non-br ♂ is like ♀. **HH** the only record is of one collected at Kakamega Forest, WKe, in Dec 1965. **Vo** not recorded in the region, but on passage elsewhere reported as a short metallic *twink.*

Plate 205

Semi-collared Flycatcher

1st year

♀

br ♂

1st year

♀

br ♂

Collared Flycatcher

1st year

1st year

br ♂

♀

Pied Flycatcher

GREY AND BROWN FLYCATCHERS

A widespread group of similar looking flycatchers: *Bradornis* are medium-sized and *Muscicapa* are small or medium-sized. Both are typical flycatchers, sitting upright for long periods and then making short flights, or dropping to ground to take food. *Myioparus* are more active, moving with a horizontal posture within the tree canopy. Take careful note of the presence or absence of crown or breast streaking, and consider voice and range. Sexes are alike. Immature *Bradornis* and *Muscicapa* are spotted and streaked above with tawny or buff, and mottled blackish below.

African Grey Flycatcher *Bradornis microrhynchus* 14cm, 5.5"

Very similar to Pale Flycatcher, but usually a little smaller and greyer: best identified by grey-brown plumage with *fine blackish streaks on the crown*, and by absence of breast streaking. Four similar races occur, but in the north smaller darker *neumanni* is sometimes considered a separate species (**Little Grey Flycatcher**). **HH** pairs are common and widespread in dry bush and open wooded acacia country from near sea-level to 2000m, and where the ranges overlap Pale occupies locally more verdant habitat. **Vo** song is rarely heard, a complex, variable and continuous warble with mostly harsh and scratchy notes. Commonly heard alarm call is a rather nasal scraping, a paired *shree-shree*.

Pale Flycatcher *Bradornis pallidus* 17cm, 6.5"

[Mouse-coloured Flycatcher]

Five races occur varying slightly in size and overall colour: all are best separated from African Grey Flycatcher by a uniform *brown crown without any streaking*. Western and southern races are generally larger and browner, while in dry scrub in NEKe *bafirawari* is paler greyish-brown; and coastal Ke and coastal NETz *subalaris* is smaller and more sandy-brown and may be a separate species. **HH** generally in lusher and more wooded habitats than African Grey from sea-level to 2000m (but see above). **Vo** call is a spitted note, extremely similar to Yellow-spotted Petronia, and often followed by a scratchy *shrehh*. Rarely heard song is a harsh rather unmusical warbled *treet-etreet-et-ti-cherr et-ti-cherr...*

Ashy Flycatcher *Muscicapa caerulescens* 14cm, 5.5"

[Blue-grey Flycatcher]

A slim ash-grey or blue-grey flycatcher with a narrow dark line through the eye, a short whitish line from base of bill to above the eye, and a small indistinct broken eye-ring. Greyish-white below, paler on the throat and belly. Very similar Lead-coloured Flycatcher (plate 207) has a horizontal posture and a white outer-tail. **HH** single birds or pairs are widespread, but only locally common in the canopy and middle levels of forest edge, clearings, and along well-wooded rivers from sea-level to 1800m. **Vo** call is a descending series of spaced, harsh but musical chips *trit tit tit it* which may break into a flourish. Song is a sweet, chat-like warble.

Spotted Flycatcher *Muscicapa striata* 14cm, 5.5"

A medium-sized slim grey-brown flycatcher which is paler below with a *streaked crown and breast* (sometimes not very distinct on the latter), and a black bill. Rear of crown seems peaked, and wing is pointed and long reaching half-way down the tail. **HH** common and widespread Palearctic passage visitor from late-Sep to Apr which may occur in any habitat from sea-level to 3000m. **Vo** song is not heard in the region, but still quite vocal: frequent call is a harsh *chick*.

Gambaga Flycatcher *Muscicapa gambagae* 13cm, 5"

Similar to Spotted Flycatcher, but the head appears rounded with a plain forecrown, an indistinctly streaked hindcrown, browner more diffuse streaking on the breast, and a *yellowish base to the lower mandible*. Closed wing does not extend beyond base of tail. **HH** solitary and very uncommon resident of dry bush and open wooded country below 1600m in NUg and NKe. Usually flicks its wings when landing after short flights. **Vo** call consists of a repeated series of paired and single clicks, like the snapping of a dry twig *t'lik t'lik...* unlike anything produced by Spotted Flycatcher.

Plate 206

African Grey Flycatcher

Ad

Imm

Pale Flycatcher

Imm

Ad

Spotted Flycatcher

Ashy Flycatcher

Imm

Ad

Ad

Imm

Gambaga Flycatcher

African Dusky Flycatcher *Muscicapa adusta* 10cm, 4"
A *small rather dumpy* brown flycatcher which is uniform dark brown above, variably paler brown or grey-brown below, with some showing a variable whitish throat and or belly. Five races occur and vary slightly in general colour, but one soon learns this common mainly highland species. **HH** very common and widespread in forest, riverine woodland and gardens from 900–3200m. Most numerous in high country, but down to 900m in WUg. Typical flycatcher in behaviour, making short flights and returning to a favourite exposed perch. **Vo** song is high-pitched, a continuous series of varied unmusical squeaks and hisses, sounding a little chat-like.

Lead-coloured Flycatcher *Myioparus plumbeus* 14cm, 5.5"
[Fan-tailed Flycatcher, Grey Tit-Flycatcher]
Blue or ashy-grey above with a blackish tail and *white outer-tail feathers*, greyish-white below. Two races occur: western nominate race is slightly darker than southern and eastern *orientalis*. General appearance is similar to Ashy Flycatcher (plate 206), but Lead-coloured moves with a horizontal posture, frequently waving and fanning its conspicuous tail. Imms are washed brownish above with small buffy spots on the wings. **HH** singles and pairs are widespread but local and generally uncommon in the canopy of a variety of woodland from sea-level to 2000m. **Vo** far-carrying song consists of long pure burry notes: coastal birds tend towards *wi-wi-oo*, the first two notes on the same higher tone. Inland birds start with a long note, followed by a higher one.

Grey-throated Flycatcher *Myioparus griseigularis* 14cm, 5.5"
[Grey-throated Tit-Flycatcher]
Behaves like a Lead-coloured Flycatcher, but overall colour is slate-grey (without any facial pattern), and the *tail is uniformly dark* (without any white edges). Imm has small tawny spots on the wings. **HH** pairs and singles inhabit primary forest and mature secondary growth in W and SUg, and extreme NWTz, from 700–1800m. **Vo** song is a set of four descending burry notes *oo-wi-wi-wooo* with a higher second note, and the last note drawn and more tremulous.

Swamp Flycatcher *Muscicapa aquatica* 14cm, 5.5"
Uniform dark earth-brown above and white below with a *broad brown breast band* and flanks: throat appears very white. Imm heavily spotted above with buff, breast band indistinct mottled brown and white. **HH** restricted to the west where pairs are common around swamps, papyrus beds and along lakeshores, from 700–1400m. **Vo** varies locally, but calls are high-pitched, chat-like, and given in snatches punctuated with short pauses: typically call a hissed *sisisi* at the end of each series, but a long, complex and sweet ramble with almost *Serinus*-like phrases is also given.

Böhm's Flycatcher *Muscicapa boehmi* 14cm, 5"
Warm brown above, finely streaked with black on the head and sides of neck, and *whitish below with small black arrow-shaped spots* on the throat, breast and flanks. Less obvious are pale lores, a narrow creamy eye-ring and black malar stripes. Imm is heavily spotted tawny above, with scaly black marks across the breast. **HH** in our area very uncommon and restricted to miombo woodland in the Tabora area of WTz, from 750–1750m. **Vo** a scratchy variable and repeated chat-like song with regular rather thrush-like phrases at the end of each series.

Plate 207

African Dusky Flycatcher

Imm

Ad

orientalis

Ad

Lead-coloured Flycatcher

Grey-throated Flycatcher

Ad

Böhm's Flycatcher

Imm

Ad

Ad

Imm

Swamp Flycatcher

WESTERN FLYCATCHERS
A varied group of grey and brown forest flycatchers restricted to the west. Sexes are alike.

Cassin's Grey Flycatcher *Muscicapa cassini* 13cm, 5"

Ad is a small grey flycatcher with a paler throat and belly, and *dark slaty-grey wings and tail*. Imm is browner above with tawny spots, and finely scalloped blackish below. Dusky-blue Flycatcher is darker with a more contrasting white throat and is found in the middle forest canopy not over water. **HH** single birds or pairs are uncommon and restricted to ponds and rivers in forest from 700–1800m, where they feed from over-hanging branches and rocks in water. **Vo** song is a long rambling, highly varied but overall scratchy warble, interspersed with high trills and squeaks that can be heard above the noise of turbulent water.

Dusky-blue Flycatcher *Muscicapa comitata* 11cm, 4.5"

Small dark slate-grey flycatcher with a short whitish line from the bill to just above the eye, a broad dark slate-grey breast band, and a dirty white belly: dark breast accentuates white throat. Bill and legs black. Imm is browner above, paler below. **HH** local within range but not uncommon from 700–1600m, preferring lower and middle canopies particularly along forest edge and in secondary growth. **Vo** calls a series of identical rather bulbul-like spitted notes and a hissed *swi chi-chi-chi...*

Chapin's Flycatcher *Muscicapa lendu* 13cm, 5"   ●●

A rather dingy flycatcher: uniform olive-brown above with an indistinct greyish loral line (hard to see on birds in the canopy), and pale greyish-brown below with a lighter throat and belly. African Dusky Flycatcher is smaller and Sooty Flycatcher is much darker. **HH** a rare and little known bird which inhabits forest tree canopies where it behaves like a typical flycatcher. Restricted to Kakamega and North Nandi forests, WKe, and the Bwindi-Impenetrable Forest, SWUg, from 1500–2150m. **Vo** rarely heard song is very lively, hurried and fairly sweet. Commonest call heard is a spitted *t't't't't't't'...* very similar to Little Grey Greenbul.

Yellow-footed Flycatcher *Muscicapa sethsmithi* 9cm, 3.5"

A very small slate-grey flycatcher with a whitish throat and belly, *yellow lower mandible and yellow feet*. From below the broad rich yellow bill is obvious. Imm spotted above and scaled below with rufous. **HH** usually solitary, sits quietly in the lower and middle levels of primary forest. In our area known only from Budongo Forest, WUg, where it is rather uncommon. **Vo** song is thin and high-pitched, the notes often being long, buzzy and insect-like.

Sooty Flycatcher *Muscicapa infuscata* 11cm, 4.5"

Often appears uniform all dark brown in the canopy, but in good light appears slightly paler below, mottled and streaked with both warm and sooty-brown. Imm has wings edged buffy, throat paler, and more streaking below. **HH** pairs or groups of 4–8 sit on the tops of tall dead trees, in or near to good forest from 900–1600m. Makes feeding sallies like a typical flycatcher, but in flight often resembles a martin. **Vo** song is a rarely heard, rather simple combination of high-pitched dry trills and his-ses, and the call is a hissed chipping given in a series or singly.

Forest Flycatcher *Fraseria ocreata* 14cm, 5.5"

A stocky species, shaped more like a puffback than a typical flycatcher. If seen well it is dark slate above and white below with distinct black crescent-shaped markings across the breast. Imm is browner above with light rufous spotting. **HH** small rather noisy flocks move through the middle and upper levels of good forest from 900–1600m. Frequently waves its tail. **Vo** unlike any other flycatcher, song is low and harsh and can easily be overlooked (since it is amazingly similar to Velvet-mantled Drongo which has more high-pitched squeaky notes in the song).

Plate 208

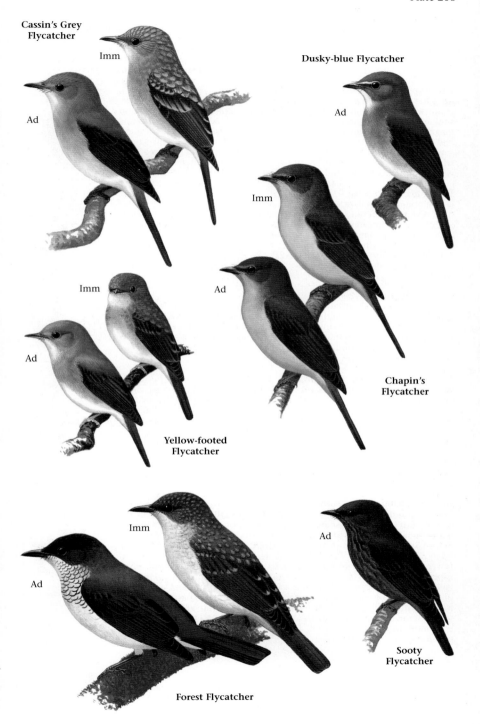

Cassin's Grey Flycatcher

Imm

Ad

Dusky-blue Flycatcher

Ad

Imm

Ad

Chapin's Flycatcher

Imm

Ad

Yellow-footed Flycatcher

Imm

Ad

Ad

Sooty Flycatcher

Forest Flycatcher

BATISES

Small neat and boldly patterned black, white and grey birds with breast bands: black on males and brown on females (except two). Many have yellow eyes. Usually found in pairs. Several are confusingly similar (and also resemble some wattle-eyes on plate 211). Colour of crown, extent of supercilium, throat and breast markings, voice and range all aid identification. Immatures are similar to females with buffy washed wing-stripes and tawny tips to the upperparts.

Chin-spot Batis *Batis molitor* 10cm, 4"

Ad ♂ has a grey crown and small white nuchal spot, a narrow white supercilium is usually prominent (narrower in similar ♂ Pale Batis). Ad ♀ has a *sharply defined dark chestnut breast band and throat spot* (paler tawny and not so defined in ♀ Pale). **HH** most common and widespread batis: pairs inhabit a wide variety of woodland, thicket and gardens from 500–3000m. **Vo** commonest song is two well spaced pure whistles *pii... poo*, the second note two tones lower. ♀ often calls in duet with snappy nasal notes and wing burring.

Pale Batis *Batis soror* 10cm, 4"

[Mozambique Batis, East Coast Batis]
Ad ♂ is very similar to Chin-spot Batis, but with a narrower breast band and slightly paler appearance overall. Ad ♀ differs in having the throat and breast band paler tawny and not so sharply defined. **HH** pairs are local to *Brachystegia* and other woodland, mainly in the coastal lowlands but up to 1000m in the East Usambara Mts, NETz. **Vo** ♂ calls a simple well-spaced piping of pure notes *pyi-pyi-pyi-pyi...*, often accompanied by the slightly nasal ♀.

Pygmy Batis *Batis perkeo* 9cm, 3.5"

A small and rather short-tailed batis: ad ♂ has a grey crown and *only a short white supraloral stripe* (sometimes hard to see in the field). Ad ♀ has a similar supraloral, a rufous-tawny breast band, and a white (or very faint buff) throat. **HH** locally common in semi-arid acacia bush country below 1200m. **Vo** song is a loud high pure piping of identical notes *hi...hi...hi...* which can recall Desert Cisticola.

Grey-headed Batis *Batis orientalis* 10cm, 4"

Ad ♂ is very similar to Black-headed Batis, but differs in having a grey crown and slightly broader breast band. From smaller Pygmy Batis by long narrow white supercilium extending back almost to the white nuchal spot. Ad ♀ has similar grey crown and long white supercilium, but the breast band is fairly broad and chestnut. **HH** owing to confusion with 'grey-crowned' Black-headed Batis the status in our area is unknown. Considered rare, it has been collected in bush country at 1200m, at Mt Moroto, Ug and in Moyale, Ke. **Vo** song is a descending series of four notes, unlike any other batis in region. ♀ often duets with accompanying short whipcrack upslurs.

Black-headed Batis *Batis minor* 10cm, 4"

Two races occur in our region: *erlangeri* in the west and *suahelicus* in the east. Crown colour is variable, usually blackish, but may be greyer (particularly on eastern birds which can then be mistaken for Grey-headed Batis). Black-crowned birds are distinctive, but greyer-crowned birds cannot be safely identified. In ad ♀ *suahelicus* the dark chestnut breast band is narrower than on ♀ Grey-headed, but both species have long narrow white superciliary stripes. **HH** ranges from sea-level to 1600m: race *erlangeri* is widespread and locally common in a variety of woodland and open bush in the west, while *suahelicus* is generally uncommon in coastal scrub and woodlands entering drier bush country further inland. **Vo** varies locally, song a series of pure pipes on an identical note *hi-hi-hi-...* at intervals of a little more than one per second. This is sometimes followed by a series of peculiar paired nasal downslurs.

Plate 209

Chin-spot Batis

Imm

♀

♂

Pale Batis

♀

♂

Pygmy Batis

♂

♀

♀

Grey-headed Batis

♂

♀

♂

Black-headed Batis

erlangeri

Forest Batis *Batis mixta* 10cm, 4"
[Short-tailed Batis]
A short-tailed, red-eyed batis with two races occurring in our area: ad ♂♂ are similar with red or orange eyes and a broad breast band: in coastal Ke race *ultima* has an indistinct white supercilium, while elsewhere the nominate has none. Ad ♀ *ultima* has a bold white supercilium and a pale cinnamon throat and upper breast; while ad ♀ nominate is darker and brown-eyed, with a short indistinct supercilium and a rich chestnut throat and breast. ♀♀ of both races have much rufous in the wing. **HH** in Ke pairs are shy (but not uncommon) in the lower stratum of thick coastal forest, while in Tz they inhabit the middle and high canopy of forest from 300–2300m. **Vo** significant local variation: commonest call of nominate is a slow monotone piping at mid-range, but *ultima* has a much lower toned piping, and some regular raspy nasal notes.

Cape Batis *Batis capensis* 10cm, 4"
In our area the race *reichenowi* occurs: it has been lumped with both Forest and Cape batises, or given specific status (**Reichenow's Batis**). Ad ♂ differs from Forest in having a narrower black breast band. Ad ♀ has a rufous-chestnut breast band merging with rufous and grey flanks: throat is washed rufous in the centre. **HH** pairs are not uncommon in the Mikindani and Lindi areas of SETz. **Vo** unknown.

Rwenzori Batis *Batis diops* 9cm, 3.5"
Similar to Ituri Batis but is larger and inhabits undergrowth at higher altitudes. Very broad black breast band and two small white spots on forecrown (like headlights) are distinctive. Sexes differ only in eye colour: yellow in ♂, orange or red in ♀. **HH** an Albertine Rift endemic: locally common in forest from 1600–2600m with a preference for undergrowth and middle level tangles. **Vo** ♂ song is a regular mid-range mournful piping on the same note *hee-hee-hee...* and the ♀ often accompanies with quick rasps.

Ituri Batis *Batis ituriensis* 8cm, 3"
Small, rare batis of forest canopy: sexes similar with black breast bands and two white supraloral spots. Similar Rwenzori Batis is larger and occurs in the undergrowth. **HH** very rare in our area and only known from Budongo and Semliki forests, WUg, where it occurs in the middle and high canopy. **Vo** song is more complex than most batises a series of short rhythmical rasps commences slowly and then speeds up, ending in 5–8 rapid, piercing high-pitched pipes on one note *trrt trrt trrt... hihihihihihi pu pu...*

African Shrike-flycatcher *Megabias flammulatus* 15cm, 6"
Ad ♂ is a striking black and white bird with red or orange-red eyes. Perches upright and gently waves its tail from side to side: similar puffbacks have white or grey on the wings and a horizontal posture. Ad ♀ is brown above washed rufous on the rump and vent, amd broadly streaked with dark brown below. Imm is like a dull ♀. **HH** pairs are rather localised and generally uncommon in the canopy of both primary forest and tall secondary growth from 700–2150m. **Vo** usual song consists of cheerful scratchy rhythmical rising or falling slurs, often given in triplets or pairs *chrerleet chrerleet*. Contact and flight-call is a repeated very high-pitched *sit-sit-sit...*

Black-and-white Shrike-flycatcher *Bias musicus* 13cm, 5"
[Vanga Flycatcher]
Ad ♂ is a stocky, rather short-tailed black and white bird with a crested head and conspicuous creamy-yellow eyes. In flight reveals large white patches in the wings. Ad ♀ is rufous above with a blackish-brown head, and whitish washed pale rufous below. Imm is like ♀ with brown mottling across the breast. **HH** singles and pairs inhabit forest from sea-level to 1500m including degraded areas, being most frequent in the open higher canopy. Locally common in parts of Ug and Tz, but inexplicably rare elsewhere. Conspicuous during slow circular display flights. **Vo** calls are explosive, loud and strident: in the east they are usually a simple see-sawing *pit-chew pit-chew pit-chew...*, but in the west they are more complex and include rising–falling series of spitted individual notes.

Plate 210

Forest Batis

♀

♂

ultima

Cape Batis

♀

♂

♂

Ituri Batis

♂

Rwenzori Batis

♀

♀

♂

African Shrike-flycatcher

Black-and-white Shrike-flycatcher

WATTLE-EYES

Two distinct genera of wattle-eyes occur: *Platysteira* are medium-sized, flycatcher-like and resemble batises, while *Dyaphorophyia* are much smaller, dumpy, and short-tailed. All have broad strong bills and conspicuous eye-wattles, several are named after the female plumage. Found in pairs, family groups, or with mixed-species flocks, usually in forest.

Brown-throated Wattle-eye *Platysteira cyanea* 13cm, 5"

[Common Wattle-eye]
Ad has a *bright red wattle above the eye and a white wing bar*. ♂ has a white throat and black breast band reminiscent of batises, while ♀ is greyer above with a dark chestnut-brown throat and upper breast. Imm is brownish-grey above with tawny-buff wing bar, throat and breast. **HH** common and widespread in the middle stratum and canopy of thick bush, woodlands and forest edge from 600–2200m. **Vo** a unique syncaphonic sound, usually three minor key descending notes precedes a series of up to five descending minor key notes. Some of the notes are burry and scratchy. Pair may duet, the ♀ giving a scratchier accompaniment.

Black-throated Wattle-eye *Platysteira peltata* 13cm, 5"

[Wattle-eyed Flycatcher]
Ad is similar to Common Wattle-eye with bright red wattles above the eye, but has *no white in the wing*. ♂ has a white throat and narrow black breast band. ♀ has the throat and breast black. Imm is browner above with tawny edges to the wings, and a buffy wash to the throat. **HH** widespread, but patchily distributed and not numerous in a wide variety of forest and woodland from sea-level to 3000m. **Vo** some variation, song is a monotonous repeated series of rhythmic scratchy notes followed by a nasal buzzy see-sawing *ch'ch'ch'ch'... in-cherin-cherin-cherin-cherinch...*, often in duet.

Chestnut Wattle-eye *Dyaphorophyia castanea* 10cm, 4"

A dumpy sexually dimorphic wattle-eye with a very short tail and purplish eye wattles (which can be difficult to see in the field). ♂ is black and white, with a broad black breast band. ♀ is distinctive, being bright chestnut with a grey crown and a white lower breast and belly. Imm is similar to ♀, but with grey and pale-chestnut mottling across the breast. **HH** unobtrusive quiet little birds of tall undergrowth and middle levels of forests from 700–1800m. **Vo** very wide vocabulary, all calls consist of identical repeated notes: can be a pinched *pee-pee-pee...*, a strange note like a distant whiplash, or a metallic tinkerbird-like *tonk-tonk-tonk...*

Jameson's Wattle-eye *Dyaphorophyia jamesoni* 9cm, 3.5"

A tiny wattle-eye, which appears black and white with *huge turquoise eye wattles*. Chestnut patch on side of neck and dark green gloss to upperparts visible in good light. Sexes are similar but ♀ is greyer above. Imm is similar to ♀, but with a pale chestnut throat. **HH** not uncommon in western forests from 700–2300m, but are always difficult to observe in the dense undergrowth. **Vo** varies locally but common call is an extremely high-pitched and piercing *pi-pi piii* often accompanied with loud wing-rattling.

Yellow-bellied Wattle-eye *Dyaphorophyia concreta* 9cm, 3.5"

Ad ♂ is dull olive-green above and bright yellow below, with *huge apple-green eye wattles*. Ad ♀ is similar, but more grey-green above with a strong wash of *orange-chestnut across the throat and upper breast*. Imm is like a pale ♂, washed grey above, with buffy tips to some wing-coverts and a greyish eye wattle. Distinctive race *kungwensis* in WTz is slate-grey above and pale yellow below with a bluish eye wattle. **HH** shy and uncommon in dense tangled vines and undergrowth in primary forest from 700–2500m. **Vo** usual call is of a very rhythmical series repeated without variation, with three higher identical notes, two descending notes, and terminating with a rising whiplash *wi-pipi wi wu kwip!*

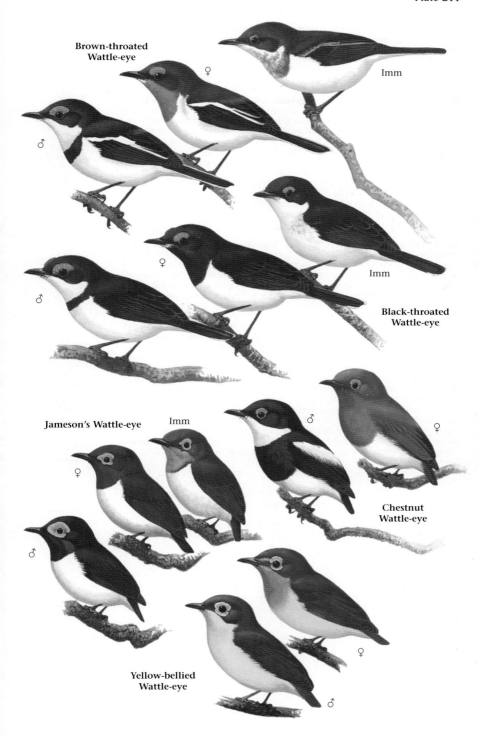

Plate 211

Brown-throated Wattle-eye

♀

Imm

♂

♀

♂

Imm

Black-throated Wattle-eye

Jameson's Wattle-eye

Imm

♂

♀

Chestnut Wattle-eye

♀

♂

♀

Yellow-bellied Wattle-eye

♂

PARADISE-FLYCATCHERS

The paradise-flycatchers are two distinctive monarchs with long rufous or white tails. Where they occur together Red-bellied is in the forest interior and African occupies the forest edge. In some areas of EUg and WKe hybrids are known.

African Paradise-flycatcher   *Terpsiphone viridis*   ♂ 36cm, 14" (with centre tail)

Highly variable with two distinct colour morphs, white and rufous, and many variations (as well as hybrids with Red-bellied Paradise-flycatcher in some areas of overlap). Of the six races occurring, a typical rufous ad ♂ has a slightly crested black or blue-black head merging into *grey underparts*, while the mantle, wings and tail are chestnut with very long central tail feathers. Typical white morph ♂ has the mantle, wings and tail white instead of chestnut. Rufous birds with partially white wings and tails are also common. Ad ♀ and imms of both sexes, are like the rufous ♂, but with shorter tails. **HH** single birds or pairs are common and widespread in forest, open woodland, gardens and bush from sea-level to 2500m. White birds are more common in dry country. **Vo** song is a loud, scratchy, nasal and cheerful warbling which sometimes breaks into a rhythmical *pi-pi-pi-pi pi-pi-pi-pi...pi-pi,* falling very slightly in tone towards the end. Common call is an abrupt and rather irritated two note *zwheet-zwhat.*

Red-bellied Paradise-flycatcher   *Terpsiphone rufiventer*   ♂ 21cm, 8" (without centre tail)

Ad ♂ has a black head (usually without a crest), *bright orange-rufous underparts,* and an orange-rufous mantle, wings and tail: length of centre-tail feathers variable. Ad ♀ is similar, but with a grey throat. Imm is like a dull ♀. Hybrids with African Paradise-flycatcher are also variable, but typically have a mixture of rufous and grey below. **HH** single birds or pairs are common in the middle levels of forest interiors from 700–1800m, often with mixed-species flocks. **Vo** call lacks the scratchy warblings of African Paradise-flycatcher: it has a rather loud nasal rising slur and then *si-si-si si-si...* notes, with a whistling-through-the-teeth quality.

Silverbird   *Empidornis semipartitus*   18cm, 7"

A distinctive flycatcher which is silvery-grey above and rufous-orange below. Sexes are alike, but imm is heavily spotted above with creamy-buff and black, and mottled and patched buff, brown and orange below. **HH** pairs or single birds are locally common in wooded acacia and bushed grassland and at the edges of cultivation from 400–2300m. Sits out in the open and drops to feed on the ground. **Vo** sings infrequently, but it is the sweetest of the flycatchers: song consists of random short phrases with a thrush-like pattern but chat-like delivery *swi-sisi sir wi-wir...*

Plate 212

**African
Paradise-flycatcher**

♀

♂

**Red-bellied
Paradise-flycatcher**

♂

Imm

Silverbird

Ad

CRESTED-FLYCATCHERS

Crested-flycatchers are dark grey or black and white monarchs with long or short crests that may be erected when excited. All are restless and frequently fan their tails. Solitary or in pairs, they often join mixed-species flocks.

Blue-mantled Crested-flycatcher *Trochocercus cyanomelas* 13cm, 5"
[Blue-mantled Flycatcher]

A black and white crested-flycatcher with white in the wings and a plain dark tail: ad ♂ has a long pointed crest, glossy blue-black head and upper breast, dark blue-grey mantle, and a white lower breast to vent. In eastern race *bivittatus* ♂ has a prominent white wing patch, while western *vivax* has two narrow pale grey wing bars. ♀♀ of both races are grey above, with mottled grey and white breasts and two narrow whitish wing bars. Imms are like ♀♀, but have buffy edges to the wing-coverts. **HH** pairs are locally common in the undergrowth and denser middle levels of forest from sea-level to 2300m. **Vo** vocal and noisy: usual call is several rising nasal and scratchy slurs (similar to African Paradise-flycatcher), often followed by a run of rapid, pure and rather hollow bell-like notes *wiu-pupupupupupupu....*

Blue-headed Crested-flycatcher *Trochocercus nitens* 13cm, 5"

Ad ♂ similar to Blue-mantled Crested-flycatcher, but entirely glossy blue-black above *with no white in wings, and a grey breast to vent*. Ad ♀ has top of the head and crest glossed dark green, and remainder of the upperparts dark slate-grey: entirely pale-grey below. Imm is similar to ♀ but washed brownish and without gloss to crown. **HH** pairs are uncommon and localised residents of forest from 700–900m, active in all canopy levels, but particularly fond of thick tangled vines. **Vo** very similar to Blue-mantled Crested-flycatcher, but lacks the introductory upslur, is less scratchy, more mellow and the bell notes are also more hollow.

White-tailed Crested-flycatcher *Trochocercus albonotatus* 13cm, 5"
[African White-tailed Flycatcher]

Ad ♂ is a blackish crested-flycatcher (greyer on back) with a white belly, and very conspicuous *broad white tips to all except central tail feathers* (obvious as it frequently jerks and fans its tail). Ad ♀ and imm are similar, but duller slate-grey. **HH** pairs are common in all levels of highland forest (mainly up to 2700m, but down to 900m in Tz). **Vo** complex warbling song consists of deliberate pure notes that rise and fall and incorporate phrases of other crested-flycatchers, and mimicry of other birds.

White-bellied Crested-flycatcher *Trochocercus albiventris* 11cm, 4.5"

Ad ♂ is dark slate-grey with a whitish belly. Sexes are similar, but ad ♀ is duller. Imm is like ♀, but washed brown on the wings. Very similar Dusky Crested-flycatcher occurs at lower altitudes and lacks the white belly. **HH** pairs are locally common within a restricted range, inhabiting the understorey and middle levels of highland forest from 1500–2400m. **Vo** similar to White-tailed Crested-flycatcher, but lacks the sweet tones and is much slower and more deliberate.

Dusky Crested-flycatcher *Trochocercus nigromitratus* 11cm, 4.5"

Ad ♂ is very similar to White-bellied Crested-flycatcher, but entirely dark slate-grey with a slightly blacker head, wings and tail, and *no white on the belly*. Sexes similar, but ad ♀ is duller. Imm is similar to ♀, but browner. **HH** shy but locally common in dense forest undergrowth from 700–2150m, where its quiet and retiring nature make it difficult to detect. **Vo** an infrequent singer, most calls are harsh and scratchy, but is also an accomplished mimic incorporating many species into a long rambling refrain.

Plate 213

**Blue-mantled
Crested-flycatcher**

♂

♀

Imm

bivittatus

**Blue-headed
Crested-flycatcher**

♂

♀

**White-tailed
Crested-flycatcher**

♂

**White-bellied Crested-
flycatcher**

♂

♂

Dusky Crested-flycatcher

BLUE-FLYCATCHERS

Blue monarchs with slightly crested heads that habitually fan their tails. Active little birds, rushing around in the canopy and middle levels searching for food. Usually solitary or in pairs. Sexes are alike.

African Blue-flycatcher *Elminia longicauda* 14cm, 5.5"
A slim caerulean blue-flycatcher with a narrow black line from bill to eye, whitish underparts with a pale blue wash across the breast, and a *plain blue graduated tail*. Imm is greyer than ad with buffy fringes to the upperparts. **HH** singles and pairs are common in the west in riverine woodland, forest, gardens and cultivation from 800–2400m. **Vo** long and complex warble of sweet and harsh, and sometimes very metallic chits and tinks and canary-like flourishes. A metallic *chink* is also used as a contact and alarm call.

White-tailed Blue-flycatcher *Elminia albicauda* 14cm, 5.5"
Very similar to African Blue-flycatcher, but more grey-blue above, and washed greyish across the breast: fanned tail shows obvious *white outer-tail feathers*. Imm is greyer than ad. **HH** behaves like African Blue-flycatcher, but is generally more restricted to forest or forest edge, and usually at higher altitudes (from 1600–2500m, but has occurred down to 1200m). **Vo** calls are drier, flatter and lack the metallic quality of African Blue-flycatcher. Canary-like flourishes are also flatter and somewhat raspier.

ERYTHROCERCUS FLYCATCHERS

Three very small monarchs with a rather warbler-like appearance. Occurring in pairs and small groups, they are lively, restless birds, constantly on the move. Sexes alike.

Little Yellow Flycatcher *Erythrocercus holochlorus* 9cm, 3.5"
Plain yellowish-olive above with a quite conspicuous dark eye (narrowly ringed with yellow), rather obvious pink lower mandible, and bright yellow underparts. Imm is very similar, but slightly paler. **HH** pairs or small flocks are common within coastal and eastern lowland forests from sea-level to 1000m, usually in the high and middle canopy, often in mixed-species flocks. **Vo** despite its diminutive size, a noisy species, with a complex and pretty chittering song which breaks into a silvery descending series of clear notes.

Chestnut-capped Flycatcher *Erythrocercus mccallii* 9cm, 3.5"
A *conspicuous streaked chestnut cap and tail* contrast with an olive-brown back and wings. Throat and upper breast are tawny-brown, but otherwise whitish below. Imm is generally similar but duller and lacks the bright chestnut forecrown. **HH** in our area only known from 1100m in Budongo Forest, WUg, where small flocks are fairly common. **Vo** a noisy species, with feeding parties constantly uttering a formless chatter interspersed with piercing squeaks.

Livingstone's Flycatcher *Erythrocercus livingstonei* 10cm, 4"
Similar to Little Yellow Flycatcher, but the *tawny-rufous tail with small black sub-terminal spots* to all but the outermost feathers is distinctive. **HH** rather local, inhabiting riverine forest and moist thickets from sea-level to 700m in SETz. **Vo** song is similar to Little Yellow Flycatcher, but there is no overlap, and it is a sweeter rising and descending *switterweedlewii*, which lacks the chittering.

Plate 214

African Blue-flycatcher

Imm

Ad

Ad

White-tailed Blue-flycatcher

Little Yellow Flycatcher

Ad

Chestnut-capped Flycatcher

Livingstone's Flycatcher

ILLADOPSES

Shy and secretive dull brown and grey babblers inhabiting leaf litter and forest undergrowth. Similar looking species are difficult to observe in the forest gloom, but voice and colour of the underparts aid identification. Sexes alike, immatures are similar to adults but with brighter upperparts.

Scaly-breasted Illadopsis *Illadopsis albipectus* 14cm, 5.5"

Underparts pale olive-brown with very narrow dark edges to the breast feathers producing (on well-marked birds) a scaly lace-like pattern. The breast markings are often difficult to see and on some individuals are not present at all: throat and belly pale grey, legs pale pinkish. **HH** solitary birds or pairs are common in the interior of good forest with ample leaf litte from 700–2100m. **Vo** distinctive song consists of a subdued chattering tⁱ it breaks into two or three slowly delivered rising notes *tiu teu tii*.

Mountain Illadopsis *Illadopsis pyrrhoptera* 13cm, 5"

Grey breast contrasts with a dirty white throat and the brown flanks and vent. **HH** common in highland forest undergrowth (including remnant patches), mainly from 1500–2800m but down to 1300m in WTz. Often in groups of 4–6, but also in pairs. Likes dense leafy undergrowth and stays within 1.5m of the ground, only occasionally venturing higher into vine tangles. **Vo** calls are similar to Brown Illadopsis but higher pitched, and the song tends to be a more rambling *trrtrrtrr...ti-ti tiyu*.

Brown Illadopsis *Illadopsis fulvescens* 13cm, 5"

Underparts are all tawny-brown except for the white throat: legs are purplish-grey. **HH** pairs and small groups are common in forest undergrowth from 700–1800m. **Vo** foraging groups utter a musical chittering, while ♂ occasionally calls a rhythmic descending *prrrrrp wiwi wiwi.....wiyu*, with a brief pause before the final two nasal notes. Similar to Pale-breasted Illadopsis but quite pure, not pinched.

Pale-breasted Illadopsis *Illadopsis rufipennis* 14cm, 5.5"

Three races occur: in the west nominate birds are pale olive-brown across the breast, flanks and vent, the throat and belly are whitish, and the legs grey or purplish-brown. In SKe and NETz the race *distans* has the breast pale grey contrasting slightly with the olive-brown flanks and vent, while in the Pugu Hills, Tz, *puguensis* is similar, but paler above. The Tz races may be specifically distinct. **HH** pairs or small groups are shy, generally uncommon and patchily distributed in dense forest undergrowth and leaf litter, from near sea-level to 1700m. **Vo** song of the nominate race is similar to Brown Illadopsis but the notes are generally higher pitched and pinched, not clear. While one bird (or the group) chatters the ♂ calls a descending series with a hiatus before the final notes *titititi titityu*. Race *distans* is quite different, the ♂ calls a rising and falling explosive nasal *tyah tya!* The voice of *puguensis* is not known.

Puvel's Illadopsis *Illadopsis puveli* 13cm, 5"

White throat and belly contrast with the buffy-brown breast and flanks. **HH** in our area only known from the northern part of Budongo Forest, WUg at 1100m. Occurs in small groups feeding on the ground. **Vo** song is a musical series of explosive hollow-sounding rising and falling notes notes *tink-tink ching ching chi chi ching*, there is some variation in the speed and number of notes but the pattern is always similar.

Grey-chested Illadopsis *Kakamega poliothorax* 17cm, 6.5"

A rather thrush-like babbler with bright rufous upperparts, medium grey underparts and a whitish throat. **HH** locally common, but shy and solitary in thick forest undergrowth from 1550–2650m (often near streams). **Vo** song is varied but typically makes an attractive rising and falling fluty *t'tyew-t-t'chloo*, and also a nasal *shrank-shrank* alarm call.

African Hill-Babbler *Pseudoalcippe abyssinica* 13cm, 5"

[Abyssinian Hill-Babbler, Rwenzori Hill-Babbler]
Three distinct races occur. Widespread nominate race has a grey head and breast, in ETz *stierlingi* has a black face with heavy black streaks on the throat, and in WUg, Rw and Bu the race *atriceps* (**Rwenzori Hill-Babbler**) has a black head. **HH** pairs and single birds are common in highland forest inhabiting tangled vines and undergrowth from 1500–3000m. **Vo** sings a variety of repeated thrush-like rich fluty warbles, but the notes are often slurred together.

Plate 215

Mountain
Illadopsis

Scaly-breasted
Illadopsis

Pale-breasted
Illadopsis

Brown
Illadopsis

nominate

Puvel's Illadopsis

Grey-chested
Illadopsis

atriceps

nominate

African Hill-Babbler

CHATTERERS AND BABBLERS

Chatterers and babblers typically occur in groups of 4–10 birds, moving together between patches of cover, and also feeding in open ground. Slim and unobtrusive chatterers make frequent contact with quiet high-pitched calls. The bulkier babblers are noisy birds, regularly calling a harsh loud babbling. Underpart pattern, eye colour and range aid identification. Sexes alike. Immatures are similar to adults but dark-eyed.

Rufous Chatterer *Turdoides rubiginosus* 19cm, 7.5″

Uniform brown above with very fine crown streaks, pale-yellow eyes, a pale-yellow or brownish bill, and bright russet-brown underparts. **HH** common and widespread in a variety of dry bushed habitats and nearby riverine vegetation from sea-level to 2000m. **Vo** chatterer calls are very unlike babblers, being quieter and higher-pitched: group members keep in contact with excited piercing squeaks. Song is similar, but many of the notes are downslurred, louder and purer with irregular chittering, and interspersed with a louder downslurred *seeeu*.

Scaly Chatterer *Turdoides aylmeri* 22cm, 8.5″

Dull brown above, with a small mask of grey skin around a yellowish eye, and a rather long and decurved pale horn bill. Throat and breast feathers have dark centres and pale fringes giving a scaly appearance. **HH** small groups are local and uncommon in thick bush country, particularly *Commiphora*, from sea-level to 1500m, usually in drier situations than Rufous Chatterer. **Vo** a high-pitched metallic, scraping and ratchet-like noise is the usual call, often given excitably by all members of the group.

Arrow-marked Babbler *Turdoides jardineii* 22cm, 8.5″

Typical grey-brown babbler with yellow eyes (in the west and north) or orange-red (more southerly). Mostly grey-brown below, *including lores and chin*, with small pointed arrow-shaped tips to feathers of the throat and breast. **HH** common within range, but with a patchy distribution, inhabiting a variety of bushed and wooded country with undergrowth from sea-level to 2200m. **Vo** call varies locally: it starts almost mechanically with alternated nasal notes, leading to all members calling a raucous crackling which develops into long nasal whining downslurs *tyah tyah tyah...*

Brown Babbler *Turdoides plebejus* 22cm, 8.5″

Very similar to Arrow-marked Babbler with yellow eyes, but *lores and chin whitish*. Pale tips to feathers of throat and breast similar to Arrow-marked, but not so pointed. **HH** groups are common in bushed and wooded country from 600–2000m, with a range to the north of Arrow-marked Babbler. **Vo** a very loud, raucous wooden-sounding chatter breaks into a scolding *k-tchah k-tchah k-tchah...*

Black-lored Babbler *Turdoides sharpei* 22cm, 8.5″

[Sharpe's Babbler]
A distinctive babbler with *white eyes and black lores*. Two races occur: widespread nominate has pale fringes to the feathers of the throat, but around Nanyuki in Ke race *vepres* is darker brown with a pure white throat (which may extend to the belly as a mixture of white and brown streaks on some birds). **HH** groups are common in a wide range of more open bushed and wooded country from 1000–2200m. **Vo** calls are higher pitched than most typical babblers with a slightly insane and hilarious laughing quality (race *vepres* sounds much the same).

Hartlaub's Babbler *Turdoides hartlaubii* 22cm, 8.5″

Easily identified by a *greyish-white rump* which contrasts with a dark grey-brown mantle and tail. Lightly scaled head markings are broader and bolder on the throat and breast and very heavy on the flanks: eyes red. **HH** groups occur in thickets and other lush vegetation from 775–2200m on the Ufipa Plateau, SWTz, and the northern shores of Lake Tanganyika in Tz and Bu. **Vo** similar to Black-lored Babbler, but slightly higher pitched with a more pinched nasal quality.

Plate 216

Rufous Chatterer

Scaly Chatterer

Arrow-marked Babbler

Brown Babbler

nominate

Black-lored Babbler

vepres

Hartlaub's
Babbler

Scaly Babbler *Turdoides squamulatus* 22cm, 8.5″

Dark grey-brown or olive-brown babbler, with very dark ear-coverts, and pale fringes to the feathers of crown, throat and breast giving a scaly appearance: eyes orange or, in extreme NEKe, creamy-white. Babblers presumed to be this species, but with variable white patches on their heads have been recorded around Rhamu, NEKe. **HH** groups are shy, keeping to coastal bush and other thick cover within its restricted range. **Vo** one of the most grating and toneless calls of any passerine, with a typical babbler pattern. Group keeps up continuous rasping noise that has a peculiar undulating quality. Single call is a *ti-yor ti-yor ti-yor...*

Dusky Babbler *Turdoides tenebrosus* 22cm, 8.5″

A dark babbler with black lores and pale yellow or whitish eyes, crown slightly paler than remainder of upperparts; chin whitish, throat to upper breast scaly, each feather with a dark centre and pale fringe, remainder of underparts plain dark brown. **HH** groups are rather shy and secretive, keeping to dense cover, often near water, from 600–1200m. **Vo** reported to call a hoarse *chow*, and a more nasal *what-cow...*

Northern Pied Babbler *Turdoides hypoleucus* 22cm, 8.5″

Two races occur: from CKe to NTz nominate is brown above with black lores and conspicuous white eyes, mostly white below with brown patches at sides of the breast and along flanks. Race *rufuensis* to the south is more grey-brown, with pale scaly fringes to the feathers of the crown. **HH** ·EA endemic: locally common in woodlands, acacia country, bush and gardens up to 1800m. **Vo** group members call single high-pitched explosive downslurs and unique long scolding nasal notes that lack the unpleasant churring of other babblers.

Hinde's Babbler *Turdoides hindei* 22cm, 8.5″ ● ●

Plumage is highly variable, but typically a very scaly looking red-eyed babbler with broad black and white fringes to the throat and breast feathers. Large areas of the plumage are often dark brown (or blackish) with smaller patches of both tawny-rufous and white. The rump, flanks and vent are frequently rufous-brown. **HH** localised and threatened Ke endemic: population is centred around Mt Kenya where it mainly survives in steep-sided valleys within cultivation from 1300–1500m. **Vo** call is similar to Scaly Babbler, a very harsh scolding chatter which breaks into a rapid downslurred *iyor-iyor-iyor...*

Capuchin Babbler *Phyllanthus atripennis* 19cm, 7.5″

Distinctive babbler with a pale yellow bill, blackish forecrown and lores, and a pale grey crown, nape and ear-coverts. Remainder of plumage is very dark chestnut-brown: eyes reddish-brown. Imm plumage is unknown. **HH** in our area restricted to the Semliki Valley, WUg from 700–900m, where it occurs in small groups in thick forest undergrowth. **Vo** nothing like a typical babbler chatter. Usual call is a clear, mournful, downslurred and thrush-like whistle *hiiiu* or *fweeu*, but it also has an explosive barbet-like *cht*, and a scolding *chrrrrrr*.

Red-collared Mountain-Babbler *Kupeornis rufocinctus* 19cm, 7.5″ ●

A distinctive tri-coloured babbler with conspicuous pale creamy eyes, a whitish bill, and a neat black cap that contrasts strongly with a cinnamon-rufous collar and breast band. Rump and vent also cinnamon-rufous, back, wings and tail blackish-brown. Imm is slightly duller with dark eyes. **HH** endemic to mountains along the Albertine Rift, and restricted, in our area, to forest above 1700m (mainly 2000–2700m) in Rw and NBu. Flocks actively forage over moss-covered branches in the middle storey and canopy of forest. **Vo** strange call is similar to a *Turdoides* babbler, but quieter with a rather rustling quality.

Plate 217

Scaly Babbler

Dusky Babbler

Northern Pied Babbler

nominate

rufuensis

Hinde's Babbler

Red-collared Mountain-Babbler

Capuchin Babbler

TITS

A well-known family, tits are very active birds working their way along branches, searching every cranny and often hanging upside down. Found in pairs and small flocks they frequently join mixed-species feeding flocks. Females and immatures duller than males, other differences in text.

White-bellied Tit *Parus albiventris* 14cm, 5.5"

Black head and breast contrast with the white lower breast and belly. Otherwise black above with white edges to wing-coverts, secondaries, tertials and outer-tail. **HH** common in a wide variety of habitats including forest edge, open woodlands and bush country from 900–3400m. **Vo** some variation, but most calls are a typically tit-like harsh, nasal and scolding *si-chah-chah-chah*, that may break into a scratchy medley.

Northern Grey Tit *Parus thruppi* 11cm, 4.5"

[Somali Tit]
Boldly marked black, white and grey tit, with a black cap, white cheeks and vertical black line down throat and breast. Differs from Miombo Grey Tit in having a *black cap encircling the white cheek patch*. **HH** locally common in a variety of dry bush country (particularly acacia) below 1600m in the north. **Vo** calls and scolds are similar to White-bellied Tit, but harsher with more a vibrating ratchet-like quality *chrrrt-chah, chrrt chah-chah*.

Miombo Grey Tit *Parus griseiventris* 11cm, 4.5"

[Northern Grey Tit in southern Africa]
Very similar to Northern Grey Tit, but the *white cheek patch joins with pale grey sides of the breast*, and is not encircled with black. Because it occurs in the northern part of southern Africa *griseiventris* is known as the Northern Grey Tit there. We prefer Miombo Grey Tit as it is restricted to *Brachystegia* or miombo woodland and is not the most northerly of the grey-coloured tits. **HH** in our area, it is locally common in the miombo woodlands of W and SWTz. **Vo** calls have a raspy quality, but contain lots of sweet notes, and are more musical than many other tits.

Dusky Tit *Parus funereus* 14cm, 5.5"

Ad ♂ is *all sooty-black* with red eyes, and the ad ♀ is slightly greyer. Imm is like ♀, but with small white tips to the wing-coverts and dark eyes. Typical tit-like behaviour helps identify this species from other black forest birds. **HH** locally common in the canopy of both primary and secondary forest from 900–2500m. **Vo** typical call is a musical *chi-chyu* with the last note down-slurred, but it also tends to babble on with a mixture of harsh tit-like notes, sweet whistles and slurs.

White-winged Tit *Parus leucomelas* 14cm, 5.5"

[White-winged Black Tit, Northern Black Tit]
Formerly considered conspecific with White-shouldered Tit and only reliably separated from it by having *dark eyes*. Imm is duller with a creamy-buff wing patch. **HH** appears to like open woodland and moist bush country below 2000m; it is locally common in SWUg and across south-central Tz, but its status is unclear elsewhere owing to confusion with White-shouldered Tit. **Vo** utters usual rasping calls, one of which sounds rather like Rattling Cisticola, but it also has sweet thrush-like phrases quite unlike other tits in the region (except White-shouldered Tit).

White-shouldered Tit *Parus guineensis* 14cm, 5.5"

Very similar to White-winged Tit, but ads have *yellow eyes*. Imm is duller with grey or brown eyes and thus similar to imm White-winged. **HH** appears to like open woodland and moist bush country and is locally common across NUg to WKe, but status is unclear elsewhere (see under White-winged Tit). **Vo** a rather un-tit-like attractive and varied song with both bunting and thrush-like qualities.

Plate 218

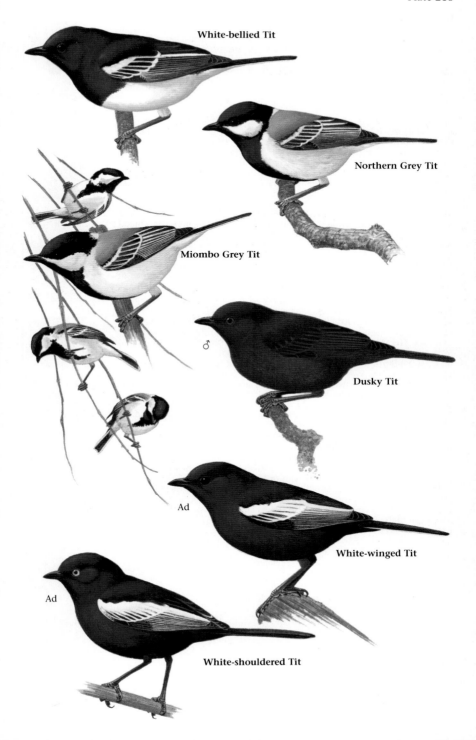

White-bellied Tit

Northern Grey Tit

Miombo Grey Tit

♂

Dusky Tit

Ad

White-winged Tit

Ad

White-shouldered Tit

Red-throated Tit *Parus fringillinus* 11cm, 4.5"

Face, nape, throat and upper breast are pale-rufous (so not very well named), contrasting with a slaty-grey crown and wings, the latter broadly edged in white. Imm is browner with a scaly rufous and grey crown. **HH** EA endemic: pairs and family parties are localised and generally not numerous residents of acacia woodland from 1000–2000m. **Vo** song contains sweet downslurs and rhythmical phrases, while the call is a rather harsh *chi-chr'chr'chr'chr'chr'chr* and *ti-tchah-tchah-tchah-tchah-tchah...*

Rufous-bellied Tit *Parus rufiventris* 13cm, 5"

Race *pallidiventris* (which is sometimes treated as a good species and called **Cinnamon-breasted Tit**) has a black head and throat, is greyer on the upper breast and *washed out pinkish-grey from the mid-breast to vent*. Grey above, with blackish wings and tail edged in white: eyes brown. Imm browner above and below. **HH** pairs and family groups are locally common residents of *Brachystegia* woodland in Tz and Bu. **Vo** song is a variety of harsh churs and rasps on different tones.

Stripe-breasted Tit *Parus fasciiventer* 11cm, 4.5" ●

A dark grey, black and white tit with black of the head extending as a broad vertical stripe down centre of breast. Grey and black above with white wing bars and white edges to the tail. Imm is browner, washed yellowish on the flanks. **HH** endemic to montane forests along the Albertine Rift from 1800–3400m, where it is common in the middle levels and canopy. **Vo** song consists of shorter churrs and a rhythmical *ch-ch ti-ti-ch-ch ti-ti-ch-ch ti-ti-ch-ch*; while the calls are obviously tit-like, but rather soft and muffled.

Spotted Creeper *Salpornis spilonotus* 15cm, 6"

A well-camouflaged mottled brown and white creeper with a decurved bill. Can be hard to see against lichen-covered branches and patchy wrinkled tree bark. **HH** solitary birds or pairs are common in *Brachystegia* woodland in the south and in large acacias and remnant woodland in the north, from 600–2300m. Birds are very active climbing up tree trunks or large limbs in the canopy, before swooping to the bottom of another tree and working upwards again. **Vo** frequently heard call is a high-pitched *si si si si...* while the song consists of different very high-pitched toneless and rhythmical slurs *si sisi siu siu seeu seeu*.

Tit-Hylia *Pholidornis rushiae* 8cm, 3"

A very small and distinctive tit-like bird with a tiny bill presently thought to be related to the penduline-tits: ad has *head and breast pale buff with heavy brown streaking, and the rump and lower breast to vent bright yellow*. Legs are bright orange. Imm is paler with less streaking on the head and breast. **HH** very uncommon in our area, and only known from Budongo, Mabira and Semliki forests in Ug. Small flocks are very active and tit-like, preferring the canopy of primary forest and secondary growth. **Vo** foraging groups maintain a continuous high-pitched chittering and spitting. Song is a series of high *si-si-si...* notes without pauses and with chittering and spitting interspersed.

Plate 219

Red-throated Tit

Ad

Rufous-bellied Tit

Ad

Stripe-breasted Tit

Ad

Spotted Creeper

Imm

Tit-Hylia

Ad

PENDULINE-TITS

Small active tit-like birds with tiny pointed bills, short tails and rather dull plumage. Solitary or in pairs, but also join mixed-species flocks. Sexes and immatures are alike.

African Penduline-Tit   *Anthoscopus caroli*   9cm, 3.5"

[Grey Penduline Tit]

Six races occur and can be assigned to four distinct groups: race *roccatii* (Ug, WKe, Rw, Bu and NWTz) has a yellowish forecrown, is olive above and pale yellow below; *pallescens* (WTz) and *rhodesiae* (SWTz) are similar, but whitish or buff on the belly; *robertsi* (coastal Ke and ETz) is greyish above and pale yellowish or buffy below; *sylviella* (CKe-NTz) and *sharpei* (SWKe-NWTz) are often considered a good species [**Buff-bellied Penduline-Tit** *Anthoscopus sylviella*] (encircled by dotted line on map). They have a buffy forecrown, are grey above and cinnamon-buff below, richer and darker in *sharpei*. **HH** localised and uncommon in a variety of open woodland from sea-level to 2200m. **Vo** typical call is a rapid high-pitched and squeaky *si-si-si-si...*, but buff-bellied races are slower and also call a rhythmical tit-like *ti-chi-wee ti-chi-wee ti-chi-wee...*

Mouse-coloured Penduline-Tit   *Anthoscopus musculus*   8cm, 3"

Similar to African Penduline-Tit, but grey-brown above and *very pale grey-brown below.* **HH** widespread but never numerous in dry bushland mainly to north and east of African Penduline-Tit from 400–1600m. **Vo** typically, call is a repeated *si si si si si si si si si*, and a more complex warbled series of high squeaky and spitted notes. **SS** imm Yellow-vented Eremomela.

WHITE-EYES

Active small birds usually found in flocks. The species and many races are confusing, but markings on the underparts, size of eye-ring, and range aid identification.

Montane White-eye   *Zosterops poliogaster*   11cm, 4.5"

Six races occur: race *kulalensis* (**Kulal White-eye** ●● on Mt Kulal, NKe) and *winifredae* (**South Pare White-eye** ●● in the South Pare Mts, NTz) are grey below with smallish eye-rings, ♂ *kulalensis* also has a yellowish ventral streak; *silvanus* (**Taita White-eye** ●● in the Taita Hills and Mt Kasigau, SEKe) is similar, but has a huge white eye-ring. The yellow-bellied races are: *kikuyuensis* (CKe) which has a yellow forecrown and a very large eye-ring; *mbuluensis* (NTz) is similar but the forecrown blends with the crown and the eye-ring is smaller; while *eurycricotus* (also in NTz) is green with a yellow throat and a large eye-ring. **HH** all occur in highland forest and forest edge, including isolated patches, gardens, and cultivation, from 1300–3400m. **Vo** calls a downslurred *seyuuu* and *piu,* while the song is a rising and falling series of slurred notes, with a rather mournful quality: race *sylvanus* has a more pinched sound.

Yellow White-eye   *Zosterops senegalensis*   11cm, 4.5"

Seven races occur: typical birds are greenish-yellow above and yellow below (sometimes greenish on sides of the breast and flanks), with a *narrow white eye-ring.* **HH** best identified by range, since it is the only white-eye in much of the west and south, occurring in a variety of habitats including forest, forest edge, gardens and cultivation. In Ke it is common in the west and in the highlands in the north. In SKe and NTz, where it overlaps with Abyssinian White-eye, it occurs at higher altitudes. Elsewhere in Tz it is common at both low and high altitudes south of the range of Montane White-eye. It can occur anywhere from near sea-level to 3400m. **Vo** an attractive songster, utters a series of typical white-eye slurry notes, but some have a rather burry quality.

Abyssinian White-eye   *Zosterops abyssinicus*   10cm, 4"

Very similar to the paler races of Yellow White-eye with clear *pale yellow underparts and a small eye-ring.* **HH** inhabits a variety of woodland and bush country from sea-level to 1800m, often in drier areas. **Vo** sings an excitable typical white-eye collection of squeaks and descending slurs put together in a random pattern, and call is a burry descending *seeu.*

Pemba White-eye   *Zosterops vaughani*   10cm, 4"   ●

A bright yellow white-eye with a narrow eye-ring and black lores. **HH** common endemic on Pemba Island, Tz. **Vo** song is a sweet refrain of varied warbled but slurred notes.

Plate 220

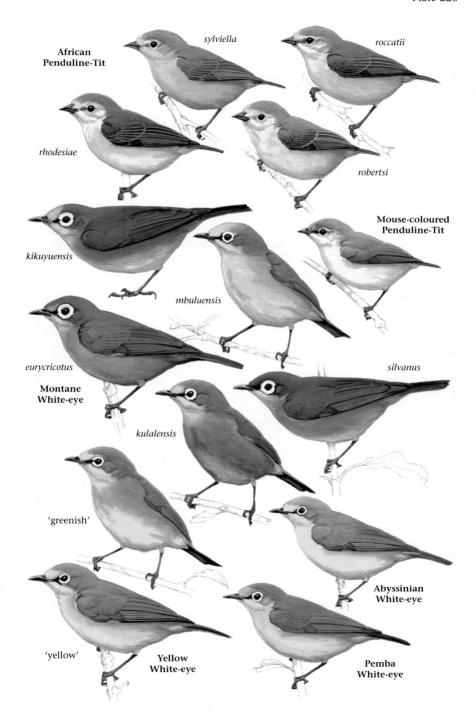

African
Penduline-Tit

sylviella

roccatii

rhodesiae

robertsi

kikuyuensis

Mouse-coloured
Penduline-Tit

mbuluensis

eurycricotus

silvanus

Montane
White-eye

kulalensis

'greenish'

Abyssinian
White-eye

'yellow'

Yellow
White-eye

Pemba
White-eye

SUNBIRDS

Males of many species are characterised by their iridescent plumages and decurved bills. Some have long central tail feathers. Many have brightly coloured pectoral tufts which are hidden apart from when used in display. Females and immatures are typically dull olive or greyish, but may have distinctive eye-stripes, breast streaking, or tail colour. Immature males often have dark throats. Constantly on the move, they feed on nectar and insects, and can hover briefly. Song is typically fast and musically complex: distinctive calls are useful for identification.

LONG-TAILED SUNBIRDS

Bronze Sunbird *Nectarinia kilimensis* ♂ 23cm, 9"; ♀ 12cm, 5"
Ad ♂ has head, back and breast predominantly *bronze-green*, but can appear blackish at first sight. No non-br plumage. Ad ♀ is dull olive-grey above with a long narrow pale supercilium, *washed yellowish below with darker streaking* and a whiter throat. Imm ♀ is similar but more mottled below. Imm ♂ is also similar but with a much darker throat. **HH** common in gardens, forest edge or open woodland from 1200–2800m (mainly above 1500m), where it often sings from tree tops. **Vo** usual call is a simple upslurred *tyuu*, but the song is one of the family's loudest and most complex: both sexes warble with an excitable rather harsh canary-like pattern that continues for long periods without pause.

Golden-winged Sunbird *Nectarinia reichenowi* ♂ 24cm, 9.5"; ♀ 13cm, 5"
Br ♂ is iridescent fiery-copper and bronze with *bright yellow edges to the wings and elongated tail*. Non-br ♂ is blacker without the fiery body plumage. Ad ♀ is dull dark olive above, mottled yellowish and olive below, *wings and tail edged bright yellow*. Imm ♀ is like ♀; imm ♂ is blackish below. **HH** common in forest edge, highland shrubs and gardens from 1800–3400m, where they may gather in large numbers at *Leonotis* flowers. Wanders down to 950m during rains. **Vo** calls a loud metallic, machine-gun-like *ri-chi-chi-chit* or *ri-chi-chit*. Song is reminiscent of a small bishop, a buzzy *chritritritrit...*, terminating in a rattling flourish that fades away with hissing squeaks.

Tacazze Sunbird *Nectarinia tacazze* ♂ 23cm, 9"; ♀ 15cm, 6"
Br ♂ often looks very dark and then shines brilliant purple, green and gold. Green head is similar to Bronze Sunbird, but *purple back, wing-coverts and breast* distinctive. Non-br ♂ loses most iridescence. Ad ♀ is dusky grey above, with a long whitish supercilium, *dark lores and whitish malar stripes;* unstreaked paler grey below. Imms are like ♀. **HH** common in montane forest edges and clearings, giant heath, cultivation, and in gardens with flowering plants from 1800–4200m, occasionally lower. **Vo** call is a simple series of 4–5 notes given as a slow and deliberate descending series, while the song is a loud, complex, rather liquid ramble centred on a few repeated notes.

Purple-breasted Sunbird *Nectarinia purpureiventris* ♂ 24cm, 9.5";
♀ 13cm, 5" ●
Br ♂ is small-bodied and very long-tailed. Shines an amazing variation of *purple, violet, gold, copper and green*. Non-br ♂ retains long tail and a small amount of iridescence on the rump and wing-coverts. Ad ♀ is dull olive above with a greyer head, and paler below with pointed central tail feathers. Imms are like ♀. **HH** endemic to montane forests along the Albertine Rift, from 1550–2500m, where it is particularly fond of tall flowering *Symphonia* trees. **Vo** unique call starts with a few introductory chips and speeds up into a rapid very dry rattle, like a bouncing ball *trt trt trt trrrrrrrrrrrrrrrrrttt* followed by a quieter hissed chatter.

Plate 221

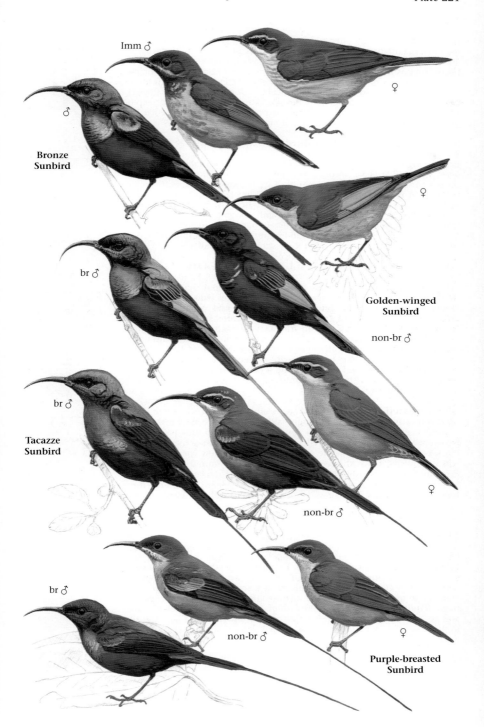

Imm ♂

♀

Bronze
Sunbird

♂

Golden-winged
Sunbird

♀

br ♂

non-br ♂

br ♂

Tacazze
Sunbird

non-br ♂

♀

br ♂

non-br ♂

♀

Purple-breasted
Sunbird

Malachite Sunbird *Nectarinia famosa* ♂ 24cm, 9.5"; ♀ 14cm, 5.5"
Br ♂ is a slim *very bright rather uniform emerald-green* sunbird with yellow pectoral tufts which are often not visible. Non-br ♂ is similar to ♀ but often retains some bright green feathers on the wings and rump. Ad ♀ and imms are dusky brown above, yellowish below, washed darker olive across the breast. Imm ♂ may have a dark throat. **HH** solitary birds or pairs are common inhabitants of moorlands, montane forest edges and high farming areas from 1650–3400m, where particularly fond of *Leonotis* flowers. Occasionally moves to lower altitudes. **Vo** call is a metallic, rather explosive *sit*, and the song consists of the *sit* note repeated and speeded up, before ending in a rattled descending flourish.

Scarlet-tufted Malachite Sunbird *Nectarinia johnstoni* ♂ 27cm, 11"; ♀ 15cm, 6"
Br ♂ is a big *iridescent dark-green sunbird with scarlet pectoral tufts and extremely long central tail feathers*. Non-br ♂ is mainly dusky brown with some green on the wing-coverts, tail long as in br. Ad ♀ is brown above, paler brown below with red pectoral tufts. Imm is like ♀ but lacks pectoral tufts. **HH** mainly restricted to alpine moorlands where it is common from 3000–4500m in areas of Giant Lobelia and *Senecio* flowers. Occasionally wanders down to 1800m. **Vo** has a variety of harsh calls including a *sit* and an arresting loud, slow wooden-sounding rattle. Song is a rasping *shree-t-shree shree shree shree shrehh shrehh* the last two notes louder.

LARGE SUNBIRDS WITH BLUE-GREEN HEADS

Green-headed Sunbird *Cyanomitra verticalis* 14cm, 5.5"
Ad ♂ has an iridescent green head which often shines blue leading to confusion with Blue-throated Brown Sunbird. Back and wings matt moss-green, lower breast to vent grey. Eyes brown. Pectoral tufts creamy-white. No non-br plumage. Ad ♀ has an iridescent blue-green cap and is grey below. Imm is dark olive above, yellowish below with a black face to upper breast. **HH** common and widespread in highland areas from 1200–2500m, inhabiting forest edge, secondary growth, gardens and cultivation. **Vo** call consists of explosive loud *chit* notes and a drawn out *chiawee*. Song starts with these notes and then breaks into a loud, energetic rolling flourish unlike any other sunbird.

Blue-throated Brown Sunbird *Cyanomitra cyanolaema* 14cm, 5.5"
Ad ♂ is mostly dark brown (although paler grey-brown below) with an iridescent steel-blue cap, throat and upper breast. Pectoral tufts pale yellow. No non-br plumage. Ad ♀ is olive-brown above with a distinctive white face mask extending back as white stripes above and below the eyes. Below whitish mottled across the breast with olive-brown. Imm ♀ is like ♀. Imm ♂ is similar but with a blackish face and breast. **HH** restricted to the west, where it is common in many forests between 700–2000m. Often sings from high up in tall trees. **Vo** like many other sunbirds, call is a harsh *zit*, but song is unique, a piercing rapid almost insect-like descending series of five to seven notes *t't't't't'tiu* which all run together.

Blue-headed Sunbird *Cyanomitra alinae* 13cm, 5" ●
Ad ♂ has the head, throat and upper breast iridescent dark blue with a violet sheen. *Mantle dark saffron-olive and belly blackish*. Eyes bright red. Pectoral tufts creamy-yellow. No non-br plumage. Ad ♀ is similar, but belly sooty-grey. Dark imm has a blackish face and breast. Similar Green-headed Sunbird has a greener head, moss-green back and is paler grey below. **HH** endemic to mountains along the Albertine Rift where it is locally common in good montane forest from 1400–2700m. Particularly fond of *Balthasarea* and *Loranthus* flowers. **Vo** call is a spitted *zit* often given in flight and the unusual song is a long loud, rolling, spitted series that undulates as a sine wave.

Plate 222

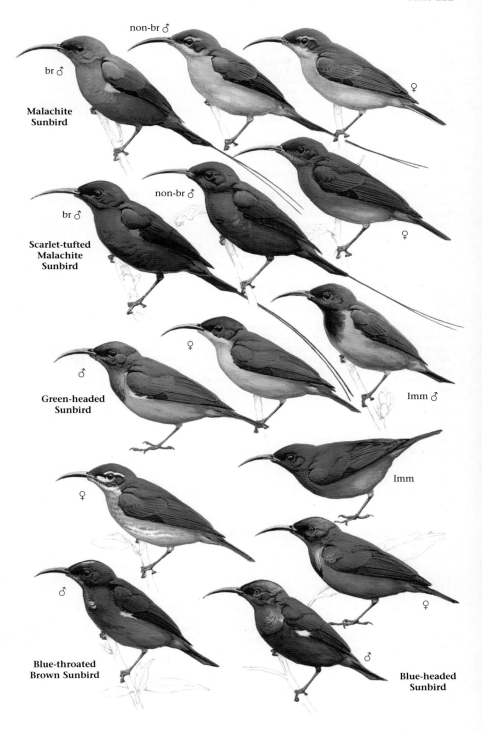

non-br ♂

br ♂

♀

Malachite Sunbird

br ♂

non-br ♂

♀

Scarlet-tufted Malachite Sunbird

♀

♂

Imm ♂

Green-headed Sunbird

Imm

♀

♀

♂

Blue-throated Brown Sunbird

♂

Blue-headed Sunbird

DOUBLE-COLLARED AND SIMILAR SUNBIRDS

A very similar looking group of sunbirds; several are separated geographically but others overlap. Best identified by width of breast bands and the colour of uppertail-coverts and belly. Males have yellow pectoral tufts which are usually concealed.

Eastern Double-collared Sunbird *Cinnyris mediocris* 11cm, 4.5"

Ad ♂ is most similar to Northern Double-collared Sunbird, but the *red breast band is not so wide* and bordered above with narrow blue band. Nominate birds in Ke and NCTz have blue uppertail-coverts, but the races *usambarica* and *fuelleborni* in NE and STz have violet uppertail-coverts. Usually shines more golden-green than Northern Double-collared. Ad ♀ and imms are dull olive above, and paler plain yellowish-green below. **HH** common in the highlands of Ke and Tz, inhabiting heath, forest, bamboo and gardens from 1800–3700m. Wanders seasonally to lower altitudes. **Vo** song commences with a few loud hissed notes, and is immediately followed by a rolling, rattled prinia-like *si-si-si turilirilirilirilirili*.

Northern Double-collared Sunbird *Cinnyris preussi* 11cm, 4.5"

Ad ♂ is very similar to Eastern Double-collared Sunbird but the *red breast band is broader* and bordered above with a narrow violet band. Uppertail-coverts violet. It often looks darker and more blue-green than Eastern Double-collared. Ad ♀ and imm are similar to ♀ Eastern Double-collared but are slightly darker overall. **HH** common in similar habitats to Eastern Double-collared, but where the two occur together usually found at lower altitudes. In the east typically 1700–2800m, but in the west from 1250m upwards. Its higher altitude limits restricted by the presence of Greater Double-collared Sunbird on some Albertine Rift mountain blocks. **Vo** a few introductory dry chipping notes precedes a sweet rolling warble that ends with a series of identical chips.

Olive-bellied Sunbird *Cinnyris chloropygia* 11cm, 4.5"

Ad ♂ is similar to the previous two species but *lacks the narrow blue or violet collar above the red breast band*: it has green uppertail-coverts and a dark olive belly. Ad ♀ is dark olive above with a short supercilium, paler yellowish-green below with indistinct streaking on the breast and a paler throat. Imm is duller and paler than ♀ with a dark throat and breast. **HH** common in a variety of lush habitats including forest edge, moist bush and cultivation from 700–1750m. **Vo** song is a dry rattle preceded by a rather tuneless warbled *trtrtrtr trilitrilitrilitrilit*.

Tiny Sunbird *Cinnyris minulla* 9cm, 3.5"

Ad ♂ is very similar to several of the double-collared sunbirds, but smaller with a *very small bill*. In good light shows tiny blue crescent-shaped markings across the red breast band. Ad ♀ and imm are very similar to ♀ Olive-bellied Sunbird but smaller and shorter-billed. **HH** in our area, known only from Kibale, Semliki and the Bwindi-Impenetrable forests in WUg from 700–1700m. **Vo** calls a loud series of spitted notes, and the frequently repeated song is a very short and tuneless descending warble.

Rwenzori Double-collared Sunbird *Cinnyris stuhlmanni*
c 14cm, 5.5"

Three races occur in our area. All are similar to Northern Double-collared Sunbird but are larger. In the Rwenzori Mts, Ug, ♂♂ of the nominate race are the largest and longest billed, the belly is olive. In SWUg and NRw, the race *graueri* has a shorter bill and a grey-buff belly, while in SWRw and NBu *schubotzi* has an intermediate length bill and a darker belly. ♀♀ are best seperated from Northern Double-collared by their larger size and longer bills. **HH** endemic to isolated high mountains around the Albertine Rift. It is locally common above 2000m, occurring at forest edge and in heath vegetation with flowering bushes. **Vo** common call is a two note *si-siii*, the second note higher. Song is not recorded in our area.

Plate 223

Northern
Double-collared
Sunbird

Eastern
Double-collared
Sunbird

♀ nominate

♂

Olive-bellied
Sunbird

♀

♂

Tiny
Sunbird

♀

♂

♀

graueri

♂

nominate

Rwenzori
Double-collared
Sunbird

Shining Sunbird *Cinnyris habessinica* 13cm, 5"
In good light ad ♂ shows a *small purple cap,* a broad red breast band some-times narrowly bordered above and below with blue, and a black belly. Ad ♀ is mostly ash-grey, with a long whitish supercilium and blackish tail very narrowly edged white. Imm is like ♀ with a blackish throat. **HH** feeds on aloes and flowering acacias in northern semi-arid bush country from 400–1000m. **Vo** call is 4–5 distinct similar or rising and then falling chips. Song is a rather monotonous but musical two-tone see-sawing like a slow trill.

Shelley's Sunbird *Cinnyris shelleyi* 12cm, 5"
Ad ♂ has a broad red breast band narrowly bordered above with blue, a black belly, and no pectoral tufts. Within range it is most similar to Marico Sunbird, but that species has a maroon breast band. Ad ♀ are olive above, paler yellowish below streaked dusky across the breast. **HH** local and generally uncommon from 500–1200m, inhabiting riverine woodland and bush country in the Morogoro area and miombo woodland near Songea, Tz. **Vo** call is a loud dry spitted chipping, and the song is a short rising and falling flourish, rather like a weaver in pattern and quality.

Miombo Double-collared Sunbird *Cinnyris manoensis* 13cm, 5"
Ad ♂ is similar to several other double-collared sunbirds with blue upper-tail-coverts and a red breast band narrowly bordered above with blue: it dif-fers in having a *pale olive-grey belly.* Pectoral tufts yellow. Ad ♀ and imm are olive-green above, paler yellowish-olive below. **HH** uncommon and gener-ally restricted to miombo woodland from 1000–1400m around Songea and north to Mikumi NP in Tz. **Vo** song is a complex and musical rising and falling series of sweet and spitted notes, often mixed with chattering between sequences.

SUNBIRDS WITH EXTENSIVE RED AND YELLOW UNDERPARTS
All have yellow pectoral tufts and there are no non-breeding plumages.

Loveridge's Sunbird *Cinnyris loveridgei* 11cm, 4.5" ●
Ad ♂ is similar to Regal Sunbird, but somewhat duller with *sides of the breast to vent olive-yellow.* Ad ♀ has a grey head contrasting with a dark olive back and blackish tail; yellow below with a pale grey throat. The form *moreaui* is now thought to be a *loveridgei* × *mediocris* hybrid. **HH** Tz endemic: Loveridge's is restricted to the Uluguru Mts where it is common in the mid-stratum and undergrowth of forest from 800–2000m, mainly above 1500m (*moreaui* is known from the Nguru, Ukaguru and Udzungwa Mts). **Vo** call is a sharp chip, while the song consists of three introductory notes (second note higher), immediately followed by a silvery rolling rattle.

Regal Sunbird *Cinnyris regia* 11cm, 4.5" ●
Ad ♂ is most similar to Rockefeller's Sunbird but differs in having extensive bright yellow to sides of breast and flanks, and a shorter bill. Ad ♀ and imm are dark olive-green above with brighter yellowish-olive edges to the pri-maries often forming a wing panel, and paler olive below with a blackish tail. **HH** an Albertine Rift endemic occurring commonly in highland forest including edge and clearings from 1550–3000m, mainly above 1800m. **Vo** has a variety of songs: one is a continuous twittering punctuated by fre-quent explosive sparrow-like chirps, another is a hissing high-pitched rapidly delivered flourish, and the strangest is a rambling low-pitched war-ble interspersed with loud chirps.

Rockefeller's Sunbird *Cinnyris rockefelleri* 11cm, 4.5" ●●
Ad ♀ is very similar to Regal Sunbird, *but has more red on breast and yellow flanks are strongly washed olive.* Ad ♀ is similar to ♀ Regal Sunbird, but has a narrow pale supercilium. **HH** a rare Albertine Rift endemic thought to pre-fer mixed bamboo and montane forest along streams. In our area it is known only from a single record at about 2500m in Nyungwe Forest, Rw. **Vo** unknown.

Plate 224

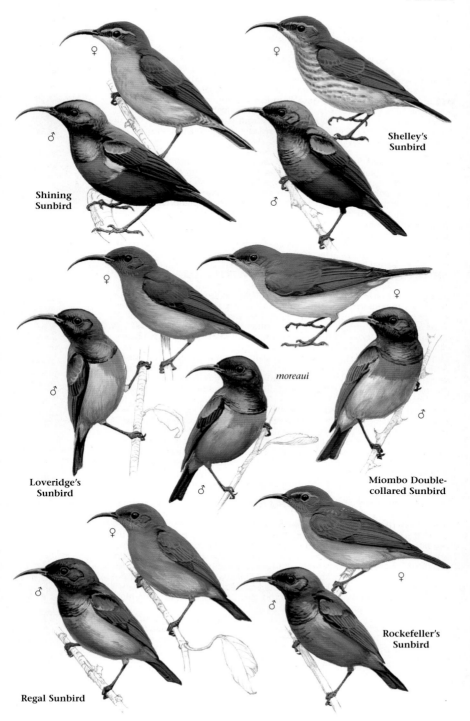

Shelley's
Sunbird

Shining
Sunbird

moreaui

Loveridge's
Sunbird

Miombo Double-
collared Sunbird

Regal Sunbird

Rockefeller's
Sunbird

BLACK SUNBIRDS

Amethyst Sunbird   *Chalcomitra amethystina*   14cm, 5.5"
[Black Sunbird]

Ad ♂ sometimes appears totally black, but in good light shows a small *iridescent blue-green cap and an amethyst-purple throat patch*. Small patch on bend of wing is iridescent fiery-amethyst. Ad ♀ has a narrow white supercilium and is streaked below: similar ♀ Scarlet-chested Sunbird lacks supercilium and is mottled below. Imm is similar to ♀ but with a dark throat. **HH** common and widespread in a wide variety of habitats including forest edge, woodland, moist bush and gardens from sea-level to 2200m. **Vo** call consists of both scratchy chirps and sweeter *seets*, and the song is not unlike a small *Acrocephalus* in quality.

Green-throated Sunbird   *Chalcomitra rubescens*   14cm, 5.5"

Ad ♂ is mostly black with a dark iridescent green cap and throat: in good light both show narrow purple borders. Ad ♀ is brown above with a narrow creamy supercilium, and pale-yellowish heavily streaked brown below. Imm is more mottled below than ♀ with a dark throat patch on imm ♂. **HH** locally common in the west, inhabiting forest and nearby secondary growth from 700–1800m, with a preference for the mid-stratum and canopy. **Vo** varied song may be a rambling mixture of sweet and harsh twittering, or 4–6 loud rising and falling chips followed by a rising rapidly spitted sequence *chu chu chu chu chi tttttt*.

SHORT-BILLED FOREST SUNBIRDS WITH GREEN UPPERPARTS

Green Sunbird   *Anthreptes rectirostris*   9cm, 3.5"

Ad ♂ has upperparts, sides of throat and breast iridescent green: *narrow orange band across breast separates green from grey lower breast and belly*. At close range small grey chin patch is visible. Pectoral tufts yellow. Ad ♀ is dull olive-green above with a yellowish supercilium, paler yellowish below. Short bill can lead to confusion with Green Hylia (see plate 185). Imm is similar to ♀ but lacks supercilium. **HH** locally common in the middle storey and canopy of forest and forest edge from 700–3150m. **Vo** calls a slow high-pitched and piercing upslurred whistle, which is sometimes repeated more rapidly, or a short repeated and monotonous downslurred *siiiiu*.

Banded Green Sunbird   *Anthreptes rubritorques*   9cm, 3.5"   ● ●

Ad ♂ is *pale-grey below with a narrow bright orange-red breast band* making it unmistakable if good views are obtained. Ad ♀ is green above and pale olive-yellow below. Imm is like ♀ but with a stronger yellowish wash below. **HH** Tz endemic largely restricted to the Usambara Mts where it is locally common from 250–1600m. Rare elsewhere with records from the Nguru, Uluguru and Udzungwa Mts. **Vo** song begins with a high *sii*, and then continues with a repeated identical note *sii siusiusiusiusiusiu*.

A DISTINCTIVE TANZANIAN ENDEMIC

Rufous-winged Sunbird   *Cinnyris rufipennis*   10cm, 4"   ● ●

Ad ♂ has a unique *orange-red wing panel*, is iridescent green above, on the throat and upper breast, with a narrow orange-red breast band, and a pale grey mid-breast to vent. Bill is long and thin. Ad ♀ is all olive with slightly paler underparts and an obvious orange-red wing panel. **HH** Tz endemic discovered in 1981. Only known from the Udzungwa Mts where it is most often seen from 1500–1700m, but occurs rarely down to 600m. **Vo** calls a descending almost two-note *see-u*, and the song is a rapid very high-pitched rattling warble.

Plate 225

♂

Imm ♂

♀

Amethyst Sunbird

♂

Imm ♂

♀

Green-throated Sunbird

♀

♂

Green Sunbird

♀

Imm

Banded Green Sunbird

♂

♀

♂

Rufous-winged Sunbird

PLAIN OLIVE OR GREY SUNBIRDS

Rather plain species that lack iridescence, and which all basically look like female sunbirds, except for Grey-headed which looks remarkably like a warbler.

Olive Sunbird *Cyanomitra olivacea* 13cm, 5"

Large long-billed all olive sunbird which is variably paler below. Bill is black but sometimes has a smidgen of orange at base of lower mandible. Eastern and southern birds have yellow pectoral tufts in both sexes, but in race *vincenti* occurring west of the Great Rift Valley only ♂♂ have pectoral tufts. Imm resembles ad. **HH** common in the forest interior, less so at edge, from sea-level to 3000m. **Vo** a very noisy and musical sunbird: in the west the songs go up and down the scale, while in the east they usually consist of a descending series of separated explosive squeaks. Calls are dry raspy chips.

Little Green Sunbird *Anthreptes seimundi* 9cm, 3.5"

A small short-tailed olive sunbird with slightly paler yellow-green under-parts, and olive-green primary edges. Sexes are alike. **HH** pairs are uncommon and patchily distributed from 700–1850m inhabiting the mid-stratum and forest canopy. **Vo** call is a fairly loud, spitted, dry series of identical notes, sometimes with a deeper more hollow sound. Song is a canary-like high-pitched twittered rising and falling series.

Mouse-coloured Sunbird *Cyanomitra veroxii* 13cm, 5"
[Grey Sunbird]

Similar to Olive Sunbird in structure, but plumage is mostly *cold grey with a darker tail*. At close range, shows an oily-blue sheen on the shoulder, a very narrow black malar stripe, and red pectoral tufts. Sexes are alike. **HH** single birds or pairs inhabit woody thickets, coastal scrub and mangroves where they are generally uncommon. **Vo** call is a harsh and tuneless scratchy note, but the song an attractive and simple refrain of well-emphasised rather indignant notes *tu-ti-tu ti-tu-tu* that rise and then fall.

Grey-headed Sunbird *Deleornis axillaris* 11cm, 4.5"

Unique, appearing *much more like a warbler than a sunbird*. Pale grey crown and sides of head contrast with a green back and wings. *Bill is pinkish and only slightly decurved*. Below yellow with a paler throat. ♂ has orange-red pectoral tufts which are usually concealed. Imm has a green head uniform with the mantle. Sometimes considered conspecific with West African Fraser's Sunbird *Deleornis fraseri*. **HH** pairs or single birds are locally common and show a preference for tangled vegetation in the middle levels of forest from 700–1550m. **Vo** distinctive song is a sine wave of rising and falling notes repeated for long periods which is very similar to Grey Longbill, but that species rolls its notes.

Copper Sunbird *Cinnyris cuprea* 13cm, 5"
[Coppery Sunbird]

Br ♂ has a *fiery-copper head, mantle and breast* with blacker wings and tail. Non-br ♂ is more like ♀ but with a few random iridescent feathers. ♀ is olive-brown above with a blackish pale, dull yellow below. Imm is like ♀ but with a dark throat on imm ♂. **HH** locally common inhabiting lightly wooded areas, bush country, the fringes of swamps and cultivation from 700–1700m. **Vo** one song is like a bouncing ball *tit tit tit tit ttttttttttt*, and there is also a similar series that breaks into a twittering flourish.

Superb Sunbird *Cinnyris superba* 17cm, 6.5"

Large with a very long bill and short tail. Ad ♂ is iridescent golden-green above with a blue cap, and has a purple-blue throat and upper breast con-trasting with a *deep maroon breast to vent*. Ad ♀ is olive above with a long pale supercilium, yellowish below washed rich orange-yellow on the belly. Imm is like a dull ♀. **HH** single birds or pairs prefer canopy at the forest edge, but also wander to visit flowering trees in cultivated areas, from 700–1700m. **Vo** call is a strident angry *tiout tiout...*, repeated for long peri-ods, sometimes slowly and sometimes more rapidly.

Plate 226

Olive
Sunbird

Little Green
Sunbird

Mouse-coloured
Sunbird

Ad

Imm

Grey-headed
Sunbird

Imm ♂

non-br ♂

Copper
Sunbird

br ♂

♀

♂

♀

Superb
Sunbird

SUNBIRDS WITH MAROON OR VIOLET BREAST BANDS

Marico Sunbird *Cinnyris mariquensis* 12cm, 5"
Ad ♂ has a *broad maroon breast band* bordered above with blue and no pectoral tufts. Crown is wholly green: northern race *osiris* has a black belly, but elsewhere *suahelica* has a greyish-black belly. It is larger and longer-billed than similar Purple-banded Sunbird. ♀ is greyish-brown above with a narrow supercilium, yellowish below with dark streaking and a paler throat. Imm is like ♀ but has a blackish throat and mottled breast. **HH** common and widespread in open woodland and bush country from 800–2000m. **Vo** strong call is a rapid nasal chipping, often given in long complaining series, while the song incorporates the call with some loud sweet warbled chipping notes.

Orange-tufted Sunbird *Cinnyris bouvieri* 12cm, 5"
Ad ♂ is similar to Marico Sunbird, but has a *small violet forecrown and orange-yellow pectoral tufts* (usually concealed). Ad ♀ is olive-brown above with a faint supercilium and blue-black tail. Yellowish below, with very indistinct dusky streaking. Imm is like ♀, but imm ♂ has a blackish throat and random iridescent feathers. **HH** rather uncommon in forest edge, secondary growth and at flowering trees in nearby cultivation from 700–1800m. **Vo** unique song commences with a long dry rattle that breaks into a sweeter *sitisitisitisiti*.

Palestine Sunbird *Cinnyris osea* 10cm, 4"
Br ♂ is a small-billed, dark iridescent blue-green sunbird with a violet-blue upper breast, small orange-yellow pectoral tufts, and a matt black lower breast and belly. Non-br ♂ is like ♀. ♀ is similar to ♀ Orange-tufted Sunbird, but paler below. **HH** vagrant: one record from Mt Kei in NWUg in 1992. **Vo** song is described as a few whistled notes followed by a rattling trill *tvui tvui tvui tirrrrrr*.

Purple-banded Sunbird *Cinnyris bifasciata* 10cm, 4"
In west and coastal Ke, br ♂ of race *microrhyncha* is extremely similar to Marico Sunbird, differing in being slightly smaller and shorter-billed. In the dry hinterland of coastal Ke and NETz race *tsavoensis* has more violet and less maroon on the breast band. Both ♀♀ are grey-brown above with a light supercilium and darker tail; underparts are pale yellowish streaked dusky. Imm is like ♀ with a dark throat. **HH** race *microrhyncha* is common and widespread in woodland, thickets and coastal scrub, while *tsavoensis* is restricted to drier habitats typical of Tsavo NP in Ke. **Vo** call is a distinctive *sip sip*, while the song commences with the call and breaks into a complex musical rolling twitter.

Violet-breasted Sunbird *Cinnyris pembae* 11cm, 4.5"
Two races occur which may be separate species: in mainland coastal areas ad ♂ *chalcomelas* (**Violet-breasted Sunbird**) has *iridescent violet from the lower throat to breast*. It is slightly larger and longer-billed than Purple-banded Sunbird, lacks maroon on the breast and has no pectoral tufts. ♀ is grey-brown above with a light supercilium and darker tail, plain grey below with a pale yellowish belly. Ad ♂ nominate (**Pemba Sunbird ●**) is slightly smaller with violet and green (not all green) lesser wing-coverts. ♀ is whiter on the breast than ♀ *chalcomelas*. Both imm ♂♂ like ♀ with a blackish throat. **HH** race *chalcomelas* is rather uncommon in coastal bush country, while nominate is common throughout Pemba Island. **Vo** call is reported as a thin high, hurried *tsewtsi-tse-tseep-sisisi-tsewtsi-tsi-tsi*.

Splendid Sunbird *Cinnyris coccinigaster* 14cm, 5.5"
Ad ♂ is highly iridescent and constantly changes colour in sunshine: brilliant green above contrasts with a purple and blue head becoming red on the breast. Ad ♀ is olive above, yellow below streaked dusky. Imm is blackish on the throat. **HH** vagrant: one record in wooded grassland in extreme NWUg in 1969. **Vo** song is a simple series of deliberate single loud, musical chipping notes falling, rising and falling again.

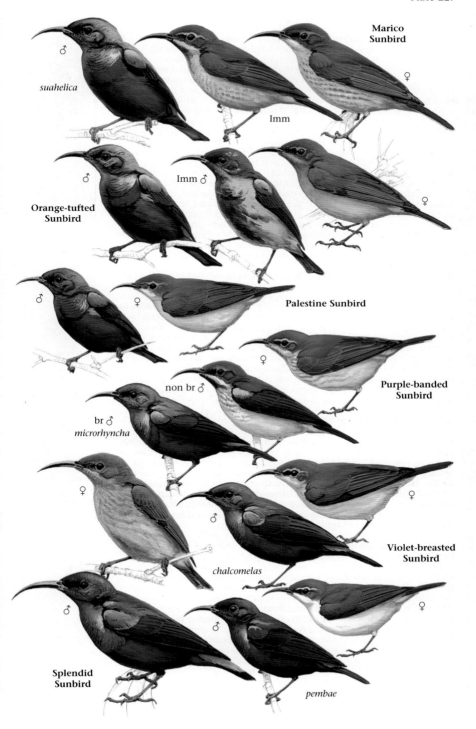

Plate 227

Marico Sunbird

♂

suahelica

Imm

♀

Orange-tufted Sunbird

Imm ♂

♂

♀

♂

♀

Palestine Sunbird

♀

non br ♂

Purple-banded Sunbird

br ♂
microrhyncha

♀

♀

Violet-breasted Sunbird

chalcomelas

♂

♀

Splendid Sunbird

♂

♂

pembae

BLACK AND RED SUNBIRDS

Scarlet-chested Sunbird *Chalcomitra senegalensis* 15cm, 6"
From Ug to CKe, ad ♂ of race *lamperti* is similar to Hunter's Sunbird with a brilliant scarlet breast and small iridescent green cap, but differs in having a *green throat* (which is sometimes difficult to see). Race *gutturalis* in Tz (except NTz) and in coastal Ke is similar, but has a small violet shoulder patch. Ad ♀ is dark brown above without a supercilium, and dirty yellowish-white below mottled brown. Imm ♂ is like ♀ but with some dull red feathers on the breast. Imm ♀ is like ♀ with a blackish throat. **HH** usually in pairs but sometimes present in large numbers at *Leonotis* flowers. Inhabits a wide variety of forest edge, wooded valleys, gardens and cultivation from sea-level to 2150m. **Vo** song is a short series of loud explosive notes, interspersed with monotonous, complex chips and scratchy notes.

Hunter's Sunbird *Chalcomitra hunteri* 15cm, 6"
Ad ♂ is similar to Scarlet-chested Sunbird but *throat is black bordered with narrow iridescent green malar stripes* (they can be very difficult to see in the field). The *purple rump* and small purple spot on shoulder of the wing can be better field marks. ♀ and imm ♀ are similar, but not as dark brown as ♀ Scarlet-chested. Imm ♂ is like ♀ but with red feathers on the breast. **HH** pairs and single birds are widespread and locally common in semi-arid bush country from 50–1200m. **Vo** song is very different from Scarlet-chested Sunbird, a rapidly delivered and energetic rolling warble.

SUNBIRDS WITH RED BREAST BANDS AND LONG TAILS

Beautiful Sunbird *Cinnyris pulchella* ♂15cm, 6"; ♀11cm, 4.5"
Br ♂ has a *red breast band bordered by large yellow patches*, and long narrow central tail feathers. Northern nominate birds have a green belly, while race *melanogastra* (mainly south of the equator) are black-bellied. Non-br ♂ is like ♀ but with a long central tail and some iridescent green feathers on the wing-coverts. ♀ is greyish-olive above with a short indistinct supercilium, and plain pale yellow below. Imm is similar to ♀ but imm ♂ has a black throat. **HH** widespread and often common inhabiting semi-arid bush country, wooded grasslands and gardens from 400–1900m. **Vo** call is a scrapy chattering, while the song consists of introductory chipping followed by short musical warbles of chips and squeaks.

Black-bellied Sunbird *Cinnyris nectarinioides* ♂13cm, 5"; ♀10cm, 4"
Ad ♂ is like a small version of Beautiful Sunbird but without large yellow patches on sides of breast. Nominate birds in SEKe and NETz have yellow pectoral tufts that the more northerly race *erlangeri* lacks. ♀ is olive above and pale yellowish below, with olive streaks and sometimes a faint patch of orange-red in the centre of the breast. Imm is like ♀ with a blackish throat. **HH** common in the dry semi-arid eastern part of our area below 1300m, where it is particularly fond of flowering *Loranthus*. **Vo** call is a loud dry repeated chipping, and the song begins with rapid higher-pitched and hissed chit notes and continues with an extraordinary and complex flourish, rather like some weaver species.

Red-chested Sunbird *Cinnyris erythrocerca* ♂14cm, 5.5"; ♀11cm, 4.5"
Similar to Black-bellied Sunbird, but ad ♂ often appears *deeper more iridescent blue above* (not green). No pectoral tufts or yellow on breast. ♀ and imm ♀ are olive-brown above with blackish tails, pale yellowish below with heavy dark mottling. Imm ♂ has a blackish throat. **HH** a western species occurring commonly in a variety of cover around lakes and marshes from 600–1800m, although often attracted away from water to flowering bushes and gardens. **Vo** calls a rapidly delivered series of spitted *chit* notes, while the song consists of these notes breaking into complex rambling warbles of harsh chips and squeaks that continue for long periods without pause.

Plate 228

Scarlet-chested
Sunbird

♂

lamperti

Imm ♂

♀

Hunter's
Sunbird

♂

Imm ♂

♀

br ♂

melanogastra

Imm ♂

br ♂

nominate

non-br
♂

Beautiful
Sunbird

♀

Imm ♂

Imm

Black-bellied
Sunbird

nominate

♀

♂

Imm ♂

♀

Red-chested
Sunbird

GREEN AND YELLOW SUNBIRDS

Variable Sunbird *Cinnyris venusta* 11cm, 4.5"
[Yellow-bellied Sunbird]

Three races occur varying in belly colour on br ♂♂: in most of Ke and Tz *falkensteini* is yellow; in the west *igneiventris* is mixed yellow and orange; and in NEKe *albiventris* is white. All three races have a *violet-blue throat and upper breast*. Pectoral tufts are either yellow or orange-red. Non-br ♂ is similar to ♀ with some iridescent feathers above. Ad ♀ and imm ♀ are olive-brown above with a blue-black tail, and plain yellow below, or white in *albiventris*. Imm ♂ is similar to ♀ with a blackish throat. **HH** the yellow-bellied races are common and widespread particularly in the highlands, and *albiventris* is restricted to semi-arid bush country in NEKe: races range from sea-level to 3000m. **Vo** calls a harsh rather nasal scraping note, while among a wide variety of songs a *si-sit-swit chichichchi* is the most commonly heard.

Collared Sunbird *Hedydipna collaris* 10cm, 4"

Ad ♂ has the upperparts, head, throat and upper breast iridescent green, the latter bordered below with a narrow violet band (can be difficult to see). Lower breast to vent bright yellow without pectoral tufts: bill short. Ad ♀ has similar iridescent green upperparts, but the underparts including the throat and breast are yellow. Imm is like a dull pale ♀. **HH** pairs are common and widespread from sea-level to 2800m in a wide range of fairly lush habitats, including forest, moist bush, gardens and coastal lowlands. **Vo** usual call is a repeated slightly lisping but penetrating *seeyu seeyu seeyu...*, while the song is a repeated *si-si-sut seeu seeu seeu seeu seeu seeu...*

Pygmy Sunbird *Hedydipna platurus* ♂ 18cm, 7"; ♀ 9cm, 3.5"

Br ♂ is like Collared Sunbird but with *very long thin tail streamers*. Non-br ♂ is similar to ♀ with some iridescent feathers above. Ad ♀ is ashy above, plain yellow below with a whitish chin. Similar ♀ Beautiful Sunbird is paler yellow below including the chin. Imm is similar to ♀, with a blackish throat on imm ♂. **HH** local in NWUg inhabiting semi-arid bush and wooded grasslands. Also occurs erratically as an occasional migrant into NWKe. **Vo** call is a downslurred very pinched *seea seea seea*, while the song begins with these notes and continues with a high-pitched series of hissed notes that break into a flourish.

WHITE-BELLIED SUNBIRDS

Amani Sunbird *Hedydipna pallidigaster* 9cm, 3.5" ●●

Ad ♂ is very dark iridescent bottle-green above including the head, throat and upper breast (high in the canopy can appear almost black), with orange pectoral tufts (very rarely seen), and the lower breast to vent white. Ad ♀ is grey above with a blacker tail and white below. Imm is like a pale ♀. **HH** EA endemic: pairs are local in the canopy of woodland and forest from sea-level to 900m, occurring in Sokoke Forest, Ke, and in the East Usambara and Udzungwa Mts, Tz. **Vo** call is a penetrating two-note *twee-twee* (first note upslurred, second downslurred), while the song is a long complex high-pitched twittering incorporating harsh chittering notes.

White-bellied Sunbird *Cinnyris talatala* 11cm, 4.5"

Ad ♂ is iridescent blue-green above including the head, throat and upper breast, with a band across the breast *shining violet-blue in good light; upper-tail-coverts green*. Lower breast to vent yellow. *Pectoral tufts are yellow*. Longer-billed than Oustalet's Sunbird. ♀ is greyish-brown above with a narrow stripe behind the eye, paler and indistinctly streaked below. Imm is similar to ♀. **HH** in our area only known from dry woodland in STz from sea-level to 1000m. **Vo** call is a hollow sounding *tik tik*, while the song consists of several introductory upslurs followed by a twittering series.

Oustalet's Sunbird *Cinnyris oustaleti* 11cm, 4.5"

Ad ♂ is very similar to White-bellied Sunbird but shorter-billed with a blackish throat, a violet and maroon band across the breast, *orange-yellow pectoral tufts* (not just yellow) and *blue uppertail-coverts*. ♀ has a plainer head than ♀ White-bellied. **HH** the few known records are from miombo woodland at about 1500m in W and SWTz. **Vo** not recorded in the region.

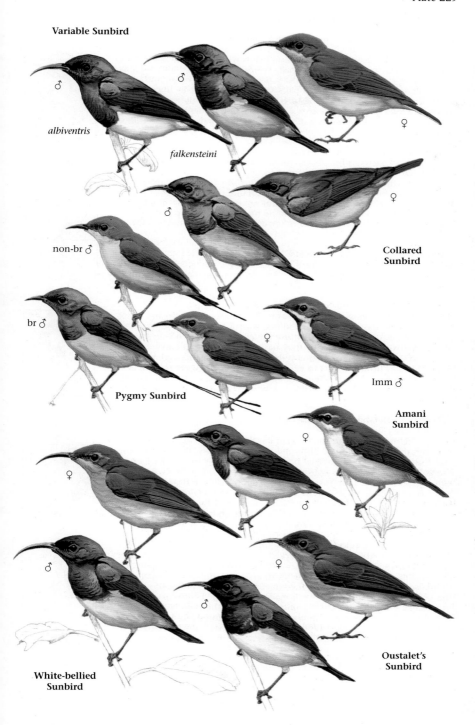

Plate 229

Variable Sunbird

♂

albiventris

♂

falkensteini

♀

♀

Collared Sunbird

non-br ♂

br ♂

♀

Pygmy Sunbird

Imm ♂

Amani Sunbird

♀

♂

♀

♂

♀

White-bellied Sunbird

Oustalet's Sunbird

TWO ANTHREPTES WITHOUT OBVIOUS CLOSE RELATIVES

Plain-backed Sunbird *Anthreptes reichenowi* 10cm, 4"
[Blue-throated Sunbird]
Ad ♂ is dull plain green above and yellow below with a dark iridescent *blue-black forecrown, throat and upper breast*. Pectoral tufts are yellow. Ad ♀ is plain olive-green above with a narrow supercilium, yellow below and paler on throat. Imm is similar to ♀. **HH** pairs are local and generally uncommon in thick coastal forest, but ascend to 1000m in the East Usambara Mts, Tz. **Vo** call is a loud nasal repeated *tyow tyow tyow...*, or a higher-pitched rapidly repeated nasal upslur. Song is a distinctive regularly repeated descending series.

Anchieta's Sunbird *Anthreptes anchietae* 11cm, 4.5"
Ad ♂ has an iridescent blue-black crown contrasting with a dark brown back, wings and tail. Below the throat to upper breast is iridescent blue-black, and centre of the breast to belly is red broadly bordered with yellow. Ad ♀ is similar but duller. Imm is mostly plain dull olive-brown, but slightly paler below. **HH** pairs are local but not uncommon in miombo woodland in SWTz. **Vo** repeatedly utters a fairly monotonous, simple and piercing sequence of 3–4 rising squeaky notes, and a very short scratchy warble.

VIOLET-BACKED SUNBIRDS
Males are all similar with violet upperparts, small turquoise patches near bend of wing, and whitish underparts. Unless males are seen well they may best be identified by range, habitat and association with more distinctive females.

Eastern Violet-backed Sunbird *Anthreptes orientalis* 12cm, 5"
Ad ♂ is violet-blue above with a contrasting turquoise-blue rump and white below. Warbler-like ad ♀ is brown above with a bold white supercilium and an iridescent dark blue tail: *entirely white below*. Beware pollen stained individuals with orange throats, they have been feeding in aloes. Imm is similar to ♀ but may have a faint yellow belly. **HH** pairs are common in semi-arid areas from sea-level to 1300m: they are particularly fond of acacia and *Commiphora* bush where aloes and *Loranthus* are plentiful. **Vo** call is a scratchy complaining downslur, given irregularly when feeding or repeatedly when excited.

Western Violet-backed Sunbird *Anthreptes longuemarei* 13cm, 5.5"
[Violet-backed Sunbird]
Ad ♂ is slightly larger than the very similar Eastern Violet-backed Sunbird, but both northern nominate birds and race *nyassae* in SETz are uniformly violet above. In WTz *angolensis* has a turquoise-blue rump like Eastern Violet-backed, but they do not overlap in range. Ad ♀ has *flanks, belly and vent yellow not white*. Imm is entirely pale yellow below. **HH** pairs occur in more verdant areas than Eastern Violet-backed Sunbird, preferring forest strips along streams, wooded grassland, and miombo woodland from 700–1850m. **Vo** call is a harsh, hollow sounding chitter, while the song is a long and complex rambling warble.

Uluguru Violet-backed Sunbird *Anthreptes neglectus* 12cm, 5"
Ad ♂ is similar to the other violet-backed sunbirds, but dark brown sides of face encircle the hindneck as a collar and the underparts are pale grey (not pure white). Both features are difficult to assess in the field. Rump shines turquoise-blue contrasting with the violet back. Ad ♀ is rather like ♂, but the belly and vent are washed yellow: lacks the supercilium of other ♀♀. Imm is like a dull ♀. **HH** pairs are quite common in the Pugu Hills and East Usambara Mts, Tz, but uncommon elsewhere in forest, forest edge and woodland from sea-level to 1200m. **Vo** call is a hissed downslurred *ssseu*, while the song consists of 5–6 similar descending hissed notes *si-siu-si-siu-siu*.

Plate 230

Imm

**Anchieta's
Sunbird**

♂

♀

**Plain-backed
Sunbird**

♂

♀

**Eastern
Violet-backed
Sunbird**

♂

♀

♀

**Western
Violet-backed
Sunbird**

♂

**Uluguru
Violet-backed
Sunbird**

♀

Imm

TRUE SHRIKES

Found singly or in small groups, *Lanius* shrikes are mostly conspicuous birds of open habitat. Plumages are bold patterns of black, white, grey and brown, several have long tails, and all have hook-tipped bills.

Common Fiscal *Lanius collaris* 23cm, 9"
[Fiscal Shrike]

Ad ♂ is a slim, narrow-tailed shrike with white scapulars forming an obvious 'V' across the back, and a grey rump. Tail is variable: either black with white tips (westerly) or black with a white outer edge and tips (on more easterly birds). Ad ♀ is similar but with a small chestnut flank patch. Imm is much browner with fine barring both above and below. Race *marwitzi* (**Uhehe Fiscal** ●) has a distinctive white forecrown and supercilium, and is sometimes considered specifically distinct. **HH** singles and pairs are very common particularly in the highlands from 500–3350m, with race *marwitzi* above 1500m in E and STz. **Vo** simple song consists of repeated mournful burry downslurs, whilst the distinct call is a repeated harsh grating *scherrrr*. The voice of race *marwitzi* is similar.

Taita Fiscal *Lanius dorsalis* 20cm, 8"

Ad ♂ appears stocky and short-tailed with a black crown and nape contrasting with a pale grey back. Very similar to Somali Fiscal, but *secondaries are all black* (without white tips). Ad ♀ has a small chestnut patch on the flanks. Imm is dark grey-brown above and white below, all with fine barring. **HH** single birds or pairs are common in dry open grassland and bush country from sea-level to 1600m. **Vo** rarely heard song is a simple but very liquid and rhythmic *wi-tirir-chh, wi-tink-tink,* repeated monotously. Alarm is a nasal buzz.

Somali Fiscal *Lanius somalicus* 20cm, 8"

Ad is slightly slimmer than very similar Taita Fiscal and best identified by *white tips to the secondaries* which appear as a narrow white trailing edge to the wing in flight. Sexes alike. Imm is similar to other fiscals with fine barring on grey-brown upperparts and whitish underparts. **HH** single birds and pairs are fairly local and not common in arid and semi-arid areas of NKe from 400–1500m. **Vo** rarely heard song is quite different from Taita Fiscal having a scratchy rather than a liquid quality *wir-chi-ri-ri;* the rising notes are repeated for long periods.

Long-tailed Fiscal *Lanius cabanisi* 31cm, 12"

Largest fiscal: ad ♂ has a *long broad all-black tail* and a white rump. Black cap contrasts with a dark grey back and scapulars: all the other similar but smaller fiscals have white scapulars. Ad ♀ is similar but has small chestnut flank patch. Imm similar to other imm fiscals but larger. **HH** common and sociable with groups of up to 10 birds interacting noisily in wooded grasslands, acacia country and coastal bush from sea-level to 1600m. **Vo** groups call noisily together from the tops of bushes. A lazy, liquid simple sequence of 3–5 notes mixed with a throaty churr.

Souza's Shrike *Lanius souzae* 17cm, 7"

Ad ♂ is a small shrike with a black face mask, pale grey crown, and conspicuous white scapulars forming a 'V' across the back. Wings are rusty brown with fine black barring. Ad ♀ is similar but with rufous wash on the flanks. Imm is finely barred with black on rufous-brown above, and white below with faint black scalloping. **HH** solitary, local and uncommon in woodland from 1000–1750m, particularly in miombo where it perches within the higher branches of small trees. **Vo** song is a simple, scraping slightly nasal downslur repeated monotonously, and the call is a harsh *schar-arrr.*

Plate 231

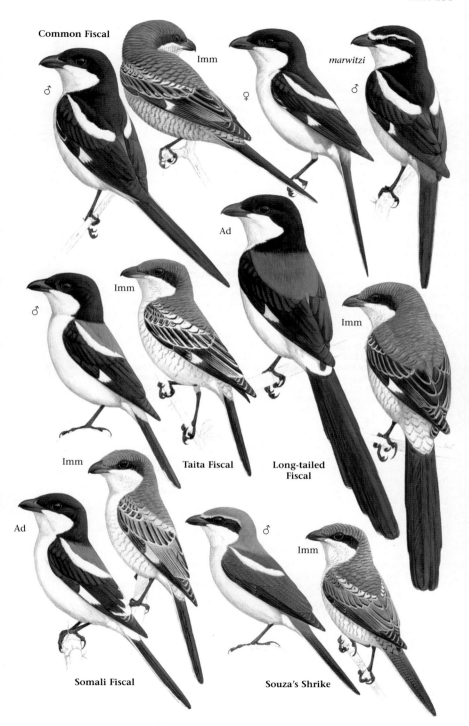

Common Fiscal
♂
Imm
♀
marwitzi
♂
Ad

♂
Imm
Taita Fiscal
Imm
Long-tailed Fiscal

Imm
Ad
♂
Imm
Somali Fiscal
Souza's Shrike

Grey-backed Fiscal *Lanius excubitoroides* 25cm, 10"
Ad ♂ is a large, bulky shrike with a broad black face mask (extending across the forecrown), grey upperparts, and *large white patches at base of the tail*. Ad ♀ is similar but with a small chestnut flank patch. Imm is grey-brown above with much fine dusky barring. **HH** locally common in open woodland, acacia country, and cultivated areas, often near water, and mainly between 600–1900m, rarely to 3000m. Small sociable groups are conspicuous and noisy, often gathering to display and wave their broad tails. **Vo** several group members sing together a sequence of liquid but raspy descending slurred scraping notes. Call is a harsh *schaah*.

Mackinnon's Fiscal *Lanius mackinnoni* 20cm, 8"
Ad ♂ is a slim narrow-tailed fiscal with grey upperparts, a white 'V' across the back, and *plain black wings* (without a white primary patch). Grey-backed Fiscal is much larger, with a black forecrown and much white in the tail. Ad ♀ has a chestnut flank patch. Imm is browner above, with light barring both above and below. **HH** solitary or in pairs, it is a quiet bird of forest edge, woodland and lush gardens from 700–2200m. **Vo** sings a quiet sometimes subdued but attractive warble which sounds rather like a slow *Sylvia* warbler.

Lesser Grey Shrike *Lanius minor* 20cm, 8"
A Palearctic migrant mainly from Mar–May when they are in very clean br plumage with dove-grey upperparts, a broad black face mask extending across the forecrown, a white throat and a *pale pink breast*. Non-br ad and imm (rare Oct–Dec) are whiter below and lack black on the forecrown. **HH** common passage migrant which can appear almost anywhere from sea-level to 3000m and like a typical shrike sits conspicuously in the open. **Vo** frequently calls a sharp scolding *chek*, but is otherwise rather quiet. From Apr–May, prior to leaving may sing a sweet *Acrocephalus*-like song with a strange throaty quality.

Woodchat Shrike *Lanius senator* 18cm, 7"
Ad ♂ is very distinctive with a black face mask, *bright chestnut crown and nape*, and white scapulars. Ad ♀ is similar but duller with more white on the face. Imm has a less defined face mask and a duller crown. **HH** uncommon Palearctic visitor from Oct–Mar, occurring in small numbers mainly north of the equator. **Vo** generally silent in the region, but occasionally calls a harsh *chhh chhh-chhh-chhh-chhhh*.

Masked Shrike *Lanius nubicus* 17cm, 6.5"
Ad ♂ is *black and white with pale apricot flanks* unlike any other shrike. Ad ♀ is similar but slightly paler and browner above. Imm is grey-brown above with scaly fringes and a pale-faced appearance. **HH** scarce Palearctic visitor from Oct–Mar, with nearly all the records from Lake Baringo, Ke. Birds are shy, sitting within the canopy of acacia trees and then dropping to the ground to feed. **Vo** usually silent in the region, but occasionally calls a harsh *tthek*.

Plate 232

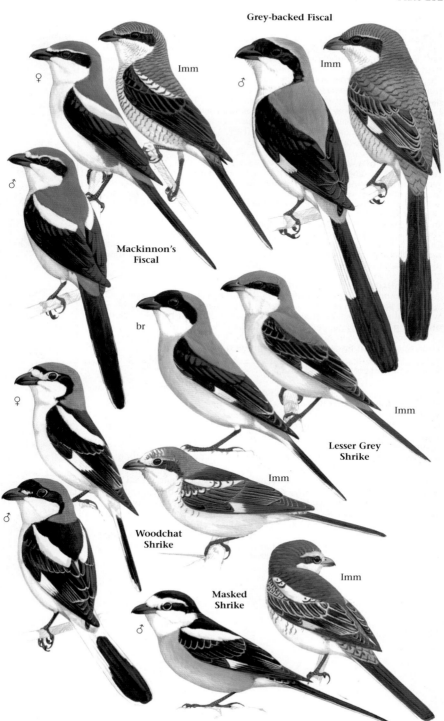

Grey-backed Fiscal

Imm

♀

Imm

♂

♂

Mackinnon's
Fiscal

br

♀

Imm

Lesser Grey
Shrike

♂

Imm

Woodchat
Shrike

Masked
Shrike

♂

Imm

Isabelline Shrike *Lanius isabellinus* 18cm, 7"
[Red-tailed Shrike]

Two races occur: ad ♂ *phoenicuroides* is reddish-brown above, particularly bright on the crown and tail; ad ♂ nominate has the crown and mantle uniform greyish-brown with a rufous rump and tail. ♀♀ and imms are similar to Red-backed Shrike, but the *tail is rufous both above and below*. Imm is also more lightly barred above than similar aged Red-backed. Their taxonomic status is controversial and they may be specifically distinct, moreover in a small area of overlap on their breeding grounds *phoenicuroides* hybridises with Red-backed Shrike. **HH** common winter visitor from the Palearctic, occurring almost anywhere on passage from Oct–Apr, but most numerous in open bush country from sea-level to 2200m. **Vo** calls a harsh *chack* or a quiet repeated *ch-ch-ch…*

Red-backed Shrike *Lanius collurio* 18cm, 7"

Ad ♂ is striking and distinctive with a blue-grey crown, neat black face mask, chestnut wings, blue-grey rump, and a *black tail with white patches at the base*. Three races occur and differ mainly in back colour: grey in *kobylini* and chestnut in nominate and *pallidifrons*. ♀♀ and imms are very similar to Isabelline Shrike, and best identified by their *grey undertail* and more heavily barred underparts. Imm is more heavily barred above than similar aged Isabelline. **HH** common, widespread and conspicuous Palearctic migrant and winter visitor from sea-level to 3000m. **Vo** makes *tak* or *chack* calls which are higher pitched than Isabelline Shrike, but may also sing a rather sweet *Sylvia*-like song prior to departure.

Emin's Shrike *Lanius gubernator* 15cm, 6"

Ad ♂ is similar but slightly smaller than Red-backed Shrike, with a *chestnut rump* (not grey), a white throat, and tawny underparts. Ad ♀ is like a dull ♂ with a smaller black face mask. Imm is much duller and barred blackish above and below. **HH** uncommon and localised resident, inhabiting open bush country between 600–1500m across NUg. **Vo** a very quiet species. Emin wrote that it has a pleasant call, but no description exists.

Magpie Shrike *Urolestes melanoleucus* 43cm, 17"
[Long-tailed Shrike]

A large and very long-tailed shrike: ad ♂ is predominantly black with white scapulars (forming a conspicuous white 'V' across the back), a greyish-white rump, and variable white wing patches. Ad ♀ is similar, but with white on the flanks. Imm is dark blackish-brown with dusky barring. **HH** highly sociable shrike usually found in small groups of up to 10 birds in open acacia woodlands from 800–1800m. **Vo** song is an attractive, extremely liquid rambling refrain, repeated for long periods without a break. Call is a harsh *chahh-chahh-chahh…*

Yellow-billed Shrike *Corvinella corvina* 31cm, 12"

A long-tailed dull brown shrike narrowly streaked throughout with black with a conspicuous *yellow bill*. Sexes alike. In flight, reveals an obvious rufous patch across the primaries. Imm is similar but duller with much barring. **HH** small groups of 4–8 are locally common in woodland and bush country from 600–2200m. **Vo** social and noisy: call is a very harsh *tik-chahh* or *tik-tik-tik-chahh* which is often repeated.

Plate 233

phoenicuroides
Isabelline Shrike

♂

Imm

♂

nominate

♂

kobylini

Red-backed Shrike

Imm

♂

nominate

Imm

♂

♀

Emin's Shrike

Imm

Magpie Shrike

♂

Imm

Imm

Ad

Yellow-billed Shrike

BOUBOUS AND GONOLEKS

Several of these bush-shrikes (genus *Laniarius*) are named after key qualities of their calls, but the terminology is not consistent. Generally speaking the all-black or black and white species are called boubous, black and red birds are gonoleks, and the black, white and chestnut species are bush-shrikes. All are rather stocky and move actively, but slowly, with a horizontal posture. They frequently draw attention to themselves with loud far-carrying calls. Sexes are alike unless otherwise mentioned.

Tropical Boubou *Laniarius aethiopicus* 21cm, 8"

A black and white boubou tinged pink below (more intense in the south). Five races occur differing chiefly in the extent of white in the wing: western and SETz birds have long white wing stripes; more northerly birds and those east of the Great Rift Valley have white on some wing-coverts only. In coastal Ke and NETz (up to 1800m in the Uluguru Mts) the distinctive race *sublacteus* has no white in the wing, and there is also a glossy all black morph. Imms are finely barred buffy above on most races. **HH** pairs are common in the undergrowth of woodlands, thick bush and gardens from sea-level to 3000m. **Vo** pairs usually call a melodic antiphonal duet, so perfectly timed as to sound like one bird: *wii-hoo wii-hoo* or *wii-hoo-hoo-hoo-hoo* are typical but there are many variations. Other calls include a harsh *tchik* and coarse scolds. **SS** Black-backed Puffback.

Lüdher's Bush-shrike *Laniarius luehderi* 18cm, 7"

Ad is a distinctive bush-shrike with a *chestnut-orange crown, throat and breast*. Imm is olive-brown above with pale yellow spots and a stripe on wing reminiscent of the nicators (plate 155), dull yellow below with fine barring. **HH** a rather secretive bush-shrike of undergrowth and tangled creepers within forest and thickly wooded valleys from 700–2400m. **Vo** usual ♂ song is a long, strange deep vibrating note *worrrrk* to which the ♀ responds with a harsh *tikk* or a long *kssshshssssh*. Also calls a variety of harsh notes.

Black-headed Gonolek *Laniarius erythrogaster* 21cm, 8"

Ads are a striking black and scarlet with creamy-white eyes and a buffy vent. Imm is blackish-brown above and pale dirty yellow below with extensive dark scaling and random red spotting. **HH** common but rather shy resident of woodland, thickets, bush country and cultivation from 600–1600m. It usually keeps low, but also ascends to canopy to call loudly. **Vo** ♂ makes a loud rather oriole-like note and the ♀ sometimes answers with a harsh ratchet-like *tchtchtchtchtch*.

Papyrus Gonolek *Laniarius mufumbiri* 19cm, 7.5"

Similar to Black-headed Gonolek but with a *golden-yellow crown, narrow white wing bar,* and orange-red underparts. Imm is much duller than ad with a dingy olive crown, dull yellowish throat and dirty pinky-orange underparts. **HH** locally common but shy and difficult to observe in dense papyrus swamps from 1100–1600m. **Vo** ♂ calls a musical *wi-onk wi-onk* or *chonk-chonk* (sometimes in a rhythmical series) and ♀ may accompany with similar antiphonal notes or a harsh *chh-t-chh*.

Red-naped Bush-shrike *Laniarius ruficeps* 18cm, 7"

A black, white and grey bush-shrike with an orange-red crown or nape. Two races occur in NEKe: *rufinuchalis* has a black forecrown and rufous nape, while *kismayensis* has an entirely rufous crown. ♀♀ are similar, but slightly duller with an olive-grey back. Imms lacks rufous on the crown, are largely dull grey above, and greyish-white below. **HH** shy and local, keeping to thick cover in semi-arid *Commiphora* and acacia bush from sea-level to 1000m. **Vo** ♂ calls a nasal, burry frog-like upslur and the ♀ answers with loud ratchet-like antiphonal notes. Other calls include harsh tiks and deep clicks.

Plate 234

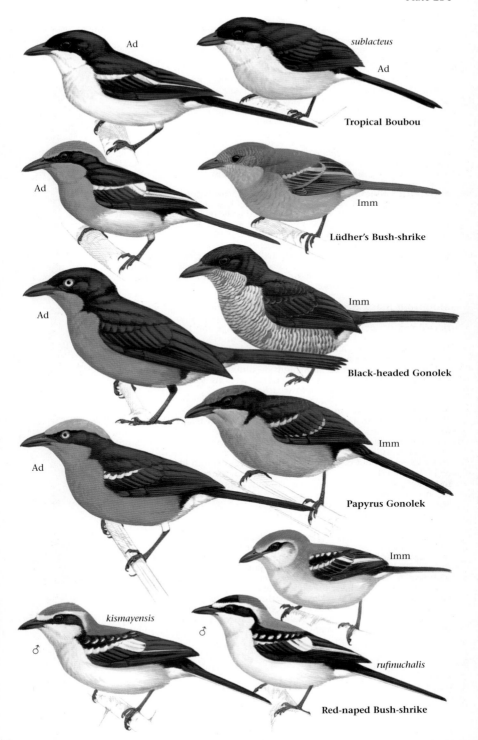

Ad

sublacteus

Ad

Tropical Boubou

Ad

Imm

Lüdher's Bush-shrike

Ad

Imm

Black-headed Gonolek

Ad

Imm

Papyrus Gonolek

Imm

kismayensis

♂

♂

rufinuchalis

Red-naped Bush-shrike

BLACK BOUBOUS

Four similar looking black boubous, which all occupy different habitats or ranges. Horizontal posture distinguishes them from drongos (plate 241) and black flycatchers (plate 204) which sit upright, and their matt plumage distinguishes them from the glossy male cuckoo-shrikes that additionally have orange gapes (plate 154). Sexes are similar.

Slate-coloured Boubou *Laniarius funebris* 20cm, 8"

Only black boubou of bush country: ad is *dull dark slate-grey*. Imm is finely barred above and below with tawny and black. **HH** common and widespread in semi-arid bush in NEUg and Ke, while in the west and most of Tz it occurs in more moist woodland, undergrowth and thickets in cultivation from sea-level to 2200m. Invariably in pairs and rather shy, often on the ground, but calls from bush tops in the early morning. **Vo** duets: ♂ most frequently calls a loud *shhhhhhh*, or a loud clicking followed by *coco-weet*, the *weet* rising as an interrogatory slur. Also makes a variety of nasal, gruff and reverberating calls accompanied antiphonally by the ♀.

Fülleborn's Black Boubou *Laniarius fuelleborni* 20cm, 8" ●

Ad ♂ is extremely similar to Slate-coloured Boubou, and ♀ differs only in having a slight olive wash over the breast and belly. Imm is also similar but slightly greyer above, with a dull olive-green wash to the underparts. Sometimes considered conspecific with Mountain Black Boubou. **HH** pairs are locally common and restricted to highland forest and nearby secondary growth in the mountains of E and STz above 900m. **Vo** a versatile songster, with a loud variety of antiphonal calls and whistles usually given from within deep cover. Calls are rather higher pitched than those of well-known Slate-coloured Boubou.

Mountain Black Boubou *Laniarius poensis* 20cm, 8"

Ad ♂ is extremely similar to Fülleborn's Black Boubou (and sometimes considered conspecific), but has a different call, range and imm plumage. ♀ and imm are slightly duller, without the olive-green wash of Fülleborn's. **HH** pairs are common and restricted to highland forests in the west. Calls frequently but is difficult to locate in the dense undergrowth and tangled creepers. **Vo** makes an exceptionally wide variety of antiphonal calls and whistles, possibly unmatched by any other *Laniarius*. Many are sequences of bell-notes followed by an explosive *tchak*.

Sooty Boubou *Laniarius leucorhynchus* 22cm, 8.5"

Slightly larger than the other black boubous with a heavier longer bill. Appears very black in the field. Imm is slightly duller black with a conspicuous whitish bill. **HH** pairs are restricted to the west where it is not uncommon in forest undergrowth and secondary growth between 700–1400m. Shy but calls throughout the day. Collected once in WKe in 1931. **Vo** song is a deep pulsating bell that throbs through the forest, either in triplets *poo poo poo* or as long regular single notes. Other calls include a harsh, crescendo of rising notes, intermixed with loud clicking and antiphonal notes from the ♀.

Brubru *Nilaus afer* 13cm, 5"

Ad ♂ is a small black and white bush-shrike with chestnut flanks. In three widespread races, ♂ has a bold white supercilium. ♀ is similar, although more blackish-brown above and some show dark streaks on the throat. Imm is dark brown heavily mottled creamy-buff and white above, whitish with brown crescentic barring below. In C and STz, ♂ of distinctive race *nigrotemporalis* lacks the white supercilium, and ♀ has a very short supercilium and some black speckles on the throat and breast. **HH** single birds or pairs are widespread, common and vocal in the canopy of open woodlands and acacia country from sea-level to 2500m. **Vo** sings a loud, very burry, gently rising and rather telephone-like slur *brrrrrrrrp*, and also utters loud scraping notes.

Plate 235

Ad

Imm

Slate-coloured Boubou

Ad

Imm

Fülleborn's Black Boubou

Mountain Black Boubou

Ad

Imm

Sooty Boubou

Imm

♂

♂

nigrotemporalis

Brubru

PUFFBACKS

A similar looking group of bush-shrikes: males are predominantly black and white, females are similar, or grey and buffy-brown. Colour of eyes, scapulars and wings, as well as range, aid identification. All are active birds usually found in pairs in the higher parts of trees (except Pringle's). They are often in mixed-species flocks. Males display by puffing out long loose back feathers and flying about calling loudly.

Black-backed Puffback *Dryoscopus cubla* 17cm, 6.5"

[Puffback]

Two distinct races occur: ad ♂ of widespread race *hamatus* is black above with a *pure white rump, scapulars and wing edgings*. Ad ♀ has a short white stripe in front of the eye and a greyer rump. Imm is similar to ♀ but duller above with buffy underparts and wing edges. Coastal race *affinis* is similar but the wings are plain black on both sexes. All ads have bright red eyes. **HH** pairs are common in forest edge, woodland and gardens from sea-level to 2200m. **Vo** ♂ calls a short click followed by a rising upslurred whiplash note, to which the ♀ frequently answers with a harsh paired *ssssshh ssssshh*. In a display flight also calls a loud abrupt *chow-chow-chow-chow-chow-...*, up to 10 times, and a rapid *tik-weeu- tik-weeu- tik-weeu...* **SS** Tropical Boubou.

Northern Puffback *Dryoscopus gambensis* 18cm, 7"

Ad ♂ is very similar to ♂ Black-backed Puffback, but is *pale grey on the scapulars and rump* with a slightly heavier bill. Ad ♀ is earth-brown above with buffy wing edges and tawny-buff below. Similar ♀ Pink-footed Puffback has a grey crown and upper back. Eyes of both sexes orange-red. Imm is similar to ♀ but with buffy fringes above. **HH** common and widespread in a variety of woodland and dry acacia country from 900–2200m. **Vo** calls are shorter, much harder and delivered more rapidly than Black-backed Puffback, often calls *tik-teek* or *tik-tik-teek*, and in a display flight a strident *chok-chok-chok-chok-chok*.

Pringle's Puffback *Dryoscopus pringlii* 14cm, 5.5"

Ad ♂ is similar to other ♂ puffbacks, but much smaller with a *pale base to the lower mandible*, pale grey scapulars and rump. Ad ♀ and imm are pale grey-brown above with a whitish loral spot, and pale dirty white underparts. Eyes bright red. **HH** in our area pairs are restricted to semi-arid and arid bush from 200–1200m, particularly in *Commiphora* and acacia woodland. **Vo** call is not well known, but the ♂ repeats a downslurred *cheow-cheow-cheow-cheow-* during the display flight, and the ♀ is known to sing a subdued and complex warble incorporating clicks and strange mewing sounds.

Pink-footed Puffback *Dryoscopus angolensis* 16cm, 6"

Ad ♂ has a black cap, grey back, and paler grey rump, all contrasting with darker grey wings: it is very pale grey below. Ad ♀ has a distinctive grey crown contrasting with an earth-brown back and wings: it is rich tawny-buff below with a white belly. *Eyes brown and legs pink*. Imm is like dull ♀. **HH** restricted to primary forests of the west where it prefers canopy and mid-stratum tangled vines from 900-2500m. **Vo** common call is a very harsh, grating and ratchet-like *trrrrrrrr*.

Red-eyed Puffback *Dryoscopus senegalensis* 17cm, 6.5"

A clean-looking, boldly marked puffback of the west. Ad ♂ is jet black above contrasting with a snow white rump and underparts. ♀ is similar. **HH** pairs occur in secondary growth and overgrown cultivation in the Semliki lowlands of WUg. **Vo** song is a repeated downslurred whiplash *t'yow t'yow t'yow...*

Plate 236

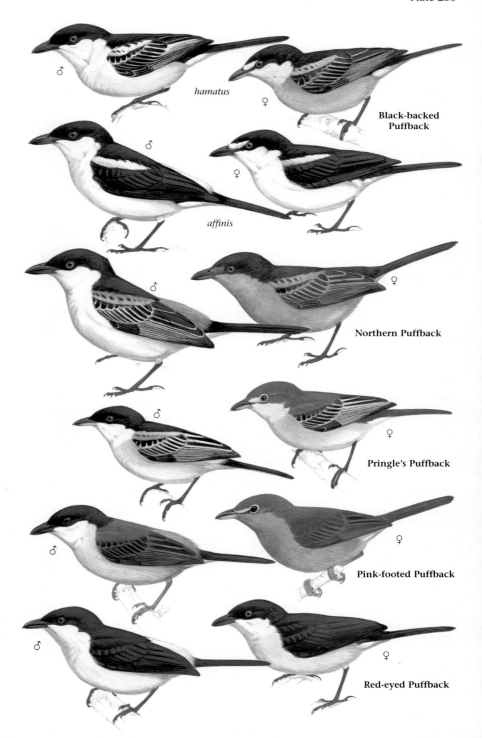

hamatus ♂ ♀

Black-backed Puffback

affinis ♂ ♀

Northern Puffback ♂ ♀

Pringle's Puffback ♂ ♀

Pink-footed Puffback ♂ ♀

Red-eyed Puffback ♂ ♀

TCHAGRAS

Rather shy grey-brown bush-shrikes with rufous wings and white-tipped tails, which are best identified by their distinctive head patterns. Inhabiting thick cover, they have slow movements, often feed on the ground and rarely ascend above eye-level. All display in flight, ascending on noisy vibrating wings and then descending into cover calling loudly.

Black-crowned Tchagra *Tchagra senegala* 21cm, 8"

Ad is larger than similar Brown-crowned Tchagra with a *broad black crown stripe*. Imm is duller with a brown crown stripe similar to Brown-crowned, but it lacks the black crown borders of that species and at close quarters usually shows some black speckling. **HH** common and widespread from sea-level to 2100m inhabiting cover within open woodland, bushed grasslands and dry country. **Vo** sings a loud far-carrying fluty and thrush-like whistled song unlike any other tchagra, and also calls a wide variety of harsh and hollow-sounding taks and churrs.

Brown-crowned Tchagra *Tchagra australis* 19cm, 7.5"

[Three-streaked Tchagra in southern Africa]
Ad has the *crown stripe brown bordered with black*, sometimes giving the impression that the bird is actually black-crowned. Imm is like ad but duller with more buffy-brown underparts. **HH** similar to Black-crowned Tchagra with no obvious habitat differences and often occurring in the same areas from sea-level to 2100m. **Vo** song, often given in a parachuting display flight, is a rapidly delivered series of sweet descending downslurs *tiu tiu tiu tiu tiu...* Also makes a variety of both harsh and musical churrs, chahs and sharp tak notes.

Three-streaked Tchagra *Tchagra jamesi* 17cm, 6.5"

A small tchagra with *three narrow black stripes on the head, one through each eye and one over the centre of the crown.* Imm is similar to ad but crown stripe is shorter. **HH** usually solitary, but may join mixed-species flocks in dense cover in dry bush and semi-desert country from sea-level to 1100m. **Vo** parachuting song-flight is similar to Brown-crowned Tchagra, but slightly higher-pitched, and the individual slurs are a more distinct *tui tui tui tui tui...*

Marsh Tchagra *Tchagra minuta* 18cm, 7"

Two distinct forms occur: in the west and north the nominate race has heavy black patches on the scapulars and mantle, forming a distinct black 'V'. In coastal Ke (rare) and Tz (except the NW) the races *reichenowi* and *anchietae* (**Anchieta's Tchagra**) occur: they lack the black 'V' on the back. *♂♂ of both forms have a solid black cap. ♀♀ have broad buff white superciliary stripes.* Imms have the crown mottled black and pale brown. **HH** thinly distributed within range, inhabiting rank vegetation along streams, tall wet grasslands and the edges of marshes from sea-level to 2000m. **Vo** nominate western birds display, usually in flight, with a bulbul-like and fairly harsh *swi'weet'weet'weer*. Calls are harsh scraping noises given slowly or rapidly in alarm. Race *anchietae* has a similar display and call, but it is a sweeter, slurred and more hurriedly delivered *siweet-wee*.

Rosy-patched Bush-shrike *Rhodophoneus cruentus* 23cm, 9"

A slender long-legged and striking bush-shrike, with distinctive patches of brilliant pink in the plumage. Two races occur: they have similar ♀ but distinctive ♂ plumages. Largely north of the equator, ♂ *hilgerti* has a brilliant pink stripe from the throat to the lower breast (without any black), while to the south and into NTz, ♂ *cathemagmena* has a similar pink stripe but also has a black band around the throat. Both have bright pink rumps. ♀♀ have a whitish throat edged with a black collar and a bright pink breast stripe. Imms are duller than ads and pale fringed above. **HH** common in pairs and small groups in semi-arid bush country from 150–1600m. Calls from open bush tops and frequently runs on the ground. **Vo** race *hilgerti* sings a loud far-carrying high-pitched and metallic *peeee-yng*, dropping and fading at the end and frequently given in duet, or sometimes with a distant ♀ replying with a lower note. Race *cathemagmena* is similar, but the call is lower pitched.

Plate 237

Imm

Ad

Black-crowned Tchagra

Ad

Imm

Brown-crowned Tchagra

Three-streaked Tchagra

♂

reichenowi

nominate

♀

♂

Marsh Tchagra

cathemagmena

Imm

♂

♂

♀

hilgerti

hilgerti

**Rosy-patched
Bush-shrike**

COLOURFUL BUSH-SHRIKES

Stunning bush-shrikes of forest and bush country. Occurring singly or in pairs, they move steathily through cover with a horizontal posture. Several attract attention to themselves with far-carrying whistled calls. Sexes similar.

Sulphur-breasted Bush-shrike *Malaconotus sulfureopectus* 17cm, 6.5"
[Orange-breasted Bush-shrike]
Ad has a *narrow yellow supercilium separating the grey crown from a black eye mask*. Bright yellow below with broad wash of orange over the breast. Imm lacks black on face, has a whitish throat, and is plain yellow below. Similar Grey-headed Bush-shrike is much larger with a huge thick bill and no black on the face. **HH** common and widespread in a wide variety of woodland, thickets and acacia country from sea-level to 3000m, often in mixed-species flocks. **Vo** varied song is a repeated series of high bell-notes which fade at the end *whi-wi-whi-whi-whi-wherrr*. Also calls *pupupupu* and an assortment of harsh scolds.

Grey-headed Bush-shrike *Malaconotus blanchoti* 25cm, 10"
A large and bulky grey-headed bush-shrike with a massive bill and yellow eyes which is yellow below with variable rufous-orange wash across the breast (virtually none in WTz, and extending onto flanks from NKe to NETz). Imm is paler with dark eyes. **HH** widespread and common at forest edge, in woodland and acacia country from sea-level to 3000m, often occurring in the same areas as much smaller Sulphur-breasted Bush-shrike. **Vo** usual call is a slowly repeated hollow whistle, either *whoo-whooik, whoo-whooik...* or either note repeated singly. Also makes loud clicks and a screeched *ereeek, ereeek, ereeek ...*

Lagden's Bush-shrike *Malaconotus lagdeni* 25cm, 10"
Very similar to Grey-headed Bush-shrike, but lacks a loral spot, the *wing-coverts and inner secondaries are black broadly edged in yellow*, and there is no rufous wash across the breast. Imm is paler below, with white in the centre of the throat, breast and belly. **HH** restricted to mountain forest along the Albertine Rift from 2200–2800m, where it can be locally common in forest undergrowth and the mid-stratum. **Vo** bell-note whistle is very similar to Grey-headed Bush-shrike, but higher pitched.

Uluguru Bush-shrike *Malaconotus alius* 22cm, 8.5" ● ●
A large green and yellow bush-shrike with a *distinctive black cap*, and yellow underparts washed green on the flanks. Imm plumage is unknown. **HH** Tz endemic which is rare and confined to the forest canopy of the Uluguru Mts from 1500–2000m. **Vo** call lacks the bell-like quality of other bush-shrikes: usually makes a rather starling-like two note *wu-chiew* (the second note a higher downslur), but this can be mixed with a rhythmic *chi toktok-chii, toktok-chii...*

Fiery-breasted Bush-shrike *Malaconotus cruentus* 25cm, 10"
A startling large bush-shrike which is brilliant orange-red below, with yellow-tipped black tertials, and a *green tail with a black sub-terminal band and yellow tips*. Imm has a brownish crown, whitish throat, and is greenish-yellow below. **HH** in our area, it is known only from the Semliki Forest, WUg, where it is a shy and uncommon bird of the forest canopy. **Vo** known to call repeatedly two far-carrying hollow and bell-like notes.

Plate 238

Sulphur-breasted Bush-shrike

Ad

Imm

Ad

Grey-headed Bush-shrike

Ad

Lagden's Bush-shrike

Ad

Uluguru Bush-shrike

Imm

Ad

Fiery-breasted Bush-shrike

Black-fronted Bush-shrike *Malaconotus nigrifrons*   18cm, 7"
Ad has a *broad black stripe through the eye and across the forecrown, without a
white upper border*. Tail is green with small yellow tips. Four colour morphs
occur, differing in the colour of the underparts, which may be yellow, red,
buffy-apricot with a white throat, or black on the throat and breast. Imm
is paler than ad without the black face mask. Sometimes considered conspecific with Many-coloured Bush-shrike. **HH** fairly common and widespread in highland forest from 900–2300m, occasionally down to 300m.
They are most frequent in the canopy often with mixed-species flocks. **Vo**
commonly calls a rising nasal snore, or varied but clear hollow ringing
notes including *whoop-wah*, with the second note lower, or a repeated *ooo*.

Many-coloured Bush-shrike *Malaconotus multicolor*   18cm, 7"
Ad has a *whitish stripe above the black face mask*. Underparts variable: yellow, yellow with orange wash, or scarlet. Ad ♀ has the forecrown white
and ear-coverts grey. Tail is mostly black with yellow tips. Imm is dull
green above, yellowish with light barring below. **HH** in our area localised
and restricted to the west, inhabiting thick tangled vines and forest
canopy from 1500–2500m. **Vo** varied calls are similar to Black-fronted
Bush-Shrike.

Doherty's Bush-shrike *Malaconotus dohertyi*   18cm, 7"
Ad ♂ is similar to Four-coloured Bush-shrike, but *the forecrown is bright red,*
with no red below the black breast band, and a black tail. Ad ♀ is similar
but the breast band is narrower and the tail is more olive-green. Imm is
mostly dull green with a yellowish-olive wash to the breast, entirely barred
blackish and buff throughout, vent dull red. Breast band begins to show
with age. A very rare morph with a yellow forecrown and throat is known.
HH reasonably common, but shy and difficult to observe in the undergrowth of highland forests from 1600–3500m. **Vo** high distinctive and far-
carrying repeated *wick, wick wick-wick-wick ...*

Four-coloured Bush-shrike *Malaconotus quadricolor*   18cm, 7"
[Gorgeous Bush-shrike]
Another beautiful bush-shrike: ad ♂ is best identified from Doherty's Bush-
shrike by a *yellow-orange forecrown*, some orange-red extending below the
black breast band and a totally different range and altitudinal limits. Ad ♀
is similar but slightly duller with a narrower breast band. Imm is dull green
above and faintly barred yellowish-green below, breast band absent or broken. **HH** pairs are secretive but call frequently from dense thickets and forest undergrowth in the coastal lowlands, mainly below 600m (but up to
2000m in NETz). **Vo** typical call is an explosive, far-carrying, rhythmical
wik-a-wik-a-wik, wik, but also utters strange, short frog-like churrs in alarm.

Bocage's Bush-shrike *Malaconotus bocagei*   16cm, 6"
[Grey-green Bush-shrike]
Very different from the other bush-shrikes and therefore not immediately
suggesting one. Ad is blackish above, greyer on the back and wings, with a
bold white forecrown and supercilium, and white below with a faint
creamy wash. An aberrant form at Kakamega, Ke had a black breast band.
Imm is barred above with buff and black, pale yellowish with grey fringing
below. **HH** locally common in canopy at forest edge, in secondary growth
and nearby forest thickets from 1100–2200m. **Vo** in the west of our region
commonly calls a repeated rhythmical *wi-chuk-a-chuk wi-chuk-a-chuk*, while
more easterly birds call a high whistled and rhythmic descending sequence
of notes *pipipipi piu piu piu piu*.

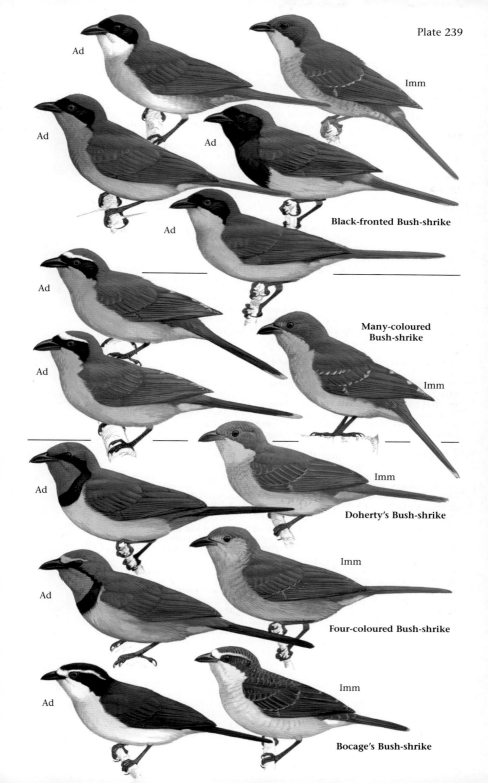

Plate 239

Ad

Imm

Ad

Ad

Ad

Black-fronted Bush-shrike

Ad

**Many-coloured
Bush-shrike**

Ad

Imm

Ad

Imm

Doherty's Bush-shrike

Imm

Ad

Four-coloured Bush-shrike

Ad

Imm

Bocage's Bush-shrike

HELMET-SHRIKES

Endemic to Africa, helmet-shrikes are active, social and vocal birds, which travel slowly in loose flocks, often snapping their bills. Northern White-crowned Shrike is more sedentary. Head and crest markings aid identification. Sexes are alike.

Northern White-crowned Shrike *Eurocephalus rueppelli* 21cm, 8"

Stocky and thick-necked with a white crown, blackish eye mask and dark brown wings and tail: white rump is conspicuous in flight. Imm is finely barred above, with a scaly brown and white crown and a buffy-brown band across the breast: bill is pinkish. **HH** small flocks are common in bush country from sea-level to 2300m, perching in small trees and flying down to the ground to feed. **Vo** group frequently calls together with a series of pinched, nasal complaining notes and harsh chattering, and also make querulous loud squeaks in flight.

White-crested Helmet-shrike *Prionops plumatus* 18–23cm, 7–9"

[White Helmet-shrike]
Four races occur: across much of Ug and NWKe races *cristatus* and *concinnatus* are large, with long curly white crests; the closed wing of *cristatus* is almost plain black; *concinnatus* shows a long white wing stripe. In EKe and NETz *vinaceigularis* has a straight white crest and no white in the closed wing; and elsewhere *poliocephalus* has a short straight grey crest and a long white wing stripe: both latter races are small. All races have yellow eyes, rich yellow eye-wattles, and in flight show a conspicuous white bar across the primaries. Imms are similar to ads but dingy, with dark eyes and no wattles. **HH** widespread and locally common inhabiting open woodland and bush country from sea-level to 2200m. **Vo** flocks frequently call long burry downslurred notes *kirro, kirro, kirro*, often accompanied with bill snaps and chattering.

Grey-crested Helmet-shrike *Prionops poliolophus* 26cm, 10" ●

Larger than White-crested Helmet-shrike with a long pointed *grey crest extending backwards from the centre of the crown, yellow eyes (with no wattles)*, and black patches on the sides of the breast. Imm is similar but with a shorter crest and dark eyes. **HH** an uncommon East African endemic, occurring in acacia and leleshwa bush country from 1200–2200m. **Vo** complex calls are deeper and more guttural than White-crested Helmet-Shrike, but also include typical helmet-shrike bill snapping and harsh churring notes.

Chestnut-fronted Helmet-shrike *Prionops scopifrons* 18cm, 7"

Mostly grey-brown, darker on the head and wings, with a whitish vent and corners to the tail. Forecrown has a rectangular patch of *velcro-like chestnut bristles*: and eyes are yellow with blue-grey wattles. Imm is rather duller brown, lacks bristles on the forecrown, and has dark eyes. **HH** groups of up to 25 birds are locally common in woodland and forest canopy, often in mixed-species flocks, from the coastal lowlands to the mountain foothills of NETz (with rare isolated populations in CKe). **Vo** very noisy, members of roving flocks give frequent high-pitched upslurred trilled rattles *trrrrrrrrrt trrrrrrrrrt*, and the song consists of these rattles mingled with tit-like whistles.

Retz's Helmet-shrike *Prionops retzii* 21cm, 8"

[Red-billed Helmet-shrike in southern Africa]
Similar to Chestnut-fronted Helmet-shrike but larger and *much blacker with a curling black crest, bright red bill and eye wattles*, and yellow eyes. Imm is duller and browner with a shorter crest. **HH** small flocks are widespread but only locally common in a variety of woodland from sea-level to 1900m. **Vo** mobile flocks give a mixed assortment of strange burry, buzzy calls and a loud descending sequence of piercing upslurred whistles *tiyui-tiyui-tiyui-tiyu-tiyui-tiyui...* accompanied by rasping notes and bill snapping.

Red-billed Helmet-shrike *Prionops caniceps* 18cm, 7"

An attractive and distinctive red-billed helmet-shrike, with a pale blue-grey head, black collar, white breast, and chestnut mid-breast to vent. Imm is generally duller, washed brownish and white on the head, with dark eyes and bill. **HH** an uncommon canopy species, in our area restricted to the forests of WUg from 700–1100m. **Vo** roving parties have loud explosive paired calls *tchew tchew tchew tchew* as well as rather querulous burry upslurs and bill snapping.

Plate 240

Northern White-crowned Shrike

Imm

Ad

Imm

cristatus

Ad

White-crested Helmet-shrike

Imm

Grey-crested Helmet-shrike

poliocephalus

Ad

Imm

Ad

Ad

Imm

Chestnut-fronted Helmet-shrike

Ad

Imm

Ad

Retz's Helmet-shrike

Ad

Imm

Red-billed Helmet-shrike

DRONGOS

Medium-sized black birds with hook-tipped bills and red or orange-red eyes. Best distinguished by tail shape, habitat, range and voice. Often sit still for long periods and then making feeding sallies. Upright posture similar to black flycatchers (plate 204), but drongos are easily separated by red eyes and thicker shrike-like bills. Black boubous (plate 235) and cuckoo-shrikes (plate 154) are more active and move with a horizontal posture. Sexes are similar.

Fork-tailed Drongo *Dicrurus adsimilis* 25cm, 10"
[Common Drongo]

Ad is glossy black (blue-black in good light) with a deeply forked tail. Moulting birds can show strange looking double-forked tails. In flight, shows a large pale window in the wing. Imm has brown eyes, some buffy speckling on the wings, is finely barred buffy-grey and black below, and has a less deeply forked tail. **HH** singles and pairs are common and widespread at forest edge, in open wooded country, semi-arid bush and cultivated areas from sea-level to 2200m. **Vo** highly variable song is a long rambling and rather coarse mixture of nasal, twangy notes, none or which are clear or pure.

Velvet-mantled Drongo *Dicrurus modestus* 28cm, 11"

Very similar to Fork-tailed Drongo, but has a *matt velvet-black mantle contrasting with the glossy wings and nape*, and a slightly more deeply forked tail. In flight, wings look blacker than in Fork-tailed, and do not show the pale windows. Imm has brown eyes and is dull grey and black barred below. **HH** pairs are rather local and uncommon, usually seen on an exposed branch below canopy in the forest interior, or in clearings within good forest from 700–1700m. **Vo** songs are not as rambling as Fork-tailed Drongo, but are more interrogatory mixing short pauses with sweet and harsh notes including a commonly heard *wichitirchi rit rit*.

Square-tailed Drongo *Dicrurus ludwigii* 19cm, 7.5"

Smaller than Fork-tailed Drongo, lacks the pale wing patches and, despite its name, the tail is not square, just *less deeply forked*. Two races occur: in WKe *sharpei* sexes are alike and the eyes are orange-red, but in eastern nominate the ♀ is more blackish-grey below and the eyes are scarlet-red. Imms are duller, with buffy speckling on the wing-coverts and light barring below. **HH** single birds, pairs, or occasionally up to six together, inhabit the forest interior and edge from sea-level to 2000m. **Vo** race *sharpei* frequently calls a short scratchy and repeated *swi-chh* or *swi-chee-chee-chee*, while eastern birds have loud, rhythmical, rapidly delivered phrases.

CROWS

Large strong and familiar black, grey and black, or black and white birds, with powerful flight and harsh voices. Easily identified by the extent of white in plumage or, in the all black species, by overall size and shape. Often unafraid of man, scavenging around villages and at rubbish dumps in towns and cities. Sexes are alike.

Piapiac *Ptilostomus afer* 36cm, 14"

An unusual crow: ads often *appear all-black with a long graduated tail*, but at close range may show dull brown wings and tail edges. In flight, pale grey-brown primaries are obvious. Bill is black in ad, but bright pink with a black tip in imm. **HH** small flocks are locally common from 600–1500m in open country and in the vicinity of *Borassus* palms in the west, invariably associating with cattle or large game, where they run about catching disturbed insects. **Vo** a noisy species especially at dawn and dusk, when parties keep up a cacophony of loud, squealing *skweeer* or *pee-ip* notes.

House Crow *Corvus splendens* 33cm, 13"
[Indian House Crow]

Slim black crow with a dark grey neck and breast, and a longish slightly decurved bill. Imm is duller than ad with a brownish cast. **HH** an introduced crow which is numerous and regarded as a serious pest along much of the coast, where it destroys the nests of smaller birds, and competes with the resident Pied Crow. **Vo** very noisy, calling a short, hurried *kwaa kwaa...*

Plate 241

Fork-tailed Drongo

Ad

Imm

Ad

Velvet-mantled Drongo

Ad

nominate

♀

Square-tailed Drongo

Piapiac

Ad

Imm

Ad

House Crow

Ad

Pied Crow *Corvus albus* 46cm, 18"
Boldly marked and distinctive black and white crow: *white hind-collar extends around sides of neck and across the breast.* Imm is similar to ad, but duller. **HH** pairs to large flocks are common and widespread occurring in all but the driest areas, as well as towns and open country from sea-level to 3000m. **Vo** variable calls include both long and short caws in flight, but while perched birds may utter a deeper call or a quiet musical hollow *clork clork ...*

Cape Rook *Corvus capensis* 43cm, 17"
[Black Crow]
Slim-looking all-black crow with a noticeably *narrow bill* and lax throat (feathers appear shaggy). Ad may show a bluish or purplish sheen in good light, but in worn plumage are often rather brown. Imm has a dull brownish wash on the head and underparts. **HH** small flocks occur commonly in the Ke highlands and parts of NTz, mainly favouring open country and farmland below 2500m, although a separate population occurs in semi-desert in NKe at about 400m. **Vo** in addition to typical crow-like caws makes a variety of strange throaty and liquid calls, in which notes tend to slur together *kwah kworlik kworlik koh.*

Fan-tailed Raven *Corvus rhipidurus* 46cm, 18"
Rather stocky glossy black crow with a thick bill and short tail that stops well before the wing tips. In flight, *tail looks very short and the wings appear broad.* Head is usually black (like the body) but may be dark brown and thus similar to Brown-necked Raven (which has a longer tail). Imm is duller and browner than ad. **HH** singles and small flocks are common across NKe from 400–2600m in dry bush country with cliffs. **Vo** typical calls are varied but rather high-pitched caws, although it also has a quiet sub-song of sweet notes usually given from shade in the heat of the day.

Somali Crow *Corvus edithae* 46cm, 18"
Formerly treated as a race of Brown-necked Raven *Corvus ruficollis*. Similar to Fan-tailed Raven, but has a slightly slimmer bill and *usually, but not always, a brown head and nape.* Separated in flight by obviously longer slimmer tail which, when perched, extends approximately to the wing tips. **HH** singles and small flocks are common in semi-desert country of NKe from 200 to around 1000m. **Vo** calls a variety of caws and *kwaar-kwaar* notes, plus a throaty rolling *krrrrrrrr.*

White-naped Raven *Corvus albicollis* 56cm, 22"
[White-necked Raven]
Very large black raven (which may be browner on the head) with a *broad white collar at base of hindneck,* and a thick white-tipped black bill. Imm is duller than ad. **HH** pairs and small flocks prefer the vicinity of cliffs and mountains but wander widely, down to 400m in EKe and as high as 5800m on Mt Kilimanjaro, NTz. **Vo** calls a rather high-pitched *kerrrrrh,* with a more purring tremulous quality than other ravens and crows.

Plate 242

Pied Crow

Cape Rook

Fan-tailed
Raven

Somali Crow

White-naped
Raven

ORIOLES
Bright yellow birds, mostly with black heads or eye-stripes, and red bills. Several are very similar and best identified by the colour of their wing edges and the uppertail, and by range and habitat preferences. All immatures have dark bills.

African Black-headed Oriole   *Oriolus larvatus*   20cm, 8"
[Black-headed Oriole]

A black-headed oriole with the *upper side of the central tail feathers olive-green*. In the wing: greater coverts are greenish-yellow, outer secondaries black edged whitish, and inner secondaries black broadly edged yellow. Imm has the head and breast streaked blackish or dark green (when it can be mistaken for Green-headed Oriole). Hybrid *larvatus × percivali* with mixed tail patterns occur occasionally in the central highlands of Ke. **HH** common and widespread in woodlands, forest edge, gardens and bush country from sea-level to 2300m. **Vo** typically calls a hurried set of 4–6 mainly slurred notes lasting about 2 seconds *tiau...tor...te...wah (wee...o)*, repeating the same sequence monotonously, and at times mimicking other species softly.

Montane Oriole   *Oriolus percivali*   20cm, 8"

Very similar to Black-headed Oriole but the *upper side of the central tail feathers is black*. In the wing: greater coverts brighter yellow, and the outer and inner secondaries are largely black with narrow yellow-olive edging. Imm is streaked blackish on the head and upper breast. **HH** common and largely replacing Black-headed within highland forest from 1500–3000m. **Vo** has a very simple repeated song of four mainly slurred notes *wi te-wor who* is typical, but also sings a long, rambling and complex whistled sequence that may be given as a duet.

Western Black-headed Oriole   *Oriolus brachyrhynchus*   20cm, 8"

Very similar to Black-headed Oriole with the *upper side of the central tail feathers olive-green*. In the wing: greater coverts dull greenish-grey, the outer secondaries are edged dark grey (not whitish), and the inner secondaries dull olive-green (not yellow). Imm is much duller than ad with a dark olive-green mottled head and breast. **HH** locally common in forest and forest edge in Ug and in the interior of forest at Kakamega, WKe, from 700–1800m. **Vo** simple song consists of 3–4 loud and distinctly separated notes *or hor wah* or *wi wor hor wah* the last note is higher.

Black-winged Oriole   *Oriolus nigripennis*   20cm, 8"

Very similar to Montane Oriole with *upper side of central tail feathers black*. In the wing: *primary coverts are black* or with just the tiniest white tips (on other black-headed orioles this is a more obvious white spot), greater coverts are yellowish-green, and the outer and inner secondaries are blackish edged yellow. Imm has a dark dull olive-green head with variable black spotting extending to the breast. **HH** in our area uncommon and only known from Semliki Forest in WUg at 700m. **Vo** song is unknown.

Green-headed Oriole   *Oriolus chlorocephalus*   22cm, 8.5"

If seen well the *plain moss-green head, throat and upper breast are distinctive*. Back, wing-coverts and uppertail are also moss green, and the wings are largely plain grey without a white spot on the primary coverts. Beware head can look dark when birds are high in the forest canopy. Imm is duller, streaked with green on the underparts. **HH** local but not uncommon within its restricted range, occurring from sea-level to 1800m in forest, mature woodland and well-established secondary growth. **Vo** call is a typical oriole-like *hor weeeu*, but also commonly makes a strange burry cat-like upslur *nraaaaaah*.

Plate 243

African
Black-headed
Oriole

Imm

Ad

Montane
Oriole

Imm

Ad

Western
Black-headed
Oriole

Ad

Imm

Imm

Ad

Ad

Imm

Black-winged
Oriole

Green-headed
Oriole

African Golden Oriole *Oriolus auratus* 20cm, 8"
Ad ♂ only really likely to be confused with Eurasian Golden Oriole from which it differs in having a *longer black streak extending behind the eye and broad yellow edges to most of the wing feathers.* Ad ♀ is similar to ♂ but is duller and washed with olive above. Imm has a dark bill, *greenish-yellow edges to the wing-coverts,* and pale yellow and whitish underparts with black streaks. **HH** seasonally common in Tz and coastal Ke Mar–Sep, occurs less commonly as a widespread migrant elsewhere throughout the year. Inhabits forest, woodland, lush gardens and moist bush country from sea-level to 1800m. **Vo** has a rather forced but typical oriole-like song *wee ah hah waah,* but also commonly calls a burry extended miaouing upslur *nahararahhhhh.*

Eurasian Golden Oriole *Oriolus oriolus* 22cm, 8.5"
Ad ♂ has a *short black eye-stripe extending from base of bill to the eye, and mostly black wings.* Ad ♀ is highly variable, either like ♂, or with white from throat to vent, or like imm with a red bill. Imm differs from imm African Golden, by having slightly darker and plainer wings. **HH** common passage migrant and less common winter visitor from Oct–Apr. Can occur anywhere on passage but may be numerous along the coast in Apr. **Vo** most frequently heard call is a harsh scolding miaowing *kree-er,* but may also gives its familiar fluty and rolling *ori-ori-ori-ole* in Apr or May.

OXPECKERS
Endemic to Africa and related to starlings the two species differ mainly in bill, eye, eye-wattle and rump colour. Often called tick birds, they are mainly seen feeding on large wild mammals or cattle. Flocks roost together in dead trees. Sexes are alike.

Yellow-billed Oxpecker *Buphagus africanus* 22cm, 8.5"
Ad has a bulbous *bright yellow red-tipped bill and bright red eyes, and a pale creamy-buff rump* that contrasts with the darker back, wings and tail (and can be obvious even at a long distance). Imm has the bill and eyes dark brown and a slightly less obvious pale rump. **HH** common, but less so than formerly away from game parks, from sea-level to 3000m. Typically occurs in small loose flocks, feeding around a variety of large mammal; they are particularly fond of buffalo, giraffe and hippo. **Vo** calls are harsh rasps *rraaah* given both perched and in flight.

Red-billed Oxpecker *Buphagus erythrorhynchus* 20cm, 8"
Ad differs from Yellow-billed Oxpecker by *entirely red bill, red eye with a bright yellow eye-ring, and a plain brown rump* (which is uniform with back, wings and tail). Imm is similar to imm Yellow-billed, but is more uniform dark brown above, and may show a reddish base to the bill. **HH** common and widespread from sea-level to 3000m wherever wild mammals and undipped cattle occur. Overlaps with Yellow-billed in many areas. **Vo** calls are softer than Yellow-billed Oxpecker, a *ssshhhhhh* all given on one tone, and often accompanied with spitted notes and clicks *tsik, tsik ...*

Plate 244

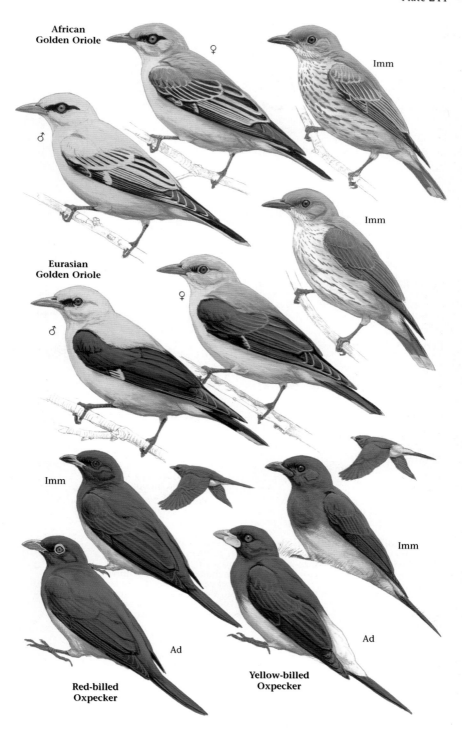

African
Golden Oriole

♀

Imm

Imm

♂

Eurasian
Golden Oriole

♀

♂

Imm

Imm

Red-billed
Oxpecker

Ad

Yellow-billed
Oxpecker

Ad

STARLINGS

In East Africa, the nine genera of starlings are a diverse group, varying from the iridescent glossy-starlings to the black and white of Magpie Starling. They include the largely similar red-winged group and singularly beautiful species like the Golden-breasted Starling. Sociable birds, they live mainly in small groups and may occur seasonally in large mixed-species flocks.

ELEGANT STARLINGS

Two very different looking slender, long-tailed and long-legged species.

Golden-breasted Starling *Cosmopsarus regius* 35cm, 14"

Stunningly beautiful starling which is iridescent blue, green and purple above, with a very long narrow graduated tail and bright golden-yellow breast and belly. Sexes are alike. Imm is much duller, with the head, mantle and upper breast mainly dull olive-brown, and breast to vent pale yellow. **HH** common in dry bush country in the east from near sea-level to 1200m. Usually in small flocks, restlessly moving through low bushes. **Vo** calls are simple: a repeated and complaining downslurred *rranyh*.

Ashy Starling *Cosmopsarus unicolor* 30cm, 12"

All brownish-grey with a long narrow tail and a pale creamy eye. In good plumage, shows a dark greenish gloss on the mantle, wings and tail. Imm is paler with dark eyes and a shorter tail. **HH** Tz endemic: small flocks are common, often feeding on the ground, in wooded grassland and bush country in N and CTz from 1000–1850m. **Vo** calls a simple, rather harsh and nasal *rannha*.

SLIM RED-WINGED STARLINGS

Poeoptera starlings are small or medium-sized with a slender build. Males are all blackish, females are greyer with dull chestnut patches on the primaries which are easily visible in flight. Can be confused with other red-winged starlings, but the *Onychognathus* group are larger and much stockier.

Kenrick's Starling *Poeoptera kenricki* 19cm, 7.5" ●

Ad ♂ is all black with grey eyes. Ad ♀ is dark slate-grey with chestnut primaries. In the field they are very difficult to identify from Stuhlmann's Starling but their ranges do not overlap. When perched high in canopy they can also be confused with Waller's Starling, but that species is larger, stockier, has chestnut wing patches in both sexes and has red eyes. Imms are duller versions of ads. **HH** EA endemic: flocks are fairly common but localised in the canopy of montane forests in NETz and CKe from 1000–2500m (but down to 450m in the East Usambara Mts, NETz). **Vo** song is a warbled drongo-like refrain, while the call is a repeated *pleep* note.

Stuhlmann's Starling *Poeoptera stuhlmanni* 19cm, 7.5"

Ad ♂ appears all black in the field (but blue-black in good light) with brown eyes and a very narrow pale yellow eye-ring. Ad ♀ is dark slate-grey with chestnut primaries. Imm is like a dull ♀. **HH** common in the canopy of highland forest in the west from 1500–2600m, but also in the Tugen Hills within the Great Rift Valley, Ke. **Vo** flocks are very vocal, especially in flight when they call a simple but musical *tuweet...*

Narrow-tailed Starling *Poeoptera lugubris* 22cm, 8.5"

Noticeably slender: ad ♂ is black (shows a violet sheen in good light), with creamy-yellow eyes, dull brown-grey wings, and a long narrow graduated tail. Ad ♀ is duller and greyer on the head with chestnut primaries. Imms are similar to ads, but duller. **HH** in our area, flocks are restricted to the far west where they are local but not uncommon residents and occasional wanderers in the forest canopy, from 700–1700m. **Vo** very noisy, both perched and on the wing, with flocks frequently calling penetrating, squealed downslurs *tyorrh*.

Plate 245

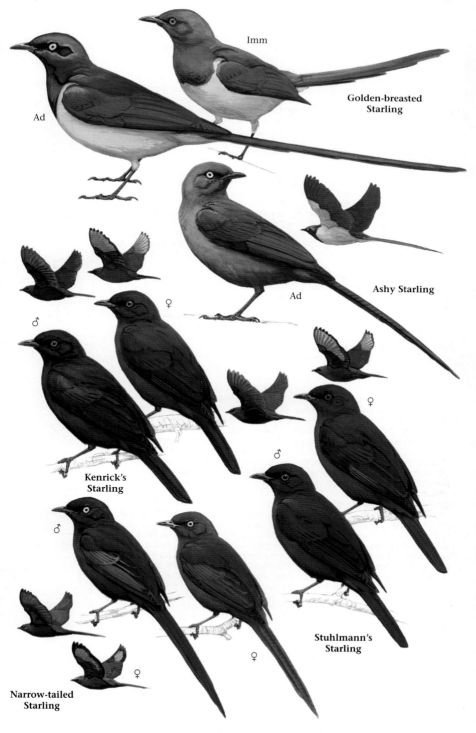

Golden-breasted
Starling

Imm

Ad

Ashy Starling

Ad

Kenrick's
Starling

♂

♀

♂

♀

Stuhlmann's
Starling

♂

♀

Narrow-tailed
Starling

♀

LARGE RED-WINGED STARLINGS
Commonly known as the red-winged group, *Onychognathus* starlings are superficially like *Poeoptera*, but larger and stockier, and both sexes have chestnut in the primaries. Most have long tails. At a distance, males look black or blue-black, and females are greyer on the head, often with a glossy blue-green sheen or streaking. Immatures are all like dull adults.

Red-winged Starling *Onychognathus morio*   31cm, 12"
Ad ♂ is a large blackish starling (shines blue-black in good light) with chestnut primaries, and a *long and pointed but not particularly well-graduated tail.* Ad ♀ has a greyer head and neck with some dark grey and violet streaking. Imm is similar, but duller. **HH** pairs and small flocks are common, usually in the vicinity of rocky hills or cliffs, but also in towns, from 500–4100m. **Vo** calls an attractive loud, oriole-like fluty note *wi-tyuor* either repeated when perched or as a single downslur in flight.

Chestnut-winged Starling *Onychognathus fulgidus*   29cm, 11"
Ad ♂ is very similar to Red-winged Starling, but appears slimmer and shows a greenish gloss to the head and violet on the mantle at close quarters. Ad ♀ has a grey head with some dark green streaks. Imm is similar, but much duller. **HH** in our area, pairs and small flocks are restricted to or near forest from 700–1300m in W and SUg. Range does not overlap with Red-winged. **Vo** usual call is a loud slightly rising and rather explosive *twee* when perched or in flight.

Waller's Starling *Onychognathus walleri*   23cm, 9"
Smaller than Red-winged Starling with a *shorter tail and red eyes.* In good light, ad ♂ shows blue-black and sometimes greenish reflections. In most of the range, the ad ♀ has a dark grey head and breast with some dark greenish-blue streaking, but on the more westerly race *elgonensis* the grey is restricted to the throat. Imm is like a dull ad. **HH** pairs and small flocks are widespread and common in the canopy of highland forests mainly between 1500–3000m, but down to 300m in the East Usambara Mts, NETz. **Vo** usual call is a loud far-carrying *wee-tyur* (the first note short and rising and the second descending and fading away), given when perched and in flight.

Slender-billed Starling *Onychognathus tenuirostris*   33cm, 13"
Similar to Red-winged Starling but slimmer with a *well graduated tail* and more slender bill. Ad ♂ has a *deep violet-blue-black gloss.* Ad ♀ is duller with grey on the head and breast. Imm is like a dull ad. **HH** small flocks are locally common, particularly around highland forest and on alpine moorlands, but are not restricted to high elevations and wander widely from 1400–4500m. **Vo** perched flocks give a loud but rather tuneless warble which may continue for long periods without a pause. In flight, flock members call harsh slurred notes *teeeo* or *teeoo.*

Bristle-crowned Starling *Onychognathus salvadorii*   42cm, 16.5"
Largest of the red-winged starlings with a *very long graduated tail and a small spiky cushion of feathers on the forecrown.* In good light shines glossy blue-black. Sexes are similar, and imms are duller. **HH** pairs and small flocks are sometimes common but rather local northern starlings restricted to semi-arid country below 1300m. They often associate with cliffs and gather to feed in Salvadora bushes. **Vo** usual flight-call is a loud, spitted, rising *swi-chit* or a more subdued but fluty *weeo* which perched birds may develop into a long but simple medley.

Plate 246

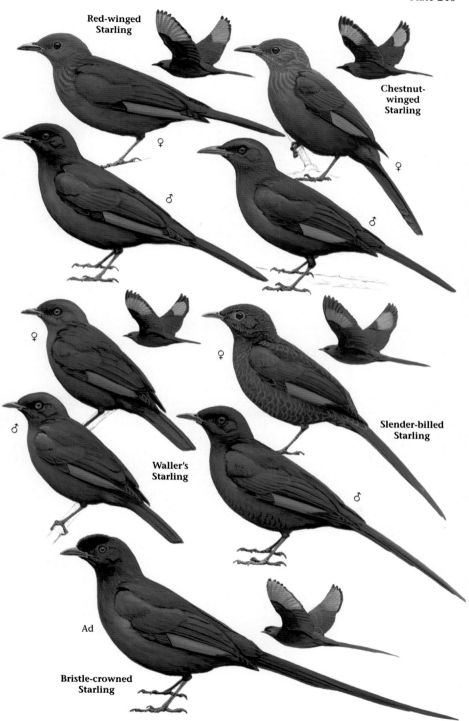

Red-winged Starling

♀

♂

Chestnut-winged Starling

♀

♂

♀

Waller's Starling

♂

♀

Slender-billed Starling

♂

Bristle-crowned Starling

Ad

GLOSSY BLUE STARLINGS
Often called glossy starlings, these birds are characterised by their highly iridescent blue-green plumage and brightly coloured (often yellow) eyes. A difficult group, but their distinctive calls and ranges help with identification. Sexes are alike.

Greater Blue-eared Starling *Lamprotornis chalybaeus* 22–24cm, 8.5–9.5"
Two distinct races occur: in NEUg, Ke (except the SE) and NCTz *cyaniventris* is all iridescent blue-green (including the tail), with matt blue-black ear-coverts and conspicuous yellow eyes. Elsewhere *sycobius* is smaller and greener with magenta-violet flanks and belly: it is very similar to Lesser Blue-eared Starling. Imm has a dark eye, is uniform dull blue-black above, and sooty-brown below. **HH** most common and widespread member of this group. Pairs and small flocks occur in a wide variety of habitats including woodland, bush country, cultivation and gardens from sea-level to 3000m. **Vo** song is a very complex and varied somewhat drongo-like warble, incorporating harsh and sweet notes. Call is a nasal cat-like mew *myaaah*, which is often given in flight.

Lesser Blue-eared Starling *Lamprotornis chloropterus* 19cm, 7.5"
Very similar to larger Greater Blue-eared Starling but *smaller-billed* and shorter-tailed. Often looks very green, but this is not a reliable field character on its own. In some light flanks and belly shine purplish-blue like the *sycobius* race of Greater Blue-eared Starling. Imm is dull sooty-brown on the head and underparts. **HH** locally common in open woodland and bush below 1600m, but also wanders to seasonally moist semi-arid areas. **Vo** groups make a continuous chattering consisting of a warbled, burry downslur, interspersed with explosive *swii* notes, which are also called in flight.

Southern Blue-eared Starling *Lamprotornis elisabeth* 19cm, 7.5"
[Lesser Blue-eared Starling in southern Africa]
Very similar to Lesser Blue-eared Starling and some authorities considered them conspecific. However, Southern Blue-eared is virtually restricted to miombo woodland, is not so green, and has a distinctive imm plumage: underparts are entirely *dull rufous with a few iridescent green spots*. **HH** small flocks are locally common in miombo woodland in C and STz but there are also old records of wanderers to SEKe. **Vo** song varies but typically consist of simple repeated phrases of harsh bugled notes *chee-chur-cheeru-chi-chi-chur-chiou*.

Bronze-tailed Starling *Lamprotornis chalcurus* 22cm, 9"
Very similar to Greater Blue-eared Starling, including blue ear-coverts and yellow eyes. Best identified by upper side of the tail which has *purple central feathers contrasting with the blue-green outer-tail*. Belly and lower flanks are also very purple. Imm is dull blackish on head and underparts. **HH** in our area generally uncommon and restricted to open woodland, bushed grassland and the edges of cultivation across NUg and NWKe from 500–2000m. **Vo** song is a rambling warble of sweet but mainly grating notes interspersed with *weert-weert-weert*. The flight-call is a repeated upslurred *swee*.

Sharp-tailed Starling *Lamprotornis acuticaudus* 24cm, 9.5"
Similar to Greater Blue-eared Starling, but tail is *slightly longer and graduated* (not particularly obvious in the field). Eyes are red in ♂, orange in ♀. In flight, shows a pale grey underwing (darker in other glossy starlings). Imm is dull dusky grey-brown on the head and underparts with dark eyes. **HH** in our area small flocks are restricted to miombo woodland near the Zambian border in extreme SWTz at about 1500m. **Vo** song consists of simple repeated upslurs, *suweet uweet* given both perched and in flight.

Plate 247

Greater Blue-eared Starling

Imm

Ad

cyaniventris

Lesser Blue-eared Starling

Imm

Ad

Imm

Southern Blue-eared Starling

Ad

Imm

Ad

Ad ♂

Imm

Bronze-tailed Starling

Sharp-tailed Starling

Black-bellied Starling *Lamprotornis corruscus* 18cm, 7"
Much darker than Greater Blue-eared Starling, often showing a dark purple and green gloss to the head, mantle and upper breast. Remainder of underparts are dark purplish-black *blending to black on the belly and vent*. No black spots on wing-coverts: eyes orange. Imm is duller with sooty black underparts. **HH** usually in flocks, they are common in forest and coastal bush in the east below 1000m. Slightly larger race *jombeni* is less common and occurs to the north of Mt Kenya between 1500–2200m. **Vo** may call for long periods, often from perches within shade, a variety of short pinched notes interspersed with a oriole-like *wi-tchew*.

Rüppell's Long-tailed Starling *Lamprotornis purpuropterus* 35cm, 14"
Large and dark-looking purply-blue starling with a *long graduated tail*, black face and a conspicuous *creamy-white eye*. Imm is similar but duller and dark-eyed. **HH** pairs are common, wide-ranging, and often on the ground in woodlands, bush country and around cultivation from sea-level to 2000m. **Vo** song is a long, complex and loud warble with both harsh and sweet notes, and mimicry. Calls *swi-chew* and a slightly tremulous *kwerr* are given both perched and in flight.

Purple Starling *Lamprotornis purpureus* 27cm, 10.5"
A fairly large starling with a rather flat-looking top to its head: ads are iridescent blue-green above and *all purple below, with an abnormally large looking yellow eye* (formed by a combination of the yellow iris and a thin yellow eye-ring). Imm is dull dark blue and green above, and blackish washed purple below. **HH** small flocks are common and widespread in remnant woodlands and isolated fruiting trees in cultivated areas from 600–1800m in Ug and uncommon in extreme WKe. **Vo** song is a musical refrain of short rising and falling notes, while an alarm call is a loud, tuneless downslur *ssshiow*, and the flight-call is a sparrow-like *shreer*.

Purple-headed Starling *Lamprotornis purpureiceps* 18cm, 7"
Blue-green with a *totally purple head, throat and upper breast, and dark eyes*. No black spots on the wing-coverts. In flight, wings look broad and rounded and the tail appears rather short. Imm is similar to the ad but duller. **HH** within range small flocks are locally common in the canopy of good forest and at the forest edge from 600–1800m. **Vo** song is a series of spaced musical *whiew* notes which are also frequently called in flight.

Splendid Starling *Lamprotornis splendidus* 30cm, 12"
The largest glossy blue starling and, in good light, a stunning bird: brilliant green and blue with golden reflections above, with black wing spots, and iridescent deep-purple, blue and coppery underparts. *Eyes are pale creamy-yellow*. Sexes are similar, but the ♀ has bluer underparts. Imm is blackish below with random blue feathers. In flight, wings look broad and make a loud swishing. **HH** small flocks occur in tree-tops at the forest edge and in remnant woodlands from 700–2300m, and are more common in the west. **Vo** unusual, rather outrageous call combines a mixture of explosive and variable gurgles, plops and creaks *krrrau kiau ko-chock wiow wi-eee* that may be delivered as a song for long periods.

Plate 248

Rüppell's Long-tailed Starling

Imm

Imm

Ad

Ad

Black-bellied Starling

Imm

Ad

Imm

Purple Starling

Ad

Purple-headed Starling

Ad ♂

Imm

Splendid Starling

BI-COLOURED STARLINGS
Four starlings with bold plumage patterns, especially in males. Easily identified if seen well.

Violet-backed Starling   *Cinnyricinclus leucogaster*   17cm, 6.5"
[Plum-coloured Starling]

Ad ♂ has *entire upperparts, throat and upper breast brilliant fiery iridescent violet and plum,* with a snowy white breast to vent. Against strong back-light may appear black and white. Ad ♀ is very different and almost pipit-like, being mottled brown and blackish above, slightly rufous on the head, and white below with numerous narrow brown streaks. Imm is like ♀. **HH** common throughout the year from sea-level to 3000m, but numbers greatly increase from Mar–Sep with the arrival of southern migrants. **Vo** song has no real pattern nor particularly sweet or harsh notes, but consists of rather rambling, slurred wails *riariarowh.*

Sharpe's Starling   *Cinnyricinclus sharpii*   17cm, 6.5"

Ad is *dark blue-black above, with a white throat and upper breast merging to tawny-apricot on the flanks and belly*: eyes are creamy-yellow. Imm is duller above and dark-eyed with small arrow shaped spots on the breast. **HH** pairs or small flocks are generally uncommon in the canopy of highland forest from 1400–3000m, where they often sit on exposed dead branches. **Vo** song is an extraordinary refrain of very high bell-like rising and falling spitted notes, then rising again, vaguely reminiscent of Dark-backed Weaver. Flight-calls include high-pitched spitted *spink* and *chin'k* notes.

Abbott's Starling   *Cinnyricinclus femoralis*   18cm, 7"   ● ●

Ad ♂ is blue-black above including the head, throat and breast *extending as a 'V' down the centre of the breast.* Lower breast to vent white with a black crescent on the lower flank. Eyes are creamy-yellow. Ad ♀ and imm plumage uncertain, but some birds are dull brown above and across the breast with extensive streaking below. **HH** EA endemic: local, uncommon, and restricted to highland forest from 1800–2500m in CKe and NETz. **Vo** very high-pitched calls include metallic spitted notes similar to Sharpe's Starling, while the song is a mixture of short musical slurs and spitted notes.

Magpie Starling   *Speculipastor bicolor*   19cm, 7.5"

Ad ♂ is *black and white with brilliant red eyes.* In flight, shows obvious white patches in the wings. Ad ♀ has similar basic plumage pattern and eye colour, but is grey on the head and upper breast. Imm is grey-brown above with dark eyes. **HH** flocks are locally common from sea-level to 1200m, mainly in the semi-arid north and east, but also wandering to moist coastal woodlands. **Vo** song is a jumble of harsh and soft squeaks, resulting in an unmusical, formless ramble. Alarm calls are harsh and loud *ti-chuk chuk-chuk.*

White-crowned Starling   *Spreo albicapillus*   27cm, 10.5"

A *large white-crowned starling* with an iridescent green sheen above, brown and white streaks below, and a white vent. Eyes white, bill black. Sexes alike. Imm is much duller brown with a black tipped bright yellow bill. In flight, white wing patches are obvious. **HH** small flocks are locally common in semi-arid and desert country, often on the ground around human habitation, from 300–1000m in extreme NKe. **Vo** song consists of various long or short rising slurs with a skirled quality, the effect being a querulous and soft sounding *krrrri-kuri-kuri-koyi.* Flight-call is a burry *koyi.*

White-winged Starling   *Neocichla gutturalis*   20cm, 8"

A unique-looking starling: ad is grey-brown above, with creamy-yellow eyes, and buffy-cream below with a *blackish stripe down centre of the upper breast.* Dark wings have large white patches in the primaries. Sexes are alike. Imm is mottled blackish on the crown with pale scalloping on the back and wings, and spotted with black below: bill is pale-yellow with a black tip. **HH** in our area small flocks are restricted to open miombo woodland in C and WTz from 1000–1500m. **Vo** song and calls consist of long complaining sequences of notes that resemble scolds punctuated by upslurred squeals.

Plate 249

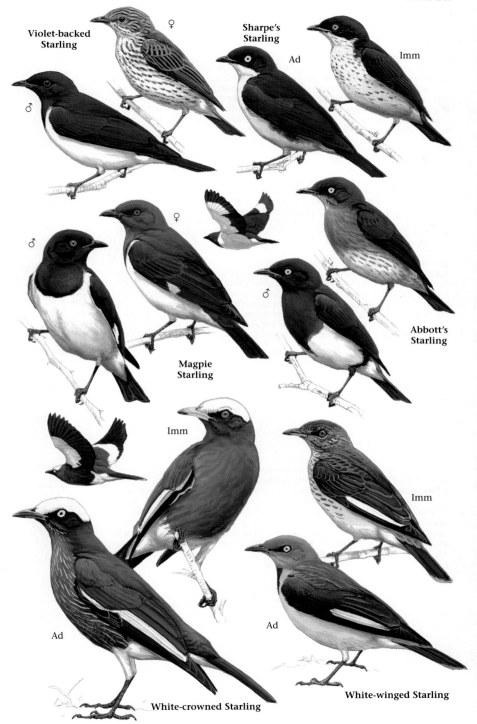

Violet-backed Starling

♀

♂

Sharpe's Starling

Ad

Imm

♂

♀

Abbott's Starling

♂

Magpie Starling

Imm

Ad

Imm

Ad

White-crowned Starling

White-winged Starling

RUFOUS-BELLIED STARLINGS

Three similar looking rufous-bellied starlings which are best identified by the presence or lack of white on the vent, and by the exact colour of the underparts and eyes. Sexes are alike.

Superb Starling *Lamprotornis superbus* 19cm, 7.5"

Ad is easily separated from similar species by its *creamy-white eyes, narrow white breast band, white underwing-coverts and vent.* Imm is duller with dark eyes and no white breast band: *white vent* is distinctive from similar imms. **HH** small flocks are confiding, common and widespread in semi-arid country, open woodland and bushed grasslands, including towns and gardens, from sea-level to 3000m. **Vo** song is a long ramble of rising and falling skirls and squeals. In flight, calls a purred *skrrrrrri.*

Hildebrandt's Starling *Lamprotornis hildebrandti* 19cm, 7.5"

Ad is *red-eyed,* and generally darker-toned than Superb Starling *without a white breast band or vent.* In flight, it reveals rufous (not white) underwing-coverts. Similar Shelley's Starling is even darker with orange eyes. Imm is dark-eyed and much duller, with paler rufous underparts. **HH** EA endemic: pairs and small flocks are common in open woodland and bush country from 500–2200m. **Vo** song is a series of short, low-toned, quite musical phrases that often end with querulous rising notes. In flight, calls a throaty *kurrrakurrrakurrra.*

Shelley's Starling *Lamprotornis shelleyi* 19cm, 7.5"

Ad is richer and darker than both Superb and Hildebrandt's starlings with *orange or orange-red eyes and a very dark rufous belly.* Imm has the head and mantle dull ash-brown. **HH** small flocks are generally uncommon wanderers in dry bush country (especially *Commiphora*) from near sea-level to 1300m, and often associate with other rufous-bellied starlings. **Vo** song is similar to Superb Starling, but louder, harsher, and broken into short phrases rather than a long continuous ramble. In flight, calls a throaty *kurrikurrikurri.*

Fischer's Starling *Spreo fischeri* 19cm, 7.5"

Ad is a rather distinctive ashy grey-brown starling with a *paler crown, black lores, white eyes and a white lower breast to belly.* Imm is browner with a yellowish bill and dark eyes. In flight, it is easily separated from Wattled Starling by its grey-brown not white rump. **HH** small flocks are locally common in dry bush country from near sea-level to 1900m. **Vo** typical song is rather burry and monotonous with some notes repeated for long periods. A striking *krrrrrrikrrrrrikrrrrrri* is commonly heard in flight.

Wattled Starling *Creatophora cinerea* 20cm, 8"

Non-br ♂, ♀ and imm are the most frequently encountered: all are *pale brown with darker wings and tail and a whitish rump.* At close range they show a small area of pale yellow skin behind the dark eyes. Greyer br ♂ has extensive yellow and black skin and wattles on the head. **HH** flocks are highly mobile, common and widespread throughout the region from sea-level to 3000m, often associating with cattle and plains game. **Vo** flocks create an unusual medley of squeals, squeaks, and hissing notes, without any really distinctive form or pattern.

Plate 250

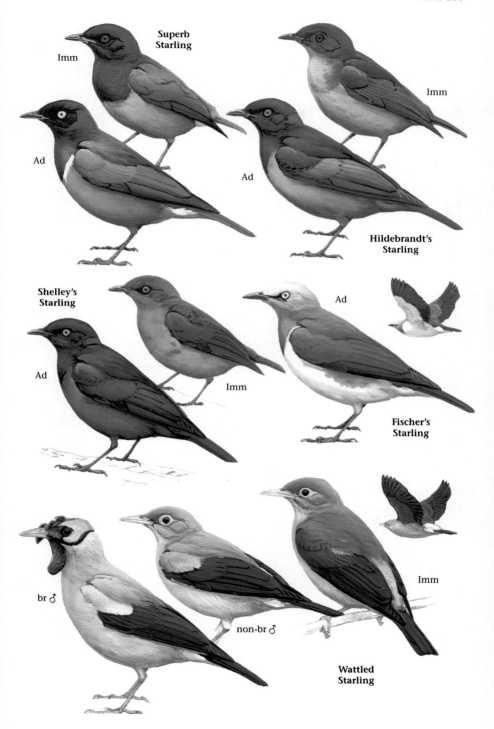

Superb Starling

Imm

Ad

Hildebrandt's Starling

Imm

Ad

Shelley's Starling

Ad

Imm

Ad

Fischer's Starling

br ♂

non-br ♂

Imm

Wattled Starling

SPARROWS

Well-known small stubby-billed birds with predominantly brown and grey plumages, some with a small amount of black on the head. All frequently feed on the ground.

Rufous Sparrow   *Passer rufocinctus*   14cm, 5.5"

Two races occur: in the highlands br ♂ nominate has a *pale eye*, small black bib, a curved rufous streak around the ear-coverts and a *rufous rump*. In Ug (and rarely NWKe) *shelleyi* is paler overall with a black line below the rusty supercilium and around the ear-coverts, and dark eyes. ♀♀ of both are duller and paler with grey (not black) throats. **HH** nominate birds are common in the highlands of Ke and NTz, inhabiting bushed grasslands, cultivation, villages and towns; while *shelleyi* is less common, and possibly prefers drier situations: they range from 1000–3000m. **Vo** a versatile sparrow, singing musical chirps and scratchy calls which are sometimes interspersed with canary-like upslurs *weeer*.

House Sparrow   *Passer domesticus*   14cm, 5.5"

Br ♂ differs from Rufous Sparrow in having a larger black bib, extensive dark chestnut on the sides of the nape, whiter cheeks and a *grey rump*. Bill and eye dark. Non-br ♂ has a greyer nape, smaller grey freckled bib and a yellowish bill. Ad ♀ and imm are buffier than ♀ Rufous with a short pale supercilium and yellowish bill. **HH** an introduced species first recorded in Zanzibar and Mombasa. Since the late 1970s it has expanded along the coast and inland. It is now common around buildings in many areas. **Vo** rather monotonous rapid chirping produces some variation and rhythm although rambles for long periods *trit treet trit tret tret...*

Somali Sparrow   *Passer castanopterus*   11cm, 4.5"

Br ♂ has *bright chestnut crown and nape*, grey mantle and rump, black bib, *yellow cheeks and underparts*. Non-br ♂ has a greyer crown and is generally paler. Ad ♀ and imm are similar to ♀ House Sparrow, but have a longer pale buffy supercilium and are washed pale yellow below. **HH** pairs and small flocks are rather localised and restricted to arid country in NKe from 300–1000m, often along tree-lined dry river beds and in villages. **Vo** typically calls a rather loud and monotonous upslurred chirping *treeet, cheritt.*

Chestnut Sparrow   *Passer eminibey*   11cm, 4.5"

Br ♂ is all deep chestnut gradually blending to a darker face with blackish wings and tail. Non-br ♂ has fine buffy edges to the feathers giving a scaly appearance. Imm ♂ is irregularly and boldly mottled chestnut and buff. Ad ♀ has typical female sparrowy plumage, but small size, pale chestnut supercilium and chestnut throat patch (if present) aid identification. **HH** common in a wide variety of bushland from sea-level to 2200m, often near water. Wanders widely, occurring in large flocks particularly after rains. **Vo** song is a continuous series of varied trills, while in flight calls *chup chup chup...* **SS** Chestnut Weaver.

Speckle-fronted Weaver   *Sporopipes frontalis*   11cm, 4.5"

Small weaver with a rather sparrow-like appearance. Forecrown black speckled with white, nape chestnut, malar stripe black. Remainder of plumage brown above and pale greyish below. Sexes are alike, imm is slightly duller. **HH** small flocks often feed on the ground and tend to be rather local in wooded grassland and semi-arid areas with bush cover from 400–2000m. **Vo** song is a rather pipit-like series of chips and trills, while flight and feeding call is a series of identical spitted notes *tsitsizizizizit...*

Plate 251

♀

Rufous Sparrow

br ♂

br ♂

shelleyi

nominate

br ♂

♀

House Sparrow

br ♂

♀

Somali Sparrow

br ♂

♀

Chestnut Sparrow

Imm ♂

Speckle-fronted Weaver

GREY-HEADED SPARROWS
Five forms are variously treated as anything from one to five species. They are similar in appearance, and are mainly separated on range. In some places, two forms overlap without interbreeding; elsewhere hybrids have been found. Sexes alike.

Grey-headed Sparrow *Passer griseus* 15cm, 6"

Classic grey-headed sparrow: rufous-brown back contrasts with a grey nape and crown. *Whitish throat is clearly separated from greyer breast and upper belly*, the lower belly is whitish. **HH** occurs mainly west and east of Swahili Sparrow in Tz, often around human settlements, and extending to the coast at Dar es Salaam. Generally prefers higher rainfall areas than Parrot-billed Sparrow. **Vo** song consists of typical sparrow-like chirping, either delivered slowly or more rapidly with a see-saw effect *chup chep chup chep...*

Parrot-billed Sparrow *Passer gongonensis* 17cm, 6.5"

Largest and darkest member of the group, which is *uniform grey below, and has a heavy conical bill*. **HH** common eastern species inhabiting a wide variety of semi-arid and bush country, and open wooded grassland. It is less fond of settlements than some other species, but does occur around Nairobi. **Vo** calls variable higher-pitched and squeakier musical chirps than its close relatives in a continuous rather monotonous ramble *chip chip tt-tt chip chet treet...* which may be rather sharp and explosive.

Swainson's Sparrow *Passer swainsonii* 15cm, 6"

Similar to Grey-headed Sparrow, but *dull brown back* contrasts with a more rufous rump: head and underparts are darker grey *with a less contrasting white throat*. Parrot-billed Sparrow is larger with a much heavier bill. **HH** in our area restricted to NKe, where it is common around Moyale. **Vo** unknown.

Swahili Sparrow *Passer suahelicus* 15cm, 6"

Very similar to Grey-headed Sparrow, but the *mantle is grey-brown more or less uniform with the nape and crown*. Darker grey below than Grey-headed. **HH** pairs and small groups are common in bushed grassland and villages throughout the central region. **Vo** typical chirps are delivered slowly, and are more downslurred and sharper than those of its close relatives *chierp... chierp...chiep...*

Southern Grey-headed Sparrow *Passer diffusus* 15cm, 6"

Very similar to Grey-headed Sparrow, but with a slightly paler grey head and underparts, and a less contrasting whitish throat. **HH** race *mosambicus* is common in coastal Tz south of Kisiju and on off-shore islands north to Pemba. **Vo** identical rapidly delivered chirps are typical of the genus *tchep tchep tchep...*

PETRONIAS
Dull grey-brown sparrows with yellow throat spots which are often extremely hard to see.

Yellow-spotted Petronia *Petronia pyrgita* 15cm, 6"

A fairly uniform pale grey-brown sparrow-like bird, typically with a *yellow spot at base of throat* which is usually concealed. *Pale bill and eye-ring* are often more obvious than the throat spot. Sexes alike. Imm is browner with a buffy supercilium. **HH** singles and pairs are common but localised, inhabiting dry bush country and open woodland from near sea-level to 2000m. **Vo** song is a repeated rising *t'chepor*, and the call is an explosive dry *chirp*.

Yellow-throated Petronia *Petronia superciliaris* 15cm, 6"

[Yellow-throated Sparrow]
Darker brown than Yellow-spotted Petronia with a well-marked *long buff-white supercilium*. Wing-coverts edged whitish forming *two short wing bars* (except in worn plumage). Dingy buff below with an inconspicuous yellow spot on the throat. Imm is similar, but lacks yellow throat spot. **HH** widespread although rather uncommon in open woodland and cultivated areas from sea-level to 1500m: favours but is not restricted to *Brachystegia*. **Vo** song is a rapidly delivered and often repeated series of 3–4 chirps *tcherp-tcherp- tcherp- tcherp...*

Plate 252

Grey-headed Sparrow

Parrot-billed
Sparrow

Swainson's Sparrow

Swahili
Sparrow

Southern Grey-headed
Sparrow

Imm Yellow-spotted
Petronia

Ad

Yellow-throated
Petronia

Ad

SPARROW-WEAVERS

Larger than the true *Ploceus* weavers with brown and white (not yellow) plumage. Breed in colonies with nests that are loosely woven balls of pale brown grasses, often with an entrance hole on both sides. Sexes and immatures are similar.

White-browed Sparrow-Weaver *Plocepasser mahali* 17cm, 6.5"
Boldly marked, brown above with a *broad white supercilium, white rump*, and white in the wings. Underparts vary from white with dark smudges at the sides of the breast in northern race *melanorhynchus*, to white with short black streaks across the breast in CTz *pectoralis*. **HH** very common in dry bush country (particularly acacia) and in wooded grasslands from 400–2000m. Highly sociable: small flocks are found at their nesting colonies throughout the year. Feeds on the ground and is often tame. **Vo** song is a musical chattering medley of chirps and throaty churrs given from the nest or on the ground.

Donaldson-Smith's Sparrow-Weaver *Plocepasser donaldsoni* 17cm, 6.5"
Medium-brown above, finely mottled with grey-brown, except for a white rump. Whitish throat has *narrow black malar stripes* running below the buffy cheeks and extending back to the sides of the neck, and is lightly mottled brownish below. **HH** locally common in semi-desert with some trees, and generally preferring drier areas than White-browed Sparrow-Weaver. **Vo** song is a continuous varied and scratchy ramble, usually delivered from the nest, a mixed medley of chirrups and nasal skirls.

Chestnut-crowned Sparrow-Weaver *Plocepasser superciliosus* 17cm, 6.5"
Slightly slimmer than the other sparrow-weavers and rusty brown above with a *chestnut crown and ear-coverts*. Bold face pattern has white superciliary stripes and black and white stripes to the sides of the throat. **HH** pairs or small groups are local and uncommon in dry bushland and woodland from 400–1800m. It is less common and much more inconspicuous than the other sparrow-weavers. They are often in rocky areas, quietly walking on the ground or under bushes feeding. **Vo** song is a very varied selection of twitters, trills, and sweet canary-like notes, while the contact call is a fast high-pitched and spitted *titititit titititit...*

Rufous-tailed Weaver *Histurgops ruficaudus* 22cm, 8.5" ●
Large, the size of a buffalo-weaver, and *entirely mottled grey-brown, with pale blue eyes and a rufous dark-centred tail*. In flight, shows much rufous in the wings. Sexes are alike. Imm is browner and dark-eyed with a pale horn-coloured bill. **HH** endemic to NTz, where it locally very common from 1100–2000m, and often seen in noisy flocks feeding on the ground. Breeds in large acacia trees, in nests like those of sparrow-weavers, and is present around its colonies throughout the year. **Vo** song is a mixture of nasal skirls and slurs strung together in an apparently random pattern, based on *skrri skrer skrah* and often sung from the nest.

Plate 253

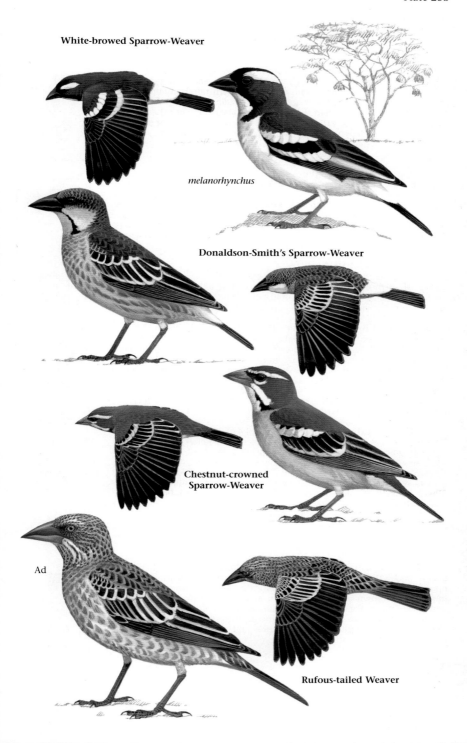

White-browed Sparrow-Weaver

melanorhynchus

Donaldson-Smith's Sparrow-Weaver

Chestnut-crowned
Sparrow-Weaver

Ad

Rufous-tailed Weaver

SOCIAL-WEAVERS

Small social weavers which occur in large flocks, often feeding together on the ground. Their nests are tightly woven balls of grass which hang from the very ends of the thinnest branches of large trees, often hundreds of pairs breeding together. Sexes are alike.

Grey-capped Social-Weaver *Pseudonigrita arnaudi* 11cm, 4.5"

Small brown short-tailed weaver with a contrasting *neat grey cap*, in flight shows a pale grey band across end of tail. Northern nominate birds have brown backs, while the more westerly race *dorsalis* has a grey back. Imm has a much browner cap than the ad, hardly contrasting with the mantle. **HH** common in a wide variety of bush and open wooded country from 500–1900m, seasonally including semi-arid areas. **Vo** song and call are a series of high-pitched piercing squeaks *tseer tseer...* given for long periods.

Black-capped Social-Weaver *Pseudonigrita cabanisi* 13cm, 5"

Small attractive weaver with a *black cap and tail* contrasting with a brown back and wings, *a white bill with a greenish tinge*, and red eyes. White below with black streaks on flanks and belly (which can be difficult to see in the field). Imm has a brown crown. **HH** flocks inhabit drier country than Grey-capped Social-Weaver from 200–1300m, including quite arid areas if large trees are present for breeding. **Vo** calls a very sparrow-like mixture of chirps and skirls, and feeding birds keep up a constant chipping.

BUFFALO-WEAVERS

Large weavers with heavy bills. *Bubalornis* are mainly black, their nests are very large constructions of dead thorn branches. *Dinemellia* is distinctly orange-red, brown and white. Its nest is smaller, includes more grass, and often has some thorny branches attached to the outside. All occur in small flocks, but *Bubalornis* may also gather in much larger numbers.

White-headed Buffalo-Weaver *Dinemellia dinemelli* 18cm, 7"

Very distinctive, particularly in flight, when white head, *bright orange-red rump* and large white wing patches are bold and distinctive. Mantle and tail are brown in the northern nominate race and black in *boehmi* in Tz, but they freely intergrade in border areas. Sexes are alike. **HH** common in acacia bush country and wooded grasslands from sea-level to 1400m. Often seen on the ground or calling loudly from their nest trees. **Vo** song and calls are slowly delivered, drawn out, and piercing nasal skirls which are variations of *skrieril skri-skril skrieril...*

Red-billed Buffalo-Weaver *Bubalornis niger* 22cm, 8.5"

Ad ♂ is *deep black with a red bill* and variable small patches of white on the sides of the breast. In flight, the wings look black, but from below can show white streaks at the base of the primaries. Ad ♀ is browner, streaked brown and white below, with a dull red bill. Imm is like ♀, but more grey-brown with heavy whitish mottling below, bill usually shows some pale red or orange colour. **HH** common but patchily distributed in dry bush country and wooded grasslands from near sea-level to 1500m, east and south of Lake Victoria. **Vo** song is usually given from the colonial nest by several members at the same time. It is a mixture of nasal skirls *chn chn chn chrerlink chrerlink...*, which may continue for long periods and becomes more excited with the arrival of a ♀.

White-billed Buffalo-Weaver *Bubalornis albirostris* 22cm, 8.5"

Br ♂ is *black with a greyish-white bill* and white streaks along the flanks. In non-br plumage, the bill is blackish. Ad ♀ is similar to ♂ in non-br plumage. Imm is dark brown above with brown and white streaked and mottled underparts, and a blackish bill. **HH** small parties and flocks favour dry acacia country from Lake Bogoria, Ke, to the northwest from 400–1300m. **Vo** song is possibly more exuberant, varied and metallic than Red-billed Buffalo-Weaver, but is still very similar.

Plate 254

Grey-capped Social Weaver

Ad
dorsalis

Ad
nominate

Imm

Ad

**Black-capped
Social Weaver**

Imm

**White-headed
Buffalo-Weaver**

Imm

♂

**Red-billed
Buffalo-Weaver**

♀

br ♂

♀

**White-billed
Buffalo-Weaver**

TRUE WEAVERS
Ploceus weavers all build tightly woven nests, varying from small onion-shapes to large round structures with long vertical entrance tunnels. Plates 255–257 illustrate some common and widespread species (plus some less common but similar looking ones). Careful attention to the exact shape of the face mask, eye colour and back pattern aid identification.

Black-headed Weaver *Ploceus cucullatus* 17cm, 6.5"
[Village Weaver, Spotted-backed Weaver]

Two distinct forms occur: br ♂♂ of both are *large with red eyes, heavy-bills and extensive black hoods tapering to a point on the breast*. Race *bohndorffi* (in most of Ug, WKe and NWTz) has *black scapulars forming two linear patches*, and shows a variable chestnut wash to the nape, breast and flanks; races *paroptus* (widespread in Ke and Tz) and *graueri* (SWUg to NWTz) have yellow backs *evenly spotted with black*, more black on the crown and a variable chestnut wash. All ♀♀ have olive-streaked backs, yellow superciliary stripes and yellow underparts when breeding. Non-br ♂♂ and ♀♀ have *greenish-yellow heads contrasting with either an olive or greyish dusky-streaked back*, a yellow breast and whitish belly. **HH** widespread and very common from sea-level to 2500m in a wide range of habitats and human settlements. **Vo** while dangling below their nests and flapping their wings, ♂♂ keep up a constant chattering punctuated with higher-pitched squeaks, strange snoring churrs and short flourishes.

Lesser Masked Weaver *Ploceus intermedius* 13cm, 5"

Br ♂ has *creamy-white eyes* standing out against a black face mask which extends over the forecrown and is variably edged with a chestnut wash: *legs blue-grey*. Bright yellow below in the east, while more widespread birds have a light chestnut wash. Similar Vitelline Masked Weaver lacks black on the forecrown, has red eyes and pink legs. Non-br ♂ and ♀ have *pale eyes, blue-grey legs* and quite a strong wash of yellow across the breast. Imm has dark eyes. **HH** common in bush country, woodland, cultivation, and a wide variety of vegetation near water from sea-level to 2000m. **Vo** song is very different from other masked weavers consisting of an accelerating series of quality of both nasal and liquid notes.

Vitelline Masked Weaver *Ploceus velatus* 13cm, 5"

Br ♂ has *red eyes and a black face mask extending below the eye with only a very narrow band above the bill*: crown is strongly washed chestnut. Lesser Masked Weaver has whitish eyes and black on the crown. Speke's and Heuglin's Masked weavers are also pale-eyed and their crowns are plain yellow. Non-br ♂ and ♀ have *red eyes, pink legs* and a yellowish breast. They are more solitary than similar Lesser Masked Weaver. Imm is browner than the ♀ with dark eyes. **HH** pairs are widespread in a variety of bush and wooded habitats including semi-arid areas from near sea-level to 1800m. Usually solitary or in pairs they build distinctive onion-shaped nests with an entrance hole at the bottom. **Vo** long rambling song is buzzy and scratchy, without any musical flourishes.

Northern Masked Weaver *Ploceus taeniopterus* 13cm, 5"

Br ♂ has *dark-brown eyes and a black face mask extending from just behind the eyes and down to the upper breast, it is broadly edged dark chestnut* (almost blackish) on the forecrown. Non-br ♂ and ♀ have dark eyes and buffy breasts. Imm is similar, but with whitish eyes. **HH** restricted range in our area: all recent records are from waterside vegetation in the Baringo district, Ke. **Vo** hesitant song is somewhat jerky and the terminal flourish is dry and unmusical.

Tanzania Masked Weaver *Ploceus reichardi* 13cm, 5" ●

Br ♂ has bright red eyes and a black face mask extending over the forecrown and ear-coverts: *crown and underparts are strongly washed orange*. Non-br ♂ and ♀ have red eyes, and a strong yellow wash to breast. **HH** inhabits a variety of bushed and wooded country, particularly near water, in SWTz. **Vo** not known.

Plate 255

Black-headed Weaver

♀

br ♂   *bohndorffi*

br ♂   *paroptus*

br ♂

♀

Lesser Masked
Weaver

♀

br ♂   Vitelline Masked
Weaver

br ♂

♀

Northern Masked
Weaver

br ♂

♀

Tanzania
Masked Weaver

Spectacled Weaver *Ploceus ocularis* 14cm, 5.5"

Ad ♂ is mostly yellow with a *green back and wings, a narrow black line through the eye and a broad black stripe down the throat.* Eyes are very pale yellow, and the bill is comparatively slender. Ad ♀ is similar, but lacks the black throat stripe. No non-br plumage. Eastern and southern birds have a rufous wash to the head. Imm is like a dull ♀. **HH** single birds and pairs are common in a wide variety of habitats from sea-level to 2200m, including forest edge, woodland, bushed grasslands and overgrown cultivation. Most often seen slowly creeping about within cover. **Vo** common and familiar call is 6–7 rapidly delivered, descending whistles *si si si si si si...* Song begins with this and then breaks into a complex, musical and buzzy flourish before ending with *cht* notes that fade away.

Black-necked Weaver *Ploceus nigricollis* 14cm, 5.5"

Ad ♂ has narrow black line through the eye and a black throat patch contrasting with a yellow (or orange-yellow) head and underparts. Ad ♀ has the black extending over the crown, a yellow supercilium and a black line through the eye. Two races occur: in western nominate, ♂ has the mantle washed brown, ♀ greenish; while both sexes in eastern and southern *melanoxanthus* are black above. No non-br plumage. Imms are like dull olive-backed ♀♀. **HH** widespread but never numerous, single birds and pairs occur in a variety of habitats from sea-level to 1500m. In the west they prefer forest, remnant woodland and secondary growth, while eastern and southern birds are in variety of woodland and thick bush including semi-arid areas. **Vo** song is a rapid, short flourish, typical of a weaver, but with a strange liquid bubbling quality. Call is a spitted *chwit chwit chwit...*

Speke's Weaver *Ploceus spekei* 15cm, 6"

Fairly large and stocky weaver with a heavy bill. Ad ♂ has the black face mask extending from the eyes downwards, edged with rufous on the underside, an *all-yellow crown, and pale-yellowish eyes. Mantle is spangled yellow and black.* No non-br plumage. ♀ is dull olive-green above with broad streaking on the mantle, a very indistinct supercilium, and pale yellow throat and breast. Imm is like ♀, but more olive-brown. **HH** common in small flocks within open woodland, acacia country, and around settlements from 1200–2200m. **Vo** breeding colonies keep up a constant chattering that lacks musical quality although individuals sing a nasal burry skirl which ends in a series of chattering notes.

Heuglin's Masked Weaver *Ploceus heuglini* 12cm, 5"

Br ♂ is very similar to Speke's Weaver, but slightly smaller with a *lightly mottled greenish-olive mantle* (not boldly patterned black and yellow), a face mask which tapers to a point on the upper breast, and pale-yellowish eyes. Non-br ♂ is quite plain olive-green above and all yellow below. ♀ is similar to ♀ Speke's, but less heavily streaked above and smaller-billed. **HH** localised and uncommon within range, breeding in small colonies in open woodland and cultivated areas from 650–1800m. **Vo** simple and monotonous song given for long periods: based on a rising *swi*, followed by a nasal *zhwee zhwee zhwee zhwee zhwee* (it is very like the call of Rattling Cisticola).

Fox's Weaver *Ploceus spekeoides* 15cm, 6" ●

Ad ♂ is similar to Speke's Weaver, but with a *very dark back*, plain yellow rump and shorter tail. ♀ is similar to ♀ Speke's, but more yellow below. **HH** Ug endemic, known only from the Lira and Soroti areas where it is not common in wooded grassland near swamps. **Vo** not recorded.

Plate 256

Spectacled Weaver

♂

♀

Black-necked
Weaver

♀

♂

melanoxanthus

♂

Speke's Weaver

♀

♀

Heuglin's
Masked Weaver

br ♂

♂

♂

Fox's Weaver

Baglafecht Weaver *Ploceus baglafecht* 15cm, 6"

Five races occur, four of which have previously been regarded as separate species. They form two distinct groups: those where ♂♂ have yellow crowns and ♀♀ black crowns, or where both sexes have black crowns. Yellow-crowned ♂♂ group includes typical *reichenowi* (highlands of Ke, N and NETz); similar *emini* which is white-bellied (NUg and WKe); and nominate which is green above (north of our area but hybridises with *reichenowi* in NWKe). The black-crowned group are: *stuhlmanni* (much of Ug, Rw, Bu and NWTz), and similar *sharpii* which is greener above (highlands of SWTz). Intermediate forms occur in many contact zones. Imms are mostly like dull versions of ♀♀, but often more olive above. **HH** pairs are very common and widespread particularly in high country, but lower in NWUg, occupying forest edge, open woodland, cultivation and gardens from 800–3000m. **Vo** typical song is a complex buzzing churr that breaks into a flourish, often then ending in another buzzy churr, and punctuated by a loud *zwink zwink* (also given as the call). There is little difference in dialect between the distinctive races.

Bertram's Weaver *Ploceus bertrandi* 15cm, 6"

Similar to some of the Baglafecht Weaver complex, but ad ♂ has a *black bar on the hindcrown, an orange washed crown and a black face mask extending on to the throat.* Eyes are pale yellow. Back, rump and tail green, wings darker with green edges. ♀ has an almost entirely black head. Imm is like ♀, but the head is mottled blackish and green. **HH** in our area pairs are restricted to the mountains of E and STz where they are rather local in wooded country along streams from 900–1800m. **Vo** fairly typical weaver-song incorporates canary-like flourishes while another song is rather chat-like. Contact call is a repeated *zwink*.

Chestnut Weaver *Ploceus rubiginosus* 15cm, 6"

Br ♂ is distinctive with a *clear-cut black head contrasting with the all-dark chestnut back and underparts.* Wings and tail blackish, edged buffy-brown or yellow. Similar Chestnut Sparrow is much smaller and has a very dark brown face blending into chestnut on the nape and throat. Non-br ♂, ♀ and imm are generally browner than similar female-type weavers, streaked with black above, and white with a broad tawny-buff band across the breast and down the flanks. **HH** wanders widely, often appearing during the rains in very large numbers. Builds hundreds (thousands) of nests together. Most frequent in dry woodland and bush country (particularly acacia), usually below 2000m. **Vo** call is similar to other weavers, but the song is unique with birds suddenly giving a very short dry fizzling call in bouts of general chattering. **SS** Chestnut Sparrow.

Grosbeak Weaver *Amblyospiza albifrons* 17cm, 6.5"
[Thick-billed Weaver]

A large stocky weaver with a *very thick bill.* Ad ♂ has variable plumage: in Ug, Rw, Bu, WKe, NW and STz, the head is brown contrasting with the blacker mantle, wings, tail and underparts. In SW and CKe, NTz and coastal areas, birds are all blackish-brown, All forms have a small white patch at the base of the primaries and often a patch of white on the forecrown. ♀ and imm have a huge yellowish bill, are brown above with no white in the wing, and heavily streaked brown and white underparts. **HH** always breeds over water: nest is a finely woven grass dome with the entrance hole near the top. Occurs in flocks in swamps, but also at forest edge, bush along rivers and in overgrown cultivation, from sea-level to 3000m. **Vo** song is a random mix of very harsh nasal skirls interspersed with loud rattles and softer twittering. **SS** White-winged Widowbird.

Plate 257

Imm

♀ *reichenowi*

♀ *stuhlmanni*

♂ *reichenowi*

Baglafecht Weaver

♂ *stuhlmanni*

♂

♀

Bertram's Weaver

♀

♀

**Chestnut
Weaver**

br ♂

♂

Grosbeak Weaver

SMALL WEAVERS
Two similar small weavers easily separated by bill shape.

Little Weaver *Ploceus luteolus* 10cm, 4"

Br ♂ has a *lemon yellow nape and underparts* (unlike the orange-yellow of so many other weavers), a small black face mask without any chestnut edging, and a *normal weaver-shaped stubby black bill*. Back, wings and tail are greenish: eyes brown. Non-br ♂ and ♀ are olive above with darker streaking, mostly yellow below, ♂ with a whiter belly. Imm is like a pale ♀, but buffy and whiter below. **HH** single birds or pairs are rather localised within range, and common but not numerous in acacia bush country, open woodland and trees within cultivation, from 400–1500m. **Vo** song is a typical weaver-buzz breaking into a flourish, with a rather nasal pinched quality. Each set is often introduced by a musical *sweetiswiswi*.

Slender-billed Weaver *Ploceus pelzelni* 11cm, 4.5"

Br ♂ is very similar to Little Weaver, but *black bill is noticeably long and slender*. Eyes are brownish. Ad ♀ is plain rich yellow on the head and underparts. Imm is like a pale ♀ with a horn-coloured bill. Spectacled Weaver also has a long bill, but has pale eyes with a distinct black eye-line. **HH** single birds or pairs inhabit swamps, papyrus, cultivation and a variety of woodland usually near water from 700–1700m. Can be very common, but is not gregarious. **Vo** song is a typical weaver-buzz breaking into a flourish with a rather nasal pinched quality, and sometimes also gives a whistled *sisisisisi* between each sequence.

CHESTNUT-BELLIED WEAVERS
Three similar weavers males of which differ mainly in the colour of the nape, mantle and underparts.

Golden-backed Weaver *Ploceus jacksoni* 13cm, 5"
[Jackson's Golden-backed Weaver]

Br ♂ has *head and nape all black, bright red eyes, a bright yellow mantle and is deep chestnut below*. Non-br ♂, ♀ and imm are olive-green above with much streaking, a yellowish supercilium, and yellowish below with buffy-orange across the breast. Imm is like a pale buffy ♀. **HH** widespread and sometimes numerous from 500–1800m, with a preference for vegetation near water, although not restricted to it, and with evidence of erratic wanderings. **Vo** song is very complex and rambling with both high hissed notes and long, deep, descending snoring notes.

Yellow-backed Weaver *Ploceus melanocephalus* 13cm, 5"

Br ♂ is similar to Golden-backed Weaver, but *black mask stops near rear of crown, and lower nape is yellow often forming a distinct collar*. Eyes brown: *underparts yellow washed with pale chestnut*. Race *dubosi* in Bu is plain yellow below. Non-br ♂, ♀ and imm are browner (above and below) than similar plumages of Golden-backed Weaver. More like ♀ Northern Brown-throated Weaver, that is in same range and habitat but which has whitish eyes. **HH** common and gregarious, inhabiting a wide range of vegetation usually near water from 600–1700m, including reed beds, papyrus, moist thickets and cultivation. **Vo** breeding colonies maintain squeaky chipping, where individuals are not discernible. The song is quite buzzing, beginning with squeaky *si si si...* notes and continuing with weaver-chatter and low nasal notes.

Juba Weaver *Ploceus dicrocephalus* 13cm, 5" ●

Br ♂ is similar to Golden-backed and Yellow-backed weavers, but the face mask is usually *black on the crown merging to blackish-chestnut on the nape and sides of face* (occasionally wholly dark chestnut). Eyes reddish-brown: washed chestnut below. Non-br ♂, ♀ and imm are similar to ♀ Yellow-backed, but more yellow below with obvious bi-coloured bill. **HH** restricted range, in our area known only from along the Daua River, NEKe, where it is common in riverside vegetation and surrounding cultivated areas. **Vo** rambling rather unmusical and slightly swallow-like song includes varied squeaks, snores and buzzes.

Plate 258

♀ **Little Weaver**

br ♂

♀

br ♂

Slender-billed Weaver

br ♂

♀

Golden-backed Weaver

♀

br ♂

Yellow-backed Weaver

♀

br ♂

Juba Weaver

MARSH WEAVERS
Three weavers mainly found in or near extensive wetlands.

Northern Brown-throated Weaver *Ploceus castanops* 14cm, 5.5"

Br ♂ has a *dark chestnut face mask tapering to a point on the upper breast* (which may appear blackish near the eyes and base of bill merging to brown on throat): *eyes whitish.* Southern Brown-throated Weaver is slightly larger and brighter, with a yellow forecrown, dark eyes and a different range. ♀ generally rather brown-toned above, within range most similar to ♀ Yellow-backed Weaver, but whitish eyes are distinctive. Imm is like a ♀, but eyes dark. **HH** common within range being particularly associated with water (but not restricted to it), and inhabiting papyrus, reedbeds, and nearby cultivation from 900–2000m. **Vo** quite a high-pitched weaver song which lacks flourishes and consists of various chattering notes and high-pitched squeaks.

Southern Brown-throated Weaver *Ploceus xanthopterus* 14cm, 5.5"

Br ♂ is very similar to Northern Brown-throated Weaver, but has *no brown on the forecrown, brown eyes*, and a different range. Non-br ♂, ♀ and imm streaked olive and brown above, buffy-yellow below with a whitish belly, and dark eyes. **HH** very local in our area, where it is occasionally found in STz. Prefers aquatic habitats, but also wanders to other vegetation nearby. **Vo** harsh, strident song: phrases are rather short ending with a bizarre and futuristic sounding *zwazwazwazwazwazwa.*

Kilombero Weaver *Ploceus burnieri* 14cm, 5.5" ●●

Br ♂ is similar to Northern Brown-throated Weaver but the *'V'-shaped mask is blacker* (narrowly edged in chestnut) and the *eyes are dark brown.* Non-br ♂, ♀ and imm are strongly washed yellow across the breast. **HH** first described in 1990, this CTz endemic is common in riverside marshes and seasonally flooded grasslands near Ifakara at 250m. **Vo** rambling song is typically weaver-like including chips and squeaks, and the call is a strong dry *chup.*

Compact Weaver *Ploceus superciliosus* 13cm, 5"

A thickset, short-tailed weaver with a rather heavy bill. Br ♂ has a yellow crown washed chestnut on forecrown, a black mask, and a streaky olive-brown nape, back, wings and tail. Br ♀ is similar to br ♂ but with a dark crown and broad rusty-yellow supercilium. Non-br birds are browner above, more buffy below, with a dark brown crown, buff supercilium and dark brown eye-lines. **HH** pairs and small flocks are rather local to damp wooded grasslands, marshy areas and nearby cultivation from 700–1700m. **Vo** feeding parties often call a buzzing twitter that is also given in flight. Song is similar, but a little more varied and burry *trrri-titi-trrrri-titi-tri.*

Rüppell's Weaver *Ploceus galbula* 14cm, 5.5"

Br ♂ has a small *chestnut face mask and orange-red eyes.* Bright yellow over crown, nape and underparts. Non-br ♂ and ♀ washed yellow above and on the throat, buffy across the breast. **HH** occurs to the north of our area where it is a gregarious species known for its erratic wanderings. Birds collected at 250m in the Garolola (Karo-Lola) area in Ke in 1901 are the only definite records. **Vo** long typical weaver-like series ends with a drawn-out snore and distinctive metallic chitter.

Plate 259

br ♂

♀
Northern
Brown-throated
Weaver

br ♂

♀
Southern
Brown-throated
Weaver

♀

♂
Kilombero
Weaver

non-br ♂

br ♀

Compact
Weaver

br ♂

Rüppell's Weaver

♀

br ♂

GOLDEN WEAVERS

Yellow weavers with some orange or chestnut on the head, the exact extent of these marks and eye colour aid identification.

Holub's Golden Weaver *Ploceus xanthops* 18cm, 7"

[Golden Weaver]
Larger and stocky: ad ♂ is mainly yellow, greener on the back and wings, with a *heavy black bill, pale yellow eyes*, and an orange wash to the throat. Ad ♀ is slightly duller without the orange throat. Imm is greener above with indistinct streaking. **HH** single birds and pairs are common in a wide variety of open wooded grassland, marshes and cultivation from 900–2300m. **Vo** song begins with a few ticking notes and then continues with a buzzy flourish *tikatikatikatika*, while the distinctive call is a loud and frequently repeated *chup*.

Golden Palm Weaver *Ploceus bojeri* 14cm, 5.5"

Ad ♂ is very bright yellow with an *orange head and throat, dark brown eyes* (often look blackish), and a black bill. Ad ♀ is yellow above with indistinct streaking, uniform yellow below, and has a bi-coloured bill. Imm is like a dull pale ♀. **HH** gregarious and common in coastal Ke in palms, wooded areas and gardens, as well as inland where it favours riverine habitat in dry country from sea-level to 1200m. **Vo** prolonged song is high-pitched and hissing, while the call is an explosive, very metallic repeated *chwenk*.

African Golden Weaver *Ploceus subaureus* 14cm, 5.5"

[Yellow Weaver]
Similar to Golden Palm Weaver, but br ♂ is a little *duller orange on the head, with pale red eyes* (not dark). Non-br ♂ has an olive wash to the head. Br ♀ similar to ♀ Golden Palm, but has reddish eyes. Non-br ♀ and imm are more boldly streaked above, with a yellow breast and white belly. **HH** gregarious and locally common from sea-level to 1800m where it prefers wetter habitats than Golden Palm Weaver. **Vo** song is rambling and usually has a winding-up series of soft squeaky *tikotikotikotiko*, before breaking into a set of complex flourishes, many with a canary-like quality.

Taveta Golden Weaver *Ploceus castaneiceps* 14cm, 5.5"

Ad ♂ has a *band of orange-chestnut across the hindcrown and another patch on the upper breast, giving it a rather yellow-faced appearance*. Eyes are dark brown. ♀ is greenish above with fairly heavy streaking, a yellow supercilium and underparts, and a bi-coloured bill. Imm is like a ♀, but more olive-brown above. **HH** a gregarious EA endemic, known only from the border area of Ke and Tz at 250–1500m where it is common but localised, foraging in a variety of woodland and breeding in swamps. **Vo** simple song is very harsh and tuneless, with many hard *chip* notes which are used as a contact call by feeding groups.

Orange Weaver *Ploceus aurantius* 14cm, 5.5"

Ad ♂ has an *orange head, breast and belly*, and grey eyes (which often look blackish and diamond-shaped, due to small patch of dark orbital skin). *Bill is pinkish with a dark ridge along the top of the upper mandible*. ♀ and imm rather plain greenish above and whitish below. **HH** locally common in lakeside vegetation and surrounding farmland at 1200m around the western and northern shores of Lake Victoria, in Ug and NWTz, but much rarer in WKe. **Vo** song is a rambling mix of smooth notes with a rather musical quality, lacking the rather harsh edge of many other weavers.

PARASITIC WEAVER

Previously considered a weaver, but is now thought to be more closely related to the whydahs. It is a brood parasite on cisticolas and prinias.

Parasitic Weaver *Anomalospiza imberbis* 11cm, 4.5"

[Cuckoo Finch]
Ad ♂ is bright yellow on the head and underparts with a *very stubby black bill*, olive back and wings heavily streaked black (all of which suggests a heavy-billed canary). Ad ♀ is very similar to ♀ Red Bishop, but with a stubbier bill. Imm is tawny-brown above with some streaking, and dull buff underparts. **HH** localised and generally uncommon in wet grasslands with scattered bushes and cultivated areas from sea-level to 2000m. **Vo** flight-call is a fast *titititit*, while the song includes a *swi-sun-suit* with a weaver-like quality and sometimes a long wheezy *vweeeeeoooooo*.

Plate 260

♂

♀

Holub's Golden
Weaver

Golden Palm
Weaver

♀

♂

♀

br ♂

African Golden
Weaver

♀

Taveta Golden
Weaver

♀

♂

Orange Weaver

♂

♀

Parasitic Weaver

FOREST WEAVERS

Nine rather similar weavers of forest or good woodland: colour of heads, backs and wings, and range all aid identification.

Dark-backed Weaver *Ploceus bicolor* 15cm, 6"

[Forest Weaver]

A white-billed dark-headed forest weaver with red eyes, blackish upperparts and a yellow breast to vent. Four races occur: in the west *mentalis* and *kigomaensis* have a dark grey mantle and wings, contrasting with a blacker head, while eastern *kersteni* has a uniform black mantle, wings and head, and *stictifrons* in SETz has a browner-backed ♂, and greyer-backed ♀ (sometimes with speckled black and white throats). Sexes are alike and imms are duller. **HH** common in a variety of forest types from sea-level to 2400m, often seen working through the middle stratum in pairs, small groups, or mixed-species flocks. **Vo** wonderfully distinct song varies regionally but typically starts with a few chips, buzzes or squeaks and continues musically with double nasal squeaks, rising and falling bell-like notes or a rhythmic and rising *wi-wi wi-chuk-chuk wi-chuk*. It may be randomly peppered with weird bleats, trumpets, and squeaky hinge noises!

Clarke's Weaver *Ploceus golandi* 14cm, 5.5"

Br ♂ is smaller than Dark-backed Weaver with a black throat that extends to the mid-breast and *yellow edges to the wings*. Eyes brown and bill black. Ad ♀ is greenish above streaked with black, very yellow on the sides of head, throat and breast, with a white belly. Imm is like a pale-billed washed-out ♀. **HH** Ke endemic: only known from a few sites near Malindi, notably Arabuko-Sokoke Forest, where fast-moving flocks occur in the canopy of *Brachystegia* woodland. **Vo** very noisy: large canopy parties forage and call together with a rolling sizzling mixed with sudden silences and bursts of their distinctive sharp *chip chip* flight call.

Weyns's Weaver *Ploceus weynsi* 15cm, 6"

Ad ♂ suggests Dark-backed Weaver but *black bill, pale yellow eyes, yellow-edged wings and chestnut flanks* are distinctive. Ad ♀ is streaked olive above, with strong yellow wing-edgings, and a wide greenish-yellow breast band. Imm is like a subdued ♀. **HH** pairs or flocks occur in the forest canopy, secondary growth and nearby clearings from 1000–1500m. Wanders erratically. **Vo** song is a very high-pitched sizzling, but flock members also call a dry chipping, when perched and in flight.

Olive-headed Weaver *Ploceus olivaceiceps* 14cm, 5.5"

[Olive-headed Golden Weaver]

Ad ♂ is mostly green above and on the throat, with a yellowish crown, and a chestnut wash in the centre of the breast. Eyes pale yellow. Ad ♀ is similar but the crown is green, and the chestnut breast-patch paler. Imm is like a dull ♀, but more yellow on the throat. **HH** restricted range in our area: pairs are uncommon in miombo woodland at 1000–1300m near Songea, Tz. They forage along branches like tits, and often join mixed-species flocks. **Vo** short scratchy song lacks the typical weaver-like fizziness and is more like a wheatear or a lark.

Usambara Weaver *Ploceus nicolli* 14cm, 5.5"

Ad ♂ has a yellow forecrown and blackish-green head merging into a black back, wings and tail. Dark green of throat blends to chestnut on the upper breast, otherwise yellow below. Eyes dark. Ad ♀ is similar but has a dark olive-brown head. Imm has no chestnut below. **HH** rare Tz endemic which occurs in pairs or as single birds in highland forest canopy and mid-levels where they work along branches tit-like. Known mainly from the West Usambara Mts, but also the East Usambara, the Uluguru and the Udzungwa mts. **Vo** song is very rhythmic repeated rising series *swi-iri t'swi–i t'swi-i t' swi-i*.

Strange Weaver *Ploceus alienus* 14cm, 5.5"

Ad ♂ is green above with a black head extending down to the upper breast where it is edged in chestnut. Ad ♀ is similar, but chestnut extends on to the throat. Imm is duller with a dark greenish head. **HH** single birds and pairs are endemic to montane forests along the Albertine Rift from 1500–2700m, where they creep about in the undergrowth and middle levels. **Vo** song is a rhythmic burry *weee chow-chow-chow*, but it also has a descending whistled series of 5–7 notes similar to Spectacled Weaver, and a short dry nasal contact call.

Plate 261

Ad *mentalis*

Ad *kersteni*

Dark-backed Weaver

br ♂ ♀

Clarke's Weaver

Olive-headed Weaver

♀

♀

♂

Weyns's Weaver

Usambara Weaver

♀

♂

♀

♂

Strange Weaver

Brown-capped Weaver *Ploceus insignis* 13cm, 5"
Ad ♂ is a *bright yellow weaver with a black head, wings and tail, and a chest-nut cap.* Ad ♀ is similar, but her crown is entirely black. Imm is paler and duller with a blackish-green head sometimes speckled yellowish. **HH** pairs and family groups are fairly common in highland forest from 1200–3000m within range, and are often seen creeping woodpecker-like along branches, or in mixed-species flocks. **Vo** usual call heard from feeding family parties is a piercing *siip siip...*, given both perched and in flight. Unique but rarely heard song is a short rapid and rhythmic sizzling ending with two punc-tuated notes.

Yellow-mantled Weaver *Ploceus tricolor* 14cm, 5.5"
Ad ♂ is black above with a *bright yellow collar on the upper mantle,* and deep chestnut below except for a black throat. Ad ♀ is all black with just a yel-low collar. Imm is mostly black above with a dull rufous head and upper mantle, and dull brown underparts. **HH** pairs are not uncommon in parts of Ug from 700–1800m in the canopy of both undisturbed and remnant forest (formerly occurred in WKe). **Vo** high-pitched song is a rising and falling sizzling, while the rasping alarm is a drongo-like but soft *chchchchchah.*

Black-billed Weaver *Ploceus melanogaster* 14cm, 5.5"
Distinctive, reverse plumage of many weavers, being *black with a rich-yellow face mask.* Ad ♂ differs from ♀ in having a black throat. Imm is a duller blackish-olive with a dingy greenish-yellow face mask. **HH** pairs are shy but fairly common in the undergrowth and tangled vines of highland forest and forest edge from 1200–3000m (usually above 1500m). **Vo** song is a rapid series of descending notes ending in a dry tuneless rattle, and sounds more like a sunbird than a weaver. Contact call is a harsh, rapidly delivered *zhink-zhink-zhink...*

BLACK WEAVERS
Two very similar black weavers best identified by size and eye colour.

Vieillot's Black Weaver *Ploceus nigerrimus* 15cm, 6"
Ad ♂ is an *all-black weaver with pale yellow eyes* (greyish in Maxwell's Black Weaver). Ad ♀ and imm are heavily streaked dull dark olive above, and are dingy-yellow below, with a strong olive-brown wash across the breast and flanks. Eyes are yellowish and darker in imm. **HH** gregarious and common within range, it occurs at the forest edge, in cultivated areas and around vil-lages from 700–2000m. **Vo** colonies maintain a constant cacophony of chattering and squeaking which is higher pitched than similar sounding weavers.

Maxwell's Black Weaver *Ploceus albinucha* 13cm, 5"
Ad ♂ is very similar to Vieillot's Black Weaver, but slightly smaller with *grey-ish eyes.* Sexes are alike. Imm is a dingy dark olive-grey with a variable oli-vaceous wash. **HH** rare in our area, and known only from the Semliki Forest, WUg, at 700m. **Vo** feeding flocks call a swizzling noise, while feed-ing in the canopy.

Plate 262

Brown-capped Weaver

♂

♀

Yellow-mantled
Weaver

♂

♀

♂

♀

Black-billed Weaver

♀

Vieillot's Black
Weaver

♂

Imm

♂

Maxwell's Black
Weaver

QUELEAS

Weaver-like birds which often congregate in large flocks. Males in breeding plumage pose no identification problems, but non-breeding males and females look very similar to each other, and also to several weavers, the widowbirds and whydahs.

Red-billed Quelea *Quelea quelea* 13cm, 5"

Br ♂ has a black face mask and red bill. Colour of crown and breast variable, either pink, tawny-yellow or buff. Non-br ♂ and ♀ have streaky sparrow-like plumage with *whitish superciliary stripes and red bills*. Imm is similar, but with a much duller, brownish-pink bill. Pin-tailed Whydah is similar in non-br plumage, but smaller and smaller-billed with a much more boldly streaked head. **HH** common, widespread, and sometimes abundant, though seasonally migratory and may be absent from apparently suitable areas for months at a time. Occurs throughout our area in bush country, grasslands and cultivation from sea-level to 3000m. **Vo** song is a medley of chipping mixed with mournful downslurs *seu seu seu seeeeu* and given from vicinity of nest. Roosting flocks keep up a continuous chipping that can be heard at a considerable distance. **SS** non-br Pin-tailed Whydah.

Cardinal Quelea *Quelea cardinalis* 11cm, 4.5"

Br ♂ has most of the head, throat and upper breast bright red. Two races occur: in Ug, much of Ke, and NWTz nominate birds have red extending on to the upper nape, while from SKe southwards *rhodesiae* is brown-naped. Non-br ♂ and ♀ have the superciliary stripes and throat washed yellowish, and a dark brown bill. Imm is like ♀ but the throat is pale brown. **HH** seasonally common, often appearing immediately after the rains in long wet grassy areas and marshland fringes from 400–3000m. **Vo** song is a series of chip notes which descend and accelerate before ending with a nasal downslurred *sheeeeu*. Other chip calls are frequently heard from feeding flocks.

Red-headed Quelea *Quelea erythrops* 13cm, 5"

Br ♂ is larger than Cardinal Quelea with a longer bill and the entire head (including the nape) is a darker red with *variable black scalloping on the throat*. Non-br ♂, ♀ and imm are extremely similar to corresponding plumages of Cardinal Quelea, but the throat is slightly whiter. **HH** less common than the other queleas with a very patchy distribution from sea-level to 1400m. It is most regular in marshy areas and wet grassland in ETz. **Vo** song is a formless, tuneless, and squealing chatter, and birds give a chipping call in flight.

RED-HEADED WEAVER

In the monospecific genus *Anaplectes*, and often considered to be a link species between the yellow weavers and black and red malimbes.

Red-headed Weaver *Anaplectes rubriceps* 14cm, 5.5"

Three distinct races occur: in widespread *leuconotus* br ♂ has a black face mask, red primary panel and a white breast to vent; in NE coastal Ke *jubaensis* is almost entirely red, while in SETz nominate is red on the head and breast, with a yellow primary panel, and a white breast to vent. Hybrids between *leuconotus* and the nominate race intergrade throughout much of STz. ♀♀ of northern races are greyish-brown with distinctive orange-red bills and orange-red primary panels, while nominate ♀ has a plain yellow head, yellow wing panel and a white breast to vent. Non-br ♂♂ are similar to ♀♀. Imms are like ♀♀ with a yellow wash to the head. **HH** solitary birds or pairs are widespread and locally common in a wide variety of woodlands, bush country, grasslands with scattered trees, and gardens from sea-level to 2000m. **Vo** song is a complex mixture of high-pitched sizzling and a little chipping, while feeding birds give a smooth *chut*.

Plate 263

Red-billed Quelea

br ♂

non-br ♂

♀

br ♂ *rhodesiae*

♀

br ♂

Cardinal Quelea

♀

nominate

br ♂

Red-headed Quelea

♀ *leuconotus*

br ♂ *jubaensis*

♀ nominate

br ♂ *leuconotus*

br ♂ nominate

Red-headed Weaver

MALIMBES
Striking red and black forest weavers that are easily identified by the extent of red in their plumage.

Red-headed Malimbe *Malimbus rubricollis* 17cm, 6.5"
Ad ♂ is all black with *bright red extending from the forecrown over the nape and spreading out slightly on to the sides of the neck*. Ad ♀ is similar, but the *forecrown is black*. Neither have any red below. Imm is a duller version of ad. **HH** single birds and pairs are widespread but not numerous in the canopy of good forest from 700–2150m, where they feed tit-like along large branches and often join mixed-species flocks. **Vo** perched or flying birds often call a few high-pitched downslurs and continue with twittering or sizzling notes and an occasional upslurred whistled *seeeu*.

Crested Malimbe *Malimbus malimbicus* 17cm, 6.5"
Ad ♂ has a small black face mask surrounded by a bright red crown, ear-coverts, throat and upper breast, with the *rear crown feathers elongated to form a short but distinct crest*. Ad ♀ is similar, but lacks the crest. Imm is duller, with the head mottled red and black. **HH** pairs occur in forests from 700–1400m in WUg, where they forage at all levels. They are only common in Budongo and Semliki forests, WUg. **Vo** song is a very varied mixture of twitters and sizzling that appears to have no pattern, and the contact call is a harsh repeated nasal *scree scree scree...*

Red-bellied Malimbe *Malimbus erythrogaster* 17cm, 6.5"
Ad ♂ is *red on the crown, nape, sides of neck and the underparts*, with a black mask extending across the throat. Ad ♀ is similar except the throat is also red. Imm has dull red and black feathering on the head, and is dull grey-brown below. **HH** restricted range, in our area only known from Semliki Forest, WUg, at 700m, where it is an uncommon bird of the canopy. **Vo** not recorded in the region.

Blue-billed Malimbe *Malimbus nitens* 17cm, 6.5"
[Gray's Malimbe]
Ad ♂ is *black with a wide red band across the lower throat and upper breast*: the *bill is grey or blue-grey*. Ad ♀ similar but with less red on the throat. Imm is generally duller black with orange-brown on the lower throat and breast. **HH** in our area, known only from Semliki Forest, WUg, at 700m, where it is uncommon in the middle levels and lower canopy of good forest, secondary growth and nearby cultivation. **Vo** feeding birds often maintain a rather rounded squarking noise *kwiekh*.

Plate 264

Red-headed
Malimbe

♂

♀

Crested
Malimbe

♂

♀

Red-bellied
Malimbe

♂

♀

Blue-billed
Malimbe

♂

Imm

WIDOWBIRDS AND BISHOPS

Related to weavers, males of both groups have distinctive breeding plumages. Breeding male widowbirds mostly have long tails and patches of red or yellow on their wings. Most non-breeding males resemble females, but are larger, and some can be identified by coloured patches in their wings. Females are extremely difficult to identify. Breeding male bishops are shorter-tailed with more extensive colour to the body plumage. Most bishops have a female-like non-breeding plumage and extreme care must be taken to identify these birds. Several occur in large mixed flocks, particularly when not breeding.

Long-tailed Widowbird   *Euplectes progne*   ♂71cm, 28"

[Long-tailed Widow]
Br ♂ is black with red and creamy-buff shoulder patches and an *exceptionally long tail*. Non-br ♂ has a streaky brown sparrow-like plumage with orange-red shoulders, but is larger than the ♀ and all other widowbirds. ♀ and imm lack the red shoulder patches and have a whitish breast to vent, and although smaller than the ♂ they are larger than most other ♀ widowbirds. **HH** common within range, inhabiting wet grassy areas from 1800–2800m. Sit on low perches or on the ground, making frequent display flights with slow laboured flapping and hovering over a territory. **Vo** calls in dramatic display flight and while perched, a loud burry *treep treep treep...* interspersed with loud descending trills.

Jackson's Widowbird   *Euplectes jacksoni*   ♂30cm, 12"

Br ♂ is all black with tawny-brown shoulders. In flight, it appears *black with brown wings, and the tail droops downwards in an even curve*, not loose and floppy as in some other long-tailed species. Non-br ♂ is similar to ♀ but larger and with tawny shoulders and feather edges. ♀ and imm often rather rich-buff below with variable streaking. **HH** EA endemic: flocks may be common in highland grasslands and wheat fields from 1500–3000m. Breeding ♂♂ display together in leks with a unique dance where they attempt to attract ♀♀ by jumping up and down repeatedly on a flattened circle of grass. **Vo** call is a repeated monotonous burry and piercing *shreep shreep shreep...*, which is similar but shorter when given in flight.

Red-collared Widowbird   *Euplectes ardens*   ♀28cm, 11"

[Red-collared Widow]
Three races occur: br ♂♂ are black and long-tailed, but vary in the amount of red on the head. Race *concolor* (**Black Widowbird**) is entirely black (WUg, Rw and Bu); *tropicus* (**Red-collared Widowbird**) has a red or orange-red collar across the lower neck (SWUg, Tz and (rarely) SEKe); while *suahelica* (**Red-naped Widowbird**) has the crown, nape, sides of the neck and collar bright red (Ke and NTz highlands). Races *tropicus* and *concolor* are known to hybridise. Non-br ♂, ♀ and imm have yellowish superciliary stripes and are rather plain below. **HH** a gregarious species occurring commonly in a variety of vegetation including tall grass, wheat fields, overgrown cultivation and rank herbage from near sea-level to 3000m. **Vo** given in both display flights and when perched, the usual song given is an insect-like *sisisisisisisisi...*, which is intermixed with dry rasps and rustling sounds when birds are excited.

Plate 265

♂ br

♀

Long-tailed
Widowbird

♂ br

♀

♂
non-br

Jackson's
Widowbird

br ♂
tropicus

br ♂
suahelica

♀

♂
non-br

Red-collared
Widowbird

Fan-tailed Widowbird *Euplectes axillaris* 15cm, 6"

[Red-shouldered Widow]

Br ♂ is a short-tailed black widowbird with deep orange-red shoulders bordered with creamy-buff: it is rather confusingly named since the tail is only fan-shaped during display. Non-br ♂ is similar to ♀ but with orange-red shoulders. ♀ and imm have typical streaky brown plumage, but with a small area of pale rusty-brown at the bend of the wing. **HH** common and widespread with a preference for marshy areas and wet grasslands from sea-level to 2300m, but also found in drier habitats (particularly in the east). ♂♂ frequently sit on reed tops and make short display flights to attract more skulking ♀♀. **Vo** song is usually heard in display flight and is a slightly variable insect-like trilling. In flight, parties maintain a constant twittering.

Hartlaub's Marsh Widowbird *Euplectes hartlaubi* ♂ 21–36cm, 8–14"

Two distinct races occur: in Ug to WKe, br ♂ *humeralis* is very similar to Fan-tailed Widowbird but larger and longer-tailed with *pale orange-buff shoulders* (not deep orange-red); while in the Ufipa area of SWTz br ♂ of the nominate race has *yellow shoulders and a much longer tail*. It is very similar to Montane Marsh Widowbird, but lacks the extensive pale buff areas in the wing-coverts and their ranges do not overlap. Non-br ♂ is like ♀, but retains the orange, or yellow, shoulders. ♀ and imm are streaked buffy-brown below. **HH** rather uncommon in wet grasslands and marshes from 1100–1800m, occurring in two widely separated locations in Ug-WKe and in the Ufipa area of SWTz. **Vo** very distinctive song is usually delivered from a perch and consists of quiet twitterings punctuated by an explosive single or double rising musical rasp *zrun-tink*.

Montane Marsh Widowbird *Euplectes psammocromius*

♂ 40cm, 16"

Br ♂ is has *yellow shoulders broadly bordered with buffy-white* and a long drooping tail. Non-br ♂ like ♀ but retains yellow shoulders. ♀ is narrowly streaked below with a whitish throat. **HH** common in high grasslands from 1800–3000m around Iringa and Mbeya in STz. **Vo** differs little from Hartlaub's Marsh Widowbird, but the explosive call is usually delivered singly.

Black Bishop *Euplectes gierowii* 15cm, 6"

Two distinct races occur: in Ug and WKe br ♂ of race *ansorgei* is a thickset black bishop with an *orange-red nape which blends into a yellowish upper back* and extends around the sides of the neck and across the upper breast as a narrow orange-red band; while in SKe and NTz br ♂ of race *friederichseni* is smaller, with a broader collar on the upper breast, and an orange-red nape, mantle and upper rump. Similar Black-winged Red Bishop has an entirely red crown. Non-br ♂, ♀ and imm are dark and very heavily streaked with black above (particularly the ♂), with black spots at the sides of the breast. **HH** local but not uncommon in tall wet grasslands and cultivated areas from 700–1600m. **Vo** very simple songs are either nasal slurs rapidly repeated in a short series, or a dry twittering.

Plate 266

Fan-tailed Widowbird

br ♂

br ♂

♀

♀

Montane Marsh Widowbird

♂ non-br

♀

♂ non-br

Hartlaub's Marsh Widowbird

♂ non-br

br ♂

humeralis

br ♂

♀

br ♂

ansorgei

friederichseni

Black Bishop

Yellow Bishop *Euplectes capensis* 15cm, 6"
[Yellow-rumped Widow]
Br ♂ is a rather stocky short-tailed bishop with *bright yellow shoulders and rump*. Non-br ♂ is like ♀, but has yellow on the shoulders and rump. Ad ♀ has a typical female-like streaky plumage, but with a dingy olive-yellow rump. Imm is like ♀, but rump is brown with darker streaking. **HH** usually solitary or in pairs, it is common and widespread in bushed grasslands and cultivation from sea-level to 2300m, particularly in the highlands (but at lower altitudes in Tz). **Vo** song is typical of a widowbird rather than a bishop, consisting of a high-pitched *sisisisisi...* with notes interspersed with insect-like trills and chittering.

Yellow-mantled Widowbird *Euplectes macrourus* ♂ 21cm, 8"
[Yellow-backed Widow]
Two distinct races (sometimes considered separate species) occur: br ♂ of the more widespread nominate race (**Yellow-mantled Widowbird**) has a yellow mantle and yellow shoulders, while br ♂ of *macrocercus* (**Yellow-shouldered Widowbird**) has the yellow restricted to the shoulders. Exact ranges and overlap between the two races is not entirely clear. Non-br ♂♂ of both forms retain yellow shoulders, and cannot be separated in the field. ♀♀ and imms may show yellow fringes at the bend of the wing. **HH** flocks are common within the range occurring in moist grasslands and cultivation from 1000–1800m. **Vo** Yellow-mantled Widowbird sings from a perch a high-pitched twitter *tzip-tzip-tzip...* followed by a louder nasal downslur *weah*, while Yellow-shouldered utters a more rapid introductory twittering, and the downslur is more subdued or absent.

Yellow-crowned Bishop *Euplectes afer* 10cm, 4"
[Golden Bishop]
Br ♂ is much smaller than Yellow Bishop with an obvious *bright yellow crown, mantle, rump and vent*. In much of the range race *ladoensis* occurs, but *taha* in STz has more extensive yellow feathering on sides of breast. Non-br ♂ and ♀ are whitish below with blackish streaking. Imm is similar, but more buffy below. **HH** uncommon resident and wanderer, sometimes occurring after rains in large numbers. It inhabits reedbeds and flooded grasslands from 400–2000m. **Vo** song is a tuneless, monotonous dry chipping with slight variation, given perched and in flight.

White-winged Widowbird *Euplectes albonotatus* ♂ 17cm, 6.5"
[White-winged Widow]
Two distinctive races occur: both have white on the primary and secondary coverts, and to the bases of the primaries (which shows *as obvious white patches in flight*), but they differ in shoulder colour which is deep chestnut-brown in the widespread race *eques* and yellow in nominate birds mainly in STz, but occasionally north to CKe. Non-br ♂♂ have streaky plumage but retain the yellow or chestnut, and white on the wing. ♀♀ and imms may show an indication of yellow or chestnut feather edgings at the bend of the wing. **HH** small and large flocks are locally common in moist grasslands and cultivation from sea-level to 2000m. **Vo** song is a repeated high-pitched insect-like buzzing *sisisisisisisisi* interspersed with a dry rasping, and the call is a repeated *twit twit*, similar to many other widowbirds.

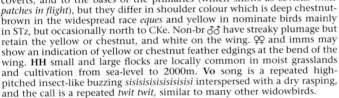

Plate 267

Yellow Bishop

br ♂

non-br ♂

♀

Yellow-crowned Bishop

taha

br ♂

br ♂

ladoensis

♀

Yellow-mantled Widowbird

macrocercus

br ♂

nominate

non-br ♂

♀

br ♂
nominate

br ♂
eques

White-winged Widowbird

non-br ♂

RED BISHOPS

An attractive group of small bishops: breeding males are often seen fluffed out and hovering over their territories like large black and red bumblebees. Some females are extremely similar and best identified by range and association with males.

Southern Red Bishop *Euplectes orix* 11cm, 4.5"
[Red Bishop]

Br ♂ is very similar to Northern Red Bishop, but black on the crown is restricted to a narrow band across the forecrown and the brown tail extends well beyond the upper and lower tail-coverts. Plumage is either bright red and black, or orange and black. Non-br ♂, ♀ and imm cannot be identified with certainty in the field, but basic description is of a small streaked bishop with buffy superciliary stripes, a whitish throat and belly, and some dark streaking across the breast. **HH** small flocks of this western and southern species are locally common in marshes, high grasses and around cultivation, often near water, from 600–1500m. **Vo** song is an exuberant dry mix of twitters and chattering interspersed with higher-pitched trills.

Zanzibar Red Bishop *Euplectes nigroventris* 10cm, 4"

Br ♂ is usually easily identified from other red bishops by being mostly black below (but can occasionally show a few red feathers on the throat). Entirely red crown further separates this species from both Northern and Southern red bishops. Non-br ♂, ♀ and imm are very similar to ♀ Southern Red Bishop, but slightly smaller. **HH** small flocks are common to the east of Southern Red Bishop, but in similar habitats from sea-level to 1000m. **Vo** song is the most complex of all the bishops: a variety of dry trills and twittering sometimes ending in a double descending, subdued and mournful piping.

Northern Red Bishop *Euplectes franciscanus* 11cm, 4.5"

Br ♂ is similar to Southern Red Bishop, but black on the crown extends to top of the nape; *exceptionally long upper and lower tail-coverts hide all but the very tip of the brown tail.* Plumage is bright red and black, except in extreme NEKe where race *pusillus* may be orange and black. Non-br ♂, ♀ and imm are like ♀ Southern Red Bishop. **HH** locally common within its range from 600–1800m and occupying similar habitats to the two previous species. **Vo** simple song is a tuneless dry chipping and trilling.

Black-winged Red Bishop *Euplectes hordeaceus* 12cm, 5"
[Fire-crowned Bishop]

Larger than the other red bishops. In flight, br ♂ shows *broad rounded black wings and tail.* Red on the crown extends to (or almost to) the bill, most like Zanzibar Red Bishop, but red collar across lower neck eliminates confusion. Non-br ♂, ♀ and imm are larger than other ♀-type red bishops with a stronger wash of tawny-brown across the breast and flanks. **HH** locally common within range inhabiting bushed grassland and cultivation in generally wet areas from sea-level to 2000m. **Vo** song is an insect-like accelerated twittering *titititititrrrrrrr* sometimes interspersed with a high-pitched musical squeaking.

Fire-fronted Bishop *Euplectes diadematus* 10cm, 4"

Br ♂ is a distinctive small bishop with a *bright red spot on the forecrown,* extensive yellow on the lower back, rump and vent, and a yellow and black streaked mantle. Non-br ♂, ♀ and imm are also small with *yellowish edged primaries.* **HH** highly migratory, it may appear in large numbers after the rains, preferring semi-arid areas from sea-level to 1000m. **Vo** reported to make a sizzling song similar to other small bishops.

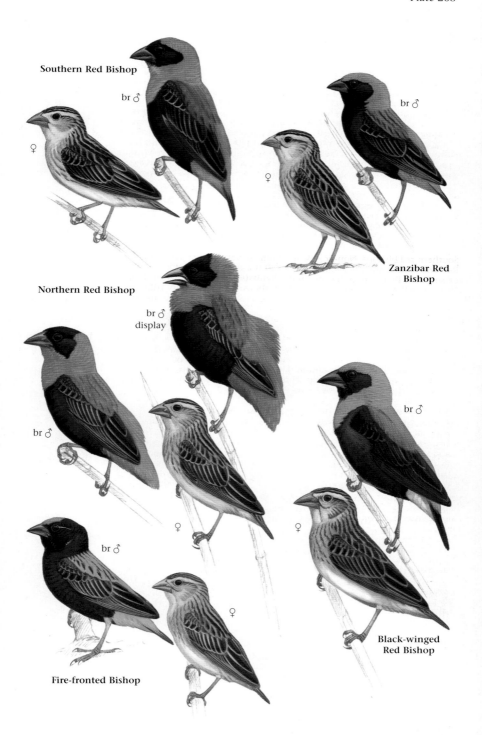

Plate 268

Southern Red Bishop

br ♂

♀

br ♂

♀

Zanzibar Red
Bishop

Northern Red Bishop

br ♂
display

br ♂

♀

br ♂

♀

Black-winged
Red Bishop

br ♂

♀

Fire-fronted Bishop

NEGROFINCHES
Two black and grey, and two very different looking finches. Solitary or in pairs, negrofinches are active birds of forest and secondary growth, often in the middle levels and canopy but also lower in fruiting shrubs and bushes.

Grey-headed Negrofinch *Nigrita canicapilla* 13cm, 5"

Ad is dark grey above and black below, with a *black forecrown*, often separated from the upperparts by a narrow white fringe. *White-spotted wing-coverts* distinguish this species from similar Pale-fronted Negrofinch. Sexes are alike. Imm is all dark grey with scaly buff edges to the wing-coverts. In the Mahali Mts, WTz, race *candida* (**Kungwe Negrofinch**) has the crown to mantle and rump whitish. **HH** common and widespread but restricted to highland forest in Ke and most of Tz, from 1700–3350m. It occurs at lower altitudes in the west, including at 700m in Semliki Forest, WUg. **Vo** song varies locally but typically is a penetrating although whistled *seeu seeu seeee* or a see-sawing *si-so-si-so-si-so* which is repeated from a high perch at irregular intervals.

Pale-fronted Negrofinch *Nigrita luteifrons* 10cm, 4"

Ad ♂ is similar to Grey-headed Negrofinch, but smaller with a *pale forecrown and plain not white-spotted wing-coverts*. Ad ♀ is all grey with a *black diamond-shaped face mask around the eyes*; and black wings and tail. Both sexes have a paler grey rump. Imm is all dull dark grey. **HH** in our area, known only from 700–800m in Semliki Forest, WUg, where it often occurs in the canopy of both primary forest and secondary growth. **Vo** song is reported to be a simple phrase of descending notes, while the call is a faint musical whistling *choo*.

Chestnut-breasted Negrofinch *Nigrita bicolor* 10cm, 4"

Dark and plain looking negrofinch, being dark brown above and deep dark chestnut-brown below. Sexes are alike. Imm is dull brown above, much paler warmer rusty-brown below. **HH** very localised in our area, it is common at Semliki, and uncommon in Maramagambo and Budongo forests, WUg, from 700–1200m. It occurs throughout the forest, but is most frequent in the middle levels and undergrowth. **Vo** songs and calls vary but are typically fairly sibilant and whistled simple phrases of three or four notes *siu-sii-siu* or *sisiswisisiswisisi*.

White-breasted Negrofinch *Nigrita fusconota* 11cm, 4.5"

A very small negrofinch with a rather waxbill-like appearance. Black cap and tail contrast with the brown back and wings and white underparts. Sexes alike. Imm has the crown, rump and tail browner. **HH** single birds and small flocks are reasonably common in western forests and forest edge from 700–1800m. They are often hard to see in the high canopy. **Vo** typical song begins with a rattle and then continues with a long descending trill lasting about 6 seconds.

Woodhouse's Antpecker *Parmoptila woodhousei* 10cm, 4"
[Red-fronted Antpecker]

An unusual bird of uncertain affinities: ad ♂ has a bright red forecrown, brown upperparts and rich rufous-brown underparts. Ad ♀ is brown above with a rufous wash to the throat, and scaled brown and white from the breast to vent. **HH** uncommon and localised in forest from 700–1800m, where it actively forages in tangled vines and creepers, or in forest undergrowth, and often accompanies mixed-species flocks. **Vo** usual call consists of fairly loud and staccato but rather variable chips and squeaks *chit chit swi...*

Plate 269

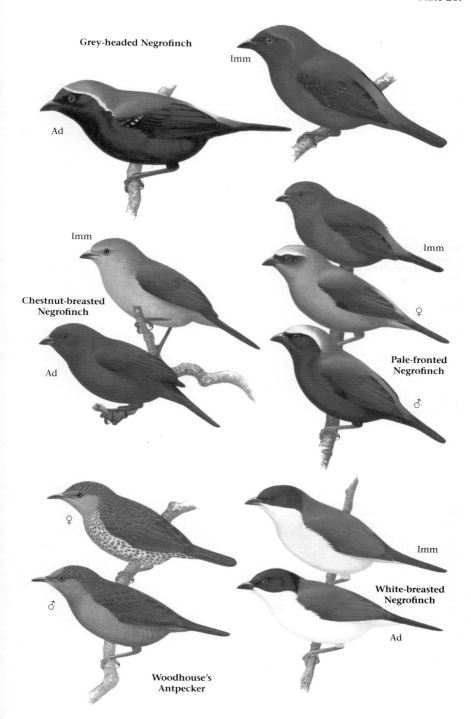

Grey-headed Negrofinch

Imm

Ad

Imm

Chestnut-breasted Negrofinch

Imm

Ad

♀

Pale-fronted Negrofinch

♂

♀

♂

Woodhouse's Antpecker

Imm

White-breasted Negrofinch

Ad

PYTILIAS

Brightly coloured waxbills found in pairs and small flocks in bush country and wooded grass-lands, often on the ground, or low down in fairly thick cover. Extent of face mask and wing colour aid identification.

Green-winged Pytilia *Pytilia melba* 14cm, 5.5"
[Melba Finch]

Four races occur: ♂♂ differ in the amount of red on the face and breast band colour. Basic ad ♂ plumage has hind part of the head grey, *mantle and wings green*, rump and tail red, breast to vent barred and spotted dark grey (or olive-grey) and white. Races in most areas have the *lores and ear-coverts grey*, and the breast band either yellow or green: race *soudanensis* from EUg to E and SKe has an entirely red face (extending back to the eye) and a yellow breast band. Ad ♀♀ are all similar, paler than ♂♂ with grey heads (lacking any red), and well barred underparts. Imms are like a dull ♀, but may have yellowish edges to wings, so beware confusion with Orange-winged Pytilia. **HH** common and widespread inhabitants of semi-arid acacia country, scrub and wooded grasslands from sea-level to 1800m. **Vo** usually sings a quite loud and persistent series of chips, squeaks and nasal notes which are well imitated by Eastern Paradise-Whydah. Call is a loud, spitted series of identical notes *spit-spit-spit.*

Orange-winged Pytilia *Pytilia afra* 13cm, 5"
[Golden-backed Pytilia]

Ad ♂ is similar to Green-winged Pytilia, but has a *smaller rounder red mask extending well back behind the eye*, and orange-edged wings. Ad ♀ is similar to ♂ with orange wing edgings, but no red on the head. Imm is like a drab ♀. **HH** local and generally uncommon in much of its range, but a widespread resident of forest edge, miombo woodland, and moist wooded grasslands from sea-level to 1800m, tends to avoid dry areas. **Vo** song is simpler than Green-winged Pytilia, a monotonous series of chips and squeaks, which is imitated by Broad-tailed Paradise-Whydah.

Red-winged Pytilia *Pytilia phoenicoptera* 13cm, 5"

Ad ♂ is all medium dark-grey with red wings, rump and tail. Ad ♀ is similar but washed grey-brown. Imm is duller and browner than ad with subdued areas of red. **HH** uncommon in wooded grasslands and bush country from 600–1200m in N and WUg. **Vo** after a few several squeaky notes calls a loud and obtrusive machine-gun-like spitted rattle *titititititititit.*

OLIVEBACKS

Distinctive olive-green, grey and black waxbills inhabiting the lower and middle levels of forest in lush vegetation. Shy and localised they occur in pairs and small flocks.

White-collared Oliveback *Nesocharis ansorgei* 10cm, 4"

A small species: ad ♂ has a *black head edged with a narrow white collar* (extending around the throat and sides of neck), a mossy olive-green mantle, wings and breast, and a black tail. Ad ♀ lacks the white collar and is entirely grey from the lower throat to vent. Imm is similar to ♀. **HH** local and rather uncommon in thick cover near water, but also at the forest edge and in overgrown cultivation from 1100–1800m. **Vo** call is harsh and wooden and sounds like the loud winding of a watch.

Grey-headed Oliveback *Nesocharis capistrata* 13cm, 5"

Larger than White-collared Oliveback with a *grey crown and nape, whitish cheeks and a black bib*, but otherwise grey below with yellow flanks. Sexes are alike. Imm is duller with grey cheeks and brownish flanks. **HH** localised and uncommon in similar habitats to White-collared Oliveback, but at lower elevations from 700–1100m. **Vo** call is a rapid metallic *titititititititititit* mixed with irregular very short pauses producing a rhythmical rather than a trilled or rattled effect.

Plate 270

Green-winged Pytilia

♂

♀

soudanensis

Orange-winged Pytilia

♂

♀

♂

Imm

Red-winged Pytilia

♂

♀

White-collared Oliveback

Ad

Imm

Grey-headed Oliveback

TWINSPOTS

Brightly coloured waxbills in four different genera. Rarely far from cover, they are usually found in pairs or groups feeding quietly on the ground or in low vegetation.

Peter's Twinspot *Hypargos niveoguttatus* 13cm, 5"
[Red-throated Twinspot]
Ad ♂ is mainly brown above with a red rump and tail base: remainder of tail black. *Sides of face to breast red, lower breast to vent black with conspicuous white spots.* Ad ♀ is similar to ♂, but more washed out, with a greyer face, and buffy-orange sides to the head and breast. Imm is dull brown with a pale buffy face, dull red rump and black belly. **HH** reasonably common but local inhabitant of forest undergrowth, thickets and dense herbage from sea-level to 2000m. **Vo** varied song is a complex mix of very high-pitched sibilant trills, mournful downslurs and single extended notes. Call is a distinctive *tit-tit.*

Brown Twinspot *Clytospiza monteiri* 13cm, 5"
Sexes are very similar with an all grey head, a dull brown mantle and wings, red rump and a black tail. Below, the *breast to vent is orange-brown heavily spotted with white.* Narrow stripe on throat is red on ♂ and white on ♀. Imm paler and duller than ad, with a brownish wash to the head: plain rusty-brown below with light barring on the vent. **HH** localised and generally uncommon in thickets, tall grass and overgrown cultivation from 1000–1500m. **Vo** an incredibly varied long and rambling song which includes mimicry is rarely heard, and the call is an explosive, nasal and clipped *cht cht...*

Green-backed Twinspot *Mandingoa nitidula* 10cm, 4"
[Green Twinspot]
Ad ♂ is a mainly green twinspot with a contrasting bright red face mask, and a black breast to vent well-spotted with white. Ad ♀ is paler than the ♂ with a buffy-yellow face mask. Imm is mostly dull grey-green with a paler area around the eyes. **HH** local and rather uncommon but also widespread from sea-level to 2150m. Particularly shy, it occurs in dense undergrowth and thick cover within forest, but also in the canopy. **Vo** song is a complex mix of very high-pitched and canary-like phrases with a variety of sibilant trills and slurs. The call is a high *zit-zit...* given perched and in flight.

Dusky Twinspot *Euschistospiza cinereovinacea* 11cm, 4.5"
Head, mantle, wings, tail, breast, and a broad stripe down centre of the belly are blackish-slate. Rump is bright red and flanks are maroon-red with small white spots on sides of the breast. Sexes alike. Imm is plain slaty-black with a dull red rump. **HH** very uncommon within its restricted range, inhabiting forest clearings and overgrown cultivation in the extreme west of our area from 1800–2300m. **Vo** pairs indulge in a twittering display while sitting side by side on an elevated and exposed perch. Call is unremarkable soft dry chip. **SS** Dusky Crimson-wing.

Dybowski's Twinspot *Euschistospiza dybowskii* 13cm, 5"
Similar to Dusky Twinspot, but with a greyer head and breast, *red mantle, scapulars and rump; and much heavier white spotting below.* Ad ♀ is paler than the ♂ with grey feathering on the red mantle. Imm is like a dingy ♀ without any white spots below. **HH** in our area, known only from Mt Kei and Otze Forest of NWUg, where it is locally common on grassy and rocky hillsides. **Vo** call is a soft *sht sht...*

Plate 271

Peters's Twinspot

♂

♀

Brown Twinspot

♂

♀

Imm

♀

Ad

Dusky
Twinspot

Green-backed
Twinspot

♂

♂

♀

Dybowski's Twinspot

CRIMSONWINGS

Mostly olive-green and red waxbills of the undergrowth in and around highland forest. Found mainly in pairs or small groups, they feed in low cover and on the ground. Generally rather shy, they quickly fly into cover if disturbed. If present, the exact extent of red on the head aids identification.

Abyssinian Crimsonwing *Cryptospiza salvadorii* 11cm, 4.5"

Sexes are very similar with a *uniform olive-green head,* and red on the back, wings and rump. In W and SWUg, the race *ruwenzori* is greyer on the head and underparts. Imm has less red above and is washed with brownish-olive. Separated from Red-faced Crimsonwing by lack of either a red or buffy face mask. ♀ Shelley's Crimsonwing has a red (not black) bill. **HH** widespread and common, but with a patchy distribution mainly from 2000-3000m, and only occasionally as low as 1500m. **Vo** calls a high sibilant *tsit-tsit...,* which can break into a rapid delivery of even higher pitched notes.

Red-faced Crimsonwing *Cryptospiza reichenovii* 11cm, 4.5"

Similar to Abyssinian Crimsonwing, but ad ♂ has a red mask around the eyes. Similarly patterned Dusky Crimsonwing is dark grey and red, not olive-green and red. Ad ♀ Red-faced Crimsonwing has a pale buffy-yellow eye mask. Imm without any indication of an eye mask is difficult to separate from imm Abyssinian Crimsonwing, but should be less grey. **HH** generally at lower altitudes than Abyssinian Crimsonwing, typically from 900–2000m, although up to 2500m in SWRw. **Vo** calls simple rattling trills and a metallic *zzzzit...*

Dusky Crimsonwing *Cryptospiza jacksoni* 11cm, 4.5" ●

Dark grey and red plumage distinguishes ads from all other crimsonwings. ♀ is similar to ♂, but with a smaller area of red on the head. Imm mostly dark grey with a variable amount of dull red on the mantle and rump. **HH** endemic and locally not uncommon in montane forest along the Albertine Rift from 1550–2700m. **Vo** call is a rather explosive *tsit-tsit...,* which is more hissed than Red-faced Crimsonwing. **SS** Dusky Twinspot.

Shelley's Crimsonwing *Cryptospiza shelleyi* 13cm, 5" ● ●

Larger than the other crimsonwings with a *distinctive red bill*. Ad ♂ has *red extending over whole crown*, nape, mantle and rump, and blackish wings and tail. Chin to vent olive-green washed orange on the flanks. Ad ♀ lacks red on the head, but also has a distinctive *red bill*: orange washed flanks and blackish wings should further identify this species from Abyssinian Crimsonwing. Imm is similar to ♀, but lacks the orange wash on the flanks. **HH** a rare endemic confined to mountain forests along the Albertine Rift from about 1550–2800m. **Vo** call is reported to be a series of rapid, high-pitched, rising and falling twittering notes *tu-tu-tu-ti-ti-ti,* similar to that of some small sunbirds.

Plate 272

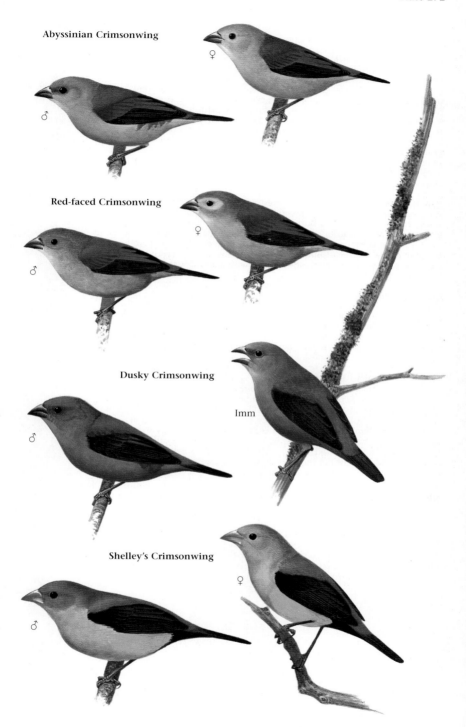

Abyssinian Crimsonwing

♀

♂

Red-faced Crimsonwing

♂

♀

Dusky Crimsonwing

♂

Imm

Shelley's Crimsonwing

♂

♀

BLUEBILLS AND SEEDCRACKERS

Heavy-billed, red and black, or red and brown waxbills. All are rather shy and quickly take to cover if disturbed. Extent of red on head and tail aid identification.

Red-headed Bluebill   *Spermophaga ruficapilla*   14cm, 5.5"

Two distinct races occur: in the west and CKe the nominate ad ♂ has the whole head, breast and flanks red, with a *red rump and black tail*. Bill blue-grey with pink cutting edges. Ad ♀ is similar but with bold white spots from the breast to vent. Imm is dark slate above with a variable red wash to the head, breast and rump, rich dark brown below, with a blue-grey bill. In the East Usambara Mts, NETz, race *cana* has the upperparts (and sometimes th nape) dark-grey, not black. **HH** pairs or family groups often feed on forε trails at dawn and dusk and are locally common in forest, secondary growth and moist thickets from 700–2150m. **Vo** whistled song is rather sibilant: it starts with a short note, then a short series of rising notes, and a longer series of rising upslurs *si-sisi-su-wii si-sis-swiswiswisiwiswi* with the emphasis on the last note.

Black-bellied Seedcracker   *Pyrenestes ostrinus*   14cm, 5.5"

Ad ♂ is similar to Red-headed Bluebill, but the *rump and tail are red* (inner webs of outer-tail are black but not visible in the field). *Bill is massive and all blue-grey*, and at close range also shows conspicuous pale-blue eyelids. Ad ♀ is red on the face, upper breast, rump and tail, with the remainder of the plumage brown (most similar to Lesser Seedcracker, but it is larger, with a different range). Imm is dull olive-brown with a dull rusty rump and central tail. Several races occur (although racial distinction is not clear), they differ in wing and bill size from race *rothschildi* in Ug which has the smallest wing and bill, through intermediate nominate birds (also in Ug), to the largest race *frommi* in Ug and SWTz. **HH** localised within range, inhabiting forest undergrowth and edges, marshy areas near forest, and moist thickets from 700–1400m. **Vo** nominate birds sing a simple, loud, and explosive phrase of four descending notes *si-si si'sa*, while race *frommi* sounds very different, singing an attractive, melodic rather greenbul-like *w'suruturo wi sisi*.

Grant's Bluebill   *Spermophaga poliogenys*   14cm, 5.5"

Ad ♂ is very similar to ♂ Red-headed Bluebill, but *black of upperparts extends further up the nape*. A blue-grey bill with a pink tip and cutting-edge and a black tail further distinguish it from ♂ Black-bellied Seedcracker. Ad ♀ is similar to ♀ Red-headed Bluebill, but the *head is largely dark grey, and red is restricted to the throat and breast*. Imm is dark dull blackish-grey with some red visible on the rump. **HH** rare in our area and found only in forest undergrowth in the Semliki Valley, WUg, at 700–800m. **Vo** song is similar to Red-headed Bluebill but includes downslurs as well as upslurs, and terminal notes climb higher *seeu-sisi-su swiswiswiswisisi*.

Lesser Seedcracker   *Pyrenestes minor*   13cm, 5"
[Nyasa Seedcracker]

Both sexes are similar to ♀ Black-bellied Seedcracker, but smaller and slimmer, with a smaller bill and a totally different range. Ad ♀ Lesser Seedcracker has slightly less red on the head than the ♂. Both sexes are separated from the bluebills by their red tails and plain blackish bills. Imm is all dull brown with some red on the rump. **HH** very local and uncommon, inhabiting dense secondary growth, thickets, and overgrown cultivation, often along streams from 100–900m. **Vo** call is a repeated and explosive *chat-chat-chat...*

Plate 273

Red-headed Bluebill

♀

Imm

♂

nominate

Imm

♀

Black-bellied Seedcracker

♂

Imm

♀

♂

Grant's Bluebill

Imm

♀

♂

Lesser Seedcracker

CORDON-BLEUS
Slim blue and brown waxbills usually found feeding on the ground in pairs or in small flocks. Head pattern identifies males: other plumages are often more difficult (see species accounts).

Red-cheeked Cordon-bleu *Uraeginthus bengalus* 13cm, 5″

Four races occur: all ad ♂♂ are easily identified by their *bright red cheek patches*. All ad ♀♀ are brown above (except for the blue rump and tail), but extent of blue on the face and underparts varies: in Ug and Rw eastwards to WKe the nominate race has the most blue, extending over sides of face, neck, breast and flanks, in N and CKe *brunneigularis* differs in having brown sides to the face and neck, while from SEKe to NETz *littoralis* and elsewhere in Tz *ugogoensis* have pale brownish cheeks. ♀ *ugogoensis* overlaps in range with Southern Cordon-bleu but that species has blue cheeks. Imms are like dull ♀♀. **HH** very common and widespread in virtually all habitats except forest interior, from sea-level to 2300m. In overlap area with Southern Cordon-bleu, Red-cheeked prefers more luxuriant habitats and miombo woodland. **Vo** rhythmic but lazy song consists of 4–6 high-pitched lispy notes with the last note lower, longer and more burry. Contact call is an often-repeated high-pitched *siii siii…*

Southern Cordon-bleu *Uraeginthus angolensis* 13cm, 5″
[Blue Waxbill]

In Tz both sexes of the race *niassensis* are almost identical with *blue on the face, breast and flanks*. They are easily separated from ♂ Red-cheeked Cordon-bleu by lack of the red cheek spot. In overlap area, the race of Red-cheeked occurring is *ugogoensis* which has pale brown cheeks. A small flock of similar looking cordon-bleus with blue cheeks would, therefore, be Southern Cordon-bleu. Imm is paler than ad. **HH** common and widespread in a variety of habitats from sea-level to 1500m, and preferring drier habitats and acacia woodland in areas of overlap with Red-cheeked. **Vo** song lacks the squeakiness of Red-cheeked Cordon-bleu and is more complex, a mixture of jumbles and slurs, usually terminating after a short pause with an upslur. Call is a smooth *seep*.

Blue-capped Cordon-bleu *Uraeginthus cyanocephalus* 13cm, 5″

Ad ♂ has an *all bright blue head*, breast and flanks, and a bright pink bill. Ad ♀ is similar to other ♀ cordon-bleus on the crown, but may show a diagnostic deep pinkish-red bill. Imm is paler, with a brownish breast and dark grey bill. **HH** widespread but never really numerous, in semi-arid country from sea-level to 1300m. **Vo** complex and varied song has a peculiar metallic twang, and its calls are stronger and less lispy than other cordon-bleus, and retain a metallic timbre.

Purple Grenadier *Uraeginthus ianthinogaster* 13cm, 5″

A brightly coloured, red-billed waxbill: ad ♂ has a russet-brown head with blue face marks, the breast to vent and rump deep violet-blue, and a black tail. Ad ♀ is similar above, but has pale blue or whitish lines over and under the eyes, and is paler russet-brown below variably barred white on the flanks. Imm is fairly uniform dull warm brown, with a plain face and a dark bill. **HH** common within range, inhabiting open woodland, bush and cultivation, as well as semi-arid areas from near sea-level to 2300m. **Vo** song often starts with a strong high trill which continues as a rising metallic squeaking *sit-t-sit sit siiiiiiii*, and the call is a metallic explosive *zeet* which may be repeated.

Black-faced Firefinch *Lagonosticta larvata* 10cm, 4″

Ad ♂ is an atypical firefinch being *grey with a black face mask* and a red rump and tail: pale lavender-grey underparts have small white spots on sides of breast. Ad ♀ is grey-brown above, with a red rump and uppertail, and buffy underparts including the vent. Bill in both sexes is dark grey. **HH** local and uncommon in tall grassland, thickets and overgrown cultivation from 700–1200m. **Vo** song is reportedly similar to African Firefinch, and the call is a weak lisping note.

Plate 274

Red-cheeked Cordon-bleu

nominate

Southern Cordon-bleu

Blue-capped
Cordon-bleu

Imm

Purple Grenadier

Black-faced Firefinch

FIREFINCHES

A similar group of small red and brown waxbills (except Black-faced Firefinch on plate 274). Different races complicate identification but they can be separated by attention to bill colour, extent of red in the plumage and presence or lack of black on the vent. Immatures are like dull, browner, or paler versions of females. Many are hosts to the nest parasitic indigobirds.

Red-billed Firefinch *Lagonosticta senegala* 10cm, 4"

Two races occur: ♂ of widespread race *ruberrima* is *mostly wine-red including the crown*, with browner wings and tail, and a *grey-brown vent*. Bill is pinkish-red on the sides with a grey culmen. ♀ is largely brown with red on the sides of face and rump, and a duller bill. Both sexes may show small white spots at sides of the breast. In SETz ♂ of race *rendalli* is more russet-brown above including most of the crown. **HH** the most common firefinch from sea-level to 2200m, occupying a wide range of habitats (including human settlements) and only really avoiding forest interiors and desert. **Vo** varied song is a mixture of chip notes and rising upslurs *chep chep de-zwiz-wi*, and also *chick-pea-pea-pea*, a song mimicked by Village Indigobird. Also utters a downslurred *seeu* both perched and in flight.

African Firefinch *Lagonosticta rubricata* 10cm, 4"
[Blue-billed Firefinch]

Two races occur: ♂♂ are similar, but ♀♀ differ. ♂♂ show more contrasting upperparts than Red-billed Firefinch, with a distinct *brown mantle, red rump and black tail*, the underparts are red with a black belly and vent. Bill is grey in both sexes. In widespread race *ugandae*, the ♀ is largely brownish except for a red rump, blackish tail, pink washed underparts and black undertail-coverts. In E and STz ♀ of race *haematocephala* is more like the ♂ but rosier below with a buff belly and black undertail-coverts. **HH** rather shy and often keeping to cover within woodland, thickets and overgrown cultivation, from sea-level to 3000m. **Vo** song varies locally but is typically consists of dry trills interspersed with bunting-like *suwee suwee suwee suwee* notes. Alarm call is a rather sharp *pit-pit-pit* which is mimicked by Variable Indigobird.

Bar-breasted Firefinch *Lagonosticta rufopicta* 10cm, 4"

Similar to Red-billed Firefinch with pink sides to the bill, but the *crown and nape are the same earth-brown as the mantle*. Small white bars on breast, or sides of breast, are highly variable and often hard to see. Rump and base of tail red. Sexes alike. **HH** locally common with a preference for overgrown cultivation and lush vegetation near water, from 600–1400m. **Vo** song is a mixture of rising and falling chipping notes, interspersed with short sibilant upslurs *chip chip weee weeee...*, the alarm call is a repeated metallic chip.

Brown Firefinch *Lagonosticta nitidula* 10cm, 4"

♂ is mostly *dark brown including the rump*, with red confined to the face and upper breast: white speckling may extend almost across the breast. Bill has pinkish-red sides and a dark culmen. ♀ is similar to ♂ but paler. **HH** in our area, known only from extreme STz where it occurs in thick cover near water. **Vo** call is a metallic yet lispy *szit* which is delivered singly or in a rapid series.

Jameson's Firefinch *Lagonosticta rhodopareia* 10cm, 4"

Two races occur: ♂♂ of both have grey bills, black tails and black vents like African Firefinch. From EKe to CTz, ♂ of race *taruensis* has the *head, back and underparts rosy-pink*, while from NEUg to NKe the nominate ♂ is extremely similar to ♂ African Firefinch, being brown above and bright red on the head and underparts. Both ♀♀ have *red lores*, greyish or pink crowns and ear-coverts, and are mostly orange-pink below with some blackish bars on the vent. **HH** local, mainly in dry bush country from sea-level to 1500m, but also in more luxuriant habitats near the coast. **Vo** song varies but is often a rather bunting-like *si..syee-syee-syee-syee-syee* all on one tone, this is frequently interrupted with a fast purring trill which is mimicked by Purple Indigobird.

Black-bellied Firefinch *Lagonosticta rara* 11cm, 4.5"

♂ is *deep wine-red including the mantle*, with brown wings and a *black lower breast, belly and vent*. Bill dark with pink base to lower mandible. *No white spots on underparts*. ♀ is browner above with a greyish head and throat and red lores, the underparts are pinkish with a black belly and vent. **HH** generally uncommon in wooded grasslands and the edges of cultivation from 800–1700m. **Vo** song begins with a sharp dry clicking, breaks into squeaky rhythmical slurs and ends with a single long note *sisisi see-susu-sisi-si weeeeeee*.

Plate 275

Red-billed Firefinch

♀

♂

ruberrima

African Firefinch

♀

♂

ugandae

Bar-breasted Firefinch

Imm

♂

Jameson's Firefinch

♀

♂

Brown
Firefinch

♂

taruensis

♂

♀

Black-bellied Firefinch

ESTRILDA WAXBILLS

A rather variable group of small waxbills, some of which congregate in large flocks. Sexes are similar.

Yellow-bellied Waxbill   *Estrilda quartinia*   10cm, 4"
[East African Swee]

A small and colourful, but *pale-toned* waxbill, with a pale grey head and upper breast, an olive-green mantle and wings, red rump, blackish tail, and a *yellow belly*. Upper mandible black, lower mandible red. Imm is similar, but paler with a dark bill. **HH** common at forest edge, in highland grasslands and around cultivation from 900–3000m. **Vo** song is a short series of slurred, whistled squeaks and nasal notes, while the call is a high-pitched lispy *siii siii siii...*

Common Waxbill   *Estrilda astrild*   10cm, 4"

Four races occur, differing in the general tone of pinks and browns, density of fine barring, and intensity of pink or red on the underparts. Basic description is *brown above including the rump and tail,* and all finely barred, with a bright red streak through the eye, and a waxy red bill. Pale brown below with a variable pink wash, or bright red streak on the belly. Imm is paler with a blackish bill. **HH** small to large flocks are very common and widespread away from forest interior and arid habitats from sea-level to 3000m, often feeding in long grass near water. **Vo** foraging birds usually keep in contact with irregular dry squeaks and chips, and the song consists of a paired *tikatik-wheez tikatik-wheez,* with the last note burry and upslurred.

Crimson-rumped Waxbill   *Estrilda rhodopyga*   10cm, 4"

Similar to Common Waxbill with a red streak through the eye and finely barred brown upperparts, but has a blackish bill, *crimson-red rump,* and red edges to the wing-coverts and tertials. Imm is plain brown, darker above than below, lacks the red eye streak and has a duller red rump. **HH** common resident and wanderer, occurring in thickets, damp grasslands and marshy shorelines from sea-level to 1800m. **Vo** song structure is similar to Common Waxbill, although the notes are nasal and more clearly defined, consisting of musical chips forming a regular rhythmic pattern *wi-chi wi-chi wi chi-chi...* Also calls a low churr and a nasal chipping in flight.

Black-rumped Waxbill   *Estrilda troglodytes*   10cm, 4"

Similar to Common Waxbill, but cleaner looking with a *jet black rump and tail,* the latter narrowly edged white. Streak through eye and bill red, faint barring above may be visible in good light. Very pale pinky-buff below, whiter on the throat. Imm is duller, with a blackish bill. **HH** common in the west, less so in Ke, inhabiting both dry country and thicker vegetation near water from 800–1400m. **Vo** call is a loud somewhat metallic chipping, and the song is similar but more subdued and punctuated by long single upslurs *soyiiiii...*

Fawn-breasted Waxbill   *Estrilda paludicola*   10cm, 4"

A rather pale looking waxbill with a bright red bill, brown back and wings, red rump and black tail. Four races occur: in SWUg to CTz birds have the crown and nape brown uniform with the mantle, and are pale grey below, elsewhere the crown and nape are grey, and the underparts are buffy-fawn (whitish on the throat). Pink on the belly or lower flanks may be present on many birds. Imms are generally paler with dark bills. **HH** common, but with a patchy distribution from 1000–2000m, preferring lush habitats, clearings in forest, wet grasslands and overgrown cultivation. **Vo** song is a loud, energetic, rolling and rhythmic nasal series of chips and squeaks, and the call is a short nasal downslurred *sieu.*

Orange-cheeked Waxbill   *Estrilda melpoda*   10cm, 4"

Rather like the grey-headed races of Fawn-breasted Waxbill, but with a *bright orange mask around the eye,* and a red bill. Imm is paler with a black bill. **HH** in our area restricted to the lowlands around Bujumbura in Bu, where it is common at about 775m. **Vo** call is a nasal piping similar to Fawn-breasted Waxbill, but it is stronger and more emphatic when the bird is agitated. Song is a simple *ti-ti-ti-siiiiia* or variants.

Plate 276

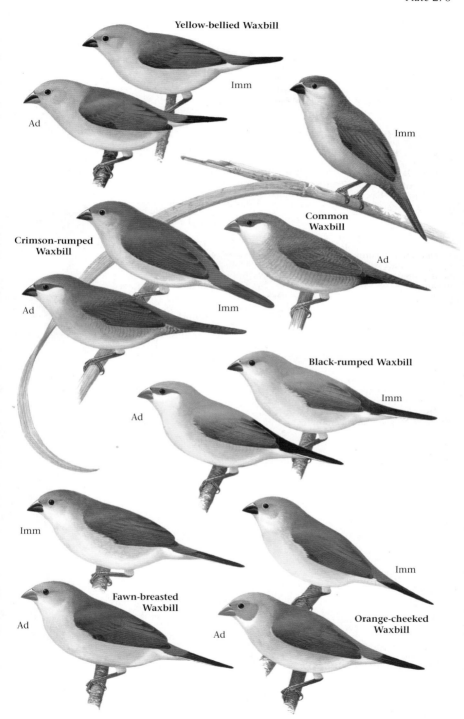

Yellow-bellied Waxbill

Imm

Ad

Imm

Crimson-rumped
Waxbill

Common
Waxbill

Ad

Ad

Imm

Ad

Black-rumped Waxbill

Imm

Ad

Imm

Fawn-breasted
Waxbill

Imm

Ad

Imm

Ad

Orange-cheeked
Waxbill

Black-crowned Waxbill *Estrilda nonnula*   10cm, 4"
Black-capped grey and white waxbill with a red rump. Very similar to Black-headed Waxbill, but has distinctive *white underparts including the vent*. At close range shows a finely barred back and wings with some red on the lower flanks. Bill red and black. ♀ has less red on the flanks. Imm is plainer and duller than ad, with a slight brownish wash and all-dark bill. **HH** common at forest edge, in secondary growth, marshy areas, and cultivation, from 800–2200m. **Vo** small flocks frequently call a high-pitched and sibilant *sii-sii-sii-sii...*, and the rarely heard song consists of rising and falling tinkling notes.

Black-headed Waxbill *Estrilda atricapilla*   10cm, 4"
Very similar to Black-crowned Waxbill, but overall appearance is much darker, especially on the underparts which are dark grey blending to *black on the vent and belly*. Also shows finely barred back and wings at close range, and red on the flanks is more extensive than on Black-cheeked Waxbill. Bill has red on lower mandible only. Imm is duller and browner without red on the flanks. **HH** a common high country species inhabiting forest edge and nearby grassy clearings from 2000–3300m. **Vo** calls a loud, persistent and slightly metallic *sii-sii-sii*, often from perches and always in flight.

Black-faced Waxbill *Estrilda erythronotos*   10cm, 4"
[Black-cheeked Waxbill in southern Africa]
Very similar to Black-cheeked Waxbill (and formerly lumped in the same species): both have pinkish-grey finely barred upperparts, black face masks, red rumps and black tails. Black-faced Waxbill differs in having a *slightly larger black area on the chin* (a black face) and an overall darker appearance: *belly to vent is black on ♂, but uniform with remainder of underparts on ♀*. Imm is like a dull version of ad. **HH** locally common within range, inhabiting open woodland, acacia country, scrub and cultivation, mainly from 1000–1700m. **Vo** call and song is a long high-pitched rising upslur *seeeeeeeii...*, and a less frequent double *tsee-tsee* and a quiet twittering.

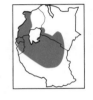

Black-cheeked Waxbill *Estrilda charmosyna*   10cm, 4"
Paler than Black-faced Waxbill, with a *black face mask mainly confined to the cheeks* (only a very narrow black line crosses the chin): *belly to vent usually pinkish-grey* in both sexes, but sometimes darker grey. Imm is less pink than ad. **HH** common in semi-arid bush country from 100–1000m, occasionally up to 1600m. **Vo** calls are much harsher than Black-faced Waxbill, and consist of repeated dry chipping and short dry rattled trills.

Black-tailed Grey Waxbill *Estrilda perreini*   10cm, 4"
[Grey Waxbill, Lavender Waxbill]
A highly distinctive lead-grey waxbill with a blackish vent (dark grey on ♀), a red rump, black tail, and dark-grey bill. Imm is duller without the black loral stripe. **HH** pairs or family groups, are shy, uncommon and localised residents of forest edge, cover within woodland and miombo woodland from 500–2100m. **Vo** call is a shrill, long and monotone *siiiiiiiir*.

Zebra Waxbill *Amandava subflava*   9cm, 3.5"
[Orange-breasted Waxbill]
A very small bright waxbill. Two races occur with distinctive ad ♂ plumages, both are olive-brown above with a red eye-stripe, red uppertail-coverts and a blackish tail. From Ug to WKe nominate ♂ is bright orange-yellow below; while from CKe to STz *clarkei* is mostly yellow: both have barred flanks. Ad ♀ is duller and paler without the eye-stripes. Imm is like a pale, drab and plain ♀. **HH** locally common in small flocks, and very active inhabitants of reedbeds, marshy grassland and cultivated areas from sea-level to 2200m. **Vo** most frequently heard calls are short repeated and complaining nasal downslurs which are usually paired, and the song mixes these notes with long decending rattled trills, or a series of random spitted metallic notes *tit tit tit tit...*

Plate 277

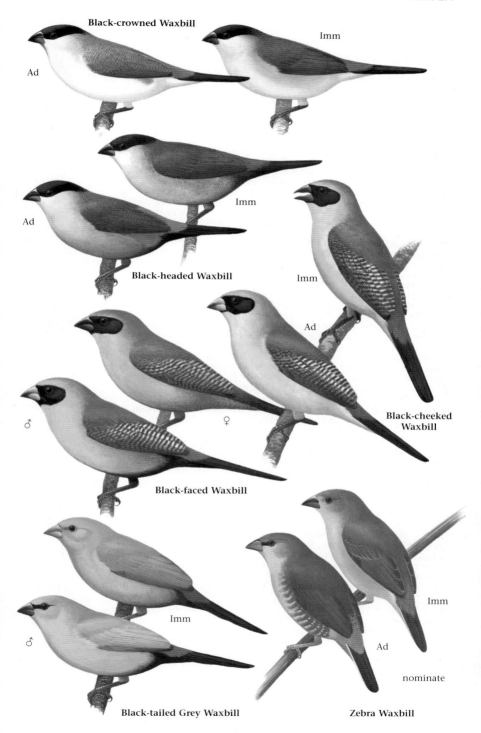

Black-crowned Waxbill

Imm

Ad

Black-headed Waxbill

Ad

Imm

Imm

Black-cheeked Waxbill

Ad

♂

♀

Black-faced Waxbill

Imm

♂

Imm

Ad

nominate

Black-tailed Grey Waxbill

Zebra Waxbill

SILVERBILLS

Two waxbills with rather stout blue-grey bills. Usually in small flocks feeding in grass on or near the ground. Sexes are alike.

African Silverbill *Lonchura cantans* 11cm, 4.5"

A *sandy-brown waxbill with blackish wings, rump and tail*, slightly paler below than above, with a rather large stubby blue-grey bill. Imm is similar but has a browner tail. **HH** locally common in semi-arid bush and dry wooded grasslands from sea-level to 1900m. **Vo** in flight calls a loud, harsh, hollow-sounding *tink-tink...*, but from a perch may utter an extended dry rattle.

Grey-headed Silverbill *Lonchura griseicapilla* 11cm, 4.5"

Larger than African Silverbill with a *grey head*, white speckled cheeks, pinky-brown upperparts, *a white rump* and a blackish tail. Washed peachy-pink below. Imm is duller than ad without white spotting on the cheeks or the peachy washed underparts. **HH** small wandering flocks are patchily distributed within range from near sea-level to 1900m, occurring in open wooded grasslands, bush, and semi-arid acacia country. **Vo** in flight utters a soft downslurred *seeu*, while the song is a series of these notes which rise and fall and are occasionally mixed with sharp metallic notes.

QUAIL-FINCHES and LOCUST-FINCH

Small short-tailed waxbills found in flocks on the ground. Often difficult to see, when they crouch motionless until flushed and then suddenly all fly away together calling.

African Quail-Finch *Ortygospiza atricollis* 9cm, 3.5"

Two races occur: in widespread race *muelleri* ad ♂ is mostly grey-brown above with a blackish face, *conspicuous white eye-lines* and a red bill. Below has a *tiny white chin patch*, barred black and white upper breast and flanks, and an orange-brown lower breast. *Shows small white corners to the tail in flight.* Ad ♀ is much duller, with a dark upper mandible. Imm is like a pale dull ♀. In WUg, ♂ of the race *uganda*, has less distinct white eye-lines (sometimes absent), a plain mantle and brighter rusty-orange underparts. **HH** common in short grasslands, ploughed fields, and along barren lakeshores from sea-level to 3000m. **Vo** when flushed, individuals within the flock utter burry and metallic *tchink-tchink...* calls.

Black-chinned Quail-Finch *Ortygospiza gabonensis* 9cm, 3.5"

Very similar to African Quail-Finch, ad ♂ has a *black chin, bright red bill, black face without the white eye-lines*, a darkish-brown slightly streaked mantle, and paler underparts. Ad ♀ and imm are not safely separated from ♀ and imm African Quail-Finch in the field. **HH** locally common, and usually occurring in wetter grasslands than African Quail-Finch, from 900–1500m. **Vo** similar to African Quail-Finch, but the notes in flight are often tripled *tri-ti-tri...*, and more spaced.

Locust-Finch *Ortygospiza locustella* 9cm, 3.5"

A tiny bright and distinctive waxbill: ad ♂ is black with a bright red face, upper breast and sides of rump, and orange-red wing patches. Two races occur: in WKe *uelensis* is uniformly blackish above, while in STz the nominate has tiny white spots on the mantle. Ad ♀ is dark brown above with rufous-orange wing patches, and whitish below with dark barred flanks. Imm is similar to ♀ but duller and browner. **HH** similar to quail-finches, with flocks unexpectedly flying up when flushed. They favour marshy grasslands, but also known from burnt areas, from 1200–2000m. **Vo** flight call is a rather mournful *tiu tiu tiu...*

Plate 278

African Silverbill

Ad

Grey-headed Silverbill

Ad

African Quail-Finch

♂

♂

♀

muelleri

Black-chinned
Quail-Finch

♂

♀

♂

Locust-Finch

♂

♀

nominate

MANNIKINS
Three similar waxbills, also known as munias. All have blackish heads and barred flanks, but the overall size and mantle colour aid identification. They occur in small flocks, feeding in long grass and on the ground. Sexes are alike.

Bronze Mannikin *Lonchura cucullata* 9cm, 3.5"

Small with a *blackish head and breast* contrasting with a *dull brown (or grey-brown) nape, mantle and wings*. In good light may show a small glossy dark-green patch at the shoulder, and western birds may also show a green sheen to the flank barring. Lower breast to vent white. Bill is stubby with a dark grey upper and pale grey lower mandible. Imm is plain buffy-brown with darker wings and tail. **HH** most common mannikin, widespread in all habitats except desert and forest interiors from sea-level to 2200m. **Vo** song and calls consist of a rapid delivery of short burry chips which rise and fall in tone, sometimes developing into a churr. Similar twittering is frequently given in flight.

Black-and-white Mannikin *Lonchura bicolor* 9cm, 3.5"
[Red-backed Mannikin]

A small mannikin with two distinct races which are sometimes considered separate species: from Ug to NWTz and WKe race *poensis is entirely black and white without any contrast between the head and mantle*; and from C and EKe to STz *nigriceps* (**Rufous-backed Mannikin**) is *chestnut-brown on the mantle, tertials and wing-coverts*. Both have barred black and white flight feathers and rumps (plain on Bronze Mannikin) and pale blue-grey bills. Imms are plain dull brown above, paler below, with the mantle washed warm brown on *nigriceps*. **HH** common at forest edge, in lush thickets and around cultivation, from sea-level to 2000m. **Vo** calls are similar to a white-eye, but are a little harsher, more mournful, whistled downslurs *tsiu tsiu…*

Magpie Mannikin *Lonchura fringilloides* 11cm, 4.5"
[Pied Mannikin]

Largest mannikin which is most similar to Bronze Mannikin but with a heavier dark grey and pale blue-grey bill. *Black on head extends over nape,* and black smudges at sides of breast are large. Black and white barred flanks may also have some rufous markings. Imm is dull brown above with a paler mantle, buff underparts and an all-dark bill. **HH** very local and uncommon resident of forest edge, secondary growth and cultivation, occurring in two widely separated areas, from sea-level to 1400m. **Vo** calls are similar to Black-and-White Mannikin, but louder with the whistled downslurs longer and not so mournful *tsiu rsii tsiu tsii…*

Cut-throat Finch *Amadina fasciata* 10cm, 4"

Ad ♂ is very distinctive with a *bright red crescent-shaped cut across the throat*, and otherwise all scaly grey-brown plumage with a variably sized patch of chestnut on the belly. Ad ♀ is entirely barred and scaly, without the red throat line or chestnut on the belly. Imm ♂ shows an indication of the red throat streak. **H** common in flocks, mainly in semi-arid country, but wanders erratically occurring less frequently in farmland and at the coast, from sea-level to 1300m. **Vo** song consists of short and abrupt phrases mixing nasal notes and squeaks.

Java Sparrow *Padda oryzivora* 15cm, 6"

Ad is distinctive with a black head, white cheeks and coral-pink bill. Otherwise blue-grey above with a blue-grey breast, pink lower breast to belly and blackish tail. Imm is dull brown with an indication of the dark crown and pale cheeks, and a pinkish base to the bill. **HH** introduced to and locally common on the islands of Zanzibar and Pemba, Tz. **Vo** contact call a liquid *t'luk* or *ch'luk*.

Plate 279

Bronze Mannikin

Ad

Imm

Imm

Ad

Ad

nigriceps

poensis

Black-and-white Mannikin

Imm

Ad

Magpie Mannikin

Cut-throat Finch

♀

♂

Imm

Java Sparrow

Ad

PARADISE-WHYDAHS AND WHYDAHS

Together with Steel-blue Whydah on plate 281, all except Pin-tailed Whydah are species-specific brood parasites, laying their eggs in the nests of a particular waxbill (see text). Within our area, breeding males have long tails and distinctive plumages. Non-breeding males and females are extremely similar to each other and also to the smaller indigobirds: careful attention to head pattern, bill and foot colour aids identifcation. All attain breeding plumage during the rains, when they display and perch prominently. They feed on the ground.

Eastern Paradise-Whydah *Vidua paradisaea* ♂ 38cm, 15"
[Paradise Whydah]

Br ♂ has a striking buffy-yellow, chestnut and black plumage with a *long tapering tail.* ♀ has a buffy crown stripe bordered with black, pale-buff superciliary stripes, *two blackish crescents behind the eye,* and usually a blackish bill. Non-br ♂ is similar to ♀, but the head pattern is bolder, more black and white. Juv is plain grey-brown with a paler belly. **HH** fairly common and widespread with a preference for semi-arid acacia country from sea-level to 2200m. Parasitic on Green-winged Pytilia. **Vo** amidst chattering, song consistently introduces the chipping and squeaky nasal phrases resembling Green-winged Pytilia and Blue-capped Cordon-bleu.

Broad-tailed Paradise-Whydah *Vidua obtusa* ♂ 31cm, 12"

Br ♂ is similar to Eastern Paradise-Whydah, but the *tail is broad throughout most of its length.* ♂♂ without tails can be identified by their *rufous hindneck* (not golden or buffy-yellow). ♀ is very similar to ♀ Eastern Paradise-Whydah, but slightly larger, with a pale or bi-coloured bill, and less distinct markings behind the eye. Non-br ♂ is like a boldly marked ♀. Juv is like juv Eastern Paradise-Whydah. **HH** occurs in moister areas than Eastern Paradise-Whydah from 300–1700m, with a preference for miombo woodland. Parasitic on Orange-winged Pytilia. **Vo** extremely unlike Eastern Paradise-Whydah, song is formless and consists of harsh chipping and chattering, suggesting some of the notes given by Orange-winged Pytilia.

Pin-tailed Whydah *Vidua macroura* ♂ 31cm, 12"

Br ♂ has striking black and white plumage, a red bill and a long narrow black tail. ♀ has a boldly patterned head and upperparts, and the bill is red in non-br, and black in br, plumage. In flight, may show white inner webs to outer-tail feathers. Non-br ♂ and imm are like ♀, but with a bolder black and white head pattern and a red bill. Juv is plain grey-brown with a whitish throat and blackish bill. **HH** commonest and most widespread whydah, inhabiting a wide variety of woodland, bush country, cultivation and gardens from sea-level to 3000m. It is not host specific, instead parasitising several Estrild waxbills including: Common, Crimson-rumped, Black-rumped, Fawn-breasted and Orange-cheeked. **Vo** song is a relatively tuneless jumble of harsh squeaks and sparrow-like chirps that form a rhythmic pattern.

Straw-tailed Whydah *Vidua fischeri* ♂ 31cm, 12"

Br ♂ has a unique yellow and black plumage, with a red bill and feet, and *long thin straw-coloured tail.* ♀ is streaked brown above, with a distinctive *plain rufous-tawny head, reddish bill and feet.* Non-br ♂ is like a boldly marked ♀. Juv is plain rufous-brown with a dark bill (similar to juv Purple Grenadier, the host species). **HH** widespread in bush country and drier cultivated areas from sea-level to 2000m. **Vo** attractive song has very lively and lark-like phrases *si-si-sit swi si swit* with bouts of song persisting for long periods.

Plate 280

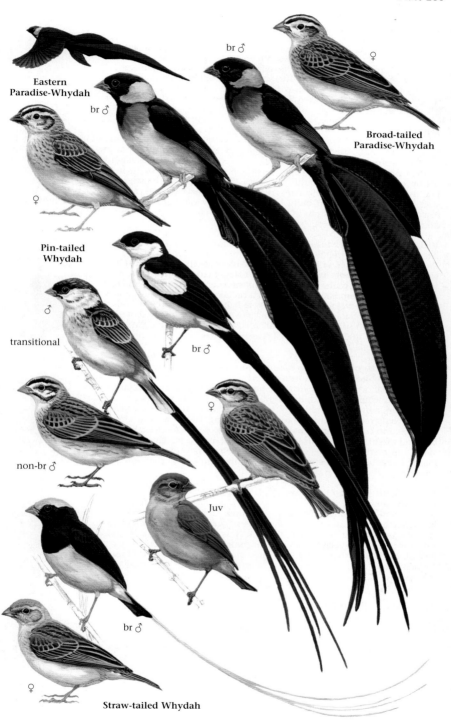

Eastern
Paradise-Whydah

br ♂

br ♂

br ♂

♀

Broad-tailed
Paradise-Whydah

♀

Pin-tailed
Whydah

♂

transitional

br ♂

♀

non-br ♂

Juv

br ♂

♀

Straw-tailed Whydah

Steel-blue Whydah   *Vidua hypocherina*   ♂ 31cm, 12"

Br ♂ looks totally blue-black in the field (but may occasionally show a white flank spot), with a *white or greyish bill.* ♀ and non-br ♂ are very similar to several other ♀ whydahs and indigobirds, but the bill is small and grey, and the feet are grey. Juv is plain brown with greyer cheeks (like juv Black-faced and Black-cheeked waxbills, the host species). **HH** rather uncommon in dry bush and bushed grassland from 500–1400m (with a curious and patchy distribution within its range). **Vo** infrequently heard song is similar to Black-cheeked Waxbill, a lazy extended medley of varied dry chips and nasal notes.

INDIGOBIRDS

Closely related to the whydahs, indigobirds are also members of the family Viduidae and parasitise Estrildid finches. Several are extremely difficult to identify. Breeding males are blackish with a blue, purple or green gloss. Bills and feet are varying combinations of red, pinkish or white. Each species is a brood-parasite, particular to one species of finch. Males sing from prominent perches and are best identified by song. In addition to their own rapid chattering, they imitate their host species, particularly its alarm calls. Non-breeding males and females are boldly streaked brown above and buffy below, and many cannot be identifed (even in the hand). Female bill and foot colour as in males. Plainer juveniles are also indistinguishable in the field. All feed on the ground.

Village Indigobird   *Vidua chalybeata*   10cm, 4"
[Steelblue Widowfinch]

Two races occur: br ♂♂ of both have a blue-black sheen, with dark brown wings and red or orange-red feet, but differ in bill colour. Widespread race *centralis* has a white bill, while coastal *amauropteryx* has a red bill. **HH** most common and widespread indigobird which occurs in a wide variety of habitats from sea-level to 2000m, closely matching the range of Red-billed Firefinch which it parasitises. **Vo** ♂♂ sing a two-tone *chick* followed by simple clear rising whistles *pea pea*, as well as *chick-pea-pea-pea* which may rise and fall. Pattern uttered frequently between phrases of its own chattering song.

Variable Indigobird   *Vidua funerea*   10cm, 4"
[Dusky Indigobird, Black Widowfinch]

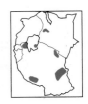

Race *nigerrima* occurs in our area: br ♂ has purplish or blue-black plumage with brown wings, a white bill and pinkish-white feet. It is virtually identical to Purple Indigobird, although some birds have a stronger blue sheen, and it is only reliably identified by its mimic song. **HH** parasitises African Firefinch and could occur throughout the range of that species (and may be overlooked). **Vo** most distinctive are *pit pit* notes, which mimic the alarm call of the firefinch, and are much slower than the rapid *purr* of Purple Indigobird. A variety of slurred whistles and *too-too* notes are also produced.

Purple Indigobird   *Vidua purpurascens*   10cm, 4"
[Purple Widowfinch]

Br ♂ is identical to Variable Indigobird with similar brown wings, but some birds may have a stronger purple sheen. ♀♀ of both species are also identical. **HH** parasitises Jameson's Firefinch which is usually in drier areas than the two preceding species. Generally uncommon, but may also be overlooked. **Vo** frequently utters a very rapid *purr* during phrases of its usual varied chatter.

Twinspot Indigobird   *Vidua codringtoni*   10cm, 4"
[Twinspot Widowfinch]

Br ♂ is distinctive with a greenish gloss to the otherwise black plumage. Bill is white and feet are orange-red. In good light there is a greyish wash across the breast. ♀ also has a distinctive greyish breast. **HH** parasitic on Peters's Twinspot, it is presently only known in our area from SC and STz (although the twinspot is far more widespread). **Vo** a variety of soft whistles, trills and chattering interspersed with high-pitched *trrrrrrreee* notes.

Plate 281

Steel-blue
Whydah

br ♂

Juv

Juv

♀

♀

br ♂
centralis

br ♂
amauropteryx

Village
Indigobird

br ♂

br ♂

Variable
Indigobird

Purple
Indigobird

Twinspot
Indigobird

CANARIES AND SEEDEATERS

Small finches with mostly green and yellow, and or brown and white plumage, with streaked upperparts and variably streaked underparts. In East Africa the yellow plumaged birds are called canaries and the browner species seedeaters.

Brimstone Canary *Serinus sulphuratus* 14cm, 5.5"

[Bully Canary]

Ad ♂ is larger than Yellow-fronted Canary with a heavier pinkish-horn bill, less distinct face pattern with an olive-green (not black) malar stripe. Rump and mantle are both green with dark streaking, and it *does not show a contrasting bright yellow rump in flight*. ♀ and imm are duller. **HH** pairs or single birds are common in wooded grassland, moist bush country and cultivated areas from sea-level to 2400m. **Vo** songs vary from a rather rapid high-pitched sparrow-like chirping (in the west) to sweeter, varied refrains (mainly in the east). The call is a loud rather gravelly trill *chrirrrrir*.

Yellow-fronted Canary *Serinus mozambicus* 11cm, 4.5"

[Yellow-eyed Canary]

Ad ♂ is quite distinctive with a bright yellow forecrown extending back as a well-marked supercilium. Narrow black line through the eye and *strong black malar stripe* create a well-marked face pattern. The bright yellow rump contrasts with a streaked greenish mantle, and the underparts are entirely plain bright yellow. ♀ is similar but paler. Imm is also paler than ad with light streaking on the sides of the breast. **HH** small flocks are common and widespread in open woodland, bush country and cultivation from sea-level to 2300m. **Vo** a rather monotonous songster, the refrain may continue for a long periods, but is broken into short phrases *si-yu sisi si yu* with embellishments.

White-bellied Canary *Serinus dorsostriatus* 11cm, 4.5"

From NEUg through N and EKe to NETz, ad ♂ of the race *maculicollis* has a distinctive *white belly and vent* and an olive-green malar stripe. In SWKe and Tz ad ♂ of the nominate race has a much smaller area of white on the belly but can be separated from very similar Yellow-fronted Canary by its olive-green (not black) malar stripe. Both races show a contrasting yellow rump in flight. ♀ *maculicollis* has a *white belly* but is paler than the ♂ with variable streaking on the breast and flanks. ♀ nominate is similar to ♀ *maculicollis* but has less white on belly. Imms like ♀♀ but paler and buffier below. Both races intergrade across a wide area in SKe. **HH** common in drier areas than Yellow-fronted Canary, usually in dry bush country from 400–1800m, but up to 2650m in NKe. **Vo** attractive song is high-pitched and continues for long periods, but is broken into complex phrases which vary a little and last about 5 seconds.

Yellow-crowned Canary *Serinus canicollis* 11cm, 4.5"

[Cape Canary]

In our area, strikingly different from the southern African Cape Canary. Two races occur: in Ke and NTz ad ♂ *flavivertex* has a *golden-yellow forecrown and two bright yellow wing bars*, and an obvious yellow rump in flight. ♀ is duller, with variable amount of white and dark streaking below. Imm is more buffy-brown with extensive streaking below. In SWUg to STz, *sassii* is similar with a more yellow tail. **HH** often in flocks, it is common at high altitudes from 1600–4300m, in cultivation, forest edge, bamboo and moorlands. **Vo** in flight, birds often give a short rapid trill of about five quite low notes *tiririririr*, while the long rambling song has a strange tinny tone.

Thick-billed Seedeater *Serinus burtoni* 15cm, 6"

Distinctive, but with some racial variation. All are basically dark brown above, with two narrow buffy wing bars, olive-green edged primaries, and a very heavy bill, and mostly dull brown below paler on the buffy belly. Most have blackish faces, some have a small area of white on forecrown, and others show crown or flank streaking. Sexes and imms are alike. **HH** rather shy but not uncommon in the undergrowth and canopy of highland forest and bamboo from 1200–3000m, mainly above 1700m. **Vo** usual call is a high thrush-like *seeep*, given perched, and in flight. The rarely heard song is a series of high-pitched hissed notes usually broken into short repeated phrases.

Kipengere Seedeater *Serinus melanochrous* 14cm, 5.5" ●

Sometimes considered a race of Thick-billed Seedeater, but smaller and smaller-billed, without white on the forecrown, or white wing bars. Buffy below with extensive heavy dark brown streaking and a whitish throat. **HH** Tz endemic restricted to Iringa and Njombe highlands. **Vo** song is very different from Thick-billed Seedeater, a long rambling series with a rattling quality.

Plate 282

Brimstone Canary

♂

♀

Imm

Yellow-fronted Canary

♂

maculicollis

♂

♀

White-bellied Canary

Kipengere Seedeater

♀

Thick-billed Seedeater

Yellow-crowned Canary

♂

flavivertex

African Citril *Serinus citrinelloides*   11cm, 4.5"

Taxonomically complex with two distinct groups in our area, each containing two races. If split into species, the two black-faced races *frontalis* (in WUg-WTz) and *kikuyuensis* (W and CKe) are known as **Western Citril** *Serinus frontalis;* while the grey-faced races *hypostictus* (SWKe-ETz) and *brittoni* (WKe) are **East African Citril** *Serinus hypostictus.* Ad ♂ *frontalis* and *kikuyuensis* have bright yellow superciliary stripes, and *frontalis* also has a broad yellow band across the forecrown, which is black in *kikuyuensis* (sometimes with a narrow yellow band). ♀ *frontalis* is distinctive as the only ♀ with a yellow forecrown and *unstreaked yellow underparts.* Both ♂ and ♀ *hypostictus* have grey faces, and indistinct or no superciliary stripes, with some streaking below. Both ♂ and ♀ *brittoni* are similar to *hypostictus*, but the face and upperparts are greener. *All forms have rather straight pointed bills.* **HH** common in small flocks, occurring at the forest edge, in moist scrub, gardens and cultivated areas from 400 to 3300m (mainly above 1000m). **Vo** song of the black-faced group is very similar to Yellow-rumped Seedeater, but more pinched, slightly nasal and has a series of diagnostic falling piped notes. The grey-faced group are basically similar, but with more variation and a little more hurried delivery.

Black-faced Canary *Serinus capistratus*   11cm, 4.5"

Extremely similar to race *frontalis* of African Citril, and occurs in the same area in Bu (but usually at lower altitudes). In overlap areas, ♂ is identified by a slightly more extensive and sharply defined black face mask, and a shorter more conical bill. ♀ lacks black face and has streaking across the breast. **HH** in our area only known from 775–1400m from around Bujumbura and Ruvubu NP in Bu. **Vo** song is high-pitched but with a typical canary-like quality.

Papyrus Canary *Serinus koliensis*   11cm, 4.5"

Very similar to race *brittoni* of African Citril, with streaking both above and below. ♂ has greenish sides to the face and dark grey lores. ♀ is similar, but has paler grey lores. In overlap area in WKe, it is best identified by a *rather short conical bill* and its preferred habitat. **HH** uncommon and restricted to papyrus beds and nearby vegetation from 900–1600m. **Vo** song is a broken series of short phrases each slightly varying but typically including a series of rattle-like identical notes *tit't't't't.* It is quite different from other African citrils.

Yellow-rumped Seedeater *Serinus reichenowi*   11cm, 4.5"

A streaky brown seedeater with a yellow rump, whitish superciliary stripes and a buff or whitish throat, the yellow rump is conspicuous in flight: density of streaking on the underparts is variable. Sexes and imm are similar. May be conspecific with Black-throated Seedeater. **HH** flocks are common and widespread in open woodland, bush country and cultivation, from sea-level to 2000m. **Vo** typical canary song is loud and continuous with little variation, the same notes and occasional trills being repeated over and over for long periods.

Black-throated Seedeater *Serinus atrogularis*   11cm, 4.5"
[Black-throated Canary]

Very similar to Yellow-rumped Seedeater, but generally darker with black mottling on the throat. Sexes and imm similar. **HH** similar to previous species, but with a more westerly and southern distribution. **Vo** song is a long rambling similar to Yellow-rumped Seedeater, but harsher and more varied.

White-rumped Seedeater *Serinus leucopygius*   11cm, 4.5"

Similar to Yellow-rumped Seedeater, but more grey-brown, with a *white rump* (not yellow). Sexes and imm are similar. **HH** in our area restricted to bushed grassland from 600–1000m in NWUg. **Vo** sings for long periods without pause, the notes are smooth and rounded and lack the scratchiness or hissed quality of some other canaries.

Plate 283

African Citril

♀

Ad

hypostictus

♂

kikuyuensis

♀

Black-faced
Canary

♀

Papyrus
Canary

♂

♂

Yellow-rumped
Seedeater

White-rumped
Seedeater

Black-throated
Seedeater

Streaky Seedeater *Serinus striolatus*   14cm, 5.5"
Widespread nominate race has a bold facial pattern with a well-defined creamy-white supercilium, heavy streaking both above and below, and variable greenish edges to the primaries. In WUg, race *graueri* is similar, but deeper buff-brown below. In the highlands of STz, distinctive race *whytii* (**Yellow-browed Seedeater ●**) has a bright yellow face, wing-edgings and tail, and underparts washed pale grey with black streaking across the breast and flanks. **HH** common and widespread in the highlands from 1300–4300m, where it inhabits moorland heath, forest edge, rank vegetation, gardens and cultivation. **Vo** song has a rather forced thrush-like quality and often ends with a soft rattle. It is sung in repeated short phrases or as an attractive continuous refrain. The cheerful call is a loud upslurred whistle *siyuya*. Race *whytii* is similar but lower pitched, and the call is *siyuuee*.

Stripe-breasted Seedeater *Serinus reichardi*   13cm, 5"
[Reichard's Seedeater]
Two races (which are almost certainly separate species) occur: in W and CKe the form *striapectus* is dark brown above, with long white superciliary stripes, brown sides to the face, and *usually fairly heavily streaked underparts*. In Tz *reichardi* (**Reichard's Seedeater**) has similar head markings, but has darker streaking on the crown and a *narrow band of short dark streaks across the breast and on to the flanks*. **HH** usually in pairs or small flocks, *striatipectus* is an uncommon rather flighty bird of wooded escarpments from 1600–1800m in W and CKe; rather more sluggish *reichardi* is locally common (especially in miombo woodland) from 500–1800m in CTz. **Vo** both forms are rather quiet although they sing from the tops of small trees when on territory: *striapectus* has an interrogatory call *siyuah*, while the song often begins with *djee t'what* or *djee tu-waa* and continues with a prolonged rambling which includes much mimicry: *reichardi* is also a fine songster, combining canary-like trills and mimicry in repeated but varying patterns.

Streaky-headed Seedeater *Serinus gularis*   13cm, 5"
In our area the form *elgonensis* occurs, it is sometimes considered a race of **West African Seedeater** *Serinus canicapilla,* or as a race of the southern African *Serinus gularis*. They are similar to the *striatipectus* race of Stripe-breasted Seedeater but have white streaks on the crown, rather plain brown upperparts and a whitish throat which contrasts with the *mainly plain brown buff underparts*. **HH** in our area only known from dry woodland in EUg and WKe where it is considered to be rare. **Vo** song is rather short and slow for a canary, commencing with three loud upslurs and terminating with a rattle *siu siu siu st st tttttttt tyo*.

Black-eared Seedeater *Serinus mennelli*   13cm, 5"
Similar to Stripe-breasted Seedeater, but has a *more striking face pattern*: the crown is streaked black and white, with bold white superciliary stripes and blackish cheeks. **HH** local, but not uncommon in miombo woodland in STz from 1100–1400m. **Vo** sings from the top of exposed branches and in flight, a short rising and falling refrain of several similar notes. The call is a rather harsh *swee'ee*.

Oriole-Finch *Linurgus olivaceus*   13cm, 5"
Ad ♂ is distinctive with a black head, yellow underparts, and a stubby orange-pink bill. Three races occur, but only vary in general tone: western *prigoginei* is more orange below, in EUg and Ke *elgonensis* is brighter yellow above, while in Tz *kilimensis* is generally greener. ♀♀ are dull olive-green with a darker face and a yellowish bill. Imms are like ♀♀ but with darker bills. **HH** pairs and small flocks are rather local but widespread in both the undergrowth and canopy of highland forest from 1700–3000m. **Vo** song is rarely heard and rather canary-like with trills and twitters, and some finch-like snoring. Call is a high-pitched *zit-zit* given both perched and in flight.

Plate 284

Streaky Seedeater

whytii

nominate

striatipectus

Streaky-headed Seedeater

elgonensis

Stripe-breasted Seedeater

reichardi

Black-eared Seedeater

♂ *elgonensis*

♀

Oriole-Finch

GROSBEAK-CANARIES
Two large canaries with heavy pinkish bills. Formerly considered conspecific, but they have different female plumages and voices.

Northern Grosbeak-Canary *Serinus donaldsoni* 15cm, 6"

Ad ♂ is similar to Southern Grosbeak-Canary, but more distinctly streaked above, with a *stronger yellow supercilium and white vent*. ♀ and imm have the crown, nape, mantle and wings brown with darker streaking, and a bright yellow rump, but are *off-white below with heavy brown streaking across the breast and flanks*. Resembles a giant version of Yellow-rumped Seedeater. **HH** pairs or family groups are uncommon in the semi-arid bush and desert country of NKe. **Vo** varied calls include a rapid *seu-seu-seu-seu-seu-seu...*, with the same note repeated 10–20 times, and also *suweer* and an upslurred *tuweeer* both of which are similar to Southern Grosbeak-Canary.

Southern Grosbeak-Canary *Serinus buchanani* 15cm, 6"

Only likely to be confused with Brimstone Canary, but larger, with a *very large pink-horn bill and contrasting yellow rump*. Sexes virtually alike, but ♀ may show more fine streaking on the breast. Imm is similar but has a duller rump. **HH** pairs are local within range, in bush and acacia scrub, especially along dry river courses. **Vo** call is a piped, loud and far-carrying *si'tiri siiyu*, and the song is a series of repeated short phrases with a mournful piping, tinny quality.

BROWN BUNTINGS
Buntings which are mostly brown and rufous with boldly marked heads. They are found in pairs or small flocks and all feed on the ground, but fly to cover when disturbed.

Cinnamon-breasted Rock Bunting *Emberiza tahapisi* 15cm, 6"

Ad ♂ is brown streaked above with a black and white striped head, *black throat and rich cinnamon breast to vent*. ♀ is duller with a subdued head pattern. Imm is plainer than ♀, with a mostly brown streaked head and duller brown underparts. **HH** widespread but seldom numerous inhabitant of rocky areas, cliff bases, and escarpments with some small trees and light cover from 400–3000m. **Vo** song is a monotonous repeated scratchy phrase of mainly falling notes, lasting about two seconds *si siri si stri*.

Cape Bunting *Emberiza capensis* 15cm, 6"

In our area, race *vincenti* is distinctive with a black and white striped head, dark brown upperparts with chestnut shoulders, and *grey underparts with a white throat*. Sexes are alike. Imm is slightly paler with a less distinct head pattern. **HH** rather local, inhabiting scrubby hillsides with rocks and boulders in STz. **Vo** song is a simple descending refrain of 5–6 almost identical chips followed by a soft and nasal, falling and rising upslur *chit chit chit chit chitchit seeeu*.

House Bunting *Emberiza striolata* 14cm, 5.5"

Ad ♂ has a bold black and white striped face pattern, but the crown, nape and upper breast are more finely streaked pale grey, black and white. Wing feathers are extensively edged with warm rufous and conspicuous in flight. ♀ and imm are largely brown, with a paler buff-brown head pattern. **HH** locally common inhabiting rocky arid and desert country between 375–800m in NKe. **Vo** song is a series of short repeated phrases *siti tiri tiri si tiou* or similar variations.

Plate 285

Northern
Grosbeak-Canary

Southern
Grosbeak-Canary

Cinnamon-breasted
Rock Bunting

Cape
Bunting

Ad

House Bunting

GOLDEN BUNTINGS

Best identified by a combination of head pattern, white on the wing, rump colour, and extent of yellow on underparts. They frequently sing from exposed perches.

African Golden-breasted Bunting   *Emberiza flaviventris*   15cm, 6"
[Golden-breasted Bunting]

Ad ♂ has white stripes both above and below the eye, a lightly mottled or plain chestnut mantle, two white wing bars, and a grey rump. Bright golden-yellow below (more orange-yellow on the breast), with whitish flanks and belly. ♀ is duller. Imm is similar, but paler and duller, with a more subdued brown and buff head pattern. **HH** single birds or pairs are common and widespread in wooded grasslands and moist bush country from sea-level to 2300m. **Vo** individual songs vary, but are typically a series of 4–5 downslurs *siu siu siu siu siu, chip-chip choo chip-chip choo* or a *cheree cheree cheree cheree cheree* all with a high-pitched and far-carrying quality.

Somali Golden-breasted Bunting   *Emberiza poliopleura*   15cm, 6"

Ad ♂ is similar to African Golden-breasted Bunting with a grey rump, white on the wings, and bright golden below with whitish flanks: *chestnut-brown mantle is broadly edged in pale buffy-grey,* creating a very scaly appearance. Imm is much paler than ad with a browner head pattern and only a hint of yellow below. **HH** common and widespread in dry bush country from sea-level to 1200m (occasionally up to 1800m) to the north and east of African Golden-breasted Bunting. **Vo** songs are similar in form and pattern to African Golden-breasted Bunting, but are hurried not relaxed in delivery *siu siu siu siu siu siu siu* and *swit swit swit chee t'choo t'choo t'choo.* Also has a distinctive piped upslur *p'yuuu* given in flight or perched.

Brown-rumped Bunting   *Emberiza affinis*   14cm, 5.5"

Ad is very similar to African Golden-breasted Bunting, but has *broader white stripes on the head, no white wing bars, a brown rump and is entirely yellow below, including the flanks.* Imm is similar but paler. **HH** uncommon in wooded and bushed grasslands in NUg, while status in NWKe is uncertain: it is presumed to be rare. **Vo** song is a warbled deliberate and scratchy *switirichiri switirichireerrr* rather like a Fawn-coloured Lark.

Cabanis's Bunting   *Emberiza cabanisi*   15cm, 6"

Two distinct races occur: from NWUg to Bu, ad ♂ nominate has a *white superciliary stripe (but no white line below the eye) and the crown and sides of face are plain black;* in Tz ad ♂ of race *orientalis* (**Three-streaked Bunting**) is similar but has an *additional narrow white streak down the centre of the crown* and is paler and more streaked above. Both races have white on the chin (and throat in nominate). ♀♀ of both are duller, with browner head patterns. Imms are like pale dull ♀♀. **HH** rather uncommon in forest edge and bushed and wooded grasslands from 300–2000m. **Vo** nominate race typically sings a fairly rapid delivery of five upslurs with a chipping quality *swi chi chi chi chi chi,* while *orientalis* has a much sweeter *swi sisi swee swee swee swee,* both of which are loud and far-carrying.

Ortolan Bunting   *Emberiza hortulana*   15cm, 6"

Ad ♂ has a greenish-grey head, a *narrow yellowish eye-ring, pink bill,* and a yellowish throat with olive malar stripes. ♀ is duller and paler with some brown streaking on the head and breast. Imm birds are even browner and more streaked above and below with a vague pipit-like appearance, but the *pale eye-ring and stubby pink bill* are conspicuous. *Broad areas of white on the outer-tail are obvious in flight* in all plumages. **HH** Palearctic vagrant with 5 records in the region, all from Oct–Jan. **Vo** call not recorded in the region.

Plate 286

Ad

Imm

**African
Golden-breasted Bunting**

Imm

Ad

Ad

**Somali
Golden-breasted Bunting**

**Brown-rumped
Bunting**

♂

♂

orientalis

nominate

Cabanis's Bunting

♂

Imm

Ortolan Bunting

INDEX OF SCIENTIFIC NAMES

Page numbers refer to text only.

575

582

INDEX OF COMMON NAMES

A term in [ ] indicates an alternative name in a species heading. A term in ( ) means that the name will be found in the species text, not as a heading. Page numbers in **bold** refer to plates.

Important Bird Areas in East Africa

All of the 182 Important Bird Areas (IBAs) identified in East Africa by are listed here and mapped on the inside back cover. These IBAs have been identified against globally agreed criteria by the BirdLife Partnership in the region. A full directory of Africa's IBAs has been been published (Fishpool, L.D.C. Ed. 2001. Important Bird Areas in Africa and associated Islands: Priority Sites for Conservation. BirdLife: Cambridge, UK).

Although a large number of these sites are nationally and internationally renowned protected areas, like the Maasai Mara Game Reserve in Kenya, or Rwanda's Akagera National Park, many are also unprotected and vulnerable. For information on the status of these areas, or about the networks of people who are involved in supporting them, please contact the relevant national NGOs in East Africa (see introduction).

Rwanda

1. Akagera National Park
2. Akanyaru Wetlands
3. Cyamudongo Forest
4. Mukura Forest Reserve
5. Nyabarongo Wetlands
6. Nyungwe Forest Reserve
7. Rugezi Marsh
8. Volcans National Park

Burundi

1. Bururi Forest Nature Reserve
2. Kibira National Park
3. Kigwena Forest Nature Reserve
4. Rumonge Forest Nature Reserve
5. Rusizi National Park
6. Ruvubu National Park
7. Rwihinda Lake Nature Reserve

Uganda

1. Mgahinga Gorilla National Park
2. Echuya Forest Reserve
3. Nyamuliro Swamp
4. Bwindi Impenetrable National Park
5. Rwenzori Mountains National Park
6. Kibale National Park
7. Queen Elizabeth National Park and Lake George
8. Kyambura Wildlife Reserve
9. Semliki National Park
10. Semliki Community and Wildlife Reserve
11. Lake Mburo National Park
12. Mabira Forest Reserve
13. Sango Bay Complex
14. Musambwa Islands
15. Sesse Islands – Lutoboka
16. Lake Nabugabo
17. Mabamba Bay
18. Lutembe Bay
19. Budongo Forest Reserve
20. Murchison Falls National Park
21. Ajai Wildlife Reserve
22. Mount Kei Forest Reserve
23. Mount Otzi Forest Reserve
24. Doho Rice Scheme
25. Lake Nakuwa
26. Lake Bisina
27. Lake Opeta
28. Mount Elgon National Park
29. Mount Moroto Forest Reserve
30. Kidepo Valley National Park

Kenya

1. Aberdare Mountains
2. Kianyaga Valleys
3. Kikuyu Escarpment Forest
4. Kinangop Grasslands
5. Mount Kenya
6. Mukurweini Valleys
7. Arabuko-Sokoke Forest
8. Dakatcha Woodland
9. Diani Forest
10. Dzombo Hill Forest
11. Gede Ruins National Monument
12. Kaya Gandini
13. Kaya Waa
14. Kisite Island
15. Kiunga Marine National Reserve
16. Mida Creek, Whale Island, and the Malindi-Watamu Coast
17. Marenji Forest
18. Mrima Hill Forest
19. Sabaki River Mouth
20. Shimba Hills
21. Taita Hills Forests
22. Tana River Delta
23. Tana River Forests
24. Tsavo East National Park
25. Tsavo West National Park
26. Chyulu Hills Forests
27. Dida Galgalu Desert
28. Lake Turkana
29. Machakos Valleys
30. Masinga Reservoir
31. Meru National Park
32. Mwea National Reserve
33. Samburu-Buffalo Springs National Reserves
34. Shaba National Reserve
35. Dandora Ponds
36. Nairobi National Park
37. Dunga Swamp
38. Koguta Swamp
39. Kusa Swamp
40. Ruma National Park
41. Yala Swamp
42. Amboseli National Park
43. Cherangani Hills
44. Lake Baringo
45. Lake Bogoria National Reserve
46. Lake Elmenteita
47. Lake Magadi
48. Lake Naivasha
49. Lake Nakuru National Park
50. Masai Mara
51. Mau Forest Complex
52. Mau Narok - Molo Grasslands
53. North Nandi Forest

54. Ol Donyo Sabache
55. South Nandi Forest
56. South Nguruman
57. Busia Grasslands
58. Kakamega Forest
59. Mount Elgon
60. Sio Port Swamp

Tanzania

1. Arusha National Park
2. Katavi National Park
3. Mount Kilimanjaro National Park
4. Lake Manyara National Park
5. Mahali Mountains National Park
6. Mikumi National Park
7. Ruaha National Park
8. Rubondo Island National Park
9. Serengeti National Park
10. Tarangire National Park
11. Udzungwa National Park
12. Mafia Island Marine Park
13. Ngorongoro Conservation Area
14. Biharamulo-Burigi Game Reserve
15. Maswa Game Reserve
16. Mkomazi Game Reserve
17. Moyowosi-Kigozi Game Reserve
18. Selous Game Reserve
19. Ugalla River Game Reserve
20. Lake Burungi
21. Dar es Salaam
22. Elenuata Dam
23. Lake Eyasi
24. Kagera Swamps
25. Kilombero Valley
26. Lake Kitangire
27. Latham Island
28. Mnazi Bay
29. Mtera Reservoir
30. Nyumba ya Mungu Reservoir
31. Lake Natron and Engaruka Basin
32. Rufigi Delta
33. Lake Rukwa
34. Singida Lakes

35. Tanga north
36. Tanga south
37. Lake Tlawi
38. Usangu Flats
39. Lake Victoria - Bumbire Islands
40. Lake Victoria - Bunda Bay
41. Lake Victoria - Mwanza Gulf
42. Lake Victoria - Mara Bay and Masisirori Swamp
43. Wembere Steppe
44. Zanzibar Island - south coast
45. Zanzibar Island - east coast
46. Bagamoyo District coastal forests
47. Kisarawe District coastal forests
48. Rufiji District coastal forests
49. Pande and Dondwe coastal forests
50. Kilwa District coastal forests
51. Lindi District coastal forests
52. Mtwara District coastal forests
53. Newala District coastal forests
54. Handeni District coastal forests
55. Muheza District coastal forests
56. Pangani District coastal forests
57. Jozani Forest Reserve, Zanzibar
58. Livingstone Mountain forests
59. Nguru Mountains
60. Nguu Mountains
61. Njombwe forests
62. Pare Mountains North
63. Pare Mountains South
64. Rubeho Mountains
65. Rungwe Mountain
66. Udzungwa Mountains
67. Ukaguru Mountains
68. Uluguru Mountains
69. Umalila Mountains
70. Usambara East Mountains
71. Usambara West Mountains
72. Uvidunda Mountains
73. Kitulo Plateau
74. Longido Game Controlled Area
75. Minziro Forest Reserve
76. Pemba Island
77. Ufipa Plateau

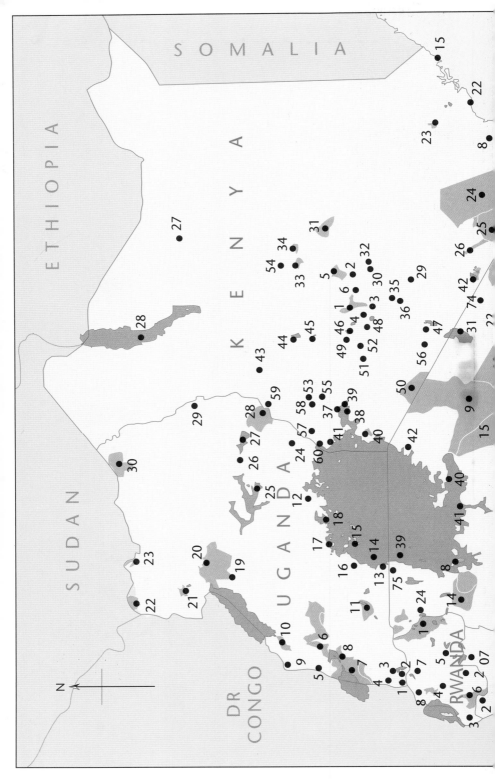